Handbook of Research on Secure Multimedia Distribution

Shiguo Lian
France Telecom R&D (Orange Labs) Beijing, China

Yan Zhang
Simula Research Laboratory, Norway

INFORMATION SCIENCE REFERENCE

Hershey · New York

Director of Editorial Content:	Kristin Klinger
Senior Managing Editor:	Jamie Snavely
Managing Editor:	Jeff Ash
Assistant Managing Editor:	Carole Coulson
Cover Design:	Lisa Tosheff
Printed at:	Yurchak Printing Inc.

Published in the United States of America by
Information Science Reference (an imprint of IGI Global)
701 E. Chocolate Avenue, Suite 200
Hershey PA 17033
Tel: 717-533-8845
Fax: 717-533-8661
E-mail: cust@igi-global.com
Web site: http://www.igi-global.com

and in the United Kingdom by
Information Science Reference (an imprint of IGI Global)
3 Henrietta Street
Covent Garden
London WC2E 8LU
Tel: 44 20 7240 0856
Fax: 44 20 7379 0609
Web site: http://www.eurospanbookstore.com

Library of Congress Cataloging-in-Publication Data

Handbook of research on secure multimedia distribution / Shiguo Lian and Yan Zhang, editors.
        p. cm.

    Includes bibliographical references and index.
    Summary: "This handbook is for both secure multimedia distribution researchers and also decision makers in obtaining a greater understanding of the concepts, issues, problems, trends, challenges and opportunities related to secure multimedia distribution"--Provided by publisher.

    ISBN 978-1-60566-262-6 (hardcover) -- ISBN 978-1-60566-263-3 (ebook)
    1. Multimedia systems--Security measures--United States. 2. Data protection--United States. 3. Copyright and electronic data processing--United States. I. Lian, Shiguo. II. Zhang, Yan, 1977-
    QA76.575.H363 2009
    005.8--dc22
                    2008030775

British Cataloguing in Publication Data
A Cataloguing in Publication record for this book is available from the British Library.

All work contributed to this book set is original material. The views expressed in this book are those of the authors, but not necessarily of the publisher.

Qibin Sun, *Institute for Infocomm Research (I2R), A-STAR, Singapore*
Jiwu Huang, *Sun Yat-Sen University, China*
John Choi, *MarkAny Corp., Korea*
Zhiquan Wang, *Nanjing University of Science & Technology, China*
Gregory L. Heileman, *University of New Mexico, USA*

List of Contributors

Table of Contents

Section I
Secure Distribution Systems

Chapter I

Pramod A. Jamkhedkar, University of New Mexico, USA
Gregory L. Heileman, University of New Mexico, USA

Chapter II

Deepali Brahmbhatt, San Jose State University, USA
Mark Stamp, San Jose State University, USA

Chapter III

Jean-Henry Morin, Korea University Business School, Korea

Chapter IV

Mercè Serra Joan, Fraunhofer Institute for Integrated Circuits IIS, Germany
Bert Greevenbosch, Fraunhofer Institute for Integrated Circuits IIS, Germany
Anja Becker, Fraunhofer Institute for Integrated Circuits IIS, Germany
Harald Fuchs, Fraunhofer Institute for Integrated Circuits IIS, Germany
Stefan Krägeloh, Fraunhofer Institute for Integrated Circuits IIS, Germany

Chapter V

Hugo Jonker, University of Luxembourg, Luxembourg & Eindhoven University of Technology,
*   The Netherlands*
Sjouke Mauw, University of Luxembourg, Luxembourg

Section III
Typical Applications

Detailed Table of Contents

Section I
Secure Distribution Systems

In this section, some secure distribution systems are presented, which provide the digital rights management (DRM) architectures for multimedia content distribution from the content producer, service provider to customer. The distribution systems include trusted and un-trusted peer-to-peer systems, video surveillance systems, hardware-based systems, and so forth.

Chapter I
Pramod A. Jamkhedkar, University of New Mexico, USA
Gregory L. Heileman, University of New Mexico, USA

Rights expression languages (RELs) form a central component of digital rights management (DRM) systems. The process of development of RELs transforms the rights requirements to a formal language ready to be used in DRM systems. Decisions regarding the design of the conceptual model, syntax, semantics, and other such properties of the language, affect not only each other, but also the integration of the language in DRM systems, and the design of DRM system as a whole. This chapter provides a detailed analysis of each step of this process and the tradeoffs involved, that not only affect the properties of the REL, but also the DRM system using that REL.

Chapter II
Deepali Brahmbhatt, San Jose State University, USA
Mark Stamp, San Jose State University, USA

This chapter presents a digital rights management (DRM) system designed for streaming media. A brief, general introduction to DRM in is also provided, along with a discussion of the some specific issues that arise in the context of streaming media. The DRM system proposed here has been implemented and some details related to the implementation are discussed.

Chapter III

This chapter introduces and discusses much needed alternatives to the traditional either/or debate on total security of secure multimedia distribution. Most DRM-based approaches rely on considering the user as untrustworthy and consequently a weak link. We argue there may be alternative ways, providing increased flexibility to users in terms of fair use and copyright balance while still maintaining a much needed level of governed usage of content. While introducing exception management in DRM environments might seam counterintuitive at first sight, we provide elements supporting the idea in the form of a model which is discussed. In doing so, we argue for the need to rethink DRM in ways that will enable both a seamless compelling user experience and the rights holder to address the issue of managed copying of content.

The Open Mobile Alliance (OMA) Digital Rights Management standard (OMA DRM) offers protection and secure access control for digital content. The OMA Mobile Broadcast Services standard (BCAST) specifies the protected content delivery for mobile broadcast applications such as mobile TV. These two standards complement each other, enabling further functionalities and use cases. This chapter provides a technical overview of the OMA DRM standard including its latest developments. Further, the OMA BCAST standard is described, focusing on the DRM profile for service and content protection.

Chapter V

The use of Digital Rights Management (DRM) systems involves several stakeholders, such as the content provider, the license provider, and the user, each having their own incentives to use the system. Proper use of the system implies that these incentives can only be met if certain security requirements are fulfilled. Much attention in literature has been devoted to specific security aspects of DRM systems. The contributions of this chapter consist of deriving a systematic overview of core security requirements for DRM systems. This chapter conducts a stakeholder analysis, gives an objective tree for each relevant stakeholder, and develops a simple, generic conceptual model to arrive at the set of core security requirements.

Chapter VI

Pallavi Priyadarshini, San Jose State University, USA
Mark Stamp, San Jose State University, USA

Peer-to-peer (P2P) networks have proliferated and become ubiquitous. A school of thought has emerged that harnessing the established user-base and ease of content dissemination of such networks presents a potentially lucrative opportunity. However, content creators have been reluctant to adopt P2P networks as a distribution vehicle since these networks are plagued with piracy. This chapter focuses on developing a solution for distributing digital content in P2P networks in a way that established businesses and amateur artists alike can profit. We propose a content distribution system that employs digital rights management (DRM) technologies and is independent of the underlying P2P network. Our system relies on innovative uses of security technologies to deter piracy. In addition, we include various non-technical features that encourage users to "play by the rules".

Chapter VII

L. Badia, IMT Lucca Institute for Advanced Studies, Italy
A. Erta, IMT Lucca Institute for Advanced Studies, Italy & Fluidmesh Networks Inc., Italy
U. Malesci, Fluidmesh Networks Inc., Italy

Traditional analog video-surveillance systems technology has recently become inadequate to face the massive demand of security systems consisting of hundreds and sometimes thousands of cameras often deployed in hostile environments miles far away from the control room. The packetized video stream can be straightforwardly conveyed to the control room relaying on common IP network infrastructures. However, the widespread adoption of IP-based solutions for video-surveillance poses serious problems in terms of required bandwidth, processing power, network security, and system dependability. This chapter first investigates the advantages of the IP-based video-surveillance systems over the traditional analog ones. Then, it describes the technical challenges and the open research issues which still lack an ultimate solution which permits to completely abandon the traditional analog technology. Finally, it proposes and verifies, by means of a case study, a methodology to address the design of video-surveillance systems in real deployment.

Chapter VIII

Ramya Venkataramu, Hewlett-Packard Company, USA
Mark Stamp, San Jose State University, USA

Apple employs a DRM system known as Fairplay in its iTunes online music store. Users communicate with the centralized iTunes server to download, purchase, play, and preview digital content. The iTunes music store has the potential disadvantage of a bandwidth bottleneck at the centralized server. Furthermore, this bandwidth bottleneck problem will escalate with increasing popularity of online music and other digital media, such as video. In this chapter we analyze the Fairplay DRM system. Then we consider a modified architecture that can be employed over existing peer-to-peer (P2P) networks. Our new system, P2PTunes, is designed to provide the benefits of a decentralized P2P network while providing DRM content protection that is at least as strong as that found in Fairplay.

Chapter IX

Nicolas Anciaux, INRIA Rocquencourt, France
Luc Bouganim, INRIA Rocquencourt, France
Philippe Pucheral, INRIA Rocquencourt, France & University of Versailles, France

The objective of this chapter is to show that new forms of Secure Multimedia Distribution cannot be tackled by existing DRM or database access control models. The chapter then suggests solutions based on secure hardware. Secure chips appear today in various form factors (smart cards, USB secure tokens, TPM, etc). They can be used to implement a Secure Operating Environment (i.e., a tamper-resistant storage and execution environment) in any device they are plugged in. This chapter will present different techniques which answer the three questions mentioned above, thanks to such Secure Operating Environment. Finally, the accuracy of these techniques will be illustrated through different commercial DRM scenarios and pervasive healthcare scenarios.

Section II
Core Techniques

In this section, some key techniques for secure multimedia distribution are presented, providing the means for protecting the confidentiality, integrity, ownership, copyrights, and so forth. These techniques include the key exchange protocol, secret sharing scheme, robust transmission technique, information hiding technique (i.e. watermarking, steganography and fingerprinting), and video authentication scheme.

Chapter X

Ionuţ Florescu, Stevens Institute of Technology, USA

Regarding fundamental protocols in cryptography, the Diffie-Hellman (Diffie and Hellman, 1976) public key exchange protocol is one of the oldest and widely used in today's applications. Consequently, many specific cryptographic implementations depend on its security. Typically, an underlying (finite dimensional) group is selected to provide candidates for the key. The study of the security of the exchange as depending on the structure of the underlying group is even today poorly understood, with the most common approaches relying on the security of the Discrete Logarithm problem or on the size of the group. Recent developments bring to attention that the relationship is not necessarily valid and that more research is needed that will relate the underlying structure of the group and the security of the Diffie-Hellman exchange. This chapter describes the problem in detail, presents the relationship with the previously studied Discrete Logarithm and Computational Diffie-Hellman problems, exposes the various concepts of security, and introduces a new statistical concept specifically designed to serve the assessment of the security of the exchange.

Secret sharing aims at distributing and sharing a secret among a group of participants efficiently. This chapter firstly proposes a plane-based access structure for secret sharing. More specifically, if any two among a set of three participants in a graph contain an edge, then these participants belong to a prohibited structure which is not able to recover the master key. Otherwise, the set of three participants belong to an access structure which can recover the master key. It then extends the plane-based scheme and proposes a generic k-dimensional secret sharing scheme. It analyzes the performance of the proposed scheme and reveals its advantages compared to existing schemes.

From all forms of digital multimedia content, video plays an increasingly important role as the emerging multimedia communication and distribution system. Regardless of its extremely large size that makes it more difficult to find effective schemes to compress and transmit flawlessly through IP and wireless medium. In this chapter, we discuss the video compression techniques, and the latest video coding standard, H.264, its implication for the wireless video transmission, and our research contribution on joint source-channel coding for wireless video transmission.

Establishing hidden communication is an important subject of discussion that has gained increasing importance recently, with the development of the Internet. One of the methods introduced for establishing hidden communication is Steganography. Steganography is a method to hide data in a cover media so that other individuals will not notice that such data is there. In this chapter, steganography is introduced and its history is described. Then the major steganography methods include image, audio, video, and text steganography are reviewed.

The digital multimedia, including text, image, graphics, audio, video, and so forth, has become a main way for information communication along with the popularization of Internet and the development of multimedia techniques. How to provide copyright protection has drawn extensive attention in recent years. As a main method for copyright protection, digital watermarking has been widely studied and applied. In this chapter we discuss the important properties of watermarks, the capacity, and the detection error rate. The watermarking system is analyzed based on the channel capacity and error rate of the communication system, and the relation between the detection error rate with the capacity and payload capacity is derived. This chapter also introduces a new analysis method of the watermarking capacity, which is based on the theories of attractors and attraction basin of artificial neural network. The attraction basin of neural network decides the upper limit of watermarking, and the attractors of neural network decide the lower limit of watermarking. According to the experimental results, the detection error rate of watermark is mainly influenced by the watermark average energy, and the watermarking capacity. The error rate rises with the increase of watermarking capacity. When the channel coding is used, the watermarking error rate drops with the decrease of the payload capacity of watermarking.

As Internet usage continues to grow, people are becoming more aware of the need to protect the display and presentation of digital documents. Digital watermarking offers a means to protect such documents. It works by embedding a piece of information into these documents – either visibly or invisibly – which can be detected or extracted from the document at a later stage to prove ownership of the document. This chapter will review, in detail, the process of digital image watermarking and evaluate the different types of watermarks which may be used and the different techniques used to embed the watermarks. An examination of the domains used to embed the watermarks and some of the techniques used for detection of the embedded watermark are provided. Finally future trends within the area of digital watermarking are outlined.

Digital video authentication has been a topic of immense interest to researchers in the past few years. Authentication of a digital video refers to the process of determining that the video taken is original and has not been tampered with. This chapter aims to provide an overview of digital video authentication systems and a universal review of the associated methods. The chapter not only establishes the importance of authenticating a video in various application scenarios; it also identifies key properties and design issues that should be considered while designing a video authentication system. The benign and tampering operations that characterize the security and robustness aspects of a typical video authentication system are described. The past works related to video authentication, based on digital signature and digital watermarking, have been described; and the emerging trends in this area of research have also been identified.

The multimedia community is moving from monolithic applications to more flexible and scalable prolif-erative solutions. Security issues such as access control and authentication of multimedia content have been intensively studied in the literature. In particular, stream authentication tends to be more complicated since a stream may be transcoded by intermediate proxies or composed by multiple sources. Traditional stream authentication schemes consider a stream as a group of packets and authenticate these packets over an erasure channel. However, by fixing the packets in transmission, any packet manipulation will cause authentication failure. In this chapter, we assume a more flexible model where a proxy, between a sender and a receiver, is able to make transcoding operations over a stream. We describe a flexible stream authentication framework that allows the so called packet independent stream authentication schemes to make transcoding operations on the packets and commit the changes, which are not appli-cable in packet-based stream authentication schemes. Such a stream authentication scheme based on the layered structure of a stream is elaborated in details w.r.t., the encoding, packing, amortizing, and verifying methods. The security and performance analysis show that the packet independent stream authentication schemes achieve higher authentication rate with less overhead per packet, as compared with that of packet based schemes.

Chapter XVIII

Media that is distributed digitally can be copied and redistributed illegally. Embedding an individual watermark in the media object for each customer will make it possible to trace pirate copies to the re-distribution source. However, digital distribution methods such as broadcast and multicast are scalable and will give all customers exactly identical copies of the media content. Distribution of individually watermarked media is more difficult to achieve. In this chapter methods for how media with individual watermarking can be distributed scalable are presented and discussed. These methods are categorized in four groups. Two groups that are based on watermark embedding in the network or client and two groups that use fragments of the media content that is unique for each customer or shared among a subgroup of customers.

Chapter XIX

Steganography is a kind of secret communication technique based on information hiding, which hides secrets into the cover media, such as image, video, audio, text, and so forth. This chapter analyzes the technique of digital steganography, including the typical algorithms for secure information hiding, the general methods for stegoanalysis, the applications, hot topics and some open issues.

Section III
Typical Applications

In this part, the secure multimedia distribution schemes for typical applications are presented. These applications include the pure peer-to-peer content distribution, value-creation chain of multimedia goods, mobile multimedia device, image steganography, video watermarking, and so forth.

Esther Palomar, Carlos III University of Madrid, Spain
Juan M. E. Tapiador, Carlos III University of Madrid, Spain
Julio C. Hernandez-Castro, Carlos III University of Madrid, Spain
Arturo Ribagorda, Carlos III University of Madrid, Spain

This chapter first describes the background and framework of content distribution in P2P and ad hoc networks. It also elaborates on the characteristics for the provision of security services, paying special attention to authentication and access control techniques suitable for self-organized networks, and summarizing the main security solutions proposed so far. In particular, the specific purpose of the present chapter is to justify the necessity of a secure content replication in such networks. It also points out some open issues and emergent trends in this research area.

Andreas U. Schmidt, CREATE-NET Research Centre, Italy
Nicolai Kuntze, Fraunhofer Institute for Secure Information Technology, Germany

Security in the value creation chain hinges on many single components and their interrelations. Trusted Platforms open ways to fulfill the pertinent requirements. This chapter gives a systematic approach to the utilization of trusted computing platforms over the whole lifecycle of multimedia products. This spans production, aggregation, (re)distribution, consumption, and charging. Trusted Computing technology as specified by the Trusted Computing Group provides modular building blocks which can be utilized at many points in the multimedia lifecycle. We propose an according research roadmap beyond the conventional Digital Rights Management use case. Selected technical concepts illustrate the principles of Trusted Computing applications in the multimedia context.

Goo-Rak Kwon, Chosun University, Korea
Sung-Jea Ko, Korea University, Korea

The objective of this chapter introduces an advanced encryption of MP3 and MPEG-4 coder with a quality degradation-based security model. For the MP3 audio, the magnitude and phase information of modified discrete cosine transform (MDCT) coefficients is encrypted. DCT coefficients and motion vectors (MVs) are used for the scrambling of the MPEG-4 video. This encryption scheme has a level of security, secures in perception, keeps format compliance, and obtains high-time efficiency though reducing the encrypted the volumes of multimedia contents. These properties make it practical to incorporate encryption and decryption process into compression and decompression process, and thus suitable for secure A/V transmission or sharing.

Chapter XXIII

Frank Y. Shih, New Jersey Institute of Technology, USA
Yi-Ta Wu, Industrial Technology Research Institute, Taiwan

Steganography is the art of hiding secret data inside other innocent media file. Steganalysis is process of detecting the hidden data which are crested using steganography. Steganalysis detects stego-images by analyzing various image features between stego-images and cover-images. Therefore, it needs to have a system that develops more critical stego-images from which steganalysis cannot detect them. This chapter presents a Genetic Algorithm (GA) based method for breaking steganalytic systems. The emphasis is shifted from traditionally avoiding the change of statistic features to artificially counterfeiting the statistic features. The idea is based on the following: in order to manipulate the statistic features for breaking the inspection of steganalytic systems, the GA based approach is adopted to counterfeit several stego-images (candidates) until one of them can break the inspection of steganalytic systems.

Chapter XXIV

Guangjie Liu, Nanjing University of Science and Technology, China
Shiguo Lian, France Telecom R&D (Orange Labs) Beijing, China
Yuewei Dai, Nanjing University of Science and Technology, China
Zhiquan Wang, Nanjing University of Science and Technology, China

Image steganography is a common form of information hiding which embeds as many possible message bits into images and keeps the introduced distortion imperceptible. The two important indices, capacity and imperceptibility, are restricted by each other. How to balance the trade-off between the two has become a very important issue in the research of steganography. This chapter discusses one kind of the solution for disposing the trade-off, named adaptive image steganography. The mechanism of adaptive steganography is to utilize the results of HVS analysis to decide how many message bits can be embedded into a target pixel or pixels in a target region.

Chapter XXV

Shiguo Lian, France Telecom R&D (Orange Labs) Beijing, China

Video watermarking technique embeds some information into videos by modifying video content slightly. The embedded information, named watermark, may be ownership information, customer information, integrity information, redundancy information, and so forth. Thus, this technique can be used for copyright protection, piracy tracing, content authentication, advertisement surveillance, error resilience, and so forth. This chapter gives an overview on video watermarking technology, including its architecture, performance requirement, typical algorithms, hot topics, and open issues.

Multiple description coding (MDC) is a promising method for robust transmission of information over non-prioritized and unpredictable networks, which has been extensively studied in recent years. As a source coding scheme, multiple description coding has been widely applied in audio, image, and video sources. It is also interesting to find that multiple description coding can be applied in multimedia watermarking. Recently, several multiple description watermarking schemes have been developed which have exhibited some advantages. In this chapter, the concept, design algorithms and some applications of multiple description coding are reviewed. Particularly, the application of MDC in watermarking, known as multiple description watermarking, is elaborated based on recent research results.

In this chapter, a pioneer concept in which multiple images are simultaneously considered in the compression and secured distribution frameworks is revealed. We have proposed the so-called fractal mating coding scheme to successfully implement the joint image compression and encryption concept through a novel design in the domain pool construction. With the exploration of the intra- and inter-image similarity among multiple images, not only the coding performance can be improved, but also the secured image distribution purpose can be achieved. The experimental results verify that the proposed methods can successfully perform both the efficient compression and secured image distribution purposes.

Foreword

I am delighted to write the Foreword to this book, as its scope and content provide commercial and government enterprises with the essential ingredients for implementing and managing secure multimedia distribution.

The recent advances in the technology, especially in the computer industry and communications, allowed a potentially enormous market for distributing digital multimedia content through the Internet. However, the proliferation of digital documents, multimedia processing tools, and the worldwide availability of Internet access have created an ideal medium for copyright fraud and uncontrollable distribution of multimedia content. Now a major challenge is the protection of the intellectual property of multimedia content in multimedia networks.

To deal with the technical challenges, two major multimedia security technologies are being developed:

1. Multimedia encryption technology to provide end-to-end security when distributing digital content over a variety of distribution systems.
2. Multimedia watermarking technology as a tool to achieve copyright protection, ownership trace, and authentication.

This handbook provides answers to many challenging questions dealing with designing modern secure multimedia distribution systems. It addresses a variety of issues related to the protection of digital multimedia content, digital right management systems, video watermarking and authentication techniques, and various applications.

The handbook is comprised of 27 chapters divided into 3 sections. Section I, Secure Systems, introduces fundamental concepts applied for digital right management. Section II, Key Techniques, includes chapters on multimedia encryption, watermarking, and authentication technqiues. Section III, Typical Applications, includes chapters that describe various application of multimedia protection schemes.

I recommend this handbook to researchers and practitioners in the field, and for scientisists and engineers involved in designing and developing systems for the protection of digital multimedia content. The Handbook can also be used for graduate students in the area of multimedia security.

Borko Furht
Chairman & Professor
Florida Atlantic University
Boca Raton, Florida, USA

Borko Furht *is chairman and professor in the Department of Computer Science and Engineering at Florida Atlantic University (FAU) in Boca Raton, Florida. He is the founder and director of the Multimedia Laboratory at FAU, funded by National Science Foundation. His research interests include multimedia systems and applications, video processing, wireless multimedia, multimedia security, video databases, and Internet engineering. He has published more than 20 books and about 200 scientific and technical papers, and holds 2 patents. His recent books include "Multimedia Security Handbook" (2005), and "Handbook of Multimedia Databases" (2004), both published by CRC Press. He is a founder and editor-in-chief of the Journal of Multimedia Tools and Applications (Kluwer Academic Publishers, now Springer). He has been program chair as well as a member of Program Committees at many national and international conferences.*

Preface

As rapid and tremendous progress in information technology is constantly being made, and, while an enormous amount of media such as text, audio, speech, music, image and video can be easily exchanged through the Internet and other communication networks, information security issues such as copyright protection, integrity verification, authentication, and access control have became exceptionally acute. As a result, the subjects of security protection in multimedia distribution have been taken as one of the top research and development agendas for researchers, organizations, and governments worldwide. Especially after 1995, multimedia distribution became more and more popular with the achievements in multimedia technology and network technology. The malicious tampering of multimedia content, such as copy, forgery, modification, illegal distribution and so on, threatens multimedia related services. Thus, secure multimedia distribution becomes necessary and urgent.

There exists some solutions for information protection, such as cryptographic techniques. However, multimedia data are different from text or binary data because of such properties as large volumes, high redundancies, and real-time interactions. Thus, multimedia protection is different from binary/text data protection. Additionally, secure multimedia distribution is in close relation with several fields, including cryptography, multimedia processing, and network communication. These properties make secure multimedia distribution a challenging research topic that has attacted more and more researchers and engineers over the past decade.

Until recently, few handbooks mentioned secure multimedia distribution. To access the latest research related to the many disciplines of secure multimedia distribution, I decided to launch a handbook project where researchers from all over the world would assist me in providing the necessary coverage of each respective discipline in secure multimedia distribution. The primary objective of this project was to assemble as much research coverage as possible, related to the disciplines selected for this handbook by defining the technologies, terms, and acronyms related to each discipline, and providing the most comprehensive list of research references related to each discipline.

In order to provide the best balanced coverage of concepts and issues related to the selected topics of this handbook, researchers from around the world were asked to submit proposals describing their proposed coverage and the contribution of such coverage to the handbook. All proposals were carefully reviewed by the editor in light of their suitability, researcher's records of similar work in the area of the proposed topics, and the best proposal for topics with multiple proposals. The goal was to assemble the best minds in the information science and technology field from all over the world to contribute entries to the handbook. Upon the receipt of full entry submissions, each submission was forwarded to at least three expert external reviewers on a peer review basis. Only submissions with strong and favorable reviews were chosen as entries for this handbook. In many cases, submissions were sent back for several revisions prior to final acceptance. As a result, this handbook includes 27 chapters highlighting current concepts, issues, and emerging technologies. All entries are written by knowledgeable, distinguished scholars from many prominent research institutions in more than 10 countries.

The handbook is composed of three sections—Secure Distribution System, Key Technique, and Typical Application. The first section, Secure Distribution System, consists of the chapters describing various secure multimedia distribution systems. The secure distribution systems include:

- *Digital rights mangement for streaming media.* Streaming media is now the most popular manners for online live TV or film services. Compared with non-streaming manners, (e.g., ftp) streaming media has strict requirements in real-time operations. In this chapter, a discussion of some specific issues that arise in the context of streaming media are given, followed by the digital rights management (DRM) system for streaming media, which is different from traditional systems.
- *Digital rights mangement for mobile communication.* Two standards are formed to protect digital rights in mobile communications, they are the Open Mobile Alliance (OMA) Digital Rights Management (DRM) standard and the OMA Mobile Broadcast Services standard (BCAST). The former one specifies offers protection and secure access control for digital content. The latter one specifies the protected content delivery for mobile broadcast applications such as mobile TV. These two standards complement each other, enabling further functionalities and use cases. This chapter provides a technical overview of the OMA DRM and OMA BCAST standards.
- *Digital rights management for peer-to-peer content sharing.* Peer-to-peer (P2P) networks have proliferated and become ubiquitous. However, secure content sharing in P2P networks is still an open issue. This chapter focuses on developing a solution for distributing digital content in P2P networks in a way that established businesses and amateur artists alike can profit. This content distribution system employs digital rights management (DRM) technologies and is independent of the underlying P2P networks.
- *Access control for content distribution.* This chapter suggests DRM solutions based on secure hardware. Secure chips appear today in various form factors (smart cards, USB secure tokens, TPM, etc). They can be used to implement a Secure Operating Environment (i.e., a tamper-resistant storage and execution environment) in any device they are plugged in. This chapter will present different techniques that answer the three questions mentioned above, thanks to such Secure Operating Environment. Finally, the accuracy of these techniques will be illustrated through different commercial DRM scenarios and pervasive healthcare scenarios.
- *Secure video surveillance systems.* This chapter first investigates the advantages of the IP-based video-surveillance systems over the traditional analog ones. Then, it describes the technical challenges and the open research issues which still lack an ultimate solution that permits them to completely abandon the traditional analog technology. Finally, it proposes and verifies, by means of a case study, a methodology to address the design of video-surveillance systems in real deployment.

Section II, Key Technique, consists of the chapters introducing various techniques for secure multimedia distribution. The mentioned techniques include:

- *Key exchange protocol.* In secure communication, key exchange is one of the key techniques. Regarding fundamental protocols in cryptography, the Diffie-Hellman (Diffie and Hellman, 1976) public key exchange protocol is one of the oldest and most widely used in today's applications. This chapter describes the security problem in existing key exchange protocols, exposes the various concepts of security, and introduces a new statistical concept specifically designed to serve the assessment of the security of the exchange.
- *Secret sharing.* Secret sharing aims at distributing and sharing a secret among a group of participants efficiently. This chapter firstly proposes a plane-based access structure for secret sharing.

More specifically, if any two among a set of three participants in a graph contain an edge, these participants belong to a prohibited structure which is not able to recover the master key.

- *Multimedia authentication.* Multimedia community is moving from monolithic applications to more flexible and scalable proliferative solutions. Security issues such as access control and authentication of multimedia content, have been intensively studied in the literature. Two chapters aim to give the overview of multimedia authentication techniques. The first one aims to provide an overview of digital video authentication systems and a universal review of the associated methods. The second one describes a flexible stream authentication framework that allows the so called packet independent stream authentication schemes to make transcoding operations on the packets and commit the changes, which are not applicable in packet-based stream authentication schemes.

- *Information hiding.* Establishing hidden communication is an important subject of discussion that has gained increasing importance with the development of the Internet. Digital watermarking and steganography are two typical techniques of information hiding. Digital watermarking embeds some information into a cover media, and the embedded information can survive some operations on the cover media. Steganography is a method to hide data in a cover media so that other persons will not notice that such data is there. Stegoanalysis is the technique to attack a steganography method. There are 3 chapters that describe digital watermarking, steganography, and stegoanalysis, respectively.

- *Wireless video transmission.* For wireless multimedia transmission, the data volumes and error-robustness are two key issues. This chapter concetrates on two techniques, source coding and channel coding. Among them, the former one refers to the multimedia compression, while the latter one refers to error-correction coding.

The final section, Typical Application, consists of the chapters describing various applications based on secure multimedia distribution. The mentioned applications include:

- *Trusted multimedia goods creation.* Security in the value creation chain hinges on many single components and their interrelations. Trusted Platforms open ways to fulfill the pertinent requirements. This chapter gives a systematic approach to the utilization of trusted computing platforms over the whole lifecycle of multimedia products. This spans production, aggregation, (re)distribution, consumption, and charging. Trusted Computing technology as specified by the Trusted Computing Group, provides modular building blocks that can be utilized at many points in the multimedia lifecycle.

- *Copyright protection in mobile multimedia device.* In mobile multimedia device, video and audio data should be protected by lightweight schemes due to the energy-limitation of mobile devices. This chapter introduces an advanced encryption of MP3 and MPEG-4 coder with a quality degradation-based security model, which keeps format compliance, and obtains high-time efficiency though reducing the encrypted the volumes of multimedia contents.

- *Image steganography.* Steganography is the art of hiding secret data inside other innocent media file. Steganalysis is the process of detecting hidden data which are crested using steganography. Steganalysis detects stego-images by analyzing various image features between stego-images and cover-images. Therefore, it needs to have a system that develops more critical stego-images from which steganalysis cannot detect them. Two chapters propose two kinds of steganography methods. The first one is based on Genetic Algorithm (GA), and the second one is based on Structural Similarity Metric.

- *Secure sharing in Ad Hoc Networks.* Secure content sharing in self-organized networks is challenging. This chapter describes the background and framework of content distribution in P2P and ad hoc networks, summarizes the main security solutions proposed so far, and points out some open issues and emergent trends in this research area.
- *Multiple Description Coding based watermarking.* Multiple description coding (MDC) is a promising method for robust transmission of information over non-prioritized and unpredictable networks. It is also interesting to find that multiple description coding can be applied in multimedia watermarking. This chapter reviews the concept, design algorithms and some applications of multiple description coding, and the application of MDC in watermarking.
- *Fractal based secure image distribution.* A pioneer concept in which multiple images are simultaneously considered in the compression and secured distribution frameworks is revealed. This chapter proposes the so-called fractal mating coding scheme to successfully implement the joint image compression and encryption concept through a novel design in the domain pool construction. With the exploration of the intra- and inter-image similarity among multiple images, not only the coding performance can be improved, but also the secured image distribution purpose can be achieved.

The diverse and comprehensive coverage of multiple disciplines in the field of secure multimedia distribution in this authoritative handbook will contribute to a better understanding all topics, research, and discoveries in this evolving, significant field of study. Furthermore, the contributions included in this handbook will be instrumental in the expansion of the body of knowledge in this vast field. The coverage of this handbook provides strength to this reference resource for both secure multimedia distribution researchers and also decision makers in obtaining a greater understanding of the concepts, issues, problems, trends, challenges and opportunities related to this field of study. It is our sincere hope that this publication and its great amount of information and research will provide a scientifically and scholarly sound treatment of state-of-the-art techniques to students, researchers, academics, personnel of law enforcement, and IT/multimedia practitioners who are interested or involved in the study, research, use, design, and development of techniques related to secure multimedia distribution.

Shiguo Lian & Yan Zhang
Editors

Acknowledgment

The editors would like to acknowledge the help of all involved in the collation and review process of the handbook, without whose support the project could not have been satisfactorily completed.

Most of the authors of chapters included in this handbook also served as referees for chapters written by other authors. Thanks go to all those who provided constructive and comprehensive reviews.

Special thanks also go to the publishing team at IGI Global, whose contributions throughout the whole process from inception of the initial idea to final publication have been invaluable. In particular to Julia Mosemann, who continuously prodded via e-mail for keeping the project on schedule.

And last but not least, special thanks go to our families for their unfailing support and encouragement during the months it took to give birth to this book.

In closing, we wish to thank all of the authors for their insights and excellent contributions to this handbook.

Shiguo Lian, P.R. China
Yan Zhang, Norway
Editors
May 2008

Section I
Secure Distribution Systems

Chapter I
Rights Expression Languages

Pramod A. Jamkhedkar
University of New Mexico, USA

Gregory L. Heileman
University of New Mexico, USA

ABSTRACT

Rights expression languages (RELs) form a central component of digital rights management (DRM) systems. The process of development of RELs transforms the rights requirements to a formal language ready to be used in DRM systems. Decisions regarding the design of the conceptual model, syntax, semantics, and other such properties of the language, affect not only each other, but also the integration of the language in DRM systems, and the design of DRM system as a whole. This chapter provides a detailed analysis of each step of this process and the tradeoffs involved that not only affect the properties of the REL, but also the DRM system using that REL.

INTRODUCTION

Every time there has been progress in the ability to make copies of some intellectual work, the need for copyright has arisen. Traditionally, copyright has been expressed using natural languages, in sufficient detail, so as to have standing in a court of law. The advent of computers, the Internet, and digital content, has created the need for management of copyright electronically, also known as digital rights management (DRM). To manage copyright electronically, it is necessary that copyright agreements be expressed in a machine-

readable form. Computers or intelligent devices can then interpret copyright agreements, and ensure that usage of copyrighted digital content is in accordance with the copyright agreement associated with the content. In DRM terminology, languages used to express copyright agreements in a machine-readable form are called rights expression languages (RELs).

Over the past several years, a number of RELs have been developed, with the eXtensible rights Markup Language (XrML) ("XrML 2.0 Technical Overview", 2002) and the Open Digital Rights Language (ODRL) (Iannella, 2002) becoming the most popular. Recently, XrML was adopted as the standard REL for inclusion in the MPEG-21 standard ("The MPEG-21 Rights Expression Language", 2003) and ODRL was accepted by the Open Mobile Alliance as the standard REL for mobile content ("Enabler Release Definition for DRM V2.0.", 2003). Nevertheless, these RELs have not been extensively used in applications, despite the fact that many businesses suffer from problems that could be solved using appropriate DRM technologies. For instance, Apple and Microsoft have created their own lightweight DRM technologies, iTunes and Windows Media DRM, respectively, that do not make use of any commercially available REL. Lack of standardized general purpose RELs has been one of the major reasons for the fragmented nature of the DRM industry.

The fragmented nature of the DRM industry, in turn has led to a lack of interoperability, and this is one of the major reasons for limited acceptance of DRM among content users. RELs play a major role in influencing the design of DRM systems. To understand the problems with DRM systems, it is therefore necessary to understand the process underlying the development of RELs, along with their role in DRM systems. There are many aspects to the process of developing a REL, which aims to map the rights requirements to a machine-readable language that is sufficiently expressive to capture these requirements. These properties include the structure, syntax, and semantics, among many other features of RELs. In this paper, we study the factors that influence the design of RELs, in terms of these properties, and how these properties, in turn affect each other and the design of DRM systems.

There has been other literature on this topic, especially ones that provide a comprehensive survey of RELs. Coyle (2004) provides an overview of the different elements of RELs along with important ways to analyze RELs. The discussion is based on four leading REL initiatives of the time, namely, ODRL, XrML, Creative Commons

and METS Rights. Guth (2003) provides a similar analysis of RELs, along with additional discussion on applications supplemented with examples on sample licenses of different RELs. Barlas (2006), similarly, provides a comprehensive discussion on the role of RELs, along with an explanation of different RELs along with various standards adopted. Wang (2005) provides an analysis on the design principles of RELs, in which several issues such as interoperability, extensibility, identification, etc. are discussed. Jamkhedkar, Heileman, and Martinez-Ortiz (2006) provide another view for the design of RELs, in which they propose refactoring and simplification of RELs to allow easy interoperability and formalization. This paper provides a different approach in which it discusses different stages in the development of RELs, along with an emphasis on formal rights expression calculus.

The rest of the paper is divided into four sections followed by the conclusions. The following section provides the history of the attempts to develop RELs, along with the current RELs developed in industry and academia. This is followed by a section that provides an overview of the process of the development of a REL. After that we discuss the development of a conceptual model for rights, and the issues involved in the process. In Section "Formalization of RELs", we discuss two types of RELs, namely XML-based and logic-based, and how formalization is achieved in these RELs. This is followed by a discussion on, how the decisions in the process of development of RELs affect the DRM system properties such as trust management, interoperability, and other system properties. Finally, we provide some useful conclusions.

AN OVERVIEW OF RIGHTS EXPRESSION LANGUAGES

Some of the earliest attempts to develop a formal language for expression of legal discourse date back to the late1980's. McCarthy (1989) proposed a Language for Legal Discourse (LLD) that was based on a logical framework. The central idea underlying LLD was to develop a deep conceptual model. Such a model is created by selecting a small set of common categories such as, space, time, action, permissions, obligations, constraints, and so on, relevant to a particular legal domain, and then developing a knowledge representation language that reflects the structure of this set.

A legal domain that gained increasing interest in the early 1990's was copyright law. Radical changes in information technology coupled with the evolution of the Internet drastically disturbed the hitherto maintained balance between intellectual property owners and consumers. Intellectual property owners pressured technologists to develop effective DRM systems to prevent violation of copyright by consumers. The central requirement of any DRM system is a machine-readable knowledge representation language for copyright contracts, known RELs (Jamkhedkar and Heileman, 2004). Rights enforcement mechanisms, operating on consumer devices, interpret copyright statements written in these languages to manage usage of intellectual property by consumers.

The precursors of the current RELs were developed in the early 1990's to address this requirement. In 1994, Stefik and Casey (1994) filed a patent for DRM technology he developed at Xerox PARC. This included the description of a "usage rights grammar" that was subsequently implemented in LISP and called the Digital Rights Property Language (DRPL). Through a evolutionary process DPRL became XrML. Specifically, in 1998, an eXtensible Markup Language (XML) implementation of DRPL (version 2.0) was released by Xerox PARC. Then, in 2000, ContentGuard, a Xerox/Microsoft joint venture, released XrML version 1.0, an evolution of DRPL 2.0. In 2002 ContentGuard released XrML version 2.0, a radical departure from all of the preceding versions. XrML 2.0 included an abstract rights

language with very few core elements. The rights elements from previous versions were carried forward in this new version via an extension called the Content Extension. Finally, In 2003, the Motion Picture Experts Group (MPEG) released MPEG-21 Part 5, Rights Expression Language (ISO/IEC 21000-5), a substantially modified version of XrML 2.0 in which the Content Extension is removed, and a MultiMedia Extension appears in its place ("Information technology—multimedia framework (MPEG-21)", 2001).

A similar evolution took place with respect to ODRL. Iannella introduced ODRL in 2000 out of concern for the closed approaches that were being used for DRM (Ianella, 2000) XML-based ODRL version 0.5 was released at that time as a work in progress, with the goals of providing clear DRM principles focused on interoperability across multiple sectors and support for fair-use doctrines. In 2001, ODRL Version 1.0 was submitted to ISO/IEC MPEG in response to a call for a rights data dictionary (RDD)--REL. By that time, Nokia's Mobile Rights Voucher and Real Networks' Extensible Media Commerce Language had been merged into the language. Then, in 2002, an Open Mobile Alliance (OMA) REL, based on ODRL 1.1, was proposed and called the OMA DRM 1.0 Enabler Release. ODRL 1.1 was also submitted to the W3C regarding possible chartering of a DRM/Rights Language activity within the W3C. By 2004, OMA released the OMA DRM 2.0 Enabler Release working drafts that addressed expanded device capabilities, improved support for audio/video rendering, streaming content, and access to protected content using multiple devices.

XrML and ODRL are the major RELs that are trying to become standardized in the digital content management industry. Each of these RELs has formed alliances with the major players in the industry and the standards bodies. Products and services companies such as Microsoft, OverDrive, Zinio Systems, DMDsecure, Integrated Management Concepts, and Content Works, have publicly announced to build products that are XrML compliant. Standards bodies such as the Motion Pictures Experts Group (MPEG) and the Organization for the Advancement of Structured Information Standards (OASIS) also endorse XrML. The International Digital Publishing Forum (IDPF), an international trade and standards organization for the digital publishing industry, has selected XrML as a basis for its rights grammar specification. The Organization for the Advancement of Structured Information Standards (OASIS), is a global consortium that drives development and convergence of open standards for global information society. OASIS has defined a token profile, which describes the syntax and processing rules for the use of licenses with the Web Services Security. It requires the processor of a license to conform to the required validation and processing rules defined in ISO/IEC 21000-5 REL, which is based on XrML ("Web services security rights expression languages token profile 1.1.", 2006). XrML is a patented technology, and ContentGuard Inc. requires a patenting license for its usage. ODRL on the other hand supports open and free standards, and aims to participate in the standards groups to achieve a royalty-free rights specification mechanism. ODRL enjoys the backing of industry players such as, Real Networks, Nokia, IBM, Panasonic, and Adobe. OMA DRM 2.0 and RSA Security also endorse ODRL.

Both ODRL and XrML are XML-based general-purpose RELs. Since these RELs are general purpose, their design is meant to be flexible and expandable. A flexible REL ensures copyright statements of different DRM environments can be expressed. Whereas, an expandable REL can be added with new types of copyright statements that may be required by DRM applications in the future. There are, however, a number of other RELs that are designed to be used for a specific application, business model, or content format.

One such example is the Adobe Lifecycle Server, which manages information access with dynamic and persistent access control over documents created in Adobe's Protable Document Format (PDF) ("Adobe® LiveCycle® ES Rights Management", 2006). The Adobe Lifecycle Server allows authors to create documents, and assign permissions that specify a recipient's level of access over the documents. It also allows authors to revoke rights, change rights, and change expiry date, without having to reissue the documents after they are distributed. The Publishing Requirements for the Industry Standard Metadata (PRISM) defines the XML metadata for managing, describing and aggregating documents related to the publishing industry. These include magazines, books, journals, news, catalog, etc. PRISM has refrained from recommending the use of any general purpose REL, because of the lack of emergence of any one REL, such as XrML or ODRL, as the accepted standard ("The PRISM Rights Language Name Space.", 2005). Therefore, the PRISM working group has created a small REL, called the PRISM Rights Language (PRL), that focuses on specifying a small set of elements that encodes the most common rights information ("The PRISM Rights Language Name Space.", 2005). Apple, with its Fairplay technology, has accomplished one of the most economically successful implementations of DRM, in the video and music industry. Apple does not make use of any commercially available general purpose REL, and instead, uses its own proprietary solution. Little information is available on how the Fairplay technology expresses and manages the usage rights of users, most of which are implicit in the system implementation.

A REL expresses statements in a copyright agreement in a machine-readable form. Most of the RELs used in the industry are based on XML. XML is a general-purpose specification for creation of specific markup languages. In an XML based REL, different terms occurring in copyright statements are represented as XML elements in a *Type-Value* form. The *Type*, which represents the semantics of different terms in copyright statements, is called *metadata*. Copy-

Figure 1. A sample XrML license. ("XrML 2.0 Technical Overview", 2002)

```
<license>
  <grant>
    <keyHolder>
      <info>
        <dsig:KeyValue>
          <dsig:RSAKeyValue>
            <dsig:Modulus>kjgHkjhsdkjG23HsdfhHkljHadff<dsig:Modulus>
            <dsig:Exponent>HJKH423HJ</dsig:Exponent>
          </dsig:RSAKeyValue>
        </dsig:KeyValue>
      </info>
    </keyHolder>
    <cx:view/>
    <cx:digitalWork>
      <cx:locator>
        <URI="http://www.ece.unm.edu/drake/samplePaper.pdf"/>
      </cx:locator>
    </cx:digitalWork>
    <validityInterval>
      <notAfter> 2008-6-15T1:00:00</notAfter>
    </validityInterval>
  </grant>
</license>
```

right statements are then expressed by storing XML elements in a tree-like structure as shown in Figure 1. For DRM to work in an open, distributed and interoperable environment, it is essential that metadata is unambiguously understood by different computers enforcing rights in a given license, and semantics of the metadata are in accordance with the meaning intended by rights issuers. To achieve this goal, it is necessary to develop a common metadata dictionary of terms involved in copyright statements, called Rights Data Dictionary (RDD). The <indecs>RDD is a consortium based initiative that aims to develop such a RDD ("<indecs>rdd White Paper.", 2002). The MPEG-21 Part 6 Standard for Rights Data Dictionary has selected <indecs>RDD as its baseline ("<indecs>rdd White Paper.", 2002). The dictionary aims to standardize the terms involved in rights expressions that can be unambiguously expressed, and applied across different domains where rights need to expressed and enforced.

Semantics of XML-based languages are informal. Hence, it is not possible to reason about rights expressed in XML-based RELs. To answer questions such as, *"Are rights statements A and B semantically equivalent?" "Is it possible to express copyright statement x, in language A?", "What is the set of all action sequences that are allowed by rights statement x?",* and so on, it is necessary to follow a more formal approach for rights expression.

To address this issue, academicians have tried to design RELs using more formal approaches such as logic, set theory, algebraic methods, just to name a few (Arnab and Hutchison, 2007; Chong et al., 2003; Gunter, Weeks and Wright, 2001; Hilty, Pretschner, Basin, Schaefer, and Walter, 2007; Holzer, Katzenbeisser, and Schallhart, 2004; Pucella and Weissman, 2002). The use of these methods not only provides a machine-readable and actionable REL, but also allows using the well-established results in these theories to reason about the resulting RELs. Such a level of formal reasoning is necessary in order to answer the kind of questions mentioned above. Later, we provide a detailed discussion on these approaches, along with the trade-offs involved in the process.

Since RELs are the communication languages of DRM systems, their design, expressive power, limitations, expression format, and other such attributes influence the structure and properties of DRM systems in a significant manner. As mentioned previously, numerous RELs have been developed in industry and academia. While the industry has taken a practical approach of using the less formal, albeit machine-readable, XML format for RELs, academicians have taken a purist approach by using a logical basis for developing RELs. The use of RELs in the industry is still fragmented and none of the general purpose RELs, such as ODRL and XrML, is used extensively in the market (Jamkhedkar, Heileman and Martinez-Ortiz, 2006). Additionally, general-purpose RELs are quite complex and bulky, which makes it extremely difficult to formalize them (Halpern and Weissman, 2004, 2008). Most of the closed DRM environments, on the other hand, use custom-made RELs that suit their application. There are a number of steps involved in transforming rights requirements into a REL and the subsequent use of REL in DRM systems. In the next section, we provide an outline of the process and design decisions in the development of RELs.

The Role of REL in DRM Systems

DRM Systems aim to manage rights associated with digital content. Content rendering environments (or machines in those environments) ensure that content is used in accordance with the rights associated with it. For DRM systems to work effectively, it is necessary for content creators and distributors to be able to expresses the intended rights associated with digital content in a machine-readable form, and digital content rendering environments must be able to interpret and enforce these rights. RELs are used for this purpose in DRM systems. This section provides an overview of the stages that are involved in the development of RELs for DRM systems. The development of a REL involves many steps that transform copyright requirements to a formal, machine-readable, and actionable language that operates within a complete DRM system.

Figure 2 provides an overview of the different stages of development of an REL. The first step is to gather the set of requirements that capture the different types of rights expression statements that are necessary in DRM systems. The set of requirements must reflect the copyright model that need to be supported by the DRM system, which will use the REL. There are many opinions regarding the types of copyright statements that need to be supported by an REL ("MPEG-21 Requirements for a RDD and an REL", 2001; "ODRL Version 2 Requirements", 2005; Parrott, 2001). It is easy to define a small set of such copyright statements for RELs that are developed for specific DRM applications, and operate within a well-defined business model. However, agreeing on such a small set for a general-purpose REL is much more difficult. A general purpose REL is expected to be flexible enough to express various types of rights expression scenarios that may be necessary in different applications. The most general requirement RELs is the ability to express rights and obligations for a given agent over a digital object under different conditions.

Once the requirements are agreed upon, the next step is to develop a conceptual model, as proposed by McCarty (1989), which comprises of a small set of common categories that are abstracted out of the requirements. For a general-purpose REL, the elements of this set need to be abstract enough to ensure that the resulting REL has enough flexibility to be used in different environments. Some of the common categories may include *rights, obligations, agents, actions, digital objects, time and space*, to name a few. The next step is to define relationships among the different entities of this set. Figure 3 shows one way to define the relationship among the set of entities defined by *Subject, Object, Operation and Constraints* (Chong et al., 2003) A conceptual model defines the scope and boundaries of the resulting REL to a great extent. Even though XrML and ODRL are XML-based RELs, they differ in their scope, and hence their expression capabilities, because they are based on different conceptual models.

Figure 2. Different stages in the development of an REL. Rights requirements are mapped to a conceptual model, which is then transformed in a language. The language is then integrated in a DRM system.

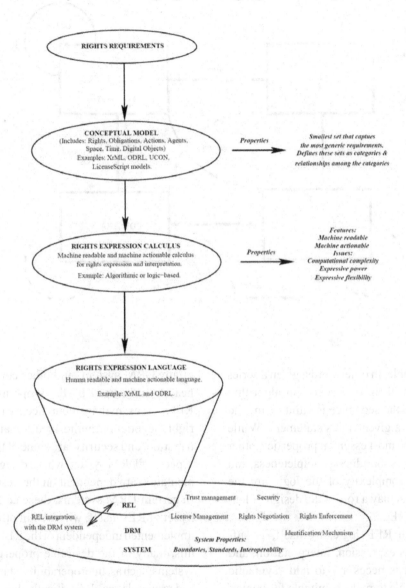

A conceptual model captures entities in the application domain along with the relationship among these entities. Once such a model is in place, a logic (or calculus) is defined over the model that allows expressing copyright statements in terms of the entities defined in the model. This is the phase that involves the design of REL grammar

and enforcement algorithm. The properties that the REL logic needs to satisfy determine the degree of formalism and expressive power of the resulting REL. The Most essential properties that need to be satisfied by all REL logics are a) the syntax must be machine readable (or map to a machine readable syntax), and b) the logic

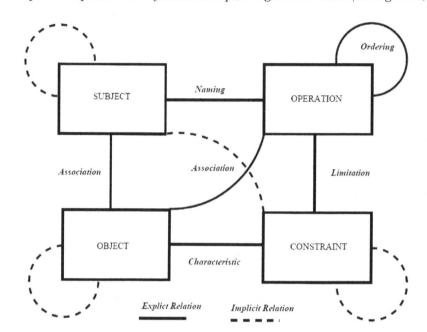

Figure 3. A simple conceptual model of LicenseScript, a logic based REL. (Chong et al., 2003)

must be actionable. In other words, given a series of user actions, there must exist an algorithm to determine if the sequence is valid or invalid with respect to a given rights statement. While these two are the most essential properties, other properties such as soundness, completeness, and computational complexity of the logic are the other factors that play a role in the design of logics underlying RELs.

Even though REL logic, by itself, is sufficient for rights expression, interpretation, and enforcement, it is necessary to add "syntactic sugar" to the logic to make it suitable for human comprehension. While this step may seem rudimentary, it is needed to enable the rights owner to specify copyright easily, and for the user to understand the rights and obligations associated with a digital object.

RELs operate in complex DRM systems, where they interact with various other components. In addition to that, RELs form a central component of any DRM system, and other components are heavily influenced by the scope and design of RELs. Trust management, license management, rights negotiation, authorized domains, superdistribution, and security, are some of the important aspects of DRM system whose design and implementation are dependent on the design of RELs. In certain DRM systems, these components are a part of REL itself, whereas, in others, they are implemented independent of the REL. Apart from this, many of the desirable properties of DRM systems, such as, interoperability, standardization, and protocols are also critically dependent on the design of RELs. RELs influence the design of DRM systems to a great extent. Therefore, while designing an REL, it is necessary to take these factors into consideration.

Many RELs have not followed all the steps mentioned above in their process of development. For example, even though XrML and ODRL have rigorously considered most of the requirements for rights expressions, they have paid little attention to the development of a solid logical basis for these languages. This has forced many researchers to reverse engineer and construct a logic based calculus for a significant portion of these languages (Halpern and Weissman, 2004, 2008; Holzer, Katzenbeisser, and Schallhart, 2004; Pucella and Weissman, 2006). There are also some greenfield attempts to construct REL logics. The focus of these attempts however has been quite narrow, and they fail to explain a sound conceptual model which captures the requirements, or discuss the boundaries of RELs, and system properties that an REL need to satisfy in order to be used in a DRM system.

All the steps mentioned above, aim to capture different aspects of RELs. Over emphasis on any particular step will influence the results in the others. For example, on the one hand, it is very difficult to create a formal logic for a highly complicated conceptual model, and on the other hand, a over simplified model is unable to capture all the requirements of rights expression. Certain RELs many not even require to undergo all the processes in order to achieve satisfactory results. In order to balance these trade-offs, it is necessary to understand the properties, requirements, goals, and trade-offs with respect to each of the steps shown in Figure 2. In the rest of the paper we will discuss each of these steps in detail, along with supporting examples, starting with the requirements and conceptual model in the next section.

Conceptual Model

A conceptual model over which an REL is based aims to capture the entities in the copyright domain and defines relationships among these entities. Since the model is created on the basis of the copyright domain, it is first necessary to define what constitutes a copyright domain. A copyright domain consists of copyright agreements over intellectual property (IP) between an IP owner

and an IP user. In traditional environments, these statements are written in natural languages. It is not possible to create a formal conceptual model based on a domain that is not well defined. It is therefore necessary to first define the scope of copyright domain over which the model will be developed. In this section, we discuss the principles over which the boundaries of this domain are determined, the trade-offs involved deciding the features included in this set, and finally the factors that are affected by the structure of the conceptual model.

The scope of the copyright domain is defined by specifying what concepts lie within the domain, and what concepts lie strictly outside the domain. Defining the scope has been a contentious subject, with a number of different opinions provided. The scope depends on a number of factors such as, type of digital objects, application environment, business model, etc. If these constraints are known, it is easier to define the scope of the domain. For example, the Open eBook Forum (OeBF) has detailed description about the requirements for rights grammar for expressing copyright over eBooks (Barlas et al., 2003). However, the task is much more difficult for general purpose RELs that are supposed to be used in all types of applications. One of the most comprehensive literatures on requirements for general purpose REL is provided in response to the call by proposals by MPEG for requirements for Rights Data Dictionary (RDD) and REL (Parrott, 2001). Requirement documents contain in detail the features that need to be supported by RELs such as, types of constraints, usage rights, obligation specification, pricing models, superdistribution, trust management, security protocols, and so on. There have also been suggestions of RELs having capabilities of carrying out rights negotiations (Arnab and Hutchison, 2005a, 2005b).

There are two dimensions to the problem deciding the scope of the copyright domain. First, what are the factors that decide whether a given feature must be included in the copyright domain or not?

Second, once the scope is defined, how does it affect the other processes in REL development such as formalization and the integration of the language within a DRM system?

The scope defines what features must be included within a given REL, and what features must be left out. To address the first problem, it is necessary to understand what happens to the features that are left out of a given REL. The features that are within an REL are expressed as rights statements, and the ones that are left out are implemented as separate protocols, or they are hard-coded within a DRM system. For example, XrML provides the facility to express security features, such as the encryption algorithm used to encrypt the content, within the language. If this feature is left out in a given REL, then it can be implemented in a DRM system as a separate protocol independent of that REL. Another example is that of authorized domains, which represent a set of devices over which a user can legally render content. This feature can be included within the language, to allow specification of devices in an authorized domain. If the feature is left out of an REL, then it can be hard coded in the system, in a manner similar to the one used by Apple's Fairplay technology, which restricts the use of a purchased song to a set of user registered devices.

Including a feature within the language offers a number of advantages. First of all it allows a more fine-grained expression of copyright statements. Any feature that is left out of the language has to be expressed over complete licenses, and cannot be expressed over parts of copyright statements in a given license. For example, if expression of authorized domain is kept out of REL, then it is not possible to specify that 2 different rights in a given license are valid over different sets of device domains. To implement a particular feature, in a DRM system, that is not a part of REL, requires development of a separate set of protocols, and mechanisms to link those features back to licenses. For example, suppose that payment obligations are not a part of RELs. In such a case, it is necessary

develop protocols to convey the payment obligation information for each license separately to the user. In addition to that, separate mechanism is necessary to track user payment actions and provide them as an input to the rights enforcement mechanisms, along with the information specifying what user actions (i.e. payments made by the user) relate to what licenses. It is much easier to make payment obligations a part of REL, where user actions can be tracked and managed by a single rights enforcement mechanism.

If a feature is included in an REL, it creates dependency of that feature on the rights enforcement mechanism, leading to lack of choice and inflexibility in the system. If any changes are desired in that feature, it requires changes to be made in the language. For example, assume that the content encryption-key exchange protocol in included in the REL. In such a situation, if a different key exchange protocol is desired, it can be implemented only by bringing about changes in the language. Such a dependency on RELs is not favorable, as it leads to rigid solutions that are incapable of rapid evolution.

The second problem is deciding how the scope of the domain affects the remaining steps of REL development. The more features an REL has, the more expressive it is, and hence can be used in different applications and business models. These qualities are desirable in general purpose RELs, which explains why languages such as ORDL and XrML have so many features. Another advantage of having a lot of features within the language makes DRM system development much easier, without having to worry about the overhead of managing the features separately, and linking them to the rights enforcement mechanisms.

However, a language having a large scope is not desirable either. Bulky languages lead to rigid, monolithic systems. In other words, the system depends too much on the language. Any changes in the system require corresponding changes in the language, as explained earlier. Another obstacle in having a language with large scope including many features is the difficulty in development of logic for a conceptual model based on such a large domain. XrML and ODRL are the general-purpose languages that have a large scope that includes features beyond rights expression. Researchers agree that formalization of all the parts of these languages is impractical and too difficult to achieve (Halpern and Weissman, 2004, 2008). Formalization and easy integration with the system are necessary REL features for DRM interoperability, as shall be shown in the following sections. Hence, on the one hand, a language with a small scope is unable to express many of the desired features of copyright statements, while on the other hand, a bulky language is difficult to formalize and manage within the system. It is therefore necessary to carefully determine the scope of the copyright domain, on which an REL is based, taking into consideration all these factors.

Once the scope is decided, most common categories within the domain must be identified to the desired level of abstraction. For example, in case of ODRL, some of the common categories identified are as follows: *rights, assets, party, permission, duty, prohibition, constraints, etc.* There are trade offs involved in the level of abstraction involved in identifying these categories. A high level of abstraction with very few categories will make the language simple, but impractical. On the other hand, a low level of abstraction with too many categories will make the language expressive, but too complex to model.

Once the categories are identified, the next step is to define relationships among these categories. The type of relationship defined among the entities determines whether the resulting language can express certain scenarios or not. The structure of the conceptual model determines the ability to capture and express aspects of copyright statements such as hierarchical relationships, sequencing of rights and obligations, inheritance semantics, matching of rights to users on the one side and digital objects on the other, matching

of constraints to rights, and so on. For example, structure of the conceptual model determines whether it is possible to express the following rights statement:

If a set of users, A enjoy rights $x_1, \ldots, x_n$ over a digital object K, then any user a belonging to A enjoys rights $x_1, \ldots, x_n$ over any part of K.

It is not possible to express this statement in an REL based on a model whose structure does not support hierarchical relationships. As mentioned earlier, the more complex the structure of a model, the harder it is to create an REL logic based on that model. RELs with XML syntax, which are less formal, can afford to have a large domain scope, and a complex structure for their conceptual model. On the other hand, logic-based RELs, which are more formal, avoid these complex relationships to keep the structure simple and easy to formalize. Figure 3 shows the complex conceptual model for ODRL, which is a XML-based REL. On the other hand, LicenseScript, a logic-based REL, has a much simpler conceptual model, as shown in Figure 4.

It is desirable to have a large scope and a complex structure for the conceptual model on which the REL is based upon. It allows including various concepts and offering versatility in REL expression capabilities. These qualities are certainly beneficial for a general purpose REL, which is used in different applications and business models. The only impediment in this approach is posed by formalization, and managing system properties, such as flexibility and interoperability. It is therefore necessary to understand the importance of these factors and the problems that might arise if they are not taken into consideration. The next section explains the importance of formalization and various approaches taken to achieve it, along with the trade-offs involved.

Figure 4. A complex conceptual model of ODRL, an XML-based REL. ("Open Digital Rights Language Version 2.0", 2008)

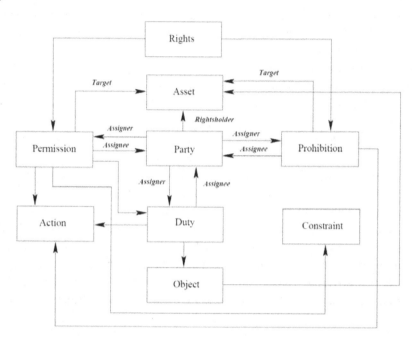

FORMALIZATION OF RELs

A conceptual model reflects the structure of the relationship among the entities that exist in a copyright domain. Such a conceptual model forms the basis upon which a rights expression language is designed to express copyright statements. Natural languages provide enough flexibility to easily express most of the copyright terms, and they are also comprehensible to the human mind. These languages, however, are not suitable for rights expression in DRM systems, where rights are managed not by humans, but by machines. Apart from power of expression, RELs need to satisfy a number of other requirements that necessitate varying degrees of "formalness". In this section, we discuss these requirements starting with the ones that are absolutely necessary to the ones that can be compromised. We will further discuss how these requirements affects the other features of REL design.

Two of the most important features of a language are syntax and semantics. Syntax decides the rules for generating the set of valid strings (i.e. grammatically correct copyright statements in case of RELs) in the language. A language is decidable if it can be determined whether or not a particular string belongs to the set of valid strings in the language. Semantics refer to the meaning behind valid sentences in a language. An REL is machine-readable if it is decidable, and a machine can interpret its semantics. Machine readability is the central requirement for RELs used in DRM systems. An REL is actionable, if it is machine readable and there exists an algorithm to determine if a sequence of actions is valid or invalid with respect to a given rights statement expressed in the REL.

Natural languages do not have a formal syntax, which rules them out as a choice for RELs. In other words, it is extremely difficult for a machine to determine if a rights statement expressed in a natural language is syntactically correct or not. Other than the syntax, the semantics of natural language can be ambiguous in certain cases, which is also a reason why they are not used for rights expression. Hence, formal approaches are taken to for rights expression, such as XML-based or logic-based, instead of using natural languages.

XML-Based RELs

The power of expression and flexibility offered by natural languages is still a major incentive to use them for rights expression. One of the ways to overcome the obstacle of informal syntax of natural languages is to restrict their expressive power, capture the most common structure of rights expression statements, and formalize the syntax. Steps 1 and 2 can be achieved by developing a conceptual model, and restricting the rights expression statements to be expressed only in terms of the categories used in the model. Once this is done, the structure of the conceptual model and that of the rights statements is captured in a formal syntax.

One of the ways to capture the structure of the rights statements in a formal syntax is to present it in a markup language whose structure reflects the structure of the conceptual model. A descriptive markup can capture the logical structure of rights statements (or a license). To create a descriptive markup, elements of rights statements are identified and tagged accordingly. For example, consider the rights statement:

Alice has the right to play the song "Hotel California".

To markup this sentence, *"Alice"* is tagged as the **USER**, *"play"* is tagged as the **RIGHT**, and *"Hotel California"* is tagged as the **DIGITAL OBJECT**. Such a tagging method allows the rights enforcement mechanism to separate and identify various elements, along with their relationship with each other. eXtensible Markup Language

(XML), allows user defined tagged elements to be represented in a unranked tree structure. XML has a formal syntax and languages based on XML are decidable (Berstel and Boasson, 2002). XrML and ODRL are two of the prominent XML-based RELs. Figure 1, shows a sample XrML license.

It is important to understand what are *not* the capabilities of markup languages. Markup languages are not a computational automaton, a data model, or a mathematical formalism (Raymond, Tompa, and Wood, 1995). Markup languages simply allow associating different elements with their respective tags, and defining relationships among these elements in terms of an unranked tree structure. Markup languages *do not* define the semantics underlying the data they present. The semantics of XML-based RELs such as XrML, are hence defined informally by means of an accompanying documentation that describes the meaning behind the tags. XrML documentation that provides prose explanation of the meaning of the tags in XrML is informal, and may lead to ambiguity. The *Authorization Algorithm* implicitly captures the formal aspects of the semantics of XrML, which is used to enforce rights. The same argument applied to ODRL.

Before discussing formal semantics, it is first necessary to define the requirements of formal semantics in terms of RELs. This is necessary, because, the nature of these requirements will decide the degree of formalism expected in the REL calculus. The most basic requirement in terms of formal semantics is: *Unambiguous interpretation of rights statements irrespective of the external conditions.* In other words, the interpretation of a rights statement is always the same, and is not influenced by, who interprets it, in what environment it is interpreted, or at what point of time it is interpreted. This means, under similar external conditions, the set of actions permitted by a given rights statement always remains the same.

As mentioned earlier, XML-based RELs do not have formal semantics. In order to have order to achieve that, one approach is to construct a layer of semantics, based on some mathematical formalism, over these languages. The main constructs available in *XML* are: "containment" (hierarchy), "adjacency" (A 'followed by' B), "co-occurrence" (if A then [also/not] B), "attribute", and "opaque reference". These constructs allow limited expressive power for modeling rights statements, however, its extensible tree structure allows tremendous flexibility. The mathematical formalism that is used to provide formal semantics to XML-based RELs must be able to capture these constructs. Flexibility provided by XML is exploited by these RELs, which has resulted in them having a large scope. Such a large scope makes it impossible to provide formal semantics to all parts of the language. As a result, researchers have been successful in providing formal semantics to only parts of XrML and ODRL. The other approach is to use mathematical logic, which provides in-built semantics to express many complex concepts and reason about them.

Logic-Based RELs

Developing a formal calculus for rights expression, interpretation, and enforcement can eliminate ambiguous syntax and semantics. Grammar of a language associates a structure for each of the strings in the language. This structure is then used to determine the semantics of those strings. A grammar that associates more than one structure for a particular string is said to be ambiguous. Since the string is associated with more than one structure, the semantics of the string also become ambiguous. Therefore, in order to avoid ambiguous semantics, it is necessary for the REL to have an unambiguous syntax.

The inherent semantic constructs available in XML are limited, and the remaining interpretation either depends on the intuition of the reader or is implicitly captured by the enforcement algorithm. Mathematical logic, on the other hand, provides tools to create languages where a significant number of deductions can be made

from the structure of the strings in the language itself. Different types of mathematical logics are available such as Propositional logic, first-order logic, modal logic, etc. Each of these logics can express different types of concepts along with precise semantics to capture these concepts. For example, Propositional logic allows to express relationship among sentences using sentential connectives, first order logic, in addition to the capabilities of Propositional logic, allows to express the fine grained structure that exists within each of the sentences, and modal logic allows to model action, temporal, spatial, deontic, and other such concepts. Since these concepts have well defined semantics in these logics, their interpretation across different systems is precise and consistent. An REL calculus must therefore aim to model the language in such a way that most of the concepts in the conceptual model are defined be means of these logics, with minimal dependence on intuition and enforcement algorithm for capturing the semantics. Once these concepts are captured in these logics, it is possible to reason about other properties of the rights statements expressed in the calculus.

The ultimate goal of a rights owner is to ensure that the user uses the content in accordance with the copyright agreement. For this purpose, rights statements in the copyright agreement are encoded in a machine-readable form by the use of an REL. It is therefore necessary to prove that the action sequences permitted conform to the ones specified in the copyright statements. Apart from this, it is also essential to be able to prove whether or not a particular rights statement can be expressed using a certain REL. While these requirements are sufficient for RELs, which are tailor-made and used in standalone DRM systems, more requirements are necessary in interoperable DRM systems. In interoperable DRM systems, it is necessary to check whether a given rights statement A in one language is semantically equivalent to another rights statement B in another REL. Also, it is also sometimes necessary to generate a rights statement in one REL, which is semantically equivalent to another statement in some different REL. In terms of semantic equivalence, it is also essential to know whether a given statement is a subset of another statement in terms of action sequences permitted. To solve this problem it must be possible to generate all the valid action sequences for a given rights statement.

It is extremely difficult to address these issues in RELs where most of the semantics are informally described or implicitly captured by an authorization algorithm. Mathematical logic, on the other hand, has precise semantics, and well-established methods for verification, a process of determining the correctness of the system built. In terms of rights expression, these methods can be employed to determine the above-mentioned properties of rights statements, which are expressed in mathematical logic. There are two approaches for verification, one is *proof-based,* and the other is *model-based.* In a proof-based approach, the license (consisting of rights statements), is expressed as a set of formulas Γ. The property to be verified is expressed as another formula φ. Formal proof techniques are used to determine if it is possible to prove that φ follows from Γ (i.e., $\Gamma \vdash \varphi$). In a model-based approach, the license is represented by a model M and the property is represented by a formula φ. Verification method consists of determining if the formula φ is satisfied by the model M (i.e., $M \vDash \varphi$).

An REL based on logic must try to capture most of the categories involved in the conceptual model. The ability to do so depends on the ability of the underlying logic to capture different semantics.

The most basic of all the types of logics is the Propositional logic. Propositional logic is a calculus for reasoning about formulas created out of simple propositions connected by sentential connectives (e.g., *and, or, implication, negation, etc.*)The grammar is defined using the standard Backaus Normal Form (BNF). Propositional logic allows to reason about compositions of different

propositions, but fails to capture the structure of the propositions themselves. For example:

If Alice is the user and Alice has made the payment, then Alice can play the song.

Let proposition x state that **Alice is the user**, proposition y state that **Alice has made the payments**, and proposition z state that **Alice can play the song.** In this case, Propositional logic can infer that for z to be true, both x and y needs to be true (i.e., **(x and y)** $\rightarrow z$). However the semantics that Alice is a user and Alice has made payments cannot be captured by Propositional logic. Hence for an REL based purely on Propositional logic, these semantics need to be conveyed to the enforcement engine by some mechanism that operates outside the REL.

These semantics can be captured within the calculus by Predicate logic, which builds upon Propositional logic. Predicate logic consists of propositions on objects of a universe. It consists of predicates that allow defining *n-ary relations* over the over the objects in the Universal set. Since the predicates are defined using variables, it is necessary to bind those variables to have definite truth-values for those predicates. This provision is made possible by the existential and universal quantifiers. A combination of predicates along with quantifiers allows Predicate logic to capture the semantics of statement x which says that **Alice is a user**. The expressive power of First Order Predicate logic is much greater than Propositional logic, and can capture the semantics of complex statements such as:

All members of group "grp" can play song "hotelClifornia" on all the devices in the authorized domain "home". Alice is a member of group "grp". Device "dev" belongs to the domain "home".

The above group of statements can be captured in Predicate logic, and it can be mathematically proved that Alice can play song *hotelCalifornia* on device *dev*.

member(Alice, grp).
belongs(dev, home).
play(M, hotelCalifornia, D) :- member (D, grp), belongs (D, home).

The First Order Predicate logic is powerful enough to capture the internal semantics sentences, and to model most of the concepts encountered in rights statements. It is possible to model concepts such as, time, actions, permissions, obligations, license states, etc., in First Order Predicate Logic. There are, however, other specialized logics, which provide inbuilt semantics to capture these concepts.

Validity of a license is, most of the times, never eternal. Actions permitted by a license depend on the state of the environment within which the license is applicable. Rights statements defined in a license are usually accompanied by a set of constraints for each right. The constraints can be defined in terms of abstract concepts such as time, space, numerical bounds, etc. Therefore, the right to exercise action on content changes, according to the changes in the state of the environment. For example, a license valid in the USA will be invalid when the user moves to a different country. Hence the change of state in the environment has been brought about by the user action of moving from one country to another. Many of the licenses are bound by the temporal constraints. A license may be valid, for instance, only during the weekends of a particular month, say January 2008. The rights in such a license change from being valid to invalid and back to valid during the month of January, as time progress, and will finally be invalid after the end of the month.

In Propositional and Predicate logic, the propositions are either true or false in a given model. Modal logic semantics, on the other hand, are able to capture different modes of truth. Semantics of Modal logic are based on Kripke structures, which

are directed graphs, where nodes represent different possible worlds, and the edges represent the accessibility relations. The validity of a proposition is never static, but changes depending on the world in question. The state and state changes in Modal logic can be used to model the change in the environment within which rights are enforced. For example, Linear Temporal Logic (LTL), which is a special case of Modal logic, can be used to model time over which the validity of licenses with respect to user actions can be studied and reasoned about.

Rights expression statements are mainly composed of permissions and obligations of a user with respect to digital content. Permissions and obligations can be modeled in Deontic logic which is also a special case of Modal logic (Huth and Ryan, 2002, p. 318-319). Deontic logic provides inbuilt semantics for *Obligation, Permission, Prohibition,* and *non-Obligation.* If these categories in rights statements are modeled in Deontic logic, it is possible to reason about them. Dynamic logic is another type of Modal logic that analyses change that occurs as a result of performing actions on the states in the world (Goldblatt, 1987; Harel, 1979). From the perspective of rights expression, interpretation, and enforcement, Dynamic logic can be used as a formal tool to model the rules of content usage, user actions on the content, and change in the environment as a result of user actions.

One of the earliest attempts to formalize RELs was proposed by Gunter, Weeks and Wright (2001). Gunter's model consists of sequence of events called realities that are checked against the language constructs, which are modeled as traces of permissible events. This mathematical model encodes simple licenses and includes payments and content rendering events. The idea is further expanded by Pucella and Weissman (2002), who propose a logic to reason about rights using trace-based semantics. The logic uses temporal operators to capture the temporal semantics such as "next time", "all times in future", "until", etc., and permission and obligation operators that attempt to capture deontic semantics. For model checking purposes, the authors reduce the logic to LTL, and apply existing verification mechanisms developed for LTL. Using this language as the basis, the authors also propose formal semantics for substantial fragments of XrML and ODRL (Halpern and Weissman, 2004; Pucella and Weissman, 2006). Another such approach to formalize ODRL, is proposed by Holzer, Katzenbeisser, and Schallhart (2004), who suggest the use of finite automata to capture a sequence of actions a user is allowed to perform according to a specific permission stated in the license.

LicenseScript is another formal REL, where licenses are represented in a multiset (Chong et al., 2003) The clauses in a license are expressed as logic programs and the state associated with these licenses are maintained as a separate set of bindings. LicenseScript is constructed over a well-defined conceptual model for rights. Licenses themselves are multiset rules, which reside in rendering devices. The communication between the device and license (i.e. the rights enforcement mechanism) is done by means of multiset rewrite rules. LicenseScript allows expression of dynamically evolving licesnses in complex environments, such as authorized domains.

Another approach to formalizing RELs has been to use and extend the well-developed concepts of access control mechanisms. Usage control is the extension of access control mechanisms that incorporates the semantics of access control, trust management, and DRM in a single framework. Park and Sandhu (2004), introduce the term "usage control", which extends traditional access control, to include trust management and DRM. They propose a usage control model, called $UCON_{ABC}$, that is based on *Authorizations, oBligations and Conditions*. Hilty et al. (2007), propose the use of usage control model as the basis for REL specification. These authors propose the Obligation Specification Language (OSL), which is based on the Z specification language for obli-

gations in policies for distributed usage control. They further define translations from OSL to a significant subset of ODRL, to provide a formal basis for the latter. Rights management is often termed as persistent access control. Arnab and Hutchison (2007) propose a language *LiREL* that uses set notion that builds upon access control mechanisms.

Other approaches in formalization of RELs involve the use of existing specification languages such as CafeOBJ. Xiang, Bjorner, and Futatsugi (2008) use CafeOBJ along with OTS (Observational Transition System) to express formal specification of RELs. OTSs are used to model transition systems in terms of equations, and CafeOBJ can be used to model abstract machines. OTS/CafeOBJ, thus provides a common framework for specifying static and dynamic properties of licenses, and existing theorem proving facilities provided by this framework is used to further reason about properties of licenses.

Role of REL in DRM Systems

RELs do not operate by themselves. An REL is a part of a complete DRM system that uses the REL for the purpose of expressing rights from a rights owner to a content user. It is the language of communication for DRM systems. The properties of an REL determine to a large extent the system properties of the DRM system that is built around it. These properties include the scope and boundaries, the structure of the conceptual model, and the format of rights expression. The design of DRM systems may include incorporation of trust management, license management, rights negotiations, superdistribution, and security. When content needs to be managed across different systems then issues such as interoperability and standardization also need to be addressed. In this section, we will analyze how the properties of REL impact these design issues concerning the DRM system that is built around it.

There is not a clear consensus in the research community over the boundaries and scope of RELs. Since REL is the communication language of DRM systems, one extreme view is to incorporate most features within the REL. XrML takes this approach, and provides features to manage trust and express security parameters. One of the reasons this approach is taken by general purpose RELs is to provide a all purpose, ready to use solution to the DRM system designers. Such an approach, however leads to a compromise in formalization, system flexibility and interoperability (Jamkhedkar, Heileman, and Martinez-Ortiz, 2006).

The bigger the scope of an REL, the more difficult it is to formalize it. For example, researchers have argued that formalization of complete XrML is too difficult to achieve (Halpern Weissman, 2008). As mentioned earlier, different organizations have adopted different RELs for their systems. Interoperability among these systems is necessary for a smooth flow of content and consumer satisfaction. Interoperability among RELs is essential to achieve DRM interoperability. As discussed in the earlier section, formalization of RELs is a prerequisite to translate licenses from one REL to another.

Another problem with the expanding scope of RELs is the flexibility of the systems that utilize such an REL. A bulky REL will force the DRM system built around it to be more monolithic and less modular. Any changes made in the system built around such an REL will mandate changes in the REL itself. For example, if security protocol parameters, such as encryption key information, encryption format etc., are included in the language, it will restrict the DRM system to follow these protocols. Bulky RELs thus undermine the flexibility of DRM systems that are built around them. While this is acceptable for standalone, closed applications, such features are undesirable in systems that are supposed to interoperate with other systems.

The categories defined in the conceptual model along with the relationship among those categories influence the design of the DRM system utilizing the REL. Enforcement of rights expressed by a given REL is possible only if the DRM system utilizing the REL is able to identify and resolve the categories and relationships defined in the conceptual model. For example, an REL with the ability to define hierarchical semantics, is not useful if the corresponding system is unable to create such hierarchies, name them, and resolve these hierarchies and their constituent elements. Consider an REL with the ability to define rights over authorized domains. Such an REL is not useful in a system that unable to create such authorized domains, name them and resolve their constituent devices. Therefore, it is necessary that the capability of rights expression is rightly matched by the DRM system using the REL.

Thus, the decisions taken in the process of design of an REL, change the properties of the language that results from such a process. These properties, in turn, determine how the REL will be incorporated in the DRM system, by influencing the DRM system properties.

CONCLUSION

The process of the design and development of RELs involves transformation of rights requirements into a machine-readable language to express rights. The central goal of this process is to create a language that is expressive enough to best reflect the rights requirements. It is pointed out in the paper, however, that the decisions taken to achieve this goal involve a number of trade-off that not only undermine other goals of REL, but also the system goals such as interoperability, and standardization. Because of these trade-offs it is not possible to create an REL, which simultaneously satisfies the goals of all the steps, which include expressive power, formalization, flexibility, etc. It will always be the case that over-emphasis on one of these properties will make it difficult for other to achieve. REL design should therefore be modularized in a manner so as to get the right balance of these properties that will eventually enable to achieve the ulterior goals of DRM systems.

REFERENCES

Adobe® LiveCycle® ES Rights Management for multiformat enterprise rights management. (2006, September). Adobe. Retrieved from http://www. adobe.com/products/livecycle/pdfs/95009150_ lc_es_rts_mngmt_multi_sb_ue.pdf.

Arnab, A., & Hutchison, A. (2005a, July). *Extending ODRL to Enable Bi-Directional Communication.* In Proceedings of the Second International ODRLWorkshop, Lisbon, Portugal.

Arnab, A., & Hutchison, A. (2005b, November). *Fairer usage contracts for DRM.* In Proceedings of the Fifth ACM Workshop on Digital Rights Management, pp. 1–7, Alexandria, VA, USA.

Arnab, A., & Hutchison, A. (2007, October). *Persistent Access Control: A Formal Model for DRM.* In DRM '07: Proceedings of the 2007 ACM workshop on Digital Rights Management, pp. 41–53, New York, NY, USA.

Barlas, C. (2006, May*). Digital Rights Expression Languages.* Rightscom Ltd. Retrieved from www. jisc.ac.uk/uploaded_documents/TSW0603.pdf.

Barlas, C., Coyle, K., Daz, T., Erickson, J., Gandee, B., Iannella, R., Kimmel, A., Mathews, R., McCoyd, E., Mooney, S., Parrott, D., Sajka, J., Samtani, R., Shaw, W., & Yaacovi, Y. (2003, March). *OeBF Rights Grammar Requirements.* OeBF. Retrived from www.idpf.org/specifications/coodinatedfiles/OeBF%20Rights%20Grammar%20Requirements. doc

Berstel, J., & Boasson, L. (2002). *Formal Properties of XML Grammars and Languages.* Acta Informatica, 38(9), 649–671.

Chong, C. N., Corin, R., Etalle, S., Hartel, P., Jonker, W., & Law, Y. W. (2003, September). *LicenseScript: A Novel Digital Rights Language and its Semantics.* In proceedings of the Third International Conference on the Web Delivery of Music, pages 122–129, Los Alamitos, CA USA.

Coyle, K., (2004, February). *Rights Expression Languages.* The Library of Congress, Retrieved from www.loc.gov/standards/relreport.pdf.

Enabler Release Definition for DRM V2.0. (2003). Open Mobile Alliance, Retrieved from http://xml. coverpages.org/OMA-ERELD_DRM-V2_0_0-20040401-D.pdf.

Goldblatt, R. (1987). *Logics of time and computation, 7.* Center for the Study of Language and Information, Stanford, CA, USA.

Gunter, C., Weeks, S., & Wright. A. (2001). *Models and Languages for Digital Rights.* In HICSS '01: Proceedings of the 34th Annual Hawaii International Conference on System Sciences (HICSS-34), 9, p. 9076, Washington, DC, USA.

Guth, S., (2003). *Rights Expression Languages.* In Digital Rights Management, *2770/2003*, pp. 101–112. Springer Berlin / Heidelberg.

Halpern, J. Y., & Weissman, V. (2004, June). *A Formal Foundation for XrML Licenses.* In Proceedings of the 17th IEEE Computer Security Foundations Workshop, pages 251–265, Asilomar, CA, USA.

Halpern, J. Y., & Weissman, V. (2008). *A Formal Foundation for XrML.* Journal of ACM, 55(1), 1–42.

Harel, D. (1979*). First-Order Dynamic Logic.* Springer-Verlag New York, Inc., Secaucus, NJ, USA.

Hilty, M., Pretschner, A., Basin, D., Schaefer, C., & Walter, T. (2007, September). *A Policy Language for Distributed Usage Control.* In Proceedings of the 12th European Symposium On Research

In Computer Security, pages 531–546, Dresden, Germany.

Holzer, M., Katzenbeisser, S., & Schallhart, C. (2004). *Towards Formal Semantics for ODRL.* In ODRLWorkshop, pages 137–148, Vienna, Austria.

Huth, M., & Ryan, M. (2000). *Logic in Computer Science: Modelling and Reasoning about Systems.* Cambridge University Press, Cambridge, England, 2000.

<indecs>rdd White Paper. (2002, May). <indecs>rdd, Retrieved from http://xml.coverpages.org/IndecsWhitePaper200205.pdf.

Iannella, R. (2000, August). *Open Digital Rights Language (ODRL),* Version 0.5, Retrieved from http://odrl.net/ODRL-05.pdf

Iannella, R. (2002, August). *Open Digital Rights Language (ODRL),* Version 1.1, Retrieved from http://odrl.net/1.1/ODRL-11.pdf.

MPEG-21 Requirements for a Rights Data Dictionary and a Rights Expression Language. (2001, July). International Organization for Standardization. ISO/IECJTC1/SC29/WG11 N4336, Sydney, Austraila.

The MPEG-21 Rights Expression Language – A White Paper. (2003, July). Rightscom Ltd. Retrieved from http://www.xrml.org/reference/MPEG21_REL_whitepaper_Rightscom.pdf

Jamkhedkar, P. A., & Heileman, G. L. (2004, October). *DRM as a Layered System.* In Proceedings of the Fourth ACM Workshop on Digital Rights Management, pages 11–21, Washington, DC, USA.

Jamkhedkar, P. A., Heileman, G. L., & Martinez-Ortiz, I. (2006, November). *The Problem with Rights Expression Languages.* In Proceedings of the Sixth ACM Workshop on Digital Rights Management, pages 59–67, Alexandria, VA, USA.

McCarty, L. T. (1989). *A Language for Legal Discourse I. Basic Features.* In ICAIL '89: Proceedings of the 2nd international conference on Artificial intelligence and law, pages 180–189, New York, NY, USA.

Information technology — multimedia framework (MPEG-21) — part 1: Vision, technologies and strategy. (2001, July). Reference number of working document: ISO/IEC JTC1/SC29/WG11 N 4333.

Open Digital Rights Language ODRL Version 2 Requirements. (2005, February). ODRL, Retrieved from http://odrl.net/2.0/v2req.html.

Park, J., & Sandhu, R. (2004). *The UCON$_{ABC}$ Usage Control Model.* ACM Transactions on Information and Systems Security, 7(1), 128–174.

Parrott, D. (2001, June). *Requirements for a Rights Data Dictionary and a Rights Expression Language.* Reuters, Retrieved from https://xml.coverpages.org/RLTC-Reuters-Reqs.pdf.

The PRISM Rights Language Name Space. (2005, February). PRISM, Retrieved from http://xml.coverpages.org/PRISM-RightsNamespaceV12.pdf.

Pucella, R., & Weissman, V. (2002, June). *A Logic for Reasoning about Digital Rights.* In Proceedings of the 15th IEEE Computer Security Foundations Workshop, pages 282–294, Nova Scotia, Canada.

Pucella, R., & Weissman, V. (2006, January). *A Formal Foundation for ODRL,* Cornell University, Ref: arxiv.org/abs/cs/0601085.

Raymond, D. R., Tompa, F. W., & Wood, D. (1995, March). *Markup Reconsidered.* Department of Computer Science, The University of Western Ontario, Retrieved from http://xml.coverpages.org/raymmark.ps

Stefik, M. J., & Casey, M. M. (1994, November). *System for Controlling the Distribution and Use of Digital Works.* Xerox Corporation, U.S. Patent No. 5,629,980.

Wang, X. (2005, July). *Design Principles and Issues of Rights Expression Languages for Digital Rights Management.* In Visual Communications and Image Processing 2005, *5960*, 1130–1141.

Web services security rights expression languages token profile 1.1. (2006). OASIS, Retrieved from http://docs.oasis-open.org/wss/oasis-wss-rel-token-profile-1.1.pdf.

Xiang, J., Bjorner, D., & Futatsugi, K. (2008, April). *Formal Digital License Language with OTS/CafeOBJ Method.* In Proceedings of the sixth ACS/IEEE International Conference on Computer Systems and Applications, Doha, Qatar.

XrML 2.0 Technical Overview, version 1.0. (2002, March). Retrieved from http://www.xrml.org/reference/XrMLTechnicalOverviewV1.pdf.

KEY TERMS

Conceptual Model: An abstract model that captures the entities, and relationship among the entities present in copyright statements.

Digital Rights Management (DRM): Management of copyright over digital content and services.

eXtensible Markup Language (XML): A general-purpose specification language that allows creating custom languages by defining language specific markups (or tags).

Interoperability: Capability of one independent DRM system to interface with other independent DRM system, and allow seamless flow of content.

Rights Expression Languages (RELs): Formal, machine-readable languages used for expressing copyright agreements in DRM systems.

Semantics: Meaning associated with the symbols and valid expressions in a language.

Superdistribution: Distribution of digital content along a chain of users, in such a way, that each user plays the role of both a consumer and a distributor.

Syntax: Structure, or form of valid expressions in a language.

Trust Management: Management of trust, in terms of rights and capabilities, among the entities in a given DRM system.

Chapter II
Digital Rights Management for Streaming Media

Deepali Brahmbhatt
San Jose State University, USA

Mark Stamp
San Jose State University, USA

ABSTRACT

This chapter presents a digital rights management (DRM) system designed for streaming media. A brief, general introduction to DRM is also provided, along with a discussion of the some specific issues that arise in the context of streaming media. The DRM system proposed here has been implemented and some details related to the implementation are discussed.

INTRODUCTION

For the purposes of this paper, digital rights management (DRM) can be viewed as an attempt to provide "remote control" over digital content. That is, DRM is supposed to make it possible to securely deliver digital content and to restrict the actions of the recipient after the data has been delivered.

Consider, for example, a digital book. Certainly, the publisher would like to deliver such a book over the Internet, since there is an enormous potential market and the costs of reproduction and delivery are negligible.

However, if an attacker can redistribute a perfect digital copy of the book, then the rate of piracy would almost certainly be intolerable—if not virtually 100%. An ideal DRM system (from the perspective of the copyright holder) would prevent the redistribution of the book in an unprotected form, and perhaps also enforce other restrictions, such as "no printing." Such an ideal DRM system is impossible, as noted in the indispensable paper by Biddle, et. al. (2002) and in Stamp (2002). The interesting question then is, what is the best practical DRM system? What is "best" depends on many factors, not all of which are strictly technical in nature. For example, the value of the content being protected, the technical sophistication of typical users, the overall business model, and the credibility of threats of legal reprisals greatly effect the utility of any DRM system; see Stamp (2003b) for a discussion of these and other non-technical DRM issues.

It is important to note a few salient issues concerning DRM. First, the fundamental requirement of a DRM system is that restrictions must be enforced after the content is delivered to the intended recipient. Since these restrictions must stay with the data wherever it goes, the buzzword for this DRM requirement is "persistent protection." This is in contrast to the usual cryptographic scenario, where the goal is simply to securely deliver the bits.

Second, the legitimate recipient is a potential attacker. This is also in stark contrast to the usual cryptographic situation, where the intended recipient (i.e., the entity that holds the corresponding decryption key) is a "good guy", not an attacker.

Third, cryptography is necessary, but far from sufficient for useful DRM. It is necessary to encrypt digital content in order to securely deliver the bits, and this is a part of any DRM system. However, securely delivering the bits is the easy part of DRM.

Cryptography alone is insufficient for effective DRM—to render the content, the recipient must access to the key, and the recipient is a potential attacker. Cryptography was not designed to solve this problem, where, in effect, we must give the attacker the key. The essence of DRM security can therefore be reduced to playing "hide and seek" with cryptographic keys, although this fundamental fact is not always clear from the descriptions of fielded or proposed DRM systems.

It has been shown that it is not trivial to effectively hide a key in data (Shamir and van Someren 1999) and that software obfuscation techniques are not sufficient to hide a key in software (Jacob, Boneh, and Felten 2003). In any event, this game of hide and seek is at the core of any DRM system. This topic is explored further in the next section.

Finally, it is important to note that there is an absolute limit on the utility of any DRM system. The digital content must ultimately be rendered, and at that point it is subject to capture in analog form. Even if a perfect DRM system were available, digital music, for example, could be recorded using a microphone when it is rendered. In our digital book example, an attacker could take digital snapshots of the pages of the book when it is displayed on a computer screen. This is the so-called "analog hole" (Doctorow 2002), which is obviously present in any DRM system. These sorts of analog attacks are beyond the scope of the DRM system. But since such attacks likely result in a loss of fidelity as compared to the original digital content, they are, perhaps, not as serious of a concern as a successful attack on the DRM system itself. Consequently, the goal of a DRM system is to prevent the attacker from obtaining an unprotected and high quality digital copy of the original.

In the next section we give a brief description of some of the techniques commonly employed in DRM systems. Our focus is on software-based systems, but we do mention some of the inherent advantages and disadvantages of hardware-based protection. Then we turn our attention to our proposed software-based DRM system for streaming media. A prototype of this proposed system has been implemented and we briefly discuss some details of the implementation. We then consider likely attacks on our proposed system as well as open problems in the field of DRM.

DRM TECHNIQUES

As mentioned in the previous section, the fundamental DRM problem is the protection of a secret, which, typically, is a cryptographic key or the equivalent thereof. The difficulty lies in the fact that the secret must be protected from the legitimate recipient, who, ultimately, must have access to the secret in order to render the digital content.

When DRM is implemented in software, the software must somehow protect itself from attack. Since the attacker is likely to have full administrative privilege, it is nontrivial to provide any meaningful software self-defense mechanisms.

Consider DRM client software executing under an attacker's control. Of course, we would like to make the attacker's job as difficult as possible. Ideally, we would like to have the challenge confronting the attacker be comparable to, say, breaking a secure cryptosystem. But, even in principle, we cannot hide a secret from a user with full administrative privileges. Furthermore, fielded DRM systems have failed so miserably and so consistently that there is now overwhelming empirical evidence that even a more modest "practical" level of protection is extremely difficult to achieve (CDFreaks 2002, Guignard 2002, "Beale Screamer" 2001, Ackerman 2003).

Today it is clearly the case that no software protection technique—or combination of such techniques—can make the attacker's job sufficiently difficult to ensure that the DRM client software cannot be broken. While unconditionally secure software-based DRM protection is unobtainable, there are techniques available that can make the attacker's job far more challenging. But since a persistent attacker will ultimately win, it may appear that software-based DRM is hopeless. Next, we argue that this is not the case, that is, software-based DRM can be of practical benefit in certain situations.

It is important to distinguish between an individual instance of DRM client software and the DRM system as a whole. We need to make it sufficiently challenging for an attacker to break a particular instance of the DRM software. We also need to be cognizant of the tradeoffs between security, usability, development, maintenance, complexity, etc. In any case, we must recognize that a persistent and dedicated attacker can, with sufficient effort, break an instance of the DRM client software. With this in mind, our goal will be to design a DRM system that remains useful even after an instance (or several instances) of the client software has (have) been broken. That is, the system as a whole should degrade gracefully under attack, instead of collapsing at the first successful attack on an instance of the client software. This system-wide DRM security is often known as "break once, break everywhere" resistance, or BOBE-resistance (Biddle, et. al., 2002).

Next, we discuss various techniques that can be used to "harden" each instance of DRM client software. Then we discuss some of the techniques that can be used to make a system more BOBE-resistant. Finally, we consider the potential benefits of hardware-assisted DRM, that is, we consider the benefits of using tamper resistant hardware as part of a DRM system.

Software Self-Defense

Software-based DRM systems can employ a wide variety of software self-defense techniques. Most of the techniques mentioned here are discussed in more detail in (Stamp 2003a); an overview of these topics can be found in (Stamp 2005).

From the DRM perspective, the fundamental weakness of software is that it is susceptible to reverse engineering. That is, even if we only provide the executable code (i.e., no source code), an attacker can analyze the software in great detail; see the excellent book (Eilam 2005) for more information on software reverse engineering. Not surprisingly, DRM protection mechanisms are squarely aimed at making reverse engineering more difficult; see (Cerven, 2002) for a discussion of several anti-reverse engineering techniques.

The essential tools of the software reverse engineer are a disassembler and a debugger. The disassembler provides a static view of the code, while a debugger provides a dynamic view. Various anti-disassembly techniques are known. For example, encrypting the executable code makes it impossible to disassemble. However, the code must be decrypted before it can be executed and an attacker may simply let the code decrypt itself before attempting to analyze it or the attacker may be able to reverse engineer the decryption routine and use it to decrypt the code.

Various "false disassembly" techniques are also used to confuse a disassembler.

Debuggers can also be confused by carefully constructed code. But, as with anti-disassembly techniques, a patient and skilled attacker can eventually remove these roadblocks.

Some fairly intricate combinations of these methods are possible. For example, Stamp (2003a) describes a method where an anti-disassembly method and an anti-debugging technique are combined in such a way that each protects the other to some extent.

Eventually, the persistent attacker will disassemble the code and run a debugger on the interesting parts of it. At this point we would like to make the code as difficult as possible to understand, thereby further delaying the attacker. Collberg, Thomborson, and Low (1997) have developed sophisticated methods of software obfuscation, which make the software difficult for an attacker to comprehend; see Eilam (2005) for a discussion of the effectiveness of such methods from a reverse engineer's perspective. The use of such obfuscation techniques is standard practice in "serious" DRM systems.

The use of proprietary algorithms is also sometimes suggested as a way to make reverse engineering more difficult (Stamp 2003a). Standard cryptographic algorithms, for example, are easy to detect and once detected, they do not need to be reverse engineered—only the key is required. On the other hand, non-standard cryptographic algorithms need to be analyzed, modified, or reverse engineered, thereby increasing the work factor for an attacker. However, Kerckhoffs' Prin-

ciple states that we can only trust cryptographic algorithms that have been publicly scrutinized by experts and such algorithms are, inevitably, well known. One solution—as suggested in Stamp (2003a)—is to use both a standard, secure cryptographic algorithm and a proprietary "scrambling" algorithm. This does not violate Kerckoffs' Principle and it should significantly increase the work for an attacker.

Another software protection technique that has been widely discussed in the literature is the use of so-called guards (Chang and Atallah, 2001; Horne , et. al., 2001). That is, parts of the code (the guards) tamper-check other parts of the code. Note that by itself this technique does not prevent an attacker from analyzing the code. Instead, guards are designed to prevent the attacker from being able to modify, or "patch" the code so that it performs a different function than the developer intended. In effect, this technique is designed to make the code fragile, which is useful for limiting attacks that make changes to the code, such as an attack that bypasses authentication.

Of course, combinations of most of these methods can be used. For example, the DRM system discussed in Stamp (2003a) uses virtually all of these techniques to some degree.

BOBE-Resistance

The goal of BOBE-resistance is to prevent one successful attack on client DRM software from breaking the entire DRM system. One step in the direction of BOBE-resistance is to "personalize" each copy of the DRM client software. That is, each instance of the software has some user-specific information embedded in it. An attacker must then determine this user-specific information in order to break a specific copy of the DRM client software.

However, personalization in this form is often very weak. For example, it may consist of nothing more than embedding a user-specific key in the software. This level of defense is unlikely to prevent an attacker from parlaying a single successful attack on a single DRM client into a system breaking attack.

For a more robust form of BOBE-resistance we turn to virus writers. Virus and worm developers have recently become infatuated with unique, or metamorphic software. In the standard software development model, each instance of a particular piece of software is identical, that is, the software is cloned from a single master copy. Virus and worm writers have recently begun to develop metamorphic software, where each copy is functionally equivalent, but the internal structure is significantly different (Stamp 2005). Malware writers are interested in metamorphism as a way to foil signature-based detection tools. In the field of DRM, metamorphism can be used so that each copy of DRM client software has a different internal structure. As discussed in (Stamp 2004), the potential benefit of such an approach is that a successful attack on one instance of the software will not necessarily succeed on any other instance of the software. In the best case, the work factor to attack N instances of the software would be N times greater than the work required to attack one instance. This would appear to be optimal with respect to BOBE-resistance.

Other approaches designed to achieve something similar to BOBE-resistance have been suggested. For example, it is possible to embed multiple security features in the software with many of these features initially dormant. Then if the DRM protection is compromised, one of the inactive security features can be activated, essentially creating a new protection scheme "on the fly." Or there may be other ways to update the software in real time. We mention one such method in the discussion of our proposed system, below.

Hardware-Assisted DRM

The discussion so far has focused on software-based protection. The fundamental problem with

any such approach is that we cannot securely hide a secret in software. On the other hand, a secret hidden in tamper resistant hardware will almost certainly present a more significant challenge to an attacker (Anderson, 2001). The benefits of a "hardware solution" can be seen in game consoles, which do a relatively good job of protecting their secrets, namely, the copyrighted software running on the system.

The potential advantages of hardware-based protection have not been lost on DRM advocates. The Trusted Computing Group (2007) is a consortium of manufacturers that produce computer chips containing special-purpose hardware that can store a secret, such as a key. This key is not directly available to a user, even if the user has full administrative privileges.

In coordination with the TCG hardware, Microsoft is developing a trusted operating system known as the Next Generation Secure Computing Base (2007). Although TCG/NGSCB is marketed today as a general-purpose security enhancing technology, the original motivation was DRM. The concern within the personal computing industry is that without a relatively strong form of DRM, the PC will lose out to closed systems, particularly in the realm of audio and video. In effect, TCG/NGSCB attempts to provide the security benefits of closed systems (e.g., game consoles) while maintaining the multitude of benefits that derive from an open platform (i.e., PCs). The details of TCG/NGSCB are beyond the scope of this paper; see Stamp (2005) for a high-level description.

DRM FOR STREAMING MEDIA

With the extensive background above, we are now ready to discuss a specific DRM system for streaming media. This system is software-based and is designed to provide simple but reasonably robust DRM protection with strong BOBE-resistance. Some aspects of this proposed system are outlined in Holankar and Stamp (2004).

First, we describe a generic streaming media application and the potential attacks on such a system. Then we describe our proposed DRM solution and we discuss the protection it provides against various attacks.

Streaming Media System

The following is a generic list of components and their functions in a (non-DRM) streaming media system; see Crowcroft, Handley and Wakeman (1999) for more information on streaming media.

1. A web server to stream the data to clients.
2. An authentication protocol to operate between the web server and clients.
3. A client side web browser, used to request the media.
4. A client application, such as Real Player Windows Media Player, to receive and render the media data.
5. A client side interface between the device driver (in kernel space) and the application (in user space).
6. A client device driver to utilize the media data.

Such an application can employ the Real-time Transport Protocol (RTP), which is a standard protocol to transport a media stream between two endpoints (RTP 2007). Secure RTP is a standard that makes use of cryptographic techniques to secure the RTP stream (Baugher 2004, Vovida 2004).

A generic streaming media system could function in the following manner.

1. The web server offers access to data.
2. A client requests a media file from the web server.

3. The web server and the user authenticate each other (mutual authentication).
4. After successful mutual authentication, the web server employs RTP to stream the data from the server to the client.
5. The client web browser opens the appropriate application (e.g., Real Player).
6. The media application removes the RTP headers and, if necessary, sequences the packets.
7. The media application uses system calls or library functions to write the data to the device that renders the data.
8. The device driver stores the data in its internal memory, writing the data to the appropriate port.

The above system has certain inherent security vulnerabilities. For example, the streamed data can be captured at any point between the two endpoints and the resulting data is subject to replay. From a DRM perspective, a more significant issue is the lack of any defense against client-side capture and subsequent redistribution of the data in an unprotected form. Below, we describe a DRM system that provides some measure of protection against the threat of data capture and redistribution.

DRM System

Our proposed security model augments the basic streaming media system described above. The two crucial DRM security components in our system are a proprietary device driver and the use of "scrambling" algorithms. Together, these features make reverse engineering any instance of the software more challenging, while also providing a reasonable degree of BOBE-resistance.

The server employs a scrambling algorithm and the client employs the corresponding de-scrambling algorithm. A scrambling algorithm should be unknown to a potential attacker. Ideally, we would like to force the attacker to "break" (by reverse engineering or other means) the scrambling algorithm in order to recover any of the unprotected data. The server must have access to a large number of distinct scrambling algorithms and the client must have access to the appropriate de-scrambling algorithm.

Scrambling serves at least two purposes. First, the scrambling algorithm creates a layer of obfuscation, making reverse engineering of the client software more difficult. Second, scrambling provides for a significant degree of metamorphism at a critical location in the client software.

Perhaps the ideal scrambling algorithm is a secure cryptographic algorithm, since the algorithm could be applied to all of the data and we could be confident that there is no simple way to de-scramble the data without access to the key and knowledge of the algorithm. However, Kerckoffs' Principle rules this out. But we will not depend on the scrambling algorithm for cryptographic strength, since we also employ standard strong encryption. Therefore, a homemade cryptographic algorithm that provides minimal cryptographic strength will serve as a scrambling algorithm.

For our prototype implementation, we employed modified forms of the Tiny Encryption Algorithm (TEA); see Wheeler and Needham (1994). From this algorithm we derived a large class of scrambling algorithms. Without extensive analysis, none of these modifications could be claimed to provide substantial cryptographic strength, but each is suitable for use as a scrambling algorithm. The rationale behind scrambling is further discussed (within the context of DRM) in Stamp (2003a).

Given a set of scrambling algorithms, each client is equipped with a subset of the available algorithms and these algorithms are compiled into the client executable. The list of scrambling algorithms known to the client is encrypted with a key known only to the server, and this client-specific encrypted list is stored on the client. After authenticating the server, this encrypted list is passed from the client to the server.

When the server receives the list, the server decrypts it and randomly chooses from among the client's known scrambling algorithms. The client's identifier of the selected scrambling algorithm is then sent from the server to the client. Note that this process eliminates the need for a database containing the mappings between clients and scrambling algorithms. This approach is analogous to that used in Kerberos to manage "ticket granting tickets" (Stamp 2005).

By having different scrambling algorithms embedded within different clients, and by randomly selecting from a client's list of algorithms, each client is unique, and each communication between client and server depends not only on different keys, but also on different algorithms. An attacker who is able to break one particular piece of content, will likely still have a challenging task when trying to break another piece of content destined for the same client. And even if an attacker completely reverse-engineers one client, it is likely that a comparable amount of effort will be required to attack any other client.

On the server side, the data is scrambled then encrypted. On the client side, the data is decrypted, and the resulting scrambled data is passed to the media application. The media application passes the scrambled data to the proprietary device driver, which de-scrambles the data. In this way, the data is obfuscated until the last possible point in the process.

Given these security features, our DRM streaming media system functions as follows.

1. The secure web server offers streaming media services.
2. A client requests a media file from the secure web server.
3. The secure web server authenticates the user and the user authenticates the web server.
4. Upon successful mutual authentication, the client sends its encrypted list of supported scrambling algorithms to the server.

5. The server generates two random keys. The first key is for secure RTP packet encryption (using a strong encryption algorithm) and the second is the scrambling key.

6. The server randomly selects from among the scrambling algorithms supported by the client. The scrambling algorithm selection and the keys are encrypted (but not scrambled) and passed to the client. The client acknowledges receipt of this information.

7. The server scrambles the data using the appropriate key using cipher block chaining (CBC) mode (per packet), with a randomly selected initialization vector (IV). The IV is included within each packet (for cryptographic terminology, see (Schneier 1996, Stallings 2003).

8. The secure RTP algorithm uses a secure encryption algorithm, such as the Advanced Encryption Standard (AES), and the appropriate key to encrypt the scrambled data in each packet. The packets are CBC encrypted with a randomly selected IV.

9. The scrambled and encrypted secure RTP packets are streamed from the server to the client.

10. The client web-browser opens the appropriate secure media application.

11. The media application requests the secure RTP decryption key. The user must authenticate in order for the client software to obtain access to the decryption key.

12. The media application strips off the secure RTP headers and sequences the packets, if necessary.

13. The media application initializes its secure device driver with the appropriate scrambling algorithm, and the algorithm is initialized with the scrambling key.

14. The media application is oblivious to the scrambling. It writes the scrambled data to the device that plays the file.

15. The secure device driver de-scrambles the data and writes the resulting plaintext to the appropriate device buffer and port.

Figure 1 gives a simplified view of the interaction between the client and server, where

1. "List" is the list of scrambling algorithms that the client supports.

2. K_{server} is a key known only to the server.

3. $E(List, K_{server})$ is the list of scrambling algorithms that the client supports, encrypted with the key K_{server}.

4. K is the cryptographic key that the server will use to encrypt the data.

5. S is the scrambling key that the server will use to scramble the data.

6. N is the identifier of the client's scrambling algorithm that the server has selected.

7. K_{client} is a key that is known to both the client and the server. This key could be shared in advance (and used for authentication) or it could be negotiated during the authentication process (in which case another method would be needed for authentication).

8. $E(K,S,N,K_{client})$ is the cryptographic key K, the scrambling key S, and the scrambling algorithm identifier N, all encrypted with the key K_{client}.

Comparison with Windows Media Player

Next, we give a brief comparison of the security features in our proposed streaming media system—as presented above—with the features available in Windows Media Player (Windows DRM 2004). The six points listed below are given on Microsoft's website (Windows DRM 2004) as the primary security features of Windows Media Player. We describe how our system implements each of these features.

Figure 1. Simplified client server interaction

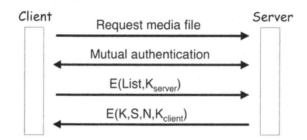

1. Persistent Protection: The protection in our system extends over the insecure network between client and server. Due to the scrambling algorithm and the secure device driver, the protection persists all the way to the client's media device.

2. Strong Encryption: Our system uses RTP with strong encryption. Our model also employs scrambling, but it does not rely on scrambling for cryptographic security.

3. Individualization: In our system, the scrambling algorithm is selected at random and the actual set of available scrambling algorithms is individual to each client. Therefore, the compromise of one client does not break the entire system. Moreover, a compromised client can easily be replaced with an upgraded device driver that employs a different set of scrambling algorithms. The secure device driver could easily be made unique in other ways as well. For example, the methods discussed in (Mishra and Stamp 2003) or methods similar to those employed by metamorphic virus writers (Balepin, 2003) could be implemented. Such protections would make the reverse engineering problem even more challenging for an attacker. We have not implemented this higher level of metamorphism, but it would certainly be feasible to do so.

4. Secure Media Path: Our system does not de-scramble the data until the last possible point in the process. The data passes through the entire system in scrambled form. When it is sent over the (insecure) network, the data is further protected by strong encryption.

5. Revocation and Renewability: In our approach, compromised players can be revoked and revoked clients will fail to authenticate. Moreover, if a particular scrambling algorithms has been compromised, the server can simply avoid using the compromised algorithm. Alternatively, all clients using the compromised algorithm can be upgraded with new device drivers that do not include the particular algorithm.

6. Secure End-to-End Streaming and Downloads: We employ secure RTP for end-to-end streaming and downloads. A strong encryption algorithm is used in secure RTP. It is worth noting that secure end-to-end transmission can also be accomplished using other well-known methods such as IPSec (Kaufman, Perlman, and Speciner 2002).

As can be seen from the discussion above, the secure device driver and the software metamorphism achieved via scrambling are the crucial security aspects of our proposed DRM system. We have developed a prototype system (in Linux) that implements the system described above. Our implementation is briefly discussed in Section 5.

ATTACKS

The obvious attacks on our proposed system include the analog hole and reverse engineering the software. Since the analog hole is beyond the scope of any DRM system, we do not consider it further here. To make the reverse engineering attacks more challenging, we could distribute the proprietary device drivers immediately before distributing the content. This would be particularly valuable for data that is somewhat "perishable", such as a live broadcast. In this way, we could limit the time available to the attacker. This could prove to be a very effective approach in certain situations.

It would also be fairly straightforward for an attacker to modify the hardware on the client so that the plaintext bits are captured directly, without attacking the software. Although a serious threat, such modifications are also beyond the scope of a software-based DRM system.

IMPLEMENTATION

This section describes in some detail various implementation issues of our secure streaming media system.

Operating System Issues

The preferred operating systems for embedded multimedia devices are Real Time-Linux, Linux and VxWorks (Yodaiken 2000). Here, we discuss implementation issues of our proposed secure streaming media model related to these three operating systems.

VxWorks does not have any memory protection between application and system tasks. This makes the device driver memory buffer in the proposed model available to any module through a simple function calls. Moreover, decryption within the device driver adds overhead, making the process not as lightweight as we would like.

On a more positive note, if the decrypted media data is made available in the memory buffer only for periodic time slices, it makes it difficult for other hacker processes to contend for the decrypted data in the same time slice. The hacker process would need to synchronize with the availability of the decrypted data. Such synchronization would be difficult in a single processor system, and it would be many times more difficult in a multiprocessor system.

RT-Linux requires the user to divide the application into two distinct parts: the real-time part and the non-real-time part. The real-time part is serviced rapidly, allowing it to meet deadlines, while the non-real-time part has the full range of Linux resources available for use, but cannot have real-time requirements. The division of multimedia data into real-time and non-real-time part must be managed carefully. The constraints increase if the media data is streamed live or it is interactive. Decryption of media data on the device driver level further increases the timing constraints of live and interactive data.

Under the Linux operating system, the implementation issues are greatly simplified. This is primarily due to the fact that Linux provides memory protection between kernel processes and user space. Linux also has non-swappable memory, which provides some protection to key material.

Open Source Resources

The following specific open source resources were utilized in the implementation of the proposed security model

- OpenSSL (OpenSSL 2007)
- Tiny httpd (Tiny httpd 2007
- Secure RTP (Secure RTP 2007)
- Linux (Linux 2007)
- Linux device drivers tutorials (Calbet 2006)

- Intel audio driver i810_audio (Audiodriver 2007)
- Crystal audio driver cs46xx (Audiodriver 2007)

Distinct Scrambling Algorithms

Our approach to BOBE-resistance requires that we have available a large selection of distinct "scrambling" algorithms. As previously noted, our scrambling algorithms consist of unique variations of the Tiny Encryption Algorithm (Wheeler and Needham 1994). Our proof-of-concept implementation supports sixteen scrambling algorithms on the server side. Of course, a far larger number of scrambling algorithms could be employed.

The scrambling and de-scrambling code is compiled as separate object code, which can be easily linked with different sender and receiver programs. In practice, it would be easy to generate multiple receivers supporting different scrambling algorithms. For demonstration purposes, we have created three receivers wherein one is totally secure, one receiver is partially broken and another one is totally broken. These receivers demonstrate the functionality of the server negotiation process in the case where some of the available scrambling algorithms have been hacked.

Hardware Requirements

To implement and test the security model proposed in this paper, the minimal configuration consists of the following:

- Two personal computers, both running Linux kernel 2.4.16 or higher, and both having sound cards and network adapters.
- Multimedia support must be enabled on the Linux operating system and sound drivers must be configured in modular mode.
- The specific sound card device driver must be available in open source.

The personal computers can be connected via a network or crossover cable. Of course, a more sophisticated network connection could be used.

It should be noted that the performance results vary depending on the available processing power as well as the network card performance at both the sender and receiver.

Implementation in Linux

This section briefly describes the implementation details in Linux using kernel 2.4.16

Server-Side Components

An HTTPS web server must be installed on the server. We employed the tiny httpd server (Tiny httpd 2000) and Open SSL (Open SSL 2000) was installed on the server side to support HTTPS. The server invokes cgi-scripts to start the secure RTP streams. The function of the cgi-script is to obtain the environment settings of the http username, the http client IP address, to locate the requested data and to invoke the sender program.

The sender program takes the following parameters

- Destination IP address
- Destination port
- Filename
- Username
- Sampling rate

The message sent by the server to the receiver includes the following parameters:

- Session key
- Server IP address
- Server port
- Scrambling key
- Sampling rate of audio file
- Total number of packets
- License Manager

As outlined above, the receiver sends an encrypted list of supported scrambling algorithms. The server randomly selects one of the supported algorithms, maps the client algorithm to its corresponding server algorithm, and sends the selected algorithm number to the receiver. The server then begins sending the streaming data (which is scrambled and encrypted) in packets of a predefined size.

The license manager maintains a list of multimedia data files and corresponding usernames and the number of times a user is permitted to invoke each file. On each invocation, the license manager decrements by one the allowed number for that particular user for the accessed file. However, if the user has no access restriction to the particular file, then the license manager will not decrement the access count. In practice this logic could be easily implemented using a secure database system.

The license manager also maintains a list of broken (i.e., hacked) scrambling algorithms. If the license manager detects that all of the supported algorithms at the receiver end are broken, it will ask the server to terminate its connection with the receiver without giving any explanation to the receiver.

Receiver-Side Components

The receiver side listens to a predefined secure RTP port. The server program sends a session key encrypted using the receiver's shared symmetric key. When the receiver receives the session key, it sends its encrypted list of supported scrambling algorithms to the sender. The sender program chooses one of the scrambling algorithms and sends the multimedia data packets. Note that the receiver application works in close communication with the receiver device driver. The receiver initializes the secure device driver using the selected scrambling algorithm and the scrambling key sent by the server. When the re-

ceiver is compiled, a private key for the receiver is built into the receiver executable file.

The receiver has an encrypted list of its supported scrambling algorithms, which the sender decrypts to determine the scrambling algorithms supported by the device driver at the receiver end. If all the supported scrambling algorithms of the device driver are found in the broken list maintained by the server, the device driver at the receiver end is considered broken. When the server receives a request from a broken receiver, it immediately terminates the connection without explanation.

Secure Device Driver

The receiver application talks directly to the secure device driver and the secure device driver in turn talks directly to the device. The Linux artsd daemon, which is used to monitor access to sound, is killed to allow direct access to the sound device. The secure device driver includes the de-scrambling algorithms and it also includes a modified write function. This modified write function enables the driver to de-scramble data before writing to the Direct Memory Access (DMA) buffer. The device reads the de-scrambled data from the DMA buffer directly.

All Linux device drivers follow a uniform structure invoking read, write and setting the parameters (also known as ioctl calls). This makes the implementation of a secure device driver on different hardware platforms relatively easy under Linux. The secure driver implements an ioctl call to initialize the selected de-scrambling algorithm with the de-scrambling key.

If any user tries to implement his or her own insecure device driver, the device driver will fail to understand the security parameters initialized by the application. The receiving application will immediately terminate, since the device driver does not understand the security parameter.

Streaming Data

The implementation on the receiver end uses two threads in round-robin mode. The receiving thread listens on a secure port for packets from the sender. The device driver thread begins writing to the sound device driver after receiving an initial buffer of data.

Our implementation of streaming uses a simple methodology. Sophisticated streaming with more control of startup latency and throughput is consistent with the proposed security techniques.

HTTPS and RTP Clients

The HTTPS protocol is used in our security model for username and password authentication, as well as for client-server mutual authentication. The client's request for a particular file is transmitted to the server using HTTPS. After user authentication, the server starts a secure RTP session, which is used for handshaking and the streaming data transmission.

In practice, multimedia transmission is usually done using the Real Time Transport Protocol (RTP) with UDP at the transport layer. Our proposed secure model uses secure RTP for transmission between the endpoints.

A comparison between the three protocols secure RTP, RTP and HTTPS, with respect to startup latency and throughput, is of interest. This comparison helps us to estimate the performance penalty of our proposed secure streaming media model. Simple HTTPS and RTP clients were implemented for the sole purpose of obtaining timing information. Details of this comparison appear below in Section 5.6.2.

Creating Receiver Components

We have developed a "create client" program, which is used to automate the process of generating a shared symmetric key for the receiver

and the encrypted list of supported scrambling algorithms. The openSSL library function crypt, which implements DES encryption (Grabbe 2003) and the MD5 hash (Rivest 2003), among other crypto algorithms, is used to encrypt the supported algorithms string in the receiver.

Deployment

This section discusses test cases, performance data, and we provide a brief analysis of the proposed system.

Performance Issues

We performed a variety of some timing tests. Our primary goal was to determine the relative cost imposed by the security measures we have adopted. The tests were performed on a 1Ghz Pentium 4 personal computer. The tests consisted of looping over many different calls of the encryption algorithms and using the "clock" C library function to make timing measurements. This method is portable, if not the most refined.

Figure 2 shows two graphs, the transmission throughput between two endpoints and the throughput using our secure device driver. Obviously that the proposed secure streaming media model is slower than the generic (no security) model but it is within reasonable limits. Primarily, the added cost results from the scrambling and de-scrambling of packets.

The time required for scrambling and de-scrambling of data packets is constant. The transmission throughput saturates as we increase the number of octets in the packet. The cryptographic mechanisms used by the server and client will be the bottleneck for performance. Crypto hardware accelerators could be used on both ends to improve performance but based on our test results, this appears to be unnecessary.

Figure 2. Performance graph

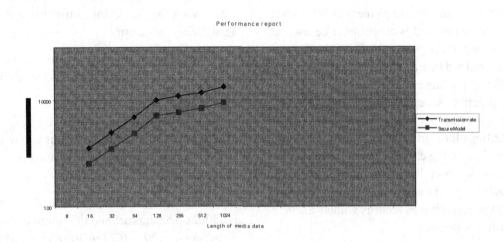

Table 1. Comparison of secure RTP, RTP and HTTPS

(Milliseconds)	Secure RTP	RTP	HTTPS
Startup time	2423.07	1616.61	2046.29
End receiving	15313.86	23305.93	5353.86

Comparison of Secure RTP, RTP and HTTPS

HTTPS and RTP clients were also implemented for the purpose of comparison to our proposed secure RTP model. Table 1 contains the startup latency and throughput times for streaming 4003604 bytes under each of the three protocols.

From the results in Table 1, it can be seen that the difference in startup latency for the three protocols is negligible. HTTPS transmission has a slight advantage over the other two protocols for transmission of longer files. HTTPS uses TCP as the transport layer protocol whereas in our implementations, RTP and secure RTP use UDP as the transport layer protocol (secure RTP allows for the usage of either UDP or TCP as the transport layer protocol). In any case, the performance penalty for secure RTP appears to be negligible.

Testing of Secure Driver

Our implementation has been successfully tested using two audio device drivers, namely, the Intel 810 audio driver and the Crystal Sound Fusion audio driver. For both of these device drivers the implementation was straightforward. The most significant driver implementation issues included compiling the de-scrambling algorithms file and modifying the write functions. The device driver maintains the initialized de-scrambling key and chosen algorithm in the current state structure.

Startup Latency and Throughput

The implementation uses a very simple streaming mode with a predefined initial buffer size. As soon as the initial buffer is filled, the receiver begins writing to the audio device driver. Depending on the available processing power and network cards, the size of the initial buffer can be increased or decreased. Currently, our implementation assumes that the network card is available to be used at its maximum throughput. Our initial buffer size was determined by trial and error using a variety of different parameters.

In practice, several streaming servers and receiver plug-ins are available which have variable settings for startup latency. Consequently, further fine-tuning can be easily determined for a specific platform. From the test cases we have conducted, it can be concluded that the proposed security model achieves security without a severe performance penalty.

CONCLUSION

In this chapter we discussed various issues concerning digital rights management in general. We then considered a software-based DRM system designed to protect streaming media. Our proposed system provides a reasonable level of robustness against attack and a high degree of BOBE-resistance.

It would be interesting to develop an analogous DRM system based on tamper-resistant hardware by making use of, say, TCG/NGSCB (Trusted Computing Group 2007, Next Generation Secure Computing Base 2007). Such a system would offer an inherently higher degree of security due to the difficulty of attacking the hardware as compared to attacking software. However, with streaming media it may be the case that a well designed, software based DRM system is sufficiently robust to be of significant practical value.

REFERENCES

Ackerman, E. (2003). *Student skirts CD's piracy guard*, http://www.newmediamusings.com/blog/2003/10/student_skirts_.html

Anderson, R. (2001). *Security Engineering: A Guide to Build Dependable Distributed Systems*, John Wiley & Sons, Inc. http://www.cl.cam.ac.uk/~rja14/book.html

Audiodriver (2007). http://community.qnx.com/sf/wiki/do/viewPage/projects.bsp/wiki/Audiodriver

Balepin, I. (2003). *Superworms and crpytovirology: A deadly combination*, http://wwwcsif.cs.ucdavis.edu/~balepin/new_pubs/worms-cryptovirology.pdf

Biddle, P., P. England, M., Peinado, & Willman, B. (2002). The darknet and the future of content distribution. *2002 ACM Workshop on Digital Rights Management*, November 18, 2002, http://crypto.stanford.edu/DRM2002/prog.html

Calbet, X. (2006). *Writing device drivers in Linux: a brief tutorial*. http://www.freesoftwaremagazine.com/articles/drivers_linux

Chang, H., & Atallah, M. J. (2001). *Protecting software code by guards*. Workshop on Security and Privacy in Digital Rights Management

Cerven, P. (2002). *Crackproof Your Software*, No Starch Press

Collberg, C., Thomborson, C., & Low, D. (1997). *A taxonomy of obfuscating transformations*. Technical Report 148, Department of Computer Science, University of Auckland, July 1997

Crowcroft, J., Handley, M., & Wakeman, I. (1999). *Internetworking Multimedia*. Morgan Kaufmann, 1999

CDFreaks. (2002). *Easy solution to bypass latest CD-audio protection*, 2002, http://www.cdfreaks.com/news/4068

Doctorow, C. (2002). EFF Consensus at Lawyerpoint, Hollywood want to plug the `analog hole', May 23, 2002, http://bpdg.blogs.eff.org/archives/000113.html

Eilam, E. (2005). *Reversing: Secrets of Reverse Engineering*. John Wiley & Sons, Inc.

Guignard, B. (2002). *How secure is PDF?* http://www.cs.cmu.edu/~dst/Adobe/Gallery/PDFsecurity.pdf

Holankar, D., & Stamp, M. (2004). Secure streaming media and digital rights management. *Proceedings of the 2004 Hawaii International Conference on Computer Science*. Honolulu, Hawaii, January 2004

Jacob, M., Boneh, D., & Felten, E. (2003). Attacking an obfuscated cipher by injecting faults. *Lecture Notes in Computer Science, 2696*, 16-31. Springer

Kaufman, C., Perlman, R., & Speciner, M. (2002). *Network Security: Private Communications in a Public World*. Prentice Hall

Linux (2007). http://www.drfruitcake.com/linux/stest.html

Mishra, P., & Stamp, M. (2003). Software uniqueness: how and why. *Proceedings of ICCSA 2003*, P.P. Dey, M.N. Amin and T.M. Gatton, editors, July 2003

Next Generation Secure Computing Base. (2007). http://www.microsoft.com/resources/ngscb/default.mspx

OpenSSL (2007). http://www.openssl.org

Real-time Transport Protocol (RTP), RFC 1889. (2007). http://www.faqs.org/rfcs/rfc1889.html

Schneier, B. (1996). *Applied Cryptography*, second edition. John Wiley & Sons, 1996

Baugher, M., et al. (2004). The Secure Real Time Transport Protocol, *RFC 3711* http://www.ietf.org/rfc/rfc3711.txt

Vovida.org. (2004). *Secure RTP,* http://www.vovida.org/protocols/downloads/srtp/

"Beale Screamer". (2001). *Microsoft's digital rights management scheme—technical details,* http://cryptome.org/ms-drm.htm

Shamir, A., & van Someren, N. (1999). Playing "hide and seek" with stored keys. *Lecture Notes in Computer Science, 1648*, 118-124. Springer

Secure RTP. (2007). http://srtp.sourceforge.net

Stallings, W. (2003). *Cryptography and Network Security: Principles and Practices*. Prentice Hall

Stamp, M. (2003a). Digital rights management: the technology behind the hype. *Journal of Electronic Commerce Research*, 4(3), 102-112, http://www.csulb.edu/web/journals/jecr/issues/20033/paper3.pdf

Stamp, M. (2003b). Digital rights management: For better or for worse? *ExtremeTech*, May 1, 2003, http://www.extremetech.com/article2/0,3973,1051610,00.asp

Stamp, M. (2005). *Information Security: Principles and Practice*. John Wiley & Sons, Inc.

Stamp, M. (2002, September). Risks of digital rights management, Inside Risks 147, *Communications of the ACM*, 45(9), 120

Stamp, M. (2004). Risks of monoculture, Inside Risks 165, *Communications of the ACM*, 47(3), 120.

Tiny httpd (2007). http://www.acme.com/software/thttpd/thttpd_man.html

Trusted Computing Group. (2007), https://www.trustedcomputinggroup.org/home

Wheeler, D., & Needham, R. (1994). *TEA, a tiny encryption algorithm*, http://www.ftp.cl.cam.ac.uk/ftp/papers/djw-rmn/djw-rmn-tea.html

Windows Media Digital Rights Management Offering. (2004). http://www.microsoft.com/windows/windowsmedia/wm7/drm/offering.aspx

Yodaiken, V. ELEC (2000). http://www.linuxde-vices.com/articles/AT3792919168.html

KEY TERMS

Break Once, Break Everywhere Resistance (BOBE): A highly desirable property of a DRM system. A system is BOBE-resistant if a successful attack on a piece of digital content does not break the entire system.

BOBE Resistance: (See break once, break everywhere resistance.)

Device Driver: Low-level software that the operating system uses to control a hardware device.

Digital Rights Management (DRM): Consists of the methods used to control access to copyrighted digital content.

Linux: On open source operating system based on Unix.

Open Source Software: Software for which the source code is freely available.

Streaming Media: Consists of digital media transmitted over a network in such a way that it can be consumed while the transmission is in progress.

Windows Media Player: A digital media player from Microsoft.

Chapter III
Rethinking DRM Using
Exception Management

Jean-Henry Morin
Korea University Business School, Korea

ABSTRACT

This chapter introduces and discusses much needed alternatives to the traditional either/or debate on total security of secure multimedia distribution. Most DRM-based approaches rely on considering the user as untrustworthy and consequently a weak link. We argue there may be alternative ways, providing increased flexibility to users in terms of fair use and copyright balance while still maintaining a much needed level of governed usage of content. While introducing exception management in DRM environments might seam counterintuitive at first sight, we provide elements supporting the idea in the form of a model which is discussed. In doing so, we argue for the need to rethink DRM in ways that will enable both a seamless compelling user experience and the rights holder to address the issue of managed copying of content.

INTRODUCTION

Having now entered the era of the so called *Read-Write Internet* and its associated culture as pointed out by Lawrence Lessig during the opening keynote of the 2006 LinuxWorld (Lessig, 2006) we are confronted with whole new challenges on how we deal with issues on copyright, neighboring rights, intellectual property and generally speaking added value creativity. For sure,

the evolution of the collaborative, user created / generated Internet combined with the broadening availability of material (hardware and software) and broadband Internet at affordable cost has enabled a new form of culture which is the basis for our emerging *mashup society*. In this context and given the tremendous amount of readily available distributed multimedia content, solutions need to be found to address some of the basic new requirements and practices in our increasingly pervasive digital world. New media warrants new thinking and consequently creativity.

The domain of multimedia content distribution, mostly driven by the entertainment industry, has triggered the need for mechanisms to ensure their secure distribution over open networks in order to enforce usage according to rules essentially drawn from the pre-Internet era. Thus giving rise to a variety of technical protection measures (TPM) among which we find watermarking, fingerprinting, access control, digital rights management, etc. mostly relying on the use of encryption.

It is now commonly agreed that TPMs such as Digital Rights Management (DRM) rarely curb those that it should (Gapper, 2007) and are for the most part considered by users as burdensome, restrictive, invasive thus preventing a smooth and enjoyable user experience which needless to say is a key aspect of entertainment.

More recent developments including Steve Jobs' open letter (Jobs, 2007) arguing to drop DRM altogether, the countless proprietary technical initiatives, the myriads of commercial initiatives each trying to lock in the consumer and the general misconceptions found among politicians trying to enact ridiculous laws such as the "three strikes and you're out" idea, etc. All these basically have lead to some form of chaos in the field, strengthening the idea of evilness of TPM.

In this chapter we propose to take a step back and rethink DRM in the context of secure multimedia distribution by considering an approach decriminalizing the user while still maintaining a level of responsibility and accountability on his side. The basic idea is to initially assume the user is trustworthy unless otherwise witnessed and consequently offload the processing weight to the parties having a justifiable interest in making sure content is not misused.

The overall objective of this chapter is to provide an argument and a discussion on why we need to revisit multimedia distribution to accommodate new and emerging practices such as exception management in DRM environments while still maintaining a much needed level of security and control. To this end we illustrate and discuss our position based on a model introducing exception management in DRM environments allowing users to claim beforehand legitimate usage situations such as fair use, private or home copy, etc.

BACKGROUND AND GENERAL PROBLEM DESCRIPTION

Starting with one of the most important problems in the field of secure multimedia distribution is probably the position and the role of the user which has largely been eluded altogether from the beginning. While such a statement might seem slightly controversial at first sight, it is supported by numerous examples mostly driven by the Majors in the music and movie industries who have at all times tried to lobby to protect their industry from the potential threats of new technologies starting with the VCR (Betamax, 1984) up to the Digital Millenium Copyright Act (DMCA, 2008) and similar laws around the world.

Consequently, technology providers have often been misled to believe that outside full protection and control of content there would be no online business in this field. With such requirements, it is in this context that DRM (Digital Rights Management) emerged based on work done initially by Mori (Mori and Kawahara, 1990) on Superdistribution for the distribution of software (Mori and Tashiro, 1987) followed shortly by Cox (Cox, 1994; Cox, 1996). In a nutshell, DRM technology allows to cryptographically associate usage rules, also called policies or rights, to digital content. These rules govern the usage of the content they are associated to. They have to be interpreted by an enforcement point prior to any access in order to determine whether or not access can be granted or denied. In the former case, the content is decrypted and rendered in a trusted interface (e.g. browser, application, sound or video device, etc.). The content being itself encrypted, it becomes persistently protected at all time and wherever it resides.

Since the mid-nineties many generations of DRM systems and approaches were developed and deployed mostly proprietary and vendor specific thus preventing interoperability among them. Detailed descriptions may be found in (Becker et al., 2003; Rosenblatt et al., 2001; Morin et al., 2007). As a result, the users have found themselves locked in situations where they couldn't take their content from one device to another or worse were denied access to the content they legitimately acquired.

Consequently, DRM has become the subject of raging debates including street demonstrations and protests such as in New-York in October 2005 (Mennecke, 2005) having potential broad societal implications on how we may experience entertainment in the future.

A *Financial Times* column by John Gapper (Gapper, 2007) on why digital music should be set free outlined that DRM does not curb those that it should and that this industry should start thinking more creatively. One couldn't agree more and assuming that users are criminals is definitely not the way to go. Recent evidence from the market actually shows otherwise.

To illustrate this point let's consider one of the most popular examples in this industry with iTunes averaging between 60 and 80 percent of the worldwide online music market depending on the sources. This platform offers legal downloading of music protected by the FairPlay DRM technology. Although proprietary and relatively easy to circumvent it is often considered sufficient by the content industry compared to an economically viable risk. The key point here is that while there will always be circumventers, most users will comply smoothly with the model provided the experience is enjoyable and the business model makes sense for them.

There are two lessons to be drawn from this case. First, that statistically, most users are not criminals (i.e., pirates in this case). Second, that total security is neither desirable nor achievable beyond a commercially viable point. Industrial piracy definitely requires other tools than consumer DRM.

As a result, we need to take a step back to rationally reconsider what is at stake. To this extent, it is striking to see that basically over the last decade the whole DRM debate has and still is only about full protection (i.e. often referred to as restriction) versus full freedom with respect to digital content and intangible assets. By ignoring the "User", especially in the entertainment industry, DRM has legitimately sparked vigorous reactions, potentially turning DRM into "evil" technology.

Early 2007, in his open letter "Thoughts on Music" (Jobs, 2007), Steve Jobs argued there were three alternatives out of which he basically favors the last one abolishing DRM entirely. This came as a wakeup call to the industry which sparked new attempts at DRM free models whether subscription based, flat fee or at a premium like with the iTunes Plus. Technically, the second alternative of licensing FairPlay being too dangerous didn't stand in the light of what is done in the field of DRM interoperability as outlined in a response (Coral, 2007; Lacy, 2007) from the Coral Consortium (a cross industry group working on DRM interoperability including IFPI, RIAA, MPAA and most of the Majors) to Steve Jobs, inviting him to join. The last option considered was the status quo but this would have forced renegotiation of the deals with the Majors at much lower margins for Apple.

There is a need for alternative ways going beyond the "either / or" debate which is by far too limitative and cruelly lacking imagination and creativity. Basically it's not really about how to "prevent" rather than how to "accommodate" legitimate use of governed electronic content. This represents a major shift towards what could emerge as a "gray zone" where statistically most users are not considered criminals "a priori".

As outlined above, Apple has played an important role in this approach (and who would dare consider this as a failure) with the FairPlay copy protection which is known to be rather easy to circumvent (at least to anyone willing to invest the time and effort). However, most users comply smoothly and enjoy the "experience" in a commercially acceptable and viable model.

Putting the User in Charge

Taking a step back looking at the CD industry, they are not protected for the most part (except for some ugly stories with rootkits and protections). In such settings, the user is in charge. He is responsible for making sure that what is done with the content falls in an acceptable usage category. In a majority of cases it consists of time shifting for playback, space shifting among a wide range of devices we use in our immediate environment or household members such as children, etc. All of which are perfectly acceptable and legal usage situations under existing practices of fair use, home copy agreements and copyright laws. In all of these common everyday examples users should legitimately be entitled to determine for themselves the scope and freedom already enjoyed in the tangible world without being considered criminals and thus prevented from doing so by some constraining piece of software.

This is especially true considering the legal hype and the numerous amendments to copyright laws throughout the world essentially criminalizing users. The French DADVSI (Jondet, 2006) debate was particularly striking in 2006 considering that most people didn't have a clue on the issues or what was going on.

The latest developments and recent events increasingly support the idea that it is still unclear how the entertainment industry and the broader society will find a viable long term solution to the problem. Among the most recent let us mention the very arguable "three strikes and you're out" laws or policies recently examined in France, the UK and Australia. The basic idea was to have ISPs monitor Internet traffic of their users for illegal use of P2P file sharing systems and to warn them twice before basically banning them form accessing the Internet.

Among the most common criticisms of such approaches we find that it isn't even clear whether such a filtering mechanism would effectively work (e.g. ability to prevent false positives like people using P2P protocols to legally share content). It is clear that it would pose serious threats to privacy. And ultimately it is arguable whether it is the role of ISPs to enforce copyright laws. Finally there is a major social and ethical question raised by potentially banning a person from the Internet. The Internet has become a commodity that can probably be classified today as a common good which is as vital as electricity and water. Nowadays, banning or preventing a user from accessing the Internet can have dramatic consequences in terms of social exclusion. Finding or accomplishing a job, communicating with administrations and relatives nowadays requires the use of the Internet.

The debate requires to further stress the Copyright Balance principle that should underlie public policy regarding DRM as discussed by Ed. Felten in the CACM Inside Risks column of July 2005 (Felten, 2005) : *"Since lawful use, including fair use, of copyrighted works is in the public interest, a user wishing to make lawful use of copyrighted material should not be prevented from doing so by any DRM system."* This sound principle should be at the forefront of rethinking the future of DRM systems and make the case for alternate approaches such as for example an Exception based Provisioning and Management system for DRM where users would basically not be given more or less liberty than previously enjoyed with traditional content. In other words, assuming by default that individuals are lawful users unless otherwise monitored is exactly what an exception based approach would enable. And current technology would allow it. Doing so would help a lot in providing the right consumer experience cruelly lacking in current DRM environments.

Moreover, assuming the kind of "always on", pervasive, ubiquitous, ambient networked economy having real-time usage metering and monitoring of content could provide valuable data to marketing specialists thus allowing fine-grained marketing campaigns and better customer service.

Obviously, DRM systems in their present form are not good at managing exceptions as it is often considered to defeat the security purpose and still remains a hard problem. At first sight, it could appear as mixing water with fire. However, giving this a second thought considering how DRM enabled systems could accommodate exception based models could lead to some new interesting approaches offering both the content industry and the consumers a commercially viable user friendly solution while still maintaining a given level of persistent protection, governed usage and control. Not to mention a whole range of emerging new business models relying on real-time monitoring and provisioning.

So what the industry needs to understand is that DRM is not about absolute and total security (which is not achievable anyway), but rather about how to offer both the entertainment industry AND the users a commercially viable solution allowing the former to develop its business and the latter a truly compelling user experience. As a result, we argue that DRM could be fundamentally compatible with legitimate user oriented principles if only the content industry and the technology providers would prove to be slightly more creative and realistic on the fact that we aren't addressing military grade security requirements. This may however force the entertainment industry to rethink its business models to finally embrace entertainment as a commodity (i.e., with a reasonable pricing strategy) like water or electricity, following a similar path as other technologies such as mobile phones, broadband Internet, etc. to name a few.

Entertainment is definitely not something one owns but rather an experience that should be enjoyed in a ubiquitous and pervasive way.

A MODEL FOR MANAGING EXCEPTIONS IN DRM ENVIRONMENTS

The proposed model presented in detail in (Morin et al., 2007) involves two additional entities to traditional DRM based environments: a Credential Manager and an Exception Manager.

The Credential Manager is an entity that emits, revokes and manages credentials. It can be any structure, such as an enterprise, an academic entity, or a national entity. It does not have to be known by the Content Owner neither at credential generation time, nor at content creation time; but it has to be able to prove its legitimate existence as well as the motivation leading to generating credentials.

The Exception Manager is an extension of the traditional License Manager found in all DRM based environments. It verifies if a credential may qualify to give access to a piece of rights enabled content. The Exception Manager checks if the credential is valid, if it has not been revoked and if it may be applicable to the content. Thus it verifies if the Credential Manager has legal existence and evaluates the reasons that led to generating the specific credential. If the credential passes these verifications, a Short-Lived License may be granted providing access to the content for a limited time. Moreover, the operation is logged as a trace for further proof of legitimate activity. Short-Lived Licenses are thus meant to give an exceptional access to content, and their validity is thus limited in time. They can give more or less rights depending on the type of the detected exception and some optional metadata information attached to the content indicating specific constraints on the Short-Lived License.

Figure 1. Eception-aware model

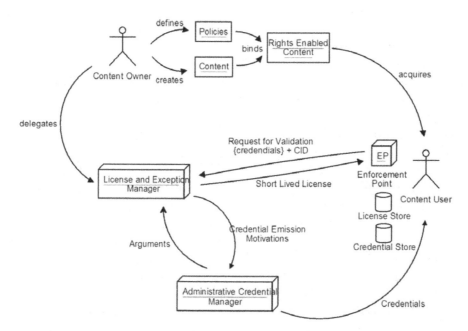

As a general overview of the model, Figure 1 highlights the main difference with a traditional DRM model. First, the content users obtain credentials from Credential Managers. These credentials are then stored in a credential store alongside the local license store to be used by the enforcement point. Compared to a classical DRM model where the enforcement point only has the choice to grant or deny access or eventually try to acquire a license, in the credential based model, credentials held by users can be sent to the exception manager and used to check if the user qualifies for an exception. If so a corresponding Short-Lived License is issued and returned for use.

As a result, content protection, credential creation, exception verification and corresponding authorization are decoupled. This approach provides greater flexibility than the classical DRM model allowing Credential Managers unknown to content owners to inform Enforcement Points

that an exceptional situation may be taken into consideration in situations where the user has no explicit rights to access the content in the form of a traditional license.

While providing flexibility to content users this approach still gives final control to the Exception Manager by allowing it to verify several points mentioned above leading to evaluating the legitimacy of the requested exception. Content Owners only have to care about the way they wish to protect their assets, ad hoc decisions being taken by the Exception Manager in case of exceptional situations. Finally, based on the logs of the credential manager the content owners can request audits of these logs either in case of fraud suspicion or simply as a regular validation procedure of the credential manager.

Lets now describe in further details the credential based model for managing exceptions in DRM systems. We first present the specifics of the content protection process when using exceptions before describing the exception management itself.

Content Protection

Content protection in the context of an exception based model differs from its traditional representation. This section explores the main differences introducing or refining the concepts of core policies, certification delegation, exception handling delegation and rights distribution.

Core Policies. At the very beginning of the content protection process the definition of policies is driven by the need to protect a content asset. But this process follows a path leading from this simple content protection to the need of having flexibility in any situation. Following this path results in producing complex policies required to deal with all particular situations that may arise.

In the proposed exception based model, only core Policies should be associated to content. Core Policies are the set of policies needed to efficiently protect the content in most situations. These policies have to reflect enterprise strategy, the most important requirements concerning the content and common usage situations. Thus policies embedded into the rights enabled content should not include other considerations, such as policies dealing with extremely rare situation which can fall under exception situations.

In this context all policies added to provide further flexibility not in the scope of usual policies are considered as potentials exceptions and should thus be handled using the credentials based exception handling model.

Credential Properties. Credentials have the following set of properties:

Known Source: Credentials must contain information about the Administrative Credential Manager who generated them, in order to be able to verify its legal existence as well as the motivations that led to credential generation.

User Bound: Each credential is bound to a single user or role, affiliated to the Administrative Credential Manager, able to prove that he is the legitimate owner of the credential.

Limited validity: Credentials are limited in time; their validity period is included in the credential.

Revocable: The Administrative Credential Manager can revoke a credential it has generated at any time.

Note that information about the nature of the credential, the reasons explaining why it has been created are not embedded into the credential. This approach allows to modify the scope of credentials generated by an Administrative Credential Manager for a single user, by widening the set of motivations, narrowing it or refining it, without having to revoke the credential and having to generate new ones. This provides additional flexibility, while retaining control over the number of credentials.

Credential Generation. In the model, generation of credentials that may lead to exceptions is delegated to Administrative Credential Managers. This indicates that credential owners can legitimately ask for the rights to access a piece of content in a given context.

Resulting credentials do not provide any direct access grant to a piece or type of content, but only indicates that even if their owner does not have the rights - in the form of a license - to access a piece of content and if the credential is recognized, he may be entitled to the right to access the content due to an exceptional situation.

Exception Handling Delegation. As stated before, the goal of the credential based model is manifold. First, it provides a way to reduce the complexity and size of rights and policy managed contents. Second it provides more flexibility in handling special or unanticipated situations as content needn't be modified to deal with such situations. Finally, it simplifies the role of content owners allowing them to produce contents and protect them with the most important and representative policies, not having to deal with all possible situations.

As a result, businesses are provided with a flexible way to delegate handling of particular situations potentially allowing exceptions. In this model, exceptions are detected, verified and handled by an Exception Manager not involving directly the content producer, nor requiring to modify the content in order to adapt to new exceptional situations. Activity logging is done for further audit by interested parties.

Exception Management

In this section we explore in further details the process of rights verification, exception detection and short lived license acquisition.

Rights Verification. A central role in the proposed exception based model is the rights verification process. As stated before, the way the enforcement point manages rights verification in our model differs from the usual way. Figure 2 depicts the underlying sequence of actions that have to be completed.

When a user wants to access content (1), the held licenses are taken from the users' license store (2) and the enforcement point tries to use them for the requested action (3). This part of the process is exactly the same as done traditionally. If existing licenses match content policies, access is granted (4a). If none of the licenses are applicable to the content, available credentials are taken from the local credential store (4b) and content identification is extracted (5). These information are signed and sent (6) with the information about the way the content is being accessed, to the Exception Manager for further verification (7). This next step tries to detect possible exceptions instead of simply denying access to the content.

The enforcement point then waits for an answer which can eventually be a short lived license, if an exception is considered, and uses it (8) to then grant access to the content (9) and store the license (10) or a deny if not (11).

Exception Detection. When the exception manager receives the credentials, as well as content identification and the usage context, it tries to detect if a suitable combination is applicable for an exception. For each credential multiple steps are involved. These are illustrated in Figure 3.

First, the exception manager has to verify if the credential has been generated by an existing and valid Administrative Credential Manager (1). To achieve this task, the credentials have to be examined in order to retrieve information about their creator, and then verify their legal existence. The next step is to verify if the credential really belongs to the user trying to access the content (2). If it is the case, the exception manager checks if the credential is still valid (3) and asks the credential manager if it has not revoked it (4). Administrative Credential Manager verifies it (5), and then sends an answer (6). Credentials not complying with any of these rules are ignored (7). Last step is then to check if the credential can be applied to the content in the context in which the content is to be used. To do so the Exception Manager asks the Administrative Credential Manager for the motivations that have led to a credential generation (8) and the Manager sends back its signed answer (9). This answer may include textual information that can be analyzed, parsed; it may also contain any other kind of information such as a certificate emitted by a content owner indicating that a contract has been signed by both parties, or even another credential emitted by another recognized Administrative Credential Manager. If this last verification succeeds - i.e. if any of the retrieved information is accepted (10) - an exception is applicable and the short lived license acquisition process can start (11). When all credentials have been verified, a short

Figure 2. Rights verification sequence diagram

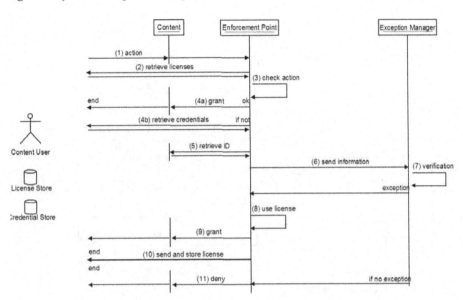

lived license or a deny message is sent back to the enforcement point depending on the result of the process (12).

Short Lived License Generation. The short lived license generation process is started when an exception has been detected and is applicable. This is a recursive process creating a license based on all exceptions that have been detected as applicable for a single access to a rights enabled content.

At this stage, the Exception Manager knows that it has to deal with an exception situation and knows what credentials have raised what kind of exception. The short lived license is built incrementally analyzing all exceptions. In order to emit such a short lived license some precautions have to be taken in order to manage issues of precedence and potential conflicting exceptions.

Figure 4 presents the different steps of this process. First, each exception has to be logged for traceability purpose (1). The log has to keep all required information to justify the exception.

This includes the identification of the content, the credentials that led to an exception, the motivations signed by the Administrative Exception Manager and the context of use, i.e. the foreseen type of content access. Once all required information have been logged, the rights this specific exception may grant to the user are compared to the rights granted by previous exceptions, and the license is refined (2). Differences may occur based on the provided reasons. For instance, a first credential may raise an exception with motivation "academic use", and a second credential may indicate that there is a "research agreement with the content owner". First credential would allow limited use, but second one would allow access to additional features, or a more detailed output. Once all exceptions have been handled, the short lived license can be generated (3).

The log of all exceptions is needed in order to be able to detect possible abuses by Administrative Credential Managers and users to blacklist them. These logs also help maintain a global trace of content usage which may be used in many ways.

Figure 3. Exception detection sequence diagram

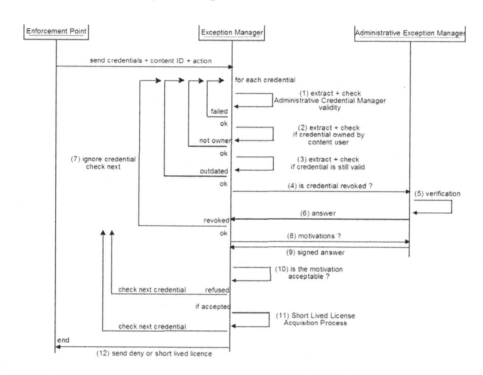

Figure 4. Short lived license aacquisition sequence diagram

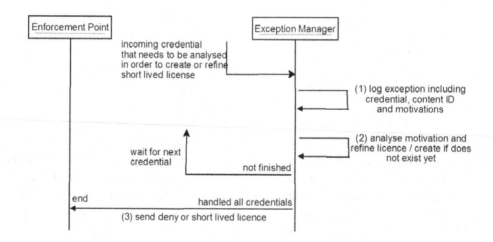

The validity of the license will usually be short (from a single access to a few days validity) or with limited use (read only) as each credential can be revoked at any time. But the effective validity is a matter of specific policies bound to the content owner which may eventually also be set as a core policy attached to the content. The final decision is thus left to the Exception Manager responsible for this task.

DISCUSSION

Let us now discusses some aspects of the proposed model based on a prototype implementation (Morin et al., 2008) highlighting the benefits and limitation of the chosen approach and trying to show the added value of the model.

Exception Manager Independence : a question raised when defining the model, was the necessity to separate the Exception Manager from the Content Producer. It appears clearly that merging these two roles may provide direct benefits such as avoiding subcontracting or trust issues which may occur when transmitting keys for generating short lived licenses. However it also appears that separating these two roles may prove to be far more efficient and provide additional benefits. These benefits mainly concern the reactivity and control over resource protection. Indeed, delegating the exception management issue enable content producers to focus on their core business of content production, not having to deal with exception management details. Let's consider some aspect further illustrating this point about Exception Manager independence:

Domain Specialization, Decoupling contextual policies from core policies provides a more detailed control over the way contextual policies are handled. This implies more precise domain knowledge. Indeed being able to evaluate if a credential applies to a particular situation requires expertise. While a content provider cannot afford

the effort to acquire and manage such knowledge, it can be far more efficient to delegate this task to a specialized entity.

Furthermore, this specialization helps handling unknown exceptions minimizing delays thus benefiting all clients of exception managers. Indeed, on the one hand the expertise gathered by the exception manager enables a fast and precise evaluation of unknown credentials. On the other hand, once evaluated, the newly gathered knowledge can be reused for other clients in similar situations. This is an important added value for content producers regarding reliability and reactivity.

Environment Knowledge, further, an independent Exception Manager can have contracts with multiple content providers. This allows to centralize effort, and build real environment or domain related knowledge. This knowledge can benefit content providers in many ways.

For instance, as information gathered about credential users and credential managers grows, this allows for better correlation and detection of abusers leading to proper actions to ban them or to take legal actions.

Finally, the role of Exception Manager may be a good argument mandating for the existence of Content Clearing Houses. These emerged in the Nineties trying to act as aggregators of License Managers and rights clearing centers. At the time, it didn't materialize as a profitable business mainly due to the fact that the market was not ready. However, looking at some of the current problems most collecting agencies are facing in the transformation of this industry, this might be an opportunity for them to also rethink creatively their role. As previously mentioned, centralizing roles may not be a good idea, thus a way to build distributed Content Clearing Houses should be explored.

Delegation implications : Now that we have seen the benefits of making use of external exception managers, we need to evaluate related implications for content producers. Basically, relying on an exception manager implies the delegation of creation of content usage rights, or licenses. The different rights to be generated may cover various levels of access to content users. These can range from full featured access to very limited access such as time based, number of uses, sample based, etc. This implies that the content producer provides some additional information as metadata in the core policies.

These information will help the exception managers in the specific exception management evaluation process. Exception managers and content producers work side by side, probably relying on a common open standard to address this issue.

Further, such a delegation implies that exception managers be able to generate licenses on behalf of content producers. To achieve this task, a primary key has to be provided to the exception manager. This key will then be used to produce valid Short-Lived Licenses for the specific content thus ensuring integrity and validity of the generated rights to be used by the enforcement point. Since such keys can produce virtually any license it is mandatory that exception manager be trusted. Tampered keys and abuses have to be detected and related licenses need to be revoked accordingly.

Managing Acceptable Risk: The proposed model improves the traditional DRM model by providing increased flexibility helping solve many current problems. The evaluation of credentials in order to detect exceptions adds the "may have rights" aspect to the traditional DRM model instead of the unrealistic either / or model of total security described above. While being a step towards copyright balance, this approach can be further improved.

Indeed, as this model decouples exception detection and validation from rights enforcement, the exception manager has to evaluate the credentials provided by content users. Until now we only

considered the situations where the credentials are approved thus leading to the generation of a short-lived license, or rejection otherwise. However, the evaluation of unknown credentials may take some time during which the user is waiting for an answer, which may take some time. This is where the model can be improved by adding the concept of acceptable risk management.

This concept aims at adding flexibility to the unknown credentials validation. This validation may require additional steps taking time. During this time the user is blocked. The idea behind acceptable risk management is that most content while definitely holding value, this value on a single item basis is minimal. For example consider the situation of listening to a song. Potentially, a single abuse will have almost no impact on the overall results. As a result, and in order to further strengthen some of the principles described above such as copyright balance and increased user experience, trusting the user a priori appears to make sense considering that most users are in legitimate usage situations. Moreover, thanks to the audit logs, abusers will be identifiable and subsequently denied and revoked. Consequently, and in addition to proper evaluation of the criticality of the content expressed as metadata, some basic or minimal rights could be granted to the users while the credential verification process is completed. This would be considered as acceptable risk in many situations and for many "commodity" like content usage situations.

The goal here is to find a tradeoff between protecting producers' rights at the price of maybe delaying legitimate access to content, and allowing smoother user experience in the case of access to individual lower value content. This approach requires a more precise classification of content. It provides flexibility but remains a choice the producer and exception manager can make on a case by case basis. Indeed, content of higher value does not have to be handled the same way more common content are. In the first case the proposed model can be applied strictly, which implies that credential verification may take some time. In the second case, an acceptable risk management approach can be applied, providing limited access to a document in order to satisfy users needs while not implying more than an acceptable risk for the producer.

Limitations: During the implementation of the model, some issues have been raised and limitations have been detected.

An interesting feature of the approach is that there is no need to modify the protected content as long as embedded core policies are not changed. However, if these core policies have to be updated former versions of the content should be retired or updated. Thus this model does not avoid the need of limiting the lifetime of released content or the model should provide enforcement points the ability to modify core policies on the fly under specific circumstances, or more likely the means to check regularly if the content has expired, and get automatically the new version of the content if needed.

Another issue concerns the multiplication of credentials implied by the model. As a single user may possess dozens of credentials requiring to be verified for exceptions, optimizations will be needed. The model already provides a way to minimize the number of credentials emitted for a single user by a given credential manager. Other optimizations could include bandwidth usage reduction only sending credentials potentially relevant to the content being used. The underlying optimization may be a structured classification of credentials allowing a smart credential filtering at enforcement point.

Also to be considered is the case of distributed exception verification. In the proposed model, the Exception Manager is presented as a unique entity. Real situations would require distribution and decentralization in order to cope with scalability issues as a large number of users may need to access simultaneously content managed by a single exception manager. Thus new issues due

to the decentralization of this role would have to be tackled. In our prototype the content includes information about the content owner, which may be contacted to obtain a list of alternate Exception Managers. However this approach is not optimal. Peer to peer approaches might be very effective in addressing such issues.

Credentials for DRM interoperability: Finally, the idea that the proposed model could be used to support DRM interoperability appeared when using the prototype. The goal here is not to provide a common model for DRM interoperability but to tackle some DRM interoperability issues from a users' rights perspective.

Let's take the example of a user buying a song using the Apple Music Store and wanting to use it on another music player, which does not support Fairplay, Apple's DRM format. While full DRM interoperability and space-shifting is a desired feature for the user, it is far from being always available and possible. In such a situation if the user really wants to listen to this song, he has to buy the song in a format compatible with his other music player.

On the one hand as using another format for the song can be seen as a new service the user want to acquire. Although slightly farfetched, paying for this new service could be considered as legitimate. On the other hand as the user has already bought the song and linked it to his identity, paying royalties each time the content format changes may be considered contrary to previously enjoyed rights.

In such situations and when applicable, credentials could be used to testify that a user has already cleared the rights. The credential could be generated when acquiring a license or at a later time and then provided when buying another license for another content format. In doing so, the user could pay only for the service providing him the new format for the content he already has the right to use.

FUTURE TRENDS AND CONCLUSION

To conclude, we highlight some key issues and their challenges in this industry for the years ahead in order to put into perspective the proposed contribution. It appears clearly that the various actors in this ecosystem have each tried to put themselves in the center of the picture thus trying to align the others. History has shown through market sanction that on the one hand the approach was wrong and on the other hand that if there should be a central actor it should definitely be the customer who happens to be the end-user. This is something the technology vendors and content holder have a hard time understanding.

More recently, this market has somewhat stabilized around a few big players and vendors upon which some integrators rely to provide often sector specific solutions as added value. However, standards are a critical success factor in this domain for the growth of this industry and its broad adoption. In a global massively interconnected society, it is definitely not reasonable to be locked in proprietary non-interoperable solutions. One cannot reasonably assume users will carry or hold as many consumer electronic rendering devices as there are incompatible competing DRM technologies. Nor is it desirable that all devices hold incompatible DRM software.

Some attempts are also being made at trying to reintroduce flat fee subscription based models together with or without DRM protection. Such models tend to be less effective as they raise many issues in terms of revenue sharing and collection, the rights that survive after the contracting period, etc. Similarly some discussions are also taking place on introducing levies on rendering devices which in turn suffer from similar shortcomings. Traditionally levies have proven to be solutions used when no other viable option is available. An approach providing support for exception management as discussed here would be a very interesting and flexible alternative to a levy model.

Not to mention the tremendous advantages for real-time monitoring for marketers and possible new business models it would enable.

Technical and semantic interoperability represents one, if not the most important challenge in this industry. Likewise, exception management in the context of DRM enabled systems is another key issue and challenge whereby all usage situations cannot reasonably be anticipated. For example, many laws still rely on often contradictory national or territorial specificities such as for example copyright exemption for the blind in certain countries.

The evolution in the field of trusted computing platforms, especially at the operating system level, is likely to be a key critical factor maybe complemented by a DRM chip as discussed for many years now. This last point remains speculative.

User centric Identity management and its corresponding usage situations for content usage will also be among the next major evolutions which should help this industry. In any case, contrary to some DRM opponents, DRM is likely to stay. Probably not in its present form but we surely need to rethink a few things such as copyright, property, technology and business. Consequently, why not attempt our best effort in shaping the kind of electronic society we want to live in.

REFERENCES

Becker, E. Buhse, W. Günnewig, D., & Rump, N. (eds.). (2003). *Digital Rights Management, Technological, Economic, Legal and Political Aspects*, LNCS 2770, Springer Verlag.

Betamax. (1984). *Sony Corp. of America v. Universal City Studios, Inc.*, 464 U.S. 417, January 17, 1984.

CORAL. (2007). *DRM Interoperability Consortium Invites Steve Jobs to Join*, Coral Consortium,

Feb. 9, 2007, http://www.coral-interop.org/main/news/pr20070209.html

Cox, B. (1994). *Superdistribution.* Wired Magazine, September 1994, pp 89.92.

Cox, B. (1996). *Superdistribution Objects as Property on the Electronic Frontier,* Addison-Wesley.

DMCA. (1998). *The Digital Millennium Copyright Act of 1998* - U.S. Copyright Office Summary. http://www.copyright.gov/legislation/dmca.pdf

Felten, E. W. (2005). *DRM and Public Policy,* Inside Risks 181, CACM 48, July 7, 2005, http://www.csl.sri.com/users/neumann/insiderisks05.html#181

Gapper, J. (2007). *Why digital music should be set free,* Financial Times, Asia edition, Comment, February 12, 2007, p. 17.

Jobs, S. (2007). *Thoughts on Music.* Apple Inc. Web site, February 6, 2007, http://www.apple.com/hotnews/thoughtsonmusic/

Jondet, N. (2006) *La France v. Apple: who's the dadvsi in DRMs?,* (2006) 3:4 SCRIPT-ed 473, http://www.law.ed.ac.uk/ahrc/script-ed/vol3-4/jondet.asp

Lacy, J. (2007). *Coral Consortium Letter to Steve Jobs,* Feb. 9, 2007, http://www.coral-interop.org/20070209_Coral_Letter.html

Lessig, L. (1996). *Opening Keynote, LinuxWorld,* San Francisco, August 15, 2006.

Mennecke, T. (2005). *Anti-DRM Demonstration Takes Place in New York City,* Oct. 28, 2005, http://www.slyck.com/news.php?story=969

Mori, R., & Kawahara, M. (1990, July). *Superdistribution: The Concept and the Architecture.* Transaction of the IEICE, E 73(7), 1133-1146.

Mori, R., & Tashiro, S. (1987). *The Concept of Software Service System (SSS).* Transaction of the IEICE, J70-D.1, Jan 1987, pp. 70-81

Morin, J.-H., & Pawlak, M. (2007) *From Digital Rights Management to Enterprise Rights and Policy Management: Challenges and Opportunities.* Advances in Enterprise Information Technology Security, F. Herrmann and D. Khadraoui (Eds), Information Science Reference, IGI Global, July 2007, pp. 169-188.

Morin, J.-H., & Pawlak, M. (2007). *A Model for Credential Based Exception Management in Digital Rights Management Systems,* First International Conference on Global Defense and Business Continuity, ICGD&BC 2007, Second International Conference on Internet Monitoring and Protection, IEEE, July 1-6, 2007, Silicon Valley, USA.

Morin, J.-H., & Pawlak, M. (2008). *Exception-Aware Digital Rights Management Architecture Experimentation,* 2008 International Conference on Information Security and Assurance, (ISA 2008), IEEE, April 24-26, 2008, Busan, Korea, pp. 518-526.

Rosenblatt, B. Trippe, B., & Mooney, S. (2001). *Digital Rights Management: Business and Technology,* New York: Hungry Minds/John Wiley & Sons, 2001.

KEY TERMS

Copyright Balance: Principle stating that since lawful use, including fair use, of copyrighted works is in the public interest, no DRM system should prevent it (Felten, 2005).

Digital Rights Management (DRM): A technical protection measure used to persistently protect digital content by cryptographically associating usage rules to the digital content. Content rendering is bound to successful interpretation of the associated rules by an enforcement point, usually a trusted piece of software.

Enforcement Point: Trusted piece of software residing on a user platform in charge of interpreting the rules associated to DRM enabled content.

Exception Management: In the context of DRM environments, model enabling users to claim legitimate and lawful usage situations by requesting unilaterally an exception based on the production of some form of credential.

Fair Use: Doctrine allowing limited use of copyrighted material without requiring permission from the rights holders, such as academic use, review, etc.

Space Shifting: Concept allowing to shift digital content among different format and devices. Commonly agreed to fall under lawful use under personal copy or home copy rights.

Superdistribution: Distribution model based on the fact that digital content being persistently protected for example with DRM, it can be freely exchanged based on the fact that access is bound to successful interpretation of the cryptographically associated rules.

Technical Protection Measures (TPM): Refers to all the techniques used to protect digital content such as DRM, watermarking, fingerprinting, access control, etc.

Time Shifting: Concept allowing to shift in time the rendering of digital content such as using VCRs for example. Commonly agreed to fall under lawful use under personal copy or home copy rights.

Chapter IV
Overview of OMA Digital Rights Management

Mercè Serra Joan
Fraunhofer Institute for Integrated Circuits IIS, Germany

Bert Greevenbosch
Fraunhofer Institute for Integrated Circuits IIS, Germany

Anja Becker
Fraunhofer Institute for Integrated Circuits IIS, Germany

Harald Fuchs
Fraunhofer Institute for Integrated Circuits IIS, Germany

Stefan Krägeloh
Fraunhofer Institute for Integrated Circuits IIS, Germany

ABSTRACT

This chapter gives an overview of the Open Mobile Alliance™ Digital Rights Management (OMA DRM) standard, which allows for the secure distribution and usage of protected digital content. Additionally, the DRM Profile of the OMA Mobile Broadcast Services standard, which is an extension of the OMA DRM standard to support mobile broadcast applications, is discussed. This chapter also introduces the associated OMA Secure Removable Media (OMA SRM) and OMA Secure Content Exchange (OMA SCE) standards, which increase the portability of DRM-protected content and offer a better user experience. The aim of this chapter is to give the reader insight in the above mentioned standards, their technical background, and possible usage scenarios.

INTRODUCTION

Digital Rights Management (DRM) is a technology that allows content and service providers to securely distribute digital content and to control its access and use.

The Open Mobile Alliance (OMA) Digital Rights Management standard (OMA DRM) offers protection and secure access control for digital content. The OMA Mobile Broadcast Services standard (BCAST) specifies the protected content delivery for mobile broadcast applications such as mobile TV. These two standards complement each other enabling further functionalities and use cases.

This chapter provides a technical overview of the OMA DRM standard including its latest developments. Further, the OMA BCAST standard is described, focusing on the DRM profile for service and content protection.

BASIC TERMS AND CONCEPTS OF DIGITAL RIGHTS MANAGEMENT

Digital Rights Management (DRM) comprises the complete process of managing and controlling the access and consumption of protected content.

In a DRM system, content is cryptographically protected and access to the content is governed through licenses issued by a license server. Licenses contain the keys to access the content and express usage rights and constraints for the content using a rights expression language (REL). Collectively, the modules that handle the license information are known as key management system (KMS).

Through the separation of protected content and controlling license, various business models are facilitated, such as superdistribution and subscription, while maintaining support for other established business models, such as pay-per-view or play-count/play-time variations. Since the protected content cannot be accessed without a license, it can be distributed without fear of misuse. Therefore content distribution is not limited to controlled networks.

The usage rules and rights are enforced at consumption time by a secure agent (secure player implementation). The agent is also responsible for secure storage of information that has to be kept secret or temper proof, like root certificates, private device keys and state information (e.g. play counts).

Cryptographically signed certificates are used to authenticate devices and to establish and verify trust between all involved parties. Trusted certification authorities that are part of a public key infrastructure (PKI) issue these certificates.

Licenses are bound to an anchor, e.g. a unique hardware property or user identification, to ensure control over the content. Providing a common anchor for a group of devices is known as domain concept. An example is the home domain, where a number of devices belonging to a single household share a common anchor allowing a single domain license to be used on any of the domain's devices.

THE OPEN MOBILE ALLIANCE™ AND OMA DRM

The Open Mobile Alliance™ (OMA) is a consortium of major companies active in the area of mobile communications. At the time of writing, OMA has about 400 members worldwide, including mobile operators, device and network suppliers, information technology companies and content providers.

The OMA DRM standard is one of the first open, standardized DRM specifications. The first version – OMA DRM v1.0 – was released in 2004. This version focuses on basic functionality: although the content is encrypted and a rights expression language is specified, the protection of the content encryption key (CEK) remains unspecified, such that the security relies on the delivery protocol of the license. Nowadays, OMA DRM v1.0 is widely supported by mobile devices and used for delivery of low-valued content such as ringtones.

OMA DRM v2.0 provides additional functionalities for a more secure and flexible solution than the previous version OMA DRM v1.0. It includes secure key exchange protocols and supports super-distribution and domains. OMA DRM v2.0 was finalized in 2006. A slightly extended version, OMA DRM v2.1, is to be finalized in 2008.

OMA DRM v2.0 is a mature, open DRM standard, which is mainly applicable for download of protected content. During the development of the OMA Mobile Broadcast Services Standard, a need was identified to protect broadcast content and services by extending the OMA DRM v2.0 standard.

After OMA DRM v2.0, the development of a number of DRM-related follow-up specifications was started. Among these are OMA Secure Removable Media (SRM) and OMA Secure Content Exchange (SCE), which are expected to be finalized in 2008.

CONTROLLED ACCESS TO DIGITAL WORKS: OMA DRM VERSION 2.0

The OMA DRM v2.0 specification is the successor of OMA DRM v1.0 and provides a complete end-to-end protection system suitable for premium content.

OMA DRM is based on the concept of separating the content and the license. Usually, content and license are delivered as separate files, possibly over separate communication channels. The content is delivered in encrypted form and the content encryption key is included in the license. The content cannot be accessed without this key.

In OMA DRM, the license is called a rights object (RO) and is represented in XML. The RO contains the content encryption key (CEK) and usage rules (permissions and constraints) for the content. "Permissions" allow certain actions related to the protected content and "constraints" limit these actions. The usage rules are expressed in a rights expression language (REL) that allows precise and individual expression of the user's rights. For example, the RO can specify that content may be played only 3 times, or until a certain date.

A license is usually generated for a particular device, in a way that it can only be used by that device. The license is said to be bound to the device. The protected content itself is not protected in a device specific way, it may be used on any compatible device if a corresponding license for that device is acquired.

General Overview of the OMA DRM Architecture

The OMA DRM v2.0 architecture consists of three main entities: the content issuer, the rights issuer and the DRM agent in the end-user's device, as depicted in Figure 1.

The content issuer distributes the content files, usually by providing a website (web shop) where the user can discover and download the content (possibly after some business transactions).

The rights issuer (RI) handles the generation and the delivery of rights objects.

After the reception of content and RO, the DRM agent in the end-user's device is responsible for the enforcement of the usage rules stated in the RO and the secure storage of information that has to be kept secret or temper proof, like root certificates, private device keys and state information (e.g. play counts).

In an exemplary scenario, the user browses the web portal (web shop) of the content issuer and acquires some content. The user can download the content directly from the web portal. The content issuer contacts the rights issuer to request the generation and delivery of an RO to the user's device. The actual communication of the content issuer and rights issuer is not specified by the OMA DRM v2.0 standard.

Figure 1. Functional architecture of OMA DRM version 2.0

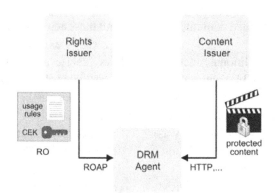

After the RI has received the request, it initiates a protocol for the secure delivery of the RO to the device. The first time that the RI and a particular device communicate, a registration protocol is performed to exchange cryptographic information, such as identities, public keys and certificates between RI and device. After the successful registration of the device, the RI delivers the RO to the device using the RO acquisition protocol (ROAP). Alternatively, ROs can be pushed to the device without the use of ROAP, e.g. in an SMS (short message service) message, and installed in the device, if the device authorizes such installations.

Rights Objects and Rights Expression Language

An OMA DRM v2.0 RO contains the content encryption key (CEK), as well as permissions and constraints. As stated above, "permissions" allow certain actions and "constraints" limit these actions. For example, the permission "play" can be constrained to a certain number of play times.

An RO can be either stateful or stateless. An RO is called stateful when the device needs to keep track of certain information, which changes every time the stateful rights are exercised. For example, an RO that allows the user to play certain content with the constraint "three times" is stateful, because the device needs to maintain a play count, which has to be decreased every time the content is played. A stateless RO is an RO that is not stateful, i.e. the device does not need to maintain state information. An example is an RO that contains a "play" permission for an unlimited time or allows playing the content until a certain date.

OMA DRM v2.0 ROs are coded in XML (extensible markup language). An XML schema defines the position and type of the different XML elements in the RO. The permissions and constraints are stored in the RO in the <rights> element. The schema for the <rights> element is based on the open digital rights language [ODRL].

The RO is integrity protected, i.e. it is protected against modifications, and is digitally signed by the RI.

Figure 2 illustrates the relationship between an RO and the protected content. The RO contains the CEK, which is needed to access the content. The CEK is cryptographically bound to a specific device, i.e. it is encrypted with the public key of that device. Only the device that possesses the matching private key can access the content.

Figure 2. OMA DRM v2 protected content is encrypted with the content encryption key (CEK). The CEK is delivered in a rights object (RO). The CEK in the RO is encrypted with the public key of the device, such that only this device can access the content with its private key.

Public Key Infrastructure and Device Binding

OMA DRM offers two different ways to ensure that protected content can only be accessed by authorized devices: a RO is either bound to a particular device, or to a group of devices, called a domain. Domains are described in the next section.

The binding of an RO to a particular device is enabled through the use of a public key infrastructure (PKI). A PKI includes a certificate authority (CA), public/private key pairs, public key certificates and revocation mechanisms. The CA is a trusted third party which is responsible for issuing and revoking public key certificates.

A PKI uses asymmetric cryptography. Each party in the PKI owns a key pair consisting of a public key, which is known by everybody, and a private key, which has to be kept secret. The public and the private key are mathematically related, but it is not possible to derive one from the other. A message is encrypted using the public key and can only be decrypted with the corresponding private key that is kept secret by the owner.

A public key certificate binds an identity to a public key via a digital signature of a trusted authority. Moreover, it specifies the permitted area of application for the public key and contains an expiry date for the certificate. A valid certificate

is taken as prove for the trustworthiness of the owner. In OMA DRM v2.0, the certificate indicates whether the entity holding the certificate is a device or an RI and contains the public key for authentication, signature verification and encryption. A central certificate authority is responsible for issuing the certificates.

In real life, a device (or in lesser extent an RI) may be compromised so that it is not compliant anymore with the DRM specifications. A compromised device could leak keys that need to be kept secret, such as the private key of the DRM agent or the domain key. A compromised device could also decrypt DRM-protected content and distribute it without DRM protection. In these cases, the device should not be trusted anymore. Especially, the device should not be able to acquire new content since it might ignore usage rules, or even distribute the decrypted content to others. Since the certificate of the device indicates that the device is trustworthy, there needs to be a mechanism to revoke certificates. An RI has to verify the revocation status of device certificates, but it is not specified by the OMA DRM v2.0 standard how this is done.

Revocation of RIs in OMA DRM v2.0 is handled via an online certificate status protocol (OCSP) responder. An OCSP responder is a server that provides information about the validity of certificates. The device can ask the OCSP responder to verify if the certificate of the RI is still valid.

The RI is the only entity that can contact the OCSP responder directly. To guarantee freshness of the OCSP response to the device, either a random number generated by the device is included in the OCSP response or a timestamp. This prevents that a revoked RI sends an old OCSP response, which it kept from the time that its certificate was still valid.

Domains

In traditional DRM systems, it is common that content is bound to a specific device. This implies that the user can only consume the content on one specific device.

To improve user experience, the domain concept was introduced. The user can group devices into a domain, and purchase a license for the domain instead of a license for a single device. The content can then be accessed by any device in that domain.

When joining a domain, a device receives a key, which is shared by all devices in the domain. This key is called the domain key and has to be securely stored by each device in the domain. The RI can issue an RO that is bound to the domain, by protecting the rights with the domain key, rather than with the public key of a particular device. Thus, content with a domain RO can be consumed on any of the devices in the domain.

Domains are flexible, i.e. devices can be added to a domain and devices can be removed from a domain. To enable this flexibility, a number of mechanisms have been specified. The most important protocols are the "join domain" protocol, which adds a device to the domain, and the "leave domain" protocol, which removes the device from a domain. A device must have a connection to the RI in order to join or leave a domain. However, once the domain is established, content can be moved within the domain without any network connection.

To ensure that devices that are removed from a domain cannot consume new domain ROs, the "domain generation" is increased and a new domain key is issued. Devices that have left the domain cannot access the ROs of the new generation.

The content and the domain RO can be combined in one file. This file can be transferred from one device in the domain to another without performing any protocol, e.g. just by a file copy. The RO does not need to be delivered using a secure protocol, because the above described methods ensure that only authorized devices, i.e. devices in the domain, are able to access the content encryption key inside the RO. This allows the user to copy and move a single file and the RO itself remains invisible to the user.

Protected Content Format

The content format defines how digital content is encoded in binary form. OMA DRM v2.0 defines two formats for protected content: the DRM content format (DCF) and the packetized DRM content format (PDCF). Both formats are based on the ISO Base Media File Format [ISOFF].

OMA DCF is used to store protected discrete media. It is especially suitable for static media like text documents, still images, computer games, applications and ring tones. In general, DCF can be used to wrap any content in a container and remains agnostic of the internal structure and layout of the data.

A multipart DCF is a DCF file that is able to contain multiple containers for multiple pieces of content. For example, a multipart DCF may contain a ring tone and a logo. The rights for the multiple pieces of content in a multipart DCF are treated independently.

OMA PDCF is used to store protected continuous media, such as audio and video. Media is protected in a packet-by-packet basis and not as a complete data block, like in DCF. In this way, PDCF supports random access to encrypted media with just-in-time decryption before decoding or rendering. PDCF is suitable for the protection of ISO File Format files like .mp4 or .3gp containing any kind of audio content, such as High Efficiency Advanced Audio Coding (HE-AAC), and video content, such as H.264/ Advanced Video Coding (AVC).

The content protection consists of encrypting the content and storing it into a (P)DCF. A (P)DCF can be either completely encrypted, or only partially encrypted. Because of the strength and implementation efficiency, OMA DRM uses the symmetric encryption algorithm Advanced Encryption Standard [DR2002] with a key length of 128 bit (AES128).

Superdistribution

The separation of license and content allows superdistribution of content. The content file can be distributed on any distribution channel, and only the license needs to be distributed in a controlled manner.

For instance, users can forward content files to other users. To consume the content, the receiving user needs to acquire the appropriate license from the RI for his device or domain.

Subscription Services

OMA DRM v2.0 enables business models based on service subscription. A user can subscribe to a service and access content for a certain time. With the subscription the user is able to consume all offered content as long as the subscription period does not expire.

Subscription is efficiently enabled with the OMA DRM v2.0 inheritance model. In this model a license is defined using a parent and a child RO. The child RO inherits permissions and constraints from the parent RO.

For example, consider a shop where the user pays a monthly fee and can download and play any content while subscribed. Every month, the

rights issuer provides the user with a fresh parent RO valid for that month. Additionally the shop provides the user with a child RO for each content that he downloads. The content is only accessible when both the parent and the child RO are valid. When the user cancels his subscription, the RI stops providing the monthly parent ROs, and all content that the user bought under the subscription becomes unusable.

Backup

OMA DRM v2.0 allows backup of purchased content and rights to an external storage. This enables the user to restore his rights on the same device if they are lost.

As the content license is cryptographically bound to the device, the rights cannot be restored to another device, even if the original device was lost. The content provider may maintain a record of the purchase data and provide a service to restore rights to other devices.

Export

OMA DRM v2.0 enables the export of OMA DRM content and rights to devices using other DRM protection schemes.

USAGE MEASUREMENT AND LICENSE TRANSFER: OMA DRM VERSION 2.1

In version 2.1 of OMA DRM two new features are available: metering and RO upload protocol.

Metering is a mechanism that enables the RI to measure the use of content in the user's device. The RI can choose to include a metering constraint to a permission, which specifies that the device must record how often and when that permission was used. For example, a piece of music can have a metering constraint on the play permission. In that case, the device keeps book of the number of times that piece was played. This information is then sent back to the RI, either on request or on a periodic basis.

The RI uses metering information to monitor the content consumption on the device. This might, for example, be used in subscription services to calculate the actual amount of royalty fees that the RI has to pay to the performance rights organization.

Metering has some privacy issues: the user might not like that his behavior is being measured and reported to the RI. OMA DRM v2.1 therefore specifies rules for user consent on metering. In the normal case, the user must give user consent via the device, on the first time that a metered RO from a certain RI is consumed. An exception is an RO, which is issued by an RI that is in the user consent whitelist. The user consent whitelist is a list of RIs that do not need user consent to perform certain actions, because the user has given his consent via another way, for example when signing his contract with his mobile phone network provider.

The RO upload protocol was introduced to enable move of ROs from one device to another device via the RI. This is particularly interesting for the mobile telecommunications business, where it is common practice that the user changes his mobile phone every two years. To ensure that the user does not lose device bound content, OMA DRM v2.1 allows uploading ROs back to the RI, such that the RI can re-issue them to the new device.

OMA DRM EXTENSIONS FOR BROADCAST SUPPORT

OMA Mobile Broadcast Services (BCAST) is a globally interoperable mobile TV standard, which enables the delivery of mobile digital broadcast services. This standard was developed within OMA in parallel to the OMA DRM standard. Part of the technologies used for the protection of broadcast content and services is based on the OMA DRM v2.0 standard described in the previous sections.

As described in section about OMA DRM v2.0, OMA DRM defines among others a protected content format, a license format including an extensive REL, and protocols to the rights issuer for device registration and acquisition of licenses. These OMA DRM protocols can be used by broadcast receivers to acquire DRM licenses for broadcast content, if they have an interactive channel at their disposal. If no interactive channel is available, extensions to DRM v2.0 have been defined to allow for broadcast-only delivery of licenses. Furthermore, broadcast receivers can make recordings of the received streams and acquire rights objects to use the recorded content later on.

OMA BCAST is agnostic to the underlying broadcast distribution scheme. At the point of writing, it defines adaptations for the following bearers that use an Internet Protocol (IP) transport layer: 3rd Generation Partnership Project (3GPP™) Multimedia Broadcast Multicast Service (MBMS), 3GPP2 Broadcast and Multicast Service (BCMCS) and Digital Video Broadcasting – Handheld (DVB®-H). The OMA BCAST specification offers the possibility of additional adaptations in the future, either to other IP-based broadcast distribution schemes, such as DVB – Satellite Handheld (DVB-SH), or for other kind of applications, such as IPTV.

OMA BCAST covers, among others, the areas of service guide (for description of services and content offerings), service and content protection, interaction between terminal and service provider, notifications (for emergency messages, general announcements, service or content associated notifications, etc.) as well as service provisioning (for requesting price, renewing or cancelling subscription, etc.) and terminal provisioning (for performing firmware upgrades, etc.). It supports streaming and file distribution over broadcast, multicast or unicast.

OMA BCAST technology allows various kinds of applications, such as interactive mobile TV and non-interactive TV-services. Interactive mobile TV is used for scheduled programs and may include a return channel (for Web access, voting, chat, etc.). Further applications are location-based applications such as navigation or information about traffic or local public transport.

The following sub-sections describe service and content protection of mobile broadcast services, focusing on the OMA BCAST DRM profile.

Key Management System

OMA BCAST uses a four-layer hierarchy for the key management (see Figure 3).

The first layer handles the registration of a device with a rights issuer. During this process the device receives the registration data encrypted with its device public key. The device registration data will allow the device to access the licenses related to subscribed services or on-demand programs.

In the second layer, the license related to a subscribed service or program is delivered to the device. Licenses are delivered within long term key messages (LTKM). A key derived from the device registration data, the Inferred Encryption Key (IEK), is used to protect the service encryption key (SEK) or program encryption key (PEK) included in the license.

In the third layer, the traffic encryption keys (TEK) protected by the SEK or the PEK, are transmitted to the device, contained in short term key messages (STKM). TEKs are the keys used to encrypt the continuous streaming data. It is common and good practice to change the TEKs periodically (e.g. every 3 seconds).

Finally, in the fourth layer, the actual broadcast stream is delivered to the device protected by the TEKs.

OMA BCAST PROFILES

OMA BCAST defines two different solutions for protecting content and services, each using a different security mechanism: the smartcard profile and the DRM profile. Both profiles are based on the four-layer key hierarchy depicted in Figure 3, but define a different key management system.

The smartcard profile uses a smartcard (e.g. the SIM card of a mobile phone) as a secure anchor

Figure 3. Four-layer hierarchy used in the key management for an OMA BCAST service or program

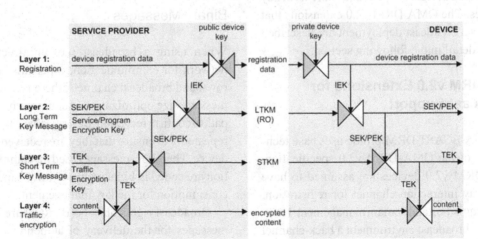

and defines a set of smartcard-based technologies to provide secure key establishment and management, as well as permissions and token handling. These technologies require that the terminal has a bidirectional channel, i.e. a cellular radio interface, at its disposal.

Registration, short-term and long-term key management are based on a generic bootstrapping architecture (GBA) [GBA] mechanism or on a shared secret key provided during the manufacturing process. GBA is a general architecture that allows the secure sharing of a secret between a server and a client.

OMA DRM rights objects are not used in the smartcard profile for the LTKMs. Instead, usage rules associated with the service and/or specific program content are delivered in LTKMs and STKMs. The description of usage rules in the smartcard profile is very limited.

The DRM profile is based on the OMA DRM v2.0 standard and the 18 Crypt Profile of DVB-H Service Purchase and Protection [DVBH-SPP] standard. As in OMA DRM, security of the system relies on a public key infrastructure.

The DRM profile extends OMA DRM v2.0 for a deployment in a mobile broadcast environment. The DRM profile supports not only devices with a bidirectional channel, but also with a unidirectional or broadcast channel. Usage rules associated with a service and/or a specific program are delivered in rights objects and short-term key messages. The OMA DRM v2.0 extensions that allow for a broadcast deployment are described in more detail in the following section.

OMA DRM v2.0 Extensions for Broadcast Support

The OMA BCAST DRM profile uses base technologies of the OMA DRM v2.0 specification. OMA DRM v2.0 devices are assumed to have a two-way interaction channel for registration, rights acquisition and domain management. However, in a broadcast environment a back-channel might not be available.

The DRM profile extends OMA DRM v2.0 to allow broadcast of DRM protected content to large mobile audiences without the need for a two-way channel, by the use of subscriber group management and broadcast encryption schemes. To allow efficient delivery and communication to devices over a broadcast channel, the DRM profile defines counterpart messages and rights objects that are optimized in size for narrow-band channels. Additionally, it extends the rights expression language to allow new types of content usage (such as recording) and new business models (such as token-based consumption).

When a device registers to a service provider, the device first has to convey its device specific data. For devices without a back-channel, this is done offline, for example via telephone, SMS message or Internet. As a next step, the service provider sends the registration data to the device, which includes the registration keys needed for the reception of broadcast rights objects, token handling and domain management.

After registration, the device has the possibility to send offline notifications to the service provider for requesting certain actions such as re-registration, join or leave domain, token requests or resend broadcast rights objects. Beside this, the service provider can broadcast a message to devices for update of important data like the RI certificate, DRM time or contact number.

Binary Messages

When using a broadcast (i.e. unidirectional) network for communication, especially for narrow-band broadcast channels, there is a need for message size optimization. As there is no return path to confirm reception, messages have to be sent repeatedly to ensure that they are received by the device. Therefore, messages used for communication are coded in binary form to limit bandwidth consumption for the key management.

Broadcast rights objects (BCROs) are binary messages for the delivery of authenticated and integrity protected rights over a broadcast channel. BCROs are the binary equivalent of ROs. BCROs can be addressed to a single device, a domain, a whole subscriber group or a subset of a subscriber group.

Subscriber Group Management

In order to receive a protected broadcast service, a user has to register the device to a service provider and subscribe for the desired service.

For the management of broadcast subscription services, all devices registered to a service provider are distributed in groups called subscriber groups. A subscriber group, labeled with a subscriber group identifier, can have a size of 256, 512 or more subscribers.

Subscriber groups are very useful to address specific devices via broadcast for conditional access purposes. Conditional access allows defining the exact group of broadcast receivers that will have access to the protected content. This is done by including the subscriber group identifier and a bit access mask to the broadcast message. The bit access mask is an array of bits that indicates to which receivers in the subscriber group the message is addressed. For each device in a subscriber group, a unique bit in the bit access mask is assigned. Only receivers in a subscriber group, whose bits in the bit access mask are set, are allowed to access the protected content. To address all subscribers in a group only the subscriber group identifier is needed.

Broadcast Encryption Schemes

A broadcast encryption scheme is used to address a subset of devices belonging to a subscriber group in a cryptographically secure way. This is necessary to allow access to content only to those devices within a subscriber group which are subscribed to a certain service. For that, BCROs are cryptographically protected with a derived key, such that only the addressed devices can compute this key and hence decrypt the BCRO for rendering the content. All other devices in the subscriber group cannot compute this key and cannot access the protected content.

OMA BCAST specifies two schemes to achieve that only addressed devices can access the content: the zero-message broadcast encryption scheme and a broadcast encryption scheme based on one-way function trees. Both schemes are based on binary trees, but differ in the way in which the node values in the tree are established and in the way these values are used to generate the BCRO encryption key.

Token-Based Consumption

For token-based consumption, the device acquires tokens from an RI or service provider and uses them as a currency to play protected content. An RO describes the amount of tokens that are required to play the RO-related content, for example 5 tokens for each content rendering, or 1 token for 30 minutes of rendering.

Tokens can be paid in advance by the user (prepaid tokens) or can be charged after consumption (post-paid tokens). To allow for post-paid tokens, the device will report periodically the amount of consumed tokens to the RI.

Transport and Recording of Broadcast Streams

OMA BCAST enables protected recordings of received broadcast streams. In principle, transmission of protected broadcast streams can be done in two different ways: link protection, if the content has to be secured only during transmission and end-to-end-protection, if content is secured during its complete lifetime. Depending on the protection mechanism used for the broadcast stream transport, two different approaches for recording are defined.

In case of link or transport protection, the content is only protected during delivery. The content is first packetized (i.e. reformatted for transport) and then encrypted. For link protection OMA BCAST is using IPSec (IP security) or SRTP (Secure Real-time Transport Protocol). For recording of such streams, the terminal needs to first decrypt the received stream in order to be able to depacketize the content. Once the stream is depacketized, the content is in the clear and the terminal is able to access and render the content. For protected storage, the terminal needs to re-encrypt the content with a single key into a (P)DCF. This key is randomly generated by the terminal itself and encrypted by the SEK or the PEK, which was used to protect the original stream.

In end-to-end protection, content encryption is applied directly after content generation using ISMACryp (see [ISMACryp]). On the server side, the content is stored in encrypted form in such a way that it can be extracted and packetized without decrypting it. In the terminal, the content is depacketized and then stored in a file. The content always remains protected after reception, without the need of re-encryption.

PORTABILITY OF PROTECTED CONTENT: OMA SECURE REMOVABLE MEDIA

In OMA DRM v2.0 and v2.1 an RO is either bound to a device or to a domain. This implies that the user can play content only on a predetermined number of devices.

The OMA Secure Removable Media (SRM) specification allows for more portability of protected content. The content is not bound to a certain device or domain, but to a portable memory card, the SRM. This card is used to store the encrypted content and ROs such that the content can be played on any SRM enabled device. From the user's perspective, the card behaves like a commonly known CD or DVD.

OMA SRM can be used to transfer protected content and ROs from one portable player to an-

other. A user may also render the content directly from the SRM: for example, a user can watch a movie stored on the personal SRM, on a friend's big TV screen.

Architecture of an SRM

An SRM is a memory card, which can store confidential information in a secure manner. The SRM contains a cryptographic processor, which enables the SRM to encrypt and decrypt data. Additionally, the SRM provides for integrity protection of the stored confidential data.

The SRM standard uses a master/slave model: the DRM agent, which is in the rendering device, controls the communication and sends commands to the SRM. For example, such a command can request a certain RO from the SRM, initiate the installation of an RO on the SRM or ask for a list of available ROs in the SRM.

Move of Rights Objects

The basic idea in OMA SRM is to use the SRM as a medium to transfer ROs between devices. To achieve this, ROs can be moved from a device to an SRM and from an SRM to another device. During a move, the content encryption keys need to be conveyed securely and, in the case of stateful ROs, the current state (e.g. the number of plays left) needs to be maintained.

In OMA SRM, there are two types of move: the move of an RO from a device to an SRM, and the move of an RO from an SRM to a device. Because of the master/slave model, both transactions are initiated by the device.

For the moving of an RO from the device to an SRM, a 4-pass protocol has been defined. In the first step of this protocol, the device informs the SRM of its intent of storing an RO in the SRM. If the SRM has enough space available, the SRM replies that it will accept the RO. The device then disables the RO, and sends a copy of it to the SRM, together with the key used to protect the rights.

The SRM then installs the RO and confirms to the device that the transaction was successful. After the device receives the confirmation, it removes the RO from its internal memory.

Notice that in the above mentioned procedure, the loss of rights can occur after the rights have been disabled. If the communication is disrupted during the delivery of the RO to the SRM, the device will never receive a confirmation from the SRM that the RO was accepted. However, the device cannot determine whether the lack of confirmation is due to the RO not being received by the SRM, or the confirmation being intercepted by an attacker.

When developing a protocol for moving rights, one has to decide whether an unexpected termination of the communication should lead to a duplication of rights or the loss of rights. For OMA SRM, it was decided that the loss of rights in case of an unexpected termination was more acceptable than the possible duplication of rights. In the latter case, an attacker might purposely interrupt the communication and thus disturb the secure protocol process to illegally gain ROs, whereas an unintentional termination is highly unusual. To minimize the chance of losing rights due to an unexpected communication failure, the SRM specification provides recovery mechanisms. These mechanisms are designed in such a way that in most cases the rights can be recovered, but they are never duplicated.

The moving of an RO from an SRM back to a device is also done over a protocol. In the first step the device requests a certain RO from the SRM. The SRM then disables this RO and sends the RO and the key protecting the rights to the device. After the device has successfully installed the RO, it informs the SRM and the SRM removes its copy of the RO.

Direct Rendering of Content

To provide a user experience similar to the use of a CD, the SRM specification allows direct rendering. The RO remains on the SRM, and the user can insert the SRM into any SRM-enabled device to consume the content.

Although SRMs have cryptographic capabilities, they are not able to enforce licenses. Hence, to perform direct rendering, the DRM agent needs to acquire the complete RO from the SRM, disable it on the SRM and enforce the rights. After the rendering is done, the DRM agent removes its copy of the RO and re-enables the RO in the SRM. In the case that the RO was stateful, the DRM agent updates the state information in the SRM.

Mutual Authentication and Revocation

To ensure that ROs are only shared between legitimate devices and SRMs, OMA SRM also provides mechanisms for mutual authentication using certificates. Certificates are issued by the certificate authority (CA) and prove that the CA initially trusted the entities.

However, the CA can stop trusting an entity. This could for example happen when a weakness in a certain type of device is detected, or when a device is discovered to be compromised. In that case, the CA needs a mechanism to revoke the device, i.e. invalidate the device certificate.

As we already discussed in section "Public key infrastructure and device binding", OMA DRM performs revocation via an OCSP responder. An SRM generally has no capability to contact a network entity and cannot send a request to validate a certificate status. Additionally, it is foreseen that mutual authentication between an SRM and a device would happen too often to allow an OCSP responder to be contacted each time.

In OMA SRM another solution was chosen: revocation is handled using certificate revocation lists (CRLs). A CRL is a list of certificates that have been revoked. Devices and SRMs keep CRLs of SRMs and devices, respectively. Whenever a device communicates with an SRM that is listed on the CRL, the device terminates the communication. Similarly the SRM terminates the communication when the device is listed on the CRL. Special protocols are defined that allow the update of CRLs in both the device and the SRM to ensure that the CRLs are up-to-date.

MORE FLEXIBILITY: OMA SECURE CONTENT EXCHANGE

The OMA Secure Content Exchange (SCE) standard is under development at the time of writing. The aim of SCE is to introduce more flexibility in content usage and sharing and to increase the user experience. Therefore, OMA DRM v2.1 is extended to enable seamless sharing of content between devices. Moreover, OMA SCE enhances the interoperability with other non-OMA DRM systems by defining a content import function.

To allow for flexible rights and content transfer between different devices as well as content exchange with non-OMA DRM devices, some new functionality is defined. In OMA SCE the concept of user domains is extended, permanent move and spontaneous sharing of content between devices is introduced and local import of non-OMA DRM content to devices and domains is enabled.

User Domains

User domains in OMA SCE are the successors of OMA DRM v2.0 domains. OMA DRM v2.0 domains have a number of limitations. For example, a user who purchases content for his domain from different RIs needs to create an OMA DRM v2.0 domain for each of the RIs. User domains in OMA SCE are independent of the RIs. In contrast to OMA DRM v2.0 domains, ROs for the same user domain can be purchased from different RIs.

Move Operation

The OMA SCE move functionality is similar to the OMA SRM move functionality, except that OMA SCE allows the direct move of content and corresponding rights between devices, without using an SRM in between. Additionally, it is anticipated that the OMA SCE specification will allow for partial move of stateful ROs: for example, a user that has an RO for playing certain content 10 times, may decide to move 5 plays to another device.

Adhoc Sharing

Adhoc sharing allows for spontaneous sharing of rights. A possible scenario may be the following: a user takes a high-definition (HD) movie on his device to a friend's home. They both watch the HD movie on the friend's HDTV. To render the movie on the HDTV the device performs adhoc sharing with the HDTV, sharing rights temporarily.

A license may specify constraints to share content adhoc with other devices. Adhoc sharing may be restricted by a proximity constraint, where e.g. the two devices have to be physically within a certain distance. Another restriction may limit the number of times the content can be shared, e.g. the recipient device is only allowed to play once or rendering rights may expire within an hour.

Import

OMA SCE specifies interfaces and entities to allow non-OMA DRM content to be converted to OMA DRM content. Import is meant to increase the interoperability with other DRM systems.

For example, the content source may be a digital video recorder, which receives content from a cable or satellite provider. The non-OMA protected content has to be transformed to (P)DCF and the appropriate rights have to be translated to OMA DRM ROs.

Together with the export functionality from OMA DRM v2.0, all necessary technical means are available to allow interoperability between OMA DRM and other DRM systems.

FURTHER DRM ISSUES

Privacy Considerations

In general, user privacy issues should be considered in the design of DRM systems. Especially in new specifications such as SRM and SCE, where content and rights can be moved between devices of different users, it is important to assure that user's private information is not conveyed to non-authorized parties. For example the Device ID or user name should not be forwarded during move operations.

DRM Interoperability

One of the major problems about DRM is interoperability. In an OMA DRM environment, this will partly be resolved by the SCE specification. However, more needs to be done.

One of the challenges is the difference in rights expression languages, i.e. available permissions and constraints. For example, an OMA DRM RO can have a permission to play the content three times. If this RO is to be exported to a DRM system that is not able to express such a count constraint, a translation rule needs to be defined. The translation rule could specify that a count constraint is translated into a time constraint, for example play three times in OMA DRM is equivalent to play 3 days in the non-OMA DRM system. Translation rules like this are business decisions involving the rights holders and therefore are out of scope of DRM standardization.

SUMMARY

In this chapter, OMA DRM and related standards have been presented to give an overview of their features and possibilities, as well as to provide technical background information.

OMA DRM is an open interoperable standard for secure delivery of protected digital content. The separation of content and license allows for new business models, such as superdistribution and subscription.

OMA BCAST is a standard for mobile broadcast. One of the OMA BCAST profiles, the DRM profile, extends the functionality of OMA DRM for broadcast specific applications. The extensions include a layered key management system, broadcast rights objects, subscriber groups and recording.

The OMA SRM specification enables the secure exchange of rights between a device and a secure memory card. This allows for more portability of content, as the user can play the protected content on multiple devices without the need to set up a domain.

OMA SCE will increase the flexibility of content usage enabling direct move of rights between devices, import from non-OMA DRM systems and spontaneous sharing of content.

REFERENCES

[DR2002]. Daemen, J., and Rijmen, V. (2002). The Design of Rijndael: AES – The Advanced Encryption Standard. Springer-Verlag.

[DVBH-SPP]. IP Datacast over DVB-H: Service Purchase and Protection (SPP), Digital Video Broadcasting™, DVB Document A100, December 2005. http:// www.dvb.org/

[GBA]. Generic Authentication Architecture. *Generic Bootstrapping Architecture (Release 6), 3rd Generation Partnership Project.* Technical

Specification 3GPP TS 33.220. http://www.3gpp.org/

[ISMACryp]. Internet Streaming Media Alliance Encryption and Authentication, Version 2.0. Release version, http://www.isma.tv/

[ISOFF]. (2005, April). Information technology — Coding of audio-visual objects – Part 12: ISO Base Media File Format. *International Organisation for Standardisation*, ISO/IEC 14496-12, Second Edition.

[ODRL]. Open Digital Rights Language (ODRL), Version 1.1. (2002, August 8). http://odrl.net/1.1/ODRL-11.pdf or http://www.w3.org/TR/odrl/

[OMABCAST10]. *OMA Broadcast Mobile Services v1.0* enabler, Open Mobile Alliance™. http://www.openmobilealliance.org/

[OMADRM20]. *OMA Digital Rights Management v2.0* enabler (2004, June 15). Open Mobile Alliance™, Approved Version 1.0, http://www.openmobilealliance.org/

[OMADRM21]. *OMA Digital Rights Management v2.1* enabler. Open Mobile Alliance™, http://www.openmobilealliance.org/

KEY TERMS

Content: Any type of information in digital format including audio files, video files, text documents, games, etc.

Content Encryption Key (CEK): Key used to digitally encrypt a piece of content.

Domain: Group of devices, usually belonging to the same user, that can share a common rights object.

DRM Agent: OMA DRM component installed in the user device, which ensures the secure rendering of the content and enforcement of the license in the device.

Mutual Authentication: Process in which two entities establish a trust relationship. Mutual authentication includes certificate exchange and revocation checking.

Public Key Infrastructure (PKI): A collective name for everything needed to perform public key cryptography, including certificates, issuing authorities, public and private key pairs, and revocation mechanisms.

Revocation: The process of ending the certification of a certain entity.

Rights Expression Language (REL): Format for describing rights, i.e. permissions and constraints, related to the use of content.

Rights Issuer (RI): A network entity that is responsible for generating and delivering rights objects.

Rights Object (RO): A data structure related to a piece of content containing information such as the content encryption key, and usage permissions and constrains. A rights object is also known as a license.

Smartcard: A card residing in the device on which information about the device is securely stored, providing a security anchor for cryptographic functionalities.

APPENDIX: USE OF TRADEMARKS AND REGISTERED TRADEMARKS

- Open Mobile Alliance and WAP Forum are worldwide trademarks or registered trademarks of Open Mobile Alliance Ltd.
- 3GPP is a registered trademark of ETSI.
- DVB is a registered trademark of the DVB Project.
- ISMA is a trademark and service mark of Internet Streaming Media Alliance.

Chapter V
Discovering the Core Security Requirements of DRM Systems by Means of Objective Trees

Hugo Jonker
University of Luxembourg, Luxembourg
Eindhoven University of Technology, The Netherlands

Sjouke Mauw
University of Luxembourg, Luxembourg

ABSTRACT

The use of Digital Rights Management (DRM) systems involves several stakeholders, such as the content provider, the license provider, and the user, each having their own incentives to use the system. Proper use of the system implies that these incentives can only be met if certain security requirements are fulfilled. Much attention in literature has been devoted to specific security aspects of DRM systems. The contributions of this chapter consist of deriving a systematic overview of core security requirements for DRM systems. This chapter conducts a stakeholder analysis, gives an objective tree for each relevant stakeholder, and develops a simple, generic conceptual model to arrive at the set of core security requirements.

INTRODUCTION

There is a precarious balance between dissemination of information (to the general public) and stimulation of innovation and art. The easier it is to spread new information, the less possibilities to profit there will be for innovators to reap the fruits of their labour. On the other hand, spreading innovation and art is considered beneficial to society.

The introduction of computers has had a profound impact on this balance. With computers, it is trivial to create a perfect copy of content – a term used to indicate a work of art, such as music, literature, movies, etc. This coupled with the widespread availability of broadband internet connections means that completely new venues for spreading content to the public at large have come into existence. This enables a business model that consists of selling and delivering digital versions of content online. The main point of concern for such a business is to prevent unsanctioned redistribution of the delivered content.

Digital Rights Management (DRM) systems have been created for this goal. The purpose of a DRM system is to protect (digital versions of) content. Content is bound to a license, and the content is only accessible under the terms stated by the license. Since the year 2000, there has been a strong push into the research and development of DRM systems. There has been work on various related security aspects such as secure storage (Shapiro & Vingralek, 2002), traitor-tracing (Kiayias & Yung, 2003; Safavi-Naini & Wang, 2003), watermarking (Cox, Bloom & Miller, 2001), fingerprinting (Haitsma & Kalker, 2002; Prechelt & Typke, 2001) and tamper resistant code (Horne, Matheson, Sheehan & Tarjan, 2002; Chang & Atallah, 2002). There have also been various proposals for models of DRM systems with specific properties (OMA, 2004; Serrão, Naves, Barker, Balestri & Kudumakis, 2003; Guth, 2003; Popescu, Kamperman, Crispa & Tanenbaum, 2004).

These proposals incorporate various security requirements. Some of these requirements assure core DRM functionality, whereas other requirements realise the specific properties for which that architecture was constructed (e.g. interoperability: MOSES (Serrão, Naves, Barker, Balestri & Kudumakis, 2003), Coral (Coral Consortium, 2006)). The emphasis of such proposals is usually on the latter type of requirements. It is not uncommon that the requirements assuring core DRM functionality receive a lesser treatment. These requirements are often not all made explicit,

nor is a justification for them provided. Which of these requirements are made explicit varies from proposal to proposal, which means that the set of requirements that assure core DRM security is scattered. There are several reasons to make this core explicit. The first and foremost reason is that security is an enabling factor for DRM systems. DRM systems are designed to provide a solution for a security problem. An understanding of (the justification for) the core security requirements is crucial for fundamental comprehension of the security of DRM systems. Moreover, knowledge of the core security requirements is instrumental in the construction and verification of DRM systems. Such knowledge enables developers to better understand the consequences of security trade offs. In practical systems, such trade offs between desired features and security requirements are not uncommon.

For example, Apple's iTunes allows the user to create a CD of protected music. Naturally, Apple realised that such a CD could be used to copy music. Nevertheless, this feature was deemed more important than the costs in terms of loss of security. In this case, an informed decision has been made. In other respects, some of the design decisions of iTunes seem less well-informed and have a negative impact on the overall security of the system. A more detailed examination of iTunes follows below.

This chapter uses a structured approach to identify core security requirements and provide a justification for them. The goal of this chapter is focused on the security aspects of the design of DRM systems and our aim is to systematically derive core security requirements for DRM systems. Although there is a wealth of methodologies supporting system analysis and design, the methodologies for deriving security requirements are only at their infancy. Therefore, our research will start by identifying some useful methodologies and combining their strengths.

In order to provide a base for the found security requirements, we describe a model which limits itself to the core processes of a DRM system. The generic nature of this core model of DRM functionality implies that requirements found for it are applicable to most DRM systems. The extensibility of this core model indicates that it can be augmented to accommodate additional functionality, and therefore that this model suffices for our needs.

The rest of this chapter is organised as follows: Section 2 details the approach we used to arrive at our security requirements, resulting in a list of security properties and a generic process model of DRM systems. These form the basis of the security requirements in Section 3. Section 4 examines the practical application of this research. And finally, we present some conclusions in Section 5.

PROBLEM ANALYSIS

To establish the core security requirements of DRM systems, we performed a problem analysis. The analysis led to a terminology and a description of the desires of the various involved parties. These desires are used in Section 3 as the foundations for the security requirements of DRM systems.

The problem analysis consisted of three steps. The first step established core stakeholders, their incentives and relevant terminology of DRM systems. The second step consisted of deriving the desired security properties from the incentives and the terminology. The third step consisted of deriving a process model. The process model captures the core operations occurring in DRM systems.

Establishing Terminology, Core Stakeholders and Their Incentives

The first step in deriving security requirements is a *stakeholder analysis*. The purpose of this step is to determine the individuals (or roles) that have an interest in using a DRM system, and their incentives for participating. This understanding of their incentives is important, as these incentives lead to security requirements.

To establish the stakeholders and their incentives, a method similar to and inspired by several existing methodologies from the field of Information Systems has been used. We based our research on a variety of methodologies, such as domain analysis (see e.g. Prieto-Díaz, 1990), stakeholder analysis (for an overview see Pouloudi, 1999), system decomposition (see e.g. Sommerville, 2004). Normally, these methods assist in designing a system. However, our goal was not to design a system, but to focus upon a system's security aspects. Parts of these methods were accordingly adapted to capture the security aspects of DRM systems.

The problem analysis leads to the following list of core stakeholders and their roles in a DRM system:

Stakeholder	Role
Media company	Creates content
User	Acquires content
Distributor	Intermediary between *user* and *media company*

Each of these stakeholders has their own, specific incentives for using DRM. DRM systems deal with providing users access to content. This observation together with a generalisation of the stakeholders' roles leads to the following formulation of the core functionality of a DRM system:

A DRM system is a system that enables users to access digital content according to access conditions as specified in a license. Licenses and content are provided by distributors, who in turn acquire content and generic access conditions from content creators.

The above description distinguishes three types of participating roles: the content creator, who creates content; the distributor, who distributes content; and the user, who desires access to content. Although developers (who create a DRM system) and network providers (who transport content) are stakeholders too, and provide essential functions for an operational DRM system, they perform no operations on the content itself. Hence, we will not study their security requirements in this chapter – network security and e-commerce security are thus beyond the scope of the current discussion.

The analysis indicates that the core roles of content creator and distributor are executed by companies (e.g. media companies). As companies are legal entities, they are firmly embedded in a legal framework and thus there exist numerous non-technical solutions to ensure that companies adhere to access agreements. This observation holds less for individual persons, which allows for an asymmetry in DRM systems: there are fewer deterrents to prevent individuals from circumventing agreements then there are deterrents preventing companies. Hence for individuals strict technological enforcement of access agreements between them and companies is necessary. This leads to a natural tendency in DRM development to focus on enforcing access control at the user's side, and to focus less (or not at all) on access control at the distributor's side.

Each of the core roles has various reasons for taking part in a DRM system, and thus related security concerns. The following outlines their incentives and security needs:

Content Creator

The role of content creator is executed by stakeholders that create content, such as media companies. They do not seek interaction with users directly, but are satisfied with leaving this to an intermediary – i.e. distributors. DRM can be used to enforce the conditions set on content by the content creator for the distributor. However, this can also be dealt with by non-digital means (contracts, agreements between companies).

Content creators use DRM technology to support new business models. For instance, they can create a bundle of desired content and other content. Such a bundle could increase the value of the content for users (e.g. by including "the making of" footage), or it could increase revenue for the content creator (e.g. by including commercials). Additionally, using DRM technology it is possible to offer a revenue-generating alternative for traditional downloading. This means that DRM technology can open a new market.

As digitised content facilitates widespread copying of content, content creators need to be assured that the DRM system that safeguards their content will only allow access to content to the right party, when conditions in the right license have been met. Hence, for content creators, the security property desired is:

c1. Content is only accessible by untampered components created by the official system developers, under the conditions of a valid license issued by a bona fide distributor.

Distributor

The distributor can use DRM technology to offer tailor-made access to content to users. On top of that, overhead compared to selling physical media is substantially reduced, because digital content requires up little physical space and the presentation of the content can also be done digitally. By offering a clearly legitimate and known-quality alternative for downloading, distributor can open up a new market. And lastly, as content is bound to a license created by the distributor, access to content distributed in this way will comply with access conditions set by the distributor.

The distributor too desires the DRM system to prevent unlicensed copying. More precisely, any content distributed by the distributor should only be accessible in accordance with the access conditions set by the distributor. Moreover, in order to compete with downloading from dubious sources, communication must be secure and reliable. And naturally, the system must secure the distributor against attacks. Hence the desired security properties for distributors are:

d1. Content is only accessible by a device with a valid license issued to that device, originating from the distributor, under the terms stated in that license.

d2. The DRM system precisely delivers the content that has been requested, with the license as requested, in the correct format, at the desired time to the user.

d3. Other parties cannot influence (hack/break) the distributor's side of the communications between the distributor and the user.

User

Users will be drawn to DRM systems because DRM systems offer a legitimate, known-quality alternative to more dubious sources of content. Ease of use is an important consideration in this regard: if use of the system or acquisition of content becomes bothersome, a user might turn back to other sources. Another advantage that DRM systems can offer users is the possibility to restrict the access to (and thus the cost of) content to precisely what the user wishes. For users, it is important that the DRM system offers an improvement over existing content distribution channels, otherwise there is no incentive for users to switch to DRM. This can, for example, be in terms of ease of use or availability. Such improvements can be offset by deterioration of other aspects – privacy concerns could turn users away from a DRM system.

The ubiquitous availability of a DRM system is thus an important property for users, as are privacy considerations. Furthermore, as the development of the DRM system in general does not involve the end-user, it is important that a user can trust

the system to act according to his wishes. Hence, users desire the following security properties:

u1. The user can precisely acquire a consumable form of the content that the user desires, at the moment the user desires it.

u2. Neither content nor licenses can be linked to the user.

u3. Conditions of and requests for content and/or licenses are fully controlled by the user.

Taken together, the above properties form a solid foundation for the core functionality of DRM systems – and therefore, they also provide sound underpinnings for the security properties of DRM systems.

Conceptual Process Model

The second step of the problem analysis consists of the development of a *conceptual process model*. This model relates the basic processes in the DRM system to each other, and can be refined to provide a basis for identifying security requirements. This process model is then combined in Section 3 with the list of security properties to establish core security requirements of DRM systems.

To ensure that the model is applicable to as many DRM systems as possible, it must be as generic as possible. In order to derive such a generic model, we start with one component for the three core roles in a DRM system: the content creator, the distributor and the user, see Figure 1. Components for non-core roles are left out as they can be introduced when necessary, as such additions constitute refinements of the core model. The resulting model is subsequently refined to incorporate various specifics of DRM systems.

The model of Figure 1 is read as follows: the content creation component creates content, which is forwarded to the distributor. The license binding component binds a license to the content, after

Figure 1. Basic process model

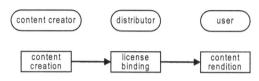

which content and license can be sent to the user. The content rendition component at the user side renders the content.

The first refinement to this model is instigated by the observation that to be perused by users, the content is eventually transformed into an analogue form. This means that there exist two variants of the content: digital content (which the system is to protect), and analogue content (which a user can consume). As all DRM systems need to convert content to a user-readable form, the generic model can be refined to incorporate this distinction without harming its genericity. Note that after conversion, more processing can be done. However, this is no longer on digital content and it is not a necessity in a DRM system. For both these reasons, we consider that a DRM system governs content until conversion to analogue.

The two types of content allow us to refine the content rendition process: one process to convert digital content to analogue content (*analogue conversion*), and one process that extracts the content from the package created by the *license binding* process from the distributor (the *content extraction* process). This refinement is depicted in Figure 2. Note that in general, analogue conversion is the final step in the process. Hence, the analogue conversion process is depicted as the last process in the model.

The next refinement is prompted by noting that DRM-protected content cannot be accessed without a license. This does not imply that a license must be bundled with the content in all cases, or even that a license must exist when the content is protected. It suffices that the resulting content is not accessible without a valid license. To express the possibility of the separate existence of licenses and protected content, the license binding component is further refined into two parts. The *content encapsulation* process provides the user with protected content, while the *license creation* process provides the user with a matching license for protected content. This leads us to the conceptual model depicted in Figure 3.

This generic process model now incorporates the core roles and models the core processes in a DRM system. The model can be refined to comply with virtually all existing DRM architectures. For example, additional roles like content issuer and license issuer can be incorporated to comply with the functional architecture of the Open Mobile Alliance DRM architecture (OMA, 2004).

The goal of this chapter is to establish core security requirements of DRM systems. As further refinements constrain the applicability of the model (i.e. they harm the genericity of the model), the model is not further refined.

Problem Analysis Results

The problem analysis has provided two results: a list of security properties desired by the core stakeholders, and a conceptual process model of the processes taking place in a DRM system. Taken together, these results elucidate security

Figure 2. Process model incorporating rendition refinement

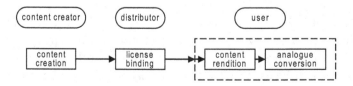

Figure 3. Generic process model of DRM systems

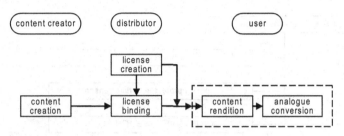

requirements of the core functionality of a DRM system.

Completeness of these descriptions can have a large impact on which security requirements are found. After all, the more complete the given descriptions are, the more complete the derived security requirements will be. The methods we adapted to arrive at the given descriptions support a systematic derivation of security requirements, but do not guarantee completeness of the results. Despite this, we believe that, due to the systematic approach, the descriptions are sufficiently exhaustive for our goals.

ESTABLISHING CORE SECURITY REQUIREMENTS USING OBJECTIVE TREES

In this section, the security properties as described before are used as a basis for establishing the security requirements per stakeholder upon the generic process model, as shown in Figure 3. In this section, these resulting properties are translated into security requirements upon the model. Both the process model and the incentives were deliberately kept widely applicable, so that the resulting security requirements will also hold in general for DRM systems. To describe security requirements on a specific setting or DRM system, the process model as well as the below requirements can be further refined. An example

of such a refinement is the inclusion of the role of Certification Authority.

The refinement of security properties was based on a technique described in Schneier (2000): attack trees. We applied this technique to systematically analyse the defensive objectives of a system – in this case, the generic process model as shown in Figure 3. In this application, the trees no longer represent attacks, but objectives, this technique is best called Objective Trees. An Objective Tree is a refinement tree, refining properties into requirements in a specific setting – the generic process model. The results of this systematic analysis are presented below.

Content Creator

Figure 4 shows the objective tree for the content creator. Objective c1 was established precisely before, and is abbreviated in the figure as "content inaccessible unless ok".

Note that the content creator requires the system to keep the content within the system, just as the distributor does (requirement d1). The difference between their respective security properties is that the content creator additionally desires content to be secured until it is handed to the distributor. From then on, their respective security properties governing accessibility of the content coincide. Hence, in Figure 4, only requirements on the system up to the distributor need to be considered. Further requirements are

Figure 4. Objective tree of security requirements for the content creator

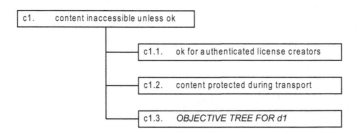

Figure 5. Objective tree with security requirements for the distributor: (a) for property d1, and (b) for property d3

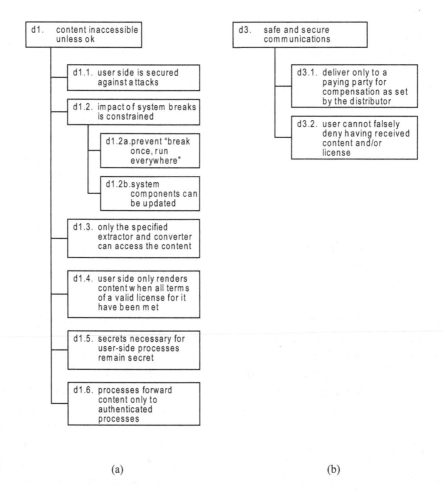

Figure 6. Objective tree for properties (a) u1,d2, and (b) u2

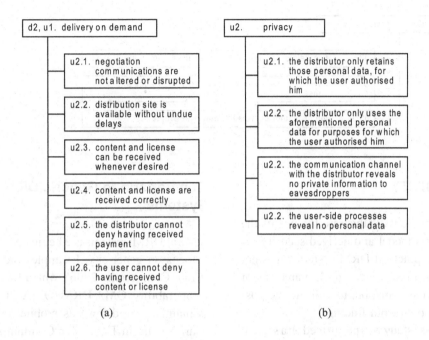

(a)   (b)

part of the distributor's objective tree and are detailed there.

Distributor

In Section 2, three desired security properties were listed for the distributor. As property d2 is the distributor's version of property u1, the objective tree for u2 serves as an objective tree for both properties. In Figure 5, the remaining properties are compactly described as "content inaccessible unless ok" (d1) and "safe and secure communications" (d3).

User

The security properties for the user are abbreviated in the objective trees of Figures 6-7 as follows: "delivery on demand" (u1), "privacy" (u2),

"order control" (u3). Note that the objective tree of Figure 6 is the objective tree incorporating the requirements for properties u1 and d2.

Consequences

The security requirements established in the previous section have some consequences, which are mentioned below.

It follows from the requirements derived from the distributor's desired security properties (d1-d3) that the components on the user's side should function as a trusted computing base. The requirements following from property u2 indicate that the distributor should provide a privacy statement. Requirement u3.3 implies that the distributor provides a security policy.

Figure 7. Objective tree for property u3

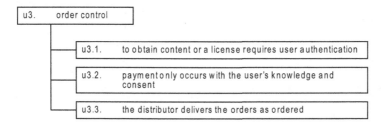

APPLICABILITY

In this section we will illustrate the use of the generic process model and derived security requirements to practical DRM systems. It is not our intention to provide a complete analysis of existing DRM systems, but to indicate the possibilities of applying our findings.

Our first case study was performed on a system from a Dutch company which develops DRM systems. This case study was based on our work, previously reported in Jonker (2004). The system matched our model very well, and our security analysis pointed out a missed requirement in the system. They took into consideration implementing a mechanism to ensure requirement u2.5 (non-repudiation for the distributor).

In the remainder of this section, we compare the results of this chapter (i.e. the generic process model and the security requirements upon it) to several high-level, generic DRM systems. This is followed by noting how to use the results in verifying DRM design. The section concludes by applying the found requirements to two popular DRM systems, *Windows Media DRM* from Microsoft and *iTunes* from Apple. These systems are interesting for a number of reasons: these systems are the most successfully deployed DRM systems in the current market, and both have been successfully attacked. Observe that both systems are refinements of the model depicted in Figure 3.

Comparison to Generic DRM Systems

Several DRM systems are being developed with a focus on genericity. Examples include Coral (Coral Consortium, 2006), which focuses on interoperability; OMA DRM (OMA, 2004), which is mainly geared towards mobile devices; and Marlin (Marlin Developer Community, 2006), which is aimed at providing DRM for content accessed using varying services and devices in the bounds of a domain. All three of these have a broad target, and thus were developed as generic DRM systems. Because of this, they are perfectly suited to illustrate how to relate our generic results to real DRM systems.

Coral

The Coral architecture is developed to act as a basic building block for DRM systems. By itself, it does not constitute a DRM system, but is intended as a core framework that enables interoperability of DRM systems. This means that content is fed to it from one DRM system, then content is processed and finally, with an appropriate set of access conditions, content is forwarded to another DRM system. As such, interoperability of DRM systems seamlessly matches our generic process model.

As Coral focuses on providing interoperability, it has a vastly expanded set of roles. Most of these roles constitute specific refinements of the distributor's role, that enable interoperability of licenses between DRM systems.

As Coral acts not as a DRM system, but an interoperability layer, the role of the content creator is not strictly necessary. This functionality is taken over by the roles of content importer and exporter.

Open Mobile Alliance DRM

The OMA DRM system's primary focus is to enable DRM on mobile devices, such as cellphones. In this context, super distribution and accessibility of content for devices grouped into domains is important. Like Coral, OMA DRM is developed for implementation. The design documentation for OMA DRM provides an architecture, which acts as the counterpart to the generic process model, and a requirements document that incorporates a counterpart to the security requirements.

The functional architecture of OMA DRM closely resembles the generic process model. It consists of a content issuer (the content creator), a rights issuer (the distributor) and a DRM agent (the user). Nonetheless, the security requirements are all aimed at protecting content while interacting with the user. The focus of the security requirements of OMA DRM is upon requirements following from properties c1 and d1. Other requirements, especially the user's security requirements, are underrepresented in OMA's DRM. OMA DRM's specifications are at an implementation level, lacking a generic nature. This has caused their security requirements to focus on implementation aspects of security, and understate other requirements.

This observation does not imply that there OMA DRM suffers from a security risk – but the set of requirements used as input for designing the system omits several requirements established in Section 3.

Marlin

Marlin is a DRM architecture being jointly developed by several large consumer electronics companies (Sony, Samsung Philips, Panasonic) with additional input from a specialised DRM company (Intertrust). Given this strong CE manufacturer backing, it comes as no surprise that Marlin is targeted at providing DRM for CE-devices, and ensuring interoperability of DRM across all devices belonging to one user. The Marlin developer community has created Octopus, a reference core impementation of a DRM system complying to the Marlin framework. Octopus, like OMA, focuses upon the user, and thus the distinction between content creator and distributor is not made explicit.

That notwithstanding, the three actors as specified in the core Marlin architecture conform to the three roles in the generic process model. Marlin's focus on CE devices and portability of content amongst devices owned by the same user has led to a refinement similar to one in OMA, namely the introduction of domains. This refinement introduces new security concerns, however, as Marlin recognises the same three core roles as the generic process model, these concerns are addressed by requirements following from the stated desired security properties. Unfortunately, Marlin security requirements are not publicly available, so a comparison between them and the stated security requirements in Section 3 cannot be made.

Verifying DRM Design

The list of security requirements can be used as a checklist when verifying security aspects of a design for a DRM system. The generic nature of the process model implies that it is applicable to most designs for a DRM system. Therefore, the requirements derived from it should be met by any matching system.

Additionally, the process model can be refined to model a specific DRM system in more detail. This refined model could be combined with the stated requirements in order to derive more detailed requirements for this specific DRM system.

Application to Popular DRM System

Both Microsoft and Apple have created DRM systems that enjoy a large use base. In this section, we take a closer look at these two systems using the established security requirements as a guideline.

Windows Media DRM

Microsoft has developed a DRM system compatible with their *Windows Media Player*. They created two file formats that can be enhanced with DRM protection: Windows Media Audio (.WMA, for audio content) and Windows Media Video (.WMV, for mixed video and audio content).

Microsoft's DRM system has a role delivering protected content to the user. This content can only be accessed with a legitimate license. This manner of operating conforms to the process model depicted in Figure 3.

There have been two well-known successful attacks on Microsoft's DRM system (described more fully by Hauser & Wenz (2003)). The first attack consisted of replacing part of the playback device that is responsible for rendering audio (the audio driver). Protected music could now be captured after it had been converted to a form understandable by the audio driver, and saved to disc.

In our proposed security requirements, this attack would have been prevented by satisfying requirements d1.3 and d1.6. The part of the DRM system on which this attack worked, was the same for each installation. This means that the attack was possible on all installed systems, which violates requirement d1.2a.

Microsoft has released a new version of Windows DRM that was not vulnerable to this attack. Naturally, content packaged under the new system was not accessible with the old system.

A tool called 'FreeMe' is available that attacks content protected for the new version. The creator of the tool has included a detailed analysis of the protection of protected files. The tool is able to determine the keys used to encrypt the content. This is a violation of requirement d1.5. The manner in which the key could be retrieved was the same for each installed system, which again violates requirement d1.2a.

Microsoft has since patched their DRM system. The patch implements measures that support requirement d1.2a and uses another method to hide the used keys. Patched systems are no longer vulnerable to this particular attack.

iTunes

iTunes is Apple's online music store. Music is sold in the Advanced Audio Coding format (AAC, see ISO (1997, 2004)). The audio data inside the AAC file is protected by encryption. The default license allows protected files to be played on up to five different computers, and to burn them to CD.

The manner in which iTunes operates, conforms to the model of Figure 3. Content is delivered to a distributor, which binds the content to a license. The user can then acquire the bound content and an appropriate license.

iTunes has suffered from two well-known attacks. The first is by Jon Lech Johansen and captures the decrypted, digital contents before it is converted into analogue form. This attack is similar to the first attack upon Microsoft's Windows DRM system, and the remarks made then apply in this case as well – this attack exploits the lack of compliance to requirements d1.3, d1.6 and d1.2a.

A second attack on iTunes bears a resemblance to the second attack on Windows DRM: keys can be learned by outsiders, which enables an attacker to compromise the encryption of protected content. The keys used by iTunes (to protect the key to the encrypted audio) are stored encrypted with a system key. It is known how to reconstruct this key[1] for the Windows platform and for Apple's portable mp3 player. This means that it is possible to remove the encryption from the audio data for these platforms. The remarks made for the second attack on MS DRM apply here as well – this attack exploits the lack of compliance to requirements d1.5 and d1.2a.

Johansen later found a third attack on the system. He created a player (called PyMusique) that replaces the iTunes player to acquire songs. According to the description of the method[2], the main difference with the official player is that it skips applying DRM to the downloaded file.

The attack thus consists of replacing a component of the DRM system by an attacker-controlled component. However, no component should send the content to another component, unless the other component identifies itself as a legitimate component. Allowing this constitutes a violation of requirement d1.6.

CONCLUSION

Digital Rights Management systems offer a method for content creators to allow their work to be spread digitally, without loss of recompensation. Security is the foremost enabling factor of DRM systems.

This chapter used a methodical way to derive security requirements from the incentives of the parties involved with a DRM system. A stakeholder analysis identified the key roles taking part in a DRM system, and the main incentives related to these roles. A domain analysis captured the core terminology of DRM systems, from which a process model was derived.

The key roles, their incentives and the core terminology together led to a description of each role's desired security properties for a DRM sys-

tem. Taken together with the process model, these security properties allowed us to establish the core security requirements of DRM systems.

The method used was justified by validation of the result of each step to known literature and comparison to a DRM system in development by a Dutch company.

The applicability of our findings was justified by comparison to several existing DRM systems. Exploited weaknesses of both Microsoft Media DRM and Apple's iTunes could have been identified in an early state using the requirements we presented. In the case of the system in development at a Dutch company, we were able to point out requirements that had been overlooked.

This chapter takes a practical stance towards security: it presents a list of requirements to be fulfilled. Compliance with these requirements may not be straightforward – see for example the second attack on Microsoft's Media DRM, which attacked a part that at first might have seem to comply to the relevant requirements presented here. This problem can be prevented using formal verification. Compliance of the used protocols with secrecy and authentication can already be formally verified. There is ongoing research into formally expressing other requirements (e.g. privacy) for protocols. Further developments can lead to establishing a theoretical basis in which it is possible to verify that a trusted computing base complies to the requirements upon it.

The process model used for establishing the requirements can be refined to include more details for a more thorough analysis of a particular system. This would then lead to further refinement in the requirements. Such a refinement requires a loss of the generic nature and therefore would result in confining the applicability of the resulting findings to systems exhibiting specific characteristics.

ACKNOWLEDGMENT

The comments and commentary of ir. Lex Schoonen and ir. Jan Verschuren were invaluable during our research, and we are grateful for their constructive commentary.

REFERENCES

Chang, H., & Atallah, M. J. (2002). Protecting software code by guards. In *Security and Privacy in Digital Rights Management, LNCS 2320*, 150-175. Springer.

Coral Consortium (whitepaper, 2006). *Coral consortium whitepaper.*

Cox, I., Bloom, J., & Miller, M. (2001). Digital watermarking: Principles & practice. *The Morgan Kaufmann Series in Multimedia and Information Systems.* Morgan Kaufmann.

Guth, S. (2003). A sample DRM system. *In Digital Rights Management, LNCS 2770*, 150-161. Springer.

Haitsma, J., & Kalker, T. (2002). A highly robust audio fingerprinting system. In *Proceedings of the 3rd International Conference on Music Information Retrieval.*

Hauser, T., & Wenz, C. (2003). DRM under attack: Weaknesses in existing systems. In *Digital Rights Management: Technological, Economic, Legal and Political Aspects, LNCS 2770*, 206-223. Springer.

Horne, B., Matheson, L., Sheehan, C., & Tarjan, R. E. (2002). Dynamic self-checking techniques for improved tamper resistance. In *Security and privacy in digital rights management*, LNCS 2320, 141-159. Springer.

ISO, International Organization for Standardization (published standard, 2004). *ISO/IEC*

13818-7:2004 Information technology – Generic coding of moving pictures and associated audio information – Part 7: Advanced Audio Coding (AAC).

ISO, the International Organization for Standardization (published standard, 1999). *ISO/IEC TR 13818-5:1997/Amd 1:1999 Advanced Audio Coding (AAC).*

Jonker, H. L. (2004). *Security of Digital Rights Management systems.* Unpublished Master's thesis. Technische Universiteit Eindhoven.

Kiayias, A., & Yung, M. (2003). Breaking and repairing asymmetric public-key traitor tracing. In *Digital Rights Management, LNCS 2320*, 32-50. Springer.

Marlin Developer Community (whitepaper, 2006). *Marlin architecture overview.*

OMA, the Open Mobile Alliance (2004). OMA-DRM-ARCH-V2 0-20040715-C DRM architecture.

Popescu, B .C., Kamperman, F. L. A. J., Crispo, B., & Tanenbaum, A. S. (2004). A DRM security architecture for home networks. In *DRM '04: Proceedings of the 4th ACM workshop on Digital Rights Management*, 1-10. ACM Press.

Pouloudi, A. (1999). Aspects of the stakeholder concept and their implications for information systems development. In R.H. Sprague (Ed.), *Proceedings of the 32nd Hawaii International Conference on System Sciences*, Los Alamitos, CA: IEEE Computer Society Press.

Prechelt, L., & Typke, R. (2001). An interface for melody input. *ACM Transactions on Computer-Human Interaction, 8*(2), 133-149.

Prieto-Digitalaz, R. (1990). Domain analysis: An introduction. *Software Engineering Notes, 15*(2), 47-54.

Safavi-Naini, R., & Wang, Y. (2003). Traitor Tracing for Shortened and Corrupted Fingerprints. In

Digital Rights Management, LNCS 2320, 32-50. Springer

Schneier, B. (2000). *Secrets & Lies: Digital Security in a Networked World*. Wiley.

Serrão, C., Naves, D., Barker, T., Balestri, M., & Kudumakis, P. (2003). Open SDRM – An open and secure digital rights management solution.

Shapiro, W., & Vingralek, R. (2002). How to manage persistent state in DRM systems. In Security and Privacy in Digital Rights Management, LNCS 2320, 176-191. Springer.

Sommerville, I. (2004). *Software Engineering*. Pearson.

KEY TERMS

Content: A work of art, such as music, a movie, literature, software, et cetera.

Digital Rights Management: Describes techniques that manage protective measures for content.

License: A virtual object granting specific rights to a specific user for accessing content.

Security Requirement: A specific prerequisite that a system needs to fulfil in order to achieve a specific security objective.

Stakeholder Analysis: A methodology to determine which parties have an interest in a given situation.

Objective Trees: A method to establish goals for stakeholders.

Open Mobile Alliance (OMA): A standardisation body comprised of most companies in the cell phone market (manufacturers as well as network operators). The corresponding DRM specifications are called OMA DRM.

ENDNOTES

[1]   e.g., see http://www.hymn-project.org/docs/hymn-manual.html#how-hymn-works

[2]   http://www.daeken.com/2004/08/24/itunes/

Chapter VI

Digital Rights Management for Untrusted Peer–to–Peer Networks

Pallavi Priyadarshini
San Jose State University, USA

Mark Stamp
San Jose State University, USA

ABSTRACT

Peer-to-peer (P2P) networks have proliferated and become ubiquitous. A school of thought has emerged that harnessing the established user-base and ease of content dissemination of such networks presents a potentially lucrative opportunity. However, content creators have been reluctant to adopt P2P networks as a distribution vehicle since these networks are plagued with piracy. This chapter focuses on developing a solution for distributing digital content in P2P networks in a way that established businesses and amateur artists alike can profit. We propose a content distribution system that employs Digital Rights Management (DRM) technologies and is independent of the underlying P2P network. Our system relies on innovative uses of security technologies to deter piracy. In addition, we include various non-technical features that encourage users to "play by the rules".

INTRODUCTION

Due to the Internet, there has been an exponential increase in the volume of digital content available to consumers. Apple iTunes (Distributed Computing Industry Association 2004) and YouTube (2006) exemplify the paradigm shift in music and video distribution. Users are increasingly obtain-

ing digital content through downloads. Given the tremendous popularity of digital content, exploring new channels to enable content distribution and creating new non-traditional marketplaces is a logical step forward.

P2P networks are currently popular vehicles for digital content distribution. With the continued proliferation of P2P networks such as Kazaa

(2006) and Gnutella (Gnutella clients 2006, Gnutella 2006), industry and academia are beginning to realize the potential of such networks in the dissemination of digital information. However, at present, P2P networks are rife with risks of copyright infringement. P2P networks lack many of the security features inherent in client-server networks that can be used to protect the rights of content owners.

This chapter focuses on exploring solutions that enable large-scale distribution of digital content in P2P networks such that intellectual property rights are not violated and the content creators are able to collect profits. We augment the basic distribution of content from creators to consumers with distribution through authorized resellers. As part of our distribution model, we apply appropriate digital rights management (DRM) technologies to the content in an effort to ensure that the P2P networks benefit creators and legitimate customers, not just pirates.

This chapter is organized as follows. Section 2 gives relevant background information on P2P networks and DRM technologies. In particular, we describe the requirements of a DRM system that is suitable for P2P networks. We also outline the design goals for our system. This section concludes with a brief review of related work.

Section 3 provides the detailed design of our proposed system. We include justification of our design decisions. We also provide a description of the system architecture and the functional flow in our proposed system. Section 4 includes the implementation details of the components of our system. We do not cover the details of the security-related features, which are discussed in the subsequent section. Section 5 covers the security features in the proposed system. We discuss the implementation aspects and analyze the strengths and weaknesses of each significant security feature.

In Section 6 we consider the testing of our working prototype system. This section illustrates the underlying functionality of the prototype by going through the steps of a sample use case in detail. We conclude the chapter with Section 7 where we summarize the achievements of the project and present various ideas that could be developed as extensions of this project.

BACKGROUND

P2P Networks

In traditional client-server network architectures, all nodes communicate to and from a central server whereas in a P2P network the nodes communicate in a relatively ad-hoc manner. Figure 1 illustrates the difference between the topologies of P2P and client-server networks.

Each P2P network has its own procedure for connecting the P2P clients. For example, the classic P2P network Napster (2006) had a central server used to index all content that peer users had to offer. This central server based approach has evolved into more decentralized networks which do not require a centralized server to connect peers in the network (Kazaa 2006, Gnutella 2006). Kazaa and Gnutella are well-known examples of decentralized P2P networks. Although Kazaa does not have any central indexing servers, it relies on a subset of peers, called supernodes, to perform the analogous function of an indexing server. Supernodes are peers with more advanced machines and faster connections which host a list of files their neighborhood Kazaa users are willing to sharing. Ordinary Kazaa users connect to the supernodes to search content. Gnutella uses a more distributed protocol (sometimes known as "pure P2P") whereby search requests are progressively routed to directly connected "neighbors" (in an overlay network), effectively creating a query flood.

P2P networks provide several advantages over traditional client-server based network model, including the following.

Figure 1. Network topology of P2P and client-server networks

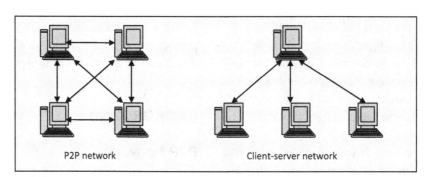

•   Scalability—P2P networks scale extremely well, since the content is exchanged directly between peers and not through a centralized server.

•   Faster response — Client-server architectures have several potential bottlenecks that are not present in P2P networks. For example, several clients in close geographical proximity to each other might all be required to download the same digital content from a central server, which may be located far away. In P2P networks, more peers will tend to offer content that is in high demand, thus improving the chances that content is downloaded from a source that is geographically closer.

•   Empowerment of peers—In P2P networks, peers can exchange files directly with other peers and, consequently, any peer can offer content. In contrast, in a client-server model, only the central server can offer content.

•   More resources—Compared to traditional systems, P2P networks can provide a significantly greater resources (computing power, available storage, overall network bandwidth, etc.) since the member peers effectively contribute resources to the network.

However, there is a dark side to P2P networks. These networks have become havens for pirates of digital content owing to the lack of central policing. Widespread piracy is the primary reason for the reluctance on part of major studios and record labels to embrace P2P networks. This reluctance, though not unfounded, probably cost these businesses dearly. Due to the growing popularity of P2P networks, the industry might be wise to adopt appropriate business models for legitimizing and monetizing content distribution on P2P networks (Distributed Computing Industry Association 2004). Apple's iTunes online music store (iPod + iTunes 2006) provides an exemplary business model, where the number of downloads after payment has exceeded one billion (iTunes 2006). To harness the advantages P2P networks have to offer with their extensive user base, industry should be the early adopters of technologies enabling legal content distribution through these networks.

Digital Rights Management

Digital Rights Management (DRM) refers to enforcement of rules and policies to control access to digital content like software, music, videos and documents (Stamp 2006). It controls not only the way a piece of digital content is delivered to legitimate end-users, but also enforces rules after the content has been delivered. For example, a particular DRM system might allow a legitimate user to access content only three times.

Like P2P networks, DRM also has its own share of detractors. Many people believe that information, especially digital, is free and they find the enforcement of rules on digital goods too restrictive. The authors in Biddel, et. al. (2002) argue that DRM has inherent technical limitations with respect to enforcement and efficient "darknets" for illegal distribution of digital goods would continue to exist. Additionally, most of the DRM products and technologies are proprietary. Given the volatile nature of business, users of any proprietary technologies are legitimately concerned about the support to the DRM products if the company providing the DRM products goes out of business. However, it is necessary to recognize that businesses need to be adequately profitable to fuel further innovations. While too many limitations on the purchase of content can understandably irritate consumers, a reasonable level of enforcement might lead to equitable profits for content creators and consequently foster creativity.

DRM for P2P Networks

Harnessing the wide user-base of P2P networks presents a huge opportunity for both established content providers and amateurs. Utilizing P2P networks for distributing content is challenging due to the lack of central control. Owing to the popularity and benefits of P2P networks, it is worthwhile to explore solutions that provide an appropriate balance between distributing content on a large-scale and preserving the right of intellectual property owners. DRM can provide a means to achieving this end (Einhorn and Rosenblatt 2005, Rosenblatt 2003).

DRM solutions make it possible to honor the rights of copyright holders. However, conventional DRM techniques would not be effective in a true P2P network owing to the decentralized nature of

distribution and complete control of peers over the network. While a typical DRM system is tailored for a client-server model of distribution, content distribution in a P2P network can lead to new requirements due to the following reasons:

- Any ordinary peer in a P2P network can be a content creator, distributor and seller.
- Content is not downloaded from a central repository in a P2P network since peers exchange content directly with each other.

To be effective, any DRM system designed for P2P network must to take into account these requirements of the P2P model of distribution.

Motivation and Design Goals

The goal of our project is to demonstrate a successful convergence of DRM and P2P. The root of this project lies in our search for a DRM solution tailored for P2P networks that enables efficient content distribution. While there are well-established DRM techniques, applying DRM to P2P networks presents complex functional and security requirements. The complexity can be exemplified by the following comparison: Apple iTunes music store has a central distribution site, and the songs are protected with proprietary DRM technology called FairPlay (2006), which can be downloaded to Apple iPods for playing. Contrast this to a P2P network, where any peer can be both creator and distributor, and the content is not accessed through any particular product. It was challenging to devise a reasonably secure architecture tailored for P2P networks where important security functions must be decentralized.

We aimed to look for a solution that would accomplish multiple design goals that we established for our system. These goals are enumerated below. Each design goal has been tagged with an identifier (DG1, DG2, etc.) for convenient cross-referencing. First, we consider usability-related design goals, i.e., design goals that are not directly related to security.

- *DG1*: Well-defined roles for peers in the system.
- *DG2*: Any peer can be content creator, copyright owner or seller.
- *DG3*: Redistribution with profit sharing by peers.
- *DG4*: Essential functions (e.g., packaging content) are decentralized.
- *DG5*: Independence from underlying peer-to-peer network.
- *DG6*: Minimal overheads for end users (e.g., no need for pre-installed client software) and convenient payments
- *DG7*: Code portability and platform independence.

Next, we consider the desired security features (within the inherent limitations of DRM).

- *DG8*: Secure transactions.
- *DG9*: Secure authentication and authorization with minimal overhead.
- *DG10*: Secure license distribution.
- *DG11*: Break once, break everywhere (BOBE) resistance, which implies that an approach used to compromise one piece of content cannot be immediately applied to compromise another piece of content.

Prior Research

In our search for existing industry and academic research, we discovered several proposed solutions that addressed some aspects of our functional and security goals.

The Music2Share (M2S) system (Kalker, et. al., 2004) proposes a P2P protocol based on audio fingerprinting and watermarking. However, the proposed protocol in Kalker, et. al., (2004) makes several questionable assumptions, the most questionable of which is that users are generally honest. In addition, many (if not most) of the crucial technologies on which the proposal rests are categorized as research problems. Conse-

quently, many critical security issues cannot be adequately addressed using available technology. Another drawback (from our perspective) is that the M2S system would not operate over existing P2P networks—according to the authors, "to date there exists no operating M2S network". Finally, M2S does not have any feature for content redistribution.

Berket, et. al., (2004) have proposed a solution using the Secure Group Layer (SGL) to achieve group communication. Their system makes heavy use of public-key infrastructure (PKI), and this reliance on PKI technologies predictably comes with considerable overhead. Also, the security ideas presented by Berket, et. al., (2004) have not been implemented. Apparently, the intent of their publication is to serve as a baseline for various types of P2P applications.

Iwata et. al. (2004) discuss the requirements of a DRM system applicable to P2P content sharing. The authors present a very high-level functional description without giving any insight into the underlying technologies. The functions identified in Iwata et. al. (2004) do not appear to meet many of our stated design goals.

CITADEL (Judge and Ammar 2003) uses the concept of "content containers" to pack role-based access control lists (ACLs) with the content being distributed. It is not clear how users obtain different roles in the system. CITADEL also makes use of digital signatures and X.509 public-key certificates for all users, which are expensive operations and, from our perspective, not particularly practical in a P2P setting.

The DiMaS system (Reti and Sarvas 2004) also proposes a solution based on distribution packages. While DiMaS is successful in eliminating the need for client software on the machines of end users, it does not incorporate reselling of content or BOBE resistance.

In fact, none of the systems described above, or any of the other systems we evaluated (Gehrke and Schumann 2002, Wierzbick 2005, Michiels, et. al. 2005), support explicit features for BOBE resistance or redistribution and profit sharing between content owners and resellers through reselling. Thus in our search for a system that would provide a solution to our design goals stated above, we did not encounter any satisfactory solution. Our objective is to design and develop a DRM system for P2P networks with both improved and new features as compared to existing designs.

DESIGN

We have designed a DRM system tailored to the needs of P2P networks. We call our system P2PRM, which is an acronym for Peer-to-Peer Rights Management. In this section, we discuss the design decisions we made and describe the architecture of the proposed system.

Design Decisions

Throughout the design of P2PRM, we attempted to keep in focus the design goals we established in Section 2.4. In each sub-heading that follows, we identify the design goals that the given design decision fulfills.

A Hybrid Approach

An overriding goal of P2PRM is to enable ordinary peers to benefit from content creation. A content creator can make his work available for download by other users on a peer-to-peer network, which provides ready access to a large potential audience-base. Creators who wish to distribute their creations free of cost do not need to take any extra step for distribution. However, if a creator wishes to charge a fee for use of his content, additional precautions need to be taken to ensure that he has a reasonable chance of collecting the desired fee.

Another overarching goal was to make P2PRM as decentralized as possible. We considered possible models for P2PRM without any central transaction server to take care of transactions and billing. In such a system, all billing related functions would be done at individual peers. Although this model is completely decentralized, it is more insecure and unreliable as compared to a model with a central transactions server. It is virtually impossible to ensure fair financial transactions when peers are tracking them, since there is no validation of the transactions by a third party. Accounting in such a system would be very difficult since, for example, a malicious peer can tamper with transaction logs stored at his terminal.

To provide a reasonable level of security, we decided to employ a central trusted peer, which we call the Secure Super-Peer (SSP), to track all transactions, maintain all billing records, validate any financial information, and provide other security related functions. Only a trusted peer can act as the SSP to enable large-scale secure distribution of content. The introduction of an SSP makes our model a hybrid model, since we have a central point of control in addition to the distributed peers. Adopting a hybrid approach fulfils the design goal identified by *DG8* (secure transactions).

Entities

As shown in Figure 2, our proposed model has four main entities, namely:

- Creator — Any peer who creates content to be distributed.
- Simple user — Any buyer in the P2P network who purchases content for his own use.
- Reseller — Any buyer in the network who purchases content not only for his own use, but also to redistribute to make a profit.
- Secure super peer (SSP) — A server that handles all transactions between other entities in P2PRM, and performs some security related tasks. We assume that the SSP is trusted by the other entities in the network.

Figure 2. Entities in P2PRM

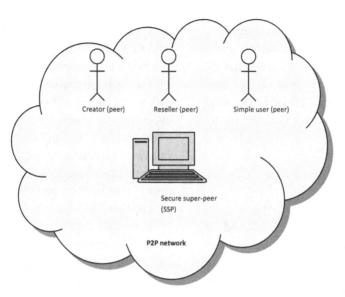

Classifying users in the system in this way fulfils the design goal identified by *DG1* (well-defined roles).

Content Distribution

Any peer who creates content can make that content available for use by other peers. If the creator wishes to charge a fee for usage of his content, the system should incorporate additional functionality to govern the entire process of creation and consumption of content. Financial transactions lead to the following requirements:

- Establishing identities of entities involved in a transaction (seller, buyer and any intermediary).
- Protecting content from unintended recipients.
- Keeping track of transaction details and preventing any illegitimate profits and transactions.

These functions are performed by different entities in P2PRM, including the creator, buyer, reseller and SSP.

Here, we introduce another entity, called the content wrapper, which works together with the other entities to make secure transactions and rights enforcement possible. As with any DRM system, in P2PRM, the content is not distributed as-is. Rather, it is packaged with some additional information and logic that plays a vital role in rights management and enforcement. We refer to the packaged content as the wrapper. Instead of distributing content, the creators distribute wrappers, as shown in Figure 3. The buyer needs to purchase access permission in order to access the content embedded in the wrapper.

The wrappers can be downloaded free of charge. Only when a buyer wishes to access the content does he need to make payment to the SSP to obtain access rights. Packaging and distribution of contents using wrappers fulfils our design goals *DG2* (any peer can be content creator and seller) and *DG6* (minimal overheads for end users).

Figure 3. Wrapper distribution environment

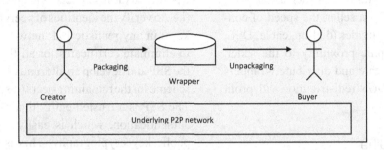

Model for Reselling

We are not aware of any DRM-enabled content distribution system for P2P networks that facilitates reselling. One of the strengths in the design of P2PRM is that it transparently enables content reselling, which can lead to larger scale distribution of content and deter piracy through profit sharing. Complexities with reselling arise for several reasons, including the following. First, resellers cannot be trusted with unencrypted content. Second, a flexible model should allow any reseller to repackage content with his own profit margin, with the new price reflecting both the creator's and reseller's markup. In this section, we describe some concepts applicable in P2PRM that focus on the area of reselling content.

A creator can decide upon a markup that he wishes to charge in the case where a reseller sells his content. Every time a reseller sells a wrapper, the creator becomes entitled to the markup he had specified during the original wrapper creation. To facilitate selling to both simple users and resellers, a creator can package his content in two forms: a user wrapper and a reseller wrapper. A user wrapper is intended for buyers who would use the content for their use only. A reseller wrapper is meant for buyers who wish to repackage the content and charge a markup for redistribution. Note that P2PRM allows a reseller to repackage a purchased content for distribution only as a user wrapper, not another reseller wrapper.

When a creator packages content, P2PRM makes a distinction between user price (price of a user wrapper) and reseller price (price of a reseller wrapper). It is generally expected that the reseller price would be higher than user price since a reseller can potentially benefit from redistributing content.

Allowing resellers to redistribute content works to the advantage the several entities in P2PRM. The content creator, simple users and, of course, resellers all can potentially benefit from reselling. By allowing resellers, a content creator can discover a larger audience for his creation. And each time the content is sold by a reseller, the creator receives his markup. In this way, the creator may obtain a larger profit as compared to selling his content by himself. Another advantage to the creator is that there may be less chance of other users compromising his content since reseller profits give an incentive for legal distribution.

For a reseller, P2PRM provides opportunities to make profits. A reseller can repackage content with a new price, which would include creator markup and reseller markup. If, for example, a reseller is on a connection that can provide faster download times for the wrapper, he can potentially charge a slightly higher price for the content.

For any buyer, P2PRM provides more choices. The buyer can choose one seller from the many sellers of content (creator and resellers). His decision to purchase a particular copy of the wrapper can be based on several factors such as the price of content offered by a seller, the speed of connection a seller is provides (dial-up, cable, DSL, T1/T3), or geographic proximity to the seller. Having resellers create and distribute wrappers fulfils design goal *DG3* (redistribution with profit sharing).

Content Packaging

One option would be to create the content wrapper at the SSP. This would require the content creator to upload the content to the SSP and the SSP would then process the content to create the wrapper. Packaging content at the SSP has some significant drawbacks, including the fact that it would make the system more centralized, and that packaging is a computationally intensive process, which would pose more computing demands on the SSP. In addition, content sizes could be very large, particularly for audio and video content. Consequently, uploads to the SSP could be very bandwidth intensive.

Since our goal is to make necessary functionalities as decentralized as possible in P2PRM without compromising security, we decided to perform content packaging at the peer. Utilizing computing power of individual peers is a cornerstone of any P2P system and we would like to retain this advantage since it will make our system more efficient overall. Creating wrappers at peers instead of the SSP falls under design goal *DG4* (essential functions decentralized).

Use of PKI

One possible approach to authenticating entities within P2PRM would be to rely on public-key infrastructure (PKI) or, more precisely, digital certificates. It is well known that public-key operations are computationally expensive. Also, the use of public key operations would require a trusted certificate authority (CA), which can grant certificates to all peers in the system. We believe it is unrealistic to expect CA to operate effectively (i.e., to verify the identities of peers before issuing keys) in any realistic P2P network. We decided to eliminate certificates for all the peers except the SSP and develop an alternative authentication scheme for the remaining peers (discussed below). The SSP is a trusted entity that requires strong authentication, which is easily achieved using public key cryptography. This is analogous to the situation on the Internet, where, for example, Amazon has a valid certificate, but ordinary users are not required to have certificates. Typically, a P2P network would require only one SSP and requiring a certificate for only the SSP would not cause significant overhead. Eliminating the need for certificates for peers in P2PRM fulfils design goal identified by *DG9* (secure authentication without excessive overhead).

License Distribution

We considered several different approaches for license distribution, including the following.

- Independent license manager — This manager would be responsible for distributing decryption keys to the buyer once appropriate payment is made at the SSP. An independent license manager would be an additional central point of control in the system.
- SSP — Without any compromise in security, we could move the functions of license manager to the SSP. The SSP would be responsible for storing the decryption keys and distributing them. While license functions would have made the SSP more complex, we did not find a significant security advantage as opposed to storing the license with the content itself.
- License with content — We decided to store the license with the content itself. To achieve security, the decryption key for the content

is encrypted with a master key known only to the SSP. We opted for this approach as it eliminates the need for the SSP to maintain a database of all decryption keys in the system and we do not envision any realistic threats beyond those involved in storing the key at the SSP. Note that this is analogous to the use of encrypted "ticket granting tickets" (TGTs) in Kerberos (Stamp 2006).

Distributing encrypted licenses with the content relates to design objective *DG10* (secure license distribution).

Independence from the Underlying P2P Network

One of our design objectives was that P2PRM should function with any underlying peer-to-peer network. That is, it should not be tied to the technologies or protocols used in a particular P2P network. To achieve this, we have made P2PRM self-contained in that it performs all functions using its own modules and standards-based protocols and it does not rely on a particular underlying P2P network in any way. Our model utilizes the P2P network only as a vehicle for distribution. Once a wrapper is created using P2PRM modules, it can be made available on any P2P network for distribution and any buyer can open the content (using out P2PRM software) upon obtaining the wrapper via the underlying P2P network. The system is independent of any specific P2P technology, which satisfies our design goal *DG5*.

Need for Client Software

Ideally, we would like to eliminate the need for peers to install any kind of client software on their terminals. However, the packaging of content wrappers by the creators on their terminals necessitates some software to do the packaging. Therefore, we require all content creators to install P2PRM client software (called wrapper creator

software). Buyers in the system (i.e., resellers and simple users) do not need any client software to repackage or access the content since all of the logic for repackaging and access is included in the wrapper itself. This logic is referred to as the wrapper access software in P2PRM. While the wrapper creator software needs to be installed on a creator's terminal, the wrapper access software is launched automatically when opening the wrapper. By doing away with client software for buyers, P2PRM is more flexible, and has reduced setup needs. This is consistent with our design objective *DG6* (minimal overhead for end-users).

Portability

P2PRM modules should be portable across platforms since all terminals active in a P2P network cannot be assumed to be uniform. Accordingly, all modules in P2PRM should be capable of executing on all platforms. As discussed in detail in Section 4, we designed P2PRM keeping in mind openness and standards-compliance for easy portability. This meets our design criteria *DG7* (code portability).

BOBE Resistance

According to our design objective *DG11* (break once, break everywhere resistance), P2PRM should foil BOBE attacks. This means that an attacker, upon compromising one piece of content, should not be able to follow an identical approach to compromise another piece of content. The purpose of BOBE resistance is to keep the amount of compromised contents in the system to a minimum by increasing the work for attackers. This can be achieved by individualizing each wrapper (which encapsulates content) using some proprietary algorithms. We designed each wrapper so that before the underlying content is encrypted with a strong cryptographic algorithm, it is "scrambled" with one of a variety of proprietary algorithms. Since these scrambling algorithms are not in the public domain, it obfuscates the wrapper code and makes system-wide reverse engineering attacks significantly more difficult.

Architecture

In this section, we discuss in detail the content of the wrapper, the processing that occurs at different entities and the interactions amongst the various entities. The process discussed here culminate in the creation of the content wrapper and, ultimately, in access of the content.

Content Wrapper

Before we delve into the functional architecture of P2PRM, it is important to know what information is included in a content wrapper. As noted above, each content wrapper is one of the following two types:

• User wrapper—These wrappers are created for simple users (i.e., users who purchase

the content for their own use, not for reselling)

• Reseller wrapper — These wrappers are created for resellers and include the capability to repackage the underlying content and sell it for a new price as determined by the reseller.

Figure 4 provides a pictorial representation of a content wrapper.

As illustrated in the Figure 4, a content wrapper has the following components:

• Unencrypted metadata — This consists of information that a potential buyer can view before paying to access the content within the wrapper. This includes a description of the content, its price and the name of the creator. For a reseller wrapper, the creator markup is also included. In addition, the URL of the SSP is included so that a connection to the SSP can be established to perform the SSP-related steps during content access.

Figure 4. Contents of a content wrapper

```
1. Unencrypted metadata
- Content description
- Price
- Creator name
- Creator markup (for reseller wrapper only)
- SSP URL
```

```
2. Encrypted information
- Creator/Reseller ID
- Price
- Content Decryption key
- Creator/reseller markup
```

```
3. Encrypted and scrambled content
```

```
4. Logic for viewing & content access
```

- Encrypted information — This includes sensitive information, which is encrypted to prevent reading or tampering by attackers. The sensitive data includes the price of accessing the content, a creator identifier and the decryption key with which the content can be decrypted. In case of a reseller wrapper, a reseller identifier and the reseller markup are also encrypted in the wrapper. The encrypted information is encrypted with a symmetric key known only to the SSP—we denote this master key by K_{master}.
- Encrypted and scrambled content — The content is scrambled and then encrypted with a symmetric key (denoted K_c) before being included in the wrapper.
- Logic for viewing and access — Since the wrapper is self-contained, it includes all logic needed for a buyer to purchase and access content. This eliminates the need

for dedicated client software on a buyer's terminal. A reseller wrapper also includes logic for a reseller to repackage content with a different price determined by the creator markup and reseller markup.

Functional Architecture

Figure 5 depicts the functional architecture of P2PRM.

Next, we discuss the interactions between the components in more detail. The "steps" below refer to the numbers that appear in Figure 5.

- *Step 1) Creator registration*—Any peer who wishes to distribute content created by him for a fee needs to register with the SSP. This SSP then generates a unique identifier for the creator. Note that the identifiers assigned to

Figure 5. Interactions between system entities

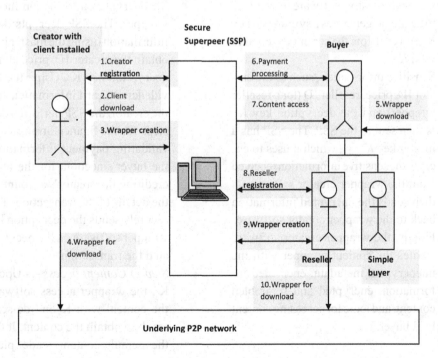

the creators and resellers are only for billing purposes. Consequently, if another dedicated server is introduced in the system to take care of all billing functionality, there is no need for the SSP to remember all these identifiers. The billing server could then track all the identifiers and transactions while the SSP would just need to perform master key encryption and decryption operations. Such an approach would make the SSP even more lightweight.

- *Step 2) Client download* — A creator needs a copy of the client software for packaging content. In P2PRM, we refer to this software as the wrapper creator software.

- *Step 3) Wrapper creation* — This step can be divided in the following sub steps:

  - A creator opens the wrapper creator software, enters details such as name, user price, reseller price, creator mark-up, content location and description.

  - The creator then chooses to create a user wrapper or reseller wrapper. The wrapper creator software scrambles the content, generates a symmetric key K_c, and encrypts the scrambled content with K_c.

  - Sensitive information, such as the creator ID, price, reseller ID (for a reseller wrapper) and the decryption key K_c, is then sent to the SSP. The SSP has a master key K_{master}, which it uses to encrypt the sensitive information received from the wrapper creator software. It then sends the encrypted information back to the wrapper creator software.

  - Finally, the wrapper creator software creates the content wrapper with the unencrypted metadata, encrypted information, encrypted and scrambled content, and logic for accessing content by a buyer.

- *Step 4) Wrapper for download* — The creator makes the content wrapper available for download by other peers, typically by hosting the wrapper on his machine and making it searchable in the underlying P2P network. Since the system allows for resellers, multiple copies of one wrapper can exist for download at a given time at different peers in the same network.

- *Step 5) Wrapper download* — A peer can obtain a content wrapper through one or more sources (i.e., the creator or any reseller) in the P2P network.

- *Step 6) Payment processing* — A peer can obtain access right to the content in the following way: The peer opens the downloaded wrapper, which launches the wrapper access software and displays information about the content, including its description, price and creator. Upon viewing the information, the user can choose to pay the required sum at the SSP by entering payment information. The wrapper access software sends the payment information to the SSP along with the encrypted information included in the wrapper. The SSP decrypts the encrypted information (using the master key, K_{master}) to obtain the creator ID, price and the content decryption key K_c. Using the buyer's provided credit card information and the ID of the creator, the SSP performs the necessary steps for the financial transaction, namely, validating payment information, charging the buyer's account for the required sum, crediting the creator's account and logging the details of the transaction. The SSP then securely sends the decryption key K_c to the wrapper software on the peer that had initiated the transaction.

- *Step 7) Content access* — Upon obtaining K_c, the wrapper access software decrypts the content with K_c and de-scrambles the result to obtain the content. It then invokes the default content reader/player on the

Table 1. Functions of entities in the system

Component	Functions
Creator	- Content creation - Content packaging - Upload content wrapper to P2P network
Reseller	- Download reseller wrapper from P2P network - Payment to the SSP - Access content - Repackage content - Upload user wrapper to P2P network
Simple user	- Download user wrapper from P2P network - Payment to the SSP - Access content
SSP	- Creator and reseller registration - Maintain billing information - Master-key encryption/decryption

buyer's terminal for the buyer to access the content.

- *Step 8) Reseller registration* — If a buyer wishes to access a reseller wrapper, in addition to payment processing, the SSP registers the user as a reseller. The SSP generates a unique ID for the reseller and passes it back to the wrapper access software for use in wrapper re-packaging.
- *Step 9) Wrapper creation* — A reseller can repackage the encrypted and scrambled content as a user wrapper with a new price. This new price, which is calculated by the wrapper access software, is the sum of the reseller markup and the creator markup. Since the creator markup is encrypted with K_{master}, it is decrypted when making a request to the SSP.
- *Step 10) Wrapper for download* — After a reseller creates a repackaged user wrapper, he can make the wrapper available for download by other peers in the network.

Table 1 summarizes the functions of different entities in P2PRM.

IMPLEMENTATION

In this section, we cover details of the implementation phase. We strived to implement P2PRM using open source and standards-based technologies. We used Java as the development tool, Eclipse as the development environment and Windows XP as the development platform.

The implementation of P2PRM is divided into three major modules: the Secure Super-Peer (SSP), wrapper creator software and wrapper access software. In the following sections, we discuss key implementation aspects and present UML (Unified Modeling Language) class diagrams for all three modules. The UML diagrams were created with the Violet UML editor (Violet 2006). All user-interfaces associated with the three modules were implemented with Java Swing (2006).

Note that security-related implementation issues of P2PRM are covered in Section 5.

Secure Super Peer (SSP)

Multiple Connections

The SSP must be able to handle concurrent connections emanating from multiple creators and buyers. Therefore, the SSP is implemented as a multi-threaded server capable of simultaneously managing multiple connections. Upon accepting a client connection request, the SSP spawns a SSP thread dedicated to service the requests associated with that connection. This allows the SSP to accept new incoming client connections while servicing prior requests.

Identification of Users

For billing purposes, the SSP assigns a unique identifier to each creator and reseller. We have used the java service java.rmi.server.UID (Class UID 2006) to generate identifiers that are unique to the host where they are generated. To ensure uniqueness, each identifier consists of the following components:

- A virtual machine (VM) identifier, which uniquely identifies the VM of the host on which the identifier is generated.
- The system time when the VM generated the identifier.

- A count to distinguish between identifiers generated by the same VM at the same time. For large-scale implementations, this identifier—which is unique per host—could be combined with a unique identifier for the host itself (e.g., IP address) to create a globally unique identifier.

User Interface

The user interface for the SSP consists of a main SSP window and one child window for each SSP thread dedicated to a client connection. The main SSP window allows a creator to register with the SSP. The main window also displays connection information such as the port number the SSP is listening on and messages about accepting client connections. When the SSP accepts a new connection and spawns a SSP thread to service that connection, a separate SSP thread window becomes active for that particular connection. This thread window displays all information exchanged with the client associated with that connection.

Class Diagram

See Figure 6.

Figure 6. SSP class diagram

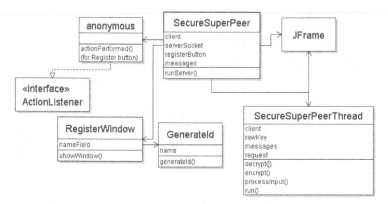

Wrapper Creator Software

Design Pattern

One of the ways to achieve modular and reusable code in software is to apply proven design patterns. We applied the model-view-controller architecture (2006) to the wrapper creator software. In conformance with this architecture, we have:

- A model class that contains all the data required by the wrapper creator software,
- A view class to display input fields that a creator needs to complete during wrapper creation,
- A controller class to handle the input entered by the creator, update information contained in the model class and start the wrapper creation process.

Wrapper as an Executable Archive

The wrapper creator software executes all the steps needed to create a content wrapper. These steps include information exchange with the SSP and encapsulating the content to include both unencrypted metadata and encrypted data. Both user wrappers and reseller wrappers have been implemented in our test implementation of P2PRM. The wrapper creation implementation for a reseller wrapper is more advanced as compared to the user wrapper, since the reseller wrapper has the capability to perform additional operations needed to repackage content.

Since our design eliminates the installation of any client software for buyers, we had to consider alternatives by which the wrapper access software could be invoked at the buyer's terminal without prior installation. The most buyer-friendly approach would be double clicking a content wrapper on the buyer's terminal, which would automatically launch the wrapper access software. To achieve this result, we have implemented the content wrapper as an executable

jar archive in Java (Jar Files 2006). The content wrapper encompasses not only the encapsulated content, but it also includes logic for completing a purchase and accessing content. The wrapper creator prepares all information to be included in the wrapper (protected content, etc.) and packs them together with the logic files (java classes) needed by the wrapper access software. Double-clicking on the archive created by the wrapper creator will automatically launch the main class of the wrapper access software. The main class specified in the archive manifest serves as the entry point into the wrapper access software (Jar Files 2006).

Format of Unencrypted Metadata

All unencrypted metadata in the content wrapper (e.g., the creator name and content description) is stored in the XML format (XML 2006). This implementation decision is consistent with our goal of implementing the system using standards-based technologies, since XML has emerged as the standard for representation and exchange of data. The wrapper creator software writes data in the XML format to be included in the content wrapper, which, in turn, is used by wrapper access software during content access processing.

Note that the wrapper creator software stores some information in the wrapper (e.g., the price) in both encrypted and unencrypted formats. While the encrypted form is tamper-resistant and used by the SSP for billing when the buyer purchases content, the unencrypted format is viewable by the buyer through the wrapper access software and can be used by a potential buyer as part of the purchase decision. In this way, during the purchase decision-making process, no connection to the SSP is required and we thereby reduce the number of connections to the SSP.

Figure 7. Wrapper creator software class diagram

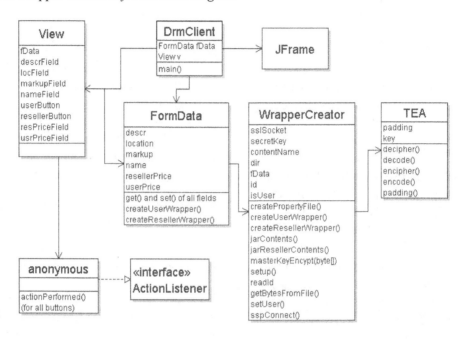

User-Interface

The wrapper creator software has a user-interface component, which enables the creator to enter information about the wrapper being created. This information consists of the creator name, content description, the price and the creator markup. The creator can choose to create a user wrapper by clicking on a create user wrapper or a reseller wrapper.

Wrapper Access Software

Archive Extraction

The wrapper access software is launched when a potential buyer double-clicks the downloaded content wrapper. During this launch, all of the files packed in the content wrapper archive are unpacked into the current directory. These files include all the data files and logic-related files (i.e.,

java classes). The wrapper access software uses the unpacked files to display relevant information to the potential buyer (content description, creator name, price). The wrapper access software gives the user the choice to purchase access rights to the content, play content or, for reseller wrappers, to repackage the content.

User-Interface

The wrapper access software has a user-interface that displays all of the details of the content when the wrapper is downloaded and double-clicked. This window also includes a button for the user to purchase access rights to content. Upon clicking the purchase button, the user enters the necessary payment information. The wrapper access software then establishes a secure communication link with the SSP to perform the transaction. The "play" button is enabled once the transaction successfully completes. The buyer can then click the play button to access the content.

Figure 8. Wrapper access software class diagram

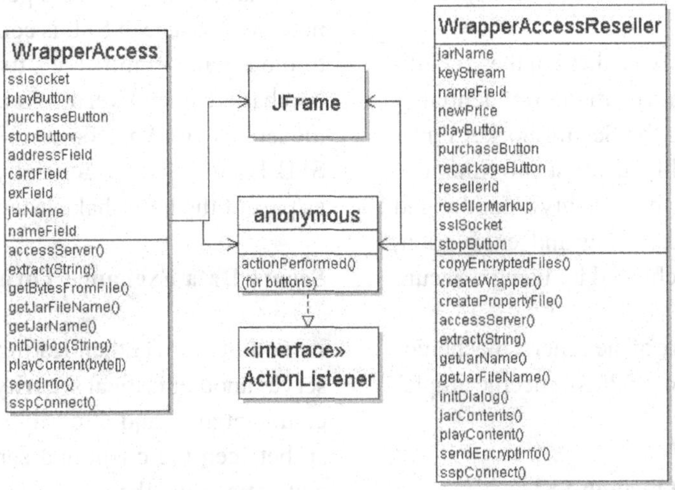

If the downloaded wrapper was a reseller wrapper, after the payment transaction is completed, the wrapper access software enables a repackage button, in addition to the play button. Using the repackage button, the buyer can repackage the underlying content. The wrapper access software allows the reseller to enter his markup and it calculates the new price of the repackaged content.

Class Diagram

See Figure 8.

SECURITY ANALYSIS

In this section, we discuss the security-critical features implemented in P2PRM. We have divided this section into the three main implementation modules of P2PRM, namely, the SSP, wrapper creator software and wrapper access software. For each feature presented, we consider possible attacks, and discuss the resilience of the system to such attacks. Note that throughout this section,

we use the terms "server" and "SSP" interchangeably, and we often use the term "client" to denote the wrapper access and/or the wrapper creator software.

SSP Security Features

Secure Sockets Layer (SSL)

A client transfers several sensitive pieces of data to the SSP. A content creator sends the content decryption key, creator ID and content price to the SSP for master key encryption while a buyer sends credit card details. Sensitive information transferred to the SSP from the client can be considered reasonably secure only when the following three conditions are met:

- The identity of the SSP is validated (authentication).
- The communication channel through which information is exchanged is protected so that only the intended recipient can view the information (confidentiality).

- The data cannot be modified without the recipient detecting the change (integrity).

In P2PRM, we satisfy all three of these conditions, namely, SSP authentication, confidentiality and integrity, by using the Secure Socket Layer (SSL) (JSSE 2006). While the first two functions of authentication and confidentiality are addressed by SSL through handshaking and encryption, message integrity is achieved by using a secure hashing algorithm.

Below we cover more of the general mechanics of SSL and the related P2PRM-specific implementation details.

SSP Authentication Through SSL

In P2PRM, the client authenticates the SSP, but not vice-versa. This requires that the SSP have a valid certificate, which, of course, involves the use of public-key cryptography. The SSP keeps its private key to itself and it distributes its public key via its certificate. A trusted certification authority (CA) digitally signs the certificate, which, effectively, vouches for the fact that the SSP holds the corresponding private key (Stamp 2006).

When the server presents its certificate in the handshake phase, the client must verify the signature on the certificate. Assuming that the client trusts the CA, once the signature is verified, the client can trust that the SSP holds the corresponding private key. Note that, among other things, SSP authentication (and subsequent confidentiality and integrity) protects the URL of the SSP, which is included in the wrapper in unencrypted form, and therefore subject to tampering. Without such protection, an attacker could modify the unencrypted URL of the SSP to his own URL in order to masquerade as the SSP and redirect all communication from the client to himself. By using SSL, if this attack is attempted it will fail at the handshaking phase since the bogus SSP will not be able to produce a signed certificate for verification by the client. That is, the SSP

certificate ensure that that a client exchanges information only with the genuine SSP. Finally, note that this use of SSL is completely analogous to the usual e-commerce situation where a user purchases content over the Web. In such situations, the server (e.g., Amazon.com) is authenticated via SSL, but the client is generally not authenticated as part of the handshake (Stamp 2006).

Secure Data Exchange Through SSL

In addition to authenticating the server, SSL serves another critical security purpose, namely, confidentiality and integrity of the data in transit between the client and server. After server authentication, the SSP and client establish a shared symmetric key that is used to encrypt and integrity protect all ensuing communication for the remainder of the session. Encryption with a symmetric key algorithm foils any attempt to eavesdropping on the information exchanged between the client and server.

SSL allows the server and client to agree upon a symmetric key for secure communication at the time of the transaction itself. No prior distribution of symmetric keys is necessary, thereby eliminating the possibility of a key being compromise during distribution.

SSL Implementation in P2PRM

For use in our P2PRM prototype, we generate the keys and certificates using a certificate management utility from Sun called *keytool* (2007). We use the RSA algorithm (RSA 2006) to generate 1024-bit key pairs for use in SSP certificates and SSL handshaking. The Advanced Encryption Standard (AES 2006) is used to encrypt SSL communication. We have used the Java Secure Sockets Extension (JSSE 2006) from Sun to implement SSL in Java. JSSE uses the term keystore to signify a repository of key information (including public-private keys and certificates belonging to an entity). In our system, the SSP stores its key information and certificate in its keystore. A truststore is a repository an entity consults when making a decision as to whether to trust another entity. The client has a truststore with public keys for various certification authorities (CAs), which is needed to verify the signature on the SSP certificate. For a client to successfully authenticate the SSP, the chain of certification authorities belonging to the SSP certificate should be a part of client's truststore. For simplicity and proof of concept, we used self-signed certificates by the SSP in our prototype and we installed the SSP public key in the client truststore. In a real-world implementation, genuine certificates, singed by a recognized CA, would be necessary.

Below we summarize the setup steps needed in our P2PRM prototype before SSL handshaking can be performed for SSP authentication and symmetric key agreement:

- Generate an RSA key pair consisting of the SSP private key and the SSP public key.
- Generate the SSP certificate, which contains the SSP public key.
- Store the SSP private key and the SSP certificate in a secure keystore.
- Extract the server public key from the keystore.
- Export the server public key to the client's truststore

Note that these steps represent a one-time setup task for the SSP. Each instance of communication between the SSP and client during wrapper creation and access can use the same SSP certificate with the same SSP public key for SSL handshaking. However, SSL handshaking in each communication instance will culminate in a different symmetric key (the session key), which is valid only during the lifetime of the specific session for which it was generated. Session keys reduce the window of any attack resulting from key compromise during a specific session.

Master Key Generation and Encryption

The SSP generates a symmetric key for use as the master key, K_{master}, to encrypt the sensitive information included in the content wrapper. The master key is known only to the SSP. We chose the Advanced Encryption Standard (AES 2006) as the algorithm for master key encryption and decryption function. An important assumption in the security of P2PRM is that the SSP maintains strict confidentiality of its master key.

Sensitive information encrypted with the SSP master key includes the decryption key, content price, creator/reseller markups, and creator/reseller identifiers. Possible attacks on this sensitive information include the following:

- Decryption key — An attacker could maliciously retrieve the decryption key of the underlying content if the key is not sufficiently secured. If possible, this would allow the attacker to gain unauthorized access to content. Alternatively, an attacker could simply tamper with the decryption key to prevent a buyer from accessing the content.
- Price — An attacker could reduce the price included in the wrapper.
- Creator/reseller identifier — An attacker can maliciously change the creator or reseller identifier included in the wrapper to his own identifier to obtain undue profits.
- Creator/Reseller markup — An attacker could maliciously change the markup of both creator and reseller to deny them of potential profits.

Encryption with the master key of the SSP prevents all of these attacks. By using master key encryption coupled with SSL, the SSP securely tracks all the transactions and sensitive billing information rather than each peer tracking their own transactions. Decentralized tracking is more prone to attack since each peer needs to be trusted, which is not a reasonable assumption. The master key security feature is critical to P2PRM for accurate billing and profit allocation. In our prototype, we have not implemented a full-blown billing and accounting mechanism at the SSP but, of course, this would be necessary for a real-world implementation.

Security Features of Wrapper Creator Software

Content Encryption

The wrapper creator software encrypts all content before packaging it into the content wrapper. For each piece of content to be packaged, the wrapper creator software generates an AES key and we encrypt the content using the AES cipher. AES is considered a strong symmetric cipher. In P2PRM, the AES key is generated and the content is encrypted without storing the key at the creator's terminal. This provides an added measure of security against key compromise at the source itself.

License with Content

The wrapper creator software stores the AES decryption key in the content wrapper. To protect the content decryption key against unauthorized use, the content decryption key is encrypted with the master key of the SSP, K_{master}. The SSP decrypts the content decryption key only after the buyer makes the required payment. An attacker cannot retrieve the content decryption key from the content wrapper without payment unless he can break the master key encryption algorithm or he obtains the master key. The use of AES as the master key algorithm renders it sufficiently secure to cryptanalytic attack and we assume that SSP securely stores the master key. Note that the SSP master key is a single point of failure for the system.

We have also includes a mechanism by whereby a successful attack on a particular content wrapper will be highly unlikely to succeed against other wrappers. This feature greatly reduces the chances

of a successful system-wide attack. This critical security feature is discussed in the next section.

BOBE Resistance

In our design, we strive to achieve "break once, break everywhere" (BOBE) resistance. The goal is to make each attack on the software a distinct challenge, as opposed to having an attack on one instance of the software, which breaks the security of the entire system. We employ unique "scrambling" algorithms, which make each wrapper somewhat unique. The scrambling algorithm is applied to the content before encryption and the scrambling algorithm is essentially a proprietary encryption algorithm. This adds an extra layer of security when an attacker tries to reverse engineer the wrapper software. That is, even if an attacker successfully recovers the AES key (or otherwise breaks the encryption) by reverse engineering, he still has to break the proprietary scrambling algorithm before recovering the actual content. The AES algorithm is well known (the key is the only secret), but our proprietary scrambling algorithms are unknown to attackers and will therefore add a degree of difficulty to reverse engineering attacks.

Any proprietary scrambling algorithm could be applied in P2PRM. We have created numerous variants of the Tiny Encryption Algorithm, or TEA (Wheeler and Needham 1994), for use as our scrambling algorithms. These different variations of TEA allow us to achieve individualization of content wrappers. Note that we do not rely on the scrambling algorithm for cryptographic strength, but instead, the scrambling is only intended to obscure the underlying code in an effective and relatively simple manner.

Secure Connection to SSP

The wrapper creator software must communicate securely with the SSP for master key encryption of sensitive information. Rather than sending this information in the clear, the wrapper creator initiates a SSL channel with the SSP, authenticates the SSP and establishes a shared symmetric key with the SSP (as described in Section 5.1). All communication between the wrapper creator and the SSP is protected with this symmetric key. This prevents any attacker from snooping data or maliciously altering data exchanged in the client-SSP interaction.

We have now discussed the general implementation aspects and security specific implementation features of the wrapper creator software. In Figure 9, we summarize the steps executed by the wrapper software when creating the content wrapper. At each step in Figure 9, we include (in parenthesis) the technology used to implement the indicated function.

Executing the steps discussed above (and illustrated in Figure 9) has the effect of encapsulating the content in a content wrapper. The underlying content is secured by the layers of protection applied by the security features provided by the SSP and the wrapper creator software. Each layer of protection adds some measure of security, translating into more work required by an attacker to recover content. The diagram in Figure 10 illustrates the levels of security features protecting the underlying content in P2PRM.

Security Features in Wrapper Access Software

Unauthorized Access

If a peer receives a content wrapper from another peer, the embedded wrapper access software will ask for payment at the SSP before the peer can get the decryption key and access the content. This is to ensure that all users of content have made the necessary payment before accessing the content.

Hard Disk Storage

The wrapper access software never stores the decrypted content on the hard drive of any peer

terminal. Instead, it directly feeds the decrypted content stream to the underlying content reader application. Although this is subject to a fairly trivial attack, there is no way to avoid it in a lightweight implementation, such as P2PRM. A more secure implementation would require hardware-based protection such as NGSCB (2006), or a comparable heavy-duty approach on each client terminal.

Secure Connection to SSP

The wrapper access software sends the buyer's payment information and the decryption key (which is encrypted with the SSP master key) to the SSP. Once the SSP processes the payment, it decrypts the content decryption key and sends it back to the wrapper access software. The payment information and decryption key are transmitted to the SSP through a secure SSL channel.

TESTING

P2PRM provides an efficient, reasonably secure, and lightweight method by which digital content can be distributed in a P2P network. Since we are not aware of any comparable system, a direct performance analysis or performance comparison of P2PRM is not feasible. Therefore, the cornerstone of our testing was verifying that the implementation meets the design objectives and functions effectively.

We tested the functionality of all of the components of P2PRM. For our testing, we used audio files as our digital content to be distributed over the underlying P2P network. In this section, we discuss a sample test case that we used to verify the implementation and demonstrate the functionality of our prototype system. We illustrate all of the steps involved in creating, selling, accessing and reselling a content wrapper. For purposes of clarity, we show the user-interfaces associated with each given step. See Exhibit A.

Figure 9. Steps in wrapper creation

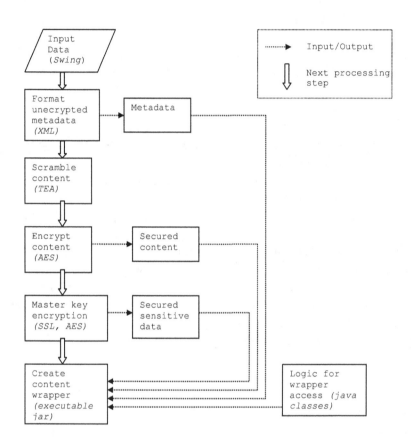

Figure 10. Layers of protection applied to content

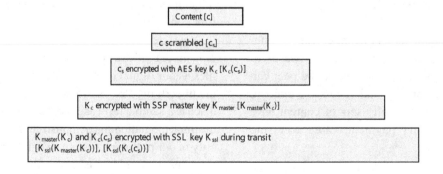

Exhibit A.

Creator registration

First, we start the SSP.

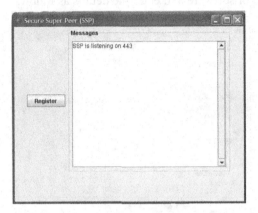

Next, we click on Register button and enter the necessary details.

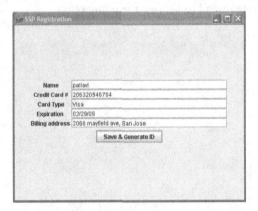

We click *Save & Generate ID* button and a confirmation window appears.

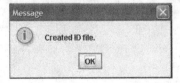

We can then verify that an ID file has been generated in the working directory and that the file contains the correct content.

continued on following page

Exhibit A. continued

User wrapper creation

We start the wrapper creator software and enter the details as follows:

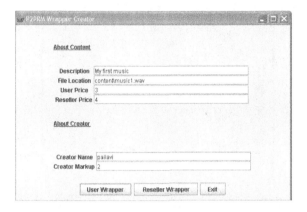

We click on the *User Wrapper* button, which creates a secure communication channel with the SSP. The SSP then spawns a separate thread to service the connection.

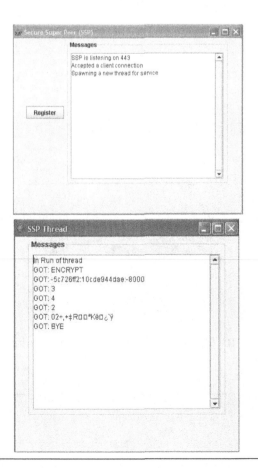

continued on following page

Exhibit A. continued

Once the creation of the user wrapper is complete, a confirmation window appears. Then we can verify that a user wrapper has been created in the working directory.

User wrapper access

To test the wrapper access, we can simply copy the generated user wrapper to a test directory and double-click the user wrapper. This launches the user wrapper access software. Double-clicking also extracts all the files needed by the wrapper access software and copies the files into the current directory.

We can then verify the content of the XML information file which is contained in the wrapper.

Address C:\Thesis\TestDir1\music1_wrapper_user\information.xml

```
<?xml version="1.0" encoding="UTF-8" ?>
<!DOCTYPE properties (View Source for full doctype...)>
- <properties version="1.0">
    <entry key="Creator_Markup">2</entry>
    <entry key="Creator">pallavi</entry>
    <entry key="Reseller_Price">4</entry>
    <entry key="User_Price">3</entry>
    <entry key="Description">My first music</entry>
  </properties>
```

It is then easy to verify that the information displayed by the wrapper access software was correct. Next, we enter all information required to purchase access rights to the wrapper as follows:

We click on the *Purchase* button from the wrapper access software. This creates a secure communication channel with the SSP, which spawns a separate thread to service the wrapper access connection.

continued on following page

Exhibit A. continued

Once the SSP and wrapper access software complete their transaction, the *Play* button in the wrapper access software is activated. We can then click on the *Play* button to play the decrypted music stream.

While the time music is playing, the *Stop* button is activated in the wrapper access software to allow the user to stop playing the music at any time.

continued on following page

Exhibit A. continued

Reseller wrapper access

The steps to create a reseller wrapper are similar to those followed when creating a user wrapper, so we omit the details here. Once a reseller wrapper has been created, we copying it to a test directory then double-click on the reseller wrapper. This launches the reseller wrapper access software. We can easily verify that the information displayed by the software is correct (e.g., reseller price). Purchasing the wrapper involves the same steps as purchasing a user wrapper, so we omit the details.

Once the transaction between the SSP and wrapper access software is completed, the *Play* button is activated and the *Repackage* button is also activated. This means that we can now repackage the underlying content.

Next, we click on the *Repackage* button and enter the reseller markup in the displayed window.

continued on following page

Exhibit A. continued

A confirmation window appears when the repackaging is complete. We can then verify that a user wrapper has been created in the current directory. Next, we launch the user wrapper. We can verify that the underlying content of the newly created user wrapper is the same as for reseller wrapper discussed above, but the price is different (as determined by the content creator's markup and the reseller's markup, which are 2 and 1, respectively, in this test case).

CONCLUSION AND FUTURE WORK

We have proposed a model and successfully developed a working prototype that enables legal and reasonably secure content distribution over an untrusted P2P network. Our system, P2PRM, includes various features to deter piracy and to enable content creators and distributors to obtain profits. Some of these features are technical, such as break-once break-everywhere (BOBE) resistance, while others are non-technical, such as reselling. We believe that the novel features of P2PRM make the system less susceptible to attacks and more conducive to legitimate use. For example, through the reselling feature, resellers can profit via content distribution, which should make potential resellers less likely to indulge in piracy.

We would argue that the features of P2PRM make it a plausible candidate for large-scale deployment over existing P2P networks. However, no system can be deemed totally secure unless it withstands the scrutiny of hackers and researchers over an extended period of time. While we do not claim that the security of our system is impregnable, we do believe that each security feature adds to the overall security. Consequently, we believe that all of the features together render P2PRM reasonably secure. In particular, even if determined hackers do succeed in compromising individual pieces of content (which is inevitable) the BOBE resistance feature should enable the system as a whole to survive.

There are several possible extensions of our basic P2PRM model. Here we outline features that could be added to P2PRM. Note that the following list is not exhaustive, and there are many other possible extensions.

- *Advanced payment system integration* – P2PRM can be integrated with an advanced payment system. Digital goods could then be offered for a very low price, or the level of access could be determined by the amount of the payment. For example, the seller could require that the buyer pay a few cents to view each page. Both low prices and the level of access can be managed by including a micro-payment capability with P2PRM (Micropayment Markup 2004, Dai 2006, Stamp and Dai 2006).

- Another payment option would be to integrate P2PRM with a subscription-based system where buyers could pay a fixed amount of money monthly to purchase access rights to a fixed amount of content or a specified number of accesses. Such a system would decrease payment-related traffic within the system.

- *Role-based Access Control* – We could incorporate role-based access control into P2PRM (Ferraiolo and Kuhn 1992, Stamp, Mathur and Kim 2006). Then all users could be classified by their roles in the system and access decisions could be based on the roles to which users are assigned. Roles in the system could be granted by the SSP or the creator based on the level of payment received from buyers. Such role-based access control could be combined with a subscription based payment strategy to significantly reduce access and payment related traffic in the system.

- *Advanced DRM capability* — P2PRM could include a finer granularity of access control techniques. A creator could specify the number of pages he wants a particular buyer to be able to read. Alternatively, a creator could specify how many times a reseller can repackage and distribute a piece of content.

- *Email support* — The SSP could send identifier files to the creators and resellers via email. This would create stronger form of authentication ("two-factor" or, more precisely, "two-channel" authentication) since the creator and reseller must be able to check their email to obtain the required ID file.

- *Content identification techniques such as audio fingerprinting* — Implementing content identification techniques (hashing, watermarking, etc.) would ensure that an attacker cannot compromise a piece of content, treat the content as his own, and then collect profits by packaging and selling the content as his own.

- *Profit through content hosting* — In order to further reduce the incentive for content piracy, an additional feature could be included in the system whereby a user would be given a share of profits when content that the user hosts on his system is purchased by a user. This would create additional incentive for peers to "play by the rules", rather than attack the system, while also reducing "free riding" on the system.

- *Integration with Next-Generation Secure Computing Base (NGSCB)* — P2PRM could utilize the inherent security offered by a trusted operating system, such as NGSCB (2006). Such a system provides hardware-based protection, which is extremely useful in securing digital content. Integration with NGSCB would offer a relatively high degree of security when the content wrapper resides on a buyer's computer or when a buyer accesses decrypted content.

REFERENCES

Kazaa. (2006). How P2P and Kazaa software works. Retrieved January 2006 from http://www.kazaa.com/us/help/new_p2p.htm

Gnutella clients. (2006). Retrieved January 2006 from http://www.gnutella.com/connect

Napster. (2006). How the old Napster worked. Retrieved January 2006 from http://computer.howstuffworks.com/napster.htm

Distributed Computing Industry Association. (2004). Proposed business models for digital music distribution. Retrieved January 2006 from http://www.dcia.info/model.ppt

iPod + iTunes. (2006). Retrieved March 2006 from http://www.apple.com/itunes/

iTunes. (2006). 1 billion served. Retrieved February 2006 from http://abcnews.go.com/Technology/story?id=1653881&technology=true

Stamp, M. (2006). *Information Security Principles and Practice*. John Wiley and Sons.

Einhorn, M., A., & Rosenblatt, B. (2005). *Peer-to-Peer networking and digital rights management*. Retrieved January 2006 from http://www.cato.org/pub_display.php?pub_id=3670.

Rosenblatt, B. (2003). *Integrating DRM with peer-to peer networks*. Retrieved January 2006 from http://www.giantstepsmts.com/drm_p2p.htm.

Kalker, T., Epema, D., H., J., Hartel, P., H., Lagendijk, R., L., & Steen, M. V. (2004). Music2Share – Copyright-compliant music sharing in P2P systems. *Proceedings of the IEEE.*

Berket, K., Essiari, A., & Muratas, A. (2004). PKI-based security for peer-to-peer information sharing. *Proceedings of the Fourth International Conference on Peer-to-Peer Computing.*

Iwata, T., Takehito, A., Ueda, K., & Sunaga, H. (2003). A DRM system suitable for P2P content delivery and the study on its implementation. *Proceeding of the 9th Asia-Pacific Conference on Communications (APCC 2003.)*

Judge, P., & Ammar, M. (2003). CITADEL: A content protection architecture for decentralized peer-to-peer file sharing systems. *Proceedings of IEEE GLOBECOM 2003.*

Reti, T., & Sarvas, R. (2004). DiMaS: Distributing Multimedia on Peer-to-Peer File Sharing Networks. *Proceedings of ACM Multimedia.*

Gehrke, N., & Schumann, M. (2002). Constructing electronic marketplaces using peer-to-peer technology. *Proceedings of the 36th Hawaii International Conference on System Sciences.*

Wierzbicki, A. (2005). Peer-to-peer direct sales. *Proceedings of the Fifth IEEE International Conference on Peer-to-Peer Computing.*

Michiels, S., Verslype, K., Joosen, W., & Decker, B. D. (2005). Towards a software architecture for DRM. *Proceedings of the Fifth ACM Workshop on Digital Rights Management.*

JSSE (2006). Java Secure Sockets Extension. Retrieved January 2006 from http://java.sun.com/products/jsse/

AES. (2006). Advanced Encryption Standard. Retrieved March 2006 from http://csrc.nist.gov/CryptoToolkit/aes/

Wheeler, D. and Needham, R. (1994). Tea, a tiny encryption algorithm. *Fast Software Encryption*, pp. 363-366

XML (2006). Extensible Markup Language. Retrieved April 2006 from http://www.w3.org/XML/

Swing. (2006). Project Swing (Java Foundation Classes). Retrieved April 2006 from http://java.sun.com/j2se/1.5.0/docs/guide/swing/

Violet. (2006). Retrieved October 2006 from http://horstmann.com/violet/

Micropayment Markup. (2006). Common markup for micropayment per-fee-links. Retrieved October 2006 from http://www.w3.org/TR/Micropayment-Markup/#Basic.

Ferraiolo, D. F., & Kuhn, D. R. (1992). Role Based Access Control. *15th National Computer Security Conference.*

NGSCB. (2006). *Next Generation Secure Computing Base.* Retrieved October 2006 from http://www.microsoft.com/resources/ngscb/default.mspx

Keytool. (2006). Key and Certificate Management Tool. Retrieved March 2006 from http://java.sun.com/j2se/1.3/docs/tooldocs/win32/keytool.html

Fairplay. (2006). Retrieved February 2006 from http://en.wikipedia.org/wiki/FairPlay

Class UID. (2006). Retrieved May 2006 from http://java.sun.com/j2se/1.4.2/docs/api/java/rmi/server/UID.html

Model-View-Controller. (2006). Retrieved March 2006 from http://ootips.org/mvc-pattern.html

Jar Files. (2006). *Packaging programs in jar files.* Retrieved April 2006 from http://java.sun.com/docs/books/tutorial/deployment/TOC.html#jar

JSSE. (2006). *Java Secure Sockets Extension Reference Implementation.* Retrieved March 2006 from http://java.sun.com/j2se/1.4.2/docs/guide/security/jsse/JSSERefGuide.html#SSLOverview

RSA. (2006). Retrieved February 2006 from http://en.wikipedia.org/wiki/RSA

Youtube. (2006). *Broadcast yourself.* Retrieved October 2006 from http://www.youtube.com

Gnutella. (2006). Retrieved January 2006 from http://en.wikipedia.org/wiki/Gnutella

Biddel, P., England, P., Peinado, M., & Willman, B. (2002). The Darknet and the Future of Content Distribution. Microsoft Corporation. *Digital Rights Management Conference*

Dai, J. (2006). QuickPay: *Protocol for online payment.* Graduate Project. Retrieved October 2006 from http://www.cs.sjsu.edu/faculty/stamp/students/QuickPayReport.pdf

Stamp, M., & Dai, J. (2006). *Micropayment token making schemes.* Retrieved October 2006 from http://www.cs.sjsu.edu/faculty/stamp/students/dai.htm

Stamp, M., Mathur, A., & Kim, S. (2006). Role based access control and the JXTA peer-to-peer network. *Proceedings of 2006 International Conference on Security & Management.*

KEY TERMS

BOBE Resistance: Refers to the ability of a DRM system to remain usable in spite of successful attack on individual pieces of content.

Content Wrapper: Consists of content that has been packaged with additional items such as authentication information and advertisements.

Digital Content: Consists of goods (such as music, video, software, books and documents) that have been converted into an electronic format (digitized) to be used on a computer and delivered via a computer network.

Digital Rights Management: Consists of the rules that can be enforced at the various stages of digital content delivery and use.

Encryption: Deals with the transformation of content into an unreadable form by using well-known algorithms based on some confidential information (i.e., a key).

License: Refers to the consent granted by an owner of an object that enables an end-user to legitimately use that object (e.g., authenticate and make payments to obtain a license to play audio file).

Peer-to-Peer Network: A network in which the computer nodes are connected in an ad-hoc manner, with each node able to act as client and server. This is in contrast to a traditional client-server network in which all computers communicate with a central server.

Reselling: The distribution of both digital and non-digital goods by intermediaries who are authorized by the original owners to re-distribute for a share of profits.

Scrambling: The transformation of content into an unreadable form by using a proprietary algorithm.

Transaction Security: Refers to the safety of confidential information when multiple entities communicate to complete a transaction (e.g., credit card payment).

Chapter VII
Pervasive Video Surveillance Systems Over TCP/IP Networks

L. Badia
IMT Lucca Institute for Advanced Studies, Italy

A. Erta
IMT Lucca Institute for Advanced Studies, Italy
Fluidmesh Networks Inc., Italy

U. Malesci
Fluidmesh Networks Inc., Italy

ABSTRACT

Traditional analog video surveillance systems technology has recently become inadequate to face the massive demand of security systems consisting of hundreds and sometimes thousands of cameras often deployed in hostile environments miles away from the control room. During the last few years, the rapid growth of the digital technology has produced sophisticated cameras which can directly record high-definition digital videos. The packetized video stream can be straightforwardly conveyed to the control room, relaying on common IP network infrastructures. This solution result is extremely flexible as the network infrastructure can be built over a wide variety of heterogeneous network technologies from the traditional Ethernet-based Local Area Networks (LANs) to the recently proposed Wireless Mesh Networks (WMNs). However, the widespread adoption of IP-based solutions for video surveillance poses serious problems in terms of required bandwidth, processing power, network security, and system dependability. In this chapter, we first investigate the advantages of the IP-based video surveillance systems over the traditional analog ones. Then, we describe the technical challenges and the open research issues which still lack an ultimate solution which permits to completely abandon the traditional analog technology. Finally, we propose and verify, by means of a case study, a methodology to address the design of video surveillance systems in real deployment.

INTRODUCTION

During the last decades, the world has become on the move. Intelligent transportation and emergency or disaster recovery facilities are more and more often integrated with remote video control. At the same time, urbanization trends combined with socio-economic changes have changed criminal and terrorism-related activities to a globalized phenomenon. As a consequence, the market for security and video surveillance systems has expanded significantly (Welsh & Ferrington, 2002). Security-system installers and integrators face several challenges in designing security and video surveillance systems that must operate in difficult and demanding settings, streaming and recording simultaneously hundreds and often thousands of video flows. In the last few years, the physical and video-security field is experiencing a massive shift from analog transmission over coaxial cables and fiber optic to digital transmission over IP networks (In-stat, 2006). In fact, until the mid-Nineties, recording was mainly performed on tapes using VHS equipments which require analog video streams as input. In the late Nineties, the majority of tape recorders have been substituted by Digital Video Recorders (DVRs) which are embedded systems that integrate hard drives with video encoding hardware. The analog video streams coming from, for example, coaxial cables to the DVR are digitized and compressed using video encoding algorithms. To this end, it is possible to subsequently transmit the video stream as a sequence of independent Joint Photographic Experts Group (JPEG) pictures, so as to realize what is informally called Motion JPEG (M-JPEG), or to utilize techniques such as Moving Pictures Expert Group (MPEG) which exploit interframe prediction; after this step, the stream is recorded on the hard drives.

The major drawback of both VHS- and DVR-based video surveillance systems is that the transmission from the cameras to the recording and viewing locations is kept analog, and therefore video quality is often directly affected by the distance between the control room and the cameras. Additionally, installing analog cameras in rural or even dense residential areas may not be feasible given the impossibility of laying long enough cables to reach the control room. Embracing the digital revolution from the camera to the head-end location and encoding the video stream into TCP/IP-like packets directly in the camera present multiple advantages (Sedky *et al.*, 2005; Cisco, 2006). In fact, the system designer can leverage existing networks and infrastructures irrespective of the specific medium used to convey the video stream (e.g., copper, fiber-optic, radio waves etc.). Furthermore, viewing and recording capabilities can be distributed by enhancing the cameras with integrated reporting and recording systems. However, the IP-based approach requires solving several additional issues in order to meet the requirements, in terms of security and reliability, of a traditional video surveillance system. For instance, the high bandwidth capacity required to transmit hundreds of video streams simultaneously (Koutsakis *et al.*, 2004) and the processing power needed to encode and decode multiple MPEG-4 streams (Ziliani, 2005) are definitely two main problems of IP-based systems which still lack a definitive solution. In this work, we describe the advantages and investigate the research open issues and technical challenges of the IP-based approach with respect the traditional analog systems for video surveillance. Furthermore, we analyze several existing IP-based solutions and develop a viable methodology to deploy efficient and effective video surveillance systems. Finally, we present, as a case study, a video surveillance system installed in a seaport in Europe where the above methodology has been successfully employed at the design stage.

BACKGROUND

In this section, we describe in detail the components of a video surveillance system. Specifically, we first analyze the video surveillance application scenarios. Then, we focus on the specific system components and we describe their characteristics. Finally, we investigate the peculiar features of IP-based video surveillance and review the enabling IP technologies for supporting IP video streaming.

A. Video Surveillance Applications

The major applications of video surveillance systems fall under the *physical* security umbrella. Every physical security system has to verify the major objectives of deterrence, detection, and verification (Smith & Robinson, 1999). The video surveillance system is usually adopted as a verification tool to reduce false positives coming out of the intrusion detection and access control systems. Typical scenarios are office buildings, banks, museums, parking lots and industrial plants. In other situations, such as municipalities and highways, video surveillance is not employed in conjunction with a detection system (e.g., perimeter protection, intrusion detection, etc.) but it is rather a standalone system managed by the local security/police personnel. In these specific contexts, the Closed Circuit TeleVision (CCTV) system plays the role of a deterrence, detection and verification means at the same time. During the last few years, due to the increasing adoption of intelligent video analysis software, video surveillance systems are becoming from passive verification systems to complete detection solutions. Video analysis is able to detect "alarm" situations by automatically analyzing the video streams. Examples of such applications are lost baggage detection in airports or the queue formation on highways (Wolf *et al.*, 2002; Bramberger *et al.*, 2006).

Both enterprise and government organizations are increasing the number of cameras on their premises to provide a 24 hours video-stream recording which helps managing security and liability threats at the same time. Thanks to extensive and pervasive video surveillance, a lot of organizations are nowadays able to decrease insurance premium and, thus, achieve more efficiency in asset management. For instance, casinos are investing huge budgets in video surveillance by installing systems with 2,000-5,000 cameras per casino. The CCTV systems help casinos to increase security, reduce frauds and solve many liability issues involved with gambling, thus, greatly rewarding the invested budget.

Other important applications for video surveillance involve monitoring specific industrial processes. However, these applications usually require special types of camera equipment which exhibit different technological challenges with respect to those for large scale physical security. For example, production plans in the pharmaceutical industry employ very high frame rate cameras (100+ frame per second) and hyperspectral imaging to monitor and certify their processes (Hamilton & Lodder, 2002). However, these special industrial applications are not the primary focus of this paper. Therefore, in the following, we will mainly refer to the physical security applications and their research challenges.

B. Video Surveillance Systems Components

Every IP-based CCTV system can be divided into 5 main components:

1. Video Capturing
2. Video Encoding
3. Video Transmission
4. Video Monitoring & Management
5. Video Recording

1) Video capturing

The video capturing component of any CCTV system is the camera, whose core is the Charged Couple Device (CCD) sensor that converts light signals in electrical signals. Traditional analog CCDs are now very often replaced with Digital Signal Processing (DSP)-based CCDs. Also, cameras usually have an analog output with a

Bayonet Neill-Concelman (BNC) connector for a coaxial cable.

2) Video encoding

As the majority of cameras installed today have digital DSP-based CCDs but still analog BNC output, a separate encoding device is required in order to streams video over an IP network. Video encoders (or video-server) are basically analog-to-digital converters that encode an analog video stream coming from a coaxial cable into a stream of IP packets usually compressed with MPEG-4 or M-JPEG. Video encoders usually have a BNC input and an IEEE 802.3 Ethernet input/output. To control motorized Pan-Tilt-Zoom (PTZ) cameras, many encoders are also equipped with a serial output which reports the telemetry readings of the electric engine. Recently, the increasing success of IP cameras, where video capturing and video encoding components are integrated into the same device, has reduced the need for separate video-encoders (Cai *et al.*, 2003).

3) Video transmission

In traditional video surveillance systems, the video stream was conveyed towards the control room through analog transmission on coaxial cables, Unshielded Twisted Pair (UTP) cables or multi-mode and single-mode fiber optic. However, in the last decade, mid to large scale video surveillance systems are migrating to wired IP-based network, and, more recently, to wireless infrastructures thanks to their increasingly lower installment and management cost (Norris *et al.*, 2004).

IP networks. As the narrow waist of the Internet, the IP protocol itself is helping also the video surveillance world in integrating different transmission technologies together. Moreover, packet switching networks allows multiple video streams to be conveyed on the same cable by sharing the available transmission capacity and leveraging the infrastructure costs with other data, video and voice flows.

Transmission Media: Copper, Fiber, Wireless. In-building IP-networks are mainly based on copper and fiber as transmission medium. Conversely, large outdoor environments are usually covered by Wide Area Networks (WANs). WANs are usually provided by large Internet Service Providers (ISPs) through high capacity leased lines or wireless technologies. A major challenge in using leased-lines and WAN technology for video surveillance is due to the high bandwidth required per video stream that dramatically bring up the leasing and operating costs.

4) Video monitoring and management

The video monitor and management system is the user interface that allows the operator to select different video streams and watch both real time and recorded video. Video monitoring and management systems are often software-based and run on generic workstation hardware. Very often the ultimate bottleneck of large video surveillance systems is the processing power required by the video monitoring workstation to decode the large number of video streams acquired. Due to the heavy hardware requirements, many custom solutions at a hybrid hardware-plus-software level are available to reduce issues related to inappropriate or insufficient general purpose hardware/software.

5) Video recording

The video recording hardware works very often in conjunction with the video management system and sometimes run even on the same server. The video recording component is usually referred to as Network Video Recorder (NVR) and tends to be a generic server with high hard disk capacity or connected to storage arrays, like Storage Area Network (SAN) or Network Attached Storage (NAS) technologies (Gemmell *et al.*, 1995). Usually, the NVR does not require extremely high processing capabilities because it does not decompress the video streams but it simply indexes the video and records the video on the network storage system.

C. Video Surveillance Over IP

Based on the above discussion, we can identify the following key advantages of video streaming over IP network with respect to traditional solutions:

- leveraging existing networks and infrastructures;
- distributing intelligence, recording and viewing capabilities;
- enhancing system flexibility in expanding the network with different transmission medium (e.g., copper, fiber-optic, radio waves etc.).

We now discuss the above key points in more detail.

Providing connectivity for multiple and diverse applications has always been among the philosophical basis of the Internet and IP networks in general. An IP network is multi-purpose in its nature (Clark, 1988). Thus, on the one hand it is possible to use existing off-the-shelf technology for the needs of our service, even though they are rather specialized, i.e., instantiating the transport flows to convey video streams. On the other hand, existing network structures deployed for data or Internet-related applications can come in handy when video flows generating from security cameras need to be transmitted across a building or even across an entire city. Moreover, thanks to the presence of large Wide Area Networks (WANs) and/or the Internet, remote monitoring of cameras hundreds of miles away is allowed without requiring any dedicated infrastructure. Finally, using IP flows is preferable from the point of view of data retrieval and storage.

From an architectural perspective, the migration of a video security system toward IP networks means that intelligence and capabilities move from the control room towards the cameras (Norris *et al.*, 2004). Compared to a traditional analog CCTV camera, an IP camera is a more complex embedded computing system, where the optical, video, encoding, and transmission components are integrated. Modern IP cameras very often include also a Web-server which allows the user to display the video stream simply through a Web-browser. Moreover, many IP cameras nowadays implement advanced artificial intelligent algorithms that make them control how and when to stream the video (Bramberger *et al.*, 2006).

Since we can regard an IP network as a distributed infrastructure that can be accessed at any point, viewing and recording can be also performed in a distributed manner. Specifically, we can have multiple viewing stations in different physical locations, each of those with different information access privileges. Additionally, each camera can locally record the video stream, both to save bandwidth and to increase the reliability and the resiliency of the overall security system.

Finally, migrating to IP networks allows for selecting the most appropriate transmission technology for every video stream and transparently switching transmission media along the path that the video stream takes to reach the control room. In this way, the IP protocol becomes also the common denominator along the path of every video streams (Saltzer *et al.*, 1984).

However, it must be observed that the usage of an all-IP structure, distributing the processing capability all over the network, can also lead to increased costs and vulnerability of the networks. For what concerns the cost increase, this is still clearly compensated by the advanced features. Given the increasing concerns about physical security, it is reasonable to assume that this additional expenditure is tolerated as long as it goes with an improved service. Still, concerns may occur about the increased safety protection required by more expensive all-IP terminals against physical damage or vandalism. From the point of view of network security and vulnerability, the challenges are different and, at the same time, more intriguing as they mainly involve the network management itself.

This point is even stronger for wireless networks, which pose additional issues to the developers, as will be discussed, together with some design guidelines, in the next subsection.

D. Migration and Extension to Wireless Networks for Video Surveillance Systems

The concept of utilizing flexible wireless interconnections in a dynamic fashion is not itself new. Already in the early Nineties, ad hoc networking became popular thanks to the diffusion of notebook computers, open-source software, and viable communication equipments based on radio frequency (RF) and infrared (Ramanathan & Redi, 2002). The concept of ad hoc network, already established for military application, moved to commercial civilian scenarios. Within 10 years, Wireless Fidelity (Wi-Fi) networks started to spread, creating a revolution in Internet service provisioning. With the increasing popularity and rising demand for more Wi-Fi connectivity, implementation problems arose. In fact, Wi-Fi typically requires extensive wired infrastructure to access the backhaul network, which is often expensive to provide and easy to damage, thus violating the security of the information delivery. To this end, the wireless mesh network (WMN) paradigm recently appeared as a valid alternative to wired connection, offering an easy and economical means to provide broadband wireless connectivity (Nandiraju *et al.*, 2007). In place of an underlying wired backbone, a WMN forms a wireless backhaul network, thus obviating the need for extensive cabling. However, WMNs are based on multihop communication to form a connected network. It is well known that multihop links are often limited in throughput and capacity in practical scenarios. For this reason we will employ the following guidelines in creating a WMN to use in video surveillance applications.

First of all, we focus on tree based solutions, because the video flow must be sent to a single data gateway, corresponding to the control room terminal. This means that we can exploit existing solutions for data collection and routing available for ad hoc and sensor networks (Al-Karaki & Kamal, 2004). However, differently from sensor networks which are commonly assumed to comprise hundreds of nodes, our video surveillance wireless network is much smaller, thus simplifying the management. Moreover, we also know the network topology in advance, which enables significant simplifications in the management of wireless communication modes. In fact, we can think of distributing a centralized management policy so as to avoid inefficiencies related to distributed and/or random access. Another guideline we will use is to limit as much as possible multihop relaying. As a rule of thumb, WMN do not work well in practice if they have to relay the traffic for more than three hops (Liese *et al.*, 2006). This limitation is relevant for our case study, since it is also reflected in bandwidth limitations.

A well known hurdle that wireless networks have to face, which very often is the ultimate limiting factor of their capacity, is the wireless interference phenomenon (Jain *et al.*, 2005). In particular, as the wireless medium is inherently broadcast, signals propagate in every direction and are virtually audible by every other terminal in the network. Apart from being a security concern, which will be discussed in the following, this also represents an inefficiency element from the propagation point of view. However, since video surveillance systems mostly consist of static terminals, we can think of using directional antennas. This, beyond decreasing interference, also improves link reliability (Ko *et al.*, 2000). However, as will be shown in the following, also radio bridges realized with directional antennas may become unreliable, especially in the presence of physical obstacles. Actually, the existence itself of the video surveillance system is justified by the desire of properly monitoring the presence of moving exogenous objects. To properly react to this case and more in general to guarantee improved reliability, we will make use of terminals with multiple antennas (usually two) so as to exploit the antenna diversity principle. In other words, we have an extremely low probability that *both* antennas fail at the same time.

For all these reasons, our scenario includes both classic wireless network characteristics but also original aspects. For what concerns network and medium access issues, it can be regarded as a standard WMN, with all the implied advantages in terms of ease of deployment and low costs. However, all the special elements described above allow solving, with limited cost increase, well known problems of wireless networks and designing a reliable system.

TECHNICAL AND RESEARCH CHALLENGES

Despite the aforementioned key advantages, the TCP/IP technology and the related IP-based networks were not intended to support the stringent requirements in terms of bandwidth and system reliability which are required by a security system. Therefore, important points must be taken into account and several issues, often in contrast with each other, arise when employing this technology in the field video surveillance:

- great amount of network bandwidth (already high even for few cameras);
- high processing capability required to encode, decode and record multiple video streams;
- network security protocols, algorithms and policies for guaranteeing the privacy and authenticity of the video streams;
- encoding algorithms designed for live streaming which offer bandwidth efficiency, low processing power requirements and whose output can be used as evidence in legal trials;

- mechanisms to detect and react to Denial of Service (DoS) attacks and guarantee service even in faulty situations.

Due to the numbers of streams involved, video-streaming and, in particular, video surveillance is among the most critical application in terms of bandwidth requirements. Every video camera usually requires between 1 and 10 Mb/s for a high quality stream with a frame rate of 25 frames per second and an image resolution of 640×480 pixels (Koutsakis *et al.*, 2005). Common enterprise and municipal networks are not designed to support tens or even hundreds of streams because the majority of currently installed Local Area Networks (LANs) only provides a maximum (theoretical) bandwidth of 10/100 Mb/s. Note that a mid-size shopping mall might easily need between 100 and 300 cameras. While for data transmission purposes a common 100 Mb/s LAN is adequate for most shopping malls, to stream high resolution video flows a 1 Gb/s network is barely sufficient and a 10 Gb/s infrastructure is clearly advisable.

There are three major approaches and techniques to cope with the bandwidth requirements of video security applications. First, *over-provisioning* of network resources can be introduced at the network design stage. Deploying high bandwidth networks by means of 1 Gb/s Ethernet standard should be a common solution for LANs. Backbones at 10 Gb/s will be necessary to guarantee a good interconnection among the LAN segments. Second, video *compression ratio* can be increased by using more efficient video compression algorithms. However, in general, the higher the compression ratio, the slower the algorithm to decode the video and, thus, the higher the computational power needed. Finally, implementing smart and efficient context-aware video *adaptation algorithms* (Ziliani, 2005) in the camera which dynamically switch from the idle to video transmission state when situations of interest are detected and vice versa.

Quite interestingly, in many video security systems, the real bottleneck is not bandwidth but the processing complexity. Although the migration to differential video encoding algorithms (e.g., MPEG-4) has greatly decreased the bandwidth required per video stream, the more complex compression schemes have dramatically increased the processing requirements and, therefore, the costs of hardware capable of simultaneously decoding multiple high resolution video streams.

As video surveillance is mostly used in crime prevention, network security, privacy and detection of faulty situations are extremely important topics (Welsh & Farrington, 2002). Furthermore, guaranteeing the video surveillance service to be always available is much more important than for other types of services. Specifically, the video surveillance infrastructure must be robust against DoS attacks and promptly report any problem (attack or fault) to the control room, along with as detailed as possible information about the location where the issue arose. Susceptibility to DoS is an intrinsic problem of any service provisioning system where events must be processed to determine their validity. As with prank telephone calls or ringing of door bells of old times, an effective means of preventing DoS attacks from occurring lies in identification of the attacker. This is also the only fundamental solution, given the intrinsic susceptibility of such service provisioning systems to DoS. If the physical source of DoS traffic can be identified, then at the very least the invaded network element can be isolated or shut down and, in some instances, the attacker's identity can be further traced back. In our video surveillance system, it may be thought of dealing with DoS by means of both proactive and reactive countermeasures. In particular, route-based packet filtering solutions (Park & Lee, 2001) may be used to this end. Indeed, observe that our WMN insulated from the external networks, the only gateway being the control room, which is assumed to be reliable enough. Thus, intrusion from external network can be easily identified and filtered at the control room terminals. Malicious data sent to the camera through the wireless links can instead be counteracted by means of the surveillance system itself. In fact, as discussed previously, directional grid antennas are used in the WMN, which are not easy to jam or maliciously disturb unless an external device is put within line of sight of transmitters and receivers. However, this would be likely detected by the surveillance system itself, thus enabling the detection of the intrusion and possibly also identifying the intruder.

VIDEO ENCODING AND COMPRESSION

The most common types of video encoding employed in video surveillance systems are M-JPEG and MPEG-4 (Halshall, 2001). M-JPEG codifies each frame as a JPEG picture, without exploiting any interframe prediction. In this manner, the resulting video stream consists of independent frames. The advantages of this approach are related to the low processing power required in compressing and decompressing the video streams. Moreover, M-JPEG is often chosen when trial evidence is the objective of the recording: M-JPEG can be divided up into separate frames that can be analyzed independently of the previous and subsequent frames. Also, since JPEG frames are themselves compressed, M-JPEG format can also be adjusted to save bandwidth.

However, with M-JPEG there is no exploitation of the inherent correlation between different frames. For this reason, differential encoding algorithms, in particular the one belonging to a MPEG format, are increasingly replacing M-JPEG due to their higher bandwidth efficiency, as they take advantage of the static nature of the scene shot during the routine cameras operations. Note also that efficient transcoding techniques are available to translate MPEG flows into M-JPEG in an efficient manner; in this way also MPEG flows can fulfill the requirement of deriving static pictures from the video flow, to be used as trial evidence.

In the following, we will focus in detail on the most recent one, MPEG-4, since to-date the majority of CCTV systems runs MPEG-4 or similar differential encoding algorithms. MPEG-4 (Fitzek & Reisslein, 2001) extends the applicability of the initial standard MPEG-1 and the more recent format MPEG-2, which is specifically targeted at high-definition television (HDTV) applications. In particular, MPEG-4 provides support for both very low bit rate encoding and for 3D content and complex video/audio objects. In this way, MPEG-4 can be said to extend the provisioning of efficient coding for video flows covering the whole range from very low bit rates up to HDTV and beyond.

Analogously to MPEG-1 and MPEG-2, MPEG-4 decomposes the video flow exploiting its redundancy by means of prediction mechanisms. However, differently from MPEG-1 and MPEG-2, the unit of representation is not called a *frame*, but rather a *video object* (VO). In the simplest case, for low bit rates, the whole scene may be a single VO. Each VO is layered into video object layers (VOLs), for example it is possible to have one base layer and several enhancement layers. VOLs are ordered sequences of snapshots in time, referred to as video object planes (VOPs). For each VOP the encoder processes the shape, motion, and texture characteristics.

The shape information is encoded by bounding the VO with a rectangular box and then dividing the bounding box into macro-blocks (MBs). Each MB is classified differently according to its position and then shape coded. The texture coding is similar to frame-based standards such as MPEG-1 or H.263, using VOPs as frames, which are classified as intracoded (I), forward predicted (P) or bidirectionally predicted (B). In an I VOP the absolute texture values in each MB are coded using Discrete Cosine Transform (DCT), whose coefficients are quantized and coded with variable length. In P VOPs each MB is predicted from the

closest match in the preceding I (or P) VOP using motion vectors. In B VOPs each MB is predicted both from the previous and the subsequent I (or P) VOPs. The prediction errors are transformed with DCT, and the coefficients are quantized, and coded with variable length. The I, P, and B VOPs are finally arranged in a periodic pattern referred to as a group of pictures (GoP). A typical GoP structure is IBBPBBPBBPBB. However, the standard leaves open the possibility of using different sequences. Note also that using a GoP structure entirely consisting of I VOP will make the MPEG-4 become a mere variant of the aforementioned M-JPEG technique. More in general, as the standard includes the possibility of regulating the GoP structure, we can fine-tune the system by trading the transmission efficiency, which increases if the exploitation of predictive VOP is pushed further, with the accuracy of VOPs taken individually, which is highest when no predictive VOP are used at all.

Additionally, MPEG-4 provides a number of error resilience and error concealment features to counteract the frequent transmission errors typical in wireless communication; the interested reader is referred to the textbook by Halshall (2001) for further details.

TRAFFIC ENGINEERING AND CENTRALIZED NETWORK DESIGN

Video traffic in a video surveillance network has a very different characterization with respect to the typical data traffic running on a common TCP/IP network. First of all, traffic in a CCTV system tends to maintain a quasi-constant rate rather than showing a bursty characterization as that of the Internet (Molina *et al.*, 2000). In fact, every video encoder streams flows towards the control room 24 hours a day, 7 days a week. The rate of each video stream is constant with the M-JPEG encoding whereas it is variable for MPEG-4. However, even though the latter usually exhibits a highly

Figure 1. IP video surveillance network topology

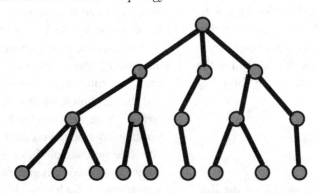

Figure 2. IP network topology with network devices representation

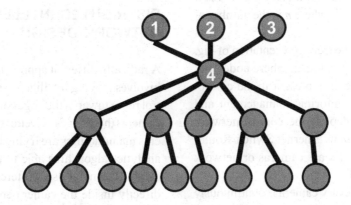

variable bit-rate with an average and maximum peak rate in common video application, the static nature of the acquired video images of a CCTV system makes the MPEG-4 video rate quasi-constant over time. Note that this consideration is also exploited for developing Object Detection Algorithms (ODA) which are able to recognize motion activity within video frames (Nascimento & Marques, 2006).

While a statistical approach based on the average and peak rate is appropriate to design a network for data and Internet applications, in video surveillance applications, network and resource provisioning should consider the requirements

of constant rate flows. Additionally, video frame loss and network congestion are definitely not acceptable for a security system. Therefore, the network must be designed assuming the worst-case scenario in terms of bandwidth requirement of every video stream.

The typical network topology of a video surveillance system is reported in Fig. 1 which represents a tree-shaped graph where edges are communication links and vertices can be considered as Ethernet switches or IP routers.

The root of the topology tree represents the control room where all the video-traffic flows converge. The video streams coming from the leaves of the tree can reach the control room if, at the network design stage, the following condition is enforced. Each sub-tree is connected to its parent node through a link whose capacity is *sufficient* to cover the bandwidth demand of the entire sub-tree. In other words, the following equation must hold:

$$B_{cr}^k = \sum_{i \in C_k} b_{i,\max} \tag{1}$$

where B_{cr}^k is the capacity available at the link connecting the sub-tree C_k to its parent node and $b_{i,\max}$ is the maximum rate required by every video stream present in the sub-tree C_k. Therefore, the overall capacity required in the control room LAN will be $B_{cr} = \sum_{k=1}^{n} B_{cr}^k$ where n is the number of root sub-trees.

More precisely, the tree representation of Fig. 1 can be modified as in Fig. 2, where nodes 1, 2 and 3 depict the devices present in the control room, i.e., video monitoring, management and recording, node 4 depicts the control network and/or the control room Ethernet Switch/Router and all the other nodes are cameras or network devices on the field.

We assume that every camera is continuously transmitting a video stream at constant rate. Video streams are usually sent as multicast UDP traffic in order to reduce the bandwidth demand when multiple video surveillance devices (viewing, recording, etc.) need to receive the same stream. However, in CCTV systems, each camera can generate more than one video stream at the same time because often the user wants to view the live streaming at a higher resolution and frame rate compared to the recording stream so as to save hard disk space. In this case we must consider the rate of each video stream to compute the total bandwidth requirements.

Advanced video surveillance cameras and recording software implement features that allow for dynamic changes in the bandwidth and/or frame-rate and resolution of each video stream. For example, when clicking or zooming on a particular video stream, the camera will automatically increase its frame rate and resolution. In other cases, the camera itself increases the frame rate and the resolution when motion in a particular area of interest is detected by performing automatic video-analysis on the video stream in real time (see for example Pelco Endura cameras, at http://www.pelco.com/endura). These advanced features make the bandwidth provisioning more complex and should be considered when designing any video surveillance system.

DISTRIBUTED INTELLIGENCE NETWORK DESIGN

A radically different approach to network design involves moving intelligence away from the control room towards the edges of the network, to the cameras themselves. Several researchers and cameras manufactures are trying to implement video analytics algorithms able to determine whether or not the image is of interest for the operator directly inside the camera encoding chip (Wolf *et al.*, 2002). With this approach, video streams are sent towards the control room only in case an alarm is generated by the camera. The most common version of this distributed architecture involves video motion detection algorithms that are able to determine if there is any movement in the scene shot by the camera. Moreover, advanced techniques perform a detailed analysis of the video stream, searching for special unusual video patterns. For example, by setting borders and virtual fences to delimit the interest scene, an alarm can be generated as soon as any object crosses these virtual borders. Different algorithms are able to determine movement of specific objects, for example if bags are left unattended, or paintings are

Figure 3. Seaport map and cameras installation points. ©2008 Fluidmesh Networks, Inc. Used with Permission.

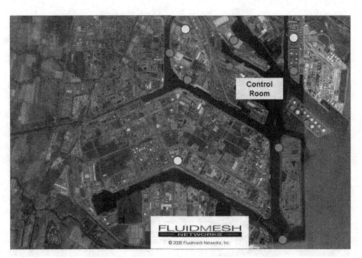

removed, generating appropriate alarms. Bringing this on-alarm only approach to the extreme, the network becomes idle most of the time and video streams are sent only in case of alarm. This approach, although extremely powerful, is usually not implemented in real life projects, mainly because video analytic algorithms are still at their infancy phase and not totally reliable.

Another distributed intelligence approach is to move video recording functionalities to the edges of the network through integration with the cameras. In this case, the operator decides which video streams are sent to the control room for live viewing. The network is never completely idle but it is designed to transmit only a subset of the entire video streams available. The major drawback of the distributed recording approach derives from the technical challenges and the costs for installing devices with high recording capacity, like hard drives, in outdoor environments, where the physical conditions and maintenance can be difficult and expensive.

REAL-LIFE CASE STUDY: VIDEO SURVEILLANCE IN A LARGE INDUSTRIAL SEAPORT

We now describe the technical challenges and design decisions made to implement a large-scale video surveillance systems for a large industrial seaport in Europe.[1] The seaport manages about 300.000 containers and more than 1.000.000 passengers per year. The purpose of the video surveillance system is mainly to comply with the international regulations regarding counter-terrorism measure that every port with international traffic must follow. The set of these regulations is often referred to as International Ship and Port Facility Security Code (ISPS).[2]

A map of the seaport is reported in Fig. 3. The seaport required a set of motorized PTZ cameras to monitor the entrances, the main canals and the premises in general. The port facility was initially equipped with a fiber optic infrastructure (the blue line in Fig. 3) connecting several buildings to a central location. However, the fiber asset was not widespread and extensive enough to be used directly to cover all the locations which are

Figure 4. Seaport video surveillance system. ©2008 Fluidmesh Networks, Inc. Used with permission.

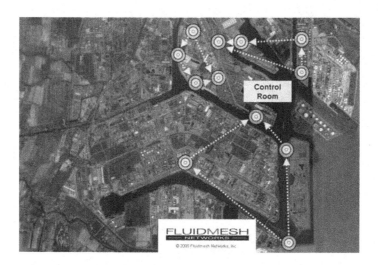

Figure 5. Temporary link unavailability. ©2008 Fluidmesh Networks, Inc. Used with permission.

represented by the red and yellow points in Fig. 3. Moreover, many cameras had to be installed on docks and on buoys at the entrance of the port. Therefore, the existing fiber-based network is extended with a wireless mesh, by means of three parallel mesh networks operating at 2.4 GHz and 5 GHz as shown in Fig. 4. The wireless mesh network employs wireless mesh routers, namely *Fluidmesh 2200*, produced by Fluidmesh Network, Inc., which mount 2 independent radios on board. Due to the distances involved between the mesh routers, directional grid antennas were installed. The use of multi-radio wireless mesh routers is not specifically used here with the goal of increasing capacity. In fact it has been shown, e.g., by Munawar & Ward (2005) that the mere use of dual-interface nodes does not necessarily increase the capacity of the WMN. Actually, dual interfaces can sometimes even lower the throughput due to higher number of transmitters and subsequent increase of interference. However, for our specific application scenario where losses should be kept at a minimum, and in this sense the use of multi-radio wireless mesh routers offers an advantage with respect to traditional point-to-point wireless bridges, which comes from the *redundancy* of wireless links. Specifically, this solution solves the problem of weak links, as it guarantees that the video stream is not interrupted in case of wireless link failure due to wireless interference or link quality degradation since multiple paths towards the control room are provided. Temporary link unavailability or quality degradation are actually rather frequent in this installation as ships can suddenly cut off the clear line of sight of a link when moving along the canals as documented by Fig. 5. A dedicated path selection algorithm automatically selects the best path based on the actual quality of the links. Importantly, this solution implements a homogenous video surveillance system by means of heterogeneous network technologies, i.e., fiber optics and wireless mesh networks.

With respect to video capturing and video encoding, the solution involved 7 PTZ and 6 fixed cameras with analog output, encoded through MPEG-4 video encoders. Every PTZ camera can be controlled from the control room and it is able to pan tilt and zoom through a telemetry serial input. The telemetry information is carried out by TCP segments. Every video encoder sends one single stream of video packets in multicast mode. Both the live viewing and the recording are performed with the same video stream. The bandwidth requirement per video stream is between 1 Mb/s and 1.5 Mb/s depending on the action in the scene shot and the noise in the image.

A major challenge in any seaport environment is the harsh atmosphere that can damage the electronics of cameras and transceivers, decreasing the Mean Time To Failure (MTTF) of every device by increasing the wear in particular of moving parts. Therefore, the cameras deployed in this specific project are pressurized cameras manufactured by Pelco. Every cameras, both PTZ and fixed, has an IP67-rated enclosure pressurized using nitrogen in order to avoid, at the same time, any leakage of the seaport aggressive atmosphere and the formation of humidity within the enclosure. In a cameras system, humidity can be very dangerous because the formation of fog within the enclosure can dramatically impair the field of view of the camera. All the external components of the enclosure are manufactured with iron specifically treated for marine use. The pressurized enclosure is extremely important in case of motorized PTZ cameras that present multiple electric servos to change the orientation of the cameras because moving parts are particularly subject to wear that can be accelerated by the direct contact with aggressive atmosphere.

Fluidmesh wireless devices are protected by polycarbonate enclosure IP68 rated. The IP68-rate polycarbonate enclosure, beyond protecting the electronics by any water or humidity leakage, offers also a very good level of protection from vandalism: it is elastic and robust enough to withstand direct attacks like hits with hammers or stones. The IP68 rating guarantees no water leakage not only in case of water splash but also in case of prolonged submersion under water up to a depth of 1 m.

The control room mainly consists of an integrated server that acts, at the same time, as video-management and video-recording unit. A separate workstation is connected to the server and works as a video-monitoring device. Due to the fairly limited number of video-streams involved in this implementation, the video-monitoring unit is able to decompress simultaneously all the 13 video-streams displaying them in real

time on multiple monitors in the control room. The operator in the control room is able to move the PTZ cameras focus through a joystick and to retrieve the recordings on the server.

Since each camera is expected to stream video at a rate between 1 Mb/s and 1.5 Mb/s, each stream is conservatively assigned with 2 Mb/s. Each red point in Fig. 3 represents one PTZ camera while each yellow point represents two fixed cameras installed on the same pole.

The yellow circles of Fig. 4 represents a Fluidmesh 2200 dual-radio wireless mesh router with two directional antennas connected. In order to reduce interference, the two radio chips of every mesh router operate on two different frequency bands, i.e., at 2.4 GHz and 5 GHz. Fig. 6 shows a sea beacon where the Fluidmesh 2200 with two grid antennas and a PTZ camera are visible. Each link in the deployment is set to a different 20 MHz wide channel and is thus independent of the other links. From a network design standpoint, we assumed that each link modulates at a *fixed* and *conservative* data rate of 18 Mb/s. Based on

that, we designed the system so that the maximum offered load injected in each wireless link does not exceed 14-15 Mb/s. Additionally, due to the unreliable and unpredictable nature of the wireless links, we exploit a heuristic to determine the maximum number of cameras N_{max} in the wireless mesh network. The objective of the heuristic is to avoid congestion in the network while, at the same time, minimizing the number of mesh nodes (gateways) connected to the fiber backbone:

$$N_{\max} = \gamma \, \min_{\ell}(C_{\ell}) / R_{\max} \qquad (2)$$

C_{ℓ} is the available capacity (in Mb/s) of a link in the wireless mesh, $R_{\max}$ is the maximum rate required by a camera and γ is a tunable parameter within the range [0.5, 1]. The latter is used to adjust the number of cameras depending on the expected wireless links conditions. For example, setting γ to 0.75 can be found to be a good compromise between performance and cost.

The heuristic is based on the assumption that a percentage of packets will be retransmitted multiple times because either the packet itself or the packet acknowledgment is lost due to channel errors. According to the above heuristic, the maximum number of cameras per wireless mesh results equal to 5.25. Therefore, to deliver to the control room the total of 13 cameras, we used three parallel mesh networks with independent gateways. In order to verify the capacity required in the fiber backbone, each mesh loop can be considered as a sub-tree whose maximum traffic load is computed according to equation . In this specific case, each sub-tree has a maximum traffic load towards the fiber backbone of about 10 Mb/s and therefore the total capacity required in the fiber backbone would be 30 Mb/s which is definitely reasonable for a fiber network. The video surveillance system has been installed at the beginning of 2006 and it has been continuously operated and extensively used. Despite the harsh and hostile environmental conditions due to the continuous exposure to salt water, no maintenance interventions was necessary thanks to the water-proof polycarbonate enclosure of the Fluidmesh wireless mesh routers and the pressurized cameras. From 2006, more than 300 Terabytes of video data have been streamed to the control room for recording. The large commercial activity of the sea-port, both in terms of goods and passengers, took remarkable advantage from the video surveillance system installation. The seaport security administrators soon decided to employ the latter in conjunction with the standard detection systems to identify anomalous conditions or dangerous situations beyond simple monitoring. In fact, despite the variable and unreliable nature of the wireless links, the network resulted highly reliable with a 99.8% average operational time per year. Three main factors guarantee this high reliability as can be drawn by the above overall discussion. First, the redundancy provided by the multiple wireless paths available from any camera to the control room is efficiently exploited by the optimized Fluidmesh routing algorithm. Second, our simple methodology for the network bandwidth

provisioning is effective in coping with the video traffic demand which can vary over time. Finally, the careful selection of material and electronic devices which are specifically suited for harsh outdoor environments contribute to absolutely increase the MTTF of the entire system.

CONCLUSION

The rising security concerns will accelerate the demand for continuous video-monitoring and the number of cameras installed in urban areas, private building, airport, seaports and industrial facilities will keep growing. On the one hand, as the number of cameras increases, the technical challenges in managing this enormous amount of information will keep researchers and practitioners busy in developing viable solutions to sustain this growth. Different solutions have been pushed forward affecting the most various system components. However, these solutions are often in contrast with each other. For example, innovative compression algorithms will decrease the bandwidth required per video stream but, at the same time, will likely increase the processing power required for compressing and decompressing the video. On the other hand, users will keep asking for higher resolution in order to obtain more and more detailed video frames. Beyond network bandwidth and processing power, other important design constraints and research topic involve video analytics and automatic video analysis which aim at decreasing the labor component in video monitoring. Due to the continuous demand for more video streams and higher resolution, large scale video surveillance will probably be among the applications that will drive most of the demand for more processing capabilities and bandwidth pushing the Moore's law limits in the coming decade. In this chapter, all these aspects are analyzed in detail, especially focusing on video surveillance over TCP/IP. In this context, a complete review of the major IP-based technologies is carried out. Additionally, we presented a simple methodology to design and dimension an IP-based video surveillance system. Based on a video traffic characterization, we developed a set of "rules of thumb" to verify whether the video surveillance system will be able to support the overall bandwidth demand. Finally, we described, as a case study, a video surveillance installation in a seaport in Europe which combines a preexisting fiber-optic asset with the wireless mesh networks technology. The above methodology is extended and applied to dimension the network in presence of wireless links.

REFERENCES

Al-Karaki, J. N., & Kamal, A. E. (2004). Routing techniques in wireless sensor networks: A survey. *IEEE Wireless Communications, 11*(6), 6-28.

Bramberger, M., Doblander, A., Maier, A., Rinner, B., & Schwabach, H. (2006). Distributed embedded smart cameras for surveillance applications. *IEEE Computer, 39*(2), 68–75.

Cai, X., Ali, F. H., & Stipidis, E. (2003). MPEG-4 over local area mobile surveillance system. In *Proceedings of the IEE Symposium on Intelligence Distributed Surveillance Systems, 15*(3), 1-15.

Cisco (2006). *Cisco Systems IP Network-Centric Video Surveillance*. White paper.

Clark, D. D. (1988). The design philosophy of the DARPA internet protocols. *ACM SIGCOMM Computer Communication Review, 18*(4), 106-114.

Fitzek, F. H. P., & Reisslein, M. (2001) MPEG-4 and H.263 video traces for network performance evaluation. *IEEE Network, 15*(6), 40-54.

Freeman, J. P. (2001). 2001 report on the closed circuit TV & video surveillance market. In A. Laurin, *Impressive CCTV growth but analog technology lags behind, Axis Company Leaflet.*

Available at: http://www.axis.com/documentation/whitepaper/video/2460_article.pdf

Gemmell, D.J., Vin, H. M., Kandlur, D. D., Venkat Rangan, P., & Rowe, L. A. (1995). Multimedia storage servers: a tutorial. *IEEE Computer, 28*(5), 40-49.

Halsall, F. (2001). Multimedia Communications: Applications, Networks, Protocols, and Standards. Reading, MA: Addison-Wesley.

Hamilton, S., & Lodder, R. (2002). Hyperspectral imaging technology for pharmaceutical analysis. In *Proceedings of the Society of Photo-Optical Instrumentation Engineers Conference, 4626,* 136-147.

In-Stat (2006). *In-Sights: Video Surveillance Systems on the Move to IP.* Industry Report.

Jain, K., Padhye, J., Padmanabhan, V. N., & Qiu, L. (2005). Impact of Interference on Multi-Hop Wireless Network Performance. *Springer Wireless Networks, 11*(4), 471-487.

Ko, Y., Shankarkumar, V., & Vaidya, N. H. (2000). Medium access control protocols using directional antennas in adhoc networks. In *Proceedings of the Annual Joint Conference of the IEEE Computer and Communications Societies (INFOCOM), 1,* 13-21.

Koutsakis, P., Psychis, S., & Paterakis, M. (2005). Integrated wireless access for videoconference from MPEG-4 and H.263 video coders with voice, E-mail, and Web traffic. *IEEE Transactions on Vehicular Technology, 54*(5), 1863-1874.

Liese, S., Wu, D., & Mohapatra, P. (2006). Experimental characterization of an 802.11b wireless mesh network. In *Proceedings of the 2006 ACM international conference on Wireless communications and mobile computing (IWCMC),* 587-592.

Molina, M., Castelli, P., & Foddis, G. (2000). Web traffic modeling exploiting TCP connections' temporal clustering through HTML-REDUCE. *IEEE Network, 14* (3), 46-55.

Munawar, M. A., & Ward, P. A. S. (2005). Are two interfaces better than one? In *Proceedings of the IEEE International Conference on Wireless And Mobile Computing, Networking And Communications (WiMob), 2*, 119-125.

Nandiraju, N., Nandiraju, D., Santhanam, L., He, B., Wang, J., & Agrawal, D. P. (2007). Wireless Mesh Networks: Current Challenges and Future Directions of Web-In-The-Sky. *IEEE Wireless Communications, 14*(4), 79-89.

Nascimento, J. C., & Marques, J. S. (2006). Performance Evaluation of Object Detection Algorithms for Video Surveillance. *IEEE Transactions on Multimedia, 8*(4), 761-774.

Norris, C., McCahill, M., & Wood, D. (2004). The Growth of CCTV: a global perspective on the international diffusion of video surveillance in publicly accessible space. Surveillance & Society. *CCTV Special. 2*(2/3), 376-395.

Park, K., & Lee, H. (2001). On the effectiveness of route-based packet filtering for distributed DoS attack prevention in power-law internets. *ACM SIGCOMM Computer Communication Review, 31*(4), 15-26.

Ramanathan, R., & Redi, J. (2002). A brief overview of ad hoc networks: challenges and directions. *IEEE Communications Magazine, 40*(5), 20-22.

Sedky, M. H., Moniri, M., & Chibelushi, C. C. (2005). Classification of smart video surveillance systems for commercial applications. In *Proceedings of the IEEE Conference on Advanced Video and Signal Based Surveillance (AVSS)*, 638-643.

Smith, C. L., & Robinson, M. (1999). The understanding of security technology and its applications. In *Proceedings of the IEEE International*

Carnahan Conference on Security Technology, 26-37.

Welsh, B., & Farrington, D. (2002). *Crime prevention effects of closed circuit television: A systematic review.* London: Home Office Research, Development and Statistics Directorate.

Wolf, W., Ozer, B., & Lv, T. (2002). Smart cameras as embedded systems. *IEEE Computer, 35*(9), 48–53.

Ziliani, F. (2005). The importance of 'scalability' in video surveillance architectures. In *Proceedings of the IEE International Symposium on Imaging for Crime Detection and Prevention (ICDP)*, 29-32.

KEY TERMS

Design Guidelines: In the chapter we identify several practical rules to use in the development of hardware and software solutions. In particular, we deal with network hierarchy, multi-hop routing and bandwidth dimensioning. Finally, we also envisioned some design choices such as multiple antennas as related to link diversity.

Multi-Hop Wireless Networks: Since the control room can be far from the area where surveillance is performed, remote control may be realized by employing multi-hop networks. This implies that the radio nodes belonging to the WMN need special procedures to work in harmony with each other and enable dedicated communications.

Network Engineering: This term implies the design of hardware and software solutions to implement a network structure, for what concerns both information exchange and physical creation of links. In particular, for video streaming this corresponds to enabling a multi-hop communication whose routes and content are predictable, yet there are several limiting factors (bandwidth, complexity) to take into account.

TCP/IP Networks: This corresponds to the realization of the Internet structure over the network of interest. In particular, TCP/IP implies a layered structure for the network, which is hence able to provide an upper-layer service (in this case, video streaming) by means of lower-layer data exchange, in particular for what concerns network routing taking place on wireless multi-hop links.

Video Streaming: This term refers to a continuous exchange of data, which can be monitored by the receiver while its transmission is ongoing, over a communication network. In particular, video surveillance pictures require an efficient streaming in order to actuate crime prevention and realize the basic functions of deterrence, detection and verification.

Video Surveillance: It corresponds to the use of video cameras to transmit signal to a specific, limited set of monitors. It is often used for monitoring and crime prevention in sensitive areas such as banks, casinos, airports, seaports, military installations and convenience stores. Note that even though wireless links may be employed, they are not intended for a broadcast audience.

Wireless Mesh Network (WMN): It is a communication network, where terminals are connected via radio to routers which are in turn interconnected via multi-hop wireless links. Its structure is entirely wireless, thus making WMNs especially applicable where cable deployment is difficult or too expensive, or the absence of cables is even recommended for security reasons.

ENDNOTES

[1]   All the material in this section is by courtesy of Fluidmesh Network, Inc.

[2]   More details can be found on IMO – International Maritime Organization website. http://www.imo.org.

Chapter VIII
P2PTunes:
A Peer–to–Peer Digital
Rights Management System

Ramya Venkataramu
Hewlett-Packard Company, USA

Mark Stamp
San Jose State University, USA

ABSTRACT

Digital Rights Management (DRM) technology is used to control access to copyrighted digital content. Apple employs a DRM system known as Fairplay in its iTunes online music store. Users communicate with the centralized iTunes server to download, purchase, play, and preview digital content. The iTunes music store has the potential disadvantage of a bandwidth bottleneck at the centralized server. Furthermore, this bandwidth bottleneck problem will escalate with increasing popularity of online music and other digital media, such as video. In this chapter, we analyze the Fairplay DRM system. We then consider a modified architecture that can be employed over existing peer-to-peer (P2P) networks. Our new system, P2PTunes, is designed to provide the benefits of a decentralized P2P network while providing DRM content protection that is at least as strong as that found in Fairplay.

INTRODUCTION

The success of the Apple iPod and associated iTunes music store has made Apple, Inc., a dominant company in both the online media distribution business and the digital media player market (Chandak 2005). The iPod is a portable digital media player which supports the Advanced Audio Coding (AAC), the Moving Pictures Experts Group (MPEG-1) Audio Layer-3 (MP3), Waveform Audio (WAV), and Audible formats (Apple 2006). The iTunes online store allows users to purchase digital media content. A proprietary software application—also known as iTunes—is used to connect to the iTunes online store to download digital content. The iTunes software is used to manage play lists among computers and iPods, and to play digital content on Windows computers, Macintosh computers, and the iPod.

Fairplay is a digital right management (DRM) technology used to protect digital content purchased from the iTunes online store. As with most DRM systems, the purpose of Fairplay is to place restrictions on the uses of copyrighted content.

For DRM, the required level of protection is much different than in most typical security applications. Many security applications simply require that data be securely transmitted from point-to-point, and for such applications, standard techniques from the fields of cryptography and security protocols suffice (Stamp 2006). However, in DRM the situation is much different, since the protection (e.g., usage restrictions) must stay with the content after it has been successfully delivered to the legitimate recipient. This additional level of security required in DRM is often known as persistent protection (Stamp 2006), since some level of protection must persist after successful delivery of the bits.

In the DRM context, the legitimate recipient is a potential attacker and, consequently, achieving any meaningful level of persistent protection is not a trivial task. In fact, it is impossible to ensure persistent protection if the content is accessible on an open platform (such as a modern PC) where the recipient has full administrative privilege. Therefore, we cannot expect a level of security comparable to, say, cryptography from a DRM system such as Fairplay. Instead, the test for such a system is whether a successful business model can be built on top of the inherently weak DRM protection (Stamp 2003). By this criteria, Fairplay is a highly successful DRM system, in spite of the known attacks that we discuss in Section 3.

The iTunes online store and Fairplay DRM employ a centralized server to distribute content and enforce the persistent protection on downloaded media. Any content distribution system based on a centralized server model has the potential disadvantage of a bandwidth bottleneck. Furthermore, as the number of users accessing the online store grows and the size of digital content increases (video requires much more bandwidth than music) additional strain will be placed on the central server (Kalker, et. al., 2004).

We believe that the centralized iTunes online music service may be improved by redesigning it to operate within a peer-to-peer (P2P) network. Such a system would make more effective use of available storage and bandwidth, since a P2P system can harness idle storage and network resources from client machines that voluntarily join the network (Rodrigues, Liskov, and Shrira 2002).

Each node in a P2P network has roughly equivalent capabilities and can initiate or service requests. This is in contrast to a client-server model, such as iTunes, where only the central server may service requests. P2P systems have emerged as a popular way to share vast amounts of data since they offer the benefits of self-organization, load-balancing, fault-tolerance, and the ability to pool and harness large amounts of resources (Daswani, et. al., 2002). Additionally, P2P networks are highly scalable and relatively easy to deploy (Tanin, Nayar, and Samet 2005). However, current P2P networks are rife with copyright violations and other security risks such as viruses, spyware, and other unwanted software (Microsoft 2007). In this paper, we present a DRM system that can be deployed over a P2P network and our proposed system enforces the same or higher level of security as iTunes. Furthermore, our proposed system, which we call P2PTunes, can operate over existing P2P networks.

In this paper, we first focus on critically analyzing iTunes and its Fairplay DRM system. We need to understand the strengths and weaknesses of this system before we can consider ways to develop a practical, efficient, and secure iTunes-like system that can function in a P2P environment.

Then we present the details of our design for a DRM system that has all of the advantages of a P2P system and provides DRM security that is as at least as strong as the highly successful Fairplay system.

This paper is organized as follows. Section 2 provides background on Apple's Fairplay DRM and iTunes. We also present a brief overview of P2P networks. In Section 3, we discuss the proposed design and architecture for our system, P2PTunes. Section 4 briefly covers a prototype implementation of P2PTunes. Section 5 deals with the security features of P2PTunes and we analyze the strengths and weaknesses of our proposed system, relative to iTunes. Finally, Sections 6 and 7 contain conclusions and ideas for future work, respectively.

BACKGROUND

MPEG-4

Fairplay DRM is built on top of QuickTime. The QuickTime file format is a "container" that can handle audio, video, images, text, and other digital formats (Apple 2006). In addition, QuickTime is adaptable—new capabilities can be added and new versions maintain backward compatibility (Apple 2006).

QuickTime is the file format of choice for Moving Pictures Experts Group (MPEG-4) standard. The MPEG-4 standard covers the entire spectrum of digital media tasks, including the capture, authoring, editing, encoding, distributing, playback, archiving, and delivery of professional-quality digital media. Since it is generally based on QuickTime, MPEG-4 inherits QuickTime's stability, extensibility, and scalability (Apple 2006).

Advanced Audio Coding (AAC) is used in the audio layer of MPEG-4 files, since AAC compresses audio data more efficiently than older formats such as MP3 (Apple 2006). Apple uses Fairplay to encrypt the AAC-encoded audio

Figure 1. MPEG-4 file structure (Anonymous 2006)

data inside an MPEG-4 file, resulting in what is known as a protected AAC files. Protected files carry an m4p extension, while unprotected files are of type m4a.

MPEG-4 files are built up of atoms, each of which stores specific information pertaining to the digital content. Every atom has an 8-byte header indicating the atom type, followed by the corresponding data field. The atom type indicates how to process the atom data.

An MPEG-4 file structure is illustrated in Figure 1. In a protected file, the audio in the AAC layer is encrypted using the Advanced Encryption Standard (AES) algorithm, which is a well-known standard (Anonymous 2006).

Various atom types are depicted in Figure 2, where, for clarity, some atoms have been omitted. Atoms generally present in a protected file appear in Table 1 (Anonymous 2006). The main difference between the protected file format discussed above and an unprotected file format is that DRM specific atoms such as drms, user, geID, priv, and name, are absent in unprotected files. As mentioned above, unprotected file carry

Figure 2. Protected AAC file structure (Anonymous 2006)

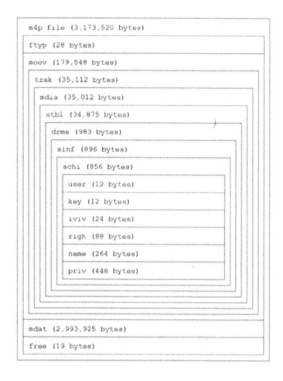

Table 1. Metadata information

Atom Name	Atom Data
moov	metadata atom
mdat	encrypted song
drms	container for user, key ,etc.
user	iTunes user ID
key	iTunes user key number
iviv	AES initialization vector
priv	encrypted AES key
name	iTunes user name
geID	watermark information

watermarking is used to embed information into the purchased file itself.

Some of the persistent protection restrictions that Fairplay attempts to enforce include the following.

- Protected tracks can only be copied to a specified number of authorized computers.
- A protected track may only be burned into a play list a specified number of times.
- Protected tracks may only be burned into an audio CD a specified number of times.
- Purchased digital content cannot be played on any dedicated digital music devices other than the iPod.
- Fairplay limits the usage of its digital content to the Windows and Macintosh operating systems. Downloaded media is not playable on other major operating systems such as Linux.
- Most audio-editing software used for editing or splicing tracks are not interoperable with iTunes content.

Predictably, these restrictions have angered many users who believe that purchased content should be free to use in any legal manner without undue restrictions (Futureproof 2006). Generally, such critics are opposed to any meaningful DRM,

an m4a extension while protected files have an m4p extension.

Atomic Parsley is a lightweight command line tool that can be used to parse the atoms from MPEG-4 files (SourceForge 2006). For our purposes, Atomic Parsley is an invaluable tool for analyzing MPEG-4 files, since it allows us to analyze the differences between protected and unprotected files and to manipulate the metadata atoms in files.

Fairplay

Fairplay DRM, which is built into the QuickTime multimedia technology, is used to protect digital content purchased from the iTunes online music store. Fairplay has several strong security features. Purchased files are encrypted to provide confidentiality and encryption also plays a role in the persistent protection mechanisms. Also, digital so these criticisms should not be considered as specific criticisms of Fairplay.

Next, we describe the Fairplay DRM system in some detail. The discussion here refers specifically to iTunes version 5, but other versions are similar.

Fairplay DRM has three levels of encryption and each level uses a different key. A system key is a symmetric key that is used by the iTunes server to encrypt user keys and is intended to be unique to a particular system. This key is known to the system and the the iTunes server. The system key is generated on a Windows machine as a hash of items from the registry including bios version, processor name, and Windows version (Anonymous 2006). For Macintosh computers, the system key hash has apparently not been reverse engineered (Anonymous 2006).

A user key database on the iTunes server contains user keys that are needed in the decryption process. Apple uses a few different user keys per iTunes music store account (Anonymous 2006). Among other things, this implies that different media purchased by one user might use the same user key for the decryption process.

The AAC audio data is encrypted with the AES algorithm. This encrypted AAC audio data forms the mdat atom. Furthermore, the AES key used to encrypt the mdat atom is, in turn, encrypted with a user key and this encrypted AES key is stored in the priv atom. The user key is itself encrypted with the system key when it is transferred from server to client.

Next, we consider the scheme used in by iTunes when a user purchases and plays content. It is important to understand this process, since we follow a similar procedure in our proposed P2PTunes system.

Purchasing and Downloading a Song

When a user purchases a song from the iTunes online music store, the following steps occur (Anonymous 2006).

1. The user chooses a song from the iTunes online music store and makes a down-load and purchase request to the iTunes server.
2. The iTunes client sends the song download request and the user's system information to the iTunes server.
4. The iTunes server sends a download URL and a download key to the iTunes client.
5. The iTunes client downloads the file from the download URL and decrypts the file using the download key. This decrypted file contains the protected song, which is then stored on the client computer.
6. The client sends a message to the server indicating success of the transaction.

Playing a Purchased Song

The following steps occur when an iTunes client plays a purchased song (Anonymous 2006).

1. The user ID and the user key index are extracted from the protected m4p file on the client, and this information is sent to the iTunes server along with the system information.
2. The iTunes server uses the user ID and the user key index to retrieve the user key from its key database. The server encrypts the user key using a system key generated from the system information and sends this encrypted key to the client.
3. Upon receiving the encrypted user key, the client decrypts it using the system key.
4. The client hashes the name and iviv atoms of the specific m4p file to obtain an initialization value.
5. The key from step 3 and the initialization value from step 4 are used to decrypt the priv atom which yields the AES key—which is the key that was used to encrypt the content.
6. The key from step 5 and the initialization value are used to decrypt the mdat atom,

which yields the audio stream that can then be played.

Watermarking

Apple inserts watermarks in protected files as an indicator of legitimate content. Apple's iTunes software looks for these watermarks to verify the authenticity of the digital content. A tampered file, which does not have a correct watermark is rendered unplayable on iTunes software. However, such content can be played on any AAC compatible hardware or software which does not look for Apple's watermark, provided the content can be decrypted (Wen 2006). Additional watermarks are cached outside the protected file, specifically, in the iTunes library database and on the iPod. These watermarks are designed to make it a harder to reverse-engineering the system (Wen 2006).

Figure 3 illustrates the interaction between the client (user) and server (iTunes).

Reverse Engineering iTunes

Apple's Fairplay DRM technology is a closed source system. Reverse engineering a closed source system is generally a difficult task since considerable effort is required to determine specific functionality. Jon Lech Johansen, who cracked the infamous Content Scrambling Scheme (CSS) encryption (used to protect DVD movies), is credited with reverse engineering Fairplay (Indigo Group 2006, Wen 2006). PlayFair, developed by Johansen, was the first successful anti-DRM tool aimed at Fairplay. Other anti-DRM software that exploits Fairplay include PyMusique, SharpMusique, JHymn, and QTFairUse6 (Indigo Group 2006, iPod News 2006).

Figure 3. iTunes protocol for purchasing and playing a song

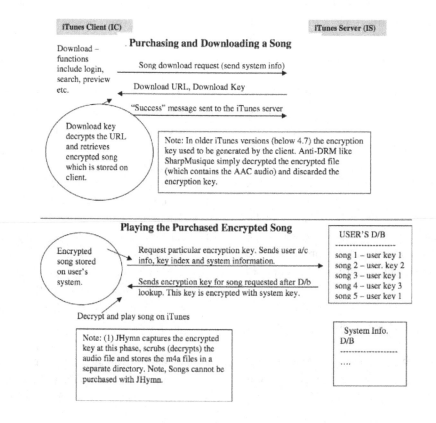

The iTunes client uses HTTP XML messages to communicate with the iTunes music store and these messages are encrypted using AES in Cipher Block Chaining (CBC) mode. This encryption is for confidentiality, that is, to prevent third parties from eavesdropping (Bornstein 2007, Indigo Group 2006). As with any DRM system, the user must be given all of the "pieces of the puzzle" (specifically, cryptographic keys) to play the digital content.

There are at least three possible ways to exploit Fairplay:

- Interface directly with the music store using a phony client similar to iTunes.
- Get the decryption key from the user's system since iTunes must give the user any keys needed to play a song.
- Let iTunes software decrypt the content, then write the content to a file in an unprotected form.

The Hymn (Hear Your Music aNywhere) project, based on Johansen's work, employs a phony client that interfaces with the iTunes online music store (Futureproof 2006, Indigo Group 2006). JHymn, which was authored by someone who uses the alias FutureProof, is a GUI implementation of the original command-line Hymn.

JHymn "scrubs" protected m4p AAC files and produces an unprotected m4a file (Wen 2006). Scrubbing removes Fairplay DRM data from the metadata atoms and leaves unprotected files free of any DRM restrictions. Scrubbed files can be played on any AAC compatible software or hardware and files scrubbed using JHymn are also playable on iTunes since the watermarking information is left intact (Wen 2006).

JHymn can be used on files that have been purchased with any iTunes version prior to iTunes 6.0 (Futureproof 2006). However, if the user performs an activity using iTunes 6.0 or later version, JHymn will not be able to scrub any more files, including files purchased using earlier versions of iTunes (Futureproof 2006).

Version 6 of iTunes remained unbroken until the anti-DRM software QTFairUse6 was released in August 2006. QTFairUse6 captures AAC frames after the song has been decrypted by iTunes, but before the decoding step. The resulting unprotected data is then copied to a file (iPod News 2006). This attack illustrates that no matter how strong the encryption scheme may be, a vulnerability almost certainly remains at the point where the song has been decoded to a format understood by a soundcard. In the case of QTFairUse6, the decoded song is captured by inserting breakpoints in the iTunes client and copying the decrypted song from the computer's memory into a new file.

Introduction to P2P Networks

A P2P network consists of a large number of networked computers or nodes, often connected in an ad-hoc fashion (Daswani, Garcia-Mollia, and Yang 2002, Peer-to-peer 2006). Each peer can function as a server (content provider) or a client (consumer), or both simultaneously (Han, et. al., 2004; Mannak, Ridder, and Keyson, 2004).

P2P systems make file sharing more efficient since the primary costs of sharing data, namely, bandwidth and storage are distributed across the peers of the network. This ensures scalability and eliminates the need for powerful and expensive servers (Daswani, et. al., 2002).

P2P architectures can be classified as either centralized or decentralized (Han, Liu, Xiao, et. al., 2004). Many real-world P2P systems combining features of both centralized and decentralized architectures.

One of the best-known centralized P2P system is Napster (France, Moore, and Dreier 2007) which uses a central server to index the content stored on peers. Kazaa could also be considered a centralized P2P system, although it is more decentralized than Napster, since the function of the centralized server is distributed among a number of peers.

In general, centralized P2P systems rely on centralized servers for specific tasks such as bootstrapping, obtaining keys for data encryption, adding new nodes to the network, and so on. The nodes in centralized systems may be involved in such tasks as locating and caching content, searching for other nodes, routing messages, encryption, decryption, and verifying content (Androutsellis-Theotokis 2004). Centralized P2P systems are vulnerable to denial of service attacks (Han, Liu, Xiao, et. al., 2004) or legal assaults aimed at shutting down the centralized server.

P2P networks that share computer resources without requiring intermediation from a centralized server are known as decentralized systems. Gnutella is an example of a decentralized P2P system. Decentralized P2P systems enjoy high fault-tolerance, good scalability, the ability to self organize (in spite of highly transient node populations), and access to resources (Androutsellis-Theotokis 2004).

There are several technical challenges that inhibit the widespread acceptance of P2P systems for legitimate content distribution. Such challenges include security, performance guarantees (e.g., atomicity and transactional semantics), and unreliable peers (Daswani, et. al., 2002).

Some of the potential security pitfalls of sharing information over a P2P network include the installation of malicious software, attacks based on the ports opened to transmit files, and denial of service attacks. Client nodes can defend themselves against some of these attacks by using antivirus software and enabling firewalls (United States Computer Emergency Readiness Team 2006).

Several techniques can be employed to address certain security issues at the P2P system level. Cryptographic techniques such as integrity checks and information dispersal algorithms or Shamir's secret sharing scheme are sometimes employed to prevent specific types of attacks. For example, nodes may be required to compute cryptographic hashes to verify the integrity of retrieved data, thereby preventing certain types of spoofing attacks (Androutsellis-Theotokis 2004). Information dispersal algorithms or Shamir's secret sharing scheme can be used to distribute files, in which case complete information cannot be obtained by any intermediate nodes in the P2P network.

"Free riding" is another common problem in P2P networks. That is, some nodes refuse to service requests for content that they are capable of providing. Nodes may misrepresent information such as available bandwidth so that they receive fewer requests and thereby save their own resources, to the detriment of the network as a whole (Saroiu, Gummadi, and Gribble 2002). This can result in fewer server nodes and more client nodes and an overall loss of efficiency in the P2P network. Several techniques are available for reducing the effect of free riding in P2P networks.

Goals of this Research

Our goal is to create a reasonably secure DRM scheme for a P2P network. Since security in DRM systems is difficult—if not impossible—to quantify, we have chosen to model our system after one of the most successful and practical DRM schemes yet developed, namely, iTunes. Our system, P2PTunes, can be viewed as a modified form of iTunes that can easily function over any typical P2P network. P2PTunes is designed to provide the following security and performance features.

- The overall level of security is equivalent to Fairplay DRM.
- The file sharing and bandwidth-related advantages of the underlying P2P net-work are not impaired.
- The confidentiality of transactions is assured.

- The integrity of digital content transferred over the underlying P2P network is verified.
- High assurance of authenticity for purchased digital content is provided.

Previous Work

In this section, we briefly review previous attempts to combine DRM and P2P networks. Perhaps the most ambitious such system to date is Music2Share (Kalker, et. al., 2004). Music2Share is a proposed P2P protocol with built-in DRM that manages legitimate music tracks using a variety of advanced technologies, with a heavy reliance on watermarking. However, many of the crucial "technologies" employed in Music2Share rely on successful resolution of difficult unsolved research problem. The authors of Music2 Share admit that the application of many of these technologies "has to be worked out and refined" (Kalker, et. al., 2004).

Our design goal for P2PTunes is, in a sense, diametrically opposed to that of Music2Share. For P2PTunes, we insist that the system can be built using technology that exists today and we want our system to be P2P-agnostic, that is, we want P2PTunes to function seamlessly within any typical P2P system. We have modeled P2PTunes on a highly successful DRM system, which provides some degree of confidence that our system would actually be viable in the real world.

Napster, a centralized P2P file sharing system, was infamous for facilitating illegal music downloads. Napster has morphed into a legal music download service, which uses Windows Media DRM. Downloads are encoded as high-quality 192Kbps Windows Media Audio (WMA) files. Napster allows registered users to stream tracks a certain number of times from its catalog to Windows, Macintosh, and Linux machines. Streamed tracks, which are encoded with a low bit rate, cannot be stored on the user's system. A Napster client is required for song purchases and downloads. Napster's online streaming works well on Windows although there appear to be some performance issues on Macintosh. Napster's client software hangs at times, not al-lowing users to adjust the volume, pause, or skip ahead. Napster does provide an innovative feature that allows users to explore other member's collections by genre; however, this feature is apparently somewhat buggy (Chandak 2005, France, Viksnins, and Kim 2007).

Rhapsody 3.0, which is owned by Real Networks, offers an on-demand streaming service and download access from its music catalog (France 2007). Purchased tracks are 192Kbps AAC files wrapped in Real Network's Helix DRM. Rhapsody allows users to listen to a certain number of tracks for free each month; these tracks are encoded at 128Kbps, which results in lower quality music as compared to purchased tracks. Rhapsody 3.0 works on Windows XP, Me, 2000, or 98SE platforms, but users have reported difficulty logging onto the service, which may be attributed to high server traffic volume (Chandak 2005, France, Viksnins, and Kim 2007). Other examples of P2P-based download services include eMusic, Yahoo Music Unlimited 1.1, Sony, etc. The eMusic scheme is noteworthy since it offers a catalog of songs from independent labels and these songs are provided in the unprotected mp3 format. There is a maximum download limit per month after which songs may be purchased (Chandak 2005, France, Viksnins, and Kim 2007).

DESIGN OF P2PTunes

Our proposed DRM system, P2PTunes, adapts the existing iTunes Fairplay DRM so that is applicable over an existing P2P network. In this section we first discuss the design and architecture of P2PTunes in general terms, then we fill in the details.

A Hybrid Approach

The strength of P2PTunes lies in obtaining the benefits of the underlying P2P system while ensuring the security aspects that are required of a viable DRM system are provided. In addition, the design of P2PTunes ensures that it functions over any typical P2P system.

P2PTunes allows users to purchase encrypted digital media such as audio and video content over the P2P network. Within the P2P network, each peer can function as both a content provider (server) and a consumer (client). Client nodes broadcast queries for specific digital content while server nodes service these requests. A node acts as a server if it has the requested content and is willing to share it. Nodes acting as client nodes in one transaction, could act as server nodes in another transaction.

In P2PTunes transactions, digital content is always transmitted in encrypted form over the P2P network. This prevents intermediate nodes and client nodes from "grabbing" the content before a payment is made. P2PTunes itself is as decentralized as the underlying P2P network, with the exception of certain transactions such as payments, billing, and content authenticity verification. These operations are performed at a centralized server to ensure the legitimacy of P2PTunes transactions. However, these centralized operations are designed so that they put only a small burden on the centralized server. The actual content is distributed entirely within the underlying P2P network.

A secure connection between the client node and centralized server is used for payment processing. In addition, the centralized server validates the authenticity of the purchased digital content. The introduction of the centralized server, in combination with a decentralized P2P network, makes P2PTunes a hybrid model. This hybrid model enables us to achieve an efficient and secure distribution system for sharing legal digital content. The resulting system provides security equivalent to iTunes together with the efficient distribution inherent in the underlying P2P network.

Entities in P2PTunes

The main entities in P2PTunes are the following.

- The originator O is a client node that initiates a request for digital content over the P2PTunes network.
- The responder R is a server node that is able and willing to service the originator's request.
- An intermediary node P is a node that forwards O's request or R's response. Such an intermediate node may or may not be a participant in the underlying P2P network.
- The P2PTunes Server (PTS) is a centralized server that handles financial and authenticity issues. Note that the PTS is a trusted component of P2PTunes.

Architecture of P2PTunes

This section describes the architecture of P2PTunes in some detail. The emphasis is on the interaction between the various entities of P2PTunes and how digital content is securely distributed over the P2PTunes network.

P2PTunes Metadata

Every protected m4p file contains priv and iviv atoms enclosed within the moov atom. The priv and iviv atoms are pivotal to the decryption process. Other atoms such as user, key, and name contain user specific information: the iTunes user ID, the user key index, and the user name, respectively. Figure 4 depicts these security-critical atoms. For a more detailed view of atoms, refer to Figure 2.

In P2PTunes, different digital content may be encrypted with the same AES symmetric key.

The AES key is used to encrypt and decrypt the mdat atom. The AES key is itself encrypted with a user key (which is user-specific so that it differs from user to user) and stored in the priv atom. The user key is, in turn, encrypted with a system key when it is transmitted from the server to the client. The system key is both user and system specific. The P2PTunes Server (PTS) uses system information from the user's system to generate the system key. The PTS stores different user keys per account and employs a user key index (found in the m4p file) to retrieve a user key from its user database. Hence, user-specific atoms play a role in retrieving the user key from the server's database. Note that this use of keys is completely analogous to the approach used in iTunes, as discussed in Section 2.2 above.

Purchasing and Playing a Song

Figure 5 illustrates a network consisting of an originator O, intermediary nodes Pi and responder nodes Rj in a simple P2P network.

The steps involved in purchasing digital content over P2PTunes are the following:

Step 1: Initiate Request — The originator O (client node) initiates a request for specific digital content, say, a song S. The request S along with O's identifier is transmitted over the underlying P2P network. The identifier ties the request to the node O.

Step 2: Respond to Query — A responder R (server node) possesses the requested digital content and is willing to share it. Upon receiving the request for S, node R sends its identifier and song information (which include title, song number, version number, etc.) to O. The identifier ties the response to R. Note that there could be more than one responder to a query.

Step 3: Select Response — Node O receives responses from n responder nodes, say, R1, R2,

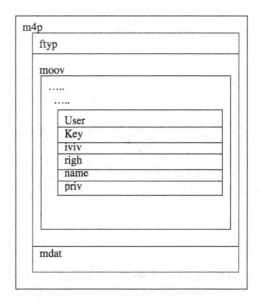

Figure 4. Key atoms in an m4p file

. . . , Rn. Then O chooses one responder, say, Ri. Depending on the underlying P2P network, choosing a responder may be based on factors such as specific digital content information (title, version number, artist, etc.), the speed of the connection between client and server, or the responder node may be known and trusted by the originator.

Step 4: Inform Responder — Node O requests the chosen Ri to deliver the song S by sending a download or "request-confirm" message to Ri.

Step 5: Transmit Encrypted Content — Upon receiving O's message, Ri encrypts its account information and a timestamp with the PTS public key. Note that the PTS employs a secure public key cryptosystem such as RSA to generate a public and private key pair. Node Ri computes the hash of the encrypted song and the encrypted account information. Node Ri strips the user-specific atoms such as those containing the name, user ID, etc., from the m4p file and sends the content byte stream to O. This byte stream contains of the following information.

Figure 5. A sample P2PTunes network

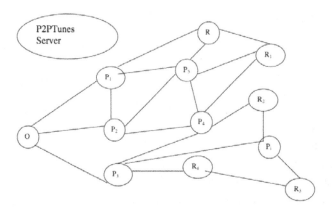

- The encrypted song (excluding the user-specific atoms).
- The node Ri's encrypted account information and timestamp.
- A CRC checksum of the encrypted song and the encrypted account information.

The purpose of encrypting Ri's account information with the current timestamp is to prevent misuse by O. Since this information is encrypted with the PTS public key, O will not be able to decrypt this message. Additionally, the timestamp allows the PTS to ensure that the transaction is current. Intermediate nodes can cache this content and later forward it over the P2P network. This process would allow for more efficient use of network bandwidth.

Step 6: Verify Integrity at O — Node O receives Ri's encrypted message. Node O verifies the integrity of the song by computing the CRC checksum of the encrypted content and verifying it against that received from Ri. Once verified, O has the encrypted song received from Ri. Note that this check is designed to detect errors in transmission. However, this check does not ensure that the received content is actually the content requested by O, since Ri could have substituted an incorrect

file for the requested file (either intentionally or accidentally).

Step 7: Verify Authenticity — It is necessary for O to verify the authenticity of the m4p file it received from Ri. To accomplish this, node O computes a hash of the non-user specific atoms in the received file. User specific atoms that vary from user to user such as priv, user, name, etc., are not present in the byte stream and hence are not part of the hash computation. Note that the atom mdat (which contains the encrypted song) is encrypted with the same AES key for every user, which implies that mdat is not user-specific. Therefore, we can (and do) include mdat in the authenticity hash computation. The computed hash value and the unique song number are sent to the PTS for verification. To verify the authenticity, the PTS simply compares the received hash value with the computed hash value of the content, which it has stored in its database. This enables the PTS to verify whether the hash value received from O matches that of the content. Note that only the hash value is sent to the PTS, not the data itself and no hash computation is required on the PTS server, since the hash has been pre-computed and stored in the PTS database. In this way, the PTS verifies the authenticity of the content with minimal overhead imposed on the PTS or the network. If the song is not authentic, the PTS informs O, and O can try another source.

Step 8: Payment Processing — To be able to play the song, O must be able to decrypt the song. The decryption key is provided to O only after O makes a payment to the PTS. To make a payment, O connects to the PTS though a secure connection, based on the system key. Then O sends the following information to the PTS.

- Node O's account information.
- The song information (including the unique song ID number).
- Node Ri's encrypted user information.

Note that this is essentially the same process used in iTunes, as outlined in Section 2.2.1, except that in P2PTunes, the responder's information is also included.

Step 9: Insert User-Specific Atoms — Upon completion of the payment step, the PTS generates all of O's user specific atoms. Node O sends its system information to the PTS, which uses this information to generate a system key. Node O's user-specific atoms are encrypted with the system key by the PTS. Note that as in iTunes, the system key is stored on the client (i.e., the originator O's system). The PTS sends the required priv atom for the content downloaded in Step 5 to O. In addition, the PTS generates and sends O's user-specific atoms pertaining to information such as the user key index and the name atoms to O. The iTunes software functionality is enhanced so that P2PTunes can add these user-specific atoms received from the PTS to the m4p file downloaded in Step 5. This step is critical since whenever O plays the song, the PTS looks up information from these atoms to retrieve the user key.

Step 10: Play Purchased Content — Each time the node O wants to play a track, it provides the

song ID, user specific information (from the m4p atoms), and its system information to the PTS. The PTS uses the song and account information sent by O as an index into its database and retrieve the appropriate user key. The user key is then encrypted with the system key generated by the PTS and sent to O. The following three levels of decryption are required to access the audio data.

1. Node O uses the system key (stored on the client) to decrypt the encrypted user key received from PTS. The decrypted user key is used to decrypt the priv atom. This retrieves the AES private key.
2. The AES private key obtained in step 2 and the initialization vector (obtained by hashing the name and iviv atoms) are used to decrypt the audio data found in the mdat atom.

Note that this is similar to the way digital content is decrypted and played in iTunes. The architecture described in this section is illustrated in Figure 6.

Advantages of P2PTunes

This section summarizes the advantages of our proposed P2PTunes system. Each of the following is an advantage of P2PTunes, as compared to iTunes.

- In iTunes, digital content purchases are made at a centralized server that services each request by providing the digital content. This consumes a great deal of bandwidth and creates a potential bottleneck. In contrast, in P2PTunes the bandwidth requirement at the central PTS server is minimal since the actual content is shared over the underlying P2P network.
- The P2PTunes design has all of the advantages of a P2P community with active user participation and community networking (Mannak, Ridder, and Keyson 2004).

- In P2PTunes, each m4p files has user-specific metadata tags pertaining to a specific user, which is identical to the iTunes system. Consequently, from a user's perspective, playing purchased content in P2PTunes is identical to iTunes. Note that in both systems, users need permission from the centralized server to play content.

- In general, P2PTunes offers a similar user experience to iTunes. The only significant difference is that in P2PTunes, a user selects the server peer from which to download the content, while in iTunes the user always obtains the content directly from the central iTunes server.

- In P2PTunes, confidentiality of the responder is protected to some degree since the responder node removes its user-specific atoms from the protected file before sending it over the P2P network.

P2P Issues

As discussed above, nodes in P2P networks may misrepresent information such as bandwidth in order to service fewer requests, or no requests at all (Saroiu, Gummadi, and Gribble 2002). This "free riding" could create an environment with a large number of client nodes and fewer server nodes which would negates some of the advantage of a P2P architecture. Taken to the extreme, this effect cause P2PTunes to degenerate into essentially the equivalent of iTunes with a centralized server (or a few such servers) distributing the content. By offering a small financial incentive to those who distribute content that results in a purchase, P2PTunes could reduce the effect of free riding.

Another issue is that participants in P2PTunes may simply share unencrypted content over the underlying P2P network. However, the equivalent of this scenario occurs with iTunes today. As

Figure 6. P2PTunes functional architecture

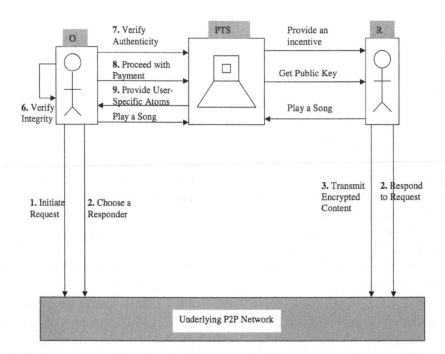

discussed above, there are many tools for scrubbing content purchased via iTunes, and there is nothing to prevent these scrubbed files from being uploaded to P2P networks. Again, in P2PTunes, we can encourage users to share encrypted content by rewarding distributors with a small financial reward from the PTS. This would create an incentive for users to "play by the rules".

IMPLEMENTATION AND TESTING

The implementation of our P2PTunes prototype is discussed in detail in (Venkataramu 2007). Here, we simply point out that such a prototype has been created and that the prototype includes the full P2PTunes functionality described above. In addition, thorough testing has been conducted to validate the functionality and security of the design. See (Venkataramu 2007) for complete details on the implementation and testing of our prototype P2PTunes application.

SECURITY

In this section we consider some security issues that arise in P2PTunes. The goal here is to illustrate that P2PTunes is as secure as iTunes. We now consider the basic steps that occur when content is purchased and played in P2PTunes. For each step, we discuss relevant security issues.

Initiate Request

An originator node O broadcasts a request for content over the P2PTunes network. At this stage intermediate and responder nodes are aware of the identity of the originator node. That is, anonymity is not provided by P2PTunes. An alternative would be to use a secret-sharing-based mutual anonymity protocol to allow peers to issue queries and responders to deliver responses anonymously (Han, Liu, Xiao, et. al., 2004). However, we do not believe this overhead is warranted, given that

legitimate content is being distributed and participants need to be identified if financial incentives are to be a part of the system.

Respond to a Request

Responder nodes send file index information containing details of the content and the identity of the responder node to the originator. The size of the file index sent is on the order of a few kilobytes which is much smaller than that of the actual audio data. Consequently, this step uses little of the P2P bandwidth. The potential security issue at this stage is that malicious nodes could bombard an originator with a large number of dummy index files which might result in the originator node's system hanging. In general, there are no easy preventative measures for this type of distributed denial of service attack.

Choose Specific Content

The originator node chooses a particular piece of content, based on details indicated in the responses. A download request is sent to the corresponding responder node over P2PTunes. At this stage, the originator can make an informed choice based on the content information and the responder's ID. We could enhance this process by employing a rating system where responders are rated by other users and by the PTS.

Content Transmitted

At this stage, the requested content is transmitted from the responder to the originator over the P2P network. The content file (a protected m4p file) consists of atoms, each of which contains information pertaining to the content (e.g., artist name), identification information (e.g., iTunes user ID), the encrypted song, and cryptographic information (e.g., encrypted keys).

The responder strips the user-specific atoms from the m4p file and prepares a byte stream. The absence of the identification atoms prevents intermediate nodes from identifying the responder and hence provides a degree of anonymity. In addition, atoms essential to the decryption process, namely the priv atom (which contains the encrypted AES key), the name atom (identification atom), and so on, are not transmitted, thereby discouraging intermediate nodes from trying to decrypt the mdat atom and recover the song in an unprotected form. Additionally, since user-specific atoms are not present in the byte stream, intermediate nodes cannot easily act as a fake responder node and request user keys from the PTS. If a node adds its user-specific atoms to the protected file and requests the user key from the PTS, the PTS would not comply since it could easily verify from its database that the particular node has not purchased the song. Hence, these security measures thwart certain attacks by unscrupulous intermediate nodes.

Note that any intermediate nodes involved in the routing are aware of the content details since the atoms of the transmitted m4p file include the artist name, the purchase date, the album name, copyright information, and the mdat atom (which contains the encrypted song). Nodes cannot decrypt the responder node's account information (consisting of its user name and user ID) from the byte stream since it is encrypted with the PTS public key. Hence, neither the intermediary nodes nor the originator node can view or alter the responder's account information.

The responder computes a CRC checksum of the byte stream, which the originator node uses to verify error-free transmission of the content. The intermediate nodes can cache the content involved in the transaction and later forward the same digital content in response to similar requests originating from different nodes. This will make more efficient use of the P2P bandwidth (Fairplay 2006).

As in P2PTunes, content cannot be played from unauthorized machines since the PTS requests system information from nodes. This system information must match that in the PTS database before the PTS will verify legitimate ownership and provide decryption keys (Apple 2006).

Originator Receives Data

The originator verifies the integrity of the content against the received checksum to be certain that the data has not been corrupted. Subsequently, the originator verifies the content authenticity with the PTS (by computing a cryptographic hash) to ensure that an unscrupulous node did not tamper with the content. The integrity and authenticity computations take place at the participating P2PTunes nodes. This leaves the centralized PTS system with few computational tasks and makes efficient use of the P2P bandwidth.

Role of PTS

The role of the PTS is to verify the authenticity of the song and to send appropriate error messages allowing the originator to choose a different source in case of a failure. Furthermore, the PTS is responsible for billing and generating user-specific atoms to be added to the purchased m4p file by the originator's software. Once the originator receives the user-specific atoms, it can request the user keys from the PTS to play any purchased content.

Authenticity verification occurs between the originator and the PTS. The originator calculates the hash value of non-user specific atoms in the digital content using a cryptographic hash. The calculated hash value, along with the content ID and encrypted account information is sent to the PTS, which validates the received hash value for the specified content. In addition, the PTS verifies whether the responder has purchased the song by decrypting the responder's account information and confirming ownership against its database. This guarantees that the digital content is from an authentic source.

The user-specific atoms generated by the PTS are small compared to the m4p content file. The PTS generates a priv atom, which contains the encrypted AES key. Additionally, the name atom (consisting of the user name) and the user atom (consisting of the user ID) are generated and sent to the originator O through a secure connection that O establishes with the PTS (based on O's system key). Then O's P2PTunes client software inserts these atoms into the MPEG-4 file, thus forming a complete protected file.

Playing Purchased Content

This step is identical to the corresponding step in iTunes, as outlined in Section 2.2.2.

CONCLUSION

The P2PTunes design is geared to efficiently utilize P2P bandwidth for content transactions and effectively delegate as much of the computational task as possible to client nodes. The role of the centralized PTS server is reduced to validating data, per-forming inexpensive computations, and handling financial transactions. This design significantly reduces the load on the PTS server since the amount of data involved in transactions between client nodes and the PTS is small in comparison to the iTunes model.

In addition, P2PTunes provides a venue for users with similar interests to inter-act and share content, fostering social networking. Rewarding participating nodes with royalty payments or other incentives could generate additional user interest and possibly reduce attacks while increasing community participation in the P2PTunes network.

In the iTunes design, the centralized server handles multiple functions and its bandwidth is occasionally under strain. For instance, swarms of online shoppers armed with iTunes gift cards overwhelmed the iTunes music store, prompting error messages and slowdowns in downloads (Montgomery Advertiser 2007). Additionally, digital distribution of video requires far more bandwidth than music and hence increases the load on the server. This potential bandwidth bottleneck is avoided in our P2PTunes system, where users of the underlying P2P network share music over the P2P network instead of approaching the centralized system.

There are many security challenges related to sharing digital content over a P2P network. Our P2PTunes design demonstrates that it is feasible to extend iTunes to a P2P system while employing sufficient security measures to make the resulting system at least as secure as iTunes.

Of course, P2PTunes is not immune to all security attacks. Reverse engineering tools like JHymn can be used to scrub protected files in iTunes as well as P2PTunes. Users could therefore make use of JHymn-like tools and share the resulting unprotected files. Installation of watermarking features such as the ge ID atom (present in m4p file) do little to deter such attacks since reverse engineering tools such as JHymn take care not to strip information that iTunes requires to play the content. This makes it a difficult task for the iTunes client to detect whether the content is in a protected or unprotected format. This same attack scenario applies to P2PTunes.

Care has been taken to make P2PTunes suitable for deployment over a P2P net-work, while having security comparable to iTunes. The P2PTunes DRM system is strong enough to withstand selected attacks but cannot be deemed totally secure, as is the case for all software-based DRM systems available today.

FUTURE WORK

The P2PTunes DRM system can incorporate numerous additional security measures and additional useful features. Some of these useful features and security measures are briefly considered in this section.

The anti-Fairplay tool QTFairUse6 captures the AAC frames after the song has been decrypted by iTunes version 6.0, but prior the decoding step, and copies the unprotected date to a file (iPod News 2006). This attack illustrates that a major vulnerability exists at the point where the data is converted to a format understood by a sound card. A trusted operating system (OS) could prevent such an attack by verifying that software running on the system is not malicious. Therefore, one way to greatly improve the security of P2PTunes—or any DRM scheme—is to implement the system within a trusted OS environment. For example, P2PTunes together with Microsoft's Next Generation Secure Computing Base (NGSCB) could provide vastly improved DRM security (Microsoft 2006).

Many additional features could be implemented to enhance P2PTunes. For example, the following features may be worth considering.

- Client nodes of P2PTunes can invite other users in their "friends" list to buy digital content from each other. A user knows her friends' music or content preferences and can suggest appropriate purchases. This might increase sales by taking advantage or social networking.
- Features could be built into P2PTunes to allow users to rate digital content and post to message boards. This would inform users of digital content available for purchase and further strengthen the social networking aspects of the system.
- In our implementation of P2PTunes, the PTS server is able to identify whether responder nodes have sent invalid content in response to an originator's request. This could be used by the PTS to blacklist misbehaving responder nodes. Then originators could avoid purchasing content from blacklisted responder nodes.

REFERENCES

Androutsellis-Theotokis, S. (2004). A survey of peer-to-peer content distribution technologies. ACM Computing Surveys, *36*, 335–371.

Anonymous. (2006). Hymn Manual, Retrieved on August 30, 2006 at http://hymn-project.org/documentation.php.

Apple Computers, Inc. (2006). MPEG-4: The container for digital media, Retrieved on August 21, 2006 at http://www.apple.com/quicktime/technologies/mpeg4/.

Bailes and Templeton. (2004). Managing P2P security. *Communications of the ACM, 47*, 95–98.

Bornstein, N. (2007). *Hacking iTunes*, Retrieved on April 5, 2007 at http://www.xml.com/pub/a/2004/11/03/itunes.html.

Chandak, G. (2005). Can iTunes be weTunes? — Is FairPlay playing fair? 20th BILETA Annual Conference, 2005.

Daswani, Garcia-Mollia, & Yang. (2002). Open problems in data-sharing peer-to-peer systems. *Proceedings of the 9th International Conference on Database Theory, 2572*, pp. 1–15.

France, Moore, & Dreier. (2007). *Napster*, Retrieved on April 7, 2007 at http://reviews.cnet.com/Napster/4505-3669_7-31302303.html.

France, J. (2007). Rhapsody 3.0, Retrieved on April 7, 2007 at http://reviews.cnet.com/Rhapsody_3_0/4505-9239_7-20050753.html?tag=also.

France, Viksnins, & Kim. (2007). *eMusic,* Retrieved on April 7, 2007 at http://reviews.cnet.com/eMusic/4505-9240_7-30974740.html?tag=also.

Futureproof. (2006*). JHymn project*, Retrieved on August 24, 2006 at http://hymn-project.org/jhymndoc/.

Han, et. al. (2004). A mutual anonymous peer-to-peer protocol design. *Proceedings of the 19th IEEE International Parallel and Distributed Processing Symposium*, p. 68.

Indigo Group. (2006). Fairplay: effectiveness and weaknesses of Apple's digital rights management technology, Retrieved on August 20, 2006 at http://www.simson.net/ref/2005/csci_e-170/p1/indigo.pdf#search=%22indigo%20fairplay%22.

iPod News. (2006). QTFairUse6 circumvents iTunes DRM, Retrieved on August 30, 2006 at http://www.ipodnn.com/articles/06/08/30/itunes. drm. circumvented/.

Kalker, et. al. (2004). Music2Share: Copyright-compliant music sharing in P2P systems. *Proceedings of IEEE, 92*, 961–970.

Mannak, Ridder, & Keyson. (2004). The human side of sharing in peer-to-peer net-works. *ACM International Conference Proceeding Series, 84*, 59–64.

Microsoft. (2006). *Next generation secure computing base*. Retrieved on March 17, 2006 at http://www.microsoft.com/resources/ngscb/default.mspx.

Microsoft. (2007). *Peer-to-peer file sharing: Help avoid breaking copyright laws and getting unwanted software*. Retrieved on April 3, 2007 at http://www.microsoft.com/athome/security/online/p2p_file_sharing.mspx.

Montgomery Advertiser. (2007). *iTunes slowdown*. Retrieved on January 3, 2007 at http://www.montgomeryadvertiser.com/apps/pbcs.dll/frontpage.

Rodrigues, Liskov, & Shrira. (2002). Peer-to-peer: The design of a robust P2P system. *Proceedings of the 10th ACM SIGOPS European Workshop: Beyond the PC*, pp. 117–124.

SourceForge. (2006). AtomicParsley, Retrieved on September 16, 2006 at http://atomicparsley.sourceforge.net/.

Saroiu, Gummadi, & Gribble. (2002). A measurement study of peer-to-peer file sharing systems. *Multimedia Computing and Networking, 153*, 156–170.

Stamp, M. (2003). Digital rights management: For better or for worse? Extreme Tech, May 20, 2003, Retrieved July 3, 2007 at http://www.extremetech.com/article2/0,3973,1051610,00.asp

Stamp, M. (2006). *Information Security: Principles and Practice*. Wiley-Interscience, 2006

Sun Developer Network. (2007). Remote method invocation, Retrieved on March 12, 2007 at http://java.sun.com/javase/technologies/core/basic/rmi/index.jsp

Tanin, Nayar, & Samet. (2005). An efficient nearest neighbor algorithm for P2P settings. *Proceedings of the 2005 National Conference on Digital Government Re-search, 89*, 21–28.

United States Computer Emergency Readiness Team. (2006). *Risks of file-sharing technology*. Retrieved on November 3, 2006 at http://www.us-cert.gov/cas/tips/ST05-007.html

Venkataramu, R. (2007). *Analysis and enhancement of Apple's Fairplay digital rights management*. Master's report, Department of Computer Science, San Jose State University, 2007, Retrieved July 3, 2007 at http://www.cs.sjsu.edu/faculty/stamp/students/RamyaVenkataramu_CS298Report.pdf

Wen, H. (2006). *JHymn goes behind atoms and Apple to bring DRM-free music*. Retrieved on September 14, 2006 at http://osdir.com/Article3823.phtml

Fairplay (2006). *Wikipedia*. Retrieved on August 21, 2006 at http://en.wikipedia.org/wiki/FairPlay

Peer-to-peer (2006). *Wikipedia*. Retrieved on October 7, 2006 at http://en.wikipedia.org/wiki/Peer-to-peer

KEY TERMS

Digital Rights Management (DRM): Consists of the methods used to control access to copyrighted digital content.

Fairplay: A digital right management (DRM) technology used to protect digital content purchased from the iTunes online store. As with most DRM systems, the purpose of Fairplay is to place restrictions on the uses of copyrighted content.

iTunes: A proprietary software application which is used to connect to the iTunes online store to download digital content. The iTunes software is used to manage play lists among computers and iPods, and to play digital content on Windows computers, Macintosh computers, and the iPod.

P2PTunes: Is designed to provide the benefits of a decentralized P2P network while providing DRM content protection that is at least as strong as that found in Fairplay. P2PTunes can operate over any existing P2P network.

Peer-to-Peer Networks (P2P): A P2P network consists of a number of networked computers, often connected in an ad-hoc fashion. Each peer can function as a server (content provider) or a client (content consumer), or both simultaneously. P2P architectures can be classified as either centralized or decentralized.

Chapter IX
A Hardware Approach for Trusted Access and Usage Control

Nicolas Anciaux
INRIA Rocquencourt, France

Luc Bouganim
INRIA Rocquencourt, France

Philippe Pucheral
INRIA Rocquencourt, France & University of Versailles, France

ABSTRACT

This chapter advocates the convergence between Access Control (AC) models, focusing on the granularity of sharing, and Digital Right Management (DRM) models focusing on conditional authorizations and obligations. The convergence is also expected in terms of control enforcement considering that both AC and DRM models must be equally protected against any form of tampering and piracy. We capitalize on the democratization of powerful secure chip platforms (e.g., smart cards, secure USB dongles) which can be plugged in a variety of client devices (PC, PDA, cell phones, consumer electronics) to design a new architecture of a trusted access and usage control system. The benefits of the proposed architecture are exemplified in two different contexts: a fair DRM scenario and a healthcare scenario.

INTRODUCTION

In computer systems, access control models are used to express who is granted privilege to execute which actions on which set of resources. Many works have been conducted on access control management in the database context, trying to provide the finest granularity of sharing. In relational database systems, privileges can be granted on virtual objects, called views, dynamically built by an SQL query (Melton et al., 1993). In XML databases, XPath expressions are usually used to delineate the objects or document parts targeted by an access control rule (Bertino et al., 2001;

Gabillon et al., 2001; Damiani et al., 2002). The reason for this granularity concern is that databases often contain sensitive information (e.g., personal, commercial, administrative, military data) shared by a large number of users playing different roles with different privileges. Digital Right Management (DRM) models are also used to regulate the access to resources. DRM models primarily target the protection of digital assets (e.g., videos and sounds). The granularity of the access control is of lesser concern here but the conditions (e.g., to pay a fee) and obligations (e.g., to increment a counter at each copy) related to how a privilege can be exercised become central (XrML; ODRL). Hence DRM models complement access control with usage control. Another major concern of DRM systems is the enforcement of the access and usage control rules to fight against a large scale piracy threatening the global multimedia content industry (IFPI).

As the information distributed to customers becomes more complex and structured (e.g., encyclopaedia, cultural collections, stock exchange databases) the need for finer granularity rules arise in the DRM context. Conversely, as database applications show an increasing concern for regulating the usage made of the information legally accessed, the need for access control rules integrating contextual conditions and obligations arises. This is particularly true for databases containing personal data (Agrawal et al., 2002). The management of Electronic Health Records illustrates this well. For example, permissive access control rules should apply to a medical folder in specific contexts like an emergency situation. Obligations like registering all accesses to a medical folder in a log are also required to allow auditing the system.

In this chapter, we advocate the convergence between the access control and DRM worlds, encompassing the expression of fine grain access control and accurate usage control. This convergence is also expected in terms of control enforcement. In database environments, the access

control is usually enforced by the database server, under the assumption that the server is trusted. Unfortunately, even the most defended servers (including those of Pentagon, FBI and NASA) have been successfully attacked, and database systems are identified as the primary target of computer criminality (Computer Security Institute, 2007). This motivated the design of new architectures where the server role amounts to deliver raw content to smart clients implementing the access control (Bouganim et al., 2004; Hacigumus et al., 2002). The question becomes how to enforce access and usage control on the client side. This question is not new in the DRM context, though no satisfactory solutions have been proposed yet. Indeed, today's DRM methods are so coercive that they do nothing but exasperating consumers and legitimize piracy (Champeau, 2004). The question is newer in the database world, people slowly becoming aware of the value of personal data and starting considering that protecting privacy is at least as important as protecting digital assets.

This chapter suggests solutions to enforce access and usage control on the client side thanks to secure hardware. Secure chips appear today in various form factors (smart cards, USB secure tokens, TPM, etc). They can be used to implement a Secure Operating Environment (i.e., a tamper-resistant storage and execution environment) in any device they are plugged in. This Secure Operating Environment is the required building block to design future trusted access and usage control systems. The suggested approach is expected to pave the way for new fair DRM models and for privacy conscious models of exchanging personal data.

This chapter is organized as follows. Section 2 presents background material on access control models, DRM models and secure hardware and sketches in this light an architecture for future trusted access and usage control systems. Section 3 summarizes two previous works related to the enforcement of XML access control policies in secure chip and the management of data embedded on chip. These works can be seen as building blocks for the aforementioned architecture. Section 4 illustrates the benefit of the suggested architecture in two different contexts: a fair DRM scenario and a healthcare scenario. Section 5 concludes discussing future trends.

BACKGROUND AND PROPOSED APPROACH

Access Control & DRM Models

Access Control Models

An access control model is a framework by which security administrators grant or revoke the right to access some data or perform some action in a system. The set of authorizations regulating the use of all resources of a system is called an access control policy. Authorizations can take different forms depending on the underlying data model. For example, an authorization over a relational database is usually expressed as granting the permission to execute a given action (e.g., Select) on a relational table or view (i.e., a virtual table computed by an SQL query) (Melton et al., 1993). An authorization over a XML document is usually expressed as a composition of positive (resp. negative) rules selecting authorized (resp. forbidden) sub-trees in the document thanks to XPath expressions (Bertino et al., 2001; Gabillon et al., 2001; Damiani et al., 2002). Another dimension of the access control model is the way by which authorizations are administered, following a Discretionary (DAC) (Harrison et al., 1976), a Role-Based (RBAC) (Sandhu et al., 1996) or a Mandatory (MAC) approach (Bell et al., 1976). In this chapter, we do no restrictive assumption on the way authorizations are actually expressed and administered, except for illustrative purposes. We also consider both the relational and XML contexts even though a large part of this chapter focuses on the XML data model. Indeed, XML

allows illustrating access control rules in a simple and intuitive way and is the preferred syntax for most existing DRM languages. We thus briefly detail below the XML and XPath syntax before presenting examples of XML access control rules.

XML has become a de-facto standard for the presentation, exchange and management of any information. Figure 1 shows a sample of XML metadata describing an MPEG-21 video. Roughly speaking, an XML document can be seen as a tree of elements, each one demarcated by an opening and closing tag (e.g., <Seq> and </Seq> for the Seq element). Attributes may be attached to elements (e.g., attribute value of the analysis element). Terminal elements (at the leaves of the tree) are represented by text (e.g., Closer).

Queries can be expressed over an XML document using the XPath language. An XPath expression allows to navigate in the document through the parent axis (denoted by /) and the descendant axis (denoted by //) and to apply predicates on elements and attributes. The result of an XPath expression is an element (or a group of elements) along with its (their) subtree(s). For example, the XPath expression /Video/Film/Seq/Key selects all the decryption keys of the sequences of the film while //Seq[SexRating>3] selects any sequence (anywhere in the document) having a direct child SexRating whose value is greater than 3.

Different authorization models have been proposed to regulate access to XML documents, tackling different facets of the problem. A particular attention has been paid on the granularity of the access control (from DTD to attribute instances) (Bertino et al., 2000; Damiani et al., 2002; Gabillon et al., 2001), on the performance of the algorithms implementing this control (Cho et al., 2002; Murata et al., 2003; Wang et al., 2001), on the distribution channel used to expose the information (pull, push, selective dissemination) (Bertino et al., 2002; Birget et al., 2001; OASIS Standard) and on the tamper-resistance of the access control (Bouganim et al., 2004; Miklau et al., 2002; Ray et al., 2002).

Figure 1. An MPEG 21 XML document

```
<Video>
<  Title> Closer </Title>
<  Film>
    <Seq>
    <    Desc> ...... </Desc>
    <    SexRating> 3 </SexRating>
    <    Key> xxxxxxxxxx </Key>
    </Seq>
    <Seq>....</Seq>
<  /Film>
<  Bonus>
    <Seq>....</Seq>
    ....
<  /Bonus>
<  Analysis Value = "Technical">
    <Seq>....</Seq>
<  /Analysis>
</Video>
```

Roughly speaking, an access control policy is composed of a set of positive (resp. negative) authorization rules granting (resp. denying) a given subject access to some nodes of the document. These nodes are usually selected thanks to XPath expressions. The descendant relationship among nodes is simply exploited as a mean to propagate authorization rules down through the XML hierarchy. There are substantial differences among the models in the way conflicts among – potentially propagated – positive and negative rules are tackled. In (Bertino et al., 2000; Gabillon et al., 2001), the complete subtree rooted at a forbidden node is forbidden. This constraint is relaxed in (Damiani et al., 2002)], allowing exceptions to a negative rule to be expressed. However, this leads to make visible the label (i.e., tag) of forbidden ancestor(s) in the path from the root to an authorized node. Replacing the node label by a dummy value has been proposed in (Fan et al., 2004; Gabillon, 2004) to reduce information disclosure in such situation.

For the sake of clarity and conciseness, we consider in this chapter a simplified access control model for XML, inspired by Bertino's model (Bertino et al., 2001) because several models share this same foundation. Subtleties of this model are ignored. In this simplified model, access control rules take the form of a 3-uple <subject, sign, object>. Subject denotes a user or a group of users. Sign denotes either a permission (positive rule) or a prohibition (negative rule) for the read operation (updates are not considered). Object corresponds to elements or subtrees in the XML document, identified by an XPath expression. The expressive power of the access control model, and then the granularity of sharing, is directly bounded by the supported subset of the XPath language. We consider in this chapter a robust subset of XPath denoted by $XP^{\{[],*,//\}}$ (Miklau et al., 2002). This subset, widely used in practice, consists of node tests, the child axis (/), the descendant axis (//), wildcards (*) and predicates or branches [...]. Attributes are handled in the model similarly to elements and are not further discussed.

For simplification purpose again, we consider that the cascading propagation of rules is implicit in the model, meaning that a rule propagates from an object to all its descendants in the XML hierarchy. Due to the rule propagation along the hierarchy and to the multiplicity of rules for a same user, a conflict resolution principle is required. Conflicts are resolved using two policies: 1) Denial-Takes-Precedence, which states that if two rules of opposite signs apply on the same object, then the negative one prevails and 2) Most-Specific-Object-Takes-Precedence, which states that a rule which applies directly to an object takes precedence over a propagated rule. Finally, if a subject is granted access to an object, it is also assumed to be granted access to the path from the document root to this object (As in (Fan et al., 2004; Gabillon, 2004), names of denied elements in this path can be replaced by a dummy value). This *Structural* rule keeps the document structure consistent with respect to the original one.

DRM Languages

Several initiatives, e.g., XrML (XRML), MPEG-REL (ContentGuard, 2004), ODRL (ODRL),

XACML (OASIS Standard), XMCL (XMCL, 2001), demonstrate the need for expressive and extensible DRM languages capable of implementing a large variety of business models. Some of these initiatives are gaining a wide acceptance. For example, XrML from ContentGuard is used by Microsoft in its DRM implementations. XrML also formed the basis for MPEG REL, the Rights Expression Language of MPEG-21. The Open Digital Rights Language has been adopted by the Open Mobile Alliance (OMA) for its DRM standard. While different in their syntax and usages, the DRM languages mentioned above share strong commonalities. To illustrate this, let us consider XrML as a reference language. The constituents of an XrML grant (the central part of an XrML license) are:

- The *principal* to whom the grant is issued.
- The *right* that the grant specifies.
- The *resource* that is the direct object of the "right" verb.
- The *condition* that specifies the terms, conditions and obligations under which the right can be exercised.

Principal, right and resource are respectively named party, right and asset in ODRL and subject, action and resource in XACML with a similar meaning. ODRL integrates conditions within the right statement while XACML distinguishes between conditions and obligations. XACML supports also denials (i.e., negative authorizations) in addition to grants. The way a right is actually exercised is implementation dependent and may differ depending on the DRM infrastructure, on the application and on the type of content to be protected.

Access & Usage Control Rules

As the two preceding sections make clear, there are strong commonalities between access control and DRM control. In both cases, the control policy grants privileges on a set of objects to a set of subjects. There are also distinctions between access control and DRM. As stated earlier, (database) access control models are highly concerned by the sharing granularity, leading to the use of assertional languages (either SQL or XPath) to identify the objects, and the subjects, targeted by a rule. Conversely, DRM is primarily concerned by the conditions and obligations related to how a privilege can be exercised on a digital asset. This lead to integrate two new concepts in the rule definition, namely *context* and *obligation*. Context is used in DRM scenarios to assess a contextual predicate (e.g., "the number of films produced by Gaumont watched in the last 7 days is more than 3") conditioning the activation of a given privilege (e.g., "to watch a free of charge film"). Obligations are mandatory actions associated to the exercise of a privilege (e.g., "append a new record to the audit trail").

For the reasons given in the introduction, we advocate in this chapter the convergence between the access control and DRM worlds, encompassing fine grain access control and accurate usage control. To this end, we consider in the sequel general Access and Usage Control (AUC) rules expressed by <subject[Q], object[Q], sign, action, context[Q], obligation>, where:

- *subject[Q]* defines the set of grantees for that rule, expressed by a qualification Q over the domain of subjects and roles;
- *object[Q]* defines the set of objects targeted by the rule, expressed by a qualification Q over the object domain;
- *sign* denotes either a permission (+) or a prohibition (-);
- *action* is the operation the subject is authorized/forbidden to exercise on the object;
- *context[Q]* defines the conditions which must be met to make the rule activable, expressed by a qualification over the set of objects materializing the subject context (history of subject's actions, audit trail, etc).

- *obligation* is the procedure the system is mandated to achieve when the subject exercises a granted action; we assume here that this procedure sums up to perform updates in the subject context (e.g., logging an action).

Secure Enforcement of Access & Usage Control

Enforcement of Access & Usage Control

In database environments, the access control is usually enforced by the database server and sometimes by the application server. In both cases, the underlying assumption is that the server is trusted. As stated in the introduction, the server security has been shown weaker than expected in a number of situations. This motivated the design of new architectures where the server role amounts to deliver raw content to smart clients implementing the access control (Bouganim et al., 2004; Hacigumus et al., 2002). In addition, important use cases (e.g., selective dissemination, parental control) require performing the control on client devices. The question becomes how to enforce AUC rules on the client side. Except in very specific situations where the client device can be trusted (e.g., an ATM terminal), the challenge is to build an incorruptible AUC rule evaluator on untrusted client devices.

This section reviews the main approaches tackling this challenge and evaluates them in the light of the following criteria: (1) tamper-resistance, (2) ease and cost of deployment, (3) platform agnosticisms (i.e., whether a subject can exercise her privileges whatever the device she is using at a particular time), (4) expressive power of the AUC model and (4) privacy preservation.

Secure software. Software-based enforcement systems consist of a secure code executed on the client device to evaluate AUC rules and render regulated contents. Representative examples are the couples *Fairplay / itunes* from *Apple* and *Windows Media Rights Manager / Windows Media Player* from *Microsoft* which both control access and usage of music files. The unquestionable advantages of software-based solutions are their low cost and ease of deployment (e.g., over the internet) and their powerfulness (there is no particular limitation of the AUC model which can be supported). The counterpart is manifold. First, the security of the enforcement process is weak, as any software is vulnerable by nature. In particular, the integrity of the secure software code (a prerequisite to a correct execution) cannot be definitely assessed in an untrusted environment (Hauser et al., 2003). This weakness is important considering that (i) any customer is a potential attacker, (ii) the attacks can be conducted with impunity from the private sphere, and (iii) a single pirate can break the security of the whole system by distributing the crack on the internet. In addition, device and software agnosticisms are difficult to achieve. The former requires developing and embedding the secure software in any rendering devices (common computers but also mp3 player, car music players, etc.) and the latter binds the consumer to the use of an exclusive software. Finally, AUC rules involving context (e.g., based on past subject actions) are either impossible to evaluate (unless all actions are performed from the same device) or require centralizing the context information on a server thereby hurting subject's privacy.

Secure hardware. Hardware solutions can be seen as trusted black boxes receiving an encrypted content and delivering the clear text of its authorized subset according to the AUC rules. For example, set-top-boxes used for decoding Pay TV in Europe are equipped with secure micro-controllers like the STi5202 decoder chip. The Microsoft NGSCB initiative[1] relies on a secure chip, called the Trusted Computing Modules (TPM), to enforce DRM on common computers). Today, standards are emerging for defining hardware-based content protection for home network devices, e.g., SVP Secure Video processor (SVP). Hardware-based solutions provide an unequalled level of security. Indeed, hardware is much more difficult to tamper than software, security protection is formally proven (and Evaluation Assurance Level can be assigned given completed Common Criteria (Common Criteria)) and large scale piracy is difficult to organize in case a chip is broken. If the secure chip comes in a portable and pluggable form factor (e.g., a USB secure token), it provides a nice answer to the platform agnosticisms (at least for devices equipped with a USB port) and privacy preservation requirements (the subject context is hardware protected and never centralized). On the other hand, hardware based solutions are more costly to deploy, linking manufacturers to higher investments and longer time to market (Grimen et al., 2006). More, current solutions largely underexploit the storage and computing capabilities of secure chips, thereby supporting only basic DRM models (raw decryption of multimedia flows).

The objective of this chapter is precisely to go one step further and show that, despite limited hardware resources, secure chip solutions can be devised to support trusted, powerful and privacy conscious AUC models. To understand how far we can go in this direction, it is mandatory to have a closer look at the current secure chip hardware constraints and at their forecast evolution.

Background on Secure Chips

The term secure chip refers to a monolithic chip providing strong anti-tampering features, whatever its actual form factor (i.e. physical sizes and shapes) ranging from the well known smart card to chips embedded in smart phones, USB keys and other forms of pluggable smart tokens. Note that powerful server-based secure coprocessors like the IBM 4758 (Dyer et al., 2001) fall outside this definition and are not discussed in this chapter. Secure chips share strong hardware commonalities and differ mainly in their interface to the host they connect to (Vogt et al., 2003).

Today's secure chips typically embed on a single silicium die: a 32 bit RISC processor (clocked at about 50 MHz), memory modules composed of ROM (about 100 KB), static RAM (some KB) and electronic stable storage (hundreds of KB of EEPROM or FLASH), and security modules enforcing physical security. The ROM is used to store the operating system, fixed data and standard routines. The RAM is used as working memory (heap and stack). Electronic stable storage is used to store persistent information, and holds data and downloaded programs. In the following, we analyze the main hardware trends for secure chips highlighting its very unique internal resource balance.

CPU resource: during the last ten years, embedded processors improved from the first 8-bit generation clocked at 2 MHz to the current 32 bit generation clocked at 50 MHz with an added cryptographic co-processor. At least two factors advocate for a continuous growth of CPU power. First, the rapid evolution of secure chip communication throughput (e.g., high delivery contactless cards, USB cards) allows secure chip applications to evolve towards CPU intensive data flow processing using cryptographic capabilities (e.g., DRM). Second, many efforts from secure chip manufacturers focus on multi-applications and multi-threaded operating systems demanding even more CPU power. In addition, note that increasing the CPU power as little impact on the silicon die size, an important parameter in terms of tamper-resistance and production cost on large scale markets.

RAM resource: secure chips hold today a few KB of static RAM, almost entirely consumed by the operating system (and the Java virtual machine in Java enabled chips). The gap between the RAM left available to the applications on one side and the CPU and stable storage resources on the other side will certainly keep on increasing. First, manufacturers tend to reduce the hardware resources to their minimum to save production costs. The relative cell size of static RAM (16 times less compact than ROM and FLASH, 4 times less compact than EEPROM) makes it a critical component, which leads to calibrate the RAM to its minimum (Anciaux et al., 2003). Second, minimizing the die size increases the tamper-resistance of the chip, thus making physical attacks trickier and more costly. RAM competing with stable memory on the same die, secure chip manufacturers favour the latter against the former to increase the chip storage capacity, thus enlarging their application scope.

Stable storage resource: the market pressure generated by emerging applications leads to a rapid increase of the storage capacity. Taking advantage of a 0.18 micron technology allows doubling the storage capacity of existing EEPROM memories. At the same time, manufacturers are integrating denser memory on chip, like NOR and NAND FLASH. NOR FLASH is well suited for code due to its "execute-in-place" property but its extremely high update cost makes it poorly adapted to data storage. NAND FLASH is a better candidate for data storage though its usage is hard. Reads and writes are made at a page granularity and any rewrite must be preceded by the erasure of a complete block (holding commonly 64 pages). Researchers in memory technologies aim at developing highly compact non-volatile memories providing fast read/write operations with fine grain access (e.g., MEMS, PCM, etc.) but this must be considered only as a long term perspective. Note that mass storage smart cards appear today in the market place, combining in a USB key form factor a smart card-like secure microcontroller connected by a bus to a Gigabyte-sized external (and then unprotected) NAND Flash module (Anciaux et al., 2007).

To conclude, secure chips appear as rather unusual computing environments and can be summarized by the following properties: (1) High processing power wrt the amount of RAM and on-chip data; (2) Tiny RAM wrt the amount of on-chip data; (3) Fast reads but slow and sometimes complex writes/rewrites in stable storage.

Trusted AUC Architecture

From the above discussion, we argue that secure chips can be a cornerstone of future trusted, powerful and privacy preserving AUC systems. This section describes such an architecture, centred on the secure chip and being agnostic with respect to the other components of a DRM system (client device and software, content server, licence server, etc). Figure 2 pictures this architecture and illustrates the software components and data which must be embedded on chip to enforce AUC rules of the form <subject[Q], object[Q], sign, action, context[Q], obligation>.

Being able to evaluate subject[Q] requires first authenticating the subject (the secure chip holder), leading to embed an authentication module and authentication data (credentials). The subject authenticates himself to the secure chip thanks to a PIN code and the secure chip authenticates itself to the other components of the system thanks to a cryptographic protocol, thereby implementing a strong authentication mechanism. Then, predicate Q can be evaluated over the subject credentials (e.g., subject.age > 18) to check whether the rule can become active.

To deliver the plaintext authorized result, the AUC engine must determine first which AUC rules are concerned by the subject request (may be more than one). Then, for each of these rules, it must (i) evaluate object[Q] and context[Q] thanks to the query processor and (ii) execute the obligation if the rule turns out to be active. The effect of this last step is in turn to update the context data (e.g., adding a record in an action trail).

Rules, objects and context data can be stored in plaintext in the secure chip (since embedded data is physically protected by the chip), encrypted on an external medium (e.g., transmitted from a remote server or stored on an insecure external memory), or both. For instance, in a DRM scenario, contextual data could be maintained on chip to protect the subject privacy, AUC rules (i.e., licenses) could be downloaded from a license server, and finally objects (i.e., the digital content) could be stored on a DVD medium or be downloaded from a content server.

Elements stored on an external medium must be cryptographically protected to protect them against any forms of attacks which could be conducted by intruders, insiders, administrators or even by the subject himself (the secure chip holder). Basically external data must be encrypted to resist to *snooping* attacks, must contain secure checksums (e.g., hashes) to prevent from *spoofing* and *splicing* attacks, and finally must include timestamps to avoid *replaying* attacks (Anciaux et al., 2006). To this end, cryptographic modules and associated keys have to be embedded on the chip. Note that embedded data (e.g., the AUC rules) can be dynamically updated through a secure channel established with a remote source.

The AUC software embedded in the secure chip acts as an incorruptible mediator between the content provider and the content consumer and protects equitably the interest of both parties. The AUC system suggested above provides the content provider with a tangible (i.e., hardware based) guarantee against piracy. Indeed, the secure chip holder himself has no access to the embedded data (except those permitted by the AUC rules) and has no way to tamper it. In commercial DRM scenarios, privacy is usually a lesser concern

and the consumer is asked to trust the server to protect data that can be gathered about him and his activity. The architecture sketched above re-establishes equity by providing the consumer with the same guarantees about the protection of his own data. To this respect, the roles of consumer and producer of information are inverted.

As section 4 will exemplify, this architecture is not tight to commercial DRM scenarios and can apply to any situation where sensitive data is exchanged between an information producer (could be a patient) and a consumer of this information (could be a physician querying the patient medical folder). The following roles can be distinguished, independently of the scenario:

- *information producer*: he is in charge of (1) protecting the storage of his data and (2) defining the adequate AUC policy to regulate the access and usage of his data. Whether obligations are integrated in the AUC policy, evidences of the fulfilment of these obligations must be given back to the producer. Data storage protection can rely on traditional server security (e.g., content servers) or on secure chip (e.g., embedded personal folders).
- *information consumer*: he can query/use the produced data according to his own privileges as defined in the AUC policy.

Figure 2. Functional architecture of a trusted AUC system. ©2008 Bouganim. Used with permission.

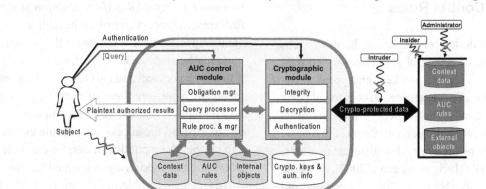

- *trusted AUC engine*: It is in charge of (1) enforcing the AUC rules, (2) checking the integrity of all incoming data, (3) securing the storage of embedded data if any, (4) supporting dynamic updates of embedded data. Whether obligations are integrated in the AUC policy, the AUC engine must build evidences of the fulfilment of these obligations. This means securing the storage of the subject context (the target of the obligations) and making this context queryable by the AUC engine, either to evaluate context dependent AUC rules or to allow the information producer auditing the AUC policy.

HARDWARE BASED SECURITY ELEMENTS

The trusted AUC architecture sketched in Section 2 needs further research efforts to become a reality. This section presents two previous works which can contribute to the definition of this architecture. The first work, presented in section 3.1, deals with the enforcement of XML access control policies over streaming documents thanks to a secure chip. The second work, presented in section 3.2, deals with the management of data embedded on chip.

Hardware Enforcement of XML Access Control Rules

When they do not rely on secure hardware, client-based access control solutions rely on data encryption. The data are kept encrypted at the server and a client is granted access to subparts of them according to the decryption keys in its possession. Sophisticated variations of this basic model have been designed in different contexts, such as DSP (Hacigumus et al., 2002), database server security (He et al., 2001), non-profit and for-profit publishing (Miklau et al., 2003; Bertino

et al., 2001; Microsoft Inc.) and hierarchical access control (Akl et al., 1983; Birget et al., 2001; Ray et al., 2002). By compiling the access control policies into the data encryption, these solutions minimize the trust required on the client at the price of a rather static way of sharing data. Indeed, whatever the granularity of sharing is, the dataset is split in subsets reflecting a current sharing situation, each encrypted with a different key, or composition of keys. Thus, access control rules intersections are precompiled by the encryption. Once the dataset is encrypted, changes in the access control rules definition may impact the subset boundaries, hence incurring a partial re-encryption of the dataset and a potential redistribution of keys.

To circumvent the drawbacks mentioned above, we designed a solution taking advantage of secure hardware on the client side (Bouganim et al., 2004). This solution is a client-based access control manager capable of evaluating dynamic access control rules on a ciphered XML document with the benefit of dissociating the access control management from encryption. The problem addressed can be stated as follows: (i) *to propose an efficient access control rules evaluator coping with the hardware constraints of a secure chip:* first, the limited amount of secured memory precludes any technique based on materialization (e.g., building a DOM (W3C DOM) representation of the document); second, the limited communication bandwidth lead to minimize the amount of data to be downloaded in the secure chip; (ii) *to guarantee that prohibited information is never disclosed:* the access control being realized on the client device, no clear-text data but the authorized ones must be made accessible to the untrusted part of this client device; and (iii) *to protect the input document from any form of tampering:* under the assumption that the chip is secure, the only way to mislead the access control rule evaluator is to tamper the input document, for example by substituting or modifying encrypted blocks.

To tackle this problem, we made the following contributions (Bouganim et al., 2007):

1. *Accurate streaming access control rules evaluator:* We proposed a streaming evaluator of XML access control rules, supporting $XP^{\{[],*,//\}}$, a robust subset of the XPath language (Miklau et al., 2002). The choice of a streaming evaluator allowed coping with the secure chip memory constraint. Streaming is also mandatory to cope with target applications consuming streaming documents. At first glance, one may consider that evaluating a set of XPath-based access control rules and a set of XPath queries over a streaming document are equivalent problems (Diao et al., 2003; Green et al., 2004; Chan et al., 2002). However, access control rules are not independent. They may generate conflicts or become redundant on given parts of the document. The proposed evaluator detects these situations accurately and exploits them to stop as soon as possible rules becoming irrelevant.

2. *Skip Index:* We designed a streaming and compact index structure allowing to quickly converge towards the authorized parts of the input document, while skipping the others, and to compute the intersection with a potential query expressed on this document (in a pull context). Indexing is of utmost importance considering the two limiting factors of the target architecture: the cost of decryption in the secure chip and the cost of communication between the chip, the client and the server.

3. *Pending predicates management:* Pending predicates (i.e., a predicate P conditioning the delivery of a subtree S but encountered after S in the document) are difficult to manage. We proposed a strategy to detect eagerly the pending parts of the document, to skip them at parsing time (whenever possible) and to reassemble afterwards the relevant pending parts at the right place in the final result.

4. *Integrity checking with random accesses:* We combined hashing and encryption tech- niques to make the integrity of the document verifiable despite the forward and backward random accesses generated by the *Skip Index* and by the support of pending predicates.

5. *Dynamic access control policy management:* The dynamicity of access control policies requires refreshing the access control rule definitions on the secure chip. We proposed a solution to ensure the confidentiality and integrity of this refreshing mechanism as well as to guarantee the consistency of the rule updates with respect to the processed document in order to avoid any unauthorized access.

The remaining part of this section summarizes the streaming evaluation of access control rules, the integrity checking and the dynamic access control policies management. A complete descrip- tion of the solution can be found in (Bouganim et al., 2007).

Streaming Evaluation of Access Control Rules

For each element of the input document, the ac- cess control rule evaluator must be capable of determining the set of rules that applies to it to determine the outcome for that element. The ac- cess control rule evaluator is fed by an event-based parser (SAX) raising *open*, *value* and *close* events respectively for each opening, text and closing tag encountered in the input document.

Each access control rule (i.e., XPath expres- sion) is represented by a non-deterministic finite automaton (Hopcroft et al., 1979), named Access control rule Automaton (ARA for short). An ARA is made of states connected by transitions (see Figure 3). Tokens traverse the ARA while transitions are triggered, at document parsing time. An ARA has one target final state (repre- senting the element targeted by the access control rule) and may have zero, one or more predicate final states (one for each predicate involved in

Figure 3. Access control rule automaton. ©2008 Bouganim. Used with permission.

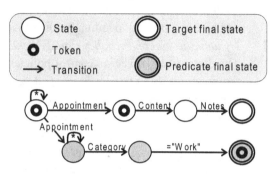

R1: ⊖ //Appointment[Category="Work"]/Content/Notes

the access control rule). When all final states of an ARA have been reached by a token, the corresponding access control rule becomes active, meaning that it applies to the forthcoming elements. Figure 3 shows the token positions in the ARA corresponding to a rule *R1* at the time the parser analyses the leftmost element of an XML document representing an agenda.

The following data structures are maintained in the secure chip to manage the set of ARA representing a given access control policy:

- *Token Stack:* The *Token Stack* memorizes the progress of tokens in all ARA and allows backtracking in the ARA.
- *Authorization Stack:* The *Authorization Stack* registers the rules having reached their target final state and is used to solve conflicts between rules. The status of a rule present in the stack can be: *positive-active* (⊕: forthcoming elements will be delivered), *positive-pending* (⊕?: the delivery of the forthcoming elements is conditioned by a predicate not yet evaluated), *negative-active* (⊖: forthcoming elements can be skipped), *negative-pending* (⊖?: the skip of the forthcoming elements is conditioned by a predicate not yet evaluated).

- *Predicate Set:* this set memorizes the predicates already evaluated.

The outcome of the current element can be easily determined from the information kept in these data structures, thanks to the conflict resolution algorithm presented in Figure 4. In the algorithm, AS denotes the Authorization Stack and AS[i]. RuleStatus denotes the set of status of all rules registered at level *i* in this stack. In the first call of this recursive algorithm, depth corresponds to the top of AS.

Integrity Checking with Random Accesses

Encryption and hashing are required to guarantee respectively the confidentiality and the integrity of the input document. Unfortunately, standard integrity checking methods are badly adapted to our context for two important reasons. First, the memory limitation of the secure chip imposes a streaming integrity checking. Second, the integrity checking must tackle the forward and backward random accesses to the document incurred by the Skip index and by the reassembling of pending document fragments. In this section, we sketch the solutions we proposed to face potential attacks on an input document.

In a client-based context, the attacker is the user himself. For instance, a user being granted access to a medical folder X may try to extract unauthorized information from a medical folder Y. Let us assume that the document is encrypted with a classic block cipher algorithm (e.g., DES or triple-DES) and that blocks are encrypted independently (e.g., following the ECB mode (Schneier, 1996)), identical plaintext blocks will generate identical ciphered values. In that case, the attacker can conduct different attacks: substituting some blocks of folders X and Y to mislead the access control manager and decrypt part of Y; building a dictionary of known plaintext/ciphertext pairs from authorized information (e.g., folder X) and

Figure 4. Conflict resolution algorithm

```
DecideElement(depth) → Decision ∈ {⊕, ⊖,?}
1: If depth = 0 then return '⊖'
2: elseif '⊖' ∈ AS[depth].RuleStatus then return '⊖'
3: elseif '⊕' ∈ AS[depth].RuleStatus and
4:        '⊖?' ∉ AS[depth].RuleStatus then return '⊕'
5: elseif DecideNode(depth -1) = '⊖' and
6:        '⊕?' ∉ AS[depth].RuleStatus then return '⊖'
7: elseif DecideNode(depth -1) = '⊕' and
8:        '⊖?' ∉ AS[depth] RuleStatus then return '⊕'
9: else return '?'
```

using it to derive unauthorized information from ciphertext (e.g., folder Y); making statistical inference on ciphertext. Additionally, if no integrity checking occurs, the attacker can randomly modify some blocks, inducing a dysfunction of the rule processor (e.g., Bob is authorized to access folders of patients older than 80 and he randomly alters the ciphertext storing the age).

To face these attacks, we exploit two techniques. Regarding encryption, the objective is to generate different ciphertexts for different instances of a same value. This property could be obtained by using a Cipher Bloc Chaining (CBC) mode in place of ECB, meaning that the encryption of a block depends on the preceding block (Schneier, 1996). This however would introduce an important overhead at decryption time if random accesses are performed in the document. As an alternative, we merge the position of a value with the value itself at encryption time. Regarding integrity checking, the document is split into chunks whose size is determined by the memory capacity of the secure chip. Each chunk contains an encrypted *ChunkDigest* computed using a technique adapted from the Merkle hash Tree (Merkle, 1989). This technique gracefully combines encryption and hashing functions to allow random accesses to any part of the document with an 8 bytes alignment. The most original part of the proposed strategy is that integrity is checked in cooperation with the untrusted terminal at the price of decrypting one digest per visited chunk in the worst case (i.e., when the chunks accessed are

not contiguous). As a conclusion, the document is protected against tampering and confidentiality attacks while remaining agnostic regarding the encryption algorithm used to cipher the elementary data. Unlike (Hacigumus et al., 2002; Bouganim et al., 2002), we do no assumption on any particular way of encrypting data that could facilitate the query execution at the price of a weaker robustness against cryptanalysis attacks.

Dynamic Access Control Policy Management

Dynamicity of the access control policies is a mandatory feature for a number of applications. This led us to design a secure mechanism to refresh the access control rules on the secure chip. Depending on the application scenarios, access control rule updates may be done pro-actively, requiring updates systematically before accessing the document, reactively when rule updates are detected, or even be disseminated jointly with the data. The update protocol must ensure three complementary properties: (i) *confidentiality* since access control rules definition may disclose unauthorized information; (ii) *integrity* since rule modification may mislead the rule processor; (iii) *consistency,* meaning that the set of access control rules stored on the secure chip must be up-to-date with respect to the processed document.

Access control rules confidentiality and integrity are enforced thanks to the encryption and hashing mechanisms presented above. Ensuring consistency is more difficult. Inconsistency between the set of access control rules and the document may appear as a result of a malicious user whom may, for instance, filter the update flow, replay the document or the update flow. In any case, the secure chip must detect it and not deliver any data. Inconsistencies appears when a new access control policy is applied to an old document, thus potentially revealing unauthorized outdated data, or conversely, when an outdated access control policy is applied to a recent version of the document, thus revealing unauthorized up to date data. Both problems are solved using a crypto-protected cross reference versioning between the document and the access control rules.

Protection of On-Board Data

Databases on Chip: Existing Approaches and Systems

The value of secure chips to manage personal folders has been recognized in several domains like healthcare (medical folder), commerce (loyalties), telecommunication (address book) or mobile computing (user's profiles containing licenses, passwords, bookmarks, etc). In this spirit, MasterCard published the MasterCard Open Data Storage (MODS) API (Mastercard Inc.), allowing retailers, banks and other organizations to access and store data on customers' smart cards with an enhanced security for the holder. This motivated the design of data management techniques dedicated to secure chips.

Historically, the first attempt towards a DBMS embedded in a secure chip is ISOL's SQLJava Machine (Carrasco, 1999)] and the ISO standard for a smart card database language, SCQL (International Standardization Organisation, 1999). Both are addressing generation of secure chips endowed with 8 kilobytes of stable memory, explaining a design limited to low data volumes and simple database techniques. Since then, more elaborated secure chip DBMS have been developed. PicoDBMS (Pucheral et al., 2001; Anciaux et al., 2001) was the first full-fledged relational DBMS embedded in a smart card. PicoDBMS supports a robust subset of the SQL standard (full relational algebra) encompassing SCQL. The PicoDBMS kernel acts as a doorkeeper that authenticates the users and solely delivers the data corresponding to their privileges. In the relational context, the powerfulness of the access control is directly determined by the complexity of the (relational) views that can be built. To provide fine grain privileges, PicoDBMS supports complex query processing including select, project, join and aggregate operations. While PicoDBMS was exclusively designed to store stable data in EEP-ROM, other works consider secure chips endowed with FLASH memory (Bolchini et al., 2003).

Recently, a benchmark called Data management in Secure Chip (DiSC) has been proposed (Anciaux et al., in press) to help designing database techniques for secure chips. In particular, this benchmark enables to (1) compare different database techniques embedded on secure chips, (2) predict the limits of on-chip applications, and (3) provide co-design hints.

Challenges Related to Data Storage and Indexation

Designing appropriate data management techniques for secure chips is not straightforward. Light versions of popular DBMS like *Sybase SQL Anywhere Studio* (Giguère, 2001), *IBM DB2 Everyplace* (Karlsson et al., 2001), *Oracle Lite* (Oracle Corp., 2002) and *Microsoft SQL Server for Windows CE* (Seshadri et al., 1999) have been developed for lightweight devices, but they do not address the more severe limitations of secure chips (see section 2.2.2). A thorough re-thinking of all database techniques is mandatory to tackle accurately the secure chip hardware constraints. We summarize below the main database challenges incurred by secure chip data management in terms of storage, indexation and query processing.

Storage and indexing challenge. Traditional (disk-based) database servers are designed to fit fast sequential and slow random disk accesses, hence data locality plays an important role. The tradeoffs introduced by electronic stable memories (mainly FLASH or EEPROM) are totally different (cf Section 2.2.2). For example, EE-PROM shares commonality with RAM in terms of access granularity (a memory word) and read performance (60-100 ns/word), but suffers from a dramatically slow write time (about 10 ms per word). Locality is no longer an issue, making disk-oriented structures irrelevant. Moreover, space consumption is an important concern in an embedded context. The challenge is then to devise compact structures for both data and indexes, adapted to the particularities of the access properties inherent to electronic memory.

Query execution challenge. Traditional query processing techniques typically resorts to materialisation (of intermediate results, hash tables, etc.) in the main memory and/or in swapping areas on disks. On the contrary, on-chip query execution strategies preclude materialisation. Within a secure chip, RAM is a scarce resource (Anciaux et al., 2003), and electronic memory is less appropriate for swapping (e.g., EEPROM exhibits a very slow write time, FLASH read/write costs exhibit a strong asymmetry and erasure is expensive). The challenge is then to devise RAM conscious query execution strategies, optimally avoiding swapping. Note that the two challenges are not independent since a lack of main memory for query processing may be compensated by a massive indexing.

EEPROM and Flash-Based Solutions

We precisely addressed these challenges when designing PicoDBMS in the particular context of a relational database and of EEPROM based secure chips. We sketch below the PicoDBMS design as an illustration of how the data management techniques required by a trusted AUC engine could be implemented. Of course, considering a different hardware platform (e.g., Flash based) or a different database model (e.g., XML) would lead to a different design.

PicoDBMS design has been driven by the following rules (Pucheral et al., 2001): *Compactness rule* (minimize data, index and code footprint), *RAM rule* (minimize RAM consumption), *Write rule* (minimize writes in EEPROM), *Read rule*

(take advantage of very fast reads in EEPROM), *Access rule* (take advantage of low granularity and direct reads in EEPROM), *CPU rule* (take advantage of the over-dimensioned CPU) and *Security rule* (never externalize private data, minimize code complexity). The resulting technical solutions in terms of storage, indexing and query execution are summarized below.

Storage and indexing model. PicoDBMS takes advantage of a compact pointer-based model to meet the *Compactness, Read* and *Access rules* altogether. This model exploits a combination of Flat storage (FS) where tuples are stored sequentially and attribute values are embedded in tuples, Domain Storage (DS) where values are grouped in domains and attribute values are replaced by pointers within tuples and Ring Storage (RS) where each domain value is linked with a ring of pointers to all tuples sharing this value. FS is adequate when the attribute does not present value redundancy. DS precludes any duplicate value to occur and then acts as a compression technique. RS plays the role of an index. It links together all tuples sharing the same attribute value through a circular chain of pointer headed by this value. This chain of pointer is stored again in place of the attribute values, providing a similar and compact implementation of both select and join indices.

Query execution strategy. PicoDBMS relies on so called *extreme right deep trees* to meet the *RAM* and *Write* rules. It executes all operators (including select, project, join, group by and aggregate computations) in a pure pipeline fashion to avoid any materialization. Pipelining join and aggregate computation is not easy. Natural joins (equijoins on key, foreign key pairs) are computed efficiently without RAM thanks to the ring index (see previous paragraph). For aggregate computation, a Cartesian product is introduced between the operands of the *group by* clause at the bottom of the tree, such that (1) the tuples sharing a same grouping value are naturally produced together at the tree leaves, (2) aggregation is computed at the tree root, one grouping value at a time. In

(Anciaux et al., 2003), we provided a more general framework for designing RAM-constrained query evaluators.

PicoDBMS has been developed on Java (Anciaux et al., 2001) and C (Anciaux, 2004), is running on different smart card platforms and it performance has been assessed using the DiSC Benchmark (Anciaux et al., in press), demonstrating that complex on chip data management techniques can be implemented today.

SCENARIOS

This section illustrates the benefits of the AUC architecture in two different contexts: a fair DRM scenario and a healthcare scenario. It reports on experiments conducted in the field, with real prototypes running on advanced smart card platforms. These prototypes are not strict implementations of the AUC architecture presented in Section 2 but rather adaptations of the main ideas.

A Fair DRM Scenario

Due to the poorness of their model and the inflexibility of their architecture, existing DRM systems badly adapt to new attractive usage scenarios. In addition, consumers are reluctant to use them for privacy preservation and fairness concerns. Indeed, exasperating coercive methods do nothing but legitimizing piracy (Champeau, 2004).

In (Bouganim et al., 2007(2)), we presented a new software and hardware infrastructure aiming at reconciling the content providers' and consumers' point of views by giving the ability to develop fair business models (i.e., that preserve the interest of both parties). The proposed infrastructure, named MobiDiQ (Mobile Digital Quietude), is an XML-based tamper-resistant right management engine embedded in a secure chip. It enforces licenses/contracts (i.e. access and usage control rules) depending both on the digital content accessed on the device (the objects) and on personal data (i.e., the context) stored securely on the chip. The MobiDiQ access right engine is embedded in the secure chip to prevent any tampering to occur, thereby giving strong anti-piracy guarantees to the content provider. Embedding personal data in the chip brings also strong guarantees about user's privacy preservation.

MobiDiQ is able to enforce versatile and powerful AUC policies required to develop fairer business models. For instance, commercial conditions can be negotiated between institutions and content providers to help some categories of citizen (e.g., students) to access valuable contents at a special rate. Parental control rules can also be set up to protect children against dangerous contents but also against a prohibitive use of legal commercial contents. Privacy preserving gifting and loaning scenarios can be supported as well (Axalto Simagine, 2005).

Let us illustrate the MobiDiQ behavior on a fair superdistribution scenario (a student accessing content negotiated by her University). Figure 1 in Section 2 showed a sample of the XML metadata attached to a given video. The video is divided into several tracks (film, bonus, analysis), each one subdivided in sequences that include descriptions, values indicated the rating in terms of violence, sex content, decryption keys, etc. Figure 5 shows the user's profile and the access control rules expressing the licenses downloaded by the user. The user's profile records the fact that this user is a master student of the University of Versailles by means of certificates (simplified in the figure).

In this example, MobiDiQ has to deal with two licenses. The first one is issued by the content provider and states that any member of the University of Versailles may have the right to play the Film (R1), Bonus (R2) and Analysis (R3) track of the video. The second license, delivered by the University of Versailles adds some restrictions, specifying that the Bonus track is restricted to students (R4) while the Analysis track is restricted to Master students (R5). Finally, the

Figure 5. Profile and licenses

```
<Profile>
    <SIM_PrivateKey> xdxdxd </SIM_PrivateKey>
    <UV_Student> xabc </UV_Student>
    <UV_Master> shqdq </UV_Master>
    <Group value = "John"> JohnGrpPrivateKey </Group>
    ....
</Profile>
                    Profile XML Data
Video License:
    Require University_Versailles License
    Rule R1: < UV_Member, play, ? , /Video/Film>
    Rule R2: < UV_Member, play, ? , /Video/Bonus>
    Rule R3: < UV_Member, play, ? , /Video/Analysis>

University_Versailles License
    Rule R4: < [not /Profile/UVStudent], play, ⊖,
/Video/Bonus>
    Rule R5: < [not /Profile/UVMaster], play, ⊖,
/Video/Analysis>
    Rule R6: < ALL, play, ⊖, //Seq[SexRating > 3]>

                    Licenses
```

last rule expresses that any sequence rated with a degree greater than 3 for sex content should not be played. The Require statement stipulates that the second license is mandatory to enable the first one. Note that a required license always restricts the possibilities of the user (Rules R4, R5 and R6 have a negative sign). Indeed, the university cannot grant more right than the one delivered by the content provider itself.

Roughly speaking, the MobiDiQ engine can be seen as a DRM virtual machine with XPath access control rules as bytecode and is nothing but a simplified instance of the trusted AUC architecture presented in Section 2.3. More precisely, the example above illustrates the enforcement of AUC rules of the form <subject[Q], object[Q], sign, action> but little effort is required to extend it with context and obligation.

Healthcare Scenario

PlugDB[2] and DMSP[3] are respectively a research and an experimental project conducted in the context of a medical-social network providing care at home for elderly people. There common objective is to improve the healthcare coordination while giving the control back to the patient over the access and sharing of her medical and social data.

Today, the coordination among the participants of this network (e.g., doctors, social workers) is organized around a paper-based folder. This folder stays at home and is consulted and updated by every participant. This solution suffers from two main drawbacks. First, the paper-based folder is the primary source of confidentiality breach since no access control can be settled but hiding the complete folder. Second, the folder cannot be accessed and filled remotely, precluding remote diagnosis and leading to incomplete content.

To solve these problems, a trusted AUC architecture is being developed and relies on a new hardware component, called Secure Portable Token (SPT). A SPT combines, in a USB key form factor, a smart card-like secure chip and an external (i.e., unprotected) Gigabyte-sized NAND Flash.

The basic idea is to place the patient in the centre of the scene, giving her the full ownership of her medical folders, as enacted by the legislation but seldom put into effect in practice. According to the AUC dialect, patients are considered as *information providers* and practitioners as *information consumers*. The peculiarity here is that the information is actually produced by the practitioners (e.g., medical prescriptions), but it remains the property of the patient who is in charge of protecting its storage and regulating access to it. Hence, in the simplest setting of the architecture, each patient is equipped with a personal SPT storing securely the patient folder (encrypted in the NAND Flash) and enforcing AUC rules (thanks to an AUC engine embedded in the secure chip), just like a trusted portable personal database server.

A more complex setting is required (1) to guarantee the durability of the patient folder in case of crash or loss and (2) to allow remote diagnosis/updates by practitioners. To this end, a central server is used and provides a permanent internet connection to the practitioners and replicates part of the patient folders. As detailed in (Anciaux et al., 2008), the patient may choose different status for different parts of her folder, the two main interesting statuses in the context of this chapter being *secret data* and *confined data*. Secret data is exclusively stored on the patient SPT and can be accessed exclusively by the practitioner physically in front of the patient, with the restrictions imposed by the AUC policy. Confined data is data a patient may want to make durable or to share among a reduced circle of trusted persons (e.g., the family doctor), with the guarantee that nobody else can access it. To do this, the patient SPT encrypts the confined data, replicates the encrypted data on the central server and shares the encryption keys with the SPTs of people belonging to this trusted circle. This sharing scheme is possible under the assumption that every participant (including the practitioners) is equipped with a personal SPT. Again, note that the SPT holder has no free access

to the SPT content and has no way to tamper it so that practitioners will still undergo the AUC control when accessing confined data.

According to Figure 2, the SPT plays a dual role. When the practitioner connects to a patient SPT and issues queries, the patient SPT acts as a trusted server guaranteeing a secure storage for the patient data and enforcing the AUC rules fixed by the patient. From the AUC engine point of view, AUC rules and context data is internal to the secure chip but patient data is stored encrypted within the SPT NAND Flash and is considered as external[4]. When the practitioner connects to the central server and issues queries over confined data, her own SPT plays the same role as above, except that (1) the AUC rules are external (even if they are cached internally, the original copy is in the patient SPT and a crypto-protected refreshing mechanism must take place through the central server) and (2) the patient data is external to the SPT, stored encrypted on the central server.

FUTURE TRENDS AND CONCLUSION

The scenarios presented above show that the trusted AUC architecture promoted in this chapter can pave the way for more powerful and versatile DRM models. DRM is no longer synonym of basic conditional access to videos and sound assets. It can be understood in a broader sense encompassing every situation where (1) sensitive information has to be shared among partners having different privileges, (2) the expression of privileges includes access and usage control with contextual conditions and obligations, (3) the enforcement of the control must be guaranteed even in untrusted client devices.

Typically, the healthcare scenario opens up interesting perspectives towards a trusted AUC management of various personal information like scholarship or insurance folders and even information captured by our ambient intelligence surrounding (e.g., electronic surveillance of elderly people at home, employees monitored at work). Nothing justify that this information is less protected today than commercial digital assets. However, several technical challenges remains to be addressed before a general, robust and efficient trusted AUC architecture becomes a reality. Some of them are sketched below.

Limited storage capacity of secure chips: the stable storage of secure chips cannot accommodate a large volume of protected data. In new hardware architectures like SPT, the secure chip is connected by a bus to an external mass storage (within the same token) where protected data can overflow. However, external storage is not tamper resistant and must be protected against *snooping, spoofing, splicing* and *replaying* attacks. Designing cryptographic protections adapted to a database usage remains an open challenge for large datasets. Moreover, data can even overflow on a central server or be hosted on a server to increase availability (cf. healthcare scenario), adding a communication overhead to the encryption/decryption cost. This means that a new memory hierarchy should be considered (on-chip RAM, on-chip stable storage, off-chip token memory and server memory) along with ad-hoc cache management strategies adapted to data access patterns, object size, availability/connectivity considerations, etc.

Context ownership and resiliency: AUC rules may be based on the context of the consumer (e.g., a condition on her past actions) and may impose the obligation to fill in an audit trail accessible by the information provider. This raises a set of problems still open in our current design. First, the context of the consumer must be complete and up-to-date. This might be achieved by forcing her to access to any content through her own token (e.g., in the healthcare scenario, a practitioner accessing a patient folder would be forced to connect her own token to activate the AUC rule). Second, the context must be made resilient to avoid the consumer intentionally loose her secure chip and thereby potentially gaining more privileges by

cleaning up her context. Third, the audit trail must be made accessible to the information provider in any situation. This introduces the problem of the audit trail location, protection and ownership and would probably lead to separate the audit trail from the context data.

Temporal AUC rules: temporal conditions have already been considered in commercial DRM models (XRML) and increase their expressive power and versatility. Typically, being able to express that a privilege can be exercised for a given duration (e.g., a one week trial), during a given time period (e.g., during working hours, during the week-end), possibly associated to a particular event (e.g., a diagnosis cannot be updated two days after an examination) is of general interest. The challenge here is that secure chips usually are not endowed with an internal clock and rely on the device they are plugged into to get time information. How to integrate a secure time server in a trusted AUC architecture is an interesting open issue.

REFERENCES

Agrawal, R., Kiernan, J., Srikant, R., & Xu, Y. (2002). Hippocratic Databases. *Int. Conf. on Very Large Data Bases*.

Anciaux, N., Bobineau, C., Bouganim, L., Pucheral, P., & Valduriez, P. (2001). PicoDBMS: Validation and Experience. *Int. Conf. on Very Large Data Bases*.

Anciaux, N., Benzine, M., Bouganim, L., Pucheral, P., & Shasha, D. (2007). GhostDB: Querying visible and hidden data without leaks. *ACM SIGMOD Int. Conf. on Management of Data*.

Anciaux, N., Benzine, M., Bouganim, L., Jacquemin, K., Pucheral, P., & Shaoyi Yin. (2008) Restoring the Patient Control over her Medical History. *IEEE Int. Symposium on Computer-Based Medical Systems*.

Anciaux, N., Bouganim, L., & Pucheral, P. (2003). Memory Requirements for Query Execution in Highly Constrained Devices. *Int. Conf. on Very Large Data Bases.*

Anciaux, N., Bouganim, L., & Pucheral, P. (2006). Data Confidentiality: to which extent cryptography and secured hardware can help. *Annals of Télécommunications, 61*(3-4).

Anciaux, N., Bouganim, L., Pucheral, P., & Valduriez, P. (in press). DiSC: Benchmarking Secure Chip DBMS. *IEEE Transactions on Knowledge and Data Engineering.*

Anciaux N. (2004). *Database Systems on Chip.* Unpublished doctoral dissertation, University of Versailles, France.

Akl, S., & Taylor, P. (1983). Cryptographic solution to a problem of access-control in a hierarchy. *ACM Transactions on Computer Systems, 1*(3), 239-248.

Axalto Simagine. (2005). Worldwide Mobile Communication and Java CardTM developer contest. 6th ed. held at 3GSM, Cannes, France. http://www.simagine.axalto.com.

Bell, D. E., & LaPadula, L. J. (1976). *Secure computer systems: Unified exposition and multics interpretation (Technical Report ESD-TR-73-306).* The MITRE Corporation.

Bertino, E., Castano, S., Ferrari, E., & Mesiti, M. (2000). Specifying and Enforcing Access Control Policies for XML Document Sources. *WWW Journal, 3*(3).

Bertino E., Castano S., & Ferrari E. (2001). Securing XML documents with Author-X. *IEEE Internet Computing, 5*(3).

Bertino, E., & Ferrari, E. (2002). Secure and Selective Dissemination of XML Documents. *ACM Transactions on Information and System Security, 5*(2).

Birget, J., Zou, X., Noubir, G., & Ramamurthy, B. (2001). Hierarchy-Based Access Control in Distributed Environments. *IEEE International Conference on Communications.*

Bolchini, C., Salice, F., Schreiber, F. A., & Tanca, L. (2003). Logical and physical design issues for smart card databases. *ACM Transactions on Information Systems, 21*(3).

Bouganim, L., & Pucheral, P. (2002). Chip-Secured Data Access: Confidential Data on Untrusted Servers. *Int. Conf. on Very Large Data Bases.*

Bouganim, L., Dang-Ngoc, F., & Pucheral, P. (2004). Client-Based Access Control Management for XML Documents. *Int. Conf. on Very Large Data Bases.*

Bouganim, L., Pucheral, P., & Dang-Ngoc, F. (2007). Dynamic Access-Control Policies on XML Encrypted Data. *ACM Transactions on Information and System Security, 10*(4).

Bouganim, L., & Pucheral, P. (2007). Fairness concerns in digital right management models. *Int. Journal of Internet and Enterprise Management, 5*(1).

Cho, S., Amer-Yahia, S., Lakshmanan, L., & Srivastava, D. (2002). Optimizing the secure evaluation of twig queries. *Int. Conf. on Very Large Data Bases.*

Carrasco, L. C. (1999). RDBMS's for Java Cards ? What a Senseless Idea !. http://www.sqlmachine.com

Champeau, G. (2004). Fnacmusic.com: Le test complet sur Ratiatum.com - Le Peer-to-Peer (P2P) au delà du téléchargement. (In French). http://www.ratiatum.com/p2p.php?id_dossier=1708&page=1.

Chan, C., Felber, P., Garofalakis, M., & Rastogi, R. (2002). Efficient filtering of XML documents with XPath expressions. *Int. Conf. on Data Engineering.*

Common Criteria. The Common Criteria for Information Technology Security Evaluation. http://www.commoncriteriaportal.org/

ContentGuard. (2004). MPEG-21 Right Expression Language (MPEG-REL), ISO/IEC 21000-5:2004 standard, http://www.contentguard.com/MPEGREL_home.asp

Computer Security Institute. (2007). CSI/FBI Computer Crime and Security Survey. http://www.gocsi.com/

Diao, Y., & Franklin, M. (2003). High-performance XML filtering: An overview of filter. *Int. Conf. on Data Engineering.*

Damiani, E., De Capitani di Vimercati, S., Paraboschi, S., & Samarati, P. (2002). A Fine-Grained Access Control System for XML Documents. *ACM Transactions on Information and System Security, 5*(2).

Dyer, J., G., Lindemann, M., Perez, R., Sailer, R., van Doorn, L., Smith, S. W., & Weingart, S. (2001). Building the IBM 4758 Secure Coprocessor. *IEEE Computer, 24*(10).

Fan, W., Chan, C. Y., & Garofalakis, M. (2004). Secure XML Querying with Security Views. *ACM SIGMOD Int. Conf. on Management of Data.*

Gabillon, A., & Bruno, E. (2001). Regulating access to XML documents. *IFIP Conf. on Database and Application Security.*

Gabillon, A. (2004). An Authorization Model for XML DataBases. *ACM Workshop on Secure Web Services.*

Giguère, E. (2001). Mobile Data Management: Challenges of Wireless and Offline Data Access. *Int. Conf. on Data Engineering.*

Green, T., Gupta, A., Miklau, G., Onizuka, M., & Suciu, D. (2004). Processing XML streams with deterministic automata and stream indexes. *ACM Transaction on Database Systems, 29*(4).

Grimen, G., Mönch, C., & Midtstraum, R. (2006). Building secure software-based DRM systems. *Norsk informatikkonferanse.*

Hauser, T., & Wenz, C. (2003). DRM Under Attack: Weaknesses in Existing Systems. *Digital Rights Management - Technological, Economic, Legal and Political Aspects.*

Hacigumus, H., Iyer, B., Li, C., & Mehrotra, S. (2002). Executing SQL over encrypted data in the database-service-provider model. *ACM SIGMOD Int. Conf. on Management of Data.*

Harrison, M. A., Ruzzo, W. L., & Ullman, J. D. (1976). Protection in Operating Systems. *Communication of the ACM, 19*(8).

He, J., & Wang, M. (2001). Cryptography and relational database management systems. *Int. Database Engineering and Applications Symposium.*

Hopcroft, J., & Ullman, J. (1979). *Introduction to Automata Theory, Languages and Computation.* Addison-Wesley Ed.

IFPI. International Federation of Phonographic Industry. http://www.ifpi.org/

International Standardization Organization. (1999). Integrated Circuit(s) Cards with Contacts - Part 7, ISO/IEC 7816-7, 1999.

Karlsson, J. S., Lal, A., Leung, C., Pham, T. (2001). IBM DB2 Everyplace: A Small Footprint Relational Database System. *Int. Conf. on Data Engineering.*

Mastercard Inc. MasterCard Open Data Storage (MODS). https://hsm2stl101.mastercard.net/public/login/ebusiness/smart_cards/one_smart_card/biz_opportunity/mods

Merkle, R. (1989). A Certified Digital Signature. *Advances in Cryptology.*

Melton, J. A., & Simon, R. (1993). *Understanding the new SQL: A Complete Guide.* Morgan Kaufmann Ed.

Microsoft Inc. Windows Microsoft Media 9. http://www.microsoft.com/windows/windowsmedia/.

Miklau, G., & Suciu, D. (2002). Cryptographically Enforced Conditional Access for XML. *Int. Workshop on the Web and Databases.*

Miklau, G., & Suciu, D. (2003). Controlling access to published data using cryptography. *Int. Conf. on Very Large Data Bases.*

Murata, M., Tozawa, A., & Kudo, M. (2003). XML Access Control Using Static Analysis. *ACM Conference on Computer and Communications Security.*

OASIS standard, eXtensible Access Control Markup Language (XACML), http://www.oasis-open.org/committees/xacml.

ODRL. The Open Digital Rights Language Initiative. http://odrl.net/.

Open Mobile Alliance. http://www.openmobile-alliance.org/

Oracle Corp. (2002). Oracle 9i Lite - Oracle Lite SQL Reference. Oracle Documentation.

Pucheral, P., Bouganim, L., Valduriez, P., & Bobineau, C. (2001). PicoDBMS: Scaling down database techniques for the smartcard. *VLDB Journal*, 10(2-3).

Ray, I., Ray, I., & Narasimhamurthi, N. (2002). A Cryptographic Solution to Implement Access Control in a Hierarchy and More. *ACM symposium on Access control models and technologies.*

Sandhu, R., Coyne, E. J., Feinstein, H. L., & Youman, C. E. (1996). Role-based access control models. *IEEE Computer*, 29(2).

SAX. A Simple API for XML. http://www.sax-project.org/.

Schneier, B. (1996). *Applied Cryptography, 2nd Edition*. John Wiley & Sons Ed.

Seshadri, P. (1999). Honey, I Shrunk the DBMS: Footprint, Mobility, and Beyond. *ACM SIGMOD Int. Conf. on Management of Data.*

SVP Alliance. Secure content anywhere, anytime. http://www.svpalliance.org/

Wang, Y., & Tan, K. L. (2001). A Scalable XML Access Control System. *Int. World Wide Web Conf.*

XMCL. (2001). XMCL - The eXtensible Media Commerce Language. http://www.xmcl.org/specification.html

XrML, eXtendible rights Markup Language. http://www.xrml.org/.

W3C DOM, DOM: Document Object Model. http://www.w3.org/DOM.

Vogt, H., Rohs, M., Kilian-Kehr, R. (2003). *Middleware for Communications, Chapter 16: Middleware for Smart Cards*. John Wiley and Sons Ed.

KEY TERMS

Access Control Models:

1. DAC: The Discretionary Access Control model (DAC) gives the creator of an object the privilege to define the policy regulating access to this object, and granted privileges can be transmitted between users.

2. MAC: The Mandatory Access Control Model (MAC) attaches security level to objects and clearance level to users in a centralized way.

3. RBAC: The Role Bases Access Control Model (RBAC) introduces the concepts of Roles and Teams to improve the administration of access control policies for a large population of cooperating users.

Access Control Policy: Set of rules regulating the use of the resources of a system, each rule granting or revoking the right to access some data or perform some action in that system.

Attackers:

1. Intruder: a person with no database privilege, who infiltrates a computer system and tries to extract valuable information from the database footprint on disk.

2. Insider: a person properly identified by the database server (i.e., a registered user) who tries to get information exceeding her own privileges. The owned privileges give her more abilities than the intruder to tamper the system and to deduce valuable unauthorized content.

3. Administrator: a person who has enough (usually all) privileges to administer a computer system (System Administrator) or a DBMS (Database Administrator or DBA). These privileges give her the opportunity to access the database files and to spy on the DBMS behavior (e.g., main memory monitoring).

Attacks:

1. Data Snooping: an attacker examines the (potentially encrypted) data, on disk, in the memory or on the communication links and deduces unauthorized information.

2. Data Spoofing: an attacker deletes or modifies (even randomly) some data, thereby potentially corrupting the evaluation of access and usage rules and/or query evaluation.

3. Data Splicing: an attacker replaces a valid data by another valid data. This attack may lead to reveal unauthorized data, corrupt the evaluation of access and usage rules.

4. Data Replaying: an attacker replaces a valid data by one of its older version. For instance, replaying old access rules may lead to disclose unauthorized data.

Secure Operating Environment: A combination of hardware and software modules providing a tamper-resistant storage and execution environment protecting against any form of snooping and tampering attacks.

Usage Control: complements access control with *contextual predicates*, conditioning the activation of a given privilege, and *obligations*, i.e., mandatory actions associated to the exercise of a privilege.

ENDNOTES

[1] Formerly Palladium, see http://en.wikipedia.org/wiki/Next-Generation_Secure_Computing_Base

[2] PlugDB is a research project funded by the French National Agency for Research (ANR). It involves the following partners: INRIA (the French National Research Institute in Computer Sciences), University of Versailles, SANTEOS (EHR provider), Gemalto (world leader in the smart card domain), ALDS (a home care association) and CoGITEY (a clinic with a section dedicated to elderly people).

[3] DMSP is an experimental project funded by the Yvelines district council in France. It experiments the PlugDB technology in the field and involves the same partners as PlugDB. See www-smis.inria.fr/~DMSP for details about these two projects.

[4] This choice has been made because the small on chip stable storage cannot accommodate a complete medical folder.

Section II
Core Techniques

Chapter X
A Summary of Recent and Old Results on the Security of the Diffie–Hellman Key Exchange Protocol in Finite Groups

Ionuţ Florescu
Stevens Institute of Technology, USA

ABSTRACT

Regarding fundamental protocols in cryptography, the Diffie-Hellman (Diffie and Hellman, 1976) public key exchange protocol is one of the oldest and most widely used in today's applications. Consequently, many specific cryptographic implementations depend on its security. Typically, an underlying (finite dimensional) group is selected to provide candidates for the key. The study of the security of the exchange as depending on the structure of the underlying group is even today poorly understood, with the most common approaches relying on the security of the Discrete Logarithm problem or on the size of the group. Recent developments bring to attention that the relationship is not necessarily valid and that more research is needed that will relate the underlying structure of the group and the security of the Diffie-Hellman exchange. In this chapter, we describe the problem in detail, we present the relationship with the previously studied Discrete Logarithm and Computational Diffie-Hellman problems, we expose the various concepts of security, and we introduce a new statistical concept specifically designed to serve the assessment of the security of the exchange.

INTRODUCTION

A key exchange protocol is any algorithm through which two parties A and B agree on a common key K_{AB}. Once the key is established, any further information shared between the parties is encoded, transmitted and decoded using the key K_{AB}. The protocol is secure if any third party C finds it extremely hard (impossible in practice) to identify the key.

In a public key exchange protocol the two parties agree on a common key pooled from a set S while communicating over an insecure channel. The difference is that all the information exchanged over the insecure channel as well as the set of possible keys S is known by the perpetrator C. If C cannot tell apart K_{AB} from any other value in the set S, given the information observed guarantees that it is computationally unfeasible to gain "any" partial information on the key.

The Diffie-Hellman key exchange protocol (Diffie and Hellman, 1976) is a primary example of a public key exchange protocol. In its most basic form, the protocol chooses a finite cyclic group $(G, \cdot)$ of order N, with generator g, where $\cdot$ denotes the group operation. In what follows we chose the multiplicative operation to denote the operation in the group, and thus the group G is generated by the powers of g (i.e., $G = \{g, g^2, ..., g^N\}$), symbolically $G = <g>$. Note that G, g and N are public information.

The participants in the information transfer, call them A and B, each randomly choose an integer $a \in \{1, 2, ..., N\}$ and $b \in \{1, 2, ..., N\}$ independently. Then A computes g^a, B computes g^b and exchange these elements of G over the insecure channel. Since each of A and B knows their respective values chosen (a and b) they can both compute g^{ab}, which, or a publicly known derivation K_{AB} of that, becomes the public key.

Any method of converting g^{ab} to K_{AB} is publicly known, and the security of the key K_{AB} is directly dependent on the security of g^{ab} thus, most articles consider g^{ab} as the established key of the exchange.

In the cryptology literature there are two concepts of security – the core security and the semantic security each leading to various security models. The semantic security and the related concepts come under the name of "provable security" Koblitz and Menezes (2004). The core security of the Diffie-Hellman key exchange protocol depends on the discrete logarithm problem, the computational Diffie-Hellman problem and the decision Diffie-Hellman problem. In this article we are concerned with the core security

of the exchange. We give a brief introduction to the discrete logarithm problem and the computational Diffie-Hellman problem, for more on these a reader can look at Koblitz and Menezes (2004) or Stinson (2005).

In the present work we are concerned with the practical security of this protocol. We investigate the various concepts of security and the known relationships between them. We interpret security in a probabilistic manner and devise a statistical test that will "assess" the security of the exchange in a given group. Our main objective is to find a test that would determine given two cyclic groups G_1 and G_2 with similar orders but perhaps different structures whether or not the security of the key exchange is the same using either group.

BACKGROUND

Traditionally the study of the security of the exchange was restricted to the verification of the following assumptions:

The Discrete Logarithm Assumption (DL): *For a cyclic group G, generated by g, we are given g and g^n, $n \in N$, the challenge is to compute n.*

The Computational Diffie-Hellman Assumption (CDH): *Given g, g^a, g^b it is hard to compute g^{ab}.*

Whether or not these assumptions are true in a given group generate the respective problems. For example we say that the Discrete Logarithm problem is hard in a given group if the DL assumption is satisfied in that group.

Clearly, if these assumptions are not satisfied then C, an adversary[1], can gain access to the key g^{ab}. The relationship between these two assumptions has been extensively studied. It is clear that the CDH assumption will not be satisfied in a group where finding the solution to the discrete logarithm problem is easy. In Maurer and Wolf (1999), Boneh and Lipton (1996), the authors show that in several settings the validity of the CDH assumption and the hardness of the Discrete Logarithm problem are in fact equivalent.

Unfortunately, the DL and the CDH assumptions are not enough to ensure security of the Diffie-Hellman key exchange protocol. Even if these assumptions are true, the eavesdropper C may still be able to gain useful information about g^{ab}. For example, if C can predict 90% of the bits in g^{ab} with high probability then for all intents and purposes the key exchange protocol is broken. Moreover, there exist protocols where the knowledge of even one bit will break its security (Casino electronic games). With the current state of knowledge we cannot be confident that assuming only CDH, a scenario like the one described above does not exist (Boneh (1998)).

It is clear that both assumptions are necessary for the security of the exchange but are they sufficient? It was evident that a new assumption needed to be formulated.

The Decision Diffie-Hellman Assumption (DDH) *Given g, g^a, g^b and an element z∈G it is hard to decide whether or not the key g^{ab} is more likely to be equal to z or to another random element of G.*

In this form the DDH assumption constitutes a sufficient condition for the security of the Diffie-Hellman key exchange protocol since it directly assesses the established key.

Furthermore, Joux and Nguyen (2003) construct groups based on elliptic curves where the DDH assumption is not satisfied while the CDH and the DL problems are proven to be equivalent and hard. This fact shows that the notions are not equivalent and prompts the necessity to directly check the validity of the DDH assumption for a given group.

The DDH assumption is assumed, either implicitly or explicitly in many cryptographic systems and protocols. Applications include: the many implementations of the DH key exchange itself (e.g., Diffie et al. (1992)), the El-Gamal encryption scheme El-Gamal (1984), the undeniable signatures algorithm Chaum and van Antwerpen (1989), Feldsman's verifiable secret sharing protocol Feldman (1987), Pedersen (1991), and most recently an implementation to the SSH file transfer protocol (Friedl et al., 2006). For a much more detailed list we point to Naor and Reingold (1997).

The DDH assumption in the form presented above is a little vague because of the use of the predicate, "hard to decide". Surprisingly, attempts to make the DDH assumption explicit were not made until late after its formulation in Diffie and Hellman (1976). The first ventures Boneh and Lipton (1996) use standard cryptographic machinery (Yao (1982); Goldwasser and Micali (1984)), to express the assumption in terms of *computational indistinguishability*. Put in this traditional cryptographic form it was discovered quickly by Stadler (1996) and independently by Naor and Reingold (1997) that if one assumes the existence of a polynomial time probabilistic algorithm which distinguishes the real key g^{ab} rom the other possible values even with a very small probability[2] (for all the possible inputs), then another polynomial time algorithm can be constructed from the first which will output g^{ab} with a very large (almost one) probability. The only requirement is that the size of the group is known, requirement lessened by Boneh (1998) which only requires finiteness of the group.

All this work points toward a more specific definition based entirely on the notion of *statistical significance*. Indeed, this fact materialized in a series of papers Canetti et al. (1999); Canetti et al. (2000); Friedlander and Shparlinski (2001); Vasco et al. (2004), which call this new form of the assumption the Diffie Hellman Indistinguishability assumption (DHI). We note that Gennaro et al. (2004); Joux and Nguyen (2003) use the same form except it continues to call it DDH. We point the reader to Håstad et al. (1999) for a detailed discussion on the concept of statistical significance versus computational significance; in the context of pseudo-random number generation.

In order to introduce this assumption we give the definition of a discrete uniformly distributed random variable.

Definition 1: *We say that a variable X has a discrete uniform distribution on the elements of a set S = {$a_1, a_2, ..., a_n$} if it can take any value in the set S equally likely, i.e.,*

$$\Pr ob(X = a_i) = \frac{1}{N}$$

for any i∈{1,2,...,N}. We will use the notation DU(S) to denote this distribution.

For the purpose of studying the security of the Diffie Hellman exchange we use:

The Diffie-Hellman Indistinguishability Assumption (DHI) *Given g, g^a, g^b the distribution of g^{ab} is indistinguishable from the Discrete Uniform distribution on the elements of G (DU(G)).*

The notion of indistinguishability used initially with this definition was the traditional, computational one. However, herein we use the statistical notion: two variables are indistinguishable if they have essentially the same distribution. Formally put, X_1 and X_1 are indistinguishable if their distribution functions $F_i(x) = \Pr ob(X_i \leq x)$ with $i=1,2$ have the property: $F_1(x) = F_2(x) \quad \forall x \in R \setminus (A_1 \cup A_2)$, where A_1, A_2 are the sets which contain the discontinuity points of F_1, respectively F_2.

In our specific case the state space is finite, therefore the distribution functions F_1 and F_2 are

just step functions with jumps in a compact set included in the real axis R, thus using the right continuity of the distribution functions, the usual definition translates here in equality everywhere. We conclude that in our context, statistical indistinguishability means that the variables have the same distribution.

We note that our version of the DHI assumption requires that the conditional distribution $g^{ab}|g^a, g^b, g$ be uniform while the previous articles Canetti et al. (1999); Canetti et al. (2000); Friedlander and Shparlinski (2001); Vasco et al. (2004); Gennaro et al. (2004); Joux and Nguyen (2003) require that the distribution of the entire triple $(g^{ab}, g^a, g^b|g)$ be Discrete Uniform on the elements of $G^3 = G \times G \times G$ ($DU(G^3)$). Given an outcome (x,y,z) we may write in Equation 1.

Under the original condition that a and b are $DU(\{1,...,N\})$ and using the fact that g is a generator for G, the distribution of $g^a, g^b|g$ is ($DU(G^2)$), thus the two formulations are perfectly equivalent.

In general it is known that *statistical indistinguishability* implies *computational indistinguishability*, but the reverse is not in general true, Goldreich (2001). The following lemma states the same result in our specific case using the assumptions presented in this section: DHI and DDH.

Lemma 2 *In a group G of order N, if the DHI assumption is true then the DDH assumption is true as well.*

Proof. Assume that DHI is true in G. Then for given g^a, g^b, the probability

$$\Pr ob(g^{ab} = z|g^a, g^b) = \frac{1}{N}$$

Equation 1.

$$\Pr ob(g^{ab} = z, g^a = x, g^b = y|g) = \Pr ob(g^{ab} = z|g^a = x, g^b = y, g) \Pr ob(g^a = x, g^b = y|g)$$

for any $z \in G$. This is the hardest possible scenario in the DDH assumption and hence the DDH assumption is satisfied.

This lemma says that in any group G, DHI is a stronger[3] condition than that of the DDH assumption. If we look at the statements in the two assumptions we find that DHI provides a statistical measure of hardness over the DDH assumption via the uniform distribution. For an additional discussion including a study of statistical independence of the established exchange key of the initial random choice we direct the interested reader to Florescu et al. (2007).

TESTING THE DIFFIE-HELLMAN ASSUMPTION

For every pair *(a,b)* there exist unique values (g^a, g^b), and correspondingly, a unique key g^{ab}. One question is: where does the probability enters into the picture?

Note that in this paper we are not considering the distribution of $(g^{ab} | g^a = x, g^b = y)$. That would be irrelevant and indeed the question above would be significant. We are instead looking at the distribution $(g^{ab} | g^a, g^b)$ and consider (g^a, g^b) as a pair of random variables.

It may be worth looking at this issue from a different perspective. Since a and b span the whole $G^2 = G \times G$ range we can see the key assigning process as a mapping from G^2 to G. Accordingly, studying the distribution of $(g^{ab} | g^a, g^b)$ and comparing it with the uniform distribution on the elements of G amounts to checking whether or not some subsets of values in G are more likely to be the key than others, as the pair *(a,b)* span the group. In other words if there exists a subset of G^2 such that the resulting key from that subset puts higher probabilities on certain values, then the conditional distribution $(g^{ab} | g^a, g^b)$ will not be uniform.

This approach is identical with the approach of Canetti et al (1999). Canetti et al (2000),

Friedlander and Shparlinski (2001), Gennaro et al. (2004) and many other papers. These papers consider the triple (g^a, g^b, g^{ab}) and its distribution in G^3. Since the key g^{ab} uniquely corresponds to (g^a, g^b) the points (g^a, g^b, g^{ab}) determine a two-dimensional surface included in a space of three dimensions. However, if this surface is randomly scattered in the cube G^3 then we can conclude that the key is secure. In other words no region in G^3 contains more points than any other similarly sized region in G^3. Owing to the equation (1) the two approaches are equivalent.

Why did we choose our approach and not the more traditional (and established) trivariate (joint) distribution approach? The answer is that our approach is more convenient for checking. It essentially amounts to verify whether a one dimensional distribution is close to the *DU(G)* while the more traditional procedure would require analyzing three-dimensional distributions.

Furthermore, for the one-dimensional distribution we have a well defined way to establish the measure of information present in the data: the entropy measure. We note that the same measure exists for three-dimensional distributions but it is more cumbersome to use in practical problems. We shall now introduce some notations and definitions.

Let X, Y, and Z be three discrete random variables taking values in the sets $\{x_1, x_2, ..., x_n\}$, $\{y_1, y_2, ..., y_m\}$, and $\{z_1, z_2, ..., z_l\}$ respectively.

Denote:

$$p(x_i, y_j, z_k) = \Pr ob\left(X = x_i, Y = y_j, Z = z_k\right)$$

the joint probability function corresponding to (X, Y, Z). We continue by using notations $p(x_i | y_j)$, $p(x_i, y_j | z_k)$, etc. for the conditional probability functions of $X|Y$, $(X,Y)|Z$, etc. Furthermore, assume that for all $k \in \{1, 2, ..., l\}$ the marginal distribution $p(z_k) = \Pr ob(Z = z_k) \neq 0$ to avoid complications conditioning on a set of measure zero.

Definition 3 (Entropy): *We define the joint and conditional* **measures of uncertainty**.

$$H(X,Y) =$$

$$-\sum_{i=1}^{n}\sum_{j=1}^{m}\sum_{k=1}^{l} p(x_i,y_j,z_k)\log p(x_i,y_j) \quad (2)$$

$$H(X,Y\,|\,Z) =$$

$$-\sum_{i=1}^{n}\sum_{j=1}^{m}\sum_{k=1}^{l} p(x_i,y_j,z_k)\log p(x_i,y_j\,|\,z_k)$$
$$(3),$$

with the convention $0(-\infty)=0$.

In the definition above we choose to work with the natural logarithm, however any other basis will be equivalent for our purpose due to the constant in the usual definition of the entropy function (see Shannon (1948)).

Remark 4 *In the definition of the entropy functions (2) and (3) we did not use the structure of the group G in any way, only the relative frequency of the elements in the group. This fact makes the methods based on the entropy function well suited for comparison between diverse groups. We will take advantage of this feature later in this work.*

The idea is to use the entropy function (3) in the sense of Kullback-Leibler divergence (Kullback and Leibler, 1951) as a measure of departure from the entropy calculated under the hypothesis of Uniform distribution. Specifically, using earlier notation, we wish to construct a statistical test that will check the validity of the following hypotheses:

H_0 : The distribution of $(g^{ab}\,|\,g^a,g^b)$ is DU(G)

H_a : The distribution of $(g^{ab}\,|\,g^a,g^b)$ is NOT DU(G)

$$(4)$$

Let us denote the elements of G as $\{g_1,g_2,...,g_N\}$. Suppose we can look at all the possible triples (g^a, g^b, g^{ab}) when $a,b \in \{1,2,...,N\}$ take all the possible values. Clearly, there are N^2 such possible triples and assuming that a and b are chosen at random, each such triple will have probability $1/N^2$. The last element in the triple g^{ab} will get mapped into N possible values (the elements of G). Thus, some values in G will be repeated. For an element $g_k \in G$ denote m_k the number of times g_k appears for g^{ab} among all the N^2 triples. We have that

$$\sum_{k} m_k = N^2.$$

For any pair (g^a,g^b) that corresponds to $g^{ab}= g_k$ we can then calculate the following conditional probability:

$$\mathrm{Prob}\big(g^a = g_i, g^b = g_j\,\big|\,g^{ab} = g_k\big) = \frac{1}{m_k}1_A(g_i,g_j,g_k),$$

where A is the set of all possible N^2 triples (g^a, g^b, g^{ab}), and we have used the notation $1_A(x)$ to denote the indicator function of the set $A \subset \Omega$, i.e., $1_A : \Omega \to \{0,1\}$ is given by:

$$1_A(x) = \begin{cases} 1 & if \quad x \in A \\ 0 & if \quad x \notin A \end{cases}$$

We can continue:

$$H\big(g^a,g^b\,\big|\,g^{ab}\big)$$

$$= -\sum_{i=1}^{N}\sum_{j=1}^{N}\sum_{k=1}^{N} p(g_i,g_j,g_k)\log p(g_i,g_j\,|\,g_k)$$

$$= -\sum_{k=1}^{N}\sum_{i,j=1}^{N} \frac{1}{N^2}\log\frac{1}{m_k}1_A(g_i,g_j,g_k)$$

$$= -\sum_{k=1}^{N} \frac{m_k}{N^2}\log\frac{1}{m_k} \quad (5)$$

Under the null hypothesis H_0, the distribution of $(g^{ab}|g^a, g^b)$ is uniform, therefore we should have all the k multiplicities equal. This automatically implies that $m_k = N$ for all k's and thus the entropy function in (5) becomes:

$$H\left(g^a, g^b \big| g^{ab}\right) = -\sum_{k=1}^{N} \frac{1}{N} \log \frac{1}{N} = \log N$$

The testing statistics is defined as:

$$T_N = H\left(g^a, g^b \big| g^{ab}\right) - \log N = \sum_{k=1}^{N} \frac{m_k}{N^2} \log m_k - \log N$$

$$(6)$$

This test is based on the whole set of values in G^2. Accordingly, if the value of the test equals zero then the null hypothesis H_0 is true, any other value of the test will support the alternative hypothesis. We summarize this result in the following:

Lemma 5 (Testing Procedure) *Using the previous notations if $T_N = 0$ then the DHI assumption is satisfied in a given group G.*

Remark 6 *In practice if we wish to calculate T_N we have to calculate all the possible values for and this will take longer than an exhaustive search. Thus calculating T_N is not practical, instead we have to estimate it. In turn this translates into calculating the distribution associated with the test statistic. We detail the estimation in the following.*

Assume that we can obtain a sample of n pairs $\{(a_i, b_i)\}_{i \in \{1,...,n\}}$ from $\{1, 2, ..., N\} \times \{1, 2, ..., N\}$. For each pair in the sample we calculate the triple $(g^{a_i}, g^{b_i}, g^{a_i b_i})$. Let n be the set of all the triplets in the sample.

Using (5) we can calculate an estimate of $H\left(g^a, g^b \big| g^{ab}\right)$ substituting the estimated probabilities:

$$\hat{p}_n(g_i, g_j, g_k) = \frac{k_{ijk}}{n} 1_{A_n}(g_i, g_j, g_k)$$

$$(7)$$

$$\hat{p}_n(g_i, g_j \mid g_k) = \frac{k_{ijk}}{n} 1_{A_n}(g_i, g_j, g_k)$$

where once again m_k denotes the multiplicity of g_k, but in the given sample of n observations. We took into account the possibility of obtaining repeated observations in the sample by multiplying with the factor k_{ijk}; which represents the number of times we see the same observation (g_i, g_j, g_k) in our sample.

The test statistic is:

$$T_n = -\sum_{i=1}^{n} \sum_{j=1}^{n} \sum_{k=1}^{n} \hat{p}(g_i, g_j, g_k) \log \hat{p}(g_i, g_j \mid g_k) - \log n$$

$$(8)$$

Now, we need to investigate the distribution of T_n under the null hypothesis H_0. Under the null, m_k's are the multiplicities of g_k's in a sample of size n drawn from the set $\{g_1, ... g_1, g_2, ..., g_2, ..., g_N, ..., g_N\}$ where each element in the group G is repeated N times.

Let us denote by $M_1, ..., M_N$ the multiplicities of the elements $\{g_1, ..., g_N\}$ in a sample of size n. It is not hard to show that the joint probability distribution of $(M_1, ..., M_N)$ is the so called *multivariate hypergeometric distribution*:

$$\mathrm{Prob}(M_1 = m_1, ..., M_N = m_N) = \frac{\binom{N}{m_1}\binom{N}{m_2} \cdots \binom{N}{m_N}}{\binom{N^2}{n}}$$

The test statistic under H_0 is:

$$T_N = \sum_{k=1}^{N} \frac{M_k}{n} \log M_k - \log n \qquad (9)$$

If we would be able to calculate the distribution of T_n knowing that $(M_1,...,M_N)$ is distributed as a multivariate hypergeometric random vector then we would be in position to reach the conclusion of the test of uniformity (4) by calculating the p-value of the test statistic (8) using this distribution.

Finding the distribution of the test statistic under H_0 in (9) is however not an easy task. This is the reason we propose the use of permutation testing for which knowledge of this distribution is not necessary.

The permutation testing procedure generates samples $(M_1,...,M_N)$ from the multivariate hypergeometric distribution. For each sample, it calculates the corresponding value of the test statistic under the null hypothesis as in (9). These values are obtained from the assumption that H_0 is true; this allow us to calculate the empirical distribution of our sample statistic T_n under the null hypothesis. The p-value of our test is given by the proportion of values as extreme or more than the one calculated in (8) using the group G.

A small p-value is evidence against the null hypothesis in (4) that the sample comes from a uniform distribution. We summarize the procedure below:

Testing procedure to determine validity of DHI for a group G

i. We take a sample of size n and we calculate the test statistic as in (8).

ii. We generate many test statistic values under the hypothesis H_0 using (9), and then we construct their empirical distribution.

iii. We calculate the p-value of the test as the proportion of values in the empirical distribution found in (ii) lower than the test value found using G in (i).

iv. If the p-value is small we reject the DHI assumption. If the p-value is big we did not find evidence that the DHI is not satisfied in the given group G.

Extension to Two or More Groups

We note that the absolute value of the test $|T_N|$ and its estimate $|T_n|$ represent a measure of departure from the Discrete Uniform distribution. The bigger the estimate the further is the distance from the uniform distribution and the weaker is the validity of the DHI assumption. Remark 4 also tells us that the nature of the group operation is irrelevant for the testing procedure. Therefore, we can use the test as a tool to compare the strength of the Diffie-Hellman key exchange protocol in two or more groups. In order to do so the order of the groups in the comparison needs to be similar and, more importantly, the sample size on the basis of which we calculate the permutation test needs to be the same. We take advantage of the ability to compare different groups in the next section.

TESTING THE DIFFIE-HELLMAN INDISTINGUISHABILITY ASSUMPTION IN THE MULTIPLICATIVE GROUP Z_p^*

We note that the simplest groups $(Z_p,+)$ cannot be tested with the current procedure since the discrete logarithm problem - a necessary condition for the security - is trivial to solve in these groups. We are going to look at the efficiency of the testing procedure for the finite groups included in Z_p^* with the multiplicative operation. We present the following examples as a way for checking the validity of the testing procedure.

Example 7 (A group where the DHI assumption does not hold.) *Consider $G = Z_p^*$ with p prime. It is known that computing Legendre symbol in this group gives a distinguisher against DDH (Gennaro et al. (2004)).*

Example 8 (A group where the DHI assumption is conjectured to hold) *We currently* *do not know any DDH distinguisher for a prime order subgroup of Z_p^*. Therefore, given p and q prime with q divisor of p−1 it is conjectured that in a subgroup of order q of Z_p^* the DDH assumption holds.*

We start with a given group G and using the test presented in the previous section we will test for the validity of the DHI assumption in that group G. This should provide a strong indication towards the security of the Diffie-Hellman key exchange protocol in that group.

The Rate of Convergence of the Testing Procedure

Firstly, we investigate the rate of convergence for our test. To do this we need to calculate the true value of T_N and thus we have to look at small groups.

We plot in Figure 1 the evolution of the test values with the size of the sample. This figure suggests that in order to get a good estimate for T_N the sample size will depend on the size of the group, e.g., we need a larger sample size for Z_{11903}^* than we need for Z_{1193}^*.

The figure points out another interesting fact. Following example we know that Z_p^* is not secure. However, it is conjectured that some groups of this type are more secure than others. It is also assumed that by increasing the size of the group one can make the group more secure.

We can see from the image presented that the second assertion is not true. Just increasing the size of the group does not make it more secure. Remembering that a smaller relative distance corresponds to closeness to the Discrete uniform distribution on the elements of G, we see from the Figure 1 that while Z_{11903}^*, the largest group, is the most secure of the three, the situation between the other two groups is not what we would have expected looking at the size of the group alone. Even though Z_{2131}^* is the larger group (almost twice the size), it is also less secure from the DHI

assumption perspective than Z_{1193}^*. This indicates that the choice of the group G rather than its size is essential for the security of the Diffie-Hellman key exchange protocol.

Comparison of the DHI Assumption Across Groups

Next we wanted to give an indication of groups that are more secure than others. It is known that considering only the Legendre symbol criterion the safest groups among Z_p^* are the ones obtained when p is a safe prime i.e., of the form $p=2q+1$ where q is another prime Menezes et al. (1996). We shall call any such group a *safe group*.

We tested this theory for a large set of Z_p^* groups with varying p's. We looked at all primes between 2000 and 4000, and again for primes between 9000 and 11000. The reason for the two separate segments of primes is that we expect some sort of consistency between them. We show the distribution of the test values for these groups separated into safe and not safe primes in Figures 2 and 3.

First, we notice that the behavior of primes in the range 2000 to 4000 is very similar with the primes for the higher range 9000 to 11000. Second, in both ranges we see the same conclusion applies, the safe prime groups are more secure than any other groups. However, the test estimate obtained for each of the safe prime groups is significantly different from zero therefore there is no safe group in the ranges given for which the DHI assumption is verified. This seems to confirm the assertion in the Example 7.

Next, we look to Example 8. We will use our test for the prime subgroups of each of the safe primes in the range 9000 to 11000. More specifically, we look at each Z_p^* with p a safe prime, and we construct the prime subgroup of order q in each such group. Then we test the DHI assumption in each subgroup thus constructed. The values obtained for the distances are plotted in the upper histogram of Figure 4. *We mention*

Figure 1. Comparison of the test values for different sample sizes and Z_p^* 's

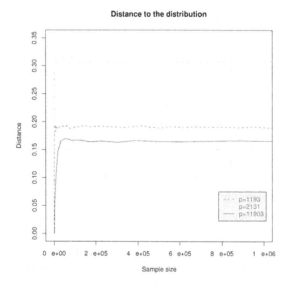

Figure 2. Histogram of all the test values for Z_p^* with 2000<p<4000. Values closer to zero represent safer groups for DH exchange.

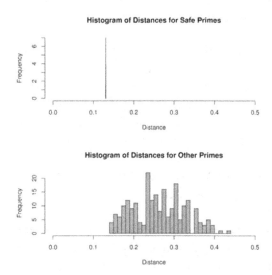

Figure 3. Histograms of test values obtained for Z_p^* with 9000<p<11000. Values closer to zero represent safer groups for DH exchange.

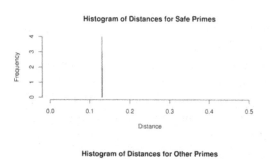

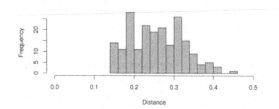

Figure 4. Comparing values of the test for different type of groups when 9000<p<11000. On top, we plot values for prime subgroups of Z_p^* when p is a safe prime. Middle, we plot values for Z_p^* when p is a safe prime. On bottom, we plot values for all the other groups Z_p^* in the range given. Values closer to zero represent better groups for DH exchange.

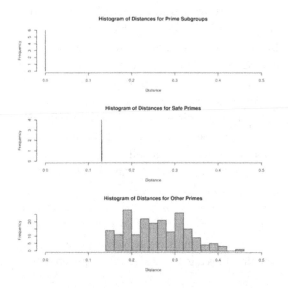

that the behavior of the test values for primes between 2000 and 4000 was very similar, and for space consideration we omit the corresponding plot. All the values are obtained using the same sample size $n = 8 \times 10^6$. The reason for this particular value is that while the groups themselves are in the range 9000 to 11000, the subgroups are of order 4500 to 5500.

It is remarkable to see that these subgroups are clearly safer for the DH exchange than any other groups plotted in the picture. The results seem to confirm the conjecture in the Example 8.. *The actual test of uniformity was rejected, but we needed a very large sample size almost equal to the maximum value N^2.*

For a better comparison we plotted in Figure 5 only the values obtained for the prime subgroups of the Z_p^* with p a safe prime (top) and the histogram of the values obtained for the Z_p^* groups, p a safe prime between 9000 and 11000 (bottom).

It is remarkable the closeness of these values to each other considering that the order of the group varies between 9000 and 11000 a 20% variation in size. This is an encouraging fact, which suggests that for even larger p's we will see the same sort of consistency in the values. This will imply that groups with the same operational structure will have similar behavior from the point of view of the Diffie-Hellman security. However, there is a variation in the values as illustrated in the Figure 6 plotting the histogram of the values obtained for the prime subgroup of Z_p^* groups, with p a safe prime varying between 9000 and 11000.

Furthermore, in Figure 7 we plot the test values versus the size of the group from which the prime subgroup originated. We can immediately see that as the size of the group increases the exchange tends to become more secure as measured by our test. This increases our belief in the test results and brings evidence that as the size of the group increases **and the structure of the underlying group remains the same** the security of the exchange increases as well.

Figure 5. A more detailed comparison of the previous image (Fig. 4). We compare the prime subgroups with the corresponding safe groups. Values closer to zero represent safer groups for DH exchange.

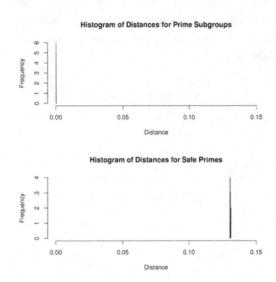

Figure 6. A blowup of the histogram of the values for the prime subgroups in the safe primes. Note the values are close to zero but not equal to zero.

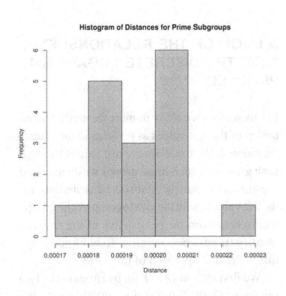

Figure 7. Here we are showing that as the size of the group increases the values of the test do in fact decrease. Here we plot the corresponding values for the histogram in Figure 6. We note that the test values for this part were estimated using the same sample size (8 million) to insure that the test values are comparable and that variability of the test values is the same regardless of the size of the group.

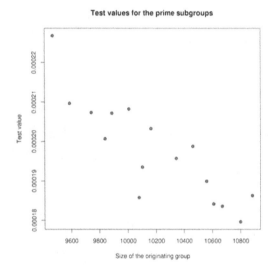

A LOOK OF THE RELATIONSHIP WITH THE DISCRETE LOGARITHM PROBLEM

In this section we study in more depth the distribution of the test values as p varies in the ranges considered. We calculate the test values for each such group (for such small groups we do not need to estimate or construct statistical distributions for the test values), with the idea to compare the groups themselves from the perspective of the test and identify (if possible) patterns. To our knowledge this is the first approach of this kind.

We first look to $\left(Z_{p}^{*},\cdot\right)$, for p primes in the two ranges $p \in (2000, 4000)$ and $p \in (9000, 11000)$. We plot the test values in the Figure 8.

It is known – due to the existence of the Pohlig-Hellman algorithm[4] that in all of these groups the Discrete Logarithm problem is easy and therefore the Diffie Hellman exchange should be breakable. It is also *conjectured* that the actual security depends on the size of the largest factor in the decomposition of $p-1$[5]. For this reason it is believed that the "most secure" groups among $\left(Z_{p}^{*},\cdot\right)$ are the ones generated by the safe primes.

In our case we consider the security of the Diffie Hellman exchange. Since the Discrete Logarithm assumption is a necessary condition for this security we expect that our test will identify these assertions and by using our test we will be able to answer questions related to the DL problem.

Figure 8 presents the test values vs. the size of the largest prime factor in the decomposition of $p-1 = q_1 q_2 ... q_k$. We can immediately see that the structure of the test values for the two ranges is very similar. In both of these images, points corresponding to values closer to 0 on the y axis represent groups that are more secure for the DH exchange.

Note that while the points in the lower right corner of the image correspond indeed to the safe primes and they are clearly more secure than the other groups as the popular belief would tell us, we can also see that there exist certain groups which have a small factor (lower left corner) and yet they are comparably secure.

This is investigated further in the Figure 9 where we plot the test values obtained for each group versus the number of factors in the decomposition of $p-1$. While we can see more clearly now that the groups corresponding to the safe primes ($x=2$ factors in the plot) are indeed more secure than all the other groups, we also find that generally as the number of factors in the decomposition increases the security decreases.

Once again we remark the closeness of the two plots in Figure 9. Based on the two pair of plots it would seem that both the number of factors and the size of the largest factor are important elements when considering the security of the exchange.

Figure 8. On the x axis we plot the biggest factor in the decomposition of p−1. Values closer to zero on the y-axis represent safer groups for DH exchange.

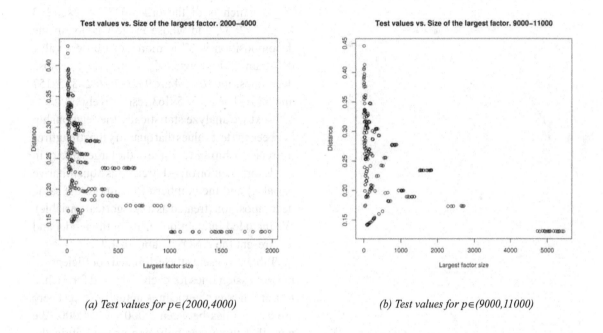

(a) Test values for p∈(2000,4000) (b) Test values for p∈(9000,11000)

Figure 9. On the x axis we plot the number of factors in the decomposition of p−1. Values closer to zero represent safer groups for DH exchange.

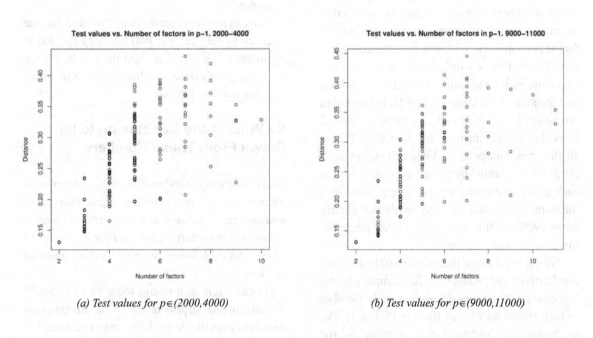

(a) Test values for p∈(2000,4000) (b) Test values for p∈(9000,11000)

Figure 10. This is the same image as Figure 8b with the respective points corresponding to number of factors in the decomposition of p−1 identified.

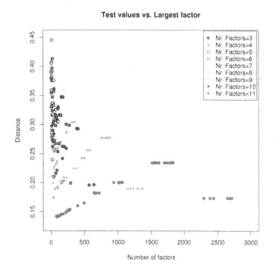

But now we are dealing with a statistical problem: trying to relate two determining factors to the variable that quantifies the security of the exchange. There probably exist other factors that are important but let us concentrate on these two for the current work. We know from the statistical theory that if there would be no interaction between the number of factors in the decomposition and the size of the largest factor then we should see points inside each category close to parallel lines. For exemplification we plotted in Figure 10 the same image as in Figure 9(b), but with the points separated by the number of factors in each group. We eliminated the safe groups from the comparison and we only made the picture for $p \in (9000, 11000)$ since for the other range the image looks very similar.

We can start to see that there must be interaction between the two factors. To exemplify better we separated the points depending on the number of factors and we plotted them in Figure 11. We see better that the determining elements for the

security of the DH exchange seem to be correlated (they are interacting).

As an example of such discrepancy the group Z_{9473} which is of the order $9473-1=2 \times 2 \times 2 \times 2 \times 2 \times 2 \times 2 \times 2 \times 2 \times 37$, and whose biggest factor in the decomposition is 37 is more secure (test value 0.2) than both groups: Z_{9421} and Z_{9781}, whose decompositions of $p-1$ are $9421-1=2 \times 2 \times 3 \times 5 \times 157$ and $9781-1=2 \times 2 \times 3 \times 5 \times 163$ respectively[6].

Next we analyze statistically the relationship between the test values that quantify the strength of the relationship and the size of the largest factor in the decomposition of $p-1$ (treated as a quantitative variable) and the number of factors in the same decomposition (treated as a categorical variable). We included interaction terms in the model and we present the ANOVA table in Table 1.

Table 2 presents the estimated coefficients of the regression lines for each level, and for each, a test of whether the mean is actually zero. There are 218 primes between 9,000 and 11,000. We note that there was only one prime within the range whose $p-1$ decomposition had 10 factors thus the interaction for that level could not be estimated.

We can see very clearly from the table that the interaction between the two factors analyzed is significant. We do not present the results for the other range of primes studied 2000−4000 since they are entirely similar.

So What is the Conclusion to be Drawn From These Numbers?

These numbers show that the interaction between the number of factors in the decomposition of p−1 and the size of the largest factor in the decomposition is statistically significant for the security of the Diffie-Hellman security as quantified by our test.

In plain terms, it would seem natural that as the size of the largest factor in the decomposition increases the group becomes more complex and therefore it is more secure. Likewise, as the

Figure 11. If the two determining elements (number of factors and the size of the largest factor in the decomposition of p−1 are independent we should see points of the same color close to parallel lines.

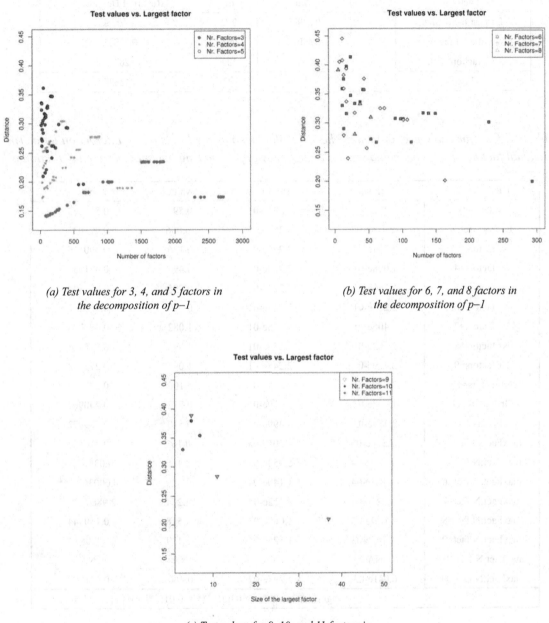

(a) Test values for 3, 4, and 5 factors in
the decomposition of p−1

(b) Test values for 6, 7, and 8 factors in
the decomposition of p−1

(c) Test values for 9, 10, and 11 factors in
the decomposition of p−1

Table 1. ANOVA table for the relationship between the size of the largest factor, the number of factors, and the test values

Factors	df	Deviance	df	Residual Deviance
Largest factor size	1	0.37997	216	0.77629
Number of factors	9	0.41977	207	0.35652
Interaction term	8	0.08881	199	0.26772
Error			217	1.15626

Table 2. Effects for each level of factor. The semicolon denotes the levels of the interaction term. The individual factors have to be included even though they appear not significant since the interaction is.

Factor levels	Estimate	Std. Error	t-values	p-values
(Intercept)	1.322e-01	2.221e-01	0.595	0.552573
Largest factor	-2.718e-07	4.353e-05	-0.006	0.995025
Nr factors=3	2.794e-02	2.223e-01	0.126	0.900116
Nr factors=4	1.098e-01	2.222e-01	0.494	0.621938
Nr factors=5	1.766e-01	2.223e-01	0.795	0.427804
Nr factors=6	2.202e-01	2.224e-01	0.990	0.323292
Nr factors=7	2.406e-01	2.225e-01	1.082	0.280778
Nr factors=8	2.462e-01	2.253e-01	1.093	0.275831
Nr factors=9	2.459e-01	2.248e-01	1.094	0.275293
Nr factors=10	2.475e-01	2.249e-01	1.100	0.272574
Nr factors=11	1.798e-01	2.329e-01	0.772	0.440964
maxFact:N.fact=3	2.375e-05	4.399e-05	0.540	0.589972
maxFact:N.fact=4	-7.348e-06	4.505e-05	-0.163	0.870586
maxFact:N.fact=5	-1.260e-04	5.954e-05	-2.115	0.035637 *
maxFact:N.fact=6	-4.137e-04	1.140e-04	-3.629	0.000362 ***
maxFact:N.fact=7	-9.027e-04	2.112e-04	-4.274	2.98e-05***
maxFact:N.fact=8	-1.609e-03	1.060e-03	-1.518	0.130544
maxFact:N.fact=9	-4.757e-03	1.525e-03	-3.119	0.002087 **
maxFact:N.fact=10	NA	NA	NA	NA
maxFact:N.fact=11	6.041e-03	1.297e-02	0.466	0.641823
Signif. codes: '***' = 0.001; '**'= 0.01; '*' = 0.05; '.' = 0.1				

number of factors in the decomposition increases, there are more equations to solve modulo each factor therefore having a larger number intuitively would also increase the security.

However, as the results in the table show that is not necessarily so, and since the interaction between the two is significant the combination of the two factors is important and the seemingly logical statements presented are not necessarily true.

FUTURE TRENDS

The papers studying statistical aspects of the distribution of the key of the Diffie-Hellmann exchange are generally concerned with the limiting distribution as the size of the underlying group converges to infinity. However, in practice we do not work with infinite groups and the question of how fast the key distribution converges to infinity is valid and of significant interest. We hope we convinced the reader that the rate of convergence is not uniform across types of the groups and that some group structures lead to a much faster convergence than others.

However, it would be much more interesting if we could follow the analysis and observe similar conclusions for very large primes, typically used in cryptography (with 2^{128}, 2^{512} or even 2^{1024} elements). The use of our testing procedure, ad-literam as in the current work prevents us from analyzing such large groups directly.

In the future, we plan to investigate directions of circumventing the permutation testing approach, thus eliminating the need for the sample generation process and transforming the methodology into a practical procedure applicable to large groups. For this purpose several directions are possible. One direction is to approximate the distribution of the test in (9) with a multinomial distribution, then use a multivariate normal distribution as a second approximation. In other words use a theoretical approximation instead of an empirical one. This would give us an approximate distribution of the test statistic under the null hypothesis, which should allow us to calculate the *p*-value of the test directly without the need of the permutation testing.

Another direction is to put together outcomes into coarser groups and look at the distribution of these groups of outcomes. This idea is similar with the approach of Canetti et al. (1999) and Banks et al. (2006), and will allow us to speed up the procedure in order to apply it to much larger groups.

A third direction is to look at the distribution of the binary representation of prime subgroups of a large group and compare the new resulting groups.

If the computing power suffices or if any of these directions would prove valid the resulting test procedure will allow a comparison between the prime subgroup of a large $\left(Z_p^*, \cdot \right)$ which we asserted to be secure and a similarly sized finite group defined using elliptical curves. This would answer a question of undeniable importance: are the groups constructed using elliptical curves potentially more secure than simpler structure groups?

CONCLUSION

This paper **does not** break or gives an algorithm to break the Diffie-Hellman exchange. What we do is analyze empirically how hard would it be to break the exchange, *on average, on any random inputs drawn from the underlying group*. The groups under study were small in order (very far from the typical cryptographic groups used in practice), but we give compelling evidence that the security of the exchange tends to be dependent on the structure of the underlying groups. That structure can be recovered and rediscovered over and over as the group size increases.

We have further studied the relationship between the security of the Diffie Hellman public key exchange protocol and the structure of the underlying group. We looked at groups were the protocol is provable not secure (of the type $\left(Z_p^*, \cdot\right)$). We have found compelling evidence that breaking it (in the sense of actually finding the key) is dependent not only on the size of the largest factor in the decomposition of $p-1$ but also on the number of terms in the decomposition. Furthermore, the relationship is not straightforward (as either one increases the security increases) since the interaction between these two determining factors is statistically significant. This means that it is entirely possible to have a group with large prime factor in the decomposition and a large number of terms in the decomposition of $p-1$ and yet to be easier to break (on average for random inputs) than another groups where both these factors are smaller but they interact in a different way.

We show using statistical arguments that the prime subgroups of the groups of type $\left(Z_p^*, \cdot\right)$ are the most secure groups we have studied. Furthermore, if one assumes that the structure of the group from which the subgroups are drawn remains the same, increasing the group's size indeed translates into increasing the security of the Diffie-Hellman exchange as well.

REFERENCES

Banks, W., Friedlander, J., Konyagin, S., and Shparlinski, I. (2006). Incomplete exponential sums and Diffie-Hellman triples. *Math. Proc. Cambridge Philos. Soc. 140*, 193–206.

Boneh, D. (1998). The Decision Diffie-Hellman problem. *Lecture Notes in Computer Science 1423*, 48–63.

Boneh, D., & Lipton, R. J. (1996). Algorithms for black-box fields and their application to cryptography (extended abstract). In *CRYPTO '96: Proceedings of the 16th Annual International Cryptology Conference on Advances in Cryptology*, London, UK, pp. 283–297. Springer-Verlag.

Canetti, R., Friedlander, J., Konyagin, S., Larsen, M., Lieman, D, & Shparlinski, I. (2000). On the statistical properties of Diffie-Hellman distributions. *Israel Journal of Mathematics 120*(part A), 23–46.

Canetti, R., Friedlander, J., & Shparlinski, I. (1999). On certain exponential sums and the distribution of Diffie-Hellman triples. *J. London Math. Soc. 59*, 799–812.

Chaum, D., & van Antwerpen, H. (1989). Undeniable signatures. In *CRYPTO '89: Proceedings on Advances in cryptology*, New York, NY, USA, pp. 212–216. Springer-Verlag New York, Inc.

Diffie, W., & Hellman, M. (1976). New directions in cryptography. *IEEE Transactions on Information Theory 22*(6), 644–654.

Diffie, W., Oorschot, P. C. V., & Wiener, M. J. (1992). Authentication and authenticated key exchanges. *Des. Codes Cryptography 2*(2), 107–125.

El-Gamal, T. (1984). *Cryptography and logarithms over finite fields*. Ph. D. thesis, Elec. Eng. Dept., Stanford Univ., Stanford, CA.

Feldman, P. (1987). A practical scheme for non-interactive verifiable secret sharing. In *Proc. of the 28th FOCS*, pp. 427–437. IEEE.

Florescu, I., A. Myasnikov and A. Mahalanobis (2007) Statistical analysis of the Diffie-Hellman key exchange protocol in a finite group. arXiv: math/0702155v1

Friedl, M., Provos, N., & Simpson, W. (2006). Diffie-Hellman group exchange for the secure shell (SSH) transport layer protocol. Internet proposed standard RFC 4419.

Friedlander, J., & Shparlinski, I. (2001). On the distribution of Diffie-Hellman triples with sparse exponents. *SIAM Journal on Discrete Mathematics, 14*, 162–169.

Gennaro, R., Krawczyk, H., & Rabin, T. (2004). Secure hashed diffie-hellman over non-ddh groups. In *Advances in Cryptology - EUROCRYPT 2004*, Lecture Notes in Computer Science, pp. 361–381. Springer Berlin / Heidelberg.

Goldreich, O. (2001). *Foundations of Cryptography: Basic Techniques*, 1. Cambridge University Press.

Goldwasser, S., & Micali, S. (1984). Probabilistic encryption. *Journal of Computer and System Sciences, 28*, 270–299.

Håstad, J., Impagliazzo, R., Levin, L. A., & Luby, M. (1999). A pseudorandom generator from any one-way function. *SIAM J. Comput., 28*(4), 1364–1396.

Joux, A., & Nguyen, K. (2003). Separating Decision Diffie-Hellman from Computational Diffie-Hellman in cryptographic groups. *Journal of Cryptology, 16*, 239–247.

Koblitz, N., & Menezes, A. J. (2004). Another look at "Provable Security". Technical report, http://eprint.iacr.org/2004/152.

Kullback, S., & Leibler, R. A. (1951). On information and sufficiency. *Annals of Mathematical Statistics,* (22), 79–86.

Maurer, U. M., & Wolf, S. (1999). The relationship between breaking the diffie–hellman protocol and computing discrete logarithms. *SIAM J. Comput., 28*(5), 1689–1721.

Menezes, A. J., Vanstone, S. A., & Oorschot, P. C. V. (1996). *Handbook of Applied Cryptography*. CRC Pr Llc.

Naor, M., & Reingold, O. (1997). Number-theoretic constructions of efficient pseudo-random functions. In *FOCS '97: Proceedings of the 38th Annual Symposium on Foundations of Computer Science (FOCS '97)*, Washington, DC, USA, pp. 458. IEEE Computer Society.

Pedersen, T. P. (1991). Distributed provers with applications to undeniable signatures. In *Advances in Cryptology - EUROCRYPT '91: Workshop on the Theory and Application of Cryptographic Techniques*. Lecture Notes in Computer Science, Brighton, UK, pp. 221–242.

Rokhlin, V. A. (1967). Lectures on the entropy theory of measure-preserving transformations. *Russian Mathematical Survey, 22*(5), 1–52.

Shannon, C. E. (1948). A mathematical theory of communication. *The Bell System Technical Journal, 27*, 379–423, 623–656.

Stadler, M. (1996). Publicly verifiable secret sharing. In *Advances in Cryptology - EUROCRYPT '96*, 1070 of *Lecture Notes in Computer Science*, pp. 190–199.

Stinson, D. R. (2005). *Cryptography: Theory and Practice* (3 ed.), Volume 36 of *Discrete Mathematics and Its Applications*. University of Waterloo, Ontario, Canada: CRC. Press Online.

Vasco, M. I. G., Näslund, M., & Shparlinski, I. (2004). New results on the hardness of Diffie-Hellman bits. In *Proc. Intern. Workshop on Public Key Cryptography*, Volume 2947 of *Lect. Notes in Comp. Sci.*, Singapore, pp. 159–172. Springer-Verlag.

Yao, A. C. (1982). Theory and application of trapdoor functions. In *Proceedings of the 23rd IEEE Symposium on Foundations of Computer Science*, pp. 80–91.

KEY TERMS

Cryptographic Key: A piece of information that controls the operation of a cryptographic algorithm.

Encryption Key: A piece of information used to specify the particular transformation of plaintext into ciphertext, or vice versa during the encryption/decryption process.

Generator of a Cyclic Group: An element *g* such that all the elements of the group are generated by successive applications of the group operation to *g* itself. Not all the elements in a group are generators.

p-Value of a Test: the probability of obtaining as extreme or more extreme values as the result of the experiment assuming that the null hypothesis is true. Numbers close to *0* are evidence against the null hypothesis (it is unlikely to see such numbers if the null hypothesis would be true).

Prime Group: A group that contains no subgroups except for the trivial subgroup. A *prime subgroup* is a subgroup of a group that contains no further subgroups except for the trivial subgroup. An example is $\{\hat{1}, \hat{4}\}$ included in $\left(Z_5^*, \cdot\right)$

Statistically Indistinguishable Random Variables: Are two or more random variable whose distribution is identical almost everywhere (with the possible exception of a set of probability measure zero).

Subgroup of a Group: A set of elements from the initial group which together form a smaller goup structure included in the original group (i.e, the operation stays in the subgroup, the identity and the inverse elements are in the subgroup) . An example is the trivial subgroup $\{\hat{1}\}$.

ENDNOTES

[1] There are various concepts of adversary in cryptographic literature, the power and authority they have. In this article we assume that our adversary is a passive eavesdropper.

[2] But not negligible. For the sake of completeness we give here the whole definition. It is presented in the footnote since it is not relevant to our approach at all. Suppose that the group *G* where the exchange takes place has order *N* and $n = \log_2 N$. It is said that a probabilistic algorithm *A* decides on the right key with small (non-negligible) probability if there exist a polynomial expression $p(\cdot)$ such that for any $r \in G$:

$$\left|\text{Pr}ob(A \quad outputs \quad g^{ab}) - \text{Pr}ob(A \quad outputs \quad r)\right| > \frac{1}{p(n)}$$

[3] or at least as strong

[4] which computes the Legendre symbol in these groups and therefore gives a distinguisher against DDH (see Genaro et al. (2004))

[5] This is due to the nature of the algorithm

[6] the test values obtained for these two later groups are very close to each other 0.3475897 and 0.3476914.

Chapter XI
Secret Sharing with k–Dimensional Access Structure

Guojun Wang
Central South University, China

Yirong Wu
Central South University, China

Geyong Min
University of Bradford, UK

Ronghua Shi
Central South University, China

ABSTRACT

Secret sharing aims at distributing and sharing a secret among a group of participants efficiently. In this chapter, we propose a plane-based access structure for secret sharing. Specifically, if any two among a set of three participants in a graph contain an edge, these participants constitute a prohibited structure which is not able to recover the master key. Otherwise, the set of three participants constitute an access structure which can recover the master key. Subsequently, we extend the plane-based scheme and propose a generic k-dimensional secret sharing scheme. Finally, we analyze the performance of the proposed scheme and reveal its advantages compared to existing schemes.

INTRODUCTION

Secret sharing is an important method of information security and data secrecy, which is a vital branch of cryptology. Moreover, it plays a key role in secure storage and secure transmission of important information. Secret sharing aims at distributing and sharing a secret among a number of participants efficiently and the secret can be recovered on condition that the pre-specified and authorized subsets of participants can pool their shares, otherwise, the secret cannot be recovered. Secret sharing mechanism is especially suitable for applications with many partners involved.

(Shamir, 1979; Blackley, 1979) respectively proposed the original mechanisms of secret sharing, both of which are (k, n) threshold schemes. The scheme in (Shamir, 1979) is based on Lagrange

Figure 1. (k, n) threshold secret sharing mechanism

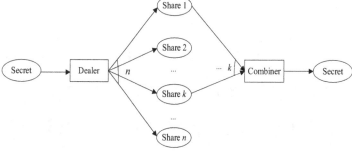

interpolation polynomial while the scheme in (Blackley, 1979) is based on projection geometry theory. In a (k, n) threshold secret sharing scheme, as shown in Figure 1, the trusted dealer delivers the distinct secret shares to n participants. At least k or more participants can pool their secret shares in order to reconstruct the secret, but only k-1 or fewer shares cannot.

The rest of this chapter is organized as follows: Section 2 introduces the research background of secret sharing, including (k, n) threshold secret sharing and general access structure secret sharing. Section 3 introduces three graph-based secret sharing schemes. A plane-based general access structure for secret sharing is proposed in Section 4. In Section 5, we propose a generic k-dimensional secret sharing scheme. Finally, Section 6 presents the conclusion and future work.

BACKGROUND: SECRET SHARING SCHEMES

In this section, we firstly introduce (k, n) threshold secret sharing schemes and then describe the secret sharing schemes based on general access structure.

(k, n) Threshold Secret Sharing Schemes

Many methods are available to implement (k, n) threshold secret sharing, such as Lagrange polynomial interpolation (Shamir, 1979), projection geometry theory (Blackley, 1979), Vector Space (Stmson, 1995; Xu, 2002), and Chinese Remainder Theorem (Pei, 2002). The commonly used scheme in (Shamir, 1979), which is based on Lagrange interpolation polynomial, is introduced as follows:

Given the master key K, the dealer selects at random a k-1 degree polynomial $f(x)=a_0+a_1x+a_2x^2+...+a_{k-1}x^{k-1}$, where $a_0=K$.

Let $x_1, x_2, ..., x_n$ be n distinct numbers which are publicly known to every participant. Then the dealer evaluates: $y_1=f(x_1), y_2=f(x_2), ..., y_n=f(x_n)$, and delivers them to each participant over a secure channel.

At least k participants are required to use the Lagrange interpolation polynomial to recover the secret. With the knowledge of the set of k points (x_i, y_i), the k-1 degree polynomial $f(x)$ can be uniquely determined below

$$f(x) = \sum_{i=1}^{k} y_i \prod_{j=1, j\neq i}^{k} \frac{x - x_j}{x_i - x_j}.$$

So,

$$K = f(0) = \sum_{i=1}^{k} y_i \prod_{j=1, j \neq i}^{k} \frac{0 - x_j}{x_i - x_j}.$$

Obviously, if only *k*-1 or fewer shares are shown, there is no information about *K* available and thus it cannot be recovered.

Secret Sharing Schemes Based on General Access Structure

With the development of secret sharing theory, (Guo, 2004; Guo 2005; Pang & Jiang, 2006; Pang & Li, 2006; Shieh, 1994; Sun, 1996; Sun, 1997) proposed many secret sharing schemes based on general access structure. For instance, (Ito, 1987) proposed a general method for secret sharing which allows a master key to be shared among a finite set of participants in such a way that only certain pre-specified subsets of participants can recover the master key. Let *P* be the set of participants. The subset of participants that can reconstruct the master key in this way is called an access structure (denoted by Γ). The subset of participants that cannot reconstruct the master key is called a prohibited structure (denoted by Δ). Obviously, Γ is monotonically increasing and Δ is monotonically decreasing. That is:

If $A \in \Gamma$ and $A \subseteq B \subseteq P$, then $B \in \Gamma$;
If $A \in \Delta$ and $B \subseteq A \subseteq P$, then $B \in \Delta$.

So, secret sharing schemes are classified into three categories:

(i) A secret sharing scheme for the access structure Γ is a method of sharing a master key among a finite set of participants in such a way that only the subsets of participants in Γ can recover the master key while others cannot. That is, $\Delta = 2^P / \Gamma$ is implied (2^P denotes the power set of *P*).

(ii) A secret sharing scheme for the prohibited structure Δ is a method of sharing a master key among a finite set of participants in such a way that the subsets of participants in Δ cannot recover the master key while others can. That is, $\Gamma = 2^P / \Delta$ is implied.

(iii) A secret sharing scheme for the mixed structure ($\Gamma = \{B \mid A \in S \,\&\&\, A \subseteq B \subseteq P\}$ and $\Delta = \{A \in R \,\&\&\, B \subseteq A \subseteq P\}$) is a method of sharing a master key among a finite set of participants in such a way that subsets of participants in Γ can recover the master key but the subsets of participants in Δ cannot recover the master key. That is, $\Gamma \cap \Delta = \varnothing \,\&\&\, \Gamma \cup \Delta \subseteq 2^P$.

It is difficult to efficiently construct a generic secret sharing scheme suitable for all access structures due to their irregular nature. Therefore, some researchers have focused only on the graph-based access/prohibited structures. In the next section, three graph-based schemes are introduced.

GRAPH-BASED GENERAL ACCESS STRUCTURE FOR SECRET SHARING

Secret Sharing in Graph-Based Access Structure

(Sun, 1996) proposed a scheme which is based on the assumptions that the pairs of participants corresponding to edges in a graph can compute the master key but the pairs of participants corresponding to non-edges in the graph cannot. The access structure contains the pairs of participants corresponding to edges, and the prohibited structure contains the pairs of participants corresponding to non-edges.

Given a graph *G* where a vertex represents a participant and an edge represents a qualified pair of participants, *P* denotes the set of *n* participants who share the master key: $K = k_1 + k_2 + ... + k_n \,(mod$

q), *E* denotes the set of edges, *S* denotes the set of pairs of participants corresponding to edges, and *R* denotes the set of pairs of participants corresponding to non-edges. So, the access structure $\Gamma = \{B \mid A \in S \ \&\& \ A \subseteq B \subseteq P\}$ and the prohibited structure $\Delta = \{A \in R \ \&\& \ B \subseteq A \subseteq P\}$.

Firstly, construct *n* conventional (2, *n*) threshold schemes, namely $TS_1, TS_2, ..., TS_n$, for each TS_i. Let k_i be its sub-master key and $s_{i,1}, s_{i,2}, ..., s_{i,n}$ be its *n* sub-shares. According to the conventional (2, *n*) threshold scheme, given any two sub-shares $s_{i,j}$ and $s_{i,k}$, the sub-key k_i can be recovered.

The share of participant P_i is given by $S_i = \{a_{i,1}, a_{i,2}, ..., a_{i,n}\}$, 1<=*t*<=*n*:

$a_{i,t} = k_t$ if $P_i P_t$ is an edge of *G*,
$a_{i,t} = s_{t,i}$ if $P_i P_t$ is not an edge of *G*,
$a_{i,t}$ is empty if *t*=*i*.

It can be validated that any subset of Γ can recover *K* while any subset of Δ cannot (Sun, 1996).

Secret Sharing in Graph-Based Prohibited Structure

In order to reduce the total number of shares held by the participants, (Sun, 1997) proposed a new scheme in graph-based prohibited structure.

This scheme is based on prohibited structure, in which the pairs of participants corresponding to edges in the graph cannot compute the master key but the pairs of participants corresponding to non-edges in the graph can. The prohibited structure contains the pairs of participants corresponding to edges, and the access structure contains the pairs of participants corresponding to non-edges.

Firstly, construct *n*+1 conventional (2, *n*) threshold schemes, named $TS_1, TS_2, ..., TS_{n+1}$, for each TS_i. Let k_i be its sub-master key and $s_{i,1}, s_{i,2}, ..., s_{i,n}$ be its *n* sub-shares. According to the conventional (2, *n*) threshold scheme, given any two sub-shares $s_{i,j}$ and $s_{i,k}$, the sub-key k_i can be recovered.

The share of participant P_i is given by $S_i = \{a_{i,1}, a_{i,2}, ..., a_{i,n+1}\}$, 1<=*t*<=*n*:

$a_{i,t}$ is empty if *t*=*i*,
$a_{i,t} = s_{t,i}$ if *t*=*n*+1 and P_t is an isolated vertex,
$a_{i,t} = k_t$ if *t*=*n*+1 and P_t is not an isolated vertex,
$a_{i,t} = s_{t,i}$ if *t*≠*i*, *t*≠*n*+1, and $P_i P_t$ is an edge of *G*,
$a_{i,t} = k_t$ if *t*≠*i*, *t*≠*n*+1, and $P_i P_t$ is not an edge of *G*.

It can be validated that any subset of Γ can recover *K* while any subset of Δ cannot (Sun, 1997).

Secret Sharing in Graph-Based Adversary Structures

The above two graph-based schemes have low efficiency. For example, *n* conventional (2, *n*) threshold schemes must be constructed, and the total number of shares held by the participants is very large. So, (Guo, 2005) proposed a new efficient scheme. In this scheme, the pairs of participants corresponding to edges in the graph cannot compute the master key but the pairs of participants corresponding to non-edges in the graph can.

Given the master key *K* and graph *G*, *m* denotes the number of edges, *m*′ denotes the number of isolated vertexes, and *I* denotes the set of isolated vertexes. The dealer generates shares as follows:

(i)   The master key *K* is divided into *m*+ *m*′ partitions: $K_1, K_2, ..., K_{m+m'}$, and satisfies

$$K = \sum_{i=1}^{m+m'} K_i,$$

(ii) $\forall P_i$:

if $P_i \in I$, then the participant of P_i,
$g(P_i) = \{K_t \mid 1 \le t \le m + m', s \ne t, if \ P_i = I_s\}$;
if $P_i \notin I$, then the participant of P_i,
$g(P_i) = \{K_t \mid P_i \notin S_t, 1 \le t \le m + m'\}$.

It can be validated that any subset of Γ can recover K while any subset of Δ cannot (Guo, 2005).

Remarks

There are some disadvantages in the above graph-based schemes. For example, the total number of shares held by the participants is large, while the threshold value is only 2. In order to overcome the drawback, we propose a plane-based scheme (Wu, 2007) in the next section.

A PLANE-BASED ACCESS STRUCTURE FOR SECRET SHARING

In this section, we propose a plane-based access structure for secret sharing. In a graph, if any two among a set of three participants contain an edge, these participants constitute a prohibited structure, which cannot recover the master key; otherwise, the set of three participants constitute an access structure, which can recover the master key.

In this scheme, let P denote the set of participants, and G be a graph where a vertex represents a participant and an edge represents a pair of participants. The graph we consider here can be a disconnected graph, possibly with isolated vertexes. The scheme is based on (Γ, Δ) mixed structure, and its access structure and prohibited structure are defined as follows:

Access Structure: if there are not any two among a set of three participants that contain an edge in the graph, then the set of three participants constitute an access structure.

Prohibited Structure: if any two among a set of three participants contain an edge in the graph, then the set of three participants constitute a prohibited structure.

Especially, if P_i, P_j and P_h contain an edge between each other, and P_i, P_j and P_k contain an edge between each other, then we assume P_h and P_k also contain an edge. In other words, if both $\{P_i, P_j, P_h\}$ and $\{P_i, P_j, P_k\}$ are prohibited structures, then $\{P_h, P_i, P_j, P_k\}$ is also a prohibited structure. So the proposed secret sharing scheme satisfies the following conditions:

if $A \in \Gamma$ and $A \subseteq B \subseteq P$, then $B \in \Gamma$;
if $A \in \Delta$ and $B \subseteq A \subseteq P$, then $B \in \Delta$.

This scheme consists of two phases: the first one is executed by the dealer and the second one is executed by a set of participants who want to recover the master key.

Shares Generation Phase

We assume that all computations are over $GF(q)$ where q is a large prime. Given a graph G and a master key K, randomly select an equation $Ax+By+Cz+D=0$, where A, B, $C \in GF(q)$ and $D=K$. The share distributed to every participant is (x_i, y_i, z_i), for $i=1, 2, ..., n$. The dealer generates shares and distributes them when visiting the graph. Given the shares of P_j and P_k, (x_j, y_j, z_j) and (x_k, y_k, z_k) respectively, the share of P_i is obtained as follows:

(i) If the set of $\{P_i, P_j, P_k\}$ constitute a prohibited structure, then $x_i=m(x_j-x_k), y_i=m(y_j-y_k), z_i=m(z_j-z_k)$, where m is a non-zero integer and its value is randomly selected by the dealer;

(ii) If the set of $\{P_i, P_j, P_k\}$ constitute an access structure, then randomly select x_i and y_i, and calculate $z_i=(-Ax_i-By_i-D)/C$.

Let

$$M = \begin{vmatrix} x_i & y_i & z_i \\ x_j & y_j & z_j \\ x_k & y_k & z_k \end{vmatrix},$$

205

and test the value of M. If $M=0$, select x_i and y_i until $M\neq0$, then calculate $z_i=(-Ax_i-By_i-D)/C$.

When three vectors from a plane are randomly selected, the probability that they are linearly independent is very high. So, the dealer only needs to select x_i and y_i once in most cases.

After generating all shares, the dealer distributes them to every participant by a secure channel. The shares generation and distribution processes are illustrated in Figure 2.

In Figure 2, since P_1, P_3 and P_5 contain an edge between each other, the set of $\{P_1, P_3, P_5\}$ constitute a prohibited structure, and their shares are linear vectors. In contrast, others are linearly independent.

Secret Recovery Phase

Without loss of generality, suppose P_1, P_2 and P_3 cooperate to recover the master key, and the share of P_1 is (x_1, y_1, z_1), the share of P_2 is (x_2, y_2, z_2), and the share of P_3 is (x_3, y_3, z_3). The master key is recovered as follows:

(i)   Let

$$M = \begin{vmatrix} x_1 & y_1 & z_1 \\ x_2 & y_2 & z_2 \\ x_3 & y_3 & z_3 \end{vmatrix},$$

and test the value of M. If $M=0$, it shows that the set of these participants constitute a prohibited structure, then stop the protocol. Otherwise, it shows that the set constitute an access structure, then continue running the protocol.

(ii)   Recover the general equation of the plane and compute:

$$n = \begin{vmatrix} i & j & k \\ x_2 - x_1 & y_2 - y_1 & z_2 - z_1 \\ x_3 - x_1 & y_3 - y_1 & z_3 - z_1 \end{vmatrix} = Ai + Bj + Ck,$$

So, the equation of the plane, $A(x-x_1)+B(y-y_1)+C(z-z_1)=0$ and the master key, $K=D=-Ax_1-By_1-Cz_1$.

Performance Comparison

We compare the performance of the proposed scheme to other existing graph-based schemes in terms of computational cost, storage cost and threshold value, as shown in Table 1.

During shares generation and secret recovery phases, the scheme in (Sun, 1997) needs to construct and recover $n+1$ conventional (2, n)-threshold schemes, and the cost to execute every conventional scheme is $O(nlog^2n)$ (Hwang, 1978). As a result, the total cost is $O(n^2log^2n)$. The scheme in (Guo, 2005) needs to execute $2(m+m')$

Figure 2. Shares generation and distribution

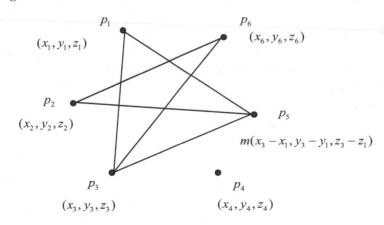

Table 1. Performance comparison

	Computations Needed in Shares Generation and Recovery Phases	Total Number of Partitions Stored by all Participants	Threshold Value of the Scheme
The scheme in (Sun, 1997)	$O(n^2 log^2 n)$	$n^2 + n$	2
The scheme in (Guo, 2005)	$2(m+m')$	$nm+nm'-2m-m'$	2
Our Proposed Scheme (Wu, 2007)	$O(n^3)$	$3n$	3

mod operations, where m denotes the number of edges and m' denotes the number of isolated vertexes. However, our scheme (Wu, 2007) needs to execute C_n^3 tests and the cost is $O(n^3)$. It is worth noting that during the secret recovery phase, our scheme only needs to compute two 3*3 determinants. Obviously, the storage cost of our scheme is lower than existing schemes. Furthermore, the threshold value of our scheme is 3 while that of existing graph-based schemes is 2.

Remarks

In this section, we have presented a plane-based access structure for secret sharing. Our scheme is superior over existing schemes in terms of both the storage cost and the computational cost. Compared to existing graph-based schemes, the main advantage of our scheme is that threshold value is improved from 2 to 3. In order to further improve the threshold value, we will extend the plane-based scheme to a generic k-dimensional access structure in the next section.

A GENERIC *K*-DIMENSIONAL ACCESS STRUCTURE FOR SECRET SHARING

In this section, we propose a generic k-dimensional secret sharing scheme. Our basic idea is: the share

distributed to every participant is a k-dimensional vector, and all vectors are linearly independent and satisfy a set of k-dimensional linear equations: $a_1 x_1 + a_2 x_2 + ... + a_k x_k + D = 0$, where D is the master key K. When recovering K, a set of k participants that constitute an access structure present their shares to construct a set of k-dimensional linear equations and thus the master key can be recovered. The access structure and the prohibited structure are defined as follows:

Access Structure: the subset which includes no less than k participants;

Prohibited Structure: the subset which includes less than k participants.

The scheme consists of three phases: system initialization, shares generation and secret recovery.

System Initialization Phase

The dealer generates a notice board (NB) to publish the open information. Only the dealer can modify and update NB, while the participants can download information from NB. Every participant has an identification mark (ID).

Shares Generation Phase

We assume that all computations are over $GF(q)$ where q is a large prime. Given a master key K, randomly select a set of k-dimensional linear equations: $a_1x_1 + a_2x_2 + ... + a_kx_k + D = 0$, where $a_1, a_2, ..., a_k \in GF(q)$ and $D = K$. The share distributed to every participant is: $(x_{i,1}, x_{i,2}, ..., x_{i,k})$, where $i = 1, 2, ..., n$, which are fixed as follows:

(i)   for $i=1$ to $i=n$ do
       $\{x_{i,1} = ID_i,$
       Randomly select $x_{i,2}, ..., x_{i,k-1}$ over $GF(q)$.
       $x_{i,k} = (-a_1x_{i,1} - a_2x_{i,2} - ... - a_{k-1}x_{i,k-1} - D)/a_k$.
       $\}$.

(ii)   let

$$M = \begin{vmatrix} x_{1,1} & x_{1,2} & \cdots & x_{1,k} \\ x_{2,1} & x_{2,2} & \cdots & x_{2,k} \\ \vdots & \vdots & \cdots & \vdots \\ x_{n,1} & x_{n,2} & \cdots & x_{n,k} \end{vmatrix}.$$

(iii) Test the value of M, if $M=0$, turn to (i).

Since the selection of n k-dimensional ($k \leq n$) vectors over $GF(q)$ is random, the probability that they are linearly independent is very high. So, the dealer only needs to select $x_{i,2}, ..., x_{i,k-1}$ once in most cases.

After generating all shares, the dealer distributes $x_{i,k}$ to a participant by a secure channel, and publishes $(ID_i, x_{i,2}, ..., x_{i,k-1})$ in NB.

Secret Recovery Phase

Without loss of generality, suppose that P_1, P_2, ..., P_k cooperate to recover the master key. Every participant downloads the information corresponding to his ID from NB, and then constructs the following equations:

$$\begin{cases} a_1x_{1,1} + a_2x_{1,2} + ... + a_kx_{1,k} + D = 0 & (1) \\ a_1x_{2,1} + a_2x_{2,2} + ... + a_kx_{2,k} + D = 0 & (2) \\ \vdots \\ a_1x_{k,1} + a_2x_{k,2} + ... + a_kx_{k,k} + D = 0 & (k) \end{cases}$$

When Eqs. (1)-(2), (2)-(3), ..., $(k-1)$-(k), (k)-(1) are applied, it can eliminate the unknown D and construct a set of k-dimensional linear equations. Since the new equations have k unknown numbers, $a_1, ..., a_k$ can be worked out and then the master key K can be recovered.

Security Analysis

A secret sharing scheme must satisfy that: (i) the set of participants constituting an access structure can recover the sharing secret, (ii) the set of participants constituting a prohibited structure cannot recover the sharing secret. In the proposed scheme, reconstructing a set of k-dimensional linear equations needs to know k k-dimensional vectors and they must be linearly independent. Obviously, the set of k participants can recover the master key. If the adversary obtains only k-1 shares, since k-1 k-dimensional vectors can not reconstruct the equation, we need to guess one more share to recover the key. The success ratio is $1/q$, and q is a large prime, therefore, it is very difficult for the adversary to be successful.

The adversary cannot obtain $x_{i,k}$ from public $(ID_i, x_{i,2}, ..., x_{i,k-1})$ in NB due to the fact that we do not know the equation, $a_1x_1 + a_2x_2 + ... + a_kx_k + D = 0$.

To sum up, our scheme satisfies the requirement and the rule of security.

Performance Analysis

During the period of shares generation, our scheme needs to select $n*(k-2)$ numbers over $GF(q)$, and evaluate one $n*k$ determinant. During the period of secret recovery phase, our scheme needs to solve a set of k-dimensional linear equations, which is equivalent to evaluate one $k*k$ determinant. Obviously, the most complicated operation is to compute $n*k$ determinant, and the cost of which is $O(kn)$, while the cost of the scheme in (Shamir, 1979) is $O(nlog^2n)$. If $k \ll n$, then $kn < nlog^2n$. That is, the above analysis reveals that the cost of the proposed scheme is much lower than the scheme in (Shamir, 1979) when the number of participants is large.

Remarks

In this section, we have proposed a generic k-dimensional secret sharing scheme. Similar to constructing and reconstructing a Lagrange interpolation polynomial in Shamir's scheme, our scheme needs to construct and reconstruct a set of k-dimensional linear equations. The analysis shows that the proposed scheme satisfies the requirement and the rule of security. Moreover, its computational complexity is not high.

CONCLUSION

In this chapter, we have investigated the issues of secret sharing and proposed a plane-based access structure scheme. As an extension, we have proposed a k-dimensional access structure scheme, which can be used in many applications, such as secure communication networks, and secure database systems. In particular, it is very important for access control in an environment where the number of participants is large.

Currently our proposed schemes cannot verify cheaters, including the dealer cheating and the participant cheating. We will propose some efficient solutions to handle the cheating problem in our schemes in the future.

ACKNOWLEDGMENT

This work is supported by the National Natural Science Foundation of China under Grant Nos. 90718034, 60503007 and 60773013, the Program for Changjiang Scholars and Innovative Research Team in University under Grant No. IRT0661, and the Program for New Century Excellent Talents in University under Grant No. NCET-06-0686.

REFERENCES

Blakley, G. R. (1979). Safeguarding *Cryptographic Keys*. Proceedings of AFIPS 1979 National Computer Conference, 48, 313-317.

Guo Y. B., & Ma, J. F. (2004). Practical Secret Sharing Scheme Realizing Generalized Adversary Structure. *Journal of Computer Research and Development, 19*(4), 564-569 (In Chinese).

Guo, Y. B., Ma, J. F., & Wang, Y. D. (2005). An Efficient Secret Sharing Scheme Realizing Graph-Based Adversary Structures. *Journal of Computer Research and Development, 42*(5), 877-882 (In Chinese).

Hwang, R. J., & Chang, C. C. (1978). An On-Line Secret Sharing Scheme for Multi-Secrets. *Computer Communications of the ACM, 21*(13), 1170-1176.

Ito, M., Saito, A., & Nishizeki T. (1987). Secret Sharing Scheme Realizing General Access Structure. *Proceedings of 1987 IEEE Global Telecommunications Conference (GLOBECOM 1987)*, 99-102.

Pei, D. Y., & Zhu, Y. F. (2002). *Algorithm and Number Theory*. Beijing: Science Press, 127-129 (In Chinese).

Pang, L. J., Jiang, Z. T., & Wang, Y. M. (2006). A Multi-Secret Sharing Scheme Based on the General Access Structure. *Journal of Computer Research and Development, 43*(1), 33-38 (In Chinese).

Pang L. J., Li, H. X., & Wang, Y. M. (2006). Secret Sharing Scheme with General Access Structures Based on LUC and its Security. *Computer Science, 33*(5), 121-123 (In Chinese).

Shamir, A. (1979). How to Share a Secret. *Communications of the ACM, 22*(11), 612-613.

Stmson, D. R. (1995). *Cryptography: Theory and Practice*. New York: CRC Press, 343-350.

Shieh, S. P., & Sun, H. M. (1994). On Constructing Secret Sharing Schemes. *Proceedings of IEEE International Conference on Computer Communications (INFOCOM 1994)*, 1288-1292.

Sun, H. M., & Shieh, S. P. (1996). An Efficient Construction of Perfect Secret Sharing Schemes for Graph-Based Structures. *Journal of Computers and Mathematics with Applications, 31*(7), 129-135.

Sun, H. M., & Shieh, S. P. (1997). Secret Sharing in Graph-Based Prohibited Structures. *Proceedings of IEEE International Conference on Computer Communications (INFOCOM 1997)*, 9-13.

Wu, Y. R., Wang, G. J., & Shi, R. H. (in press). Designing Secret Sharing Scheme with a Plane-Based General Access Structure. *Computer Engineering* (In Chinese).

Xu, C. X., Chen, K., & Xiao, G. Z. (2002). A Secure Vector Space Secret Sharing Scheme. *Acta Electronica Sinica, 30*(5), 715-718 (In Chinese).

KEY TERMS

Access Structure: The subset of participants that can recover the master key.

(k, n) Threshold Secret Sharing Scheme: The trusted dealer delivers the distinct secret shares to n participants. At least k or more participants can pool their secret shares in order to recover the secret, but only k-1 or fewer shares cannot, where $1 <= k <= n$.

Linearly Independent: If a determinant consists of n vectors, and its value is non-zero, then the n vectors are linearly independent.

Master Key: Master key is the secret shared by all participants in the system.

Participant: A member in secret sharing scheme in the system.

Prohibited Structure: The subset of participants that cannot recover the master key.

Secret Sharing: Secret sharing aims at efficiently distributing and sharing a secret among a number of participants, and the secret can be recovered on condition that pre-specified and authorization subsets of participants can pool their shares, otherwise, the secret cannot be recovered.

Threshold Value: In (k, n) threshold secret sharing scheme, k is the threshold value.

Chapter XII
Wireless Video Transmission

Supavadee Aramvith
Chulalongkorn University, Thailand

Rhandley D. Cajote
Chulalongkorn University, Thailand

ABSTRACT

Presently, both wireless communications and multimedia communications have experienced unequaled rapid growth and commercial success. Building on advances of network infrastructure, low-power integrated circuits, and powerful signal processing/compression algorithms, wireless multimedia services to support digital video applications such as videophone, video conferencing, video streaming, video on demand (VoD), and video surveillance, likely finds widespread acceptance. Many wireless multimedia applications require video coding schemes and underlying transport that can provide acceptable quality of service to the end users. Due to the burst errors nature of wireless channels and the error propagation property of compressed video, suitable source and channel coding schemes are required to handle such conditions. This chapter provides overview of video compression techniques, and the latest video coding standard, H.264/AVC, its implication for the wireless video transmission, and our research contribution on joint source-channel coding for wireless video transmission.

INTRODUCTION

Multimedia is defined as media that utilizes a combination of different content forms (http://en.wikipedia.org/wiki/Multimedia). Those forms are regarded as text, audio, still images, animation, video, and interactivity. To exchange those data among humans or among humans and machines, the field "multimedia communication" is estab-

lished. Multimedia communication refers to the representation, storage, retrieval, distribution of machine-processable information expressed in multiple media. It can be divided according to the type of media such as data, text, audio, image and video communications. Some example applications are data transfer and fax. For audio communication example applications are telephony and sound broadcasting. For video communication example applications are video conferencing, television, and high-definition television.

The elements of multimedia communication system are divided into person-to-person and person-to-machine communication. Person-to-person communications are systems where humans are the end users of the system connected through telecommunication networks. This kind of system enables interactive and real-time multimedia data to flow between parties. Examples are MSN messaging, Skype, and video conferencing system. Another kind of system is a person-to-machine communications where humans interact with computer servers such as music server, video server, or a simple text information server. The computer servers perform the task of processing, storage, and retrieval of multimedia data. The example scenario is when users browse through the web page and decide to stream the video clips to their computer terminals. To develop such a system, careful considerations should be taken into account; those include users and network requirements and specification of multimedia terminals. From the user's point of view, the capabilities of dynamically controlling the multimedia information in terms of connection interaction, quality on demand, and friendly user interfaces are important as well as the ability to prepare and present different multimedia information according to time budget constraints and available terminal resources. Standardization of multimedia representation is also a necessary component in multimedia services. The key requirements of new multimedia services would involve instant availability, real-time information transfer, and universal access from any terminal. The network technology needs to be continuously developed to support high speed, varying bit rates and the ability to synchronize different types of information. In the end, there are still many issues that need to be addressed in developing multimedia terminals: basic techniques for compression and coding various multimedia data, basic techniques for organizing, storing, and retrieving multimedia signals, basic

technique for accessing, searching and browsing individual multimedia documents.

In the above mentioned digital multimedia content, speech, audio, and video are the most widely researched in terms of applications areas such as internet telephony, streaming video and audio, digital audio and video broadcasting, etc. Nevertheless, the bit rate required to make such applications possible ranges from the order of kilobits for speech to gigabits for video. Thus to realize these, a lot of research and standardization effort have been aimed at the efficient transmission of these digital multimedia content. The signal processing community has devoted a lot of effort in developing efficient multimedia source coding techniques. The communication community has also devoted efforts in terms of channel coding techniques and efficient method of multimedia transmission and distribution. Nevertheless, joint efforts from research communities are presented today. From all the forms of digital multimedia content, video plays an increasingly important role as the emerging multimedia communication and distribution system. Regardless of its extremely large size that makes it more difficult to find effective schemes to compress and transmit flawlessly through IP and wireless medium.

In this chapter, we discuss the video compression techniques, and the latest video coding standard, H.264/AVC, its implication for the wireless video transmission, and our research contribution on joint source-channel coding for wireless video transmission.

BACKGROUND ON VIDEO CODING STANDARDS

Today most of the information are represented and stored in digital format. The digital format has several advantages such as flexibility in processing, storing, and manipulating multimedia data, reproducible accuracy and fidelity, and can be easily integrated for multimedia applications.

Nevertheless the amount of multimedia data, especially images and videos, are extremely large. For example, the amount of bits needed to represent a BT.601 video format that is the typical size of standard television format, 24-bit color 720x576 pixels, at frame rate of 30 frames/sec of length 2 hours is 2,150 Gbits. To store this large file would require up to fifty-eight 4.7- Gbyte DVDs. This large amount of data would require an extremely long download time if it will be streamed from a server. The required rate to download video without compression is far beyond the capacity of any practical communications channel. From this example, it is clearly seen that it is not possible at all to develop successful multimedia applications, services, or consumer electronics if the compression technology is not invented. Thus multimedia compression technology is important and vital to several related applications. Compression methods can be divided into lossless and lossy compression schemes. Lossless compression exploits statistical properties of input data to remove statistical redundancy. On the other hand, lossy compression exploits the spatial and temporal redundancies within image and video frames and finds ways to remove those redundancies such that they are least perceptible to human visual/hearing system. Text compression is the good example of lossless compression while the rest of multimedia data employs both lossy and lossless compression techniques. Multimedia compressions techniques are defined in several international standards. The well-known image coding standard includes JPEG (ITU, Sept. 1992) and JPEG2000 (ISO/IEC, 2002). Examples of video coding standards are MPEG-1 (ISO/IEC, 1998), MPEG-2 (ISO/IEC, 1995b), MPEG-4 (ISO/IEC, 2003), H.261 (ITU, 1993), H.263 (ITU, 1995), and H.264/MPEG-4 Part 10 (ITU, March 2005). Examples of audio coding standards are MPEG-1 Layer 3 (MP3) audio (ISO/IEC, 1995a), MPEG-2 Advanced Audio Coding (ISO/IEC, 1997), High Efficiency Advance Audio Coding (HE-AAC) (ISO/IEC, 2004). More details about multimedia compres-

sion standards can be founded in (Rao, Bojkovic, & Milovanovic, May 2002).

Video Compression Concepts

One way to compress video is to compress each image picture separately, just like compressing several images. The most popular compression scheme for digital image is JPEG. In the JPEG scheme, the picture is segmented into 8x8 blocks of samples. These blocks are transformed using discrete cosine transform (DCT) to reduce spatial redundancy. The DCT coefficients are quantized and entropy coded using variable-length codes to reduce statistical redundancy to achieve higher compression ratio. This kind of coding schemes is referred to as Intra-picture or Intra-coding, since the picture is coded without reference to other pictures.

Improvement in coding performance can be achieved by exploiting the large amount of temporal redundancy in the video content. Much of the depicted scene is essentially repeated in succeeding pictures with small significant change, except in significant scene changes. By sending only the changes in the scene, a video can be represented more efficiently as compared to coding each picture separately. The difference or change in a scene is referred to as the amount of *residual* information. This technique of coding only the *residual* information is called Inter-picture or Inter-coding.

Further improvement in coding efficiency can be done by exploiting the temporal dependence in the video signal. This technique is called motion-compensated prediction (MCP). The motivation for using MCP is that most changes in video content are typically due to the motion of objects in the depicted scene relative to the image plane. A small amount of motion can result in a large difference in values of the samples in the picture, especially near the edge of the object. By predicting an area of the current picture from a region of the previous picture that is displaced

Figure 1. Hybrid video encoders

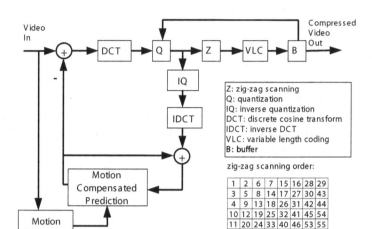

by a few samples in spatial location can reduce the amount of residual information. The use of a spatial displacement motion vectors to form a prediction is known as motion compensation. The encoder's search for the best motion vector (MV) to use is known as motion estimation (ME). The coding of the resulting difference signal is known as MCP residual coding. The use of two redundancy reduction techniques, using prediction and transformation, leads to the basic design of hybrid video codecs.

The subsequent improvements in the MCP techniques are the main reason for the improved coding efficiency in modern video coding standards from generation to generation. The disadvantage in using MCP is the increase in complexity for the use of more sophisticated MCP techniques. The improvements in MCP that eventually found their way into the latest video coding standard, the H.264/AVC, are fractional-sample-accurate MCP, MV's over picture boundaries, Bi-predictive MCP, Variable block size MCP, multi-picture MCP and multi-hypothesis and weighted MCP (ITU, March 2005).

Figure 1 shows an example hybrid video encoder that has been used as the basis of many video coding standards.

The operations of the hybrid video encoder are as follows. Each picture is split into blocks. The first picture of a sequence, or a random point, is encoded in Intra mode. Each sample of a block in an Intra picture is predicted using spatially neighboring samples of spatially coded blocks. For all remaining pictures of a sequence, or between random points, typically Inter coding is utilized. The process of Inter prediction (ME) consist of choosing motion data comprising the selected reference picture and MV to be applied to all samples of each block. The motion and mode data are transmitted as side information and are used by the encoder and decoder to generate identical Inter prediction signals using MC.

The residual of the Intra or Inter prediction, the difference between the original block and its prediction, is transformed by a frequency transform. The transform coefficients are scaled, quantized, entropy coded and transmitted together with the prediction side information.

The encoder contains a model of the decoding process so that both will generate identical prediction values computed in the decoder for the prediction of subsequent data. The quantized transform coefficients are reconstructed by inverse-scaling and are then inverse-transformed to generate the decoded prediction signal. The residual is then added to the prediction and the result the reconstructed picture. An optional deblocking filter, not shown in the Figure 1, is used in newer standards such as H.264/AVC to improve the visual quality of the output. The final picture provides the decoded video output and is then stored for the prediction of subsequent encoded pictures.

H.264/AVC MPEG-4 PART 10 ADVANCED VIDEO CODING STANDARD

H.264/AVC is a new video coding standard recommendation of ITU-T also known as International Standard or MPEG-4 part 10 Advanced Video

Coding of ISO/IEC. These previous standards reflect the technological progress in video compression and the adaptation of video coding to different applications and network environments. The potential application area for H.264/AVC ranges from video telephony (H.261) to consumer video on CD (MPEG-1) and broadcast of standard definition or high definition TV (MPEG-2). H.264/AVC is a standard for high quality encoding that is resilient to poor network conditions, but still provides high enough quality to serve as the basis for HDTV and HD-DVD encoding. H.264/AVC provides enhanced video compression performance that makes it suitable for interactive such as video telephony that requires a low latency. It is also equally applicable for non-interactive applications such as storage, broadcast and streaming of standard definition TV where focus is on high coding efficiency.

H.264/AVC has the same basic building block as the hybrid standard video encoder as described in Section 2.1 with some improved functionalities as shown in Figure 2. Some of the main features of H.264/AVC that contributed to its increased

Figure 2. Generalized block diagram of a hybrid video encoder with motion compensation The adaptive deblocking filter and Intra-frame prediction are two new tools in H.264/AVC.

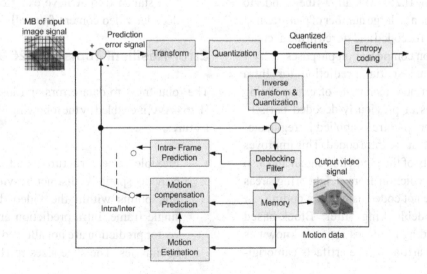

coding efficiency are discussed here. This is not a comprehensive list, but only some representative features of the Video Coding Layer. Detailed discussion of the source coding tools in H.264/AVC can be found in (Wiegand, Sullivan, Bjontegaard, & Luthra, 2003). It should be noted that there is no single component of the H.264/AVC coding tools that we can attribute to the dramatic increase in coding performance compared to previous standards. Rather it is due to the combination of small performance improvements of the different components of the system.

The improvements in the prediction methods are as follows:

- Adaptive block size for motion compensation: the standard supports more flexibility in the selection of motion compensation block sizes and shapes, with a minimum luminance motion compensation block size as small as 4x4
- Quarter-sample-accurate motion compensation: The prior standards enable half-sample motion compensation; the H.264/AVC improves on this by allowing quarter-sample motion vector accuracy, and also further reduces the complexity of the interpolation process compared to previous standards.
- Multiple Reference Picture Motion Compensation: The H.264/AVC allows the encoder to select among a large number of pictures that have been decoded and stored in the decoder for motion compensation purposes.
- Directional spatial prediction for Intra coding: a new technique of extrapolating the edges of previously-decoded parts of the current picture is applied in regions of pictures that are Intra coded. This improves the quality of the prediction signal and also allows prediction from neighboring areas that were not coded using intra coding.
- In-loop deblocking filter: Block-based video coding produces artifacts known as blocking artifacts. The artifacts can origi-

nate from both the prediction and residual difference coding stages of the decoding process. Application of a deblocking filter is a well-known method of improving the quality of the decoded signal. The H.264/AVC deblocking filter is brought within the motion-compensated prediction loop, so that the improvement in quality can be used in inter-picture prediction to improve the ability to predict other pictures as well.

Other improvements that contribute to improved coding efficiency are the following:

- Small block-size transforms: the H.264/AVC design is based on 4x4 transform, this allows the encoder to represent signals in a more locally-adaptive fashion.
- Short-word length transform: prior standards designed generally require that encoder and decoder use 32-bit processing, the H.264/AVC only requires 16-bit arithmetic.
- Exact-match inverse transform: In previous video coding standards, the transform used for representing the video was generally specified only within an error tolerance bound, due to the impracticality of obtaining an exact match to the ideal specified inverse transform. The H.264/AVC is the first standard to achieve exact equality of decoder video content from all decoders.

Error-Resilient Tools in H.264/AVC

The robustness to data errors and losses of the H.264/AVC is enabled by the following highlighted features.

- Flexible slice structured coding: Slices provide spatially distinct resynchronization points within the video data for a single frame. Intra prediction and motion vector prediction are not allowed over slice boundaries. The slice sizes in H.264/AVC are highly flexible as compared to the rigid slice structure found in MPEG-2.

- Flexible Macroblock Ordering (FMO): A new ability to partition the picture into regions called slice groups, and each slice becomes an independently-decodable subset of the slice group. When used effectively (especially in conjunction with an appropriate error concealment method), FMO can significantly enhance the robustness of data losses by managing the spatial relationship between regions that are coded in each slice.

- Arbitrary Slice Ordering (ASO): Since each slice of a coded picture can be decoded independently of the other slices of the picture, the H.264/AVC design enables sending and receiving the slices of the picture in any order relative to each other.

- Redundant pictures: To enhance the robustness to data loss, the H.264/AVC design contains a new ability to allow the encoder to send redundant representation of regions of pictures, enabling a course representation of regions of pictures for which the primary representation has been lost during data transmission

- Data partitioning: Since the coded information for representation of each region is more important than other information for purposes of representing the video content, H.264/AVC allows the syntax of each slice to be separated into up to three different partitions for transmission.

- SP/SI synchronization/switching pictures: A new feature in H.264/AVC consisting of picture types that allow exact synchronization of the decoding process of some decoders with an ongoing video stream produced by other decoders without penalizing all decoders with the loss of efficiency resulting from sending an I picture. This can enable switching a decoder between representation of the video content that used different data

rates, recovery from data losses or errors as well as enabling fast-forward and fast-reverse playback functionality.

Rate Control Scheme in H.264/AVC

Compressed video are variable rate in nature because of several reasons. One is because video compression standards allow different coding frame types. Frames that are encoded in intra or inter mode will result in different bit rates. The characteristics of the input video also leads to variable bit rate. If we consider a single coding type and fixed coding parameters, different scene changes in the video will result in bit rate variations. Finally, the output rate depends on the selection of the coding parameters. The different coding parameters that specify quantization step size, coding modes and motion compensation modes can be used to modulate the output rate.

Because of the variable-bit rate nature of the compressed video frames, using a fixed quantization step-size results in a relatively constant video quality but variable bit-rate streams. To transmit the video over a constant bit rate channel, a buffer is used at the encoder to smooth out the variations in the bit rate and also to match the required channel rate for successful transmission. To prevent the buffer from overflow or underflow, and to achieve good over-all video quality, a rate-control scheme is applied to adjust the quantization step size. By varying the quantization step size for each frame results in variable PSNR. So a constant bit-rate video will result in variable video quality per frame.

The challenge of the rate control is to determine the suitable quantization step sizes for each macroblock that achieves the best overall video quality and at the same time satisfy the network and application constraints. The rate control algorithm usually determines the quantization step size based on the buffer fullness, the available channel bandwidth and the video frame complexity. The operations of the rate control is not specified in the video standards, so flexibility in implementing efficient rate control algorithms is left to the designers. The performance of the rate-control algorithm to determine the quantization step size and at the same time satisfy the given constraints have a large impact on the resulting video quality.

To achieve the good video quality, one method used in the rate control algorithm is to implement a rate-distortion optimization technique to find the optimal quantizer that satisfies the given constraints (Ortega, Ramchandran, & Vetterli, 1994). Langrangian formulations and dynamic programming are two popular techniques used to find the optimal or nearly-optimal bit allocation for each macroblock. One difficulty in this method is the computational complexity involved in finding the optimal solutions. Another type of approach for rate-control is through mathematical modeling (Chiang & Zhang, 1997; Ribas-Corbera & Lei, 1999). Based on the rate and distortion models, mathematical formula are derived from optimization based on the statistical properties of the input. With information such as current buffer fullness and the variance of the residual prediction errors as inputs, mathematical formulas are used to determine the quantization step-sizes for rate control. Many rate-control schemes in previous standards use this type of strategy for rate control due to its simplicity. The disadvantage is that if the models do not fit the input statistical distributions well, the resulting video quality is not as good.

In H.264/AVC rate control, a quantization parameter is determined by using linear and quadratic rate – distortion models. The rate control in H.264/AVC is composed of Group of picture (GOP) layer, frame layer and basic unit layer. When encoding the current frame, the rate control will compute the occupancy of encoder buffer by using fluid traffic model as shown in eq. (1). The initial buffer fullness is set to zero. The N_{gop} denotes the total number of GOP, $n_{i,j}$ (i=1,2,...: j=1,2,..., N_{gop}) denotes the jth frame in the ith GOP,

$B_c(n_{i,j})$ denotes the occupancy of encoder buffer before coding the jth, $A(n_{i,j})$ denotes number of bits generated by the jth frame in the ith GOP, F_r denotes the target frame rate and $u(n_{i,j})$ denotes the available channel bandwidth.

$$B_c(n_{i,j}) = B_c(n_{i,j-1}) + (A(n_{i,j-1}) - (\frac{u(n_{i,j-1})}{F_r}))$$

(1)

If the occupancy of encoder buffer is larger than the maximum encoder buffer size, B_S, the rate control will skip encoding the frame and release the accumulated bit in the encoder buffer to the channel. The determination of a target bit for each P frame is composed of two steps.

Step 1.1 Budget allocations among pictures. The bit allocation is implemented by predefining a target buffer level, $Tbl(n_{i,j+1})$, for each P picture, as shown in eq. (2), where N_p is the number of P frames in GOP.

$$Tbl(n_{i,j+1}) = Tbl(n_{i,j}) - \frac{B_c(n_{i,2}) - B_s / 8}{N_p - 1}$$

(2)

Step 1.2 Target bit rate computation. The target bit rate, $f(n_{i,j})$, for the jth P frame in the ith GOP is scaled based on the target buffer level, current buffer level, frame rate, and channel bandwidth. It is given in eq. (3),

$$\tilde{f}(n_{i,j}) = \frac{u(n_{i,j})}{F_r} + \gamma (Tbl(n_{i,j}) - B_c(n_{i,j}))$$

(3)

where γ is a constant weighting factor and its default value is 0.75.

Further adjustment by a weighted combination of the average number of remaining bits for each frame is given, as shown in eq. (4),

$$f(n_{i,j}) = \beta * \frac{T_r(n_{i,j})}{N_p - j} + (1 - \beta) * \tilde{f}(n_{i,j})$$

$$(4)$$

where $T_r(n_{i,j})$ is the total number of remaining bits left to encode the jth frame onwards in the ith GOP, and β is a constant weighting factor. Its default value is 0.5. Note that the detailed information about the H.264/AVC rate control can be found in (JVT, 2003).

WIRELESS CHANNEL CHARACTERISTICS

Radio Channel Parameters

In this section some important radio channel parameters are presented. The understanding of these parameters is essential to the understanding of the characteristics of the wireless channel.

Time Delay Spread and Coherence Bandwidth

The two parameters that are often used to characterize multipath wireless channels are the time delay spread and the coherence bandwidth. The time delay spread, T_{delay}, is a measure of the length of the impulse response for the multipath wireless channel. Time delay spread leads to intersymbol interference (ISI) and degrades the performance of the wireless communication system. One way to define the impulse response of a multipath wireless channel is by its maximum time delay spread, $T_{D,max}$, defined as the range of delays over which the delay peaks of the channel power delay profile is not less than 30 dB from the peak of the first received pulse (Ngan, Yap, & Tan, 2001). An illustration of a typical power delay profile of an indoor wireless channel showing maximum time delay spread is shown in Figure 3.

As a measure of fading correlation between frequencies, the coherence bandwidth is directly related to the time delay spread. For an exponentially distributed delay spread power profile, the coherence bandwidth is given as:

$$B_{coherence} = \frac{1}{2\pi T_{delay}}$$

$$(5)$$

Two frequencies lying within the coherence bandwidth are likely to experience correlated fading. Such a channel is frequency non-selec-

Figure 3. Maximum time delay spread of a typical indoor wireless channel power delay profile

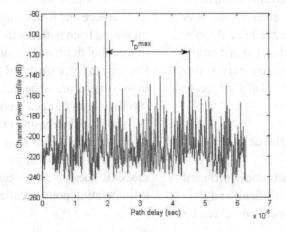

219

tive and all frequency components are subject to the same attenuation, phase shift and time delay. Narrowband wireless channels are usually characterized as a frequency non-selective channel, because the bandwidth of the transmitted signal is less than the coherence bandwidth of the channel. On the other hand if two frequencies are separated by more than the coherence bandwidth, they are affected differently by the channel. When the coherence bandwidth is small compared to the bandwidth of the transmitted signal, the channel is frequency selective. This is usually the case for wideband wireless channels.

Doppler Spread and Coherence Time

Another channel phenomena associated with wireless communications is the Doppler spread. Doppler spread may be interpreted as the measure of the variation of the shift in carrier frequency, or the measure of the rate at which the channel changes. Small Doppler spreads imply a large coherence time, $T_{coherence}$, or a slowly changing channel. Wireless channel characterized by small Doppler shifts ($0.3 - 6.1$ Hz) are often called slow fading channels. If the wireless communication channel symbol duration, T_{symbol}, is large compared to the coherence time then the channel is subject to fast fading.

The change in the carrier frequency because of the Doppler spread (or Doppler shift) is mainly due to the mobility of the receiver relative to the transmitter. A fast moving receiver (mobile user in a car, or train) will experience high Doppler frequency shifts and hence subject to fast fading channel conditions. While slow moving receiver (walking or in an elevator) are usually subject to slow fading channel conditions.

Wireless Channel Simulator

Wireless channel measurements under different possible environments can be difficult and time consuming. However, a wireless channel can be reasonably modeled using a multipath Rayleigh fading model. The effects of the channel under different environments can then be easily studied through computer simulations and varying the appropriate parameters. An example of the wireless channel simulator that can be used for this purpose is (T.-C. Chen, Chang, Wong, Sun, & Hsing, April 1995). A schematic of the wireless channel simulator is outlined in Figure 4.

The parameters that can be changed in the simulation are the maximum Doppler frequency f_D, the propagation power delay profile (modeled as n-rays with different inter-path delay and power), signal power and antenna diversity. The data rate is fixed at 256 kbps. A coherent receiver, with optimal symbol timing recovery and perfect carrier recovery is assumed. An ideal maximal ratio combiner for antenna diversity combining is used.

The wireless channel simulator is used to study the average bit-error rates (BER) at different signal-noise-ratios ranging from 17 to 23 dB, and the effects of different Doppler frequencies (f_D = 1Hz, 2Hz, 5Hz, 16Hz and 40 Hz), inter-path delay (τ=0, T/16, T/8 and T/4) and diversity (no diversity, two-branch and three-branch) are investigated.

The inter-path delay is due to the different distances traveled (multi-path) by the scattered rays received at the receiver. The effect of this delay is to increase the spread of the channel impulse response which leads to increased intersymbol interference and hence increases the BER as τ is increased from 0 (flat fading) to $\tau = T$, where T is the symbol duration, as can be seen in Figure 5. One way to decrease the BER at a given inter-path delay is to increase the transmitted signal power (SNR), as can be seen from Figure 5 at $\tau = T/4$, T/8 and T/16. Increasing the signal power (SNR) also has limited effect for a certain value of τ. For example in Figure 5 at $\tau = T/2$ and T, increasing the SNR does not significantly reduce the BER, this operating point is called irreducible BER.

Figure 4. Schematic of the wireless channel simulator

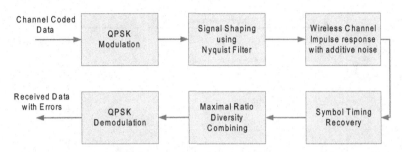

Figure 5. Effect of interpath delay and SNR on BER

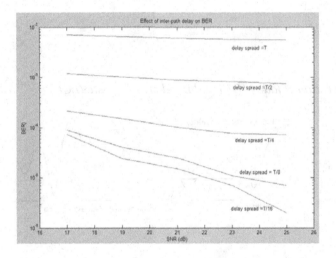

One way to improve the BER when τ is at the point of having an irreducible BER even at increased SNR is to increase the diversity of the antenna. Increasing the number of receiver antennae that are spaced at a certain distance apart (antenna array) from each other is a well-known technique (space diversity combining) to combat the effects of multi-path fading. In the absence of antenna diversity, only one antenna at the receiver, the rate of fading is highly dependent on the Doppler frequency (f_D). So if we have more than one antenna at the receiver, the received signal strength at different antennae is relatively uncorrelated. The probability that the signals received in the antenna array being under fade decreases as the number of antenna in the array increases. A maximal ratio combining of the different signals received at the antenna array is a good strategy to reduce the BER. The BER of an N-array antenna (diversity N) is of the order $(P_e)^N$, where P_e is the BER of one antenna. Figure 6 show the effect of increasing the antenna diversity on the BER at τ = T/4.

The level crossing rate (LCR) is the rate where the fading signal crosses a specified threshold L in a positive going direction. $LCR = n / T$, where n is the number of fades and T is the duration of the fade as illustrated in Figure 7. The average

Figure 6. Effect of antenna diversity on BER

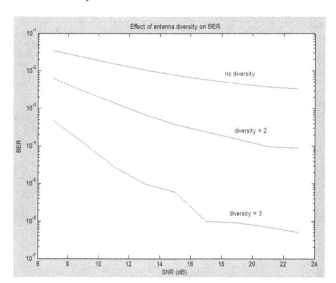

Figure 7. Average duration of fade (ADF) and Level crossing rate (LCR)

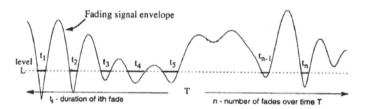

duration of fade (ADF) is a measure of the average amount of time the fading signal stays below a certain threshold L,

$$ADF = \frac{1}{n}\sum_{i=1}^{n} t_i .$$

The average BER is proportional to the product of the ADF and LCR at a given power level. The ADF is inversely proportional to the Doppler frequency f_D, as illustrated in Figure 8, at different antenna diversity. On the other hand, the LCR is directly proportional to f_D, as illustrated in Figure 9, at different antenna diversity.

Hence at a given power level, it is possible that f_D has no effect on the BER. However since the ADF corresponds to the length of burst errors and the LCR corresponds to the frequency of the burst, the Doppler frequency plays an important role in understanding the nature of errors in wireless channel. For small values of f_D, slow fading channel (slow moving receivers), the frequency of the fades are lower but the duration of the fades are longer. Thus error burst does not occur frequently in slow fading channel conditions but the errors burst have very long durations. For high values of f_D, fast fading channel (fast moving receivers), error burst occur more frequently but the duration

Figure 8. Effect of Doppler frequency f_D on ADF

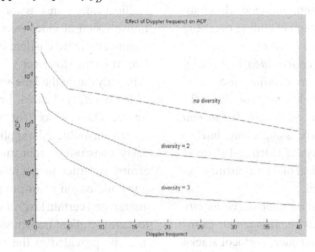

Figure 9. Effect of Doppler frequency f_D on the frequency of error burst

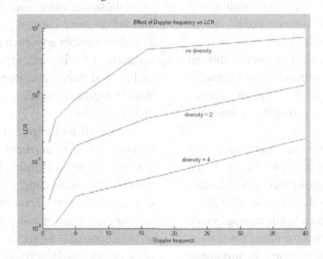

of the error bursts are shorter. These effects are illustrated in Figure 8 and Figure 9, the figures also shows that increasing the antenna diversity can help reduce the number of deep fades.

ERROR RESILIENT VIDEO TRANSMISSION SYSTEM

The basic problem in any communication system may be posed as conveying data with the high-est fidelity possible within an available bit rate. Or it can be conveying the source data with the lowest bit rate possible for a given reproduction quality (Shannon, 1959). The ability of a source coding system, or codec, to make this trade-off is called its coding efficiency or rate-distortion performance. In practical video transmission systems, video codecs are primarily character-ized in terms of:

- *Throughput of the channel*: A characteristic of transmission systems influenced by channel bit rate and amount of coding overhead due to protocols and error-correction.
- *Distortion of the decoded video*: Induced by the imperfections source coding process and channel errors introduced by the channel.
- *Delay (start-up latency and end-to-end delay)*: Includes processing delay, buffering, structural delays of video and channel codecs, and the speed of data transmission through the channel.
- *Complexity (computation, memory capacity and memory access requirements)*: Complexity of the video codec, protocol stacks and network

Taking all the above mentioned things into consideration, the practical source coding design problem for communication is given as: Given a maximum allowed delay and a maximum allowed complexity, achieve an optimal trade-off between bit rate and distortion for the range of network environments envisioned within the scope of the applications.

In communication system, information may be altered or lost during transmission due to the imperfections of the signal processing schemes and transmission errors due to noise. The effect of errors can be detrimental to compressed video streams not only because of the visual distortions introduced but also because errors can propagate spatially and temporally in motion compensated based video compression algorithms. Errors can be classified as either *random bit errors* or *erasure errors*. Random bit errors are caused by imperfections of physical channels and results in bit inversion, bit insertion and bit deletion. Erasure errors can be caused by packet loss in packet-based transmission or burst errors in wireless channels. The effects of erasure errors are more destructive due to loss of contiguous segment of bits.

To ensure the acceptable quality of video transmitted through time varying communica-tion channel especially, wireless channel, error resilient video transmission system is needed. The transmission of video over wireless channels is technically more challenging and more difficult than transmission over wired channels. This is primarily due to the time-varying characteristics of the wireless channel, limited bandwidth and limited QoS support for reliable transmission. Moreover, multimedia applications demand strict delay constraints, robustness and tolerance to errors. In order to guarantee successful video transmission on error-prone channels and still guarantee a certain level of video quality, support for error-resilient transmission and error control must be provided in the encoder, decoder and transmission control. There are several techniques developed for such scenarios. One approach is to make the source video more resilient at the encoder and utilize error concealment techniques at the decoder. Another approach uses channel coding methods, i.e., forward error correction (FEC) coding and Automatic Repeat reQuest (ARQ). Recent approach moves toward the joint source channel coding.

Figure 10 and Figure 11 show an example diagram of error resilient video transmission system. The main building block consists of error resilient video codec, efficient rate control, channel coding, and error concealment.

The error resilient video encoder (or transmitter) is responsible for the efficient representation of the compressed video signal with error resilient tools available at the encoder. An example is the H.264/AVC with data partitioning, FMO and redundant slice option enabled on the encoder. In order to match the output bit rate of the encoder with the available channel rate a rate-control buffer is included and the managed by the rate-control algorithm. In order to better estimate the conditions of the wireless channel and to efficiently modulate the output rate of the encoder, the rate-control algorithm must have knowledge of the current channel condition to predict future channel behavior. This can be accomplished by

Figure 10. Error-resilient video transmission system

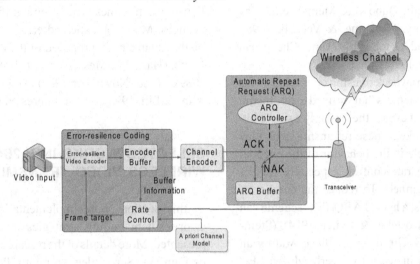

Figure 11. Error resilient video receiver system

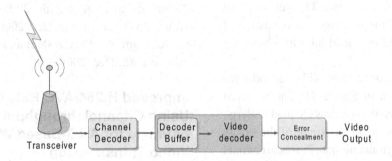

providing feedback from the link layer control in the form of ACK and NAK acknowledgement reports to indicate if a packet has been successfully received at the decoder. The prediction of future channel condition in order to estimate the future channel rate or fading condition a priori channel model is used. To protect the video packets from channel errors, channel coding schemes are provided such as FEC. Usually FEC is combined with bit-interleaving to improve the effectiveness of the FEC scheme against burst errors at the cost of additional delay in the interleaving buffer.

In contrast with FEC, ARQ requires a feedback channel from the receiver to the transmitter. For ARQ, the incoming bitstream is grouped into packets; each packet is extended by a header including a sequence number (SN) and error detection code-often a cyclic redundancy check (CRC) at the end of each block. This information is used at the receiver for error detection and to request the retransmission of the corrupted packets using positive acknowledgements (ACKs) and/or negative acknowledgements (NAKs), which are sent back via the feedback channel. Usually, retransmissions are repeated until error-free data are received or a time-out is exceeded. Several research works related to ARQ and video transmission could be found in (Heron & MacDonald,

1992) (Hsu, Ortega, & Khansari, May 1999), (Khansari, Jalali, Dubois, & Memelstein, May 1999), (Podolsky, McCanne, & Vetterli, 1998), (Farber & Girod, October 1997) and (Cherriman & Hanzo, June 1998).

The main drawback of using only ARQ as the error-control scheme is that we need to retransmit the whole packet even if there is only a single bit-error in the packet. These retransmissions play a significant role in the behavior of the encoder buffer and the rate-control, especially for the low bit-rate channels. To reduce the number of retransmissions, a hybrid ARQ/FEC scheme can be used (Lin, Costello, & Miller, 1984), (Steinbach, Farber, & Girod, Dec. 1997). Adding an FEC code will increase the overhead. An FEC code with a stronger error-correction capability will save more retransmission bits but will incur more transmission overhead. The scheme will be better only if the retransmission bits saved are more than the overhead bits introduced by the FEC code.

The typical error resilient video decoder (or receiver) is shown in Figure 11. The received video packets from the wireless channel undergo channel decoding to correct some of the errors introduced during transmission. Practical channel encoding and decoding schemes for video transmission do not provide perfect error recovery from transmission errors because this would require large bandwidth overhead. In practice a certain amount of error can be tolerated in the decoder since the human visual perception can tolerate some degree of distortion and visual artifacts. In order to mitigate some objectionable effects of distortions in the decoder, error concealment algorithms are used the last stage in the error recovery process. The choice of error concealment techniques used would contribute to the improvement of the received video quality. The simplest error concealment technique is the non motion-compensated error concealment where a lost block is simply replaced by the co-located block from the previous frame. Nevertheless, the

method does not work well when there is large motion between frames or between significant scene changes. More sophisticated error concealment methods have been proposed in (C. Chen, Sept. 1995), (Haskel & Messerschmitt, 1992), (Wada, 1989), (Tzou, November 1989) and (Lam, Reibman, & Lin, 1993), for the interested reader.

SELECTED WORKS IN H.264/AVC WIRELESS VIDEO TRANSMISSION

In this section some implementations of the error-resilient coding strategies discussed are presented. More details of the research works can be found in (Supavadee Aramvith, Pao, & Sun, May 2001), (S. Aramvith, Lin, Roy, & Sun, June 2002), (Hantanong & Aramvith, August 2005), (Srisawaivilai & Aramvith, 2005), (Supavadee Aramvith & Hantanong, Dec. 2006), (Eiamjumrus & Aramvith, Dec. 2006a) and (Eiamjumrus & Aramvith, Dec. 2006b).

Improved H.264/AVC Rate Control Using Channel throughput Estimate for ARQ-Based Wireless Video Transmission

One effective method of error control for wireless video transmission is to jointly design data link layer control mechanism and source coding techniques. Data link layer solutions such as forward error correction (FEC) and automatic repeat request (ARQ) have been shown to be effective when combined with rate-control algorithms to modulate the output bit rate. While FEC may incur some unnecessary overhead and thus reduces effective channel throughput, ARQ can be more effective method of error control if the delay requirements are not too strict to allow retransmission. It has been shown that using ARQ-based transport protocols and by carefully monitoring the rate of encoder buffer fill-up can

Figure 12. Simulation of "Foreman" sequence, using H.264/AVC with ARQ

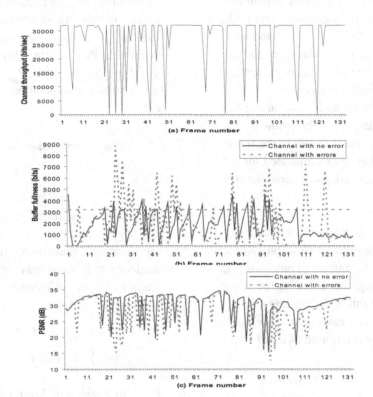

effectively improves video quality and reduces the number of skipped frames.

The scenario of using selective-repeat ARQ control and an improved rate-control scheme that estimates the effective channel throughput is investigated. By using the default rate-control mechanism in H.264/AVC and a selective-repeat ARQ control, a low bit-rate wireless video transmission system is simulated. The H.264/AVC codec is JM 9.0 and the wireless channel simulator described in Section 3 is used with the following parameters. The maximum Doppler frequency is set to 1Hz to simulate slow fading channel conditions, constant bit-rate of 32 kbps and target frame rate of 10 frames per second. The result of the simulation of the "Foreman" sequence is shown in Figure 12.

Figure 12(a) shows that the channel throughput is reduced if there are a lot of packets that needs to be retransmitted. Figure 12(b) illustrates the buffer fullness level, if there are packets that need to be retransmitted the number of bits in the buffer is much higher compared with having an error-free channel. Figure 12(c) shows the effect of the retransmission to the PSNR.

In order to reduce the number of frames skipped and improve PSNR, an improved rate-control mechanism is implemented. In order to improve the bit-allocation scheme of the H.264/AVC rate control some additional information about the condition of the channel is needed to. A two-state markov Gilbert channel (Gilbert, Sept. 1960) model simplified at the packet level is used to predict the condition of the wireless channel. This model has been shown to provide a course but sufficient approximation of the packet error behavior of slow fading channels (Supavadee Aramvith, Pao, & Sun, May 2001). The channel model is used to estimate the channel throughput and use this as a priori information for the bit-allocation scheme of the rate-control algorithm.

The improved-rate control algorithm at the frame level is summarized in the below by the basic unit rate control mechanism. In the frame level the target number of bits allocated for the current frame, $f(n_{i,j})$, is adapted using channel information.

1. Determine current channel state by calculating the ratio of the retransmission bits, *RBits*, to the number of transmitted bits, *AveBits*, collecting during the encoding of three previous frame intervals, as shown in eq. (6). If this ratio is greater than a threshold, H, then the state is declared as a bad state.

$$if(\frac{RBits}{AveBits}) > H; \text{ then State } = S_1. \text{ Else State } = S_0$$

(6)

2. Determine the model parameters, γ, and β to use in the H.264/AVC rate control algorithm in eq. (7) and eq. (8). If the buffer occupancy, $B_c(n_{i,j})$, is higher than half of the maximum buffer size, B_s, both model parameters will be set empirically as shown in eq. (7).

$$if\left(B_c\left(n_{i,j}\right) > 0.5 \times B_s\right); \quad \gamma = 1.0, \beta = 0.1$$
$$else \quad\quad\quad \gamma = 0.0, \beta = 0.5$$

(7)

3. Calculate the target bits for the current P frame $f(n_{i,j})$, as stated in eq. (2).

4. Calculate the estimated average number of successful bits per frame-interval, $f_{est}(n_{i,j})$. This is done by adjusting target

bit rate, $f(n_{i,j})$, with the estimated channel throughput, i.e., the average probability of correct packets transmitted in the ith packet interval, $p(i \mid Current\_State = S_n)$ (Supavadee Aramvith, Pao, & Sun, May 2001), where $i = f(n_{i,j}) / Psize$, and P_{size} is a packet size, set to 80 bits. Computation is shown in eq. (8).

$$f_{est}(n_{i,j}) = f(n_{i,j}) \times (p(i \mid Current\_State = S_n)$$

(8)

5. Adjust the new frame target bits to be $f_{est}(n_{i,j})$, which is generally less than the computed frame target, if there is high tendency that there may be a chance of frames skipped, otherwise, use the same frame target, $f(n_{i,j})$, as in eq. (9).

$$if(B_c(n_{i,j}) + f(n_{i,j})) > 1.5 \times B_S)$$
$$f\left(n_{i,j}\right) = f_{est}\left(n_{i,j}\right)$$

(9)

6. Perform basic unit layer rate control as describe in this section.

7. Update buffer occupancy, as shown in eq. (2). If there are more frames to be encoded, go to step 1, otherwise, stop.

The basic unit layer rate control is responsible for computing a suitable quantization parameter for each basic unit. The computation of the quantization parameter for the first basic unit (case 1) and when there are enough bits to encode the rest of the basic unit in a frame (case 3) is done according to the original H.264/AVC rate control algorithm. For case 2 when there is not enough bits to encode the rest of the basic unit, the method of selecting a quantization parameter by monitoring the buffer fullness level at the basic unit layer is used (Navakitkanok & Aramvith, 2004).

The results of using the improved rate control algorithm tested using three video sequences are shown in Figure 13 below. The encoder parameters

Figure 13. Comparison of improved rate control with H.264/AVC rate control

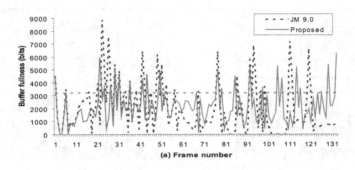

(a) buffer fullness

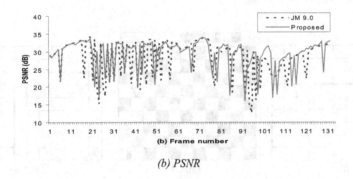

(b) PSNR

are defined in the H.264/AVC extended profile, the maximum encoder buffer size is set to 3200 bits and the PSNR computation when frames are skipped is done according to the rate control test in MPEG-4 (ISO/ICE:JTCI/SC29/WG11, 1997).

The comparison with the H.264/AVC rate control and the improved rate control scheme shows that an improvement of 0.8dB and a reduction in the number of skipped frames of up to 32%. This shows that a selective-repeat ARQ scheme with improved rate-control algorithm that takes into consideration channel information in the buffer level monitoring are effective in improving the PSNR and reducing the number of skipped frames for wireless video transmission.

Using FMO for H.264/AVC Wireless Video Transmission

In this section we present some methods on how to effectively use FMO as an error-resilient tool for wireless video transmission.

Flexible Macroblock ordering (FMO) is a MB-level interleaving tool in the H.264/AVC standard. It allows flexible transmission of MBs in a non-raster scan order by grouping macroblocks into *slice groups*. The H.264/AVC allows what is called *slice structured coding* as mentioned. A *slice* provides spatially distinct synchronization points within a frame to allow the encoder and decoder to synchronize their state and prevent spatial propagation of errors. To enhance the flexibility of slice structured coding FMO allows mapping of MB's to *slice groups*. A slice group

Figure 14. A slice is a sequence of MBs within the same slice group

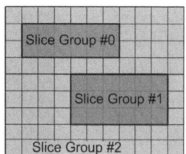

Figure 15. H.264/AVC FMO Map types

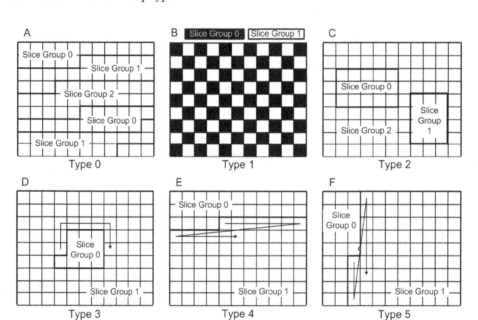

in itself may contain several slices. An example of a slice group is shown in Figure 14.

Slice groups can be thought of as a separate entity similar to pictures consisting of slice in the case when FMO is not used. The H.264/AVC standard provides seven FMO map types. Six of the map types are predefined by the standard, as shown in Figure 15, and the seventh type is the explicit FMO map type. The explicit type allows full flexibility in assigning MB to slice groups.

The current H.264/AVC standard supports a maximum of up to eight slice groups per picture (Wenger & Horowitz, May 2002).

Grouping MBs into slice groups have several advantages. One advantage is that using FMO actively helps the decoder in the error concealment process. Most error concealment algorithms rely on the availability of correctly received MBs in the neighborhood of the MB to be concealed in order to provide good estimate of the lost information. Using FMO to interleave the MB somehow increases the probability that neighboring MB will be received without error and can be used for error concealment. Using FMO is most effective when error concealment algorithms at the decoder are taken into consideration. Another advantage is when there is a Region of Interest (ROI) within the frame, like objects of interest in a relatively static background. Such regions can be mapped to a separate slice group than the background and provide better protection for ROI in image frames. The MB-to-slice group mapping is indicated in the Picture Parameter SET (PPS) header of the frame. The disadvantage of using FMO is the slight reduction in coding efficiency because motion prediction is limited to one slice. The advantage is the added error-resiliency because using FMO effectively stops spatial propagation of errors at the slice boundary. The slight overhead in the PPS header when using FMO has been found to be less than 10% (Y. Dhondt, Lambert, & Walle, 2006).

One issue that arises in the use of FMO is how to group the MB's into slice groups. One idea is to group seemingly important MB's into separate slice groups in order to provide better protection. Many researchers have developed different criteria in assessing the relative importance of a MB. In (Lie & Ngan, 2005), the importance of a MB is determined by computing a MB PSNR. In (Y. Dhondt, Lambert, & Walle, 2006), a MB *impact factor* is computed to determine the slice group mapping. In (Thomos, Argyropoulos, Boulgouris, & Strintzis, Nov. 2005), a MB importance factor is computed based on distortions of the coded MB and distortions if a MB is lost and concealed. In (Hantanong & Aramvith, August 2005) and (Supavadee Aramvith & Hantanong, Dec. 2006), the MB coded bit-count is used to determine the MB-to-slice group mapping, the bit-count information is regarded as a spatial indicator of MB importance because it depends on the nature of the motion compensated prediction. In (Panyavaraporn, Cajote, & Aramvith, Nov. 2007) and

(Cajote, Aramvith, Guevara, & Miyanaga, May 2007), a *distortion-from-concealment* and *distortion-from-propagation* measure is computed to determine the MB-to-slice group mappings. The distortion is regarded as a temporal indicator of MB importance because it depends on the interframe dependence of video sequence.

In most cases using only FMO provides only marginal improvements in video quality when video is transmitted over wireless channels. FMO is usually combined with other error-resiliency techniques to improve its performance. FMO is usually combined with unequal error protection techniques (UEP), data partitioning, error concealment techniques, FEC and interleaving.

Joint FMO and FEC Coding for H.264/AVC Wireless Video Transmission

In this section we investigate the effectiveness in using MB coded bit-count as a spatial indicator of MB importance in finding a suitable MB-to-slice group mapping. More details of the research work can be found in (Supavadee Aramvith & Hantanong, Dec. 2006) and (Hantanong & Aramvith, August 2005). The idea is that bit-count can be used as a spatial indicator of MB importance due to the properties of the motion-compensated prediction. So in order to mitigate the loss of seemingly important MB, the MBs with high bit-count are interleaved in consecutive slices. The steps in interleaving MBs using bit count are: (1) collect MB bit count information from the first pass encoding process and sort the MB in descending order and (2) map each macroblock in the sorted list to eight different slice groups.

The performance of the explicit FMO map using bit count is compared against the *interleaved* (Type 0) and *dispersed* (Type 1) map types of H.264/AVC. The H.264/AVC codec (JM 9.2) was modified to make use of the MB bit-count in generating the explicit FMO slice group mapping.

A simulation of the transmission system was done in order to investigate the effects of different

Table 1. Summary of MB loss count for slow and fast fading

Sequence	FMO Maps							
	Slow fading				Fast Fading			
	One slice	Interleave	Dispersed	Bit count	One slice	Interleave	Dispersed	Bit count
Akiyo	1547	812	836	**720**	5367	1535	1355	**1205**
bridge close	1028	458	462	**387**	4398	972	789	**710**
carphone	1380	888	790	**615**	5634	1390	1233	**1113**
foreman	1235	858	719	**668**	5903	1337	1232	**1193**

Figure 16. Summary of MB loss count for FMO with FEC, slow and fast fading

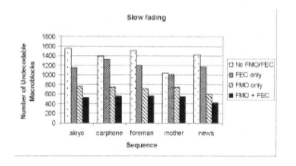
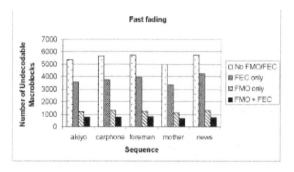

fading conditions, different FMO map types and FEC coding on the quality of video sequences under test. The wireless channel simulator with characteristics described on page 221 was used to generate the bit error patterns with random and burst errors. To simulate different fading conditions the maximum Doppler frequency is set to 1 Hz and 40 Hz for fast and slow fading conditions respectively. The packetization of the video packets follows the Personal Access Communication Services (PACS) standard which is a low-bit rate standard for wireless communications and uses fixed packet size of 80-bit. The resulting bit error rate (BER) and packet error rate (PER) are 0.06 and 0.09 respectively, both for slow and fast fading conditions. The average PSNR and number of undecodable MB are used as performance metrics.

The summary of the number of undecodable MBs for slow and fast fading conditions are summarized in Table 1. By using explicit FMO using bit-count information, the number of undecodable MB can be reduced by up to 20% as compared with the predefined map types of H.264/AVC.

To further improve the error resiliency of the video packets against channel errors, FMO is combined with FEC coding (Supavadee Aramvith & Hantanong, Dec. 2006). For simplicity, the Bose, Chaundry, Hocquengham (BCH) code is used, although other FEC coding methods can also be used. The BCH(25,20) that is capable of correcting 1-bit error is used in the simulations. The summary of the number of undecodable MBs and average PSNR for slow and fast fading conditions are summarized in Figure 16 and Figure 17.

Figure 17. Average PSNR for FMO with FEC, slow and fast fading

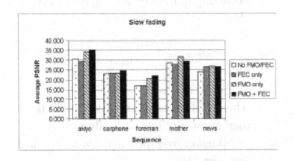
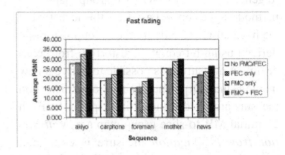

The combination of FMO and FEC can reduce the average number of undecodable MB of up to 60% for slow fading and up to 86% for fast fading. The improvement in average PSNR is up to 5 dB for slow fading and up to 7dB for fast fading respectively. This shows that using FMO with FEC outperforms other methods that use FMO only or FEC only.

Joint FMO Using Spatial and Temporal Indicators, FEC Coding and Interleaving for Wireless Video Transmission

In addition to using bit-count as a spatial indicator of MB importance, temporal indicators of MB importance were also investigated. In (Panyavaraporn, Cajote, & Aramvith, Nov. 2007), a *distortion-from-concealment* measure was used as a temporal indicator of MB importance to generate explicit FMO slice group maps. The idea is that if groups of MB contains error and are concealed at the decoder, a certain amount of distortion is incurred depending on the difference in pixel values between frames.

Given a packet corresponding to an area of pixels in macroblocks that has an error, the undecodable macroblock at the decoder will then be concealed using non motion-compensated error concealment method. The *distortion-from-concealment* due to the error concealment process,

D_{CE}, based on the sum of absolute difference (SAD) can be computed at the encoder during the first pass encoding, as shown in eq. (9),

$$D_{CE} = \sum_{(x,y \in L)} \left| f_k(x,y) - f_{k-1}(x,y) \right| \qquad (9)$$

Frame k and k-1 are the current frame and previous frame, respectively, $f(x,y)$ is the reconstructed pixel value at the coordinate (x, y), and L is the damaged area due to the error packet. The computed *distortion-from-concealment* error per macroblock is then sorted in descending order. The macroblocks with high *distortion-from-concealment* measures are assigned to different slice groups, in order to interleave the seemingly important macroblock into different slice groups, to generate the explicit FMO slice group mapping using temporal information of the MBs.

The same simulation scenarios as described on page 232 are used in order to provide fair comparison with the previous works that use explicit FMO map types. From Table 2 and Table 3 that using *distortion-from-concealment* error performs slightly better if not comparable to the method that uses bit count information both for slow and fast fading conditions.

In order to further improve the performance of using FMO for wireless video transmission, a method that combines the spatial and temporal information of the MBs is suggested in (Cajote,

Aramvith, Guevara, & Miyanaga, May 2007) to generate explicit FMO slice group maps. The method suggested is based on the idea that if we have an initial MB-to-slice group mapping, derived using bit-count or distortion from concealment measure, it is possible to derive a new mapping that can potentially have lower distortion measure provided by the initial mapping. So from an initial MB-to-slice group map a new *distortion-from-propagation* measure is computed using three parameters: 1) the individual *distortion-from-concealment* measure of that MB, 2) the distortion measure of the MB belonging to the same slice group, the *distortion-from-propagation,* and 3) the estimated probability that a MB will have an error within the slice, derived from the bit-count information.

The new distortion measure is called *distortion-from-propagation* because the location of the MB within a slice is taken into consideration. The location of the MB within the slice determined the severity of spatial error propagation when the MB is corrupted with errors. In effect, new information is combined with the *distortion-from-concealment* measure, in order to consider the location of the MB within the slice. The new information is in the form of the *location* of the MB within the slice, provided by the initial slice group mapping and the *probability* that an error will occur in the MB, provided by the bit-count information. The resulting explicit FMO map type is called STI-FMO map to indicate that it uses both spatial and temporal information in generating the MB-to-slice group maps.

The procedure for computing the *distortion-from-propagation* measure is as follows.

1. An initial slice group mapping is generated based on the *distortion-from-concealment* measure using eq. (9).
2. The probability that a given MB_j in a slice will be in error is computed by using the bit count information of the MB and the location of the MB in the initial slice group

mapping. The probability of a single bit error occurring in the MB is computed as in eq. (10),

$$P\left(MB_j \text{ error} \mid \text{single bit error}\right) = \frac{P\left(\text{single bit error} \mid MB_j \text{ error}\right)P\left(MB_j \text{ error}\right)}{P\left(\text{single bit error}\right)} \approx \left(\frac{m}{k}\right)$$

(10)

where m is the bit-count of MBj and k is the total number of bits in the slice.

3. A *distortion-from-propagation* is computed using eq. (11).

$$D_{prop} = \sum_{i=j}^{N} \left(D_{CEi} \cdot P\left(MB_i \text{ error} \mid \text{single bit error}\right)\right)$$

(11)

where i denotes the set of MBs in slice group position j up to N, and N is the last MB in the slice. D_{CEi} is the individual distortion of MB computed from eq. (9) and $P(MB_i error \mid single bit error)$ is the probability the MBs will be in error as computed from eq. (10).

The same simulation scenarios described on page 232 were used to evaluate the performance of the STI-FMO method. The summary of the results in comparing the PSNR and number of undecodable MBs are shown in Table 2 and Table 3 respectively.

It can be shown that using STI-FMO performs well in reducing the number of undecodable MB under fast fading conditions. This is because the *distortion-from-propagation* measure correlates well with the effects of error propagation under fast fading conditions.

Some improvements in the PSNR can also be obtained when using the STI-FMO scheme. Figure 18 and Figure 19 shows the comparison of PSNR plots for the carphone sequence under slow and fast fading conditions respectively.

The previous results show that using STI-FMO performs better, in terms of PSNR and number of undecodable MBs, than the previously reported works in (Hantanong & Aramvith, August 2005)

Table 2. Comparison of number of undecodable MB, using FMO

Loss MB	Akiyo		Foreman		Claire		Carphone	
	slow	Fast	slow	Fast	slow	fast	slow	Fast
No FMO	1547	5367	1499	5740	1346	5269	1380	5634
Bit count	758	1210	**712**	1243	**780**	1257	742	1329
Distortion	**701**	1210	746	1187	833	1182	651	1202
STI-FMO	750	**1153**	734	**1185**	833	**1147**	**622**	**1176**

Table 3. Comparison of average PSNR, using FMO

PSNR (dB)	Akiyo		Foreman		Claire		Carphone	
	slow	fast	slow	fast	slow	Fast	slow	fast
No FMO	30.71	27.63	17.11	15.12	30.82	24.31	23.04	19.01
Bit count	34.46	32.17	20.61	18.19	31.12	**30.07**	23.29	21.94
Distortion	34.75	31.58	**20.62**	**19.81**	30.66	29.59	25.49	22.62
STI-FMO	**35.03**	32.37	20.34	19.40	**31.79**	29.89	**26.45**	**23.06**

Figure 18. Comparison of PSNR for Carphone sequence, slow fading

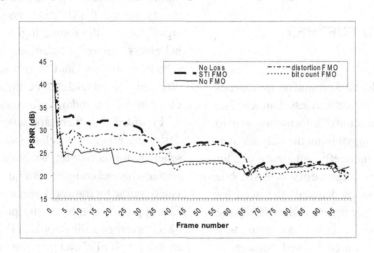

Figure 19. Comparison of PSNR for Carphone sequence, fast fading

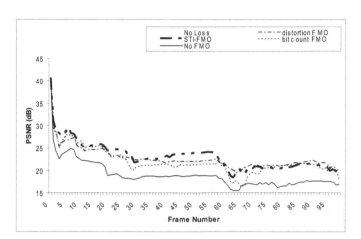

and (Panyavaraporn, Cajote, & Aramvith, Nov. 2007). The new *distortion-from-propagation* measure is more accurate in assessing the relative importance of a MB because it combines the spatial and temporal information of MBs.

SUMMARY AND FURTHER READINGS

This chapter provides background on approaches for video transmission over wireless channels. The need to reduce the amount of information used to represent the video signal is not the only motivation for developing more efficient algorithms for video transport. The emergence of wireless mobile communication systems demands the need for more efficient multiple access and multiplexing schemes. Users have to share a common radio space often with resource limited constraints due to the need for mobility, low complexity and power constrained mobile devices. In addition, radio transmissions over wireless mobile channels are highly prone to errors due to multipath effects and deep signal fading due to interference. Because of the hostile propagation environments

inherent in mobile radio link channels, video compression algorithms must be error-resilient as well. The requirements of high compression efficiency often conflicts with robust error-resiliency in video transmission. This is due to the limited bandwidth and error-prone characteristics of the wireless channel. Efficient encoding of the video signal renders the source highly-prone to channel errors. Although traditional channel coding schemes can detect and correct some errors, this often leads to reduced channel throughput because of the added redundant information.

Provided that there are several tradeoffs in designing efficient wireless video transmission scheme, in this chapter, we have presented joint source-channel coding technique for H.264/AVC video coding for transport over wireless channels. The approach combines the proposed Explicit FMO as error-resilient tools in H.264/AVC video encoder with FEC and interleaving such that the number of macroblock errors is reduced. Another approach explores the intelligent rate control algorithm utilizing wireless channel model and feedback from wireless channel with ARQ as channel coding scheme. This also helps in video quality improvement. The works toward the integration of error-resilient video transmission system are still quite challenging research areas in the wireless video research community.

To further explore more reading in research literatures, the authors would recommend the reader to refer to (Ogunfunmi & Huang, May 2005), (Katz, Greenberg, Yarkoni, Blaunstien, & Giladi, March 2007) and (Yves Dhondt, Mys, Zutter, & Walle, June 2007) for some recent works about FMO in H.264/AVC. For some recent work on Rate Control and Rate-Distortion in H.264/AVC the interested reader can refer to (Eiamjumrus & Aramvith, Dec. 2006b), (Yi & Ling, May 2005), (Ming & Hong-yuan, 2006), (W. Wang, Lu, Cui, & Tang, 2006), (Liu, Li, & Soh, January 2007), (Jeong & Choe, Feb. 2007), (Tu, Yang, & Sun, May 2007), (Kwon, Shen, & Kuo, May 2007), (Hassan & Krunz, August 2007), (H. Wang & Kwong, January 2008) and (Ates & Altunbasak, February 2008).

REFERENCES

Aramvith, S., & Hantanong, W. (Dec. 2006). Joint Flexible Macroblock Ordering and FEC for H.264 Wireless Video Transmission. *Paper presented at the IEEE Symposium on Intelligent Signal Processing and Communications (ISPACS).*

Aramvith, S., Lin, C.-W., Roy, S., & Sun, M.-T. (June 2002). Wireless Video Transport using Conditional Retransmission and Low-Delay Interleaving. *IEEE Trans. on Ckts. and Sys. for Video Tech, 12*(6), 558-565.

Aramvith, S., Pao, I.-M., & Sun, M.-T. (May 2001). A Rate-Control Scheme for Video Transport over Wireless. *IEEE Trans. on Ckts. and Sys. for Video Tech, 11*(5), 569-580.

Ates, H. F., & Altunbasak, Y. (February 2008). Rate-Distortion and Complexity Optimized Motion Estimation for H.264 Video Coding. *IEEE Trans. on Ckts. and Sys. for Video Tech, 18*(2).

Cajote, R. D., Aramvith, S., Guevara, R. C. L., & Miyanaga, Y. (May 2007, May 2007). *FMO Slice Group Maps Using Spatial and Temporal Indicators for H.264 Wireless Video Transmission.* Paper presented at the Int'l Symposium in Ckts. and Systems (ISCAS), Seatle, Washington.

Chen, C. (Sept. 1995). Error Detection and Concealment with Unsupervised MPEG2 Video Decoder. *Journal of Visual Communication and Image Representation, 6*(3), 265-278.

Chen, T.-C., Chang, L.-F., Wong, A. H., Sun, M.-T., & Hsing, T. R. (April 1995). Real-time software-based end-to-end wireless visual communications simulation platform. *Paper presented at the Proc. of SPIE: Visual Comms and Image Processing.*

Cherriman, P., & Hanzo, L. (June 1998). Programmable H,263-based video transceivers for interference-limited environments. *IEEE Trans. on Ckts. and Sys. for Video Tech, 8*(3), 275-286.

Chiang, T., & Zhang, Y.-Q. (1997). A new rate control scheme using quadratic rate distortion model. *IEEE Trans. on Ckts. and Sys. for Video Tech, 7*(1), 246-250.

Dhondt, Y., Lambert, P., & Walle, R. V. d. (2006). A Flexible Macroblock Scheme for Unequal Error Protection. *Paper presented at the Int'l Conf. on Image Processing.*

Dhondt, Y., Mys, S., Zutter, S. D., & Walle, R. V. d. (June 2007). An Alternative Scatter Pattern for Flexible Macroblock Ordering in H.264/AVC. *Paper presented at the International Symposium on Image Analysis and Multimedia Interactive Services.*

Eiamjumrus, N., & Aramvith, S. (Dec. 2006a). New Rate-Control Scheme based on Cauchy Rate-Distortion Optimization Model for H.264 Video Coding. *Paper presented at the IEEE International Symposium on Intelligent Signal Processing and Communication Systems*, Japan.

Eiamjumrus, N., & Aramvith, S. (Dec. 2006b). Rate-Control Scheme based on Cauchy Rate-Distortion Optimization Model for H.264 under Low Delay Constraint. *Paper presented at the IEEE International Conference on Intelligent Information Hiding and Multimedia Signal Processing*, USA.

Farber, N., & Girod, B. (October 1997). Robust H.263 compatible video transmission for mobile acess to video servers. *Paper presented at the IEEE Conf. on Image Processing (ICIP)*, Santa Barbara, CA.

Gilbert, E. N. (Sept. 1960). Capacity of Burst-noise Channel. *Bell Systems Technical Journal, 39*, 1253-1266.

Hantanong, W., & Aramvith, S. (August 2005, August 2005). Analysis of Macroblock-to-slice Group Mapping for H.264 Video Transmission over Packet-based Wireless Fading Channel. *Paper presented at the 48th Midwest Symposium on Circuits and Systems.*

Haskel, P., & Messerschmitt, D. (1992, 1992). Resynchronization of motion compensated video affected by ATM cell loss. *Paper presented at the ICASSP.*

Hassan, M., & Krunz, M. (August 2007). Video Streaming over Wireless Packet Networks: An Occupancy-Based Rate Adaptation Perspective. *IEEE Trans. on Ckts. and Sys. for Video Tech, 17*(8).

Heron, A., & MacDonald, N. (1992). Video Transmission over a radio link using H.261 and DECT. *Paper presented at the IEE Conference.*

Hsu, C.-Y., Ortega, A., & Khansari, M. (May 1999). Rate Control for robuts video transmission over burst-error wireless channels. *IEEE Journal on Selected Areas in Communications, 17*(5), 756-773.

http://en.wikipedia.org/wiki/Multimedia. Multimedia.

ISO/ICE:JTCI/SC29/WG11. (1997). *Text of ISO/ICE 14496-2 MPEG-4 Video VM ver. 8.0.* Stockhome: Video Group.

ISO/IEC. (1995a). Coding of moving pictures and associated audio for digital storage media at up to about 1.5 Mbit/s – Part 3 Audio: ISO/IEC 11172-3.

ISO/IEC. (1995b). MPEG-2 Standard: Generic coding of moving pictures and associated audio information: Video: ISO/IEC 13 818-2.

ISO/IEC. (1997). Generic coding of moving pictures and associated audio information - Part 7: Advanced Audio Coding (AAC): ISO/IEC 13818-7.

ISO/IEC. (1998). Coding of Moving Pictures and Associated Audio and Digital Storage Media of up to about 1.5 Mbit/s: ISO/IEC 11172.

ISO/IEC. (2002). International Standard Coding of Still Pictures (JPEG 2000): ISO/IEC 15444-1:2004.

ISO/IEC. (2003). Information technology -- Coding of audio-visual objects -- Part 14: MP4 File Format: ISO/IEC 14496-14.

ISO/IEC. (2004). MPEG-4 High Efficiency AAC (HE AAC): ISO/IEC 14496-3, Amd.2.

ITU. (1993). Video codec for audiovisual services at p x 64 kbit/s ITU-T Recommendation: H.261.

ITU. (1995). Video Coding for Low Bit Rate Communications: ITU-T Recommendation H.263.

ITU. (March 2005). Advanced Video Coding for generic audiovisual services: ITU-T Recommendation H.264.

ITU. (Sept. 1992). Digital Compression and Coding of Continuous-Tone Still Images - Requirements and Guidelines: ITU-T Recommendation T.81.

Jeong, J., & Choe, Y. (Feb. 2007). A Rate Control Scheme for H.264/AVC CBR Transmission. *Paper presented at the Fourth International Conference on Signal Processing, Pattern Recognition and Applications.*

JVT. (2003). *Proposed Draft of Adaptive Rate Control.* Geneva: Inst. of Computer Technology.

Katz, B., Greenberg, S., Yarkoni, N., Blaunstien, N., & Giladi, R. (March 2007). New Error-Resilient Scheme Based on FMO and Dynamic Redundant Slice Allocation for Wireless Video Transmission. *IEEE Trans. on Broadcasting, 53*(1), 308-319.

Khansari, M., Jalali, A., Dubois, E., & Memelstein, P. (May 1999). Low bit-rate video transmission over fading channels for wireless microcellular systems. *IEEE Trans. on Ckts. and Sys. for Video Tech, 6*(1), 1-11.

Kwon, D.-K., Shen, M.-Y., & Kuo, C.-C. J. (May 2007). Rate Control for H.264 Video with Enhanced Rate and Distortion Models. *IEEE Trans. on Ckts. and Sys. for Video Tech, 17*(5).

Lam, W.-M., Reibman, A. R., & Lin, B. (1993). Recovery of lost or erroneously received motion vectors. *Paper presented at the ICASSP.*

Lie, J., & Ngan, K. N. (2005, 2005). An Error Sensitivity-based Redundant Macroblock Strategy for Robust Wireless Video Transmission. *Paper presented at the Int'l Conf. on Wireless Networks, Comms. and Mobile Computing.*

Lin, S., Costello, D. J., & Miller, M. J. (1984). Automatic repeat error control schemes. *IEEE Communications Magazine, 22,* 5-17.

Liu, Y., Li, Z. G., & Soh, Y. C. (January 2007). A Novel Rate Control Scheme for Low Delay Video Communication of H.264/AVC Standard. *IEEE Trans. on Ckts. and Sys. for Video Tech, 17*(1).

Ming, Y., & Hong-yuan, W. (2006). A rate-control scheme for H.264 video under low bandwidth channel. *Journal of Zhejiang University SCIENCE A, 6.*

Navakitkanok, P., & Aramvith, S. (2004). Improved Rate Control for Advanced Video Coding (AVC) Standard under low-delay contraints. *Paper presented at the Intn'l Conf. on Info. Tech.: Coding and Computing* (ITCC'04).

Ngan, K. N., Yap, C. W., & Tan, K. T. (2001). *Video Coding for Wireless Communication Systems.* New York: Marcel Dekker, Inc.

Ogunfunmi, T., & Huang, W. C. (May 2005, May 23-26). A Flexible Macroblock Ordering with 3D MBAMAP for H.264/AVC. *Paper presented at the IEEE International Symposium on Circuits and Systems.*

Ortega, A., Ramchandran, K., & Vetterli, M. (1994). Optimal trellis-based buffered compression and fast approximations. *IEEE Trans. on Image Processing, 3*(1), 26-40.

Panyavaraporn, J., Cajote, R. D., & Aramvith, S. (Nov. 2007, Nov. 2007). Performance Analysis of Flexible Macroblock Ordering using Bit-count and Distortion Measure for H.264 Wireless Video Transmission. *Paper presented at the Int'l Workshop on Smart Info-Media Systems,* Bangkok, Thailand.

Podolsky, M., McCanne, S., & Vetterli, M. (1998). Soft ARQ for layeres streaming media, *Technical Report UCB/CSD-98-1024.* University of California, Berkeley: Computer Science Division.

Rao, K. R., Bojkovic, Z. S., & Milovanovic, D. A. (May 2002). *Multimedia Communication Systems: Techniques, Standards and Networks*: Prentice Hall PTR.

Ribas-Corbera, J., & Lei, S. (1999). Rate Control in DCT Video Coding for Low-Delay Video Communications. *IEEE Trans. on Ckts. and Sys. for Video Tech, 9*(1), 172-185.

Shannon, C. E. (1959). Coding Theorems for a discrete source with a fidelity criterion.

Srisawaivilai, N., & Aramvith, S. (2005). Improved H.264 Rate-Control using Channel

Throughput Estimate for ARQ-based Wireless Video Transmission. *Paper presented at the IEEE Symposium on Intelligent Signal Processing and Communications,* Hongkong.

Steinbach, E., Farber, N., & Girod, B. (Dec. 1997). Standards compatible extension of H.263 for robust video transmission in mobile environments. *IEEE Trans. on Ckts. and Sys. for Video Tech, 7*(6), 872-881.

Thomos, N., Argyropoulos, S., Boulgouris, N. V., & Strintzis, M. G. (Nov. 2005). Error Resilient Transmission of H.264/AVC streams using Flexible Macroblock Ordering. *Paper presented at the EWIMT05,* London, UK.

Tu, Y.-K., Yang, J.-F., & Sun, M.-T. (May 2007). Rate-Distortion Modeling for Efficient H.264/AVC Encoding. *IEEE Trans. on Ckts. and Sys. for Video Tech, 17*(5).

Tzou, K. (November 1989). Post filtering for Cell loss Concealment in Packet Video. *SPIE Visual Communications and Image Processing IV, 1199,* 1620-1628.

Wada, N. (1989). Selective Recovery of video packet loss using error concealment. *IEEE Journal on Selected Areas in Communications, 7,* 807-814.

Wang, H., & Kwong, S. (January 2008). Rate-Distortion Optimization of Rate Control for H.264 with Adaptive Initial Quantization Parameter Determination. *IEEE Trans. on Ckts. and Sys. for Video Tech, 18*(1).

Wang, W., Lu, Y., Cui, H., & Tang, K. (2006). Rate control for low delay H.264/AVC transmission over channels with burst error. *Paper presented at the IMACS Multiconference on Computational Engineering on Systems Applications.*

Wenger, S., & Horowitz, M. (May 2002). *FMO: Flexible Macroblock Ordering.* Fairfax (USA).

Wiegand, T., Sullivan, G. J., Bjontegaard, G., & Luthra, A. (2003). Overview of the H.264/AVC video coding standard. *IEEE Transactions on Circuits and Systems for Video Technology, 13*(7), 560-576.

Yi, X., & Ling, N. (May 2005). Improved H.264 Rate Control by Enhanced MAD-based frame complexity prediction. *Journal of Visual Communication and Image Representation.*

KEY TERMS

ADF: Average Duration of Fade, the average amount of time that a fading signal stays below a specified threshold.

ARQ: Automatic Repeat Request, a system of transmission protocols for error control.

BER: Bit Error Rate, the percentage of bits that have errors relative to the total number of bits received during transmission.

FEC: Forward Error Correction, system of error control schemes for data transmission which adds redundant information in order to provide robustness to channel errors.

H.264/AVC ITU-T: Standard for advanced video coding, also known as MPEG-4 Part 10.

LCR: Level Crossing Rate, the rate (or frequency) that a fading signal crosses a specified threshold in the positive going direction.

MPEG-4 Part 10: The same as H.264.

PSNR: Peak Signal to Noise Ratio, a measure of signal fidelity by computing the ratio the peak signal power and the corrupting noise power.

Chapter XIII
A Survey of Information Hiding

M. Hassan Shirali-Shahreza
Amirkabir University of Technology, Iran

Mohammad Shirali-Shahreza
Sharif University of Technology, Iran

ABSTRACT

Establishing hidden communication is an important subject of discussion that has gained increasing importance recently, particularly with the development of the Internet. One of the methods introduced for establishing hidden communication is Steganography. Steganography is a method to hide data in a cover media so that other persons will not notice that such data is there. In this chapter steganography is introduced and its history is described. Then the major steganography methods include image, audio, video, and text steganography are reviewed.

INTRODUCTION

Today the Internet is a tool for the human life while being a necessary means of living in many developed countries where it is used for shopping, communicating with others, carrying out transactions, etc. Although hidden exchange of information has been an important issue since old times, today in the age of the communications and information (ICT) and esp. with the development of the Internet and its use in information systems, the issue of information security has become increasingly important. One of the grounds for

discussion in the field of information security is the hidden exchange of information. To this end, various methods such as cryptography, *steganography*, coding, etc have been used.

To fight back against such people as hackers, intruders, sniffers and those stealing information usually we use the cryptography method. In cryptography, the information is encrypted with a key and only the person who has the key can decrypt and read the information. So without the key, nobody has access to that information. But encrypted data will attract the attention.

In recent years, *steganography* is widely used for hidden exchange of information. The word *steganography* is a Greek word that means 'hidden writing'. While implementing this method, the main purpose is to hide data in a *cover media* so that other persons will not notice that such data is there. This is a major distinction of this method with the other methods of hidden exchange of data because, for example, in the method of cryptography, individuals see the encoded data and notice that such data exists but they cannot comprehend it. However, in *steganography*, individuals will not notice at all that data exists in the sources (Judge, 2001).

Most *steganography* jobs have been performed on images (Chandramouli, and Memon, 2001), video clips (Doërr, and Dugelay, 2003), text (Alattar, and Alattar, 2004), music and sound (Gopalan, 2003). It has also been implemented on such varying systems as computers and mobile phones (Shirali Shahreza, 2005, July).

Nowadays, however, information security has improved considerably with the other mentioned methods. The *steganography* method, in addition to application in cover exchange of information, is also used in such other fields as copyright protection, preventing e-document forging, etc (Hartung, and Girod, 1997).

In the followed sections after explaining the *steganography* history, we will discuss about the major *steganography* methods: *Image Steganography*, Video *Steganography*, Audio *Steganography* and *Text Steganography*. In sections 7 and 8 Black & White *Steganography* and Webpages *Steganography*, which are subcategories of image and *text steganography*, are reviewed. In the last section we have drawn the final conclusions.

BACKGROUND

In this section some of the *steganography* methods which are done until today are reviewed.

- In the era of Darius the Great [Iranian king, 500 A.C.] a Greek prisoner shaved head of a slave to tattoo a message for his son-in-law over his head. After the slave's hair grew again, the prisoner sent him to Greece. There the message was extracted after the slave's head was shaved again.

- A Greek commander who wanted to send a colleague some information wrote them on a wooden tablet and impregnated the surface of the tablet with white solid oil and then sent it as a white tablet (Saha, 2000).

- Romans used to use invisible ink in text writing. The hidden text reappeared by heating.

- John Trithemius carried out the first researches on *steganography*. He has provided tables of figures in his book in which messages are hidden. It was only recently that the messages were discovered.

- The first book which really dealt with *steganography* was written by Gaspari Schotti which is titled Steganographica. The book was written in 1665 (Judge, 2001).

- In the centuries 15 and 16, historians used to hide their names within their books in fear of rulers (Rabah, 2004).

- Bach, the renowned musician, hid his name by special musical notes.

- Shakespeare hid the name of Bacon in his plays (Rabah, 2004).

- Scottish queen used to hide confidential letters in the holes of beverage barrels.

- In Peru, there are designs on the ground that conveys special concepts if seen from the sky.

- During the World War II, Nazis used to downsize confidential messages by two hundred times to resemble just a point. They also used hide messages within a paragraph so that the real message would appear only after juxtaposing the second letters of the paragraph words (Jamil, 1999).

Figure 1. The sign used to guide slaves in American Civil War (Judge, 2001)

- In Vietnam War, American seized soldiers shaped their hand in particular forms in their pictures to send messages.
- In America's civil war slaves were guided to escape through messages hidden on quilts' designs and drawings. In order to put the quilts on display for the slaves, they were washed and hanged. The figure 1 shows one of these signs advising the slaves to follow the bear tracks over the mountain (Judge, 2001).

IMAGE STEGANOGRAPHY

The most *cover media* used for *steganography* is image. As a result, numerous methods have been used to this end. The reason is the large redundant in the images and the possibility of hiding information in the images without attracting attention to human visual system.

Work performed on *steganography* in image can be classified into three major groups: temporal method, spatial domain method and fractal method.

A. Temporal Method

In this method, the data in question is added to quantities of luminosity of pixels in the image. One of the commonest methods of temporal method is the least significant bit (LSB) method, in which information is hidden in one to four least significant bits (Curran, and Bailey, 2003). Figure 2 shows a sample of LSB *steganography*.

In RGB images, every pixel consists of three separate colors of red, green and blue. Each bit of data is put in the least significant bit of a color. As change of the value of the least significant bit

Figure 2. An example of LSB steganography

A) Original image

B) Stego image

has no tangible effect on the color of the image, the hidden information, therefore, is not disclosed. Indeed more bits of information can be hidden in each color, thus increasing the amount of information that can be hidden in the image. However, this will make the changes more tangible.

The advantages of this method include:

1. Because of its simple performance and implementation, this method can be used for hiding information by the beginners.
2. In this method, because of *steganography* of information in the image, the size of the image is not change. In addition, as the volume of the image remains fixed even by changing *steganography* information inside the image and further *steganography* of information in the images, as a result one image can be used for several exchanges of information.

B. Spatial Domain Method

Another method is the calculation of conversion of frequency of the image and adding information in the frequency domain. A well-known method is to use the Discrete Fourier Transform (DFT) or the Discrete Cosine Transform (DCT) (Provos, and Honeyman, 2003). Considering the use of exchange of cosine transform in JPEG image format, this method is good for said format. However, it also entails problems as provided below:

*   If information is hidden in the image before frequency exchange, considering the loss of information in the JPEG algorithm, the retrieval of information embedded in the image faces some difficulty. Therefore, it is necessary for the information in the coefficients to be embedded after conversion.
*   The low-frequency DCT coefficients in the JPEG images show the areas with a similar color in the image and the change of these coefficients is very tangible. In addition, the data is not saved in coefficients with quantities of 1, 0 and -1.

The capacity of *steganography* in spatial domain method depends on the apparent features of the image and the variety of colors used in it while, in temporal method, capacity relates to the number of pixels and the number of bits allocated to each pixel for display of color.

C. Fractal Method

The other method of *steganography* is based on fractal compressing. In this method, blocks of the image that contain repeated patterns are selected and information is saved in them.

In this method, a little amount of information can be hidden in the image. Moreover, this method is very error-sensitive and also costly in terms of calculation (Marvel et al., 1999).

VIDEO *STEGANOGRAPHY*

As little work has been carried out on video *steganography*, in this section we survey various video *watermarking* methods.

Watermarking is a branch of data hiding close to the *steganography*, which has common usage in the protection of copyrights of digital media, such as art images, music, and video. The main idea of *watermarking* is that a unique piece of data is embedded within a media without noticeably altering it. At any time we can extract the secret data from the media to prove their originality. The conceptual difference between the *steganography* and *watermarking* is the object of the communication. In *watermarking* the carrier data are the communication, while the hidden data provide copyright protection; on the contrary, in *steganography* the secret is the communication, while the carrier data are a cover. Moreover, the *steganography* should be undetectable, while the presence of *watermarking* is often declared; any attempt of remove a watermark leads to a deterioration of the quality of the carrier (Amoroso, and Masotti, 2006).

While in 1995 only two papers were presented on *watermarking*, this reached 376 in 2001, which indicates a rapid growth in the use of *watermarking* (Doërr and Dugelay, 2003). There has also been a considerable increase in video *watermarking*.

However, one should know that the methods used for video *watermarking* are different from those used for image *watermarking*. There are three major differences between these two methods:

- Because of much processing that is carried out on video clips for different purposes -such as video show, video quality improvement, video compressing, etc- there is the possibility of deleting the information hidden in the video while such a problem is not so important for images.
- Because of continuity and connection of video frames, change of the contents of a frame and hiding information in it may be noticeable.

- Videos broadcast nowadays are usually real-time, such as live sports broadcast. This creates many problems for hiding data in video. For example, the time available for *steganography* calculations is very limited or the incorrect broadcast of a frame will create numerous problems.

The result is that one cannot use the algorithms used for images the same way for videos. Therefore, appropriate methods have been provided below for video *watermarking*:

A. Considering Video as Separate Images

In this method (Doërr and Dugelay, 2004), each video frame is considered as a separate image, in which images information is hidden. This is the most simple and straightforward method (Figure 3).

The main advantage of this method is the possibility of using the algorithms used in image

Figure 3. Three consecutive frames from "Table Tennis": Original (top), watermarked (middle), absolute frame difference (bottom) (Ge et al., 2003)

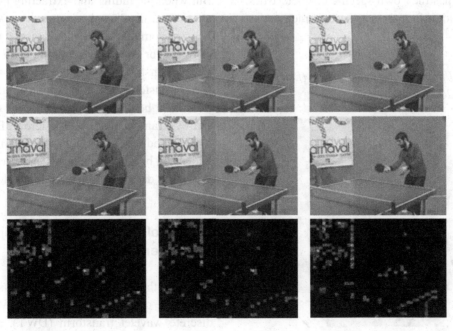

watermarking for video, but it requires a large amount of computation.

B. Finding New Dimensions in Video

Videos have potential characteristics and dimensions, in which dimensions, if identified, one can hide information (Ge et al., 2003; Wang et al., 2005). For example, one can use special characteristics of the human visual system to hide information in the video so that the human eye cannot identify the changes made in the video. Or one can consider the video as one dimensional signal -like the one received by the TV- to hide information in the signal (Hartung and Girod, 1998; Kalker et al., 1999) (Figure 4).

With this method, we will be able to provide powerful watermarks in video. Unfortunately, however, this method, like the previous method, requires a great deal of computations.

C. Using the Special Characteristics of Video Saving Formats

Each of these video saving formats, like MPEG, AVI, etc, has their own specific characteristics. One can hide information in these characteristics.

Figure 4. Line scan of a video stream (Doërr and Dugelay, 2003)

For example, some formats benefit from special conversions, where information can be hidden (Lu et al., 2002).

The main advantage of this method is having simple algorithms that can be used real-time. Unfortunately, however, the *watermarking* in this method totally depends on the video saving format.

AUDIO *STEGANOGRAPHY*

In this section we will review some of the works which has been done on audio *steganography*.

Time domain is one of the common domains used for *steganography* (Bender et al., 1996). While time domain *steganography* is usually simple and fast (Cvejic and Seppanen, 2004), other domains can also be used for *steganography*. For example wavelet domain (Cvejic and Seppanen, 2002) and Fourier domain (Gang et al., 2001) are used to hide information in audio signals.

Different domains have special features which made them suitable for different application. Most time domain methods have zero error rates. But when the hiding and extracting procedures are done in another domain such as wavelet or Fourier, some error are introduced. The source of this error is usually rounding error occurred during transform or when the signal is saved as a file or transferred via a communication channel. So it must be considered to know the error rate (Kirovski and Malvar, 2003). There are Error Correction Coding (ECC) (Sweene, 1991) methods which can be used to achieve zero error rate but it is more desirable to have a method with low error rate.

A. Wavelet Domain LSB (Cvejic and Seppanen, 2002)

In this method, the wavelet coefficients of audio signal are calculated using Haar wavelets and discrete wavelet transform (DWT). Then the coefficients are scaled and converted to integers. Now the information is hidden in the LSB of the coefficients. Then the coefficients are scaled back to original scale and the inverse DWT is done to generate the stego audio. The extracting procedure is similar to hiding procedure. This method has high capacity and also good SNR. The listening tests also show good *perceptual transparency* (which means that nobody will notice the existence of hidden information).

B. Audio-to-Image Wavelet Domain Steganography (Santosa and Bao, 2005)

In this method, first the wavelet transform of the audio is calculated. Then some of the details coefficients are chosen and sampled at a defined interval. The sampled coefficients are arranged to form an image. Then the data is hidden in the image using an *image steganography* method. After that the *stego image* (image containing *steganography* data) is decomposed to a set of details coefficients. Then the stego audio is constructed by performing the wavelet reconstruction transform.

This method has low hiding capacity (for example 256 bps), but has resistance to MP3 compression. The parameters of wavelet transforms such as the type of wavelet which is used, the level which wavelet transform is done and the selected coefficients used for hiding data can be used as a secret key to gain more security.

C. Comparing Wavelet and Fourier Transforms for High Rate Steganography (Cvejic and Seppanen, 2004)

In (Cvejic and Seppanen, 2004), a comparison is done between wavelet transform and Fourier transform for high capacity *steganography*. They use LSB method to hide data in an audio signal in Time domain, Wavelet domain and Fourier domain. Their results show that hiding in wavelet or Fourier domain has better *perceptual transparency* and SNR (Signal to Noise Ratio). And between Fourier and wavelet, wavelet has small advantages in SNR.

TEXT STEGANOGRAPHY

A few works have been done on hiding information in texts. Following is the list of eleven different methods of the works carried out and reported thus far.

A. Steganography of Information in Random Character and Word Sequences

By generating a random sequence of characters or words, specific information can be hidden in this sequence (Bennett, 2004).

In this method, the characters or words sequence is random; therefore it is meaningless and attracts the attentions too much. It seems to be that this method is not *steganography*, but it is a kind of encryption.

B. Steganography of Information in Specific Characters in Words

In this method (Moerland, 2003), some specific characters from certain words are selected as hiding place for information. In the simplest form, for example, the first words of each paragraph are selected in a manner that by placing the first characters of these words side by side, the hidden information is extracted. This has been done by classic poets of Iran as well.

This method requires strong mental power and takes a lot of time. It also requires special text and not all types of texts can be used in this method.

C. Creating Spam Texts

This method is based on the Internet (Bennett, 2004). Based on the piece of information aimed for hiding, a number of spam emails are selected and some phrases appropriate to the concerned piece of information are chosen from among these letters, so that the concerned piece of information might be extracted from these phrases later. As 82 percent of emails in the United States are spam, this method does not attract too much attention.

However, the created text has no specific meaning in this method. On the other hand, the same as in the system which is described in previous method, using any kind of text is not possible. Furthermore, as email service providers filter spam, there is the risk of losing the email in the communication process.

D. Line Shifting

In this method (Alattar, and Alattar, 2004; Low et al., 1995), the lines of the text are vertically shifted to some degree (for example, each line shifts 1/300 inch up or down) and information are hidden by creating a unique shape of the text. This method is proper for printed texts.

However, in this method, the distances can be observed by using special instruments of distance assessment and necessary changes can be introduced to destroy the hidden information. Also if the text is retyped or if OCR (Optical Character Recognition) programs are used, the hidden information would get destroyed.

E. Word Shifting

In this method (Low et al., 1995; Kim et al., 2003), by shifting words horizontally and by changing distance between words, information are hidden in the text. This method is acceptable for texts where the distance between words is varying. This method can be identified less, because change

of distance between words to fill a line is quite common.

But if somebody was aware of the algorithm of distances, he can compare the present text with the algorithm and extract the hidden information by using the difference. The text image can be also closely studied to identify the changed distances. Although this method is very time consuming, there is a high probability of finding information hidden in the text. The same as in the previous method, retyping of the text or using OCR programs destroys the hidden information.

F. Syntactic Methods

By placing some punctuation signs such as full stop (.) and comma (,) in proper places, one can hide information in a text file (Bennett, 2004).

This method requires identifying proper places for putting punctuation signs. The amount of information to hide in this method is trivial.

G. Semantic Methods

In this method (Bennett, 2004; Niimi et al., 2003), they use the synonym of words for certain words thereby hiding information in the text. A major advantage of this method is the protection of information in case of retyping or using OCR programs (contrary to line shifting or word shifting methods).

However, this method may alter the meaning of the text.

H. Feature Coding

In this method (Rabah, 2004), some of the features of the text are altered. For example, the end part of some characters such as h, d, b or so on, are elongated or shortened a little thereby hiding information in the text. In this method, a large volume of information can be hidden in the text without making the reader aware of the existence of such information in the text.

By placing characters in a fixed shape, the information is lost. Retyping the text or using OCR program (as we mentioned in line shifting and word shifting methods) destroys the hidden information.

I. Abbreviation

Another method for hiding information is the use of abbreviations (Bender et al., 1996).

In this method, very little information can be hidden in the text. For example, only a few bits can be hidden in a file of several kilobytes.

J. Open Spaces

In this method (Bender et al., 1996; Huang and Yan, 2001), hiding information is done through adding extra white-spaces in the text. These white-spaces can be placed at the end of each line, at the end of each paragraph or between the words. This method can be implemented on any arbitrary text and does not raise attention of the reader.

However, the volume of information hidden under this method is very little. Also, some text editor programs automatically delete extra white-spaces and thus destroy the hidden information.

K. Persian/Arabic Text Steganography

In this method (Shirali-Shahreza and Shirali-Shahreza, 2006), data is hidden in Persian and Arabic texts by using a special characteristic of these languages.

Considering the existence of too many points in Persian and Arabic phrases, in this approach by vertical displacement of the point (see figure 5), we hide information in the texts.

Although this method doesn't attract attention and can hide a large volume of information in text, it can be only applied to Persian and Arabic and similar languages and for example can't be used

Figure 5. Vertical displacement of the points for the Persian letter NOON (Shirali-Shahreza and Shirali-Shahreza, 2006)

for hiding data in English texts, because only two English characters "i" and "j" have dot.

STEGANOGRAPHY IN BLACK & WHITE IMAGE

As mentioned before, most *steganography* work so far carried out on pictures has been on color or grayscale pictures and little work has been done on B&W pictures, because B&W pictures are sensitive to changes and, for example, change in one pixel of the picture in a white area would be quite visible while, in color pictures, if the color of a pixel is changed slightly, this would not be tangible. In this section, we study work carried out on *steganography* of B&W pictures.

A. Using Dithered Images

In this method, data are saved in dithered images. In old newspapers, the dithered method in the form of B&W dots were used for printing color or grayscale pictures and the pictures looked grayscale from a distance. The problem with this method is that it cannot be used for normal two-color pictures and, on the other hand, a small number of data can be saved in the picture (Tanaka et al., 1990).

B. Method to Displace Words and Lines

In this method, by displacing the text or changing the distance between words, data are hidden in the printed picture of a text. The problem with this method is that it can only be used for pictures of text and cannot be used for regular pictures (Low et al., 1995).

C. Changing Two Bits in Each Block

In this method, the input picture is divided into m×n blocks. Then each block is changed by apply XOR with a key on that block, so that the block is encoded. Considering the weight matrix, at most 2 bits of each block are changed. In this method, if the block dimensions are m×n, each block can hide $\log_2(mn+1)$ bits of data. The main advantage of this method is the high hiding capacity of this method. However, its major drawback is the tangible changes in the output picture (Tseng et al., 2002; Chen et al., 2000; Tseng and Pan, 2001).

D. Changing One Bit in Each Block

In this method, the B&W pictures are first divided into m×n blocks and then, in each block, at most one bit of information is hidden. For each block, the possibility of saving is calculated and, if the possibility exceeds a certain limit, the middle point in that block is changed according to the data in question. The major advantage of this method is the intangible changes in the resulting pictures. The drawback of this method is the low *steganography* capacity of the pictures. The more the edges of the picture, the higher the *steganography* capacity will be (Wu et al., 2000; Wu and Liu, 2004).

STEGANOGRAPHY IN WEB PAGES

This section reviews some works that have been done on HTML document *steganography* as a subcategory of *text steganography*.

A. Hiding in Comments

We can add comments on HTML pages as with other languages. On HTML pages, the comments begin with this symbol "<!--" and end with this symbol "-->". An easy way of *steganography* on HTML pages is to place data as comments.

As the browser does not show such information, the regular user cannot view the comments. However, by seeing the source of HTML document, he will be able to see the comments (HIPS 2005).

B. Hiding at the End of HTML Files

HTML pages begin with an <html> tag and end with an </html> tag. One of the other simplest methods for *steganography* on HTML pages, similarly to the method used in *steganography* at the end of images and documents (Camouflage, 2008; Arefin, 2004), is to place them after the </html> tag at the end of the page (Pinet, 2007). As the browser does not show such information, the user cannot see the information. However, if the user refers to the contents of the HTML document, he can easily see the information at the end of the document.

C. Steganography by Creating White Spaces

On HTML pages, the existence of space in tags is not important and the browser does not pay attention to such spaces. This feature is used for hiding information by placing certain white spaces among tag members (NeoByte 2008). Then, while extracting information from the page, information is extracted by calculating the amounts of spaces and by using the appropriate function. In this method, the document size increases considerably because of the many spaces in the document. Also, the HTML document loses its normal form and may attract attention.

D. Hiding by Changing the Case of the Letters

A method that we used for *steganography* in HTML documents was *steganography* by change of case. From among the other features of HTML documents is their case-insensitivity of tags and their members. For example, the three tags <BR>, <Br> and <br> are equally valid and are the same. As a result, one can do information *steganography* in HTML documents by changing the case of the letters in document tags. To extract information, one can extract information by comparing words in normal case and by using the appropriate function.

Since it is very difficult (and even impossible!) to type letters in lower cases and upper cases, the presence of information on the page will be noticed and the page will attract attention, esp. because typing words in lower cases and upper cases has become common among hackers.

E. Hiding by Permuting Tags' Attributes

One of the features of HTML documents is the insensitivity of such documents to the order of the tag members. Therefore, one can hide information in HTML documents using the same feature (Forrest, 2006; John, 2004).

To extract information from the document, the order of the tag members is compared with the sorted state of the members and the hidden information is thus extracted.

Despite the advantages of this method, such as no change of the document size, very little information can be hidden in this method.

F. Steganography in Tags' ID

One of the attributes being present in nearly all tags of the HTML pages is the Identity Code. In this attribute a unique ID code is given to each object which is a combination of letters and digits. In this method (Shirali-Shahreza,2005, December; Shirali-Shahreza, 2006, February), data is placed as the ID code of the tags which don't have ID codes after being changed into a combination of letters and digits. These codes are created in a particular format in order to tell them and ID codes having no hidden data apart.

Although this method is able to hide a great deal of data without drawing any attention but causes the volume of the page to increase.

G. Steganography by Adding Pseudo-Spaces

This method (Chang and Tsai, 2003) hides data in webpages by adding some extra spaces. It is similar to HTML method which hides data by adding whitespaces, but this method using pseudo-spaces instead of whitespaces and adding extra spaces into the main text of webpages not in tags.

Pseudo-space or non-breaking space is a special space character that prevents an automatic line break at its position. This space is shown by " " in HTML files.

In this method, two spaces, which are composed of one pseudo-space and one real space, between words and sentences are interpreted as 1 and a single real space is interpreted as 0.

The advantage of this method is that the spaces are not changed by saving, copying or editing the page, so the hidden data won't be lost. But this method is also increasing the size of webpages. The other problem is that some browsers collapse multiple, concurrent non-breaking spaces into a single space.

H. Steganography in HTTP Protocol

HTTP (Hyper Text Transfer Protocol) is a protocol used to transmit webpages over the Internet. This method (Bao, and Wang,2002) hides secrets into the HTTP protocol responds instead of hiding messages into the webpages. Some information in HTTP responds are optional, therefore can be changed and hide the message into them.

Because a normal user-visit session (to a website) is composed by a lot of HTTP request/response pairs, a large amount of information can be hidden by only embedding a little information into each HTTP request. Therefore it is hard to detect the hidden message. But if the HTTP respond is not processed at the time of receiving, the hidden data will be lost.

I. Steganography by Chaning Page Elements' Color

In that paper (Shirali-Shahreza, 2007), the authors propose a method for *steganography* in artistic websites with HTML format. To achieve this goal the method changes the color of elements of the page through LSB (Least Significant Bit) method. This way the data are hidden in the page. This method keeps the size of the HTML documents unchanged.

CONCLUSION

Steganography is a method for hidden information exchange that has received attention in recent years. In this chapter the major methods of *steganography* are surveyed. Also two subcategories of these methods – *steganography* in binary images and *steganography* in webpages – are reviewed.

Because *steganography* is relatively new, it has more rooms to expand.

Among the *steganography* methods, less work has been done on text and audio and they need more attention. However, the *image steganography* methods need to be improved to become more resistance.

In addition to desktop computer, *steganography* methods are applied to other devices, such as mobile phones (Shirali Shahreza, 2005, July). Also some methods are specially developed for

new technologies like SMS (Shirali-Shahreza, 2006, April), MMS (Amoroso and Masotti, 2006; Papapanagiotou et al., 2005) and WAP (Shirali-Shahreza, 2006, February).

REFERENCES

Alattar, A. M., & Alattar, O. M. (2004). Watermarking electronic text documents containing justified paragraphs and irregular line spacing. *Proceedings of SPIE, vol. 5306, Security, Steganography, and Watermarking of Multimedia Contents VI,* 685-695.

Amoroso, A., & Masotti, M. (2006). Lightweight Steganography on Smartphones. *Proceedings of the 2nd IEEE International Workshop on Networking Issues in Multimedia Entertainment - Consumer Communications and Networking Conference 2006 Satellite Workshop, vol. 2,* (pp. 1158-1162), Las Vegas, Nevada.

Arefin F. (2004). *Information hiding in images: Implementing a steganographic application for hiding information in images,* B.S. Thesis, Computing and Information Systems, University of London, London, England.

Bao, F., & Wang, X. (2002). Steganography of Short Messages through Accessories. *Proceedings of Pacific Rim Workshop on Digital Steganography 2002 (STEG'02),* (pp. 142-147), Kitakyushu, Japan.

Bender, W., Gruhl, D., Morimoto, N., & Lu, A. (1996). Techniques for data hiding. *IBM Systems Journal, 35*(3-4), 313-336.

Bennett, K. (2004). *Linguistic Steganography: Survey, Analysis, and Robustness Concerns for Hiding Information in Text* (CERIAS Technical Report 2004-13). Purdue University.

Camouflage (2008), CamouflageSoftware, http://camouflage.unfiction.com, last visited: January 23, 2008.

Chandramouli, R., & Memon, N. (2001). Analysis of LSB based image steganography techniques. *Proceedings of the International Conference on Image Processing, 3,* 1019-1022.

Chang, Y. H., & Tsai, W. H. (2003). A steganographic method for copyright protection of HTML documents. *Proceedings of National Computer Symposium 2003,* Taichung, Taiwan.

Chen, Y. Y., Pan, H. K., & Tseng, Y. C. (2000). A Secure Data Hiding Scheme for Two-Color Images. *Proceedings of the Fifth IEEE Symposium on Computers and Communications (ISCC 2000),* (pp. 750-755), Antibes, France.

Curran, K., & Bailey, K. (2003). An Evaluation of Image Based Steganography Methods. *International Journal of Digital Evidence 2(2),* 1-40.

Cvejic, N., & Seppanen, T. (2002). A wavelet domain LSB insertion algorithm for high capacity audio steganography. *Proceedings of 10th IEEE Digital Signal Processing Workshop and 2nd Signal Processing Education Workshop,* 53- 55.

Cvejic, N., & Seppanen, T. (2004). Channel capacity of high bit rate audio data hiding algorithms in diverse transform domains. *Proceeding of 2004 IEEE International Symposium on Communications and Information Technology (ISCIT 2004), vol.1,* 84- 88.

Doërr, G., & Dugelay, J. L. (2003). A Guide Tour of Video Watermarking. *Signal Processing: Image Communication, 18(4).* 263-282.

Doërr, G., & Dugelay, J. (2003). Video Watermarking: Overview and Challenges. *Handbook of Video Databases: Design and Applications, Chapter 42,* by Furht, B., & Marques, O. (Editors), CRC Press.

Doërr, G., & Dugelay, J. (2004). Security Pitfalls of Frame-by-Frame Approaches to Video Watermarking. *IEEE Transactions on Signal Processing, Supplement on Secure Media,* 52(10), 2955-2964.

Forrest S. (2006). *Introduction to Deogol.* http://www.wandership.ca/projects/deogol/, last visited: January 23, 2008.

Gang, L., Akansu, A. N., & Ramkumar, M. (2001). MP3 resistant oblivious steganography. *Proceedings of 2001 IEEE International Conference on Acoustics, Speech, and Signal Processing (ICASSP'01), 3,* 1365-1368.

Ge, Q., Lu, Z., & Niu, X. (2003). Oblivious Video Watermarking Scheme with Adaptive Embedding Mechanism. *Proceedings of the Second International Conference on Machine Learning and Cybernetics,* (pp. 2876-2881), Xian, China.

Gopalan, K. (2003). Audio steganography using bit modification. *Proceedings of the IEEE International Conference on Acoustics, Speech, and Signal Processing, (ICASSP '03), 2,* 421-424.

Hartung, F., & Girod, B. (1997). Copyright Protection in Video Delivery Networks by Watermarking of PreCompressed Video. *Proceedings of the Second European Conference on Multimedia Applications, Services and Techniques, Springer Lecture Notes in Computer Science, 1242,* 423436, Springer, Heidelberg, Milan, Italy.

Hartung, F., & Girod, B. (1998). Watermarking of uncompressed and compressed video. *Signal Processing,* 66(3), 283–301.

HIPS (2005), HIPS Systems, ShadowText, http://home.apu.edu/~jcox/projects/HtmlStego1, last visited: 29 July 2005.

Huang, D., & Yan, H. (2001). Interword Distance Changes Represented by Sine Waves for Watermarking Text Images. *IEEE Transactions on Circuits and Systems for Video Technology,* 11(12), 1237-1245.

Jamil, T. (1999). Steganography: The art of hiding information in plain sight. *IEEE Potentials 18(1),* 10-12.

John, C. (2004), Steganography - Hiding messages in the Noise of a Picture, http://www.codeproject.com/csharp/steganodotnet.asp, last visited: January 23, 2008.

Judge, J. C. (2001). Steganography: Past, Present, Future. *SANS white paper,* November 30, 2001. Retrieved January 23, 2008, from http://www.sans.org/rr/papers/index.php?id=552

Kalker, T., Depovere, G., Haitsma, J., & Maes, M. (1999). A video watermarking system for broadcast monitoring. *Proceedings of SPIE, 3657, Security and Watermarking of Multimedia Content,* 103–112.

Kim, Y., Moon, K., & Oh, I. (2003). A Text Watermarking Algorithm based on Word Classification and Inter-word Space Statistics. *Proceedings of the Seventh International Conference on Document Analysis and Recognition (ICDAR'03),* (pp. 775–779), Edinburgh, Scotland.

Kirovski, D., & Malvar, H. S. (2003). Spread-spectrum watermarking of audio signals. *IEEE Transaction on Signal Processing, 51*(4), 1020-1033.

Low, S. H., Maxemchuk, N. F., Brassil, J. T., & O'Gorman L. (1995). Document marking and identification using both line and word shifting. *Proceedings of the Fourteenth Annual Joint Conference of the IEEE Computer and Communications Societies (INFOCOM '95),* 2, 853 - 860.

Lu, C., Chen, J., Liao, H. M., & Fan, K. (2002). Real-Time MPEG2 Video Watermarking in the VLC Domain. *Proceedings of 16th International Conference on Pattern Recognition, 2,* 552-555.

Marvel, L. M., Boncelet, Jr. C. G., & Retter, C. T. (1999). Spread spectrum image steganography. *IEEE Transactions on Image Processing,* 1075-1083.

Moerland, T. (2003). Steganography and Steganalysis, *Leiden Institute of Advanced Computing Science,* Retrieved January 23, 2008, from www.liacs.nl/home/tmoerlan/privtech.pdf

NeoByte Solutions (2008). *Invisible Secrets 4.* http://www.invisiblesecrets.com, last visited: January 23, 2008.

Niimi, M., Minewaki, S., Noda, H., & Kawaguchi, E. (2003). A Framework of Text-based Steganography Using SD-Form Semantics Model. *IPSJ Journal, 44*(8).

Papapanagiotou, K., Kellinis, E., Marias, G. F., & Georgiadis, P. (2005). Alternatives for Multimedia Messaging System Steganography. *Proceedings the IEEE International Conference on Computational Intelligence and Security (CIS 2005), Part II, LNAI 3802,* (pp. 589-596), Xian, China.

Pinet, A. (2007), SecurEngine Professional 1.0, http://securengine.isecurelabs.com, last visited: 12 January 2007.

Provos, N., & Honeyman, P. (2003). Hide and Seek: An Introduction to Steganography. *Security & Privacy Magazine,* 32-44.

Rabah, K. (2004). Steganography-The Art of Hiding Data. *Information Technology Journal, 3(3),* 245-269.

Saha, S. (2000). Image Compression - from DCT to Wavelets: A Review. *ACM Crossroads Magazine, 6(3),* 12–21, Retrieved January 23, 2008, from http://www.acm.org/crossroads/xrds6-3/sahaimgcoding.html

Santosa, R. A., & Bao, P. (2005). Audio-to-image wavelet transform based audio steganography. *Proceedings of 47th International Symposium ELMAR,* 209- 212.

Shirali Shahreza, M. (2005, July). An Improved Method for Steganography on Mobile Phone. *WSEAS Transactions on Systems, 4(7),* 955-957.

Shirali-Shahreza, M. (2005, December). A New Method for Steganography in HTML Files. *Proceedings of the International Joint Conference on*

Computer, Information, and Systems Sciences, and Engineering (CISSE 2005), (pp. 247-251), Bridgeport, CT.

Shirali-Shahreza, M. (2006, April). Stealth Steganography in SMS. *Proceedings of the third IEEE and IFIP International Conference on Wireless and Optical Communications Networks (WOCN 2006)*, Bangalore, India.

Shirali-Shahreza, M. (2006, February). Steganography in Wireless Application Protocol. *Proceedings of the IASTED International Conference on Internet and Multimedia Systems and Applications (EuroIMSA 2006),* (pp. 91-95), Innsbruck, Austria.

Shirali-Shahreza, M. (2007). Steganography in Artistic Websites. *International Reviews on Computers and Software (IRECOS),* 2(1), 25-29.

Shirali-Shahreza, M. H., & Shirali-Shahreza, M. (2006). A New Approach to Persian/Arabic Text Steganography. *Proceedings of the 5th IEEE/ACIS International Conference on Computer and Information Science (ICIS 2006),* (pp. 310-315), Honolulu, HI, USA.

Sweene, P. (1991). *Error Control Coding (An Introduction),* Prentice-Hall International Ltd., Englewood Cliffs, NJ.

Tanaka, K., Nakamura, Y., & Matsui, K. (1990). Embedding secret information into a dithered multi-level image. *Proceedings of IEEE Military Communications Conference,* 216-220.

Tseng, Y. C., & Pan, H. K. (2001). Secure and Invisible Data Hiding in 2-Color Images. *Proceedings of Twentieth Annual Joint Conference of the IEEE Computer and Communications Societies (INFOCOM 2001) Vol. 2,* (pp. 887-896), Anchorage, Alaska, USA.

Tseng, Y. C., Chen, Y. Y., & Pan, H. K. (2002). A Secure Data Hiding Scheme for Binary Images. *IEEE Transaction on Communications,* 50(8), 1227-31.

Wang, H., Lu, Z., Pan, J., & Sun, S. (2005). Robust Blind Video Watermarking with Adaptive Embedding Mechanism. *International Journal of Innovative Computing, Information and Control,* 1(2), 247-259.

Wu M., & Liu, B. (2004). Data Hiding in Binary Image for Authentication and Annotation. *IEEE Transaction on Multimedia,* 6(4), 528-538.

Wu, M., Tang, E., & Liu, B. (2000). Data hiding in digital binary image. *Proceedings of IEEE International Conference on Multimedia & Expo 2000 (ICME 2000), vol. 1,* (pp. 393 – 396), New York, USA.

KEY TERMS

Copyright Protection: Mechanisms that prevent data, usually digital data, from being copied.

Cryptography: In cryptography, the information is encrypted with a key and only the person who has the key can decrypt and read the information. So without the key, nobody has access to that information.

DCT: A discrete cosine transform (DCT) is a Fourier-related transform similar to the discrete Fourier transform (DFT), but using only real numbers.

Digital Watermarking: A digital watermark is a message which is embedded into a digital content (audio, video, images or text) that can be detected or extracted later.

HTML: HyperText Markup Language (HTML), is the publishing language of the World Wide Web.

Information Hiding: The science of hiding a secret message in another file. It provides a means to describe the structure of text-based information in a document.

Internet Security: Techniques for ensuring that data stored in a computer cannot be read or compromised by any individuals without authorization.

LSB Method: Replacing the Least Significant Bit of signal with the data.

Steganography: Steganography is a method to hide data in a cover media so that other persons will not notice that such data is there.

Stego Media: A media such as an image containing steganography information.

Chapter XIV
Digital Watermarking Capacity and Detection Error Rate

Fan Zhang
Henan University, China

ABSTRACT

The digital multimedia, including text, image, graphics, audio, video, and so forth, has become a main way for information communication along with the popularization of Internet and the development of multimedia techniques. How to provide copyright protection has drawn extensive attention in recent years. As a main method for copyright protection, digital watermarking has been widely studied and applied. In this chapter we discuss the important properties of watermarks, the capacity, and the detection error rate. The watermarking system is analyzed based on the channel capacity and error rate of the communication system, and the relation between the detection error rate with the capacity and payload capacity is derived. This chapter also introduces a new analysis method of the watermarking capacity, which is based on the theories of attractors and attraction basin of artificial neural network. The attraction basin of neural network decides the upper limit of watermarking, and the attractors of neural network decide the lower limit of watermarking. According to the experimental results, the detection error rate of watermark is mainly influenced by the watermark average energy and the watermarking capacity. The error rate rises with the increase of watermarking capacity. When the channel coding is used, the watermarking error rate drops with the decrease of the payload capacity of watermarking.

INTRODUCTION

Digital representations of copyrighted material such as movies, songs, and photographs offer many advantages. However, the fact that an unlimited number of perfect copies can be illegally produced is a serious threat to the rights of content owners. Until recently, the primary tool available

to help protect content owners' rights has been encryption. Encryption protects content during the transmission of the data from the sender to receiver. However, after receipt and subsequent decryption, the data is no longer protected and is in the clear. Watermarking compliments encryption. A digital watermark is a piece of information that is hidden directly in media content, in such a way that it is imperceptible to a human observer, but easily detected by a computer. The principal advantage of this is that the content is inseparable from the watermark.

Until the early nineties, digital watermarking techniques had received very much less attention from the research community and from industry than cryptography, but this has changed rapidly since. The first academic conference on the subject was organized in 1996. It was followed by several other conferences focusing on information hiding as well as watermarking.

The main driving force is concern over protecting copyright; as audio, video and other works become available in digital form, it may be that the ease with which perfect copies can be made will lead to large-scale unauthorized copying which will undermine the music, film, book and software publishing industries. There has therefore been significant recent research into watermarking (hidden copyright messages) and fingerprinting (hidden serial numbers or a set of characteristics that tend to distinguish an object from other similar objects); the idea is that the latter can be used to detect copyright violators and the former to prosecute them. But there are many other applications of increasing interest to both the academic and business communities, including anonymous communications, covert channels in computer systems, detection of hidden information, steganography, etc.

Today, cryptographical techniques have reached a level of sophistication such that properly encrypted communications can be assumed secure well beyond the useful life of the information transmitted. In fact, it's projected that the most powerful algorithms using multi kilobit key lengths could not be comprised through brute force, even if all the computing power worldwide for the next 20 years was focused on the attack. Of course the possibility exists that vulnerabilities could be found, or computing power breakthroughs could occur, but for most users in most applications,

current cryptographic techniques are generally sufficient.

Watermarking is very similar to steganography in a number of respects. Both seek to embed information inside a cover message with little to no degradation of the cover-object. Watermarking however adds the additional requirement of robustness. An ideal steganographic system would embed a large amount of information, perfectly securely with no visible degradation to the cover object. An ideal watermarking system however would embed an amount of information that could not be removed or altered without making the cover object entirely unusable. As a side effect of these different requirements, a watermarking system will often trade capacity and perhaps even some security for additional robustness.

A digital watermark embeds an imperceptible signal into data such as audio, video and images, for a variety of purposes, including captioning and copyright control. As watermarking is increasingly used for a wide variety of applications, various properties of watermarks, such as how they respond to common signal transformations or deliberate attack, have become important considerations. In this chapter we discuss the important properties of watermarks, the capacity and the detection error rate.

The watermarking capacity of digital image is the number of bits that can be embedded in a given host image. The performance of watermarking detection is measured by the bit error rate (BER) or probability of error PB. The bit error rate is the number of error bits in the total length of information messages bits. The detection reliability of watermarking closely correlates to two other parameters, which are the watermarking capacity and robustness. The robustness denotes the performance towards intentional and unintentional attacks. The main requirement of robustness is to resist different kind of distortions introduced by common processing and/or malicious attacks while satisfying the imperceptibility criteria.

The watermarking can be considered as a communication process, and the Gaussian probability distribution is a popular model for the watermarking channel. This model gives rise to closed form solutions for the watermarking capacity. The image in which the watermark messages are embedded is the communication channel. The watermark messages are transmitted over the channel (Cox, 1999). The watermarking capacity corresponds to the communication capacity of the "watermarking channel".

Recently, a few models on the watermarking capacity have been proposed. Servetto (1998) considers each pixel in the image as an independent communication channel and calculates the capacity according to the theory of Parallel Gaussian Channels (PGC). Barni's research focuses on the watermarking capacity in the DCT and the DFT domain (Barni, 1999). A game-theoretic approach for the evaluation of watermarking capacity is introduced by Moulin (Moulin, 2002). Lin (2001) presents zero-error watermarking capacity analysis in the JPEG compression domain using the adjacency-reducing mapping technique.

The content of image influences the watermarking capacity in two aspects. The content of image is the carrier of watermarking, but in the blind watermarking, they become the obstacles in the watermark detection or extraction. Obviously, more watermarks can be embedded in the complex images than in the flat images, such as a pure white image. We suggest that the watermarking capacity should be associated with the content of image. The watermarking capacities of images differ from each other. However, in some previous works on the watermarking capacity, the capacity is calculated using a given power signal-to-noise ratio (PSNR), and the same watermarking capacity is designated to different images with the same size.

This chapter discusses the watermarking capacity of digital images in the spatial domain and wavelet domain. Most of these works discuss watermarking in the spatial domain. Recently, the wavelet transform became widely applied in watermarking research due to its excellent property of multi-resolution analysis. Watermarking algorithms based on the wavelet transform became the major direction of watermarking research. In these algorithms, watermark is embedded and extracted in the wavelet transform domain. The content of image in the wavelet domain differs from that in the spatial domain. It would be proper to discuss the watermarking capacity in wavelet domain. The capacity and reliability are two important properties of the digital watermarking. The research on the relation between watermarking capacity and reliability will help us find ways to transmit more watermark information while keeping an acceptable watermark detection bit error rate.

The rest of this chapter is organized as follows. In Section 2, a watermark algorithm is introduced. In Section 3, the watermarking capacity of digital images is discussed in the spatial domain and wavelet domain. Watermarking capacity based on neural network is analyzed in Section 4. In Section 5, we analyze the relationship between the watermarking capacity and the watermark detection error rate, and derive the relation between the capacity and the bounds of error rate. When the channel coding is used, the relationship between the watermarking payload capacity and the watermark detection error rate is discussed in Section 6. The experimental results are shown in Section 7. The conclusions of this chapter are drawn in Section 8.

ADAPTIVE WATERMARKING ALGORITHM

Spatial Domain

The Human Vision System (HVS) models have been studied for many years. These works describe the human vision mechanism such as the spatial frequency orientation, the sensitivity on local contrast and the masking. Noise Visibility Function (NVF) is the function that characterizes local image properties. It identifies the texture and the edge regions of an image where the watermark should be more strongly embedded (Voloshynovskiy, 2001). It can be used in either the spatial domain or the wavelet domain.

The Noise Visibility Function is derived based on the mathematic statistics model of images. Comparing with other human experience based perceptual models, the NVF is more appropriate to the theoretic analysis, such as the analysis of the watermarking capacity. We think that the NVF is the best bridge that connects the watermarking capacity to the content of images.

There are two kinds of the NVF, based on either a non-stationary Gaussian model of the image, or a stationary Generalized Gaussian model. Because watermarking problem has a close relationship with the local properties of image, we think that the NVF based on non-stationary Gaussian model more suits for watermarking problem. In this case, the NVF of each pixel can be expressed as,

$$NVF(i,j) = \frac{w(i,j)}{w(i,j) + \sigma_x^2(i,j)} \quad (1)$$

Where $\sigma_x^2(i,j)$ is the local variance of the image in a window centered on the pixel with coordinates (i,j), $1 < (i,j) < N$. $w(i,j)$ is weighting function which depends on the shape parameter γ. $w(i,j)$ can be written as:

$$w(i,j) = \gamma \left[\eta(\gamma)\right]^\gamma \frac{1}{\|r(i,j)\|^{2-\gamma}} \quad (2)$$

where

$$r(i,j) = \frac{x(i,j) - \bar{x}(i,j)}{\sigma_x}, \quad \eta(\gamma) = \sqrt{\frac{\Gamma(\frac{3}{\gamma})}{\Gamma(\frac{1}{\gamma})}},$$

and

$$\Gamma(t) = \int_0^\infty e^{-u} u^{t-1} du$$

is the gamma function. The parameter γ is called the shape parameter, and $\bar{x}(i,j)$ is the local mean of the image.

If we assume that the original image subjects to the generalized Gaussian distribution, the NVF of each pixel can be expressed as,

$$NVF(i,j) = \frac{1}{1 + \sigma_x^2(i,j)} \quad (3)$$

The maximum allowable distortion of each pixel can be calculated as follows,

$$\Delta(i,j) = (1 - NVF(i,j)) \cdot S_0 + NVF(i,j) \cdot S_1 \quad (4)$$

where S_0 and S_1 are the maximum allowable distortion in the textured and the uniform regions of image respectively. Typically S_0 is as high as 30, while S_1 is usually about 3 (according to experience) (Pereira, 2001). In the uniform regions of the image, the NVF tends to 1, so the first term of Eq. 12 tends to 0, and consequently the allowable distortion is determined by S_1. Intuitively this makes sense, since we expect that the distortion is more visible in the uniform regions and less visible in the textured regions. According to Eq. 12, the watermark in the textured or the edge regions is stronger than that in the uniform regions.

Wavelet Domain

Watson proposed a mathematical model about noise detection thresholds for the Discrete Wavelet Transform (Watson, 1997). Watson presents a quantization matrix for the perceptually lossless compression. The quantization matrix is composed by the quantization factor of each wavelet levels and orientations. It can be expressed as follows,

Table 1. The quantization factors for four-level DWT. (The display resolution is 32 pixel/degree)

| Orientation | Level | | | |
| | λ | | | |
θ	1	2	3	4
1	14.049	11.106	11.363	14.5
2	23.028	14.685	12.707	14.156
3	58.756	28.408	19.54	17.864
4	23.028	14.685	12.707	14.156

$$Q_{\lambda,\theta} = \frac{2}{A_{\lambda,\theta}} a 10^{k\left(\log \frac{2^\lambda f_0 g_\theta}{r}\right)^2},$$

(5)

where λ and θ is wavelet level and orientation respectively, γ is display resolution, $A_{\lambda,\theta}$ is the basis function amplitudes, and a, k, f_0, g_θ are constant. The quantization factors of four-level DWT are shown in Table 1. If the distortion is lesser than the quantization factors, the distortion will be invisible.

Watson's perceptual model is human experience based; it satisfies the requirements of Human Vision System (HVS). It is also independent of the content of image. During image compression in the wavelet domain, the wavelet coefficients are quantized using the same quantization factor in a sub-band. And if we control the watermark amplitude (distortion) below the quantization factor in a wavelet sub-band, the watermark will be invisible. But if the watermark strength is the same in all wavelet sub-bands, the watermarking capacity is only one bit in each sub-band. Almost no information is thereby transmitted. In order to achieve the maximum information in the watermark, we should design the watermark strength according to the content of wavelet sub-bands.

Kim presents an adaptive digital watermarking based on the wavelet transform using the successive sub-band quantization and the perceptual model (Kim, 2002). In this chapter, the quantization factor of Watson's perceptual model represents the visual threshold in a wavelet sub-band. It can be used as the maximum allowable distortion of the wavelet coefficients. Let $S_0 = Q_{\lambda,\theta}$, then the maximum allowable distortion of each coefficient in the wavelet domain can expressed as follows,

$$\Delta(i, j) = (1 - NVF(i, j)) \cdot Q_{\lambda,\theta} + NVF(i, j) \cdot S_1$$

(6)

WATERMARKING CAPACITY

In the watermarking schemes, the process of watermarking can be considered as a communication problem. The image is the channel in which the watermark messages are transmitted. The watermarking capacity corresponds to the communication capacity of the "watermark channel". The Gaussian probability distribution is a popular model for the watermarking channel. This model gives rise to closed solutions for the watermarking capacity.

A block diagrams is shown in Figure 1 to illustrate the process of watermarking. In Figure 1, the stego image is the watermarked image. A

Figure 1. Block diagrams of watermarking

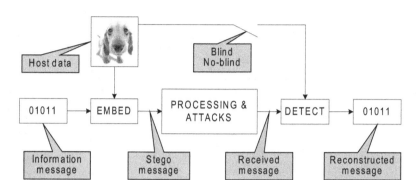

switch is designed to show the different conditions of the blind and the non-blind watermarking. The blind watermarking means that the information are detected or extracted without the original image, and the non-blind watermarking means that the original image is needed during the watermark detection or extraction.

Consider the original image as an independent Additive White Gaussian Noise (AWGN) channel. Let P_S denotes the watermark power constraint and P_N denotes the noise power constraint. Then, according to the well-known Shannon channel capacity formula, the watermarking capacity is:

$$C = W \log_2 \left(1 + \frac{P_S}{P_N} \right),$$

$$(7)$$

where W is the bandwidth of channel. Assume that the size of an image is $N \times N$, the number of pixels is $M = N \times N$. According to Nyquist sampling theory, if we want to express all the pixels correctly, sampling points should be $2W$ at least. So the bandwidth of an image is $W = M/2$.

We suggest that the watermark power constraint P_s should be associated with the content of image. We have introduced a content adaptive watermarking algorithm. This algorithm can obtain the strongest watermark while keeping watermarks invisibility. We define the strongest watermarked image as the Maximum Watermark Image (MWI). Mathematically, MWI is the image for which the amplitude of each pixel is the maximum allowable distortion $A(i,j)$ of the corresponding wavelet coefficients. We can calculate the watermark power constraint according to the MWI, which depends on the content of the image. Assuming σ_w^2 denote the variance of the MWI and σ_n^2 denote the variance of noise, then, in non-blind watermarking scenario, image watermarking capacity can be written as:

$$C = W \log_2 \left(1 + \frac{\sigma_w^2}{\sigma_n^2} \right).$$

$$(8)$$

Costa (1983) presents a "dirty paper" communication model to study the channel capacity problem. The capacity problem of blind watermarking is the same as the dirty paper communication problem described by Costa. According to Costa's work, the capacity of blind watermarking is the same as the non-blind watermarking cases. So, in both cases, the watermarking capacity is the same.

WATERMARKING CAPACITY BASED ON NEURAL NETWORK

Almost all previous works on watermarking capacity used the information theoretic model. Those researches focus on the maximum information that can be hidden in an image, which is the upper limit of hidden information. But the lower limit of watermarking, the minimum detectable information capacity is also an interesting problem. It is difficult if we analyze the minimum detectable information capacity based on information theory, so few works are proposed in this field.

Watermarking process can be modeled as a communication task, consisting of two steps: information embedding, in which the information or watermark is transmitted over the channel (watermarking channel), and information detection, in which information is received and extracted from data. Usually the watermarking channel is modeled as an AWGN (additive white Gaussian noise) channel, so that the corresponding capacity of information theory can be used. The AWGN channel capacity is the maximum mutual information between input and output, which mainly depends on the signal to noise rate (SNR). In watermarking scenarios, the noise is the time-varying attack, which includes the deterministic and the random components. To get the upper bound on the watermarking capacity, we should calculate the deterministic attack, the content of image, which is usually modeled as Gaussian distribution. To get the lower bound on capacity, we should also calculate the random attack. In real scenarios, we may not know the probability distribution of it. So, it is difficult to analyze the minimum detectable information capacity according to the information theoretic model.

This section proposes a new analysis method of the watermarking capacity bounds, which is based on the theories of attractors and attraction basin of artificial neural network. The upper limit and lower limit of watermarking, namely the maximum information capacity and the minimum

detectable information capacity are unified in a same theory frame.

Algorithm

The inspiration of information hiding capacity analysis based on neural network comes from three points. Firstly, some neural networks (such as associative memories) also have capacity problems. So we want to know if we can associate the capacity of watermarking with the capacity of neural networks. Secondly, almost all previous works on watermarking capacity used the information theoretic model, but information coding theory can also apply to study the capacity of the associative memory. Thirdly, information theory based capacity analysis is hard to analyze the minimum detectable information capacity. So, this chapter proposes a new analysis method of the watermarking capacity bounds, which is based on the theories of attractors and attraction basin of artificial neural network.

The Hopfield neural network is a recurrent neural network that stores information in a dynamically stable configuration (McEliece, 1987). An interesting property of recurrent type networks is that their state can be described by an energy function. The energy function is used to prove the stability of recurrent type networks. The local minima of the energy function correspond to the energy of the stored patterns. An energy function is used to evaluate the stability property, and the energy function always decreases to a state of the lowest energy. Hopfield has shown that the energy of the discrete Hopfield model decreases or remains the same after each unit update. Therefore, the neural network will eventually converge to a local minimum that corresponds to a stored pattern. The stored pattern to which the network converges depends on the input pattern and the connection weight matrix.

Attractors of Hopfield network represent the stored patterns. The basin of attraction is the set of states in the system within which almost all states flow to one attractor. For a trained neural network, the attraction basin gives a measure of neural network error-correcting capability. Once a pattern is stored, the Hopfield network can reconstructs the original pattern from the degraded or incomplete pattern.

A computational energy function is used to evaluate the stability property in Hopfield neural network. The energy function always decreases toward a state of the lowest energy. Starting from any point of state space, system will always evolves to a stable state, an attractor. The Neurons state of Hopfield neural network is usually binary +1, -1. For the sake of neural network can store a standard gray-scale test image, we separate image into eight of the bit planes. The pixels of bit planes are 0 or 1. The number of neurons equals to the number of pixels. So, we input one of the bit planes into the Hopfield neural network for training. After some times iterative process (usually twenty or more times), system will evolves to a stable state. We say the neural network have remembered or stored this bit plane. Other bit planes are also stored by neural network in same way. When all eight of the bit planes are stored, the neural network have remembered or stored the original gray-scale image. In data extracting, the network can associative recall the host image (original image) form a stego image (information hidden image) or a noised image, do not need the host image.

The trained neural network model is needed at the extraction side. The memory size equals to the number of pixels. If the size of image is 256×256, training time of neural network is about one second in a computer with Intel Pentium 4 2.9G CPU and 1G memory. We assume that the trained neural network model is available at the extraction side. The original image and the hidden information are not needed during the detecting or extracting. This is a kind of blind detection.

Capacity Based on Neural Network

The Hopfield network is a recurrent neural network that stores information in a dynamically stable configuration. Attractors represent the stored patterns. The basin of attractor is the set of states in the system within which almost all states flow to one attractor.

Usually the basin of attraction is measured by Hamming distance. Hamming distance is the number of components that differ between two vectors. The distance between two vectors S^1 and S^2 is $d_h (S^1, S^2)$. The Hamming distance can be used to measure the basin of attraction.

Let P denotes the number of stored patterns and N denotes the number of neurons. The Hopfield network model can be expressed as,

$$x_i^{t+1} = \text{sgn}\left(\sum_{j \neq i}^{N} w_j x_j^t\right),$$

(9)

where x_i^t is the state of neurons at time t; *sgn* is the sign function. The weight matrix can be computed according to the Hebb rule,

$$w_{ij} = \frac{1}{N}\sum_{\mu=1}^{P} \xi_i^\mu \xi_j^\mu,$$

(10)

where $\xi=(\xi^1,\xi^2,...,\xi^P)$ denote the stored patterns of the neural network. Let $X^0 =\{x_1^0, x_2^0,..., x_N^0\}^T$ denotes the initial state of neural network, $X^t =\{x_1^t, x_2^t,..., x_N^t\}^T$ denotes the state at time t. If assume that the probe pattern is one of the stored patterns, then,

$$\sum_{j \neq i}^{N} w_{ij} x_j^0 = \sum_{j \neq i}^{N}\frac{1}{N}\sum_{\mu=1}^{P} \xi_i^\mu \xi_j^\mu x_j^0$$

$$= \frac{1}{N}\sum_{\mu=1}^{P}\left[\left(\sum_{j=1}^{N}\xi_i^\mu \xi_j^\mu x_j^0\right)-\xi_i^\mu \xi_j^\mu x_i^0\right]$$

$$= \frac{1}{N}\left[\xi_j^{\mu}(\xi^{\mu})^T X^0 + \sum_{\upsilon \neq \mu}^{P} \xi_i^{\upsilon}(\xi^{\upsilon})X^0 - Px_i^0 \right]$$

(11)

Because $(\xi^{\mu})^T X^0 = N - 2d_h(X^0, \xi^{\mu})$ and $(N-P)/2P < N/2$, if assume x_i are orthogonal to each other, then,

$$-2d_h(X^0, \xi^{\mu}) \leq (\xi^{\upsilon})^T X^0 \leq 2d_h(X^0, \xi^{\mu}).$$

(12)

When $d_h(X^0, \xi^{\mu}) < (N-P)/2P$,

$$N - 2d_h(X^0, \xi^{\mu}) - 2(P-1)d_h(X^0, \xi^{\mu}) - P > 0$$

(13)

So, when $\xi_i^{\mu} = +1$,

$$\sum_{j \neq i}^{N} w_{ij} x_j^0$$

$$= \frac{1}{N}\left[\xi_j^{\mu}(\xi^{\mu})^T X^0 + \sum_{\upsilon \neq \mu}^{P} \xi_i^{\upsilon}(\xi^{\upsilon})X^0 - Px_i^0 \right]$$

$$> \frac{1}{N}\left[N - 2d_h(X^0, \xi^{\mu}) - 2(P-1)d_h(X^0, \xi^{\mu}) - P \right] > 0$$

(14)

When $\xi_i^{\mu} = -1$,

$$\sum_{j \neq i}^{N} w_{ij} x_j^0$$

$$= \frac{1}{N}\left[-N + 2d_h(X^0, \xi^{\mu}) + 2(P-1)d_h(X^0, \xi^{\mu}) + P \right] < 0$$

(15)

So,

$$\xi_i^{\mu} = \text{sgn}\left(\sum_{j \neq i}^{N} w_{ij} x_j^0 \right),$$

and then,

$$x_i^{\upsilon} = \text{sgn}\left(\sum_{j \neq i}^{N} w_{ij} x_j^0 \right) = \xi_i^{\mu}.$$

(16)

According to Eq. 16, if the Hamming distance between the probe pattern and a stored pattern,

$$d_h \leq \frac{N-P}{2P},$$

(17)

the neural network will converge to this stored pattern. In the Hopfield neural network, if the stored patterns are orthogonal and $N > P$, the attraction basin of each stored pattern can be expressed as the Hamming distance shown in Eq. 17.

In the watermarking schemes, hidden information can be viewed as noise which pollutes the original image. The amplitude modification of some pixels occur some changes in the image. This means that the image is polluted. The more information data are hidden, the bigger Hamming distance between the stego image and the original image is. When the Hamming distance is out of the bounds of the attraction basin, the neural network can not retrieve the original image correctly. So, the basin of attraction restricts the number of points that can be modified in an image, therefore, restricts the capacity of watermarking.

Hopfield neural network is a single layer network which each neuron is connected to every other neuron. The number of neurons equals to the number of pixels. Of course, if the number of neurons equals to the number of pixels, the computation will be very complex. We should reduce the dimension of neural network to reduce the commutative complexity. The NVF is calculated in a local image region, a window centered on a pixel. We can divide image into many non-overlap regions according to the window size of the NVF. Each region corresponds to a neuron. If the NVF calculation region is a window of size 5×5, then a 256×256 image can be divided into 51×51 regions, and the dimension of neural network is 51×51.

If the size of a test image is 256×256, and the image is a uniquely stored pattern, according to Eq. 17, $d_h \leq 32{,}768$. The maximum number of points that can be modified should be less than 32,768. If modified points in the original image are less than 32,768, the neural network can reconstruct this image correctly.

In proposed information-hiding algorithm, the hidden information is a binary sequence. Each bit of the sequence is random (0 or 1). There are 2^n combinations in an n-length binary sequence. The probability of each combination is $1/2^n$. According to the information theory, the information of an n-length binary sequence is,

$$C = -\log_2(1/2^n). \tag{18}$$

So, at most 32,768 bits information can be hidden in the image.

Because of the different analytical methods used, and the different experimental conditions or parameters, the results of watermarking capacity of those works are quite diverse. In (Servetto, 1998; Moulin, 2002; Lin, 2001; Barni, 2000), the watermarking capacity of a 256×256 image is from about 20,000 bits to 80,000 bits. The result of our capacity (upper bound) is relatively small comparing with those results. We think that the smaller hidden information is due to the limited competence of a neural network.

The Minimum Capacity

Almost all previous works on watermarking capacity used the information theoretic model. Those researches focus on the maximum information that can be hidden in an image, which is the upper limit of hidden information. It is difficult to analyze the minimum detectable information capacity according to information theory. The proposed analysis method is based on the capacity theories of neural network.

The concept of capacity in the neural network is different to the capacity concept of information

theory. In the Hopfield neural network, a pattern is stored if it is a fixed point of the retrieval dynamics. The storage capacity can be understood as the maximum number of patterns that can be stored in the Hopfield neural network. The storage capacity in this concept is defined as the number of patterns that can be permitted such that they (one or all of them) are fixed points of the retrieval dynamics (Hopfield, 1982). The other approach to storage capacity takes into account small errors that we are willing to accept in the restoration of the patterns (with the idea to increase the storage capacity) (Newman, 1988). So we are satisfied if the retrieval dynamics converges to a configuration, which is not too far away from the original patterns.

Assume that the set of P stored patterns is given by $\xi = (\xi^1, \xi^2, \ldots, \xi^P)$, the nodes in the network are labeled 1, 2, ..., N. If an input pattern ζ is same as one of the stored patterns ξ^υ, then the stability condition of Hopfield model is:

$$\text{sgn}(\zeta_i^{\upsilon}) = \xi_i^{\upsilon}, \forall i, \tag{19}$$

where

$$\zeta_i^{\upsilon} = \sum_{j=1}^{N} w_{ij}\xi_j^{\upsilon} = \frac{1}{N}\sum_{j=1}^{N}\sum_{\mu=1}^{P}\xi_i^{\mu}\xi_j^{\mu}\xi_j^{\upsilon}$$

$$= \xi_i^{\upsilon} + \frac{1}{N}\sum_{j=1}^{N}\sum_{\mu=1,\mu\neq\upsilon}^{P}\xi_i^{\mu}\xi_j^{\mu}\xi_j^{\upsilon}. \tag{20}$$

The second term is called the crosstalk term. If it is zero, the network has stability. But even if it is not zero, the network can still has stability if its magnitude is smaller than 1, in which case it cannot changes the sign of ζ_i^{υ}. It turns out that if this is the case, and the initial state of the network is near one of the stored patters (in Hamming distance), the network moves towards ξ_i^{υ}. The ξ_i^{υ} is an attractor. The more patterns are stored, the lower the chances that the crosstalk term is sufficiently small.

Lets

$$C_i^\upsilon = -\frac{1}{N} \sum_{j=1}^{N} \sum_{\mu=1, \mu \neq \upsilon}^{P} \xi_i^\mu \xi_j^\mu \xi_j^\upsilon. \qquad (21)$$

The sign of crosstalk term is same as the sign of ξ_i^υ if $C_i^\upsilon < 0$. Thus, ζ_i^υ always has the same sign as ξ_i^υ. We can define the error probability that some bit in the pattern will not be stable (because in this case the crosstalk term changes the sign and the bit is flipped) as follows.

$$P_e = P(C_j^\mu > 1). \qquad (22)$$

The quantity C_i^υ has a binomial distribution since they are the sum of random numbers ($-1, +1$). For P random patterns and N units, the distribution of values for the quantity C_i^υ closes to Gaussian distribution with variance $\sigma^2 = P / N$. Thus,

$$P_e = \frac{1}{\sqrt{2\pi}} \int_1^\infty \exp\left(-\frac{x^2}{2\sigma^2}\right) dx$$

$$= \frac{1}{2}\left[1 - erf(\sqrt{\frac{N}{2(P-1)}})\right] \qquad (23)$$

where $erf(x)$ is the Complementary Error Function that is defined as,

$$erf(x) = \frac{2}{\sqrt{\pi}} \int_0^x \exp(-u^2) du. \qquad (24)$$

For example, if the error is less than 0.01, then the maximum number of patterns that can be stored is $0.185N$. Now we consider this problem again in an opposite position. If we want to the neural network store some patterns, the minimum number of nodes $N_{min} = P / 0.185$. In proposed information-hiding algorithm, the minimum number of nodes are 6, namely at least 6 neurons are needed. Each neuron corresponds with a point that the information data is hidden, so at least 6 pixels will be modified. In the proposed information-hiding algorithm, each of the embedded points corresponds with one bit information messages.

So, when $P_e < 0.01$, the minimum detectable information messages is 6 bits.

In the capacity analysis of watermarking, the concept of game theory can be applied to data hiding as, information hider tries to embed as much information as he can constrain to maximum allowable distortion and the attacker tries to remove the embedded information by attacking the watermarked data constrained to maximum allowable distortion. So, in the information theory based capacity analysis, the capacity is determined by the statistical model used for the host image and by the distortion constraints on the data hider and the attacker. The proposed method abandons the information-theoretic model. The capacity of watermarking is analyzed based on the theories of attractors and attraction basin of neural network. In the Hopfield neural network, the error rates but not the distortion constraints decides the capacity and attraction basin of neural network. In this scheme, the error rates of bounds actually depend on the error rates of Hopfield neural network, which is defined as the probability that some bit in the pattern will not be stable. The error rates of Hopfield neural network subject to a binomial distribution.

DETECTION ERROR RATE

In this section, we analyze the relation between the watermarking capacity and the watermark detection error rate, and derive the relation between the capacity and the bounds of detection error rate.

Capacity and Detection Error Rate

The correlation test method is usually used in the watermark detection. Let w_0 denotes the host (original) image, w_1 denotes the stego (watermarked) image, and the test statistics are $z = n$ and $z = n + w$ respectively, where n denotes the noise subject to the Gaussian distribution with zero mean and variance σ_n^2, w denotes the information messages. Then the conditional probability density functions $p(z \mid w_0)$ and $p(z' \mid w_1)$ are,

$$p(z \mid w_0) = \frac{1}{\sigma_n \sqrt{2\pi}} \exp\left[-\frac{1}{2}\left(\frac{z}{\sigma_n}\right)^2\right]$$

$$p(z \mid w_1) = \frac{1}{\sigma_n \sqrt{2\pi}} \exp\left[-\frac{1}{2}\left(\frac{z-w}{\sigma_n}\right)^2\right]$$

(26)

There are two types of testing errors in information hiding detection. The first error is false negative (failing to detect the presence of a hidden information when it should) and its probability is,

$$p(e \mid w_1) = \int_{-\infty}^{\gamma_0} p(z \mid w_1)dz,$$ (27)

where γ_0 is the optimization test threshold.

Another error is false positive (detecting the presence of a hidden information when it should not) and its probability is,

$$p(e \mid w_0) = \int_{\gamma_0}^{\infty} p(z \mid w_0)dz$$ (28)

Assume that the priori probabilities are $P(w_0) = 1/2$ and $P(w_1) = 1/2$ respectively. If the conditional probability density function is symmetrical, then the optimization test threshold is $\gamma_0 = \mu + \mu_w/2$, where μ is the mean of noise, μ_w is the mean of hidden information messages. The sum error rate can be expressed as follows,

$$P_B = p(e \mid w_0)P(w_0) + p(e \mid w_1)P(w_1)$$

$$= \int_{\gamma_0}^{\infty} p(z \mid w_0)dz.$$ (29)

Combining Eq. 25 and Eq. 29, we obtain

$$P_B = \int_{\gamma_0 = \mu_w/2}^{\infty} \frac{1}{\sigma_n \sqrt{2\pi}} \exp\left[-\frac{1}{2}\left(\frac{z}{\sigma_n}\right)^2\right]dz$$

(30)

Let $v = z/\sigma_n$, $dv = dz/\sigma_n$, then:

$$P_B = \int_{v = \mu_w/2\sigma_n}^{\infty} \frac{1}{\sqrt{2\pi}} \exp\left[-\frac{v^2}{2}\right]dv = Q\left(\frac{\mu_w}{2\sigma_n}\right)$$

(31)

where $Q(x)$ is the Complementary Error Function that is defined as,

$$Q(x) = \frac{1}{\sqrt{2\pi}} \int_x^{\infty} \exp\left(-\frac{v^2}{2}\right)dv$$

(32)

Consider

$$\frac{\mu_w^2}{\sigma_n^2} = \frac{E(w^2) - \sigma_w^2}{\sigma_n^2}$$

(33)

then,

$$P_B = Q\left(\frac{1}{2}\sqrt{\left(\frac{E(w^2)}{\sigma_n^2}\right) - \left(\frac{\sigma_w^2}{\sigma_n^2}\right)}\right),$$ (34)

Finally, from Eq. 8 and Eq. 33, the error rate can be expressed as follows,

$$P_B = Q\left(\frac{1}{2}\sqrt{\left(\frac{E(w^2)}{\sigma_n^2}\right) - 2^{C/W} + 1}\right).$$

(35)

Eq. 35 shows the relationship between the watermarking capacity and the detection error rate. Where $E(w^2)$ is the average energy of the watermark. From Eq. 35, we can see that the watermark detection error rate decreases with the increase of average watermark energy but rises with the increase of watermarking capacity.

The Bounds of Error Rate

According to the result of Eq. 4, we calculate the watermark amplitude by:

$$w = (1 - NVF(i,j)) \cdot S_0 + NVF(i,j) \cdot S_1$$

$$= \left(1 - \frac{1}{1+\sigma_x^2(i,j)}\right) \cdot S_0 + \frac{1}{1+\sigma_x^2(i,j)} \cdot S_1$$

$$= \frac{\sigma_x^2(i,j) \cdot S_0 + S_1}{1+\sigma_x^2(i,j)}$$

$$(36)$$

Since σ_x^2, S_0, S_1 are positive, and $S_1 \leq S_0$,

$$\sigma_x^2 \cdot S_0 + S_1 \leq \sigma_x^2 \cdot S_0 + S_0. \qquad (37)$$

Thus we can deduce:

$$\frac{\sigma_x^2(i,j) \cdot S_0 + S_1}{1+\sigma_x^2(i,j)} \geq S_1 \qquad (38)$$

$$\frac{\sigma_x^2(i,j) \cdot S_0 + S_1}{1+\sigma_x^2(i,j)} \leq S_0 \qquad (39)$$

Because $S_1 \leq w \leq S_0$, $E(S_1^2) \leq E(w^2) \leq E(S_0^2)$, then:

$$S_1^2 \leq E(w^2) \leq S_0^2. \qquad (40)$$

Applying Eq. 40 to Eq. 35, and considering the properties of Complementary Error Function, we derive the expressions as follows:

$$P_B \geq Q\left(\frac{1}{2}\sqrt{\left(\frac{S_0^2}{\sigma_n^2}\right) - 2^{C/W} + 1}\right) \qquad (41)$$

$$P_B \leq Q\left(\frac{1}{2}\sqrt{\left(\frac{S_1^2}{\sigma_n^2}\right) - 2^{C/W} + 1}\right) \qquad (42)$$

In the wavelet domain,

$$w = (1 - NVF(i,j)) \cdot Q_{\lambda,\theta} + NVF(i,j) \cdot S_1$$

$$= \frac{\sigma_x^2(i,j) \cdot Q_{\lambda,\theta} + S_1}{1+\sigma_x^2(i,j)} \qquad (43)$$

and

$$S_1^2 \leq E(w^2) \leq Q_{\lambda,\theta}^2. \qquad (44)$$

So the low bounds of watermark detection error rate is,

$$P_B \geq Q\left(\frac{1}{2}\sqrt{\left(\frac{Q_{\lambda,\theta}^2}{\sigma_n^2}\right) - 2^{C/W} + 1}\right). \qquad (45)$$

Then we derive the bounds of watermark detection error rate in the spatial domain and wavelet domain. The result shows that the bounds of error rate also relates to the watermarking capacity.

PAYLOAD CAPACITY

The watermarking capacity is the number of bits that can be hidden in a given host image. In spite of the definition is simple, we have to distinguish between two different concepts of the watermarking capacity:

1. Payload capacity C_{PL}. It is the size (in bits) of the watermark messages actually embedded, associated to a certain decoding error rate.
2. Theoretical capacity C. It is a theoretical limit on the amount of error-free emendable watermark messages, or inversely, on the minimum probability of error attainable for the given messages.

Therefore, the capacity is the maximum possible messages length for errorless decoding. But because of the involuntary attacks or noises, the zero error rate is not attainable even the input messages length (payload capacity) less than the channel capacity. According to Shannon second coding theorem, when the information transfer rate R is lesser than the channel capacity C, we can find a code, so that the average decoding error is small enough. If the information transfer rate R is greater than the channel capacity C, no matter how the codeword length is, we cannot find a code so that the average decoding error is small arbitrarily. The channel coding can be used to reduce the error rate P_B. Channel coding theorem does not tell us how to find good codes but it gives us the direction, it gives us confidence to find the suitable codes. In recent year Turbo code may be is a good code. The RS code and the Revolution code also are good codes (Perez-Gonzalez, 2001; Pereira, 2000).

The bit error rate of channel decoding is the quotient of the number of erroneous bits divided by the total number of bits transmitted in a channel. We denote the bit error rate of channel decoding as P_b. In the condition of no channel coding is used, the error rate is decided by the watermarking detection error rate P_B. The watermark messages are embedded in images after the channel coding is used. In the watermarking detection, the probability of error for transmission is P_B. The channel coding will decrease P_B. So, P_B and P_b decide the total error rate of watermarking.

The channel coding means the increase of redundancy data, but the increase of redundancy data needs the higher information transfer rate. This means the greater bandwidth of channel is needed. According to Shannon second coding theorem, no matter what channel code we used, the bit error rate P_b can not be zero when the input energy ratio $E_b/N_0 \leq$ -1.6db. We should decrease the payload capacity C_{PL} to decrease P_b. But if the payload capacity C_{PL} is too small, we can only embed few watermark messages in images. Our goal is to embed more watermark messages while keeping acceptable detection bit error rate.

When the information transfer rate is lesser than the channel capacity, we can decrease the bit error rate by increasing the codeword length n. When $R < C$, P_b can be expressed as,

$$P_b = \exp[-n \cdot E_r(R)] , \qquad (46)$$

where R is the information transfer rate, $E_r(R)$ is the random-coding exponent (Gallager, 1965),

$$E_r(R) = \max_{0 \leq \rho \leq 1} \max_{p(x)} \{E_0[\rho, P(x)] - \rho R\}, \qquad (47)$$

where ρ is the correction coefficient, $0 \leq \rho \leq 1$. The function $E_0[\rho, P(x)]$ is,

$$E_0[\rho, P(x)] = -\ln \sum_Y \left[\sum_X p(x_i) \cdot p(y_j \mid x_i)^{\frac{1}{1+\rho}} \right]^{1+\rho} \qquad (48)$$

According to Eq. 47, the random-coding exponent $E_r(R)$ is the maximum of function $\{E_0[\rho, P(x)] - \rho R\}$ to ρ, under the condition as,

$$\frac{\partial E_r(R)}{\partial \rho} = \frac{\partial [E_0(\rho, P(x)) - \rho R]}{\partial \rho} = 0. \qquad (49)$$

According to above equation,

$$R = \frac{\partial E_0[\rho, P(x)]}{\partial \rho}. \qquad (50)$$

If $\rho = 0$, $R=C$. While when $\rho = 1$, $R=R_{CR}$. R_{CR} is called the Critical Rate,

$$R = \frac{\partial E_0[\rho, P(x)]}{\partial \rho}\bigg|_{\rho=1}. \tag{51}$$

According to Eq. 47,

$$\frac{\partial E_r(R)}{\partial R} = -\rho. \tag{52}$$

We can see from above equations, the random-coding exponent $E_r(R)$ decreases with the rise of the information transfer rate R, and according to Eq. 46, the bit error rate P_b raises with the rise of the information transfer rate R when the codeword length is fixed. On the other hand, $E_r(R)$ increases with the drop of the information transfer rate R and the bit error rate P_b decreases. In the information-hiding channel, the bit error rate P_b will raise with the increase of the payload capacity C_{PL}. The error cannot be corrected if the payload capacity exceeds the bound of channel capacity.

In the general communication channel, if we wand to decrease the bit error rate by using channel coding, we should increase the codeword length, and the added information messages can be performed by enlarging the bandwidth or increasing the transfer time. While in the information hiding channel, the bandwidth is fixed, and no transfer time can be used. So we should analyze Eq. 46 according to the properties of the information-hiding channel.

Assume that the maximum length codeword is used in order to get the optimum error rate. The maximum length of codeword is decided by the capacity of information hiding.

$$n_{max} = \log_2 C. \tag{53}$$

In this case, according to Eq. 46, the random-coding exponent $Er(R)$ decides the error rate. The information messages are hidden in images after the channel coding is used, and the detection error rate is P_B. We view the process of information messages hiding and detection is a binary symmetric channel (BSC) communication. Assume that the hidden information messages include two kinds of letters with the same probability, $p(0) = p(1) = 1/2$, then the cross transition probability is P_B.

Table 2. The experimental results of watermarking capacity of Fishingboat and Lena images in the spatial domain and the wavelet domain

σ_n^2	Spatial domain		Wavelet domain	
	Fishingboat (bits)	Lena (bits)	Fishingboat (bits)	Lena (bits)
1	128032	80599	84813	66243
2	110410	65541	68364	54447
3	98309	55724	57914	46953
4	89214	48677	50543	41642
5	82005	43319	45006	37622
6	76088	39082	40664	34439
7	71106	35635	37151	31842
8	66833	32768	34239	29669
9	63113	30344	31783	27817
10	59835	28263	29677	26215

For example, according to the experimental results of the reference (Zhang, 2005), the information hiding capacity of Lena image is 27,789 bits when the variance of Gaussian noise is 4, and P_B is 0.00885. According to Eq. 48, we can calculate the function $E_0[\rho, P(x)]$ in above conditions,

$$E_0[\rho, P(x)] = -\log_2 \sum_Y \left[\sum_X p(x_i) \cdot p(y_j \mid x_i)^{\frac{1}{1+\rho}} \right]^{1+\rho}$$

$$= \log_2 \left\{ \left[\frac{1}{2} p(y_0 \mid x_0)^{\frac{1}{1+\rho}} + \frac{1}{2} p(y_0 \mid x_1)^{\frac{1}{1+\rho}} \right]^{1+\rho} \right.$$

$$+ \left. \left[\frac{1}{2} p(y_1 \mid x_0)^{\frac{1}{1+\rho}} + \frac{1}{2} p(y_1 \mid x_1)^{\frac{1}{1+\rho}} \right]^{1+\rho} \right\}$$

$$= -\log_2 \left\{ 2 \times \left[\frac{1}{2}(1-P_B)^{\frac{1}{1+\rho}} + \frac{1}{2} P_B^{\frac{1}{1+\rho}} \right]^{1+\rho} \right\}$$

$$= \rho - (1+\rho)\log_2 \left[P_B^{\frac{1}{1+\rho}} + (1-P_B)^{\frac{1}{1+\rho}} \right]. \quad (54)$$

When $\rho = 1$,

$$E_0[1, P(x)] = 1 - 2\log_2(\sqrt{P_B} + \sqrt{1-P_B}) = 0.351 \quad (55)$$

From Eq. 20 and Eq. 17, we can calculate the Critical Rate, $R_{CR} = 0.209$. And the random-coding exponent $Er(R)$ is,

$$E_r(R) = E_0[1, P(x)] - R = 1 - 2\log_2(\sqrt{P_B} + \sqrt{1-P_B}) - R \quad (56)$$

Combining Eq. 56 and Eq. 53 to Eq. 46, we get the decode error rate of watermarking channel as follow,

$$P_b = \exp\{-n_{max} \times [1 - 2\log_2(\sqrt{P_B} + \sqrt{1-P_B}) - R]\} \quad (57)$$

RESULTS

In the experiments, 256×256 test image Peppers, Lena and Fishingboat are used. A bi-orthogonal 9/7 DWT is used to decompose the host image into four levels. The NVF is computed in 3×3 image windows. The noises are assumed to be the white Gaussian noises.

According to Eq. 12, we can calculate the maximum allowable watermark amplitude of

Figure 2. The relationship between the watermark detection error rate and the average watermark energy E(w2)

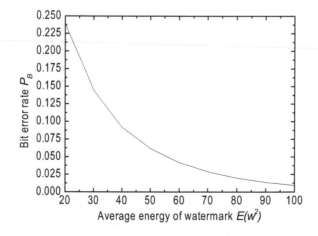

Figure 3. The relationship between the watermark detection error rate and the normalized watermarking capacity C=W

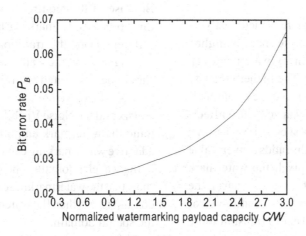

Figure 4. The error rate and the information transfer rate of Lena image

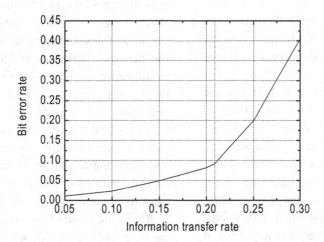

each pixel while keeping watermark's invisibility. Similarly, we can calculate the maximum allowable watermark amplitude of each wavelet coefficient according to Eq. 14. In the complex texture regions or in the edge regions, for example, the regions of Lena's hair, allow the bigger amplitude of watermark to embed.

We calculated the variance of the MWI, and finally we calculated image's watermarking capacity according to Eq. 16. The noises are assumed

to be the white Gaussian noise. Table 2 shows the watermarking capacity experimental results of Fishingboat and Lena images respectively in the spatial domain and the wavelet domain. The experimental results show that the watermarking capacity in the wavelet domain is lesser than the watermarking capacity in the spatial domain.

Figure 2 shows that the watermark detection error rate decreases with the increase of average watermark energy ($C/W = 2$, $\sigma^2_n = 4$). Figure 3 shows that the error rate rises with the increase of normalized watermarking capacity ($E(w^2)$ / $\sigma^2_n = 16$).

The results can be comprehended easily. If the average energy of the watermark is higher, it means that a higher intensity watermark can be embedded in the image. The higher intensity watermark is easy to extract, and the error rate is smaller. The watermarking capacity also affects the error rate. For the simplest case, if we assume that a watermarking algorithm adds a given value to the amplitude of each pixel, the watermark information is only one bit. In this scenario, the watermark detection is very easy and the error rate is the smallest. If we want to transmit more information, the modification to the host image must be more complex, and the detection error rate will rise with the increase of watermarking capacity.

The limit of watermark information is surely existent, but the precise bounds are unknown. This work and other previous works on image watermarking capacity try to find how much information can be hidden in a digital image or try to approach the unknown limit. Because of the different capacity analysis methods, different experimental methods and parameters, watermarking capacity results of those works quite diverse form each other. According to the results of our method, Lena image watermarking capacity is about 20,000 bits to 80,000 bits. Table 3 is the experimental results comparison of watermarking capacity of Lena image between proposed methods with other works in the spatial domain.

Figure 4 shows the relationship between the error rate of channel decoding and the information transfer rate (payload capacity) of Lena image. The Critical Rate R_{CR} is 0.209. From the figure we can see that when the payload capacity is lesser than the Critical Rate R_{CR}, the channel decode error rate is smaller, and if the payload capacity is greater than the Critical Rate R_{CR}, the channel decode error rate increases rapidly.

CONCLUSION

Because of the requirements of robustness and invisibility, watermarking has some properties different from the traditional communication. We suggest that the watermark power constraint should be associated with the content of image. In this article, we combine Watson quantization matrix and the Noise Visibility Function to determine the watermark amplitude, and propose an adaptive watermarking capacity analysis method in the wavelet domain. The experimental results show that the watermarking capacity in the wavelet domain is less than the watermarking capacity in the spatial domain.

This chapter intrudes a new analysis method of the watermarking capacity bounds, which is based on the theories of attractors and attraction basin of artificial neural network. The proposed method abandons the information-theoretic model. The capacity of watermarking is analyzed based on the theories of attractors and attraction basin of neural network. The results of research show that the attraction basin of neural network decides the upper limit of watermarking. The minimum detectable information capacity problem is analyzed in this paper. The upper limit and lower limit of watermarking, namely the maximum information capacity and the minimum detectable information capacity are unified in a same theory frame.

The neural network based watermarking capacity can be applied in almost all watermarking scenarios, such as Covert Channels, Steganography, Anonymity and Copyright Marking. The proposed capacity analysis is applicable to any image watermarking schemes based on artificial neural networks. We think that the proposed method is a helpful work to the capacity analysis of watermarking. And it is surely a helpful complement to the capacity analysis based on information theory. We will continue work on it and try to apply this capacity analysis to all watermarking schemes.

We also analyze the relationship between the watermarking capacity and the watermark detection bit error rate, and derive the relation between the capacity and the bounds of BER. The detection error rate of watermark is mainly influenced by the watermark average energy and the watermarking capacity. The error rate rises with the increase of the watermarking capacity. In the condition of no channel coding is used, the watermarking error rate is decided by the detection error rate. When the payload capacity C_{PL} lesser than the channel capacity, the error rate drops with the increase of payload capacity. Because the signal-noise rate of the watermarking channel is smaller, the detection error rate P_B is higher. So, it is difficult to get arbitrary small error rate if no channel coding is used. If the channel coding is used, the watermarking error rate is decided by P_B and by the channel decode bit error rate P_b. The error rate drops with the decrease of the payload capacity. If the payload capacity C_{PL} is lesser than the channel capacity, the error rate will keep in a lower lever.

REFERENCES

Barni, M., Bartolini, F., De Rosa, A., & Piva, A. (1999). Capacity of the watermarking-channel: how many bits can be hidden within a digital image. In *Security and Watermarking of Multimedia Contents, Proceedings of SPIE, 3657,* 437–448. USA: SPIE Press.

Barni, M., Bartolini, F., De Rosa, A., & Piva, A. (2000). Capacity of full frame DCT image watermarks. *IEEE Transactions on Image Processing, 9* (8), 1450–1455.

Costa, M. (1983). Writing on Dirty Paper. *IEEE Transactions on Information Theory, 29*(3), 439–441.

Cox, I. J., Milller, M., & McKellips, A. (1999). Watermarking as communications with side information. *Proceedings of the IEEE, 87*(7), 1127–1141.

Gallager, R. (1965). A simple derivation of the coding theorem and some applications. *IEEE Transactions on Information Theory, 11*(1), 3–17.

Hopfield, J. (1982). Neural networks and physical systems with emergent collective computational abilities. *Proceedings of the National Academy of Sciences. USA, 79*(4), 2554–2558.

Kim, J., Kwon, S., Hwang, H., Kwon, K., & Kim, D. (2002). Adaptive Digital Watermarking Based on Wavelet Transform Using Successive Subband Quantization and Perceptual Model. In *The International Technical Conference Computers and Communications, 1,* 1240–1243. USA: SPIE Press.

Lin, C. Y., & Chang, S. F. (2001). Zero-error Information Hiding Capacity of Digital Images. In *IEEE International Conference on Image Processing, 3,* 1007–1010. USA: IEEE Press.

McEliece, R., Posner, C., Rodemich R., & Santosh, R. (1987). The capacity of the Hopfield associative memory. *IEEE Transactions on Information Theory, 33*(4), 461–482.

Moulin, P., & Mihcak, M. (2002). A Framework for Evaluating the Data-Hiding Capacity of Image Sources. *IEEE Transactions on Image Processing, 11*(9), 1029–1042.

Newman, C. (1988). Memory capacity in neural networks, *Neural Network, 1*(1), 223–238.

Pereira, S., Voloshynovskiy, S., & Pun, T. (2000). Effective channel coding for DCT watermarking. In *Proceedings of the IEEE International Conference on Image Processing, 3,* 671–673. USA: SPIE Press.

Pereira, S., Voloshynovskiy, S., & Pun, T. (2001). Optimal transform domain watermark embedding via linear programming. *Signal Processing, 81*(6), 1251–1260.

Perez-Gonzalez, F., Hernandez, J., & Felix, B. (2001). Approaching the capacity limit in image watermarking, A perspective on coding techniques for data hiding applications. *Signal Processing, 81*(6), 1215–1238.

Servetto, S. D., Podilchuk, C. I., & Ramchandran, K. (1998). Capacity Issues in Digital Image Watermarking. In *IEEE International Conference on Image Processing, 1,* 445–449. USA: IEEE Press.

Voloshynovskiy, S., Pereira, S., Iquise, V., & Pun, T. (2001). Attack modelling: towards a second generation watermarking benchmark. *Signal Processing, 81*(6), 1177–1214.

Watson, A. B., & Yang, G. Y. (1997). Visibility of wavelet quantization noise. *IEEE Transactions on Image Processing, 6*(8), 1164–1174.

KEY TERMS

Attractors: Attractors of Hopfield network represent the stored patterns.

Basin of Attraction: The basin of attraction is the set of states in the system within which almost all states flow to one attractor.

Bit Error Rate (BER): The bit error rate of watermarking detection is the number of error bits in the total length of information messages bits.

Digital Watermark: A digital watermark embeds an imperceptible signal into data such as audio, video and images, for a variety of purposes, including captioning and copyright control.

Hopfield Neural Network: The Hopfield neural network is a recurrent neural network that stores information in a dynamically stable configuration.

Human Vision System (HVS): The Human Vision System (HVS) describes the human vision mechanism such as the spatial frequency orientation, the sensitivity on local contrast and the masking.

Payload Capacity: It is the size (in bits) of the watermark messages actually embedded, associated to a certain decoding error rate.

Theoretical Capacity: It is a theoretical limit on the amount of error-free emendable watermark messages, or inversely, on the minimum probability of error attainable for the given messages.

Watermarking Capacity: The watermarking capacity of digital image is the number of bits that can be embedded in a given host image.

Chapter XV
Digital Watermarking

Aidan Mooney
National University of Ireland Maynooth, Ireland

ABSTRACT

As Internet usage continues to grow, people are becoming more aware of the need to protect the display and presentation of digital documents. Digital watermarking offers a means to protect such documents. It works by embedding a piece of information into these documents – either visibly or invisibly – which can be detected or extracted from the document at a later stage to prove ownership of the document. This chapter will review, in detail, the process of digital image watermarking and will evaluate the different types of watermarks which may be used and the different techniques used to embed the watermarks. An examination of the domains used to embed the watermarks and some of the techniques used for detection of the embedded watermark are provided. Finally future trends within the area of digital watermarking are outlined.

INTRODUCTION

As the number of people who wish to display, sell and distribute their work via the Internet continues to grow, a number of issues arise. Such people may wish to post images on personal or business websites to promote a product or service or to increase sales, but they do not want their images stolen, posted on a rival's sites, or claimed by others as their own personal images. Since a digital copy is an exact replica of the original, the problem of document protection in the digital world is one of enormous importance. A person will be much more comfortable conducting work in the digital world if the documents security and identity can be protected. This identity protection is the goal of steganography, cryptography and watermarking.

This chapter will examine in detail digital watermarking for digital images. It will not look at digital video or digital audio watermarking. However, a lot of the ideas and implementations discussed here for image watermarking may also be applied to these other types of digital watermarking. First some related concepts to digital watermarking will be reviewed and examination of the differences and similarities between them presented. Watermark embedding and detection and the different types of watermarks used in watermarking systems will also be presented. Finally an introduction on the concept of watermark attacks and a look at future trends in the field will be examined.

BACKGROUND

Digital watermarking aims to embed a piece of information in some cover document without affecting the overall appearance of the image. Before going into detail on digital watermarking we will first look at some similar techniques, namely Steganography and Cryptography.

Steganography

Steganography is a term derived from the Greek words *steganos*, which means "covered", and *graphia*, which means "writing". Steganography is the art of concealed communication: the very existence of the message is a secret. An often used example of steganography is a story from the histories of Herodotus, which tells of a slave sent by his master, Histiaeus, to the Ionian city of Miletus with a secret message tattooed on his scalp. After tattooing, the slave grew his hair back in order to conceal the message. He then travelled to Miletus and, upon arriving, his hair was shaved to reveal the message to the city's regent, Aristagoras. The message encouraged Aristagoras to start a revolt against the Persian king. In this case the message is of primary value to Histiaeus and the slave is simply the carrier of the message. In steganography, the message being hidden is of upmost importance and the document it is hidden within (the carrier) is of minor importance (de Sélincourt, 1954).

Steganography is the study of techniques for hiding the existence of a secondary message in the presence of a primary message. The primary message is referred to as the *carrier signal* or *carrier message*; the secondary message is referred to as the *payload signal* or *payload message*. Arnold (2003) states that classical steganography (i.e., steganographic techniques invented prior to the use of digital media for communication) can be divided into two areas; *technical steganography* and *linguistic steganography*. Examples of technical steganography include the above mentioned story about Histiaeus and the use of invisible ink. Examples of linguistic steganography include marking specific characters with punctuation or lowering certain characters and using spacing between letters in a word to hide a secret message.

Cryptography

Cryptography is the process or skill of communicating in or deciphering secret writings or ciphers, (Cryptography, 2008). Cryptography encodes information using a secret key in such a way that nobody can read it, except the person who holds the key. This provides security, whereby, if someone intercepts the communication or accessed the server, they would be unable to read any of the encrypted messages. One of the main reasons why cryptography is not used more widely is attributed to it being a very complex and broad topic, (Cole, 2003).

One of the most famous examples of cryptography was the Enigma machine used by the German army during World War II. The machine was a cipher machine used to encrypt and decrypt secret messages. It is predicted that the ability of Allied forces to decrypt messages sent using the Enigma helped to shortly the war dramatically, with some sources claiming the war to have been shortened by two years. Examples of modern day cryptography are elliptical curve techniques, Cramer-Shoup encryption and the RSA encryption algorithm.

Digital Watermarking Reviewed

While steganographic techniques are usually not robust to modification of the data being protected, watermarking schemes are developed to take into account some possible attacks and modifications which the cover document may be subjected to. Cryptographic techniques have the purpose of protecting information as it is being transmitted prior to decryption. Once a message is decrypted it is no longer "protected". It is here that watermarking has an advantage as the watermark is present within the document at all times (unless removed by stealth).

Both watermarking and steganography describe techniques that are used to imperceptibly convey information by embedding information in the cover data. However, steganography typically relates to covert point-to-point communication between two parties. Thus, steganographic methods are usually not robust against modification of the data, or have only limited robustness and protect the embedded information against technical modifications that may occur during transmission and storage, like format conversion, compression, or digital-to-analogue conversion. Steganography and watermarking describe methods to embed information transparently into a carrier signal, while steganography establishes a covered information channel in point-to-point connections, watermarking does not necessarily hide the fact of secret transmission of information from third parties (Arnold, 2003).

Watermarking, unlike steganography, has the additional notion of resilience against attempts to remove the hidden data. Thus, watermarking, rather than steganography principles, are used when cover-data is available to parties who know the existence of the hidden data and may have an interest in removing it. A popular application of watermarking is to give proof of ownership of digital data by embedding copyright statements. It is obvious that for this application the embedded information should be robust against manipulations that may attempt to remove it (Johnson, 2000).

This makes watermarking appropriate for applications where the knowledge of an existing hidden message should not be sufficient for the removal of the message, without knowledge of additional parameters such as secret keys. The insertion of the watermark into some cover data should not affect the perceptual quality of the cover data. The fact that the embedding should be robust implies that the data cannot be stored in a file header but rather in the actual data values of the cover data. This requires a certain perceptual threshold allowing the insertion of additional information and hence distortions of the carrier signal without incurring unacceptable perceptual degradation of the original carrier signal (Arnold, 2003).

Watermarking

Although paper was invented in China over a thousand years earlier, paper watermarking first appeared in 1292 in Italy, (Katzenbeisser, 2000). The marks were made by adding thin wire patterns to paper moulds. The paper would be slightly thinner in these areas and thus more transparent and the mark visible when held up to the light.

By the eighteenth century, watermarks on paper made in Europe and America became popular. They had many uses, including trademarks, to record the date the paper was manufactured and to indicate the sizes of the original sheets. It was also around this time that watermarks began to be used as anticounterfeiting measures on money and other documents. The term *watermark* appears to have been coined near the end of the eighteenth century and may have been derived from the German term *wassermarke* (although the reverse could also be true). The term is actually a misnomer, in that water was not used in the creation of the marks.

With the uptake of watermarking in bank notes, pirates then turned their emphasis to de-

Figure 1. Watermarks present in the twenty and one hundred Euro banknotes

veloping techniques to forge the watermarks used in paper money. In turn others began developing more complex and sophisticated techniques for the generation of watermarks, some of which form the basis of today's models for watermark generation. Watermarks are still used in modern day to form part of the security measures present in bank notes. For example, the Euro banknotes, employed in the majority of Europe, contain a watermark along with holograms, checksums, security thread, colour-shifting ink and bar codes to provide security for its bank notes. An example of the watermark present on a twenty Euro note and one hundred Euro note are shown in Figure 1. These watermarks are only visible when the bank notes are held up to the light (ECB, 2002).

The analogy between the paper watermarks and digital watermarking is obvious: paper watermarks in bank notes or stamps inspired the first use of the term "watermark" in the context of digital data. In 1954 the first example of a technology, similar to some of the digital methods frequently discussed in the literature, was discussed by Emil Hembrooke, in which he filed a patent for "watermarking" musical works (Hembrooke, 1961).

It appears that digital watermarking was first discussed in 1979 by Szepanski (1979) in which a machine-detectable pattern could be placed on documents for anti-counterfeiting purposes. Nine years later, Holt *et al.* (1988) described a method for embedding an identification code in an audio signal. However, it was Komatsu and Tominaga (Komatsu, 1998) in 1988, who first appear to have coined the term *digital watermarking*. It was not until the mid 1990's that interest in digital watermarking began to soar and this interest has continued until the present day (Cox, 2002).

A watermark is a piece of information that is permanently embedded in some digital document. Some desirable features of a watermark include that it be:

- robust/resilient to standard manipulations,
- redundantly distributed over many samples,
- statistically irremovable, or better, undetectable,
- able to withstand multiple watermarking to facilitate the tracking of subsequent transactions to which an image is subject (Hernández, 1999).

WATERMARKING TRADEOFFS

In every watermarking system there is a tradeoff between the imperceptibility, the robustness and the capacity of the system. This tradeoff can be represented as shown in Figure 2. It can be seen from the figure that imperceptibility, robustness and capacity are conflicting properties of a watermarking system. If one property is determined, the other two parameters are inverse-proportional. For example, a specific application may determine how many message bits are needed, copyright protection may need to embed about 10 bytes and authentication may need anywhere from 100-1000 bytes for a 256 * 256 pixel image. After the embedded amount is decided, there always exists a trade-off between visual quality and robustness. Robustness refers to the extraction of embedded bits with an error probability equal to or approaching zero. Visual quality represents the quality of watermarked image (Lin, 2000).

Figure 2. Tradeoffs present in any watermarking system

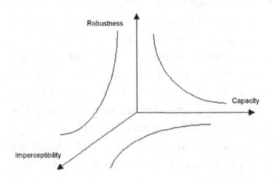

In general, if one wants to make the watermark more robust against attacks, then a longer or larger amplitude mark will be necessary to provide better error-resistance. However, visual quality degradation can be expected. Another scenario may be that with a default visual quality, there exists a trade-off between the information quantity of embedded message and robustness. For instance, the fewer the message bits that are embedded, the more redundant the watermark can be. Therefore, the mark has better error correction capability against noises (Lin, 2000).

The capacity of a system refers to the number of bits of a watermark that may be encoded within a document. For an image, the capacity refers to the number of bits encoded within the image. For audio, the capacity refers to the number of embedded bits per second that are transmitted. For video, the capacity refers to either the number of bits per frame or the number of bits per second. A watermark that embeds N bits is referred to as an *N-bit watermark*. Such a system can be used to embed any one of 2^N different messages (Cox, 2000). Image watermarking capacity is a complex problem and is influenced by the image content. Every image will have a different watermark capacity, with more complex images having the ability to hold more information compared to a flat image, for example, a pure white colour image (Fan, 2004).

Most of the early research on watermarking capacity (Barni, 1999; Ramkumar, 1999) directly applied information-theoretic channel capacity bounds without considering the properties of multimedia data. Shannon's well-known channel capacity bound,

$$C = \tfrac{1}{2}\log_2(1+\frac{S}{N}) \qquad (bits\,/\,sample)$$

(Equation 1)

is a theoretic capacity bound of an analog-value time-discrete communication channel in a static transmission environment, i.e., where the (codeword) signal power constraint, S, and the noise power constraint, N, are constants (Shannon, 1948). When transmitting a message rate at this bound, the probability of decoding an error can approach zero if the length of the codeword approaches infinite, which implies that infinite transmission samples are expected.

More recently work on analysing the visibility or noticeability of changes made to a digital image has been carried out. This work can be broadly categorised into three types, which vary with the extent of utilisation of the Human Vision System (HVS) model. Works of Type I consider that the just-noticeable changes are uniform in all coefficients in a specific domain, such as the spatial domain, frequency domain, or some transform domain. Works of Type II apply the human vision model to some extent. Works of Type III attempt to fully apply the HVS model to predict the visibility of changes. The fact that some coefficient changes are not noticeable is due to some masking effects. The maximum un-noticeable changes (or equivalently the minimal noticeable changes) are sometimes called the Just-Noticeable Distortion (JND) (Lin, 2000). It is thus the goal of all watermarking systems to establish a compromise between the three watermark tradeoff parameters of the system, namely, imperceptibility, capacity and robustness to improve the system performance.

KERCHOFF'S ASSUMPTION

In the case of systems requiring high levels of security the assumption that the pirate knows nothing about the watermarking algorithm is generally considered unsafe, as it is often impossible to keep the algorithm completely secret. Also, if the algorithm is kept secret, serious flaws may pass unnoticed as the larger community is not able to inspect the algorithm. For these reasons, the cryptographic and watermarking community's advocates that the adversary knows almost everything about the algorithm used, with the exception of perhaps a secret key. This is known as *Kerckhoff's assumption*, and may be stated as: *If you depend on keeping an algorithm secret to ensure security, the security is very fragile and will eventually be discovered* (Kerckhoff, 1883). It is often the case that developers not only assume the pirate knows the algorithm used but they actually ensure he does by publishing it. This also allows other developers to view and study the algorithm and find flaws in it and thus improve the algorithm (Cox, 2000).

APPLICATIONS OF WATERMARKING

Three of the most common application of watermarking are Watermarking for copyright protection, Fingerprinting for traitor tracking and Watermarking for copy protection. Each is briefly described next.

- *Watermarking for Copyright Protection*: For the protection of intellectual property, the data owner can embed a watermark representing copyright information in their data. This watermark can prove their ownership

in court when someone has infringed on their copyright (Langelaar, 2000).

- *Watermarking for Owner Identification*: In certain jurisdictions, the creator of a painting, story, song or any other original work automatically holds copyright to it the instant that the work is recorded in some physical form. Copyright on works may last for the creator's lifetime plus seventy years. The trouble with textual copyright symbols on images is the ease with which the image can be cropped to remove the copyright symbol.

o Perhaps the most famous example of this is a photograph of Lena Sjööblom which appeared in an edition of Playboy magazine. When this image was used as a test image most of the image was cropped, leaving only Lena's face and shoulders (see Figure 4). Unfortunately the copyright information of Playboy was also lost. Since then, the image has been distributed electronically and used in numerous publications. Watermarking can be used in a case like this to embed an imperceptible watermark in the cover image which stays with the image even after cropping (Cox, 2000).

- *Fingerprinting for Traitor Tracking*: The term *fingerprinting*, in a watermarking context, refers to a digital watermark uniquely identifying the intended end user of a work which is embedded in the creation's carrier signal as a payload. The fingerprint watermark can be embedded at the time of distribution to a specific customer. This requires a considerable computational overhead for the generation of unique watermarks for each user. There is also a distribution overhead for the generation of watermarks as well as a distribution medium that permits the efficient creation of distinct copies of the work (Arnold, 2003).

- *Watermarking for Copy Protection*: The information stored in a watermark can directly control digital recording devices for copy protection purposes where the watermark represents a copy-prohibit bit and watermark detectors in the recorder determine whether the data may be recorded or not (Langelaar, 2000).

COMMERCIAL WATERMARKING

Perhaps the best known commercial digital watermark product is Digimarc (Digimarc, 2007). Currently Digimarc provides a commercial watermarking system used by many of the image processing software packages. Digimarc provides digital watermarking software that embeds a watermark into digital content, including images, audio and video. Digimarc's subscription-based software allows customers to control copyrights, license online content, and manage their digital assets. A program like Adobe Photoshop can read this special embedded watermark and link the user back to Digimarc's website, and confirm if it is a watermarked image. In October 1996, Adobe launched the first digital watermark-enabled application, Photoshop 4.0. Today, Adobe ships numerous digital watermark-enabled applications. Jasc Corporation integrated Digimarc digital watermarking with Paint Shop Pro while Corel Corporation also included Digimarc's digital watermarking software in CorelDRAW and Corel Photo-Paint (Digimarc, 2005). Corel' Paint Shop ProX2 also incorporates Digimarc watermarks. When an image with one such watermark is opened in Paint Shop Pro or Photoshop the software flags that the image is watermarked.

Another example of commercial watermarking products are provided by Sarnoff. Sarnoff (2005) developed watermarking and data hiding technologies for both commercial and government clients. This work spans many application areas including authentication, tracking, copy control and prevention, device control, owner identification, and steganographic communication. Post Logic Studios announced in November 2004 that it was collaborating with Sarnoff Corporation to help benchmark and roll out Sarnoff's new digital cinema watermarking technique for digital cinema. The anti-piracy technology, named *iTrace*, lets a movie studio reliably trace a pirated copy of a film back to its source, even after the copy has been captured by a camcorder in a theater and then compressed at low bit-rates for illegal digital redistribution, such as over the Internet. *iTrace* includes watermarks that are invisible to the human eye, but easily recovered by machine analysis. These marks are embedded in each copy of a distributed motion picture, allowing identification of the last legal owner (Sarnoff, 2005). For further insight into the trends within the overall commercial watermarking industry the reader is directed to the Future Trends section of this chapter.

THE WATERMARKING PROCESS

The watermarking process consists of three main tasks: watermark generation, watermark embedding and watermark detection. Watermark generation is the process of generating a watermark, which may be embedded within an image. This image may then be available in the public domain where it may be subject to both intentional and unintentional attacks. The watermark embedded within an image may need to be detected at a later stage using some detection technique. This process is shown in Figure 3.

Watermark generation relates to the process of creating or selecting the watermark which will be used in the embedding process. The simplest case of watermark generation is where the user places an already created image or logo in the image to be watermarked, also known as the *cover image*.

Figure 3. Generic watermarking scheme

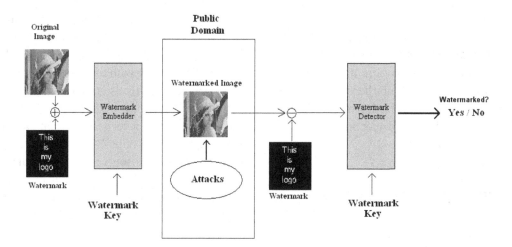

The user may also decide upon some technique to generate a watermark, for example, the user may use a random number generator to generate a sequence of numbers which may be used to construct the watermark or the use of a chaotic function to generate a watermark. The user also needs to decide on whether the watermark should be visible or invisible and also the effect the watermark has on the cover image. Watermark embedding relates to the placing of the watermark within the cover image and the user must decide on whether the watermark should be embedded in the spatial domain or in some transform domain. Watermark detection is the process of determining if a particular image contains a certain watermark and relaying this information back. We will now examine the main processes involved in the watermarking process.

Watermark Types

Robustness refers to the ability to detect a watermark after common signal processing operations. Robust watermarks are designed to withstand attacks on an image such as common image processing operations. Fragile watermarks are watermarks which are designed to ensure the credibility of the image, i.e., they can detect any changes made to the image as well as localising the changed areas (Inoue, 2000). Digital watermarks have been generated in numerous ways, including the use of personal logos (Mohanty, 1999), the use of text (as used in Adobe's PhotoShop and Corel's Paint Shop Pro), the use of pseudorandom sequences of numbers (Barni, 2001; GUI, 2006) and the use of chaotic functions (Tefas, 2003; Mooney, 2003; Mooney, 2008).

There are two main categories of watermarks, namely, visible and invisible ones. Visible watermarks are also referred to as perceptible watermarks and are visible to the human eye. By the nature of these watermarks they are very intrusive to the media they are embedded in and thus act to deter theft. They tend to reduce the commercial value of the media and make it obvious to criminally inclined people that the documents ownership has been definitively established. An example of a perceptible watermark is shown in Figure 4(c) and Figure 4(d), where the image shown in Figure 4(b) is watermarked perceptibly with the

Figure 4. (a) Watermark to be embedded, (b) original image, (c) and (d) visibly watermarked images. The watermark is stronger and thus more perceptible in (d).

(a)

(b)

(c)

(d)

image in Figure 4(a). The embedded watermark is clearly visible within the watermarked cover images and it can be seen that the watermark is more perceptible in Figure 4(d). This is due to the fact that the watermark has more precedence in the embedding process than in the case of Figure 4(c).

Visible watermarks are useful for protecting images in the public domain due to their ability to discourage unauthorised copying. Several visible watermarking techniques have been proposed, with the most famous and most cited being the techniques developed by IBM, which have been used by the Vatican Library (Mintzer, 1996) and the National Gallery of Art (USA) (Mintzer, 1998; Stewart, 2007). Visible watermarks are subject to removal attempts and even proving that the visible watermark in an image is an original watermark is often a challenge (Hu, 2004).

Invisible watermarks, also referred to as imperceptible watermarks, are invisible to the human eye. They have an advantage over perceptible watermarks in that their location is not known to an attacker. However, the less perceptible a watermark is, the more vulnerable it is to manipulation, as it may be removed by a user who is unaware of its presence. When an image is watermarked imperceptibly there should be as little difference as possible present between this image and the original cover image.

WATERMARK EMBEDDING

A watermark embedding technique is an algorithm for inserting a watermark into a cover work; for example, an image. Watermark embedders take at least two inputs: the message to be embedded

Figure 5. Generic watermark embedding and detection scheme

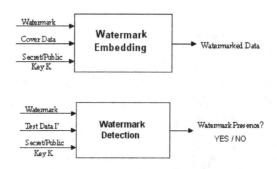

as a watermark and the cover image in which to embed the mark, as shown in Figure 5. The output is referred to as the watermarked work. Watermark embedders may also employ a watermark key for added security, which is known only to the person embedding the watermark (Cox, 2002).

The two most common embedding techniques used for watermark embedding are the additive and multiplicative embedding techniques. Additive techniques enjoy popularity due to their simplicity and are mainly used in the spatial domain.

The form of an additive embedding technique is:

$$I' = I + \gamma x \qquad \text{(Equation 2)}$$

where I' is the watermarked image, I is the image to be watermarked, x is the watermark and γ is the embedding factor.

The form of a multiplicative embedding technique is (Hartung, 1999):

$$I' = I(1 + \gamma x) \qquad \text{(Equation 3)}$$

where the symbols have the same meaning as in Equation 2. The embedding factor, γ, plays an important role in watermark embedding. The embedding factor, also known as the scaling factor, controls the intensity of the embedded watermark within the cover image.

Watermark embedding relies on "Weber's Law", which indicates that the change in a stimulus (the amount the cover image is modified) that will be just noticeable is a constant ratio of the original stimulus (Britannica, 2007), and may be expressed as:

$$\frac{\Delta I}{I} = k \approx 0.02 \qquad \text{(Equation 4)}$$

where I represents the initial intensity of a pixel, ΔI is the change in the intensity of the pixel and k signifies that the proportion on the left hand side remains constant despite the value of I changing. Another way of stating this, is that the human eye is less sensitive to brightness changes in higher luminance values, than it is in lower luminance values.

Spread Spectrum Watermarking

In the study of communications, the term *spread spectrum* refers to a secure signal that is transmitted in such a way that the bandwidth used is much larger than the bandwidth of the source itself (Eggers, 2002). Spread spectrum communications were developed by the United States military to provide resistance to jamming and interference of signals. The exact spreading technique used is known only by the transmitter and receiver (Cox, 2002). Frequency hopping, direct sequence, pseudorandom-noise (PN) spreading and combinations of these are all forms of spread spectrum. Watermarking can be seen as a form of communicating, in that, we wish to communicate a message from the watermark embedder to the watermark receiver.

In spread spectrum watermarking, a narrow signal (watermark) is modulated by a broad carrier signal (cover image), which broadens the original narrow signal. For security reasons, the carrier signal is normally generated from a pseudorandom sequence, which has statistical properties similar to a truly random signal, when spread spectrum watermarking is performed.

The following properties of spread spectrum are well-suited for watermarking:

- Anti-Jamming: The attacker does not know the information being conveyed in the watermark. As a result the attacker must jam the whole spectrum of the signal, therefore not only distorting the watermark but also the entire cover image.
- Low probability of interception: As the watermark is spread over the image, only a small amount of power is added to each frequency. This level of power may be unnoticeable in the image and thus the attacker may not even notice the change.
- Pseudo-noise: The majority of watermark systems use a pseudorandom-noise watermark, meaning it has statistical properties similar to that of a random system, but it can be easily regenerated (Meerwald, 2001a).

Pseudorandom Watermarks

There are many different types of watermarks used. The most common types used in visible watermarking systems are logos and images. In invisible watermarking systems the most commonly used watermarks are those generated from pseudorandom generators.

Much of the work to date on digital watermarking is based on spread spectrum principles. In general, the watermark used in these cases are pseudo-randomly generated white noise signals. According to Simon *et. al* (Simon, 1995) the term "pseudonoise" and its abbreviation "PN" were first used in internal reports of the Jet Propulsion Lab of California I. T., Pasadena in 1953.

The PN number sequences used for watermarking are either monopolar or bipolar after quantifying the sequence – see Equation 5. A monopolar sequence has elements with the values 0 and 1 whereas a bipolar sequence has elements with the values 1 or −1. There is a "near" balance in the spread of the values within a PN number sequence as each of the values can occur with equal probability. All frequencies in the Discrete Fourier Transform of the sequence are equally represented within the PN number sequence, which is why it is also called a white pseudonoise sequence (Van Schyndel, 2003). Since the pseudorandom noise sequences are white in nature they do not possess lowpass or highpass characteristics without applying some filter to the sequence. These systems generate a unique sequence of numbers based on a function seed. This function seed is chosen in such a way as to provide a certain level of security to the watermark generated.

Chaotic Watermarks

Chaotic watermarks have been proposed as an alternative to the more commonly used pseudorandom watermarks. The process of generating a watermark derived from a chaotic map involves several steps. A value for the function seed and an initial starting value must be first selected. The function y_n is iterated n times (after allowing initial "ringing" to dissipate), where n is the number of watermark bits required, by successively passing in the generated value, y_{n+1} as the new input.

The resultant sequence, y_n, is a sequence of real numbers. A chaotic binary sequence is quantified from the real sequence generated using:

$$w_n = \begin{cases} 0 & y_n \le 0.5 \\ 1 & y_n > 0.5 \end{cases} \qquad \text{(Equation 5)}$$

where 0.5 is chosen as the cutoff threshold in assigning the binary values.

To date, a number of chaotic functions have been proposed in the literature for the purpose of watermark generation; the three most prominent are the *skew tent map* (Tefas, 2001; Tefas, 2003), the *Bernoulli map* (Tsekeridou, 2001a; Tsekeridou, 2001b) and the *logistic map* (Xiang, 1999; Mooney, 2003; Dawei, 2004; Mooney, 2005).

The Bernoulli map has been shown to produce lowpass watermarks and also white watermarks. These white watermarks are similar to those generated by a pseudorandom number generator. The skew tent map has been shown in the literature to generate both lowpass and highpass watermarks dependant on the function seed. It can also generate white watermark sequences. The logistic map has also been shown to generate white watermarks and lowpass watermark sequences. Watermarks generated in this way offer an effective alternative to more traditional watermarks, in that they can generate a white sequence, and also that their spectral properties may be controlled to produce varying types of watermarks (Tefas, 2003). Care must be taken in particular when using the logistic map for watermark generation as there are regions of periodic behaviour within the so-called chaotic region of the map (Mooney, 2004; Mooney, 2006).

This control of spectral properties of the generated sequences of these chaotic functions offers a distinct advantage over the sequences generated by the pseudorandom generators. For example, if we know that our watermarked image will be subjected to attacks which are lowpass in general we can generate a lowpass watermark which will be more robust to these attacks. By simply altering the function seed in these chaotic function one can generate watermarks with different spectral properties. In comparison, if we wanted to generate a watermark with particular spectral properties using a pseudorandom generated watermark one would need to colour the watermark using some filter.

In applications where no severe distortions are expected, e.g. in captioning or indexing applications, highpass spectrum watermarks can be used since they guarantee superior performance (Tefas, 2001). Watermark signals generated by the iterating of a chaotic function have an advantage over signals generated by colouring white noise in that these signals are much easier to create and re-create. Rather than having to seed a pseudorandom number generator and then apply a filter to the resultant signal to generate coloured noise, a single seed can determine the properties of the generated sequence from the chaotic function. Highpass sequences are typically less robust to lowpass filtering and small geometric deformations of the image than lowpass sequences. They are however extremely robust with respect to noise addition, nonlinear deformations of the grayscale, such as contrast/brightness adjustment and gamma correction (Fridrich, 1998).

Embedding Domains

In order to use the additive or multiplicative embedding equations one must decide on the domain the watermark will be embedded in. All images in the spatial domain may also be represented in other domains, for example, the discrete Fourier domain, the discrete cosine domain and the discrete wavelet domain. It is possible to add a watermark to the image either in the spatial domain or some transform domain using an additive or multiplicative embedding technique described.

The simplest watermarking techniques involve embedding a watermark in the spatial domain of an image. The most common method of watermark embedding used in early watermarking schemes embedded the watermark in the Least Significant Bits (LSB) of the cover image. Since these bits have little overall influence on the image quality, modifying them will not degrade the image quality (Johnson, 1998). These techniques showed little robustness to common watermark attacks and interest in it within the field of digital watermarking declined. Some more recent work has looked at using the local image characteristics for watermarking but this is a complicated technique in the spatial domain and may be performed much easier in some transform domain (Kuo, 2007).

Although transform domain watermarking schemes require higher computational complexity than spatial domain schemes they are generally regarded as more desirable due to the increased robustness offered in these domains (Lee, 2005). Transform domain watermarking techniques apply some invertible transform to the cover image before the watermark is embedded. The transform domain coefficients are then modified as the watermark is embedded, usually in a multiplicative manner, before the inverse transform is applied to obtain the watermarked image. The most commonly used transforms for transforming an image prior to embedding are the Discrete Cosine Transform, the Discrete Fourier Transform and the Discrete Wavelet Transform. There are also other domains used such as the Fourier-Mellin transform (Ó Ruanaidh, 1998) the Fresnel transform (Aoki, 2001), the complex wavelet transform (Kumgollu, 2003) which have been used as embedding domains.

The discrete wavelet domain has proved to be one of the most popular transform domains used for watermarking recently. The wavelet transform enables high compression ratios with good quality reconstruction along with excellent spatial localization and frequency distribution. The JPEG2000 compression technique is based on the wavelet transform standard and this provides techniques based on the wavelet transform to have a certain level of robustness against an attack made using JPEG2000 (Meerwald, 2001b). Another major advantage afforded by wavelets is the ability to perform local analysis, i.e., to analyse a localized area of a larger signal. If one considers a sinusoidal signal with a small discontinuity – one so tiny that it is barely visible, a plot of the Fourier coefficients of the signal shows little of interest. However, a plot of the wavelet coefficients clearly shows the exact location in time of the discontinuity. Wavelet analysis is capable of revealing aspects of data that other signal analysis techniques miss, aspects like trends, breakdown points, discontinuity in higher derivatives and self-similarity. It affords a different view of data that those presented by traditional techniques, because wavelet analysis can often compress or denoise a signal without appreciable degradation.

The wavelet transform can be taken as one special type of pyramid decomposition. It retains most of the advantages for image fusion but has much more complete theoretical support. After one level of decomposition, there will be four frequency bands, namely Low-Low I_0^3, Low-High I_0^2, High-High I_0^1 and High-Low I_0^0. The next level of decomposition is just applied to the I_0^3 band of the current decomposition stage, which forms a recursive decomposition procedure. Thus, an N-level decomposition will finally have *3N + 1* different frequency bands, which include *3N* high frequency bands and just one low frequency band. The 2D DWT will have a pyramid structure. The frequency bands in higher decomposition levels will have a smaller size.

The wavelet transform consists in a multiscale spatial-frequency decomposition of an image as shown in Figure 6. The lowest frequency band at the lowest scale factor is found at the top left corner I_3^3. At the same resolution level, the block I_3^0 contains information about the highest horizontal and lowest vertical frequency band. Similarly, the block I_3^2 contains information about the lowest horizontal and the highest vertical frequency band at the lowest scale factor. The same process is

Figure 6. A4-level wavelet decomposition scheme

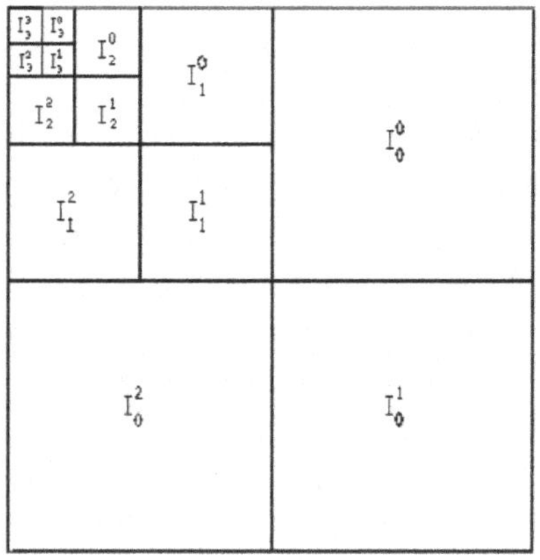

repeated for the intermediate and highest resolution levels (Katzenbeisser, 2000).

The selection of the coefficients that are manipulated in the watermarking process is determined by the embedding technique and the application. The main distinction is between the approximation image I_3 which contains the low-frequency signal components and the detail sub-bands (I_j^2, I_j^1, I_j^0, where j is the resolution level) that represent the high-frequency information in horizontal, vertical and diagonal orientations. One does not want to embed entirely in the low frequency components as this introduces artefacts in the image being watermarked. However, embedding in just the high frequency components does not afford good robustness to the watermark. Therefore it is advisable to find a balance between low and high frequency components by embedding in the middle frequency components – a straightforward task using the wavelet transform.

The wavelet transform has linear computational complexity, O(n), as opposed to

$$O(\frac{n}{\log n})$$

for the DCT (where n is the length of the watermark to be embedded). The difference is only important when watermark embedding occurs over the entire image and not in a block-based format (Meerwald, 2001b).

Watermark Detection

A watermark detector is a hardware device or software application that detects and decodes a watermark. A watermark decoder is the portion of the watermark detector that maps extracted marks into messages. In most cases, this is the entire operation of the watermark detector. In general, no distinction is made between a watermark detector and watermark decoder (Cox, 2002). In some watermarking applications, the original unwatermarked cover work is available during detection. This is referred to as informed detection or as a private watermarking scheme. However, in other applications, detection must be performed without access to the original cover work. These applications are known as blind detectors or as a public watermarking scheme. Figure 5 shows the generic watermark detection technique.

The detection region for a given image, I', and watermark w, is the set of works that will be returned by the detector as works containing that message. The detection region is often (but not always) defined by a threshold on a measure of similarity between the detector's input and the possibly watermarked image Cox, 2002). If an image I' is watermarked by a watermark w in either an additive or multiplicative manner, watermark detection can be treated as a hypothesis test where the hypotheses are:

- Hypothesis A: image I' is not watermarked (w is not present),
- Hypothesis B: image I' is watermarked but not with w (w is not detected),
- Hypothesis C: image I' is watermarked with w (w is detected).

Hypothesis A and B are equivalent in the sense that the specific watermark w is not present and these can be grouped together:

- H_0: The possibly watermarked image, I', does not contain the watermark w
- H_1: The possibly watermarked image, I', contains the watermark w,

where the watermark w_d is not embedded if $w \neq w_d$ (event H_0) and w_d is embedded in the work if $w = w_d$ (event H_1) (Tefas, 2001).

Thus, detection performance can be characterised by the false alarm errors and their corresponding probability, P_{fa}, and the false rejection errors and their corresponding probability, P_{fr}. The P_{fa} is the probability to detect a watermark in an image that is not watermarked or is watermarked with a different watermark than the one being tested, and, P_{fr} is the probability of not detecting a watermark in an image which has been watermarked (Tefas, 2001).

For example, a false alarm probability of 10^{-3} indicates that one expects, on average, one false positive for every 1,000 detection attempts. It is an easy task to guarantee no missed detection, by setting the threshold value to the lowest possible value, i.e. zero. However, by doing this the probability of false alarms increases as even unwatermarked images are passed through as being watermarked.

To determine whether a particular image is watermarked the output from a watermark detector is usually compared to a threshold and if the result is greater than the threshold value one can say the image is watermarked, otherwise, it is not watermarked. By setting the threshold value to the lowest possible value one can ensure that there are no missed detections, however, unwatermarked images are also assumed to be watermarked. By setting the threshold to the highest possible value one can ensure that there are no false alarms as no image, either watermarked or unwatermarked, returns a positive detection. The value of the

threshold needs to be selected such that the system correctly determines that watermarked images are watermarked (Hypothesis C), and that the number of false alarms is minimised.

Piva *et al.* (Piva, 1997) were amongst the first to look at the selection of a threshold as crucial in a watermarking system employing a correlation detection technique. They stated that the threshold may be evaluated using:

$$T = \frac{\gamma}{3M} \sum_{i=1}^{M} |w_i| \qquad \text{(Equation 6)}$$

where γ is the watermark embedding strength, M is the number of pixels watermarked and w_i are the watermarked pixels. Later, the authors (Piva, 1998) improved this threshold by analysing similar probability density functions (PDFs) to those in Figure 7, where they found the optimum threshold to be halfway between zero and the mean of $f_c(x)$ (the PDF generated from the detection of watermarks; Hypothesis C). However, this threshold is only suitable when the watermark system does not undergo any attacks and thus the authors set a constraint on the maximum false positive probability (for example, $\leq 10^{\wedge -6}$) such that the threshold moves leftward in the presence of attacks. The new threshold was found to be:

$$T = 3.3\sqrt{2\sigma_C^2} \qquad \text{(Equation 7)}$$

Barni *et al.* (Barni, 2001) later set the constraint that the maximum false positive probability should be $\leq 10^{-8}$ and thus the threshold could be calculated as:

$$T = 3.97\sqrt{2\sigma_C^2} \qquad \text{(Equation 8)}$$

The detection value returned by the watermark detector is compared against a suitably selected threshold T and if the value of the correlation is

Figure 7. False alarm and false rejection probabilities

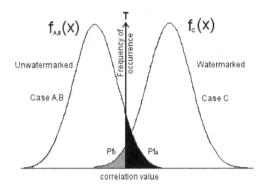

greater than the threshold, positive detection of the watermark is assumed (Barni, 2001; Tsekeridou, 2001b).Once a cover image has been watermarked it may be made available in the public domain. While here the image may be subjected to some form of attack which aims to remove the embedded watermark from the cover image.

Attacks

An attack is any attempt to inhibit a watermarking system. A malicious attack aims to remove, alter or weaken the embedded watermark. A coincidental attack is an attack which may occur during common image processing and is not intentionally aimed at corrupting the watermark The security of a watermark refers to its ability to resist hostile attacks. Depending on the application and the watermarking requirements, a list of distortions and attacks which may take place are (Katzenbeisser, 2000):

- Signal enhancement (sharpening, colour correction, gamma correction),
- Additive and multiplicative noise (Poisson, Gaussian, uniform, speckle),
- Linear filtering (lowpass, highpass, bandpass),

- Nonlinear filtering(median filtering, morphological filtering),
- Lossy and lossless compression (images: JPEG2000, video: MPEG-7, audio: MP3),
- Local and global affine transforms (rotation, scaling),
- Data reduction (cropping, clipping),
- Embedding multiple watermarks.

There are also attacks known as ambiguity attacks. These attacks aim to discredit the authority of a watermark within an image by placing additional watermarks within the host image or placing a watermark from one image into another without the consent of the legitimate watermark owner. Robust watermarking systems should be able to correctly detect the presence of a particular watermark after multiple watermarks have been embedded in the image. Removal attacks attempt to analyse the watermarked data, estimate the watermark and then remove this watermark from the image. These attacks include the collusion attack, denoising and non-linear filtering (Meerwald, 2001a; Hartung, 1999). In the collusion attack, many instances of different watermarked image containing the same watermark are available and the attacked image is generated by taking only a small part of each image and rebuilding a new attacked image from these parts (Kutter, 2000).

FUTURE TRENDS

Digital watermarking has progressed considerably from an immature technology in a relatively short time period to a state of the art technology. The outlook for digital watermarking is promising with watermarking applications having recently been successfully deployed in billions of objects, including motion pictures, music and broadcast TV programming, along with the more mature areas of print and digital images. There is significant research and development in the watermarking area, with a massive increase in research in the areas of motion picture, TV programming and music.

In late 2007, Nielsen, the media measurement company, and Digimarc, the leader in watermarking patents, teamed up to introduce an online content identification scheme for the US television industry based on watermarking technology – called the Nielsen Media Manager. Digimarc is licensing digital watermarking patents from its patent portfolio to Nielsen for these new solutions. The Nielsen solution will use a combination of digital watermarking and fingerprinting and aimed at social networking sites, peer-to-peer sites and file-sharing sites to aid in the identification of video data on such sites (Rosenblatt, 2007).

Digital television and IPTV (Internet Protocol Television) have recently received a lot of interest and attention in the digital watermarking field. Some set-top box vendors have now incorporated watermarking technologies with their existing encryption technologies. The leaders in this market are seen to be Verimatrix and Cinea. Some of the other giants have also begun looking at this area, Philips and Thomson for example, and research in this area is set to expand in the following years.

There is considerable interest in music watermarking in recent times and this has led to many major companies joining the watermarking path. In 2007 Microsoft received a patent for audio watermarking technology for inserting and detecting watermarks in audio signals. Recently all of the Big Four record labels (Universal Music Group, Warner Music Group, EMI and Sony BGM) discarded digital rights management solutions. Sony and Universal have both experimented with watermarks as an alternative to digital rights management systems (Rosenblatt, 2007). One can be fairly certain that the other two giants of the music industry will soon follow suit and invest a lot in digital watermarking for their audio content.

CONCLUSION

Digital watermarking is a technique that aims to embed a piece of information permanently into some digital media, which may be used at a later stage to prove owner authentication and attempt to provide protection to documents. Watermarking, unlike steganography, has the additional notion of resilience against attempts to remove the hidden data. Digital watermarking is a three step process: (1): generate a watermark, (2): embed a watermark, and, (3): detect a watermark. In this chapter image watermarking was examined but the same criteria and ideas can be implemented for audio and video watermarking.

A watermarked document may be subjected to attacks, either malicious or coincidental, where the attack is aiming to remove the watermark or inhibit its detection. All watermarking systems should be robust to attacks, especially ones which will be known to occur. The majority of watermarks used to date have been generated from a pseudorandom number generator. However, it has been shown that chaotic watermark offer an alternative to these watermarks and provide an extra degree of robustness.

The interest in digital watermarking has increased dramatically since it first came into the public domain in 1979. This interest is continuing to grow with more and more research into the area. Large multinationals have invested deeply in this field and one can be sure that this interest will continue for a long time yet.

REFERENCES

Aoki, Y. (2001). Fresnel Transform of Images for Applications to Watermarking. *Electronics and Communications, Japan, 82*, 1612-1622.

Arnold, M., & Schmucker, M. (2003). *Techniques and Applications of Digital Watermarking and Content Protection*. Artech House.

Aubrey de Sélincourt. (1954). *The Histories of Herodotus*. London, Penguin Books.

Barni, M., Bartolini, F., De Rosa, A., & Piva, A. (1999). Capacity of the Watermark-Channel: How Many Bits Can Be Hidden Within a Digital Image? *Proceedings of SPIE Conference on Security and Watermarking of Multimedia Contents, 3657*, 437-448.

Barni, M., Bartolini, F., & Piva, A. (2001). Improved Wavelet Based Watermarking Through Pixel-Wise Masking, *IEEE Trans. on Image Processing, 10*, 783-791.

Britannica. (2007). *Encyclopedia Brittanica Online*, Retrieved December 12, 2008 from http://www.britannica.com.

Cryptography. (2008). Retrieved January 8, 2008, from http://dictionary.reference.com/browse/cryptography.

Cole, E. (2003). *Hiding in Plain Sight: Steganography and the Art of Covert Communication*. London: Wiley Publishing Incorporation.

Cox, I. J., Miller, M. L., & Bloom, J.A. (2002). *Digital Watermarking*, London: Morgan Kaufmann.

Dawei, A., Guanrong, C., & Wenbo, L. (2004). A chaos based robust wavelet-domain watermarking algorithm. *Chaos, Solitons and Fractals, 22*, 47-54.

Digimarc Corporation. (2007). *Digimarc (DMRC)*, Retrieved December 12, 2007, from http://www.digimarc.com/.

Rosenblatt, B. (2007). DRM: 2007 Year in Review, Part 2. Retrieved December 12, 2008 from http://www.drmwatch.com/watermarking/article.php/3718651

ECB – European Central Bank. (2002). *The Euro – Our Money*. Retrieved December 20, 2007 from http://www.ecb.int/pub/pdf/other/eurobren.pdf.

Eggers, J., & Girod, B. (2002). *Informed Watermarking*. Boston, MA: Kluwer Academic Publisher.

Fan, Z., & Hongbin, Z. (2004). Capacity and Reliability of Digital Watermarking. *Proceedings of the International conference on the Business of Electronic Product Reliability and Liability*, 162-165.

Fridrich, J. (1998). Combining low-frequency and spread spectrum Watermarking. *Proceedings of SPIE Symposium on Optical Science, Engineering and Instrumentation, 3456*.

GUI, G.-F., JIANG, L.-G., & Chen, H. (2006). A New Asymmetric Watermarking Scheme for Copyright Protection. *IEICE TRANS. FUNDAMENTALS, 89*, 611-614.

Hartung, F., & Kutter, M. (1999). Multimedia Watermarking Techniques. *Proceedings of the IEEE, 87*, 1079-1107.

Hembrooke, E. F. (1961). *Identification of sound and like signals*. United States Patent, 3,004,104.

Hernández, J. R., & Pérez-González, F. (1999). Statistical Analysis of Watermarking Schemes for Copyright Protection of Images. *Proceedings of IEEE, Special Issue: Identification and Protection of Multimedia Information*, 1142-1166.

Holt, L., Maufe, B. G., & Wiener, A. (1988). *Encoded Marking of a Recording Signal*. U.K. Patent GB 2196167A.

Hu, Y., Kwong, S., & Huang, J. (2004). Using Invisible Watermarks to Protect Visible Watermarked Images. *Proceedings of the IEEE International Conference on Circuit and Systems*, 584-587.

Inoue, H., Miyazaki, A., & Katsura, T. (2000). Wavelet-Based watermarking for Tamper Proofing of Still Images. *IEEE International Conference on Image Processing, 2*, 88-91.

Johnson, N. F., & Jajodia, S. (1998). Steganalysis: The investigation of Hidden Information.

Proceedings of IEEE Information Technology, 113-116.

Johnson, N. F., Duric, Z., & Jojodia, S. (2000). *Information Hiding: Steganography and Water-marking - Attacks and Countermeasures*, London: Kluwer Academic.

Katzenbeisser, S., & Petitcolas, F. A. P. (2000). *Information Hiding Techniques for Steganography and Digital Watermarking*. London: Artech House.

Kerckhoff, A. (1883). La cryptographie militaire. *Journal des sciences militaires, 9*, 5-38.

Komatsu, N., & Tominaga, H. (1998). Authentication System Using Concealed Images in Telematics. *Memoirs of the School of Science and Engineering, Waseda University, 52*, 45-60.

Kumgollu, F., Bouridane, A., Roula, M. A., & Boussaktd, S. (2003). Comparison of Different Wavelet Transforms for fusion based watermarking applications. *Proceedings of IEEE International Conference on Electronics, Circuits and Systems, 3*, 1188-1191.

Kuo, C. –T., & Cheng, S. -C. (2007). Fusion of color edge detection and color quantization for color image watermarking using principal axes analysis. *Pattern Recognition, 40*, 3691-3704.

Kutter, M., Voloshynovskiy, S., & Herrigel, A. (2000). The Watermark Copy Attack. *Proceedings of SPIE, Security and Watermarking of Multimedia Content, 3971*, 1-10.

Langelaar, G., Setyawan, I., & Lagendijk, R. (2000). Watermarking digital image and video data: a state of the art overview. *IEEE Signal Processing Magazine, 17*, 20-46.

Lee, C. –H., & Lee, H. –K. (2005). Geometric attack resistant watermarking in wavelet trasform domain. *Optics Express, 13*, 1307-1321.

Lin, C.-Y. (2000). *Watermarking and Digital Signature Techniques for Multimedia Authen-tication and Copyright Protection*, PhD Thesis - Columbia University.

Meerwald, P. (2001a). Digital Image Watermarking in the Wavelet Transform Domain, *PhD Thesis: Univeristy of Salzburg*.

Meerwald, P., & Uhl, A. (2001b). A Survey of Wavelet domain Watermarking Algorithms. *Proceedings SPIE, Electronic Imaging, Security and Watermarking of Multimedia Contents III, 4314.*

Mintzer, F. C., Boyle, L. E., Cazes, A. N., Christian, B. S., Cox, S. C., Giordano, F. P., Gladney, H. M., Lee, J. C., Kelmanson, M. L., Lirani, A. C., Magerlein, K. A., Pavani, A. M. B., & Schiattarella, F. (1996). Toward on-line, worldwide access to Vatican Library materials. *IBM Journal of Research and Development, 40*, 139-162.

Mintzer, F. (1998). Developing Digital Libraries of Cultural Content for Internet Access. *IEEE Communications Magazine*, 92-98.

Mohanty, S. P., Ramakrishnan, K. R., & Kankanhalli, M. (1999). A dual watermarking technique for images. *Proceedings of the seventh ACM International Conference on Multimedia*, 49-51.

Mooney, A., & Keating, J. G. (2003). An Optical and Digital Technique for Watermark Detection. *Proceedings of SPIE International Symposium on Optical Science and Technology, 5202*, 97-105.

Mooney, A., & Keating, J. G. (2004). The impact of the theoretical properties of the Logistic Function on the generation of optically detectable watermarks. *Proceedings of SPIE, Technology for Optical Countermeasures, Optics/Photonics in Security and Defence, 5615*, 120-129.

Mooney, A., & Keating, J. G. (2005). Generation and Detection of Watermarks Derived from Chaotic Function. *Proceedings of Opto-Ireland, Proceedings SPIE, 5823*, 58-69.

Mooney, A., & Keating, J. G., & Heffernan, D. M. (2006). A Detailed Study of the Generation of Optically Detectable Watermarks using the Logistic Map. *Chaos, Solitons and Fractals, 30,* 1088-1097.

Mooney, A. & Keating, J. G., & Pitas, I. (2008). A Comparative Study of Chaotic and White Noise Signals in Digital Watermarking. *Chaos, Solitons and Fractals, 35,* 913-921.

Ó Ruanaidh, J. J. K., & Pun, T. (1998) Rotation, scale and translation invariant spread spectrum digital image watermarking. *Signal Processing, 66,* 303-317.

Piva, A., Barni, M., Bartolini, F., & Cappellini, V. (1997). DCT-based watermark recovery without resorting to the uncorrupted original image. *Proceedings IEEE International Conference on Image Processing, 1,* 520-523.

Piva, A., Barni, M, Bartolini, F., & Cappellini, V. (1998). Threshold Selection for Correlation-Based Watermark Detection. *Proceedings of COST254 Workshop on Intelligent Communications,* 67-72.

Ramkumar, M., & Akansu, A. N. (1999). A Capacity Estimate for Data Hiding in Internet Multimedia. *Symposium on Content Security and Data Hiding in Digital Media,*

Sarnoff Corporation. (2005). *Sarnoff Watermarking Technologies,* Retrieved December 12, 2007, from http://www.sarnoff.com/products_services/video_vision/digital_watermarking/index.asp.

Shannon, C. E. (1948). A Mathematical Theory of Communication. *Bell System Technical Journal, 27,* 373-423.

Simon, M. K., & Hinedi, M. K., & Lindsey, W. C. (1995). *Digital Communication Techniques: Signal Design and Detection.* London: Prentice-Hall.

Stewart, D., & Lerner, E. A. (2007). *IBM - Think Research,* Retrieved December 20, 2007 from http://domino.watson.ibm.com/comm/wwwr_thinkresearch.nsf/pages/solutions299.html.

Szepanski, W. (1979). A Signal Theoretic Method for Creating Forgery proof Documents for Automatic Verification. *Carnahan Conference on Crime Countermeasures,* 101-109.

Tefas, A., Nikolaidis, A., Nikolaidis, N., Solachidis, V., Tsekeridou, S., & Pitas, I. (2001). Performance Analysis of Watermarking Schemes based on Skew Tent Chaotic Sequences, *NSIP'01, 51,* 1979-1994.

Tefas, A., Nikolaidis, A., Nikolaidis, N., Solachidis, V., Tsekeridou, S., & Pitas, I. (2003). Markov Chaotic Sequences for Correlation Based Watermarking Schemes. *Proceedings of Chaos, Solitons and Fractals, 17,* 567-573.

Tsekeridou, S., Solachidis, V., Nikolaidis, N., Nikolaidis, A., Tefas, A., & Pitas, I. (2001). Theoretic Investigation of the Use of Watermark Signals derived from Bernoulli Chaotic Sequences, *SCIA2001.*

Tsekeridou, S., Solachidis, V., Nikolaidis, N., Nikolaidis, A., Tefas, A., & Pitas, I. (2001). Bernoulli Shift Generated Watermarks: Theoretic Investigation. *Proceedings of IEEE International Conference on Acoustics, Speech and Signal Processing, 3,* 1989-1992.

Van Schyndel, R. G. (2003). Digital Watermarking and Signal Delay Estimation Using Pseudonoise Sequences. *PhD thesis, School of Physics and Material Science, Monash University, Australia.*

Xiang, H., Wang, L., Lin, H., & Shi, J. (1999). Digital watermarking systems with chaotic sequences. *Proceedings of Security and Watermarking of Multimedia Contents,* 449-457.

KEY TERMS

Capacity: The capacity of a system refers to the number of bits of a watermark that may be encoded within a cover document.

Chaotic Watermark: A watermark generated by iterating a chaotic function. These watermarks offer the user more control over the spectral properties of the generated watermarks.

Cryptography: Cryptography is the process or skill of communicating in or deciphering secret writings or ciphers.

Digital Watermarking: Digital watermarking is a technique that aims to embed a piece of information permanently into some digital media, which may be used at a later stage to prove owner authentication and attempt to provide protection to documents. Watermarking, unlike steganography, has the additional notion of resilience against attempts to remove the hidden data.

Pseudorandom Watermark: A watermark generated by iterating a pseudorandom number generator. These watermarks are generally white in nature.

Robustness: Robustness refers to the ability to detect the watermark after common signal processing operations and attacks.

Steganography: Steganography is the art of concealed communication: the very existence of the message is a secret. Steganography is the study of techniques for hiding the existence of a secondary message in the presence of a primary message.

Watermark Attacks: An attack is any attempt (malicious or coincidental) to inhibit a watermarking system.

Watermark Detection: A watermark detector is a hardware device or software application that detects and decodes a watermark.

Watermark Embedding: A watermark embedding technique is an algorithm for inserting a watermark into a cover document.

Chapter XVI
Digital Video Authentication

Pradeep K. Atrey
University of Winnipeg, Canada

Abdulmotaleb El Saddik
University of Ottawa, Canada

Mohan Kankanhalli
National University of Singapore, Singapore

ABSTRACT

Digital video authentication has been a topic of immense interest to researchers in the past few years. Authentication of a digital video refers to the process of determining that the video taken is original and has not been tampered with. This chapter aims to provide an overview of digital video authentication systems and a universal review of the associated methods. The chapter not only establishes the importance of authenticating a video in various application scenarios; it also identifies key properties and design issues that should be considered while designing a video authentication system. The benign and tampering operations that characterize the security and robustness aspects of a typical video authentication system are described. The past works related to video authentication, based on digital signature and digital watermarking, have been described; and the emerging trends in this area of research have also been identified.

1. INTRODUCTION

The last decade has witnessed a tremendous growth in the use of digital video in various applications such as electronic media, surveillance, advertising and the entertainment industry. Digital video has many advantages over its counterpart, analog video, such as better picture quality, sharper images, better color reproduction, and better immunity to signal problems in recording. In digital form, a video can be easily transported over the Internet and it facilitates easy editing and copying. On the other hand, the ease of modifying a digital video is sometimes considered as a disadvantage since a video in digital form is so vulnerable that it can be easily tampered with.

Moreover, detecting manipulations in a video is often found difficult. This concern has generated significant interest among the multimedia research community to focus on investigating techniques for authenticating a digital video.

By definition, authentication is a process that provides some means to guarantee that the entities are who they claim to be (i.e. entity authentication), or that the information has not been manipulated by unauthorized parties (i.e. data authentication) (Menezes, 1997). In the context of multimedia, video authentication refers to a process that ascertains the integrity of a given digital video and detects if it has been tampered with in any way. In other words, a video authentication system ensures the integrity of digital video, and verifies that the video taken into use has not been corrupted.

The need for authenticating a digital video is further argued by providing the following examples:

a) In the recent years, several cases have been reported where a video recording of a political leader receiving a bribe was made public. However, in the absence of a foolproof method to authenticate the video, it is hard to trust such reports. On the other hand, criminals get away from being punished because the video showing their crime can not be proved conclusively in the court of law.

b) In surveillance camera systems, the video captured by the cameras are often used as evidence in the post-incident investigation process. In such scenarios, it is hard to ascertain that the digital video produced as evidence is the one that was actually shot by the camera.

c) In a sensitive scenario where a video is produced as a witness in the court of law, even a small alteration may not be acceptable. However, there are some scenarios where some editing also may be allowed while keeping in tact the authenticity of the video.

For example, a journalist, after shooting a video, may need to perform some editing before broadcasting it on a news channel. In such a case, a video-authentication system should be able to allow editing on the video up to a certain level ensuring the authenticity of the video.

d) A video viewer (or a consumer) who receives video through a communication channel cannot ensure that the video being viewed is really the one that was transmitted (by a producer). There may be eavesdroppers who can alter the video content intentionally to harm the interest of both the producer and consumer.

e) Video authentication is also important in an advertisement monitoring scenario where a commercial company or an individual can automatically identify, in real time, whether or not a specified TV channel is playing their video advertisement for the stipulated time. A TV channel may cut a few frames to gain more time and money.

The above examples establish that there is a compelling need that videos, wherever they are and in whatever form, should be made authenticable before use.

The goal of this chapter is to provide readers with a good understanding of a typical video authentication system, its properties and design issues, and a review of video authentication techniques. An ideal video authentication must be able to detect tampering. In addition, it should also be able to localize the altered regions and recover the losses due to tampering (Celik, 2002; Sun, 2002). The tampering could be of two types: *spatial tampering* and *temporal tampering*. *Spatial tampering* refers to spatial attacks such as region tampering, whereas inter-frame alterations such as frame adding, replacement, dropping, or reordering are *temporal attacks*. In addition to the detection of tampering, a video authentication system should be robust to benign operations such as affine transformation and compression.

This chapter is organized as follows. Section 2 describes a typical video authentication system, its properties, and various design issues associated with it. In this section, we also present two types of classifications: first, a classification of the benign and tampering operations that can be performed on a digital video; and second, a classification of authentication scenarios based on whether the authentication of the video is performed in an offline or online manner. In Section 3, we present a state of the art video authentication technique. Finally, Section 4 concludes the chapter with some general remarks and further sources of information.

2. A TYPICAL VIDEO AUTHENTICATION SYSTEM

A typical video authentication system is shown in Figure 1. The figure shows two steps: authentication (Figure 1a) and verification (Figure 1b). In the authentication step, for a given video V,

the authentication data S is computed using an authentication algorithm. The authentication data S is encrypted using private key k and packaged with the video in two forms. It can be kept as a *signature* in the header of the video file; or alternatively, it can be embedded as a *watermark* into the video content. The video integrity is confirmed in the verification step by computing the new authentication data S' for the given video V using the same authentication algorithm. The new authentication data S' is compared with the original authentication data S that is decrypted using private key k. If they do not match, the video is treated as tampered otherwise it is considered to be original. The selection of authentication method is an important aspect of a video authentication system. The method should be robust to normal video processing operations but must be sensitive to tampering.

In the subsequent subsections, we discuss the following: first, properties of an ideal video authentication system; second, a classification of benign and tampering operations that can be

Figure 1.

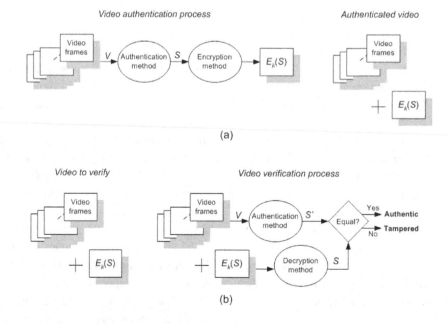

(a)

(b)

performed on a video; and finally, a classification of authentication scenarios based on whether authentication and verification are performed online or offline.

2.1 Properties and Design Issues

There are various issues that affect the methodologies and design of a video authentication system in the practical scenarios. For instance, in a surveillance scenario, authentication is required at the video camera level; while in a video streaming scenario; the video frames should be authenticated and verified at the transmitting and receiving ends, respectively. Therefore, the design of a video authentication system depends on the needs of a specific scenario. However, any generic video authentication system, to be efficacious, must live up to the following criteria:

- Sensitivity to alterations
  A video authentication system must uncover the malicious manipulations performed on the video. It should not only detect the manipulations but also the type of alteration. The possible alteration may include spatial as well as temporal tampering at the frame level, shot level, or video level. We further discuss all benign and tampering operations in Section 2.2.
- Localization and self-recovery of altered regions
  The system must be able to precisely locate any malicious modification made to a frame or video. By localizing the altered region(s), it should also be able to reconstruct the loss occurred due to alterations (Celik, 2002; Sun, 2002). The location or the level of tampering in a video may be at the intra-frame level, i.e. within only a frame; or the video may also be altered at the inter-frame level, i.e. by dropping and replacing a few frames or by changing the sequence of frames.

- Robustness to benign operations
  Robustness is a real concern in developing a video authentication system. There are several operations like image enhancement, image/video compression, rotation, scaling, flipping, filtering, format transformations, etc. that are performed on a video. An authentication method should be robust enough to distinguish the benign operations from the manipulations done with a bad intention.
- Tolerance against the loss of information
  The authentication system should be able to tolerate some loss of information due to non-malicious operations like lossy compression, etc. The degree of tolerance may vary from application to application.
- Compactness of signature
  The digital signature should be small in size compared to the original video data. The signature should not be a burden to deliver. On the other hand, small signatures are susceptible to loose their uniqueness property. So there must be a tradeoff between the size of signature and its uniqueness.
- One-way property of signature
  Given a video, one should be able to compute the signature but not vice versa. It must be computationally infeasible to devise a video that has the same signature.
- Sensitivity against false alarm
  The false alarm refers to a situation when the tampering is detected even if the video is not actually modified. An ideal scheme should be able to correctly identify between a false alarm and tampering.
- Computational feasibility
  The signature computation should be feasible under the given requirements. For instance, for a real time video-on-demand scenario, the signature computation process should be fast and should meet the real-time requirements. For other cases like the journalist case where the authentication can be performed offline,

the security is considered more important than the computational requirement.

In addition to the properties discussed above, there are various issues that should be taken into account while designing a video authentication system. These are as follows:

- Authentication objective: Complete vs. Content verification

  The techniques, which consider the whole piece of video data as input and do not allow any manipulation, are classified in the *complete verification techniques* group. In complete verification, the video data is considered as untouchable messages. It is like the message authentication in the cryptography field. On the other hand, in the *content verification techniques group*, the authentication data is generated using invariant video features so that even small manipulations may be detectable (Lin, 1999; Lin, 2000).

- Authentication source: Uncompressed vs. Compressed data

  The source of the authentication system may be raw or compressed data. For example, video frames stored one by one in an uncompressed form are raw data. In practical applications, video data is hardly found available in raw format. In general, due to the large volume of data, video is kept in a compressed form. So most of the video authentication systems are designed and developed for compressed data as input (Lin, 1999).

- Authentication approach: Digital signature vs. Digital watermarking

  An important aspect in the design of an authentication system is how to package the authentication data in the original video. The authentication data may be kept separately as a file or in the header of a video. Alternatively, it can be embedded into the content of the original video. The former mode is called *digital signature* and the latter is *digital watermarking*. Various techniques proposed by researchers based on these two approaches will be described in detail in Section 3.

- Authentication data: Content dependent vs. Content independent

  The authentication data (i.e. digital signature or watermark) may or may not be content dependent. Since any alteration generally causes changes in the content, hence it is reasonable to have authentication data that is dependent on content so that any change in content also affects the authentication data.

- Authentication scenario: Offline vs. Online

  Online video capturing is required in the live transmission of an event. In this real time scenario, the video authentication needs to address issues like efficiency of the algorithm in addition to accuracy. On the other hand, offline video capturing refers to a situation where video recording is done first and then edited. Once the video package has been edited, it can be used for transmission or for storage. A classification of the authentication scenarios based on offline and online cases will be described shortly in Section 2.3.

- Encryption algorithm: Symmetric vs. Asymmetric encryption

  The authentication data such as digital signature is encrypted with a symmetric algorithm or an asymmetric encryption algorithm. In symmetric encryption, the authentication data is decrypted at the verification time by using the same key. On the other hand, in asymmetric encryption such as Public Key Cryptography systems (Sun, 2002), the authentication data is encrypted using a private key authenticator and is decrypted by the private key of the verifier while the public key is made open.

- Authentication data: Visibility vs. Invisibility

  Since the visibility of authentication data can help an attacker, it is preferred that the authentication data should be invisible under normal observation. For example, the visual impact of watermarking should be as week as possible (Du, 2002). In other words, watermark embedding should not introduce distortions to the video.

2.2 Classification of Benign and Tampering Operations

The operations that do not modify the content of a video semantically are considered as benign operations. For example, the video undergoes several image/video processing operations such as image enhancement, changing luminance or contrast, changing hue and colors, and compression. The geometric transformations such as scaling, rotation, translation, shearing, and flipping are also considered as permissible operations (Atrey, 2007; Dugelay, 2000; Niu, 2002).

The benignity of the operations also depends upon the application scenario. For instance, in a surveillance camera scenario, no editing is allowed because the recorded event can be used as evidence in the court of law. However, in this scenario, the video authentication scheme must be robust against image enhancement. The pictures received by the surveillance camera may be in foggy or poor lighting conditions, and therefore, the images need to be processed for quality improvement. On the other hand, in a journalist scenario, once a video is recorded, the editing of video is allowed to prepare it for a news channel. However, in this case, the semantic meaning of the video should not change and the relative order of the frame-sequences should be preserved.

In the scenario of streaming a video (either live or recorded), due to the large size of video data, the network often suffers from a congestion problem at the bottlenecks. To overcome the network congestion problem, some data loss (for example, the loss of a few video frames) is inevitable. In such cases, the video transcoder or the designated router intentionally may drop frames to avoid buffer overflow. So the dropping of a few frames may be allowed in the streaming video scenario except in highly sensitive applications such as military surveillance. In essence, a video authentication system specific to an application must be robust against its benign operations.

In addition to the benign operations, it is very important to consider all possible attacks while designing an authentication system. The basic objective of a video authentication system is to make a given video resistant against all possible attacks and to verify whether a given video has been tampered with or not. It is useful to find where (i.e. localization of alterations) and how the tampering has been done (Celik, 2002; Yin, 2002).

Based on the dimension, tampering is divided into spatial tampering and temporal tampering. These are described in the following.

- Spatial tampering

  Spatial tampering, also called intra-frame tampering, refers to the manipulations in a video frame. The manipulations include cropping, replacement, content adding and removing at the pixel level, block level, frame-level, sequence of frames level, and shot level. The type of manipulation includes spatial cropping in a specified region of a frame, several frames, or even an entire shot/video. These operations change not only the semantic meaning but it can also hide some important content in video. For instance, if a face is replaced with another face in a video frame, it completely changes the semantic meaning.

- Temporal tampering

  Temporal tampering is an inter-frame jittering. It refers to the manipulations performed with respect to time. The pos-

Table 1. Classification of benign and tampering operations (Atrey, 2007)

Benign operations	Tampering operations

• *Spatial operations*
     ▪ Geometric transformations: scaling (resizing), rotation, flipping and shearing.
     ▪ Image enhancement: changing intensity/ contrast/ grayscale range.
     ▪ Color converters.
     ▪ Changing hue and saturation.
 • *Temporal operations* such as frame dropping up to an extent temporally.
 • *Global loss of spatial detail due to compression*: brightness and resolution reduction.
 • Compression and quantization.
 • Transmission error and noise.
 • Data storage error.
	• *Spatial tampering*: Localized intra-frame attacks such as spatial manipulations through the temporal axis-frame level, the GOP (Group of Pictures) level, shot level, and video level.
	 • *Temporal tampering*: Localized inter-frame attack on a sequence of frames such as adding, dropping, and reordering at the GOP level, shot level and video level.

sible manipulations are frame dropping (or removing), replacing, adding extra frames and reordering (also called a re-indexing attack) video frames (or a sequence of frames). These manipulations can be performed on the sequence of frames level, shot level or the video level. Major dropping of frames may lead to hiding of some important part of a video. Similarly, frame reordering may change the meaning of the video with respect to time. Replacing and/or adding frames may contribute to false information in a video, which is extremely undesirable taking security into consideration.

As video data contains a large amount of temporal redundancy, dropping of a few adjacent frames does not affect the visual appearance and semantic meaning substantially. Therefore, it is affordable to drop or reorder the frames up to a certain extent if the application so demands. On the other hand, in applications such as advertisement monitoring, frame dropping is treated as tampering. However in most cases, the replacing, inserting, and reordering of frames in a

video significantly alters its semantic meaning; therefore, it should be treated as tampering with a high degree of sensitivity.

Although benign and tampering operations are application specific, a general classification of benign and tampering operations with respect to a generic video authentication system is provided in Table 1.

2.3 Classification of Authentication Scenarios

In the following, a classification of the video authentication scenarios will be presented. This classification is based on whether the authentication and the verification processes are performed in an online or offline manner. The four categories are: Online authentication: and online verification; Online authentication and offline verification; Offline authentication and online verification; and Offline authentication and offline verification. We describe them as follows.

• Online authentication and online verification

In online authentication of a video, the authentication of a video sequence is performed at the source (camera) level in real time. For instance, in the scenarios such as live broadcast and video-conferencing, the authentication is needed online at the source camera level. In online verification, the verification at the receiver end is also performed in real time to ensure the authenticity of a streaming video. In such scenarios, the authenticity of a video is not only verified whether it is really the one shot by the camera, but it is also verified against possible tampering done by an eavesdropper on the communication channel. The real time efficiency issues are of utmost importance in these cases. In a scenario such as online video conferencing, delay or jittering is usually not acceptable. Therefore, the network issues such as bandwidth (broadband or wireless), jittering, and latency are very important in designing a video authentication system for such video streaming scenarios. Also, no editing or manipulation is tolerated. The video should be transmitted or received as it is captured by the camera.

- Offline authentication and online verification

The offline-authentication refers to an authentication process that is performed on a ready-to-use video. Here, ready-to-use video refers to the video that has been shot, edited and made available for use. In case of streaming of a recorded video, the ready-to-use video is authenticated offline before broadcast. At the receiver end, the verification is performed in an online manner. The viewer should be able to ensure, in real time, whether or not s/he is receiving an authentic video. Note that in this scenario the authenticity of the ready-to-use video is verified for its completeness and against the possible tampering on the channel. For example, in an advertisement monitoring

scenario, the advertising video should be verified in real time to check whether the advertisement is played in full and whether it is played a specified number of times for which it is paid.

- Online authentication and offline verification

This category consists of all those scenarios that require authentication at the camera level in real time, but the verification is performed in an offline manner, and hence, does not have real time computing requirements. For instance, in the journalist scenario, when a journalist records an event, the authentication is needed at the camera level so that the recorded video can be verified offline whenever required. In such cases, the editing of the video sequences may be allowed up to the extent that the editing process ensures the authenticity of the report. In another scenario of face tampering disputes, the recorded video shot must be made authentic at the camera level by the private keys of the artists involved so that no face tampering can be done at the time of editing.

- Offline authentication and offline verification

The final category is the one in which both authentication and verification processes are performed in an offline manner. For instance, a buyer buys a movie from a video shop. The buyer can buy it in two ways: either by ordering and receiving it online (i.e. Online shopping of a video); or by personally going to the shop and then receiving it by hand in a compact disk (i.e. manual or offline shopping). Initially, the movie is authenticated offline by the seller. Then in the first mode of buying, since the buyer buys it online, the network issues, such as data loss, should be considered in verifying the authenticity of the received video. While in the second case, since the buyer himself manually receives the video, the authenticity should be checked against disk errors, etc. However in both the cases, completeness and originality of the movie should be ensured in the verification process.

3. VIDEO AUTHENTICATION TECHNIQUES

In this section we intend to draw up an overview of video authentication techniques. Two different areas of study have mainly contributed to the development of video authentication methods: *Cryptography* and *Signal processing*. The cryptographers have used the *digital signature* as authentication data; and the signal processing researchers utilized the spatial and frequency transform methods to compute the *digital watermark* for ensuring the video integrity. However, the researchers from both of these disciplines have exploited the inherent features of video in order to compute the authentication data. Due to the fact that the video data is generally huge in volume, the content authentication (i.e. computing authentication data) is preferred over complete authentication (such as encryption of whole video data) (Shi, 1998).

In a digital signature approach, the authentication data is computed based on the content (feature) of the original video data. The digital signature can be saved in two different ways. If the header of the compressed source data remains intact through all processing stages, then the digital signature can be saved in the header. Otherwise, it can be saved as an independent file (Lin, 1999). However, in both the cases, old and new signatures are compared to authenticate the video data. The digital signature should be sensitive enough to detect the malicious alterations and should also be robust against the benign operations like compression, transformation, etc.

The digital watermarking approach works as follows. We embed the authentication data into the video bit stream in a manner that its semantic meaning does not change. Digital watermarks can be categorized into *fragile*, *semi-fragile*, and *infragile*. The fragile watermark breaks even with a small change in the video data; hence it is not robust to benign operations on the video. The infragile watermark becomes too rigid and does not react to the undesired changes in the video data. Therefore, a semi-fragile watermark is considered the best for authentication purpose as well as for performing the benign operations (Tzeng, 2001; Yin, 2002). Although, in general, digital signature and digital watermarking approaches have been used independently; in some cases, these two approaches have been combined to produce the authentication data (Dittman, 1999).

The *cryptographic hash function* has been very well utilized by the researchers for computing compact size signatures and/or watermarks. A cryptographic hash function must follow the properties such as one-way, strong collision, and week collision. Due to these properties, the authentication data computed using a hash function is considered highly secure. The simplest approach is to hash the whole video data. This approach appears clumsy because it does not provide robustness, and the authentication data drastically changes even with a single bit change in the video data. As a change in the hash output is non-linear to the change in the video, it is very difficult to quantify tampering. However, in practical scenarios such as video streaming, some data loss is inevitable. To overcome this problem, the researchers have worked towards the development of *visual hash* functions (Fridrich, 2000; Radhakrishnan, 2003) that are robust to some allowable operations in specific scenarios. The video features invariant to these benign operations are used as input to the hash function. The hash output should not change with the change in these invariant features. A visual hash function should:

- Be invariant against the benign video processing operations.
- Change drastically with the malicious operations.

- Degrade gracefully with a slight change in the content.

The researchers have used inherent features of the compressed video to compute the digital signature (Dittman, 1999; Lin, 1999; Tzeng, 2001) and the digital watermarks (Celik, 2002; Daniel, 2002; Du, 2002; Lin, 2000; Mobasseri, 2001; Mobasseri, 2000; Yin, 2001; Yin, 2002) in order to authenticate a video. To compute the digital signature, most of them have used hash functions that are robust to some benign operations. The invariant features include DCT coefficients in the compressed domain video (Du, 2002; Lin, 1999; Yin, 2001; Yin, 2002); and edges at the block level (Dittman, 1999; Tzeng, 2001), key frames (Yan, 2003), MSB of blocks (Celik, 2002), and Angular Radial Transformation (ART) coefficients of a Visual Shape Descriptor (He, 2003) in the uncompressed domain. The methods have also been proposed for lossless authentication (Du, 2002), localization of tampering and self-recovery (Celik, 2002).

In the following, we describe the past works related to video authentication done by researchers. The works are described in two categories: digital signature and digital watermarking.

3.1 Digital Signature Schemes

- *Camera-level Video Authentication*: Cryptographers Quisquater and Joye (1997) have proposed a framework for the authentication of video sequences with a secure camera system. Their functional model consists of a TTP (Trusted Third Party), Secure Camera, Journalist, Editor, Verifier and most importantly the Pirate (Quisquater, 1997a; Quisquater, 1997b). The authentication is performed at the time of recording and editing. At the time of recording, an image is divided into 128 blocks. Each block is associated with a hash value $h_{i,j}$. The *succession witness* (sequences) Z_i of images

are computed until the ith image I_i i.e. $Z_i = H(Z_{i-1}, I_i)$, $(1 \le i \le k)$, where H is a hash function and $Z_0 = 0$. Z_i is used to calculate GQ-signature; i.e. $(d_i, D_i) = GQ(Z_i)$ for $1 \le i \le k$. This process authenticates the image sequencing at the time of recording. At *editing* time, the editor is allowed to remove some images from the original recording $(I_1, I_2, \ldots, I_k)$ by respecting their relative order so that the edited sequence can be made authentic. So, if a sequence from image l to image $l+m$ is removed, the new Z_{l+m} is computed to reinitialize the succession witness computation for the next sequence Z_{l+m+1}, and so on. After editing, the final image sequence (e.g. from p to q) is written on the tape. The authentication data written on the tape consists of the following:

o The compressed image $B_{i,j}$ for $p \le i \le q$, $1 \le j \le 128$;
o The hash value of the 128 blocks of the images p to q, i.e. $h_{i,j}$, $p \le i \le q$, $1 \le j \le 128$;
o The GQ-signature of the succession witness until the qth image, i.e. (d_i, D_i).

The editor also authenticates himself by applying his signature to the video by using the Tillich-Zemor hash function. This work is useful in authenticating a video at the time of its capture. However, the real timeliness remains a concern in such cases. Moreover, since each image is hashed individually and saved on to the tape, the temporal relationship between the images has not been utilized to further reduce the size of the signature.

- *A Video Authentication Scheme Robust to Transcoding and Editing Operations*: Lin and Chang (2000) have proposed a video authentication technique that is robust against five transcoding operations (Lin, 1999; Lin, 2000). These are dynamic rate shaping, rate control without drift error correction, rate control with drift error correction, editing with mostly consistent picture types, and editing or transcoding with inconsistent picture types. The first three operations are used for bit rate changes and the latter two are used to edit or cut the video. In operation 4, the GOP is preserved; while in operation 5, it is not preserved. In the first four processes, the motion vector is also preserved, but in process 5, it changes. The authors proposed two robust signatures. For the first four transcoding operations, signature I is proposed while signature II is robust against the fifth operation.

Robust signature I is based on the observation that the relationship between a coefficient pair (i.e. two DCT coefficients of the same coordinate position) in any two 8×8 blocks of an image should be the same. The quantized (intra or non-intra) DCT coefficients of the luminance and chrominance matrices in each macroblock are used to form the comparison pairs to compute the feature code Z_c. To protect the other information including motion vectors and control codes, the hash values Z_m of the bit streams in the video sequence is added to the feature codes. Finally, the digital signature DS is computed by encrypting (Z_c, Z_m) with a private key where $Z_c = \forall_{\text{Pictures}} VLC (\forall_{MBs}, z_c)$ and $Z_m = Hash (GOP\_Header, z_{m,1}, z_{m,2}, ..., z_{m,N})$; where *VLC* is the Variable Length Coding.

Robust signature II is used where the GOP structure, motion vectors or DCT residual coefficients are changed. The signature is generated picture by picture based on their pixel values. Therefore, first the compressed video sequence is decoded and pixel values are reconstructed of the pictures of any kind of picture type ('I', 'P', 'B'). The feature codes from the pictures are computed by forming the block pairs and comparing the DCT coefficients at the block pair using

one bit to represent each comparison. After getting the feature codes from each picture, the time code is added and then a private-key encryption is used to form the digital signature.

Although the method is robust against transcoding operations and editing operations, it has a drawback. The relative differences between DCT coefficient pairs are prone to an attack if the value of each DCT coefficient pair is significantly modified while keeping their relationship preserved. Also, in signature II, the temporal redundancy could have been better utilized.

- *Edge-based Signature Schemes*: Dittman (1999) have utilized edges as features to compute the digital signature. Canny edge-detectors have been used to detect the edges in a video frame. Later, Tseng and Tsai (2001) also proposed an edge-base scheme. However, their edge-based methods can be easily attacked since the content of a video frame can be changed while preserving the edge's information. Therefore, this scheme is vulnerable to a cropping attack.

- *Motion Trajectory based Signature Scheme*: A video authentication based on motion trajectory has been proposed by Yan and Kankanhalli (2003). In this scheme, the signature is computed using cryptographic secret sharing (Shamir, 1979). Given a video, first it is segmented into shots. For each shot, the key frames are identified using motion trajectory. The color histogram energy is used as a feature of the video frame to determine the key frames. Then the signature is computed using secret sharing, which considers the key frames as the shares. However, they used secret sharing here with a fundamental difference. In secret sharing, one holds the secret and computes the shares lying on an interpolating polynomial. In their scheme, the key frames of the video are treated as shares and the secret is computed using these shares. The secrets are computed for all the shots. A master secret is then computed using all shot secrets. The master secret is treated as the signature of the video.

This scheme is vulnerable to spatial as well as temporal attacks. Considering only key frames for signature computation is not enough. If a smart attacker replaces all non-key frames in such a way that key frames remain unaffected then all the frames except key frames are changed and still the signature remains the same. Also, the key frames are determined based on the color histogram energy of the video frames, which is susceptible to spatial attacks because an attacker can modify the frame content while preserving its color histogram energy.

• *A Scalable Signature Scheme*: Recently, Atrey et al. (2007) have proposed a scalable signature scheme that is robust against frame dropping in a video streaming scenario. The proposed method is an extension of (Yan, 2003) with some differences. They identified key frames based on block-wise differences between the two video frames. Moreover, they also considered non-key frames in computing the signature, which made their scheme resistant to several attacks such as spatial cropping and temporal tampering. They demonstrated the sensitivity and robustness of their scheme in three different scenarios: (i) Robustness against dropping a few frames in a video streaming scenario; (ii) Sensitivity against frame dropping in an advertisement monitoring scenario; and (iii) Sensitivity against face tampering in video frames.

3.2 Digital Watermarking Schemes

• *A Semi-fragile Watermarking Scheme Robust against Transcoding*: Yin and Yu (2002) have proposed a semi-fragile watermark technique that is robust to transcoding with consistent picture types where the picture types ('I', 'P' and 'B') are kept unchanged in the process of transcoding. They used two types of watermarks: robust and fragile. For robust watermark, the features used are randomly shuffled and then hashed. The authors have used a DC-DCT coefficient of 'I' pictures because the DC coefficients are kept unchanged during transcoding operations. Due to the limited embedding capacity, the 'I' picture's blocks were shuffled with a secret key for hashing. The fragile watermark is also computed by combining the features along with the private key and then encrypting using a public key. The fragile watermark is embedded by modifying the LSB of the quantized AC-DCT coefficients. Both robust and fragile watermarks were added to compute the final watermark.

To prevent the counterfeiting attack, the authors have proposed to embed a GOP's authentication bits into its next GOP. Adding a watermark in the 'I' picture results in drift errors for the following 'P' or 'B' pictures in the same GOP.

Adding a DC-DCT coefficient at the block level may provide robustness but it is not sensitive against spatial manipulations. Since the DC-DCT coefficient is computed using a linear combination of the pixel values, it can be compromised. An attacker can replace a block of 8×8 pixels by another 64 pixels retaining the same DC-DCT coefficient. Successive repetitions of this operation on different blocks of a video frame may lead to major cropping.

• *Lossless Watermarking Scheme*: Using the concept of invertible authentication, Du and Fridrich (2000) have proposed two lossless watermarking methods for the authentication of a digital video. In the first method, the authentication code includes a hash of the frame content and the frame index.

Each frame contains its hash and its frame index embedded losslessly. The chrominance blocks of both intra and non-intra macroblocks are used for embedding. The hash value is computed from non-zero DCT coefficients instead of pixel values from the whole frame. Then a selected quantization factor is halved and the Least Significant Bits (LSB) of those coefficients is made into zero by multiplying the corresponding DCT coefficients by 2 to embed the authentication bits. By using DCT coefficients instead of pixel values is advantageous in the sense that the authentication of 'P' or 'B' frames does not depend on the authentication result of previous reference frames.

In the first method, the distortion due to data embedding becomes perceptible when the distance between two 'I' frames is too large. To avoid the spread of distortion, the second method has been proposed. In this method, a hash group of frames is embedded in 'B' frames only. This is because 'B' frames are not used as reference frames for encoding other frames, and the distortion in 'B' frames due to data embedding will not spread to subsequent frames. A group of frames includes 'B' frames and their reference frames. All non-zero DCT coefficients from a group of frames form the input for the hash computation. The authentication data is formed by the index of the group of frames and the hash value, which are both embedded into the 'B' frames. Only chrominance blocks of non-intra macroblocks are used for data embedding.

- *Video Authentication with Self-Recovery*: A secure and flexible fragile video-authentication watermark with spatio-temporal localization and self-recovery properties has been proposed by Celik (2002). In their method, the watermark payload has two parts: *Authentication Packet* and *Recovery Packet* (Celik, 2002; Celik, 2003). The basic concept in generating the recovery packet is to embed the compressed copy of the video into itself so that during the recovery phase the tampered regions may be reconstructed using this embedded copy. Since it is not always possible to embed the full description of content into itself, the key frames of the video are selected. The key frames are divided into blocks. A *Multiple Description Coding* scheme is used that provides a graceful tradeoff between resilience against the packet loss and recovery quality. Using this coding scheme, it is possible to recover a low quality version of the key frame even if some of the recovery packets are lost during tampering. Then, a one-dimensional interleaving strategy is applied to blocks in the video sequence to achieve better error resilience on information networks.

For the authentication packet, the authentication information is formed by first hashing the Most Significant Blocks (MSB) of the block and the recovery packet, then XORing the hash value with the localization information, and finally encrypting the result. The localization information consists of a unique *Video ID* that differentiates between different video sequences, the *frame number*, and the *block's spatial position*. The encrypted recovery packet and the authentication packet both constitute the final watermark that is inserted in video frames by *LSB modification*. The scheme is good because it localizes the tampering and also performs its recovery, but the major disadvantage of the method is that it is not suitable for real time applications. The multiple passes are required to diffuse the recovery information throughout the sequence. Even if the diffusion is limited in a certain group of frames, the algorithm has substantial delay and buffering requirements.

- *Watermarking for Self Authentication of Compressed Video*: Daniel and Bijan (2002) have proposed a watermarking scheme for self-authentication of a compressed video. They used a compressed 'I' frame to watermark the following GOP based on a GOP-unique key. The method is sensitive to tampering at the GOP level. Since the watermark is derived from the frame content, it cannot be pirated and used elsewhere. The GOP-specific keys used for watermarking allows for the identification of the missing, removed or altered GOPs by monitoring the keys needed for authentication. The method is robust against compression; however, it is fragile to re-encoding and bit-rate control.

- *Object-based Watermarking Scheme*: An object-based video authentication scheme has been proposed by He (2003). Their proposed method is robust to video processing operations such as translation, scaling, rotation, and lossy compression. The authors have used content-based watermarking to authenticate the foreground objects in a video. First, the raw video is segmented into foreground objects and background video. Then the feature extracted from the foreground objects and the background video is used to construct a watermark. The watermark is embedded into foreground objects in order to establish a relation between the background and foreground of a video. To generate the watermark, a set of *Angular Radial Transformations* (ART) coefficients is selected as a robust feature of the video objects. *Error Correction Coding* (ECC) is employed to encode the feature vector. The ECC codeword with a user key and the background feature code is hashed by a typical cryptographic hash function (such as MD5). To improve the security of the watermark, the hashed value of two consecutive frames are XORed. Finally, this watermark is encoded again by another ECC scheme called *message ECC encoding*.

The strategy of embedding background features into the foreground objects can be attacked if both the foreground and background of a video frame are changed. Also, it can be attacked if the authors embed the watermark in each frame and have not utilized the temporal redundancy in video.

4. CONCLUSION

In this chapter, we have presented an overview of the video authentication techniques proposed over the past few years. We identified the properties of an ideal video authentication system. We also discussed various technique issues related to video authentication. We categorized benign and tampering operations that are performed on video.

From the past works, it has been observed that the researchers have proposed various methods to authenticate video in both compressed and uncompressed domains. There are two major goals of video authentication: security and robustness. It is difficult to achieve security and robustness together. A highly secure scheme provides only a little robustness against benign operations, whereas increasing robustness opens the door for various attacks. Therefore, in the past, the researchers attempted to have a balance between the two, and proposed methods that provide robustness against some operations in specific scenarios.

The selection of features for computing the authentication data (digital signature or watermark) is very crucial. It is required that, in the chosen features, a threshold can be identified in order to distinguish between benign and tampering operations. In other words, the features should be invariant such that they remain unchanged during a benign operation and change drastically on tampering.

Although the existing video authentication methods have been reported as successful in specific scenarios, they have some weaknesses. In particular, the robustness against several benign operations still remains a concern. Therefore, it is expected that the robustness is the fundamental issue in video authentication, which needs to be explored in future.

Last but not least, video authentication is an important aspect of digital media forensics, which is an emerging area nowadays. There are two aspects of forensics (Van, 2007) - source identification (Lukas, 2006) and tampering (Ye, 2007). The robust authentication techniques will be the key factor in detecting a possible tampering in the different types of media including video.

5. REFERENCES

Atrey, P. K., Yan, W.-Q., & Kankanhalli, M. (2007). A scalable signature scheme for video authentication. *Springer Journal of Multimedia Tools and Applications*, 34(1), 107–135.

Celik, M. U., Sharma, G., Tekalp, A. M., & Saber, E. S. (2002). Video authentication with self-recovery. In *SPIE Security and Watermarking of Multimedia Contents IV, Vol. 4675.* (pp 531–541), San Jose, CA, USA.

Celik, M. U., Sharma, G., Tekalp, A. M., & Saber, E. S. (2003). Localized lossless authentication watermark. In *SPIE Security and Watermarking of Multimedia Content V 2003,* Santa Clara, CA, USA.

Christian, R., & Dugelay, J. L. (2002). A survey of watermarking algorithms for image authentication. *Journal of Applied Signal Processing,* (6), 613–621.

Daniel, C., & Bijan, M. (2002). Watermarking for self-authentication of compressed video. In *IEEE International Conference on Image Processing 2002, Vol. II,* (pp 913–916), Rochester, New York, USA.

Dittman, J., Steinmetz, A., & Steinmetz, R. (1999), Content based digital signature for motion pictures authentication and content-fragile watermarking. In *IEEE International Conference on Multimedia Computing and Systems, Vol. II, 1999,* (pp 209), Firenze, Italy.

Du, R., & Fridrich, J. (2002). Lossless authentication of MPEG-2 video. In *IEEE International Conference on Image Processing, Vol. II,* (pp 893–896), Rochester, NY, USA.

Dugelay, J. L., & Petitcolas, F. A. (2000). Possible counter-attacks against random geometric distortions. In *SPIE Electronic Imaging, Security and Watermarking of Multimedia Contents II, Vol. 3971.* (pp 338–345), San Jose, CA, USA.

Fridrich, J., & Goljan, M. (2000). Robust hash functions for digital watermarking. In *International Conference on Coding and Computing.* (pp 178–183), Las Vegas, USA.

He, D., Sun, Q., & Tian, Q (2003). A semi-fragile object based video authentication system. In *IEEE International Symposium on Circuits and Systems, Vol. III,* (pp 814–817), Bangkok, Thailand.

Lin, C. Y., & Chang, S. F. (1999). Issues and solutions for authenticating MPEG video. *SPIE Electronic Imaging, Vol. 3657,* (pp. 54–65), San Jose, CA, USA.

Lin, C. Y., & Chang, S. F. (2000). Semi-fragile watermarking for authenticating JPEG visual content. In *SPIE Security Watermarking of Multimedia Contents IV, Vol. 4675.* (pp 512–519). San Jose, CA, USA.,

Lukas, J., Fridrich, J., & Goljan, M. (2006). Digital camera identification from sensor pattern noise. *IEEE Transactions of Information Forensics and Security*, 1(2), 205–214.

Menezes, A. J., van Oorschot, P. C., & Vanstone, S. A. (1997). Handbook of Advanced Cryptography. CRC Press.

Mobasseri, B. G., & Evans, A. E. (2001). Content-dependent video authentication by self-watermarking in color space. In *SPIE Security and Watermarking of Multimedia Content III, Vol. 4314*, (pp 35–44), San Jose, CA, USA.

Mobasseri, B. G., Sieffert, M. J., & Simard, R. J. (2000). Content authentication and tamper detection in digital video. *IEEE International Conference on Image Processing, Vol. I,* (pp 458–461), Vancouver, BC, Canada.

Niu, X., Schmucker, M., & Busch, C. (2002). Video watermarking resisting to rotation, scaling, and translation. In *SPIE Security Watermarking of Multimedia Contents IV. Vol. 4675*, (pp 512–519), San Jose, CA, USA.

Quisquater, J.-J., & Joye, M. (1997). Authentication of sequences with the SL_2 hash function: Application to video sequences. *Journal of Computer Security, 5(3)*, 213–223.

Quisquater, J.-J., & Joye, M. (1997). Practical solutions to authentication of images with a secure camera. *SPIE 97*, Dallas, Texas. In: *SPIE International Conference on Storage and Retrieval for Image and Video Databases, Vol. 3022*, (pp 290–297), San Jose, CA, USA.

Radhakrishnan, R., Xiong, Z., & Memon, N. D. (2003). On the security of visual hash functions. In *SPIE International Conference Annual Symposium on Electronic Imaging: Science and Technology, Vol. 5020*, (pp 644–652), Santa Clara, CA, USA.

Shamir, A. (1979). How to share a secret. *Communications of the ACM, 22(11)*, 612–613.

Shi, C., & Bhargava, B.(1998). A fast MPEG video encryption algorithm. In *The Sixth ACM International Conference on Multimedia,* (pp 81–88), Bristol, UK.

Sun, Q., Chang, S. F., Kurato, M., & Suto, M. (2002). A new semi-fragile image authentication framework combining ECC and PKI. In *IEEE International Symposium on Circuits and Systems, Vol. 2,* (pp 440–443), Phoenix, USA.

Tzeng, C. H., & Tsai, W.-H. (2001). A new technique for authentication of image/video for multimedia applications. In *ACM Multimedia and Security Workshop,* Ottawa, Canada.

Van, L. T., Chong, K.-S., Emmanuel S., & Kankanhalli M. (2007). A survey on digital camera image forensic methods. In *IEEE International Conference on Multimedia and Expo,* pp 16–19, Beijing, China.

Yan, W.-Q., & Kankanhalli, M. S. (2003). Motion trajectory based video authentication. In *IEEE International Conference on Acoustics, Speech, and Signal Processing, Vol. III,* (pp 810–813), Bangkok, Thailand.

Ye, S., Sun, Q, & Chang, E.-C. (2007). Detecting digital image forgeries by measuring inconsistencies of blocking artifact. In *IEEE International Conference on Multimedia and Expo,* pp 12–15, Beijing, China.

Yin, P., & Yu, H. H. (2001). Classification of video tampering methods and countermeasures using digital watermarking. In *SPIE's International Symposium: ITCOM 2001,* Denver, CO, USA.

Yin, P., & Yu, H. H. (2002). A semi-fragile watermarking system for MPEG video authentication. In *International Conference on Acoustic, Speech and Signal Processing, Vol. IV,* (pp 3461–3464), Orlando, FL, USA.

KEY TERMS

Benign Operations: Tasks that are allowed to be performed on a digital content.

Digital Signature: Cryptographic means to determine the integrity of a digital content.

Digital Watermark: A message which is embedded into digital content that can be detected or extracted later.

Spatial Tampering: Spatial attacks such as region tampering.

Temporal Tampering: The process of performing inter-frame alterations such as frame adding, replacement, dropping, and reordering.

Video Authentication: A process that ascertains the integrity of a given digital video and detects if it has been tampered.

Visual Hash Function: A cryptographic transformation method that takes digital content as an input and returns a fixed-size string and that is robust to some benign operations.

Chapter XVII
Flexible Multimedia Stream Authentication

Tieyan Li
Institute for Infocomm Research (I2R), Singapore

ABSTRACT

The multimedia community is moving from monolithic applications to more flexible and scalable proliferate solutions. Security issues such as access control and authentication of multimedia content have been intensively studied in the literature. In particular, stream authentication tends to be more complicated since a stream may be transcoded by intermediate proxies or composed by multiple sources. Traditional stream authentication schemes consider a stream as a group of packets and authenticate these packets over an erasure channel. However, by fixing the packets in transmission, any packet manipulation will cause authentication failure. In this chapter, we assume a more flexible model where a proxy, between a sender and a receiver, is able to make transcoding operations over a stream. We describe a flexible stream authentication framework that allows the so called packet independent stream authentication schemes to make transcoding operations on the packets and commit the changes, which are not applicable in packet-based stream authentication schemes. Such a stream authentication scheme based on the layered structure of a stream is elaborated in details w.r.t., the encoding, packing, amortizing, and verifying methods. The security and performance analysis show that the packet independent stream authentication schemes achieve higher authentication rate with less overhead per packet, as compared with that of packet based schemes.

1 INTRODUCTION

Multimedia data, such as image, audio and video, come fast and furious in everyone's life, thanks to the advances in digital signal processing and inter-networking technologies. End users are experiencing innovative streaming applications (*e.g.*, video-on-demand, IPTV) effectively and benefiting more from the widely adopted pervasive architectures. As multimedia data are being disseminated anywhere, a number of security issues are arisen as the major concerns on protecting such digital assets. One research trend is on protecting the media content from being disclosed to the unauthorized users, *w.r.t.*, "the secure media transmission" problem, which addresses the "*confidentiality*" security property. All major Digital Right Management (DRM) solutions are providing this security function via hardware or software protection techniques. While this is important, another trend on authenticating the media content is even more important, as it is more dangerous to receive a tampered (or misleading) message than a scrambled (or unreadable) message in a security sense. Thus, both the security properties, media origin "*authenticity*" and media data "*integrity*", are to be addressed in multimedia authentication. In this chapter, we concentrate on the stream authentication techniques in particular and present a generic flexible stream authentication framework.

Message authentication has been intensively studied in traditional cryptographic research field for more than twenty years. Typically, a message, no matter how long it is, is first compressed into a fixed length digital digest. The digest is then signed using some digital signature scheme that generates a signature based on the digest. In transmission, both the message itself and its signature are to be bundled together and sent to the receivers. On receiving the message, a receiver computes the digest with the same way as the originator does and uses the verification algorithm to verify the digest against the signature. An illustrative example is

given in Section 2.1. It is nature to think of using the similar authentication scheme on multimedia data, as one just treats the multimedia data as an ordinary message. However, it turns out to be inconvenient, if not impossible, to authenticate multimedia data in this way. In fact, multimedia data have some unique features compared with messages, and thus deserve specially designed and dedicated authentication techniques.

Firstly, representing multimedia data requires a large amount of information and sometimes, there is no clear ending (*e.g.*, of real-time streaming). In case of multimedia stream, instead of authenticating the whole stream at once, a stream is divided into various blocks and these blocks are to be authenticated one by one. As a result, only part of a stream is authenticated at certain time and the authentication process is a progressive procedure until the last block is verified. Secondly, the dominant requirements for bandwidth and energy consumption on stream transmission cause the significant bottlenecks. To improve the quality of a multimedia service, transcoding is required to adapt a stream with various multimedia communication conditions, which is possible to help overcome the bottlenecks. Hence, some portions of the original stream content arc to be abandoned due to the limitations (*e.g.*, narrow bandwidth). Therefore, one can not tell whether a stream is authenticated or not as a single unit, but how much percentage of a stream is authenticated, or what is the authentication probability of a received stream. Thirdly, even there is no obvious manipulation on original multimedia content, there might still be partial content being lost in the delivery channel. For example, Internet is such a lossy channel as it loses IP packets from time to time. Some researchers proposed to use erasure code to tolerate arbitrary patterns of packet loss. However, there are intentional attacks on the delivery channel where data might be intercepted, altered and injected. How to authenticate a stream in a malicious channel is still being studied intensively. Last but not least, many multimedia applications allow multiple streams to be composed into a single stream (*e.g.*, movie advertisement, multi-screening and digital art creation), which are called "Stream Composition". How to authenticate multiple sources in a composite stream and how to maintain the integrity of those media content are the ongoing research directions. To address these challenges, the multimedia security community is working very hard on providing the authentication techniques that are secure, effective and flexible.

In this chapter, we start by introducing several basic techniques on authenticating messages and media streams. These are the building blocks on constructing complex multimedia stream authentication schemes. We then introduce various stream authentication techniques in the literature and identify the weaknesses in existing packet based stream authentication schemes (P-SASes). Next, we promote the contemporary packet independent stream authentication schemes (PiSASes) and present a generic and flexible stream authentication (FSA) framework. Although the framework works on any formats of multimedia streams, we take as an example, the layered stream format, to elaborate the detailed processes of a PiSAS. Step by step, we describe how to encode a raw stream in a flexible way; how to prepare the authentication data over the stream; how to amortize the authentication overhead; how to process the stream with various transcoding operations; and finally how to verify such a composite stream. Strict security and performance analysis show that the PiSASes are significantly better than any P-SASes.

Chapter organization: Section 2 introduces basic message authentication and multimedia authentication techniques. Section 3 reviews some of the related works on packet based stream authentication schemes and packet independent stream authentication schemes. We depict a generic and flexible stream authentication framework in Section 4. In Section 5, we elaborate the core operations of our flexible stream authentication scheme on a layered streaming format. Following on, we analyze the security and performance issues in section 6. We point out future trends in Section 7. At last, we conclude the chapter.

2 AUTHENTICATION BASICS

From the introduction, we know that there are subtle differences on the authentication techniques for messages and multimedia data. Fundamentally, the same basic authentication mechanisms are used for authenticating multimedia data as for authenticating messages. In this section, we describe the basic message authentication techniques and show how they can be deployed into multimedia authentication.

2.1 Message Authentication

Message authentication and digital signature are two mechanisms to provide the authenticity of a message, of which message authentication is a procedure to verify that a message comes from the alleged source and has not been altered during transmission. Digital signature is an authentication technique that can counter repudiation of a message by either the source or destination. Here, we briefly introduce two typical authentication techniques: Message Authentication Code (MAC) and Digital Signature Scheme.

Assume that the two communicating parties are **A** (the sender) and **B** (the receiver). They share a common secret key K. When **A** sends a message to **B**, it calculates the MAC as a function of the message M using K: $MAC=C_K(M)$. The MAC is actually a fixed length bit string, also known as a cryptographic checksum of the message. **A** appends the MAC on the message and sends them to **B**. Upon receiving the message, **B** performs the same calculation on the message using the same key K, to generate a new MAC. The received MAC is then compared to the calculated MAC. If there is a match, **B** is assured that the message comes

Figure 1. Message authentication using MAC

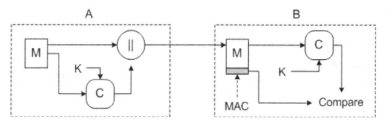

from **A** and has not been altered in transmission. The process is illustrated in Fig. 1.

A variation of the message authentication code is the one-way hash function (H) (SHA-1, 1995), which takes as input a variable length message (M) and produces a fixed length message digest D ($D=H(M)$) as output. Other than the one-way property, a secure hash function must have other properties like weak or strong collision resistance.

Using hash function alone can only provide message integrity, since there is no shared key between two communicating parties involved in the calculation. To provide message authentication, a hash function can be used as the first step to generate an authenticator of a message, which is further processed using symmetric ciphers or asymmetric ciphers.

Message authentication can authenticate a message against any third party, but it can not distinguish a message sent or received by any one of the two communicating parties. For example, one party of them can deny the fact of having sent or received a message; it can even forge a message and claim that it comes from another party (by holding the same secret key). To solve the problem, one can use a digital signature scheme. For instance, a public key encryption algorithm (Rivest R. L., et al., 1978) can also be used as a digital signature algorithm. In an RSA signature scheme, a message to be signed is first hashed and the hash code $H(M)$ is signed using the signing function (S) with the private key (KP_A) of the signer to produce the signature $\sigma = S_{KP_A}[H(M)]$. Both

the message and the signature are transmitted to the receiver. Similarly, the receiver hashes the message to produce the hash code. It then works on the signature using the verification function (V) with the public key (KU_A) of the signer. The result is compared with the hash code. If there is a match, the signature is accepted as valid. Because only the signer knows the private key, it must be the signer who produces the signature, which is non-repudiable. The RSA digital signature scheme is illustrated in Fig. 2.

2.2 Multimedia Authentication

Multimedia, as the name suggests, means multiple media formats being integrated together to represent rich media information. Their authentication techniques are also in a variety. According to (Sun Q. & Chang S., 2004), there are generally two categories: content authentication and complete authentication. In content authentication, the meaning or representation of the content are the dominant metric on justifying the authenticity of the content. As long as the represented multimedia content is not changed so much, no matter how many intermediate processes or transformations are performed, the content is regarded as authentic. For example, a video stream can be encoded in one way or another, delivered over a lossy channel and decoded before it is shown to the end user. In this procedure, not 100% of the stream is presented at the user interface due to bit losses in delivery or bit changes in coding. Thus, whether the stream is accepted as authentic or not mainly

Figure 2. Message authentication using RSA digital signature scheme

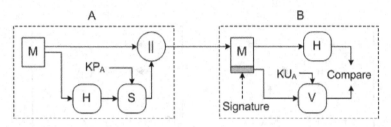

Figure 3. Media signature scheme for content authentication

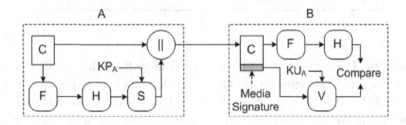

depends on the tolerability on its (displaying) quality. As different applications allow different distortion rates on a stream, the received stream could be regarded as unauthentic in some situations and authentic in other cases. Thus, there is no unified authentication definition on content authentication. A media signature working on the features of the media data is popularly used as the authenticator of the media data in content authentication (Sun Q. & Chang S., 2004).

In Fig. 3, a media signature scheme is illustrated. At the sender side (**A**), the media content (C) is first processed by some feature extraction function (F), which can produce some media features. Only the features are hashed into a digest using a hash function (H) and signed using a signing function (S). The media content, being attached with the signature, are ready to be sent out. Similarly, a receiver (**B**) extracts the features with (F) and hashes them. The result is compared with the output of the signature verification function (V). If there is a match, the media content is considered as authentic. Otherwise, the authen-

tication fails. Apparently, as long as the features are extracted the same as that of the original media content, an intentionally (or not) distorted media content, can always be authenticated. While content authentication is reasonable and tolerable due to the fuzzy requirements in most realistic applications, it is totally unacceptable in a strict security sense, where a single bit flip will make the authentication result negative.

Complete authentication resembles message authentication much, which cares more about bit-level digital security rather than the meaningfulness of the content. As stated in Section 1, the authentication techniques for them are different. In Fig. 4, a conceptual complete authentication scheme is illustrated.

Suppose a sender (**A**) will be sending some media content to a receiver (**B**). The media content can be treated as one authentication block and be prepared as a group of packets {P1, P2, ..., Pn}. All of the packets are hashed individually, which produce n hash values. These hash values are to be computed in some way (see Section 3.1) to gener-

Figure 4. Typical complete authentication scheme

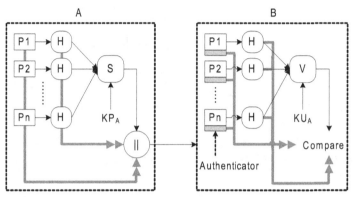

ate a fix-length digest. The digest is then signed using a signing function (S). The signature and all the hash values are to be attached on the original n packets. When the packets are received, they are hashed again and the calculated hash values are compared with the received hash values. If they match, then the integrity check is done. If not, either the packets or the hashes must have been altered due to some reason. Further on, the signature is verified using a verification function (V). In this way, the integrity of the media content can be verified and the originator of the media content can be authenticated. How to organize the hash values and how to append them on the packets will be introduced in the next section. Without loss of clarity, we refer to complete authentication throughout this chapter.

3 PRIOR ART ON STREAM AUTHENTICATION TECHNIQUES

The research works on authenticating a digital stream were started in late nineties, when a group of researchers in security community were studying methods on signing a flow of continuous packets (or a stream). The very first model was proposed by Gennaro and Rohatgi in their pioneer work "How to sign digital streams"

(Gennaro R. & Rohatgi P., 1997), in which the sender signs the first packet in a group of packets and then ties in subsequent packets to guarantee non-repudiation. Following the initial work, many research approaches were proposed and they are currently known as a class of packet based stream authentication schemes (P-SASes). The essential methodology with P-SAS is that each packet in a group is processed individually with the integrity unit appending on some other packets, the integrity units (such as one time signatures, hash values) of the packets are maintained in some way and finally the only digest of the group is signed/verified once using some signature scheme. Obviously, the "sign-once" approaches are much more efficient for verifying each packet in a whole group than the typical "sign-each" approaches.

In parallel, the researchers in multimedia community have come out of a number of approaches on authenticating multimedia streams, of which content (or fuzzy) authentication schemes (see Section 2.2) are the main trend. Fortunately, researchers at both sides recognized that traditional digital stream authentication techniques can also be used in the context of multimedia streams. If we divide a multimedia stream into a group of packets, we can directly apply any of the packet based stream authentication schemes. But a subtle difference hinders the direct adoption of the

P-SASes. All P-SASes assume a stream being delivered in a sender-receiver (**S-R**) model where any intermediate alteration of the packets would cause the failure of stream authentication. In multimedia delivery, however, it has unique benefit to allow a proxy to tailor part of the media content, either to block improper content,

or to meet some (*e.g.*, narrow bandwidth) limitations. Therefore, multimedia stream authentication should work under the Sender-Proxy-Receiver (**S-P-R**) model, where a proxy performs a more active role as not only storing and forwarding packets, but also manipulating the packets. Some stream authentication approaches in S-P-R model are proposed to allow adaptive streaming and are regarded as packet independent stream authentication schemes (PiSASes).

3.1 Packet Based Stream Authentication Scheme (P-SAS)

Of all the packet based stream authentication schemes (P-SASes) (Gennaro R. & Rohatgi P., 1997; Wong C. K. & Lam S. S.,1998; Perrig A. et al., 2000; Golle P., & Modadugu N., 2001; Miner S. & Staddon J., 2001; Park J. M. et al., 2002; Pannetrat A. & Molva R., 2003), some of them (Gennaro R. & Rohatgi P., 1997; Perrig A. et al., 2000; Golle P., & Modadugu N., 2001; Miner S. & Staddon J., 2001} are further categorized into a sub-class of graph based stream authentication schemes (GP-SASes) and others (Wong C. K. & Lam S. S.,1998; Park J. M. et al., 2002; Pannetrat A. & Molva R., 2003) are categorized as the tree based stream authentication schemes (TP-SASes).

3.1.1 Graph Based Stream Authentication Scheme (GP-SAS)

Gennaro and Rohatgi (Gennaro R. & Rohatgi P., 1997) proposed a simple hash chaining scheme, in which the hash of a packet is inserted into its preceding packet and only the first packet of a group is signed. But the backward chaining is not robust at all, as a single packet loss can break the connectivity and cause all subsequent packets non-verifiable. To provide a robust authentication scheme, Perrig et al. proposed an Efficient Multi-chained Stream Signature (EMSS) scheme in (Perrig A. et al., 2000). In EMSS, the hash of a packet is appended to a number of (more than one) other preceding packets which are decided a priori at random. By adding redundant paths, the EMSS scheme is more robust as a randomly lost packet may only affect the verifiability of itself, not others. Taking it further, if several packets are lost in a burst, above scheme may not be able to handle it. The augmented chaining technique was then proposed by Golle and Modadugu (Golle P., & Modadugu N., 2001) to resist against a single burst of packet loss, in which the hash of a packet is appended not only on a packet close to it but on a packet at longer distance. Clearly, a burst may drop several continuous packets, but the hash value of a retained packet can be found at a remote position. More seriously, in some extreme network conditions, multiple bursts of packet loss could happen. To address the worst case, Miner and Staddon (Miner S. & Staddon J., 2001) presented a unified graph based approach to represent the relationships of the hash of a packet linking to multiple other packets. So, all above methods are the special constructions of the generic framework. It can tolerate many bursts with minimized overhead and guarantee high burst tolerance for some packets. In addition, the burst tolerant constructions incur no receiver delay and make them resistant to denial of service (DoS) attacks.

With all graph based authentication schemes (GP-SASes), whether a packet is verifiable depends on two receiving items: the packet itself and its hash value. A packet can not be verified if its hash value is not obtainable from any other packets due to some packet loss. The reliance between pairs of packets makes GP-SASes unattractive in some delay-sensitive cases where a packet, once received, can be self-authenticated immediately (without waiting for other packets) . Note that the "sign-each" approach can achieve this feature with significant computation and communication overhead.

3.1.2 Tree Based Stream Authentication Scheme (TP-SAS)

Wong and Lam (Wong C. K. & Lam S. S., 1998) worked out a *Merkle hash tree* based integrity mechanism to enhance the "sign-once" authentication schemes. The hash values of a group of packets form the leaf nodes and parent nodes are computed as the hashes of their children, and a hash tree is constructed with the root being signed. Each packet contains extra information including the (root) signature, the hash value of the packet and the siblings of the nodes in tree to reconstruct the root. A packet can be self-authenticated by verifying the signature and the related integrity units, and caching is used to make the verification process more efficient. The scheme has no receiver authentication delay, but suffers from a high amount of overhead on each packet (as O(log n) extra pieces of information are appended, where n is the number of packets in the stream).

Park et al. (Park J. M., et al., 2002) described an authentication scheme-SAIDA by encoding the hash values of packets and the signature on the whole block with information dispersal algorithm. By amortizing the authentication data into the packets and deploying erasure codes, the method reduces the storage overhead and tolerates more packet loss. Later, Pannetrat et al. (Pannetrat A. & Molva R., 2003) improved SAIDA by constructing a systematic code to reduce the overhead. All of above schemes are tree based stream authentication schemes (TP-SASes), where a group of n packets is processed in a batch and the authentication data are constructed as a tree and amortized onto the packets.

Nonetheless, the sender-receiver (**S-R**) transmission model allows no intermediate processing

of the stream in term of packet manipulation. Researchers tend to assume the Sender-Proxy-Receiver (**S-P-R**) model for multimedia stream authentication and propose packet independent stream authentication schemes (PiSASes) for adaptive stream applications.

3.2 Packet Independent Stream Authentication Scheme (PiSAS)

The first work, of claiming to concurrently achieve multimedia content adaptation and end-to-end authenticity, was done by Suzuki et al. in (Suzuki T., et al., 2004). The authors assumed a multimedia streaming system where meta-data specifying how media components are handled is provided prior to actual content delivery. However, the paper only focused on the meta-data level adaptation, where one may manipulate the composition of audio and video components in the scene according to user preferences or service contexts, not on media-data level adaption, where one may apply transcoding techniques such as multi-rate switching or scalable compression. Moreover, the paper does not assume an erasure channel where packets are lost arbitrarily. In a later work (Gentry C. et al., 2005), Gentry et al. proposed two media-level authentication schemes, LISSA and TRESSA, which ensure secure streaming media authentication with adaptive proxies. However, similar to (Suzuki T., et al., 2004), it does not apply an erasure code directly and only treats streaming multimedia content simply as message blocks being sent in frames, instead of real streaming media format like MPEG-4 (ISO/IEC 14496-1:2001).

In (Li T., et al., 2004), the authors proposed the first packet independent stream authentication scheme (PiSAS) that allows a proxy to transcode streaming content flexibly while they can still be verified by the final receiver. The so called Unequal Loss Verification (ULV) scheme works on MPEG-4 streaming format, and is secure, efficient and error resilient. Its sister paper (Li T., et al., 2005) further provides additional features like multi-source stream authentication for composite streams. In this chapter, we elaborate in detail such a flexible stream authentication scheme in favor of all above valuable features.

4 FLEXIBLE STREAM AUTHENTICATION FRAMEWORK

The flexible stream authentication framework borrows many building blocks from aforementioned stream authentication schemes (P-SASes and PiSASes). Generally, a stream has a number of objects/layers (according to a specific multimedia streaming format) and is divided into a group of packets. We assume an erasure channel without "pollution attacks" (Karlof C. et al., 2004; Krohn M. N., et al., 2004) throughout this chapter. The objects/layers of a stream at different priority levels are given unequal protection levels via erasure correction coding (ECC) (Mohr A. E. et al., 2000). The group hash is generated, signed and appended onto the packets using the amortization mechanism of SAIDA (Park J. M., et al., 2002). It is generally believed that by amortizing the authentication data over a group of packets the authentication overheads are much smaller than that of signing on each packet.

Unlike traditional erasure channel in the **S-R** model where no packet modification is allowed, the proxy in the **S-P-R** model is not only working on Internet Protocol (IP) layer as a packet forwarder, but also working on application layer that can actively transcode the stream and then redistribute it into the end network. The transcoding mechanism allows a proxy to discard data layers from the lowest priority layer to higher layers until the resource restrictions are met. For example, Fine Granular Scalability (FGS) (Li W., 2001) is such a scalable mechanism to distribute a stream efficiently and flexibly over heterogeneous wired and wireless networks. An illustrative example of transcoding operation is given in Fig. 5. Here, we use structured packet group of a stream with unequal loss protect scheme in (Mohr A. E. et al., 2000). A stream is divided into several sub-streams (A, B, C), each sub-stream is encoded differently with different priorities. Note that the transcoding strategy differs from packet dropping strategy, as the transcoded stream can tolerate the same number of packet loss as the original stream, thus the error-resilience capability is not decreased. To this end, a receiver is able to verify authenticity of a transcoded stream (*w.r.t.*, P1', P2', ..., Pn') using the authentication units (s1', s2', ..., sn').

We further identify two types of transcoding operations:

Figure 5. Transcoding by a proxy. Sub-stream A is retained and sub-streams B and C are removed. The updated patches (s1', s2', ..., sn') are attached to the new packets, while the packet size is significantly reduced.

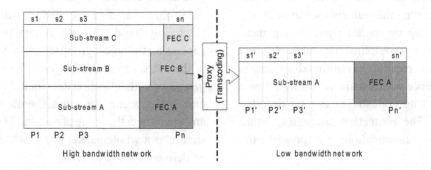

Figure 6. Flexible stream authentication (FSA) framework

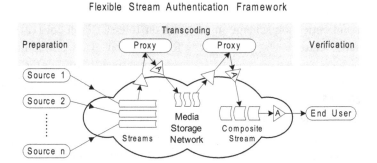

Type-1 transcoding operation, *w.r.t.* trunca-tion-only: A proxy is only allowed to truncate one or multiple sub-streams from an original stream. That is to say, there is only one valid stream source.

Type-2 transcoding operation, *w.r.t.* grafting: A proxy can selectively truncate one or multiple portions of an original stream, and insert one or more portions from multiple stream sources. All of them form a new stream with multiple sources.

Note that for type-1 transcoding operation, a verifier might verify not only the stream source's signature, but also the signatures from the prox-ies for committing their transcoding operations. For type-2 transcoding operation, a verifier has more complex verification procedures involving multiple stream sources and proxies.

In Fig. 6, we sketch the overall flexible stream authentication (FSA) framework. One critical concern is whether the framework can be incor-porated into legacy digital right management (DRM) systems, as complimentary authentication mechanisms. Typically, raw multimedia stream is compressed once with a scalable coding scheme and the resulting codestream can be decoded accordingly. The protection strategies, either encryption or authentication, must preserve the scalability of the codestream. Current DRM systems are focusing on protecting illegal ac-cess to the content, where end users download content from content distributors and separately, obtain the decryption keys from a license server. Authentication could be applied after the coding phase and normally before the encryption process. Note that authentication and encryption are two separate processes since they are based on dif-ferent (asymmetric/symmetric cipher) techniques, although in a shared key case, it is also possible to combine them by using authenticated encryp-tion schemes.

We assume all media content are stored in a media storage network. To process stream authentication, the framework consists of three main parts: stream preparation by sources, stream transcoding by FSA proxies and stream verifica-tion by end users. We describe them as follows:

Part 1: PiSAS Preparation The streaming video objects are first encoded according to some streaming standard. Each source prepares the packets for the object group based on the priorities of the video objects and layers. The source then generates authentication data including integrity units and its signature. The authentication data is amortized over the group of packets. The protected stream as a whole packet group is then ready to be delivered to the proxies.

Figure 7. Flexible stream authentication (FSA) framework

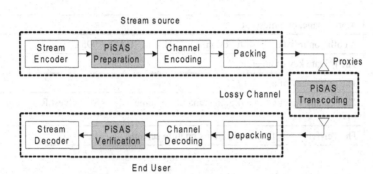

Part 2: PiSAS Transcoding On receiving the protected stream, a proxy can either apply type-1 transcoding operations to fit the stream into some narrow bandwidth, or employ another protected stream and apply type-2 transcoding operations. In either case, or combined transcoding operations, the proxy needs to sign the new stream with some signature scheme. The process can be repeated at some proxies and finally, the constructed stream is ready to be downloaded by the end users.

Part 3: PiSAS Verification The verification procedure is actually reversing the above two processes. Suppose a receiver retrieves a stream as well as its authentication data from some proxy. It then unpacks, decodes the packets. With recovered authentication data, the receiver can verify the stream integrity and signatures with the proper verification scheme.

The system diagram of such a PiSAS is shown in Fig. 7. Within this framework, we enable secure and efficient stream authentication in the existences of flexible transcoding operations and multiple stream sources.

5 PiSAS OVER LAYERED STREAM

In this section, we elaborate the components in a PiSAS system based on a layered streaming format. Since raw streams are encoded in different ways, without loss of generality, we assume a common layered streaming format (*e.g.*, ISO/IEC 14496-1:2001) in this chapter.

5.1 Notations and Preliminaries

We first list some notations (in Table 1) that are frequently used in this chapter. We then introduce some useful tools like Merkle hash tree (MHT) (Merkle R. C., 1989), erasure correction coding (ECC) (Luby M., et al., 1997), and a flexible encoding technique (Mohr A. E., et al. 2000) as well.

Merkle hash tree (MHT) has been widely used in many security applications, since it has good security property as committing on one hash digest over a set of data items. In this paper, we use MHT for generating the integrity data in section 5.3. Fig. 8 illustrates the construction of an MHT, in which $h(.)$ is a collision-resistant hash function and $D = \{d_1, d_2, ..., d_8\}$ is a set of data items. The constructed MHT is a 3-level complete binary tree.

The root node G with value h_G is normally signed by its owner to commit the entire data set. For example, to authenticate the data item d_6, the verifier can authenticate it with a small amount of auxiliary information (the shadow nodes in

Table 1. Notations

m	A pre-image, or a message.
$h(.)$	A collision resistant hash function, e.g., SHA-1 (SHA-1, 1995).
KP_X	The private key of an entity X.
KU_X	The public key of an entity X.
$Sign(.)$	The signing function in a digital signature scheme, e.g., RSA (Rivest R. L., et al., 1978).
$Vf(.)$	The verifying function in a digital signature scheme.

Figure 8. Merkle hash tree with 8 leaf nodes. The hash values are computed as hi=h(di || i), i=1, 2, ..., 8. For a non-leaf node, the value is hashing on the concatenation of its two child node values, e.g. node A, hA = h(h1 || h2); node G, hG = h(hE || hF).

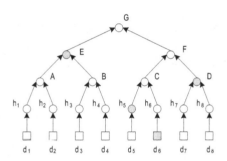

Fig. 8, which is actually the path from leaf node d_6 to root G, i.e., h_5, h_D and h_E. In this case, the verifier computes $h(h_E || h(h(h_5 || h(d_6 || 6)) || h_D))$ then checks if the value equals to the root value h_G. If yes, the verifier accepts d_6. In general, the verification requires O(log(n)) (or the height of the tree) hash operations given n data items.

Erasure correcting codes In erasure channel, a systematic ECC is a good means for error resilience in content dissemination. An ECC system with symbols in finite field GF(2^w) includes two modules: encoding $Enc_{n,k}(.)$ and decoding $Dec_{n,k}(.)$, where n is the codeword length and k is the message length. In ECC, an appropriate $n \times k$ matrix **G** is selected such that any k rows of **G** form a non-regular matrix. A systematic code $Enc_{n,k}(.)$ requires the first k rows of **G** forms an identity matrix. Denote a message as m=(m_1, m_2, ..., m_k)^T, $m_i \in$ GF(2^w) for all i, and the corresponding codeword as $C = Gm = (c_1, c_2, ..., c_n)^T$. Given any k elements $\hat{C} = (C_{\tau 1}, C_{\tau 2}, ..., C_{\tau k})^T$ of the codeword C, the decoder selects the corresponding k rows $\tau_1, \tau_2, ..., \tau_k$ of **G** to form a $k \times k$ matrix $\hat{G}$, then the recovered message is $m = \hat{G}^{-1}\hat{C}$.

Flexible encoding and packing We depict a flexible encoding and packing scheme for preparing stream data to be delivered in a lossy network. Fig. 9 illustrates the layered structure of a video sequence with $l+1$ layers. For example, an MPEG-4 (ISO/IEC 14496-1:2001; ISO/IEC 14496-2: 2003) stream can be encoded in a layered structure. The base layer, enhancement layers are assigned with different parity units based on predefined priority levels. Then the object group is encapsulated into n packets vertically {P1, P2, ..., Pn}, where the packet Pi consists of data units Pi_j, $j \in$ {0,1, ..., l}, with l being the number of layers. Refer to (Mohr A. E. et al. 2000) for details of unequal loss protection scheme.

Figure 9. Packing an object sequence. Data units in the same column form a packet, while data units in the same row form a layer. A layer j includes all the data units Pij, i ∈ {0,1, ..., n} with unequally assigned FECs, where higher priority layers have more parity units, and lower priority layers have less parity units.

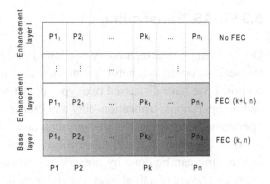

5.2 PiSAS Preparation

5.2.1 Generating Authentication Data

Above we introduced flexible encoding of an object group with layered structure. Our authentication scheme works on flexible encoding scheme for any layered stream. For example, an object based MPEG-4 stream, as a layered structure, can be divided into video sequences (VSs) includes a series of video objects (VOs). In our scheme, one VS, as one object group, is processed as one authentication block (*w.r.t.*, "sign-once" for each VS), while each VO can be one layer in our encoding scheme (*e.g.*, VO_1-the base layer and VO_2-the first enhancement layer, *etc.*). Each layer will have only one root such as EL_i. Secondly, these roots construct another high level hash tree as shown. At last, the final tree root is to be signed by the producer as a commitment. By signing once only, the producer actually commits a whole object group to the receivers. Suppose a stream consists of *s* video sequences, *s* signatures are to be generated to authenticate the stream. To sim-

plify the presentation, we describe only one video sequence (with several layers) hereafter. Follow on, we elaborate the procedures of generating the hash values and signatures, which are denoted as the authentication data of a video sequence.

Inside a layer, we can use any hash generation methods to prepare the basic layer hash values. For example, a hash tree can be generated bottom up based on the MPEG-4 stream structure. Otherwise, given any layered stream structure, we can use a method similar to the LISSA or TRESSA hashing schemes in (Gentry C. et al., 2005). The details on generating hash values inside a layer are ignored here, without loss of generality; we assume each layer has a unique root associated with a hash value. Thus, for a video sequence with *l+1* layers, we get *l+1* subroots as $BL\ (EL_0)$, EL_1, ..., EL_l as in Fig. 10. We now construct the final tree with those layer roots as leaf nodes:

$$h_{L_i} = h(h_{E_i} \mid h_{L_{i+1}}) \ (i=0, 1, ..., l-1) \qquad (1)$$

where $h_{EL_i} = h_{L_i}$. To this end, the final tree root is L_0. We now compute the VS hash as:

$$h_{VS} = h(h_{L_0} \parallel ID_{VS}) \qquad (2)$$

The stream source, assuming it is Alice (**A**), now signs the group hash h_{VS} using its private key KP_A and gets the signature as:

$$\sigma = Sign(KP_A, h_{VS}) \qquad (3)$$

Now, we have one part (the signature unit) of the authentication data (denoted as λ). Suppose we take all layer hash values as evidence of integrity unit (Since we do not know the network conditions beforehand, in the stream preparation phase, we just simply take all values as the evidence and assign them with the highest priority. Another assumption is that the number of layers is much less than the number of packets in any layered stream, so the overhead of taking all hash values is much less, too.), we can compose its integrity unit as

Figure 10. A hash tree construction over an object group (BL, EL1, ..., ELl), where a square denotes the hash tree construction inside a layer. Based on their priority levels, the tree is constructed bottom up from the lowest priority layer (ELl)to the highest priority layer (BL).

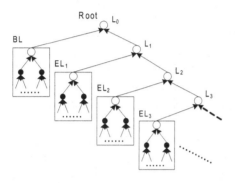

$\phi = \{h_{VS}, h_{EL_0}, h_{EL_1}, ..., h_{EL_l}\}$. Thus, we combine them and get the authentication data $\lambda = \{\sigma, \phi\}$. Note that the integrity unit size $|\phi|$ can be chosen flexibly depending on the network conditions. For example, in case of a heavy traffic delivery channel, the producer can generate authentication data only on the most important portion to reduce the authentication overheads.

5.2.2 Amortizing Authentication Data

After generating the authentication data, we employ ECC encoders to encode them and amortize them onto the packets (with packets structure shown in Fig. 9) before sending them out over an erasure channel (We use the method introduced in Pannetrat A. & Molva R., 2003). For simplicity, we treat the authentication data uniformly with the same encoding rate as of the highest priority layer. The encoding procedure is described as follows:

- Divide the authentication data λ into k symbols λ_i of the same size (i=1,2,..., k),

$\lambda_i \in GF(2^w)$. Then encode it to produce a codeword $C_c = Enc_{n,k}(\lambda_1, \lambda_2, ..., \lambda_k)$. Denote the n symbols in the codeword C_c as authentication units $c_1, c_2, ..., c_n$.

Next, we append the authentication units c_j on packet Pj, for all j=1, 2, ..., n. That is, the packet Pi now consists of c_i and $Pi_1, Pi_2, ..., Pi_l$.

5.3 PiSAS Transcoding

On receiving a stream, a proxy is allowed to do transcoding operations before retransmission. In section 4, we have discussed two types of transcoding operations: truncation-only and grafting operations. Regarding the tree presentation of a video stream in Fig. 10, the truncation-only transcoding can be done by preserving certain important layers of a final hash tree and truncating other (unimportant) layers. For example, to meet a narrow network bandwidth, we preserve the base layer EL_0 and one enhancement layer EL_1, and truncate other layers EL_j (j=2, ..., l) as shown in Fig. 11.

In this case, when we discard the subtree rooted at (L_2), we need to provide a proof that the proxy makes this operation. Thus, the proxy needs to retain the hash value of L_2 as h_{L_2} and sign on this value using its private key KP_p, $\sigma_p = Sign(KP_p, h_{L_2})$. Apparently, the original authentication data λ has to be changed to a new one λ_p. The new data should contain the original signature σ, the new signature σ_p and the new integrity unit ϕ_p. Thus, we get the new authentication data $\lambda_p = \{\sigma, \sigma_p, h_{VS}, h_{EL_0}, h_{EL_1}, h_{L_2}\}$. Using the amortization method described in Section 5.2, we can append λ_p onto the packets and send them out. Recall that the packet size is reduced as for each Pi (i $\in$ {1,2,...,n}) in Fig. 9, it consists of c_{pi} (the new codeword unit) and Pi_1, Pi_2 only, other packet data Pi_j ($3 \leq j \leq l$) are removed. The verification process is presented in next section, while a receiver has to verify an additional (recovered) signature $\hat{\sigma}_p$ with $Veri(KU_p, \hat{\sigma}_p, \hat{h}_{L_2})$ where KU_p is the public key of the proxy.

Figure 11. Truncation-only transcoding

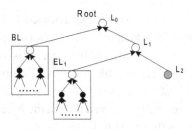

Figure 12. Grafting transcoding, in which in which BL and EL1 are retained. EL' is grafted on L2'.

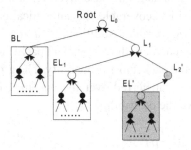

Besides truncation-only transcoding, the proxy can do grafting operations as well. I.e., a local news channel, which is authorized to broadcast a live news from CNN, may change the English subtitle with the local language. The channel must make new commitment on the changed parts. The unchanged parts are verified as usual, while the changed parts are verified based on the new commitment. Now suppose we replace the layers EL_i (i=2, ..., l) with the new layer EL', as shown in Fig. 12. Inside the packets, we actually remove Pi_j (j=2, ..., l) and append Pi_2' (for i={1,2,...,n}) as of the data representing EL'. To commit the change, the proxy can use several signing methods. One naive method could be signing on the new layer only, $\sigma'_p = Sign(KP_p, h_{EL'})$. However, this is not secure since an adversary can simply move the changed content to another layer and claim the change. One secure way of signing on the *meaningful* changes is to sign as $\sigma'_p = Sign(KP_p, h_{L_2'})$ (where $h_{L_2'} = h(h_{L_2} \mid h_E \cdot)$). Another secure way is to re-construct the hash tree and sign on the new

root. Whatsoever, the new authentication data is $\lambda'_p = \{\sigma, \sigma_p', h_{VS}, h_{EL_0}, h_{EL_1}, h_{L_2}, h_{EL'}\}$. Additionally, to process hybrid transcoding operations like truncating, grafting and truncating again, *etc.* the commitment scheme could be more complicated, but the rule of thumb is to let all sources or proxies commit all *meaningful* actions.

Note that as the above processes continue, the signature size will be linearly increased and proportional to the number of signing parties. The overheads of these signatures will soon become unaffordable after several transcoding operations. Fortunately, there are two methods to reduce the size of the authentication data. Firstly, we can reduce the size of integrity unit by dropping some hash values of the subtrees. Support we generate a hash tree over totally n leaf nodes. If we cut off all hash values of those leaf nodes, we remain $n-1$ hash values. Bottom up, if we cut off lower m levels of the tree, we have only $n/2^{m-1}-1$ hash values. However, the tradeoff of using this method is that it can not refine the verification. Thus, we hereby concentrate on reducing the signature size without losing any verification granularity as well as security. For this, one can employ new cryptographic primitives-aggregate signature schemes such as (Boneh D. et al., 2003; Lysyanskaya A. et al., 2004), to significantly reduce the size of multiple signatures into one only.

One special variant-a sequential signature scheme (Lysyanskaya A. et al., 2004) (Since the scheme is built on standard primitives like RSA, that is widely adopted.) can be applied into our type-1 transcoding operation for reducing the signature size. Here, a proxy p_i takes as inputs the signature σ_{i-1} from its predecessor and all integrity data ϕ_i as a whole, and outputs aggregate signature σ_i ($\sigma_i = AggSign(KP_{p_i}, \sigma_{i-1}, \phi_i)$). Thus, $\lambda_i = \{\sigma_i, \phi_i\}$. The new authentication data is amortized onto the packets and sent to the end users.

5.3 PiSAS Verification

At the end user, the verification process reverses the preparation process including unpacking, decoding and verifying operations. Based on the erasure coding, at least k out of n packets of a group should be received in order to recover the authentication data. Suppose k packets $\hat{P}1, \hat{P}2,..., \hat{P}k$ are received successfully. The authentication units $\hat{\lambda}_1, \hat{\lambda}_2,..., \hat{\lambda}_k$ are recovered from the received packets. With the decoder $Dec_{n,k}(.)$, the authentication data is reconstructed as $\hat{\lambda} = \{\hat{\sigma}, \hat{\phi}\}$. Then, the signature can be verified with algorithm $Vf(KU_A, \hat{\sigma}, \hat{\phi})$, where KU_A is the public key of the signer. If $Vf(.)$ is true, then continue to verify the integrity unit $\hat{\phi}$; if not, the object group is bogus and discarded. To this end, the client reconstructs the hash tree ϕ' according to formulas (1)-(2). The extracted integrity unit $\hat{\phi}$ is now compared with the constructed unit $\phi' = \{h'_{VS}, h'_{EL_0}, h'_{EL_1},..., h'_{EL_l}\}$, which is actually the comparison of two hash tree constructions. If there is no transcoding operation, we require $h'_{VS} = \hat{h}_{VS}$, $h'_{EL_i} = \hat{h}_{EL_i}$ (for all i $\in \{0,1\}$) for a successful verification. If there are transcoding operations, the signatures and integrity units are verified one by one in descendent order. If the recovered signature $\hat{\sigma}$ is an aggregate signature, it can be verified with $AggVf(\hat{\sigma}, \hat{\phi})$ sequentially with the corresponding public keys $\{KU_{p_1}, KU_{p_2}...\}$ of all signing parties. If $AggVf(.)$ is true, then continue to verify the integrity unit as above; if not, the object group is bogus and discarded.

6 SECURITY AND PERFORMANCE ANALYSIS

The primary goal of our flexible authentication scheme is to provide the maximal authentication probability with minimal packet overhead over a lossy channel. First of all, the security of our scheme relies on the security of the Merkle hash tree. Fortunately, Merkle hash tree has very nice security properties (Merkle R. C., 1989). Secondly, we focus on the authentication probability of a meaningful stream in a lossy channel. Then, we analyze the computational cost and communication overheads of each role in the scheme.

6.1 Authentication Probability

Recall the amortization method in section 5.2, the authentication data has the same priority level as the base layer of a stream, that means as long as the base layer is receivable, the authentication data can also resist the heaviest packet losses (A stream is not successfully received if even the base layer is not correctly recovered, and no verification is available in this condition.). In our scheme, we attach the same number of parity units for authentication data as of the base layer. Assuming the base layer is recoverable, the authentication data is also recoverable. Additionally, assuming an erasure channel with independent packet losses, given ρ the packet loss probability. The group of *n* packets transferred over the erasure channel may have the probability:

$$\binom{n}{k} \rho^{(n-k)}(1-\rho)^k$$

of receiving k packets. Thus we have the authentication probability as

$$\Lambda = \sum_{i=k}^{n} \binom{n}{i} \rho^{(n-i)}(1-\rho)^i.$$

The simulation is setup assuming different bit-rates at 256kbps, 512kbps and 1Mbps, respectively. To simplify the presentation, we take uniform packet loss rate at ρ = 0.02. Suppose all packets are of the same size (1.5k bytes), and a video stream VS is grouped and processed based on one second time period. Thus, for different bit rates, VS is composed of different number of packets. I.e., for 256kbps network channel, there are totally 21 packets processed in a group. The authentication probability is plotted in Fig. 13. It shows that the more the parity units, the higher the authentication probability. For a fixed parity unit point (X=2), the 256kbps and 512kbps network channels can provide higher than 95% authentication probability. This is because their group sizes

Figure 13. Authentication probability vs. packet redundancy (in number of parity units)

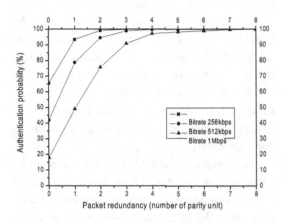

(packet numbers in a group) are relatively smaller (than 85 packets per group as of 1Mbps). Given the fixed error rate, the higher bit rate channels need more parity units.

6.2 Computational Cost

We study the computational cost related to security and ignore object encoding/decoding. Firstly, if there is no transcoding operation at the proxy, the signature is generated once for a group of packets by the producer only. The computational cost for signature generation and verification depends on the signature scheme selected. However, the signature verification can be much faster than signature generation. Secondly, based on equations (1)-(2), verifying the integrity unit depends on how many hash operations are required in generating the hash tree. For a special Merkle hash tree as in Fig. 10 with l+1 leaf nodes, the total number of hash operations is roughly 2(l+1). Thus, both the signer and the verifiers are required to perform 2(l+1) hash operations.

Last, when there are u (u<l+1) transcoding operations, the cost of generating and verifying the signature is proportional to the number of transcoding operations (assuming one transcod-

ing operation results in one signature generation/ verification operation). However, for signature generation, the cost at the producer is fixed by one; the cost at the proxies is proportional to the number of signature generations. For signature verification, the final receiver has to verify all the signatures, but at relatively lower cost (than generation). The receiver will also spend time on reconstruct the (probably partial) hash tree over the object group. A partial hash tree means that the receiver spends less time on constructing the tree at the cost of verifying more signatures.

6.3 Communication Overhead

Besides the packet redundancy discussed above for tolerating packet loss, for each packet consisting of contents from different layers, we obtain the overhead of a single packet in a group regarding authentication data as: $|\omega| = |\lambda| / k$. Suppose the number of layers is fixed in the encoding/decoding phase, we set l=3 for 4 layers. We select 1024 bits as a signature size and 160 bits as a hash size. We consider 3 scenarios: A0: no transcoding; A1: type-1 transcoding by truncating EL_2 and EL_3 only; and A2: type-2 transcoding with replacing EL_1. We get $|\lambda_{A0}| = 1024 + (160 * 5) = 1824$ (bits); $|\lambda_{A1}| = 1024 + 1024 + (160 * 4) = 2688$ (bits) and $|\lambda_{A2}| = 1024*2 + (160 * 6) = 3008$ (bits). For different network channels 256kbps, 512kbps and 1Mbps, the overhead per packet for A0 is roughly 91 bits (0.76%), 46 bits (0.38%) and 23 bits (0.19%), respectively. The results can be compared with the overhead in packet based stream authentication schemes (case B), where generally n packet hashes are carried as integrity units. Their overhead per packet is 1.76%, 1.55%, and 1.44% for different network channels (256kbps, 512kbps and 1Mbps). We show in Fig. 14, that the PiSASes have much less overhead than that of P-SASes. The overhead reduction is originated from the hashing schemes: layers' hash values (l) vs. packets' hash values (n); where l is fixed at encoding phase, but n is fluctuated with the

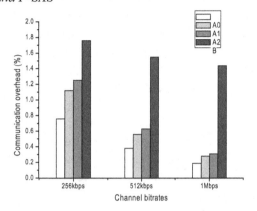

Figure 14. Communication overheads of PiSASes and P-SAS

transmission rate. Another observation is that the more the packets grouped into one video stream, the less the overhead per packet. That is why the curves of all PiSASes decline faster than that of P-SAS. Moreover, the overhead for A1 and A2 is more than that of A0, since transcoding operations produce additional signatures (sometimes more or less hash values).

7 FUTURE TRENDS

We introduced a flexible stream authentication (FSA) framework, under which we elaborated such a flexible authentication scheme for a layered stream. We also described the authentication techniques for transcoded stream and multi-source stream. We briefly analyzed the security and performance issues with the sample stream metrics in FSA, but we have yet given a full comparison on various encoding, packing, amortizing and verifying mechanisms over a number of different stream types. A lot of research works are to be done on investigating their variety, while we only focus on the security properties (e.g., authenticity) of a stream authentication scheme, so far. In reality, streams have many form factors and other stream properties like delivery quality, display distortion, etc. might be (more) important. Thus in the

near future, we will be witnessing two potential research trends: security-oriented approaches and quality-oriented approaches.

The security-oriented approaches will be providing multiple security properties such as confidentiality, authenticity, availability and right management as well. All these features are to be combined together to build a synthesis media security framework. Under which, media publishers and media consumers would share media contents securely.

The quality-oriented approaches will be focusing on end-to-end media transmission scheme with more balanced quality and security properties. We will be expecting more innovative quality guaranteed techniques, for example, the rate-distortion-authentication (R-D-A) optimized streaming for authenticated video will be on demand soon.

8 CONCLUSION

In this chapter, we introduced the basic techniques of multimedia authentication, as a comparison with message authentication. The multimedia stream authentication schemes are categorized into two classes, namely packet based stream authentication schemes (P-SASes) and packet independent stream authentication schemes (PiSASes). We proposed a generic and flexible stream authentication (FSA) framework under the S-P-R model, which applies to any stream supporting transcoding operations. Further on, a PiSAS based on a layered stream structure is elaborated in detail. The scheme is flexible on verifying transcoded or multi-source streams. It is secure in terms of high authentication probability and cost effective in terms of low packet overhead as analyzed in Section 6. The PiSAS assumes an "erasure channel", but can be adapted to "polluted erasure channel" (Lysyanskaya A., et al., 2004) (*e.g.*, by using "distillation code" Karlof C., et al., 2004).

REFERENCES

ISO/IEC 14496-1:2001 Information Technology - Coding of Audio-Visual Objects- Part 1: Systems

ISO/IEC 14496-2:2003 Information Technology - Coding of Audio-Visual Objects- Part 2: Visual

Boneh, D., Gentry, C., Lynn, B., & Shacham, H. (2003). Aggregate and Verifiably Encrypted Signatures from Bilinear Maps. In Eli Biham (Ed.): *Advances in Cryptology - EUROCRYPT 2003.*

Gennaro, R., & Rohatgi, P. (1997). How to sign digital streams. In Burton S. Kaliski Jr. (Ed.): *Advances in Cryptology – CRYPTO 1997.*

Gentry, C., Hevia, A., Jain, R., Kawahara, T., & Ramzan, Z. (2005). End-to-End Security in the Presence of Intelligent Data Adapting Proxies: The Case of Authenticating Transcoded Streaming Media. *Journal of Selected Areas of Communication, Q1, 2005.*

Golle, P., & Modadugu, N. (2001). Authenticated streamed data in the presence of random packet loss. In *Proceeding of Network and Distributed System Security Symposium (NDSS)*, San Diego, CA, Feb. 2001.

Karlof, C., Sastry, N., Li, Y., Perrig, A., & Tygar, J. (2004). Distillation codes and applications to DoS resistant multicast authentication. In *Proceeding of 11th Network and Distributed Systems Security Symposium (NDSS'04)*, San Diego, CA, Feb. 2004.

Krohn, M. N., Freedman, M. J., & Mazires, D. (2004). On-the-Fly Verification of Rateless Erasure Codes for Efficient Content Distribution. *IEEE Symposium on Security and Privacy (S&P'04)*, California, USA.

Li, T., Wu, Y., Ma, D., Zhu, H., & Deng, R., (2004). Flexible Verification of MPEG-4 Stream in Peer-to-Peer CDN. *6th International Conference on Information and Communications Security (ICICS'04)*, LNCS 3269, Spain, 2004.

Li, T., Zhu, H., & Wu, Y., (2005). Multi-Source Stream Authentication Framework in case of Composite MPEG-4 Stream. *Seventh International Conference on Information and Communications Security (ICICS'05)*, December 10-13, 2005, Beijing, China. LNCS 3783, 389-401.

Li, W. (2001). Overview of fine granularity scalability in MPEG-4 video standard.

IEEE Trans. on Circuits and Systems for Video Technology, 11(3), 301-317.

Lysyanskaya, A., Micali, S., Reyzin, L., & Shacham, H. (2004). Sequential Aggregate Signatures from trapdoor one-way permutations. In Christian Cachin, Jan Camenisch (Eds.): *Advances in Cryptology - EUROCRYPT 2004.*

Lysyanskaya, A., Tamassia, R., & Triandopoulos, N. (2004). Multicast Authentication in Fully Adversarial Networks. *IEEE Symposium on Security and Privacy (S&P'04)*, California, USA.

Luby, M., Mitzenmacher, M., Shokrollahi, A., Spielman, D., & Stemann, V. (1997). Practical loss-resilient codes. In *Proceeding of 29th Annual ACM Symposium on Theory of Computing (STOC)*, El Paso, TX, May 1997.

Merkle, R. C. (1989). A certified digital signature, Crypto'89, *Lecture Notes on Computer Science, Vol. 0435*, pp. 218-238, Springer-Verlag, 1989.

Miner, S., & Staddon, J. (2001). Graph-based authentication of digital streams. In *Proceedings of the IEEE Symposium on Research in Security and Privacy,* pages 232-246, May 2001.

Mohr, A. E., Riskin, E. A., & Ladner, R. E. (2000). Unequal loss protection: Graceful degradation of image quality over packet erasure channels through forward error correction. *IEEE Journal on Selected Areas in Communications,* 18(6), 819-828.

Pannetrat, A., & Molva, R. (2003). Efficient multicast packet authentication. In *Proceeding of Network and Distributed System Security Symposium (NDSS)*, San Diego, CA, Feb. 2003.

Park, J. M., Chong, E. K., & Siegel, H. J. (2002). Efficient multicast packet authentication using signature amortization. In *Proceedings of the IEEE Symposium on Research in Security and Privacy,* pages 227-240, May 2002.

Perrig, A., Canetti, R., Tygar, J. D., & Song, D. (2000). Efficient authentication and signature of multicast streams over lossy channels. In *Proceedings of the IEEE Symposium on Research in Security and Privacy*, pages 56-73, May 2000.

Rivest, R. L., Shamir, A., & Adleman, L. M. (1978). A method for obtaining digital signatures and public-key cryptosystems. *Communications of the ACM, 21(2),* 120-126.

SHA-1 (1995). National Institute of Standards and Technology. *Secure Hash Standard (SHS)*, FIPS Publication 180-1, 1995.

Sun, Q., & Chang, S. (2004). Signature Based Media Authentication. In *Multimedia Security Handbook*, CRC Press, 2004.

Suzuki, T., *et al.*, (2004). A system for end-to-end authentication of adaptive multimedia content. *Eighth IFIP TC-6 TC-11 Conference on Communications and Multimedia Security (CMS'04)*, Sept. 2004.

Wong, C. K., & Lam, S. S. (1998). Digital signatures for flows and multicasts. In *Proceeding of IEEE International Conference on Network Protocols*, Austin, TX, Oct. 1998.

KEY TERMS

Amortization: The technology to divide a message into multiple parts and assign them over different packets.

Message Authentication: Refers to the procedure to verify that a message comes from the alleged source and has not been altered during transmission.

Multimedia Authentication: Refers to the technology to verify that the multimedia content comes from the alleged sources and has not been altered illegally in transmission.

PiSAS: Refers to Packet independent Stream Authentication Scheme, the method to generate authentication data based on the multimedia content. Thus, the authentication data can be generated and amortized onto original multimedia content, which is independent of the packing process.

P-SAS: Refers to Packet based Stream Authentication Scheme, the method to generate authentication data based on the packets. Thus, only after packets are produced, the authentication data can be generated and amortized back onto those packets.

Sign: The algorithm in a digital signature scheme used to generate a cryptography value-signature over a message using one's private key.

Transcoding: The method to remove part of the stream content to adapt to the bandwidth of the transmission channel.

Verify: The algorithm in a digital signature scheme used to verify a cryptographically generated signature using the signer's public key.

Chapter XVIII
Scalable Distribution of Watermarked Media

K-G Stenborg

Swedish Defence Research Agency, Sweden
Linköping University, Sweden

ABSTRACT

Media that is distributed digitally can be copied and redistributed illegally. Embedding an individual watermark in the media object for each customer will make it possible to trace pirate copies to the redistribution source. However, digital distribution methods such as broadcast and multicast are scalable and will give all customers identical copies of the media content. Distribution of individually watermarked media is more difficult to achieve. In this chapter, methods for how media with individual watermarks can be distributed scalable are presented and discussed. These methods are categorized in four groups. One group that is based on watermark embedding in the network, another group for embedding in the client, and two groups that use fragments of the media content that are unique for each customer or shared among a subgroup of customers.

INTRODUCTION

Distribution of digital media can be done in many different ways. TV can for example be distributed through internet, cable, satellite and terrestrial transmission. The media can be transmitted using unicast, multicast or broadcast. Terrestrial and satellite distribution of TV are broadcast where all receivers are reached by the media stream (even thou they may not be able to see it if the media is encrypted). Unicast are used for pay-per-view and similar services over cable and internet. Finally multicast can be used for scalable distribution over networks.

A distributor has one or many customers to which the media is transmitted. In the middle of the distribution chain we have some kind of network consisting of nodes. The number of nodes can be very different between different methods of distribution. Satellite distribution will probably only have one level of nodes (the satellites), terrestrial distribution maybe at most three (relayed signal over two extra transponders) while for large network, the media may pass through many routers before it reaches the customer.

If one of the customers retransmits the media illegally he is a pirate. One way to trace the source of such pirate copies is to use watermarks. Watermarks are embedded in the media content and every customer will get an individual watermark in the media that is distributed to him. If then a pirate copy is found by the distributor he can extract the individual watermark from the media and use it to identify the pirate. The distributor can then decide to take legal actions against the pirate or just stop the distribution to that customer. If it is known that the media contains individual watermarks it will deter customers from becoming pirates.

Pirates may try to remove the watermark by using different attacks that alter the media slightly. If two or more pirates collaborate they can try to blend their individual copies and in that way corrupt the watermarks. A good watermarking algorithm should be robust against such attacks.

Scalable distribution like multicast and broadcast are desired since they require less bandwidth. For broadcast the distributor will only transmit the media one time and all customers will get identical copies of the media. But if the distributor wants the media to contain individual watermarks, the received copies by the customers will no longer be identical. Can individually watermarked media be transmitted by broadcast? Is that not a contradiction?

How individual watermarks and scalable distribution can be combined is the topic of this chapter. Different methods will be described and discussed. These individual watermark distribution methods are categorized as being Network Based Watermarking, Unique Fragments Distribution, Shared Fragments Distribution or Client Based Watermarking. For some of these methods there exists another type of attack known as the test pattern attack. This attack is described and which methods that are robust against it.

BACKGROUND

In this section the background to watermarking is given. Compression and distribution algorithms are also discussed.

Watermarking

Watermarking is a term borrowed from the water coated stamp that can be impressed on paper, an invention first done in Fabriano, Italy in 1292 (Hartung and Kutter, 1999). During the last twenty years watermarking of digital media objects such as images, audio and video have been a research topic. The watermarks should be embedded in the media in such a way that the original media and the watermarked media should be undistinguishable from one another for human eyes and ears. This type of perceptually disguised watermarks is called invisible. Another type of watermark is visible and can for example be a logotype or copyright information that is written on an image. In this chapter only invisible watermarks are described.

The watermarks can be used for many different purposes but we will only deal with methods for finding the pirate responsible for redistributing pirate copies. For that case the media object that is distributed is embedded with watermarks in such way that the individual copy for each customer contains a unique individual watermark. Individual watermarking is sometimes known as fingerprinting but in this chapter we will refer to them as individual watermarks or simply watermarks.

Note that watermarking is not an alternative but a complement to cryptology. By encrypting a media object the distributor can control the initial distribution of the media so that only authorized customers will be able to use the data. Cryptology can also be used to try and protect the possibility to make illegal copies. If illegal copies of a media object, despite the cryptology, are re-distributed the encryption will no longer be able to control the pirate copying. For that case the individual watermarking will come into use.

From a watermarked media object, the watermark can be identified. For public watermarking (Kutter and Petitcolas, 1999) only the media object is needed for the extraction. In the case of private watermarking the original (non-embedded) media object is also needed for the extraction. If the distributor or someone trusted by him gets hold of a pirate copy and extracts the individual watermark the pirate is identified among the customers.

A pirate that does not want to be identified can try and attack the media object and in that way try and remove the watermark. If the media object is an image possible attack methods are cropping, scaling, skewing, filtering, noise addition and quantization among many more. A good watermarking method should be robust against these attacks. The attacks will distort the watermark but at the same time the media object will also be distorted. Ideally the watermarking algorithm should be able to withstand attacks, so that the watermark is recognizable, as long as the quality of the media object makes it usable for its purpose. For a given embedding method the more robust the watermarking is the more distortion the embedding of the watermark will give the media object. To find a good robust watermarking algorithm that at the same time gives perceptually invisible watermarks in the embedded copies can be difficult.

For individual watermarks another type of attack is possible. If two or more customers are pirates and collaborate they can try and use their copies (with different individual watermarks) to remove the watermarks or even try to create another watermark so that an innocent customer will be blamed for pirate coping. This is an attack that the watermarking algorithm must be robust against if the legitimacy of extracted watermarks from pirate copies should be trusted.

Sometimes it is desirable to be able to embed more than one watermark in the same media object. For such cases it is important that the embedding

is robust so that we do not destroy the first watermark when the second watermark is embedded. For some embedding methods it is possible to use the same embedding method for all watermarks while other methods only can embed one watermark and then the second watermark must be embedded with another method. The first case with the possibility to embed many watermarks is desirable since that method will be robust against collaborating attacks such as taking the mean of several individually watermarked images.

Compression

Media objects that are distributed are usually compressed with a lossy compression method (Sayood, 2006). That means that the compression has added distortion so that the media is no longer exactly the same as the non-compressed media. For a good image compression method with a fair compression ratio the non-compressed and compressed media should be perceptually equal. Both the compression and watermarking algorithm try not to distort the media more than needed. Some watermarking methods are also very similar to compression algorithms.

A difference between compression algorithms and watermarking is that in lossy compression redundant data is removed while for watermarking redundant data is added to the media. Therefore, a compression algorithm will act as an attack if it is applied to a media object that contains a watermark. Watermark algorithms must therefore also be robust against lossy compression.

For images, compression is usually done with DCT-transform coding (JPEG) or wavelet coding (JPEG2000). For video, the different frames of the stream is arranged in sequences as I-, P- and B-frames (MPEG-2, AVC). The I-frames (I for intra) are coded separately similar to still images while the P-frames (predictive) and B-frames (bidirectionally predictive) are coded using motion-compensated prediction from neighboring frames.

The Embedding of Watermarks

If a video object is going to be embedded with a watermark it must be decided where the embedding should be done. Should both frames and audio be embedded? Is the embedding done before or after the compression? If the embedding is done after compression, should the embedding be done in only the I-frames or all frames?

Another similar question is how much data that is needed for one watermark to be embedded. Does every frame in the video stream contain the watermark or do we need several frames (say 10 seconds of video) to extract the watermark? This depends on whether the watermark is dense or sparse. For dense watermarks only a small amount of data (for example one frame) is needed to extract the watermark while for sparse watermarks a large amount of data is needed for extracting the watermark.

A simple example of a sparse watermark is a book that on each page has one word that either is one of two synonyms (for example "sample" or "specimen"). If the book has 100 pages we end up with 2^{100} possible watermarks. From this algorithm we construct a number of copies with individual watermarks. To extract the individual watermark from one of these books all pages are needed.

Let another book be embedded such that all spaces between letters are slightly altered given a pseudorandom noise. The same noise is used to alter each page of the book and the noise is individual to each book copy. These books will then contain dense watermarks since only one page will be needed to extract the individual watermark.

One often used dense watermark embedding algorithm is spread spectrum watermarking (Cox, Leighton and Shamoon, 1997). Spread spectrum watermarking for images are embedded as a noise that is added in a transform domain. The watermark can be adapted to the image characteristics so that suitable transform coefficients are embedded with stronger watermark signals.

For sparse watermarking the number of positions that is embedded is sparse and often the amount of possible values for these positions is also small. Sparse watermarks are usually built from codes and to be robust against collaborating pirates these codes needs to be long (Boneh and Shaw, 1998).

Distribution

For digital distribution the media stream is usually split into small IP packets. These packets can be transmitted through a network using three different ways: unicast, multicast and broadcast (Stevens, 1994).

In unicast one packet is sent from the server to the client in the network. If the distributor wants to send the same information to ten customers the server has to send the same packets ten times, once to every client. So this is not a very efficient way to transmit the same data to many customers. Unicast is the transmission method that is most frequently used today but in the future more efficient methods will hopefully be used.

For multicast distribution the server will only need to send each packet once. The clients of authorized customers will belong to a multicast group. In the network the routers will know which of its downstream branches that contain members in the multicast group. A router will multiply the packets and transmit them on all branches with clients in the multicast group. In that way all authorized customers will receive the same packets that the distributor transmits.

In broadcast situations the server will only send each packet once. The routers in the network will multiply and forward the packet downstream so all routers and eventually all clients will get it. It does not matter if the customers are subscribed to the distributor or not, they will all get the packet. If the packet is encrypted non-subscribed customers will not be able to decrypt it.

SCALABLE WATERMARK DISTRIBUTIONS

The distributor wants to use multicast or broadcast to transmit the media object to the customers. At the same time he wants to individually water-mark each copy, so that every customer will get a unique copy. But in multicast and broadcast the packets that reach the customers are the same. Is it possible to distribute individually watermarked media content in a scalable way?

Different approaches for doing this will be presented in this section. The methods are described in four different categories presented in four different subsections: Network Based Watermarking, Unique Fragments Distribution, Shared Fragments Distribution and Client Based Watermarking. An early version of some of this was described in Stenborg (2005).

Network Based Watermarking

In this category the individual watermarking is done in the network. To achieve this smart overlay

network needs to be implemented. Some methods for doing this are presented below.

Watercasting

Brown, Perkins and Crowcroft (1999) introduced Watercasting as a distribution method. This combination of individual watermarking and multicast uses an overlay network with special routers to handle the watermarking. Each packet that is going to be a watermarked position is made into n different copies. Each of these packet copies are embedded with an individual mark but contains the same basic information (no perceptual difference). All of these copies are then transmitted from the server to the network. The overlay network routers will not act like ordinary routers since they will not forward all packet copies. Instead the routers will forward all but one of the packets to each downstream router. In this way all underlying routers will receive different set of packet copies. Figure 1 describes the method in more detail. From the last overlay router only one copy of each packet is transmitted to the subnet of customers.

Figure 1. Watercasting. At the server the packets are copied and embedded with different marks, A1, A2 and A3. In the network the first router forwards packet A1 and A2 to the second router and packet A2 and A3 to the third router. From the last router to the customer only one packet of each copy is transmitted. The same is done with packet B but now other packets are dropped. Customers on different subnets will receive different sets of packets.

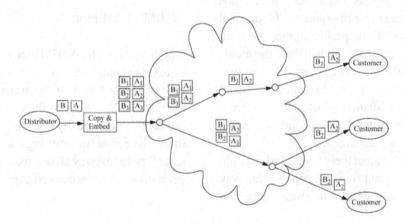

For the next packet the same thing is done but now other packet copies are intentionally dropped in the network. It is this dropping of copies that result in an individual watermarked set of packets giving a unique media object. Even if the watermark embedding is done at the server it is the active network that gives the individual watermarking.

If the depth of the tree of overlay routers is d the minimum numbers n of copies for each packet is $n \geq d$. If that is fulfilled all last hop routers will receive at least one copy of each packet. The needed bandwidth will be larger at the beginning and will then decrease during transmission and finally only one packet from each set of packet copies are transmitted to the customer.

The tree topology must be stored and also the information about which packet copies that were dropped for every packet. The dropping can be done in a repeated way so that information will be easier to store.

One problem with this method is that all customers on the same subnet will receive the same packets. Another problem is that the method does not seem to be able to handle collaborating pirates from different subnets.

Hierarchical Tagging

Caronni and Schuba (2001) described two different methods for distributing individual watermarks in an efficient way. One of the methods called Hierarchical tagging is based upon the idea that there is more than one distributor. The original distributor has to his help a hierarchical network of sub-distributors that will distribute the media object until it reaches the customer. These sub-distributors will be required to embed individual watermarks for all of their sub-distributors. From the last sub-distributor to the customer the media is individually watermarked.

The idea is that all of these watermarks should be possible to extract from the copies. That way the distributor can extract the watermark that tells him who his sub-distributor was. The sub-distributor can extract the information about the next hand in the transmission chain and so on until the customer is identified. This method is dependent on the existence of a network of distributors. The next method will use a similar method and implement it in a network.

WHIM - Backbone

Judge and Ammar (2000) created a system that "watermarks in a hierarchy of intermediaries", WHIM. This method contains two parts: the Backbone (WHIM-BB) and the Last Hop (WHIM-LH).

For WHIM-BB an overlay network is created that contains special routers that can embed watermarks. The network is adapted for multicast. If for example images are transmitted each of these overlay routers will embed a watermark in the image. The watermarks are unique for the routers and each router will always embed the same watermark in the images. In that way an image will contain identification watermarks from all routers that it passed during transmission from the distributor to the receiver. This can be used to trace the transmission chain from the server to the last router.

Similar to Watercasting the individual watermarks will only be able to identify the subnet of the receiver. This will be fixed by WHIM - Last Hop.

WHIM - Last Hop

Another part of the WHIM method is the WHIM - Last Hop (Judge and Ammar, 2000). This takes care of the last part of the transmission, from the last overlay router to the customer. The last router will individually watermark and encrypt the media before transmitting it to the subscribed receivers. In that way all receivers in a subnet will get individual watermarked copies.

If a WHIM-LH watermarked copy is found it might be a problem to locate the subnet that the receiver belongs to. By combining WHIM-LH with WHIM-BB information about the whole transmission chain from the distributor to the receiver will be embedded in the media. Both of these methods use dense watermarking and can be made robust against collaborating pirates.

One of the big problems with the WHIM methods are that all the embedding will probably make the network slow. However, the main problem is that a special overlay network is needed for the distribution. These methods are therefore dependent on the network and can for example not be used for TV broadcasting. If WHIM-LH is used for all overlay routers we will end up with a method similar to the Hierarchical Tagging.

Unique Fragments Distribution

The methods in this section are all based on the idea that the media object is split into two parts. One part of the media object is the same for all customers and can therefore be distributed scalable and another part is unique for each customer.

Combined Unicast and Multicast

Wu and Wu (1997) described a method to transmit individually watermarked data to many customers without all of the data being transmitted by unicast. The solution is simply to split the data into one multicast part (or broadcast part) and one unicast part. The packets in the multicast part can be read by all customers while the packets in the unicast part are only transmitted to and read by one customer. The unicast part is embedded with an individual watermark and encrypted in the server before it is transmitted to the corresponding client. Figure 2 describes the method.

The watermarking method used is an extension of the spread spectrum embedding. The authors have tested seven different locations for the mark from only the DC part of the luminance in I-frames to both luminance and chrominance of I-, P- and B-frames. They use dense watermarks and only one embedded frame is needed to extract the watermark.

For this method to be scalable over a network with many customers only a small part of the data can be transmitted by unicast. The smallest embedding results in less than 1% being transmitted with unicast while the largest embedding gives that 90% of the stream for each customer are transmitted with unicast. If we have 1000 customers the smallest embedding would still give a total data expansion of 10 times compared to video distribution without any individual watermarking. Therefore this method will only work for transmission to a small number of customers.

Joint Source Fingerprinting

Luh and Kundur (2005, June) propose a similar scheme called Joint Source Fingerprinting. They split the video stream into a semantic class and a feature class. The semantic class is encrypted and transmitted with broadcast so that all customers receive and decrypt the same data. The feature class is made into multiple copies, one for every customer. The feature class is then used for the individual watermarking and the embedding is done at the distributor. The feature class for all customers is also encrypted and transmitted by broadcast. Every customer has only one decryption key so he can only decrypt his own feature class part. In that way every user will get an individual watermark. The authors also discuss how the distribution of the feature class can be done by unicast in cases where unicast transmission is possible.

In the algorithm the semantic part has a low frame rate and will therefore have a choppy motion that will give it no commercial value on its own. When combined with the feature class the video will not contain any visual degradation compared to the original non-watermarked video. The authors claim that the method will be robust against

Figure 2. Combined Unicast and Multicast. In this example the distributor has two customers. Some packet (B and C) are transmitted using multicast. Packet A is made into two copies embedded with individual watermarks. These packet copies are encrypted with individual keys and transmitted by unicast to one customer each. That way part of the stream will be individual for each customer.

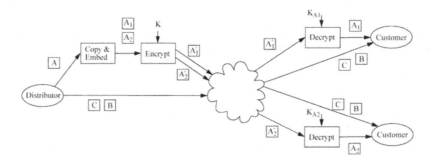

collaborating pirates because the quality of the video will be distorted by colluding attacks.

One problem when using broadcast is that the number of possible customers must be small enough to let the individual information be part of the broadcast stream. The amount of data in the feature class is claimed to be small but if we are aiming for distribution to millions of customers the bandwidth needed for the feature class will be huge. No description of how to combine the algorithm with a video coder to get compression is given.

Shared Fragments Distribution

In the methods described below unicast is not used for the distribution. These methods use other means of distribution and decryption to give the customers unique sets of watermarked media objects.

Packet Based Embedding

Parviainen and Parnes (2001) described a method that uses multicast to transmit individually watermarked radio. For every packet that is transmitted

two copies (with different watermarks) are made. The packet copies are encrypted with different keys and all packets are transmitted with multicast. Every customer has a unique set of decryption keys. These keys can only decrypt one of the two copies of every packet. That way every customer will get access to different sets of watermarked packets, i.e. individually watermarked radio streams. See Figure 3 for more details.

Compared to Joint Source Fingerprinting the amount of transmitted data is not increased when the number of customers increases. The needed bandwidth will always be double compared to a system what have no individual watermarking. For the system to work well a good way of distributing the decryption keys is needed.

The watermarking will be sparse since the watermarks from many packets must be extracted before the individual set of marks can be identified. The system is not very robust against collaborating pirates since the position of the individual watermark (every packet is one position) is known.

We can also expand the number of copies of each packet so that less amount of data is needed to identify the pirate. Such extension will demand

Figure 3. Packet Based Embedding. In the server the packet A is duplicated and the copies are individually watermarked. The packet copies A1 and A2 are encrypted with different keys and transmitted. The customer can only decrypt one of the packet copies. After more packets are distributed the customers will get different sets of packets combined to unique watermarks.

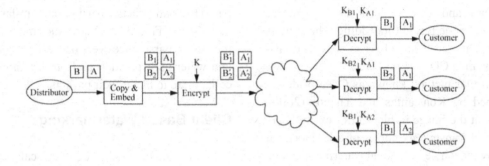

higher bandwidth. The main drawbacks of this method are the increase in transmitted data and the fact that we need a large part of the video before a pirate can be identified.

Frame Based Embedding

Chu, Qiao and Nahrstedt (2002) introduced a similar idea to Packet Based Embedding. Instead of using different copies of packets they use different copies of each frame. So every frame in a video stream exists in two versions embedded with different watermarks. The frames are encrypted with different keys. The video stream that is distributed will then contain two versions of each frame. Each customer will be able to decrypt only one of these frames and the decrypted video stream will then contain an individual watermark.

The main problem with this method is that in video coders such as MPEG there is dependence between the frames (P- and B-frames). Since the frames will be different the distortion will propagate. To solve this problem the coder can be constructed to transmit only I-frames but that will give low compression. Another possibility

is to only embed in the I-frames but then the watermark will be even sparser.

The sparse watermark is otherwise also a problem. The authors need between 14 minutes and 1939 minutes of video for the embedding of one watermark. The length depends on number of customers and how many colluding pirates the mark should be robust against. If the number of copies of each frame is increased to 8 instead of 2 the needed length of video for embedding one watermark will be between 4 minutes and 443 minutes. If eight copies are used the needed bandwidth will also be eight times larger compared to video with no watermark and four times larger than the binary watermark.

The method can be extended so that the watermark that is embedded in every frame contains information about the copyright holder. That way each frame contains a watermark with information about the distributor and the video stream contains an individual watermark.

Bulk Tagging and COiN-Video

Caronni and Schuba (2001) did not only describe Hierarchical tagging but also a method called Bulk tagging. This is a method with many similarities to Packet Based Embedding and Frame Based Embedding. One of their ideas is to transmit two versions of image blocks. In that way one image can contain many positions for the individual watermark and the method is therefore not as sparse as Frame Based Embedding. The authors discuss that the scheme also can be used in distribution on a CD.

A similar method known as COiN-Video is described by Konstantas and Thanos (2000). They split the image in blocks (for example six parts) and transmit six copies of each block. In this way the whole individual watermark can be contained in one frame of the video.

Joint Fingerprint Design and Distribution

Zhao and Liu (2006) describe an embedding and distribution scheme called Joint Fingerprinting Design and Distribution. This method contains similar element from Unique Fragments Distribution but instead of unique distribution of parts of the media to one customer the distribution is done over multicast to subgroups of the customers.

A video is split into two parts. One part is distributed to all customers by multicast and the other part will contain the watermark. In the second part watermark elements are embedded in different positions of the video. Then a tree-based structure is used to combine different watermarked elements for the positions so that a number of unique individual watermarks are created.

Every watermark element is placed in one packet. The tree structure is used to build multicast groups that are subgroups of all customers. These multicast groups will then change for each watermark position. The copies containing different watermarks for a position is distributed through these multicast groups so that every customer receives one copy of each packet.

The tree-based distribution will give a more efficient distribution compared to if the watermark part of the video would be distributed through unicast. The authors show that the bandwidth requirement can be reduced by up to 87% compared to an all unicast distribution. Similar to the other Shared Fragments Distribution methods this method is sparse since every packet only contains one watermark position and pirates can easily collaborate to blend their packets.

Client Based Watermarking

In this section the final category of scalable individual watermark distribution is described. For these methods all customers receive the same data and the individual watermarks become apparent first after the data have been retrieved at the client.

Chameleon

Anderson and Manifavas (1997) describe a method called Chameleon. This method is based upon a stream cipher and was originally developed for audio. The idea is that all customers have different decryption keys. The encrypted audio is transmitted using broadcast and the decryption keys will decrypt it in different ways. After the decryption the stream has been slightly distorted and it is this distortion that is the individual watermark.

The authors work with 16-bit audio signals and the watermark is embedded into the least significant bits. Their example is not so good since the embedding is not robust against attacks on the least significant bits. No compression is used so they need a lot of bandwidth to transmit the audio signal.

An extension of how to implement the Chameleon cipher is given by Luh and Kundur (2005). Tamper proof smart cards are used to contain the key. This improves the security by making it difficult for the customers to make their own keys. Another implementation of Chameleon is given by Briscoe and Fairman (1999).

Mask Blending

Emmanuel and Kankanhalli (2003) developed an interactive protocol that addresses security issues for both the distributor and the customer. Contained in their DRM scheme is a simple and efficient way of embedding and distributing individually watermarked video. The idea is to mask the video at the distributor and transmit the same material to all customers. To be able to view the masked video properly the customer will need to unmask it. The unmasking frame is slightly different for all customers and therefore the unmasked video will contain an individual watermark that can be traced back to a pirate.

The masking of the frames is done in the transform domain of the MPEG stream for faster embedding in already compressed video. The unmasking will be done in the spatial domain by the client. An unauthorized customer that tries to view the masked video will only see a distorted version of it.

In this scheme two marks are actually embedded. One watermark is used to trace pirates and another watermark is for the customer's concerns. How the masking affects the compression ratio is not mentioned in the article. The data expansion will probably not be large compared to coding without Mask blending.

Joint Fingerprinting and Decryption

Kundur and Karthik (2004) created Joint Fingerprinting and Decryption which is also an extension of the Chameleon algorithm. For this method the whole image is transformed using DCT. A set of perceptually significant regions in the low- and mid-frequency domains are identified. These sets are portioned into subsets. During encryption these subsets are sign scrambled, meaning that the sign of the coefficients are changed depend-

ing on a key. This encrypted image is transmitted using multicast or broadcast. The customer will only be able to decrypt a portion of the encrypted subsets. The remaining scrambled subsets are then the embedded watermark. Every customer has individual decryption keys that descramble different coefficients and therefore the copies will have individual watermarks. The individually watermarked copies will contain some distortion but they will all be close to the original image. The encrypted image is still possible to receive and view by an unauthorized customer but the scrambling makes the image quality poor and therefore of little commercial value.

The method is not adapted for video compression since it is the whole image that is DCT transformed in the embedding. Therefore the embedding will probably affect the compression ratio in a negative way during video encoding.

Modified Transform Watermarking

A generalized version of Mask Blending and Joint Fingerprinting and Decryption is given in Stenborg (2005). In the server the media object is scrambled (i.e. masked) by the embedding of an offset watermark. The media object containing the offset watermark is distributed in a scalable way to all customers. If an unauthorized customer tries to view the media it will be scrambled and heavily distorted. Every authorized customer has a unique key that is used to descramble the media. The individual key is a combination of the offset watermark and an individual watermark. By applying the key to the media the offset watermark is removed and at the same time the individual watermark is embedded in the media object. The generalized method is illustrated in Figure 4.

For the Modified Transform Watermarking the embedding is done during the compression of the media object. If the media object is an image and a transform compression method is used, the transform is modified in the encoder by adding a pseudo random noise V_j to the elements in the

Figure 4. Client Based Watermarking. The offset watermark V is embedded at the server. If an unauthorized customer U tries to view the image it will be distorted. Authorized customers will use their individual keys Vi to remove the offset watermark. Their images Fi will then contain an individual watermark.

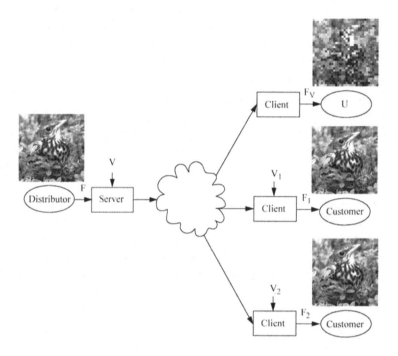

transform matrix. Thereafter the encoder with the modified transform is used to compress the image. The image is distributed and a customer *i* receive it. To be able to decode the compressed image correctly the transform matrix in the decoder needs to be the same as in the encoder. But the pseudo random noise V_{ij} that is added to the transform matrix in the decoder is not exactly the same as in the encoder. A small difference W_{ij} exist between the offset watermark V_j and the individual key V_{ij}. This difference is the individual watermark. By decoding the compressed image using this transform matrix the image will be embedded with the individual watermark.

During the transform compression the image is split into small blocks of size *8x8* pixels. If a special offset watermark is used for each block *j* all transform matrices will be different. In a similar way the transform matrices in the decoder are different for each block that is decoded.

This embedding method does not embed in the spatial domain and not in the transform domain either. Instead the embedding is done during the transform between the transform domain and spatial domain.

Since the transform matrices in the encoder have been modified the efficiency of the compression have changed. Tests gives a decrease of the compression ratio by about 5 % for an image compressed with modified transform compared to an image compressed with a regular DCT transform encoder. By optimizing the parameters of the offset watermarks the compression ratio can be increased and still give a scrambled media object.

FUTURE TRENDS

Of the four categories described in the previous chapter two are more promising for future studies: Shared Fragment Distribution and Client Based Watermarking. Compared to the other two categories they perform better for a number of issues.

Network Dependence

For Network Based Watermarking methods a special network is needed. Therefore, it will be expensive to use this type of watermarking in already existing networks. These methods are not suitable for satellite or terrestrial distribution since they need a network with a larges depth of nodes. The methods in the other categories are not dependent of the network and are therefore easier to implement using existing network infrastructure.

For new networks that needs high security (for example military networks) Network Based Watermarking can still be a suitable part of the overall security solution. If media objects are not deliberately redistributed by a customer but instead intercepted during initial transmission, the network embedded watermark will make it possible to identify in which part of the network that the interception of a redistributed media object was done.

Data Expansion

One of the most important issues for digital distribution is the amount of data needed to transmit a specific media object. By introducing the uniqueness of the individual watermarks most distribution methods need more bandwidth compared to distribution without individual watermarking. Therefore it is desired to use distribution methods that achieve independent watermarking without increasing the overall amount of distributed data.

Methods that use Unique Fragments Distribution or Shared Fragments Distribution will all expand the amount of distributed data from the distributor. For large sets of customers Unique Fragments Distribution will be especially bandwidth inefficient.

Network Based Watermarking methods such as Hierarchical Tagging and WHIM-BB will not increase the transmitted data much. Watercasting on the other hand will have an increased amount that is transmitted from the distributor. But the distributed data will decrease during the transmission and in the end be small when it reaches the customers.

The methods that are most adapted to the data expansion problem are those in the Client Based Watermarking category. While some of the other methods need double or more bandwidth during transmission the only increase that may occurs during Client Based Watermarking methods are introduced because of the fact that the efficiency of the compression method has been slightly degraded.

If the keys needed for decryption of the media objects are distributed on the same network as the media itself the bandwidth increase caused by the key distribution must also be taken into account when the required bandwidth is calculated. For higher security these keys should not be the same for long amounts of time. The more often the keys are changed the more bandwidth is required.

Secure Hardware

It would be possible to make a distribution solution with clients that are based on secure hardware. First the media is encrypted and transmitted using broadcast or multicast to all clients, i.e. all clients receive the same encrypted media. Inside these trusted clients, the decryption of the transmitted data could be followed by the embedding of the individual watermarks (see Figure 5). This method has many similarities to the methods in Client Based Watermarking. But for this method no extra modulation in the server is needed since the watermark embedding is done on the received media object. The method is not dependent on the network or any special distribution method.

Figure 5. Secure Hardware. The media is encrypted in the server. After transmission the client will decrypt the media and thereafter embed the individual watermark Wi.

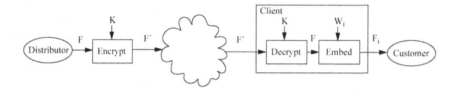

The difference compared to Chameleon, Mask Blending, Joint Fingerprinting and Decryption and finally Modified Transform Watermarking is that they perform the embedding at the same time as the encryption or decoding. For the trusted client method there is a weakness that the non-embedded media object can be extracted if the client is cracked. To only relying in secure hardware is always dangerous and therefore we expect that type of security to be less used in the future.

The methods categorized and described in Client Based Watermarking do not rely on secure hardware at the client. Instead the security is achieved by the use of keys that in many cases are unique for each customer.

Collaborating Pirates

The attacks that collaborating pirates can perform is another important issue. The pirates can use many different methods to blend the content of their copies. Sparse watermarks are more sensitive to collaborating attacks than dense. From dense watermarks there will be more difficult to totally remove the unique trace that the individual watermarks leave if many pirates collaborates and also smaller parts of the media object is needed for the identification.

Watercasting will not be efficient against collaborating pirates that are located at different parts of the network. The other methods in Network Based Watermarking will on the other hand be dense. Methods that use Unique Fragments Distribution will be sparse since the individual watermarks only consist of a small part of the media. But these watermarks can still be robust against collaborating attacks. The problem is that a lot of media content is needed to retrieve the watermark. Methods in the Shared Fragments Distribution category are sparse while some of the Client Based Watermarking methods are dense. In the future more dense watermarking methods will probably emerge.

The individual keys that are used by in Client Based Watermarking can also be used for collaborating attacks. It may be so that it is possible to create a new key from the knowledge of two or more pirate keys. Therefore the keys also needs to be robust against collaborating pirates so that either it is not possible to create new keys by blending two existing keys or that the media that have been extracted using a new pirate key should contain watermark information that can be traced to one or more of the pirates.

Test Pattern Attack

Another attack that has not been discussed earlier is the test pattern attack. This attack method is of concern for Client Based Watermarking methods.

If the media object is video, a section M_{w1} (one or several frames) of the individually watermarked video stream M_w will be available to the customer.

The non-embedded original section M_I of the video stream is kept by the distributor. Consider the case where M_I is known. This is possible if the video section M_I for example contain a test pattern, a black frame video or a movie that is available to buy without the embedding. For that case both M_{wI} and M_I is available to the customer. If the customer is a pirate he can take advantage of this knowledge. With the use of M_{wI} and M_I it may be possible to reverse engineer the embedding and remove the watermark w so that the whole video object M_w will become non-embedded $\dot{M}$. If such a watermark removal scheme is possible the watermarking method is not robust against the test pattern attack.

For Client Based Watermarking the Mask Blending, Chameleon and Joint Fingerprinting and Decryption methods are all sensitive to the test pattern attack. For Mask Blending the test pattern attack will find the mask and the pirate will therefore be able to remove the mask from other frames. For the Joint Fingerprinting and Decryption method and Chameleon the test pattern attack will find the locations of the positions where the individual embedding is done. Thus a pirate can concentrate his next attack to those positions and probably be able to remove the individual watermark.

Modified Transform Watermarking is more robust against the test pattern attack. This comes from the fact that it is not possible to know exactly how a transform matrix will affect the frames since there is dependence between all pixels in the blocks that are transformed.

Note that the test pattern attack also can be performed by an unauthorized viewer since it may be possible to descramble the video using a known video section and a scrambled version of the same section. That way the pirate that uses the test pattern attack does not even have to be one of the customers!

One way to deal with the test pattern attack is to avoid transmitting known frames. Another way is to often change the embedding by changing the scrambling and therefore the descrambling will only work for a short time. A third method is to add a small random noise to the transmitted media so that the difference between M_w and M does not only depend on the watermark but also the random noise.

CONCLUSION

In this chapter individual watermarking that makes it possible to detect pirates that redistributes media content have been described. The main topic has been scalable distribution of individual watermarked media in multicast- or broadcast-type environments. A number of distribution methods have been presented and categorized as being Network Based Watermarking, Unique Fragments Distribution, Shared Fragments Distribution or Client Based Watermarking.

For the methods categorized as being Network Based Watermarking a special overlay network is implemented and used for the embedding of the individual watermark. For methods using Unique Fragments Distribution parts of the media stream is transmitted uniquely to each customer. For Shared Fragments Distribution no parts of the stream are unique for each customer but instead parts of the stream are unique for different subgroups of customers. By changing the subgroups for different parts of the stream each customer receives an individual watermark. Finally, for Client Based Watermarking the received media stream is the same for all customers but to be able to view the media a unique key is needed. When using the key an individual watermark is embedded in the media content.

If two or more pirates collaborate they can use their individually watermarked media content to try and remove the watermarks. Another type of collaborating attack can be used on the individual keys. This new blended pirate key is intended to be able to retrieve the media content in such way that the individual watermarks are corrupted so that the pirates can not be identified. A pirate can also use the test pattern attack to try and remove the watermark by using knowledge of existing non-watermarked media such as test patterns.

For a good distribution method of individual watermarked media the required bandwidth should only be slightly increased compared to broadcast distribution of non-watermarked media. If the network already exists distribution methods that are network based will be expensive to implement. The watermarking method should not rely on secure hardware and be robust against attacks such as the test pattern attack and attacks made by collaborating pirates.

The methods in the Client Based Watermarking do not give any major data expansion during transmission and are not network dependent. As long as they do not rely on secure hardware and are robust against the test pattern attack and collaborating attacks these methods are the ones that seem to be most promising for the future.

REFERENCES

Anderson, R., & Manifavas, C. (1997, January). Chameleon - A new kind of stream cipher. In *Proceedings of the Fourth International Workshop on Fast Software Encryption FSE'97* (pp. 107–113).

Boneh, D., & Shaw, J. (1998, September). Collusion-secure fingerprinting for digital data. In *IEEE Transactions on Information Theory, 44*(5), 1897–1905.

Briscoe, B., & Fairman, I. (1999). Nark: Receiver-based multicast nonrepudiation and key management. In *Proceedings of the First ACM conference on Electronic commerce* (pp. 22–30).

Brown, I., Perkins, C., & Crowcroft, J. (1999, November). Watercasting: Distributed watermarking of multicast media. In *Proceedings of the First International COST264 Workshop on Networked Group Communication* NGC'99, (pp. 286–300).

Caronni, G., & Schuba, C. (2001, December). Enabling hierarchical and bulk-distribution for watermarked content. In *Proceedings 17th Annual Computer Security Applications Conference ACSAC'01*, (pp. 277-285).

Chu, H. H., Qiao, L., & Nahrstedt, K. (2002, April). A secure multicast protocol with

copyright protection. *ACM SIGCOMM Computer Communications Review, 32*(2), 42–60.

Cox, I., Kilian, J., Leighton, T., & Shamoon, T. (1997, December). Secure spread spectrum watermarking for multimedia. *IEEE Transactions on Image Processing, 6*(12),1673–1687.

Emmanuel, S., & Kankanhalli, M. S. (2003). A digital rights management scheme for broadcast video. *Multimedia Systems Journal, 8,* 444–458. ACM-Springer Verlag.

Hartung, F., & Kutter, M. (1999, July). Multimedia watermarking techniques. In

Proceedings IEEE: Special Issue on Identification and Protection of Multimedia Information, 87(7), 1079–1107.

Judge, P., & Ammar, M. (2000, June). WHIM: Watermarking multicast video with a hierarchy of intermediaries. In *Proceedings of the International Workshop on Network and Operation System Support for Digital Audio and Video NOSSDAV'00, 39*(6), 699-712.

Konstantas, D., & Thanos, D. (2000). Commercial dissemination of video over open network: Issues and approaches. *Technical report, LAND, Center Univeritaire d'Informatique of University of Geneva*, Object Systems Group.

Kundur, D., & Karthik, K. (2004, June). Video fingerprinting and encryption principles for digital rights management. *Proceedings of the IEEE, 92*(6), 918–932.

Kutter, M., & Petitcolas, F. A. P. (1999, January). A fair benchmark for image watermarking systems. In *Proceedings of the SPIE Security and Watermarking of Multimedia Contents, 3657,* 226–239.

Luh, W., & Kundur, D. (2005, June). New paradigms for effective multicasting and fingerprinting of entertainment media. In *IEEE Communications Magazine, 43*(6), 77–84.

Luh, W., & Kundur, D. (2005). Digital Media Fingerprinting - Techniques and Trends. In Furht B., & Kirovski D. (Ed.), *Multimedia Security Handbook - Techniques and Trends* (pp. 577–603). CRC Press.

Parviainen, R., & Parnes, P. (2001, May). Large scale distributed watermarking of multicast media through encryption. In *International Federation for Information Processing Communications and Multimedia Security Joint working conference IFIP TC6 and TC11.*

Sayood, K. (2006). Introduction to Data Compression – Third Edition, San Francisco/CA, Elsevier/Morgan Kaufmann.

Stenborg, K-G. (2005). Distribution and Individual Watermarking of Streamed Content for Copy Protection, Licentiate thesis, Department of Electrical Engineering, Linköping University, Sweden.

Stevens, W. R. (1994). TCP/IP Illustrated, Volume 1 - The Protocols. Addison-Wesley.

Wu, T-. L., & Wu, S. F. (1997, June). Selected encryption and watermarking of MPEG video. In *International Conference on Image Science, Systems, and Technology CISST'97.*

Zhao, H. V., & Liu, K. J. R. (2006, January). Fingerprint Multicast in Secure Video Streaming. In *IEEE Transactions on Image Processing, 15*(1), 12-29.

KEY TERMS

Broadcast: The distributor transmits one packet that reaches all customers.

Compression: Decreasing the amount of data needed to describe a media object. If distortion is added to the media during compression the method is lossy.

Dense Watermark: Watermarks that are embedded in such way that only a small part of a large media object is needed to extract the watermark.

Individual Watermarking: The embedding of a unique mark for each copy of a media object, also known as Fingerprinting.

Multicast: The distributor transmits one packet that reaches all customers belonging to a multicast group.

Scalable Distribution: A distribution method that does not need to transmit the same content many times to reach all recipients, like multicast and broadcast.

Sparse Watermark: Watermarks that are embedded so that a large part of the media object is needed to extract the watermark.

Unicast: The distributor transmits one packet to each customer.

Watermarking: The embedding of a mark within a media object. The mark can later on be retrieved from the media.

Chapter XIX
Critical Analysis of Digital Steganography

Hafiz Malik
University of Michigan, Dearborn, USA

ABSTRACT

This chapter provides critical analysis of current state-of-the-art in steganography. First part of the this chapter provides the classification of steganography based on the underlying information hiding methodology used and covert-channel type, and desired features of the information hiding used for covert communication. This chapter also discusses various known steganalysis techniques developed to counteract the covert-communication and highlights limitations of existing steganographic techniques. Performance analysis of commonly used shareware/freeware steganographic tools and steganalysis tools is also provided in this chapter. Some open problems in covert-communication are also discussed.

INTRODUCTION

The explosive growth of the Web, digital content generation, deployment of ultra high speed networks, and development of P2P technologies to the exchange information has created both tremendous opportunities and new security threats. Advances in digital content generation, manipulation, and distribution technologies have completely changed the way we used to sharing information, do business, market new products, make social networks, etc. Today, marketing a new product, sending pictures, sharing videos etc. is just a matter of few mouse-clicks, which was impossible few years ago. At the same time, however, advances in these technologies have also made covert-communication *drag-and-drop* easy, which poses new security threats; *digital steganography* is one of these treats.

Steganography deals with hiding information into a cover (host or original) signal such that no one other than the intended recipient can detect or

Figure 1. Secret key steganography in the presence of a passive warden (top) and an active warden (bottom)

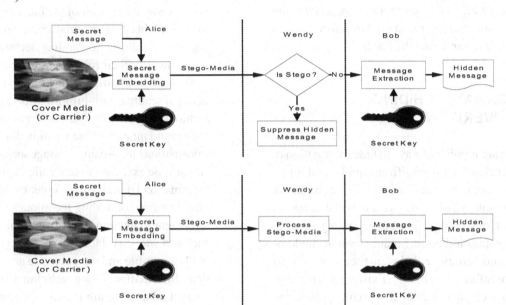

extract the hidden message. The steganographic encoder embeds a message into the cover-signal using a secret key such that perceptual and other distortion constraints are satisfied. A statistical dissimilarity measure between the cover and the stego-signal is generally used to measure the security of a given steganographic method (Cachin, 1998; Zollner et al., 1998; Chandramouli & Memon, 2003).

Steganography can be modeled as a prisoner's problem (Simmons, 1984). For example, consider two prisoners, Alice and Bob, who want to secretly exchange information regarding their escape plan. However, the warden, Wendy, examines every communication between Alice and Bob, and punishes them if steganographic covert communication is detected. In a standard steganographic framework, Alice sends a secrete message, M, to Bob by embedding her secret message into the cover-signal, S, to obtain the stego-signal, X.

Alice then sends X to Bob using a public channel. The warden, who examines the communication channel between Alice and Bob, can be passive or active. A passive warden attempts only to detect a steganographic covert channel. An active warden, on the other hand, deliberately alters every signal exchanged between Alice and Bob, to foil any covert communication between them. The allowable distortion the warden can introduce in the stego-signal depends on the underlying model and the cover-signal used. Figure 1 illustrates secret key steganography for active and passive warden scenarios.

Clearly, Alice and Bob attempt to design the steganographic channel (encoder, secret key, and decoder) such that the warden is unable to distinguish in any sense (statistically as well as perceptually) between the cover-signal and the stego-signal. On the other hand, Wendy tries to detect or estimating the hidden message, M, from the stego-signal, **X**, by using one or several stega-nalysis algorithms. In general, steganalysis must not make any assumption about the underlying steganographic algorithm used to embed a secret message (Chandramouli, 2002).

INFORMATION HIDING: AN OVERVIEW

There are number of ways to hide information in digital content, ranging from simple random bit replacement to sophisticated one based on content adaptation. All of them offer some stealth, but not all of them are equally strong. Exiting existing information hiding techniques exploit random-ness, uncertainty, or "holes" in the cover (or host) file for information hiding. Existing information hiding techniques for steganographic applications can be classified into the following categories:

1. Information Hiding using Noise Replace-ment: Information hiding using *noise replacement* is the simplest technique that replaces noise with the hidden information. The digital media files (audio, video, and images) consists of numbers that represent intensity of light, or sound pressure at a particular point in time or space. These techniques exploit extra precision (usually least significant bits) in these numbers to hide information. Information hiding techniques based on least significant bit substitution, quantization index modulation (QIM) etc. belong to this category.

2. Information hiding using Message Spread-ing: Unlike LSB embedding, these tech-niques spread message information over a number of data points of the cover-file. This makes hidden message less susceptible to detection, either by visual or by statistical attacks. Information hiding techniques that fall in this category use theory of spread-spectrum for message embedding. The

spreading based information hiding tech-niques generally distribute information in such as way that not all of the bits required to reassemble this original data. Spread-ing based information hiding techniques are known for their robustness to active as well as passive warden attack models. Ex-isting spreading based information hiding techniques generally hide information in the redundant part of the multimedia files. Information hiding using message spreading can also be extended to other file formats.

3. Information Hiding using Content Adapta-tion: Information hiding techniques based on content adaptation, embed information in such as a way that statistical characteristics of the stego-file and the cover-file are iden-tical. Information hiding techniques based content adaptation are robust to statistical steganalysis attacks.

4. Information Hiding using Content Structural Adaptation: Content structural adaptation based information hiding is an advanced version of statistical adaptation based information hiding. These techniques use advanced data modeling tools to model hid-den information look like a cover-file; for example, information can be embedded by making secret message look like the tran-script of a cricket match. The message can be embed by selecting between the verbs, nouns, and other parts speech to generate text-file. Data can be recovered by sorting through the text that used to select these words during embedding process.

Data hiding also has several other ap-plications such as copyright protection, ownership protection, fingerprinting, etc. Robustness against active warden attacks is a desirable feature of these applications. In this chapter, however, we shall focus on message embedding for covert com-munication only. This chapter will also highlight weaknesses of commonly used steganographic techniques. In addition, we shall also provide brief overview of existing steganalysis techniques developed to defeat existing steganographic techniques. The following section presents an overview of desirable features and requirements of information hiding for steganographic applications.

INFORMATION HIDING: REQUIREMENTS

An information-hiding scheme is characterized by a number of defining properties. In general, an information-hiding scheme should combat common data manipulations such as lossy compression, A/D and D/A conversions, rescaling, requantization, resampling, filtering, data format conversion, encryption, decryption, and scrambling. In addition, it is also desirable that information hiding technique should also combat active adversary attacks. Following are the desirable features of information-hiding scheme for steganographic application.

- Fidelity: Fidelity of the hidden information is the most important property of information hiding schemes for steganographic application. Fidelity measures the perceptual similarity between the cover-signal and the resulting stego-signal. To achieve this goal, perceptual based information hiding scheme ensures that perceptual distortion, introduced due to information embedding, is kept below human perceptual level, that is, distortion due to information hiding is below the masking threshold of the human auditory system (HAS) for audio data, and the human visual system (HVS) for video and images.
- Capacity: Information hiding capacity for steganographic application refers to the amount of information hidden without be-

ing detected. Information hiding capacity is an application dependent feature, for example, a information hiding schemes developed for copyright protection or copy control applications do not require high data embedding capacity, whereas, information hiding schemes for covert-communication generally require high capacity.

- Blind Detection: Blind detection means cover-signal is not used during information detection/extraction process. If the cover-data is available at the detector during information detection/extraction process, this is referred as *informed* detection. Information hiding technique developed for steganographic application use blind detection.
- Robustness: Robustness measures the ability of embedded data to withstand active warden attacks. Steganographic techniques developed for real-world applications should combat active warden attacks that include lossy compression, A/D and D/A conversions, rescaling, requantization, resampling, filtering, data format conversion, encryption, decryption, and scrambling etc. This is important to mentions that robustness of the hidden information is achieved at the cost of either capacity or fidelity.

STEGANOGRAPHY: STATE-OF-THE-ART

Rapid proliferation of digital multimedia signals on the Internet makes them good candidates as cover-signals. Existing steganographic techniques can be broadly classified into the following major classes:

1. Steganography using LSB Embedding: Rapid proliferation of digital media and the high degree of redundancy in digital representation (despite compression) are the main

Table 1. LSB embedding

Input Sample Value		Message Bit	Output Sample Value	
Decimal	Binary (8 bit rep.)		Decimal	Binary (8 bit rep.)
149	10010101	0	148	10010100
12	00001100	1	13	00001101
201	11001001	0	200	11001000
203	11001011	1	203	11001011
150	10010110	0	150	10010110
15	00001111	0	14	00001110
159	10011111	1	159	10011111
32	00010000	1	33	00010001

motivations for using multimedia data as a cover-signal for steganographic applications. The simplest of the existing steganographic techniques is the LSB steganography. The steganographic techniques based on LSB embedding exploit the fact that in general, multimedia objects are perceptually insensitive to the distortion introduced in the least significant bit plane. These techniques embed the secret message in the cover-signal by replacing (or substituting) the LSB plane of the cover-signal in the spatial/time domain or in the transformed domain. Table 1: LSB Embedding illustrates LSB embedding with an example. Here, an 8-bit secret message "01010011" is embedded into eight samples of the cover-signal.

There exist more than 100 steganographic tools, freely available on the Web, ranging from freeware to user-friendly and more sophisticated commercial products. Most of these steganographic tools use LSB substitution for message embedding. For example, *Stegotif*[1], *Blindside*[2], *Steganos*[3], *S-Tools*[4], etc. embed message in digital images using LSB replacement in pixel domain. Steganographic tools like *EzStego*[5], *Hide and Seek*[6], *GIF-Shuffle*[7], *Gif-It-Up*[8], etc. embed a message in GIF images using LSB substitution of the color palette indices. Whereas, steganographic tools such as *JSteg*[9], *OutGuess*[10], *StegHide*[11], *JP Hide and Seek*[12], *Invisible Secrets*[13], etc. embed secret message in JPEG images by LSB substitution in the quantized coefficients in discrete cosine transform (DCT) domain.

In contrast to the standard LSB embedding, steganographic tools such as *F5*[14], *Hide*[15], etc. increment or decrement the sample/coefficient values to match the LSB plane of the cover to embed secret message. These steganographic methods can also be treated as LSB steganography.

Steganographic techniques based on LSB substitution can only withstand passive warden attacks therefore these techniques may not withstand active warden attacks. This mean in case of LSB steganography, warden can disrupt covert communication between Alice and Bob by simply introducing imperceptible distortion in the stego-media.

2. Steganography using Cover Modeling: Researches in the steganographic community have also developed few complex and more sophisticated steganographic techniques, robust to an active warden as well as statistical attacks. For example, Sallee et al in (Sallee, 2003) and Fridrich et al in Fridrich & Goljan, 2003) have proposed model based steganographic techniques. These techniques insert secret message into the cover-image without perturbing statistical features such as density function of the cover-image. Westfeld et al's in (Westfeld & Pfitzmann, 1999) have shown that the model based steganographic techniques are robust to statistical steganalysis attacks.

3. Steganography using QIM-based Embedding: The quantization index modulation (QIM) based data hiding and its extensions (Chen & Wornell, 2001, 2000) are commonly used for steganography applications due to salient features such as high embedding capacity and direct handle to control robustness of the hidden message and resulting embedding distortion due to message embedding. In addition, QIM based data hiding can also be used for joint compression and message hiding applications, e.g., Jsteg, JP Hide and Seek. The QIM steganography is robust to active warden attacks as long as attack channel distortion is below quantization step used for message embedding.

4. Steganography using Message Spreading: Spread spectrum based steganographic techniques (Marvel, Boncelet, & Retter, 1999; Matsuoka, 2006) take advantage of robustness of the spread spectrum communications against antijamming and de-lectability attacks to embed secret message into the cover-signal. Robustness to active warden attacks is an attractive feature of the spread spectrum steganography. The spread spectrum steganography achieve robustness at the cost of embedding capacity therefore low embedding capacity is one of the limitations of spread spectrum based steganography.

5. Steganography using Network Protocols: The network protocol suit, e.g. Transmission Control Protocol (TCP)/Internet Protocol (IP), also has number of holes in it that can be used as a cover-channel. A number of steganography techniques (Rowland, 1997) have been designed to insert a covert channel into seemingly random TCP/IP fields, such as the IP ID, TCP initial sequence number (ISN) or the least significant bits of the TCP timestamp. While compliant with the TCP/IP specifications, these steganographic techniques generate output is not similar to that an unmodified operating system would generate.

6. Steganography using Executable Files: Covet-communications is not limited to multimedia files or network protocol suit, other files types such as executable files also have "holes" in them that can be exploited for information hiding. For example, Rakan El-Khalil and Angelos D. Keromytis have developed steganographic tool, Hydan[16] that can hide text messages in Windows/DOS. EXE files. Steganographic tool Hydan exploits redundancy in the i386 instruction set and inserts hidden message by defining sets of functionally equivalent instructions, i.e. conceptually grammar-based mimicry. It offers very low embedding capacity, that is, it can embed approximately one byte per 200 instruction bytes while maintaining the original size of the application file. It also supports message encryption feature using Blowfish algorithm.

There exit many steganographic programs that can be used to hide information in wide rage of file format and data types, for example, BMP, GIF, JPEG, MP3, Painbrush (PCX), Portable Network Graphics (PNG), Tag Image File Format (TIFF), WAV, VOC, TXT, etc. A very good list of freeware, shareware, and commercial steganographic tools for DOS, Linux/Unix, MacOS, Windows, OS/2, and other operating systems can be found on StegoArchive.com[17]. In this chapter however we shall consider steganographic tools that embed secret message in digital images and audio files.

ATTACKS ON STEGANOGRAPHY: STEGANALYSIS

Steganalysis refers to detection of the presence of hidden information in the stego-object. Several approaches have been proposed for passive steganalysis. These techniques exploit embedding induced statistical anomalies to discriminate between the stego- and the cover-signal. Next we describe some steganalysis approaches.

Visual Steganalysis

LSB embedding algorithms assume that the LSB plane of the luminance channel in digital images is completely random. However, Westfeld et al (Westfeld & Pfitzmann, 1999) have shown that this assumption is not always true, especially for images containing reasonably large uniform areas (or low-texture images). For example, consider Figure 2 of the cover **Windmill** image (a low-texture image) and the corresponding stego-image. The stego-image was obtained by embedding 11.3K bit message using the steganographic software *Stego*. Figure 3 shows the LSB plane of these two images.

Similarly, LSB planes of the **Baboon** image (a rich-texture image) and the corresponding stego-

image are shown in Figure 5. Here the stego-image was obtained by embedding 2.6 KB of data using the software tool *Stego*. Figure 3 shows that message embedding in low-texture images using LSB embedding method introduces noticeable visual artifacts in the LSB plane of the corresponding stego-image. Therefore, visual inspection of the LSB plane of the test-image can be used to distinguish between the cover- and the stego-image. Westfeld et al in (Westfeld & Pfitzmann, 1999) have shown that visual attacks can successfully detect the stego-image obtained using software, which embed message in pixel domain, e.g., *EzStego*, *Hide and Seek*, *Stego*, and *S-Tools*. We note that even though visual attacks are simple they are highly unreliable especially for rich-texture images. For example, Figure 5 shows that a visual attack will be unable to detect the hidden message by just inspecting the LSB plane of the stego-image. One reason for this is that for rich-texture images the LSB plane is pseudorandom (i.e. $\Pr[x = 1] \approx \Pr[x = 0] \approx \frac{1}{2}$, where x denotes that the values in the LSB plane).

Statistical Learning Based Steganalysis

Universal steganalysis techniques make no assumption about the statistical properties of the stego-signal. Instead statistics of some features are learnt using a large training data set of cover and stego signals. Some metric that is a function of the feature statistics is used to discriminate between cover and stego. Therefore, universal steganalysis techniques, in general, consist of two major stages:

1) feature generation and feature selection stage to extract feature vectors from the training data set based on some feature selection criteria, and

2) classification stage that uses the extracted feature vectors learn a classifier for cover-stego discrimination.

*Figure 2. Windmill cover (left) and the corresponding stego-image (right) carrying 11.2K bit message and obtained using steganographic software **Stego***

Figure 3. Least significant bit (LSB) plane of the cover (left) and the corresponding stego-image (right). Here black pixel stands for LSB = 0 and white for LSB = 1

Some universal steganalysis techniques (Farid, 2002, 2001; Avcibas, Celik, Sharma & Tekalp, 2004; Lyu & Farid, 2002, 2004, 2006) can detect steganographic tools such as *S-Tools, F5, OutGuess, Hide, JP Hide and Seek, EzStego,* etc. with reasonable accuracies.

Universal steganalysis techniques generally use supervised learning to train a statistical classifier. First, a *k*-dimensional feature vector is estimated from the training data set during the learning phase. Many of these techniques (Farid, 2002, 2001; Celik et al., 2004; Lyu & Farid, 2002, 2004, 2006) select this *k*-dimensional feature vector heuristically. Feature vectors that consist of higher-order statistics are widely used. The classifier then learns the best classification rule using the input feature vectors for each steganographic method. These techniques use sophisticated machine learning tools such as linear regressions analysis based on Fisher linear discriminant (FLD), support vector machine (SVM), principal component analysis (PCA) (Duda & Hart, 1973),

*Figure 4. Baboon cover (left) and the corresponding stego-image (right) carrying a 16K bit message obtained using steganographic software **Stego***

Figure 5. LSB plane of the cover (left) and the corresponding stego-image (right)

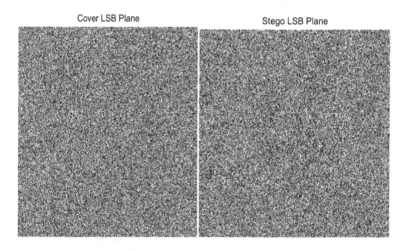

etc. for the classification stage. Therefore, to design a universal steganalysis technique based on feature selection and classification involves independent problems: good feature selection and classifier design to obtain a low stego classification rate. Obviously, choosing features capable of accurately capturing the statistical irregularities introduced by an embedding algorithm is critical. The chosen features must have good prediction accuracy and a monotonic relationship with the embedded message size. Recently, Wang et al (Wang & Moulin, 2006) have proposed a feature selection criterion for learning based steganalysis.

Some learning based steganalysis approaches include the following.

- Farid's steganalysis (Farid, 2001) is an early work based on universal steganalysis. This technique uses a $24(n - 1)$-dimensional feature vector, where n is the number of muli-resolution decomposition scales. The feature vectors consist of first- and higher-order statistics and the transform co-efficient prediction error of a multi-resolution decomposed natural image. It is shown these features computed for natural images are relatively consistent. Steganographic tools such as *JSteg, OutGuess, StegHide, JP Hide and Seek*, and *EzStego* have been found to affect these features in the discrete wavelet transform (DWT) domain. The $24(n-1)$-dimensional feature vector consists of $12(n-1)$-dimensional coefficient statistics and $12(n-1)$-dimensional linear prediction error statistics. The feature vector is then used to train a linear FLD classifier.

Lyu and Farid (Farid, 2002; Lyu & Farid, 2002, 2004, 2006) later extended the learning based steganalysis scheme using higher-order image statistics. Advanced classifiers such as linear SVM, non-linear SVM, and one-class SVM are used. For example, Lyu et al's proposed technique (Lyu & Farid, 2006) uses a 432-dimensional vector estimated from the four level wavelet decomposition and three-level local angular harmonic decomposition (LAHD) of color images in the RGB color space. Feature vector used in (Lyu & Farid, 2006) consists of 108 magnitude statistics (e.g., mean, variance, skewness, and kurtosis), 108 error statistics and 216 phase statistics. Comparisons of the detection performances of the proposed stegnalysis methods for linear SVM, non-linear SVM and one-class SVM, to detect steganographic tools such as *JSteg, OutGuess, StegHide, JP Hide and Seek*, and *F*5 are presented. It is observed that a non-linear SVM classifier performs better than a linear SVM classifier for a given steganographic algorithm. In addition, one-class SVM classifier results in modest performance degradation while offering a simpler training stage. The results also indicate that at low embedding rates the detection performance deteriorates significantly irrespective of the underlying

steganographic algorithm used for message embedding. It is interesting to notice that a larger feature space yields only a marginal improvement in the stego detection rate.

- Celik et al (Celik et al., 2004) propose another supervised learning based steganalysis technique to detect LSB embedding. A rate-distortion feature vector is used. They assume that rate required to represent the seven most significant bits (MSB), R_{7MSB}, of a cover-image, I_c, is approximately equal to the rate required to represent 7 MSB plus the LSB plane with all ones, $R_{7MSB}(I_c+\mathbf{1})$, that is,

$$R_{7MSB}(I_c) \approx R_{7MSB}(I_c+\mathbf{1}) \qquad (1)$$

where $\mathbf{1}$ is a matrix of all ones. But, Eq. (1) may not necessarily hold for a stego-image I_s, as in case of stego-image following inequality is likely to hold,

$$R_{7MSB}(I_s) \le R_{7MSB}(I_s+\mathbf{1}) \qquad (2)$$

Therefore a normalized difference between these rates can be used as the distinguishing feature, that is, the feature is

$$\Psi R(I_c) = \frac{\Delta R(I_c)}{\Delta R(\tilde{I}_c)} \qquad (3)$$

where $\Delta R(I_c)$ is defined as,

$$\Delta R(I_c) = \left| R_{7MSB}(I_c) - R_{7MSB}(I_c+\mathbf{1}) \right| \qquad (4)$$

Here, $\tilde{I}_c$ denotes the modified image obtained by randomizing the LSB plane of the test-image to combat false positives due to under/over exposed regions in the cover-image. The estimated feature vector is projected onto a low dimensional subspace using the Karhunen-Loeve (KL) transform.

Feature vector in the subspace is then used to train a Bayes classifier. As observed from the simulation results presented in (Celik et al., 2004) the detection performance of this technique depends on the embedding rate.

- Fridrich et al (Fridrich, 2004) propose learning based steganalysis to detect JPEG stego-images. They use a 23-dimensional feature vector to train a linear LFD classifier. Feature vector used during the training phase consists of the following: 1) local and global first- and second-order statistics of discrete cosine transform (DCT) coefficients, 2) "*blockiness*" (or artifacts) in spatial domain, and 3) pair-wise correlation in neighboring blocks (or *co-occurrence factor*) estimated from the difference between the stego-image and an estimate of cover-image. The decompressed stego-image is cropped by 4 pixels from the top and left. The resulting cropped image is then recompressed using same JPEG quantization table to obtain an estimate of the cover image. It is seen that the detection performance of this technique depends on the hidden message length.

- Sullivan et al (Sullivan, Bi, Madhow, Chandrasekaran, & Manjunath, 2004) have proposed supervised learning based steganalysis technique to attack QIM steganography. Empirical probability mass function (PMF) estimated using a histogram with 300 bins from the test-image in the DCT domain acts as a feature vector. However, details about the classifier are not presented in their paper. It is seen that the detection performance depends on:
  1. quantization step-size used to embed the message using QIM steganography, and
  2. the embedding rate.

Model Based Steganalysis

Model based steganalysis generally assumes a suitable statistical non-parametric or parametric model for the cover and stego signals. Detection statistic is then derived using these models (Fridrich & Goljan, 2002; Malik, Subbalakshmi, & Chandramouli, 2008). Statistical analysis based on first- and second-order statistics of the test-image (i.e. mean and variance), Chi-square (χ^2) tests, etc. are commonly used to distinguish between the stego and the cover-signals.

Some non-learning and parametric model based steganalysis techniques can be found in (Westfeld & Pfitzmann, 1999; Fridrich, Goljan, Hogea, & Soukal, 2003; Malik, Subbalakshmi, & Chandramouli, 2007a; Malik et al., 2008; Trivedi & Chandramouli, 2005). A brief overview of some of these techniques is described below.

- Trivedi et al (Trivedi & Chandramouli, 2003, 2004, 2005) propose a steganalysis technique to detect sequential steganography (Marvel et al., 1999). They discuss a theoretical framework to detect abrupt changes in the stego-image statistics, which can be used to distinguish between the cover- and the stego-images. A locally most powerful (LMP) sequential hypothesis is designed to detect the secret key.

- Malik et al (Malik, Subbalakshami, & Chandramouli, 2007a, 2008) proposed a technique nonparametric steganalysis of QIM based embedding (Chen & Wornell, 2001, 2000). This paper proposes a nonparametric steganalysis method for quantization index modulation (QIM) based steganography. The proposed steganalysis method uses irregularity (or randomness) in the test-image to distinguish between the cover- and the stego-image. They have shown that plain-quantization (quantization without message embedding) induces regularity in the resulting quantized-image; whereas message embedding using QIM increases irregularity in the resulting QIM-stego image. *Approximate entropy*, an algorithmic entropy measure, is used to quantify irregularity in the test-image. Simulation results presented in (Malik, Subbalakshami, & Chandramouli, 2007a, 2008) show that the proposed steganalysis technique can reliably distinguish between the cover- and the stego-image with low false rates. In addition, the proposed scheme in (Malik, Subbalakshami, & Chandramouli, 2007a, 2008) can also be used to detect stego-images obtained using dither modulation (Chen & Wornell, 2001, 2000).

- Malik et al in (Malik, Subbalakshami, & Chandramouli, 2007b, 2007c, Malik 2008) also proposed steganalysis technique to attack QIM steganography. The proposed scheme is based on the observation that message embedding using QIM introduces local irregularity (or randomness) in the cover-object. The proposed steganalysis technique exploits rich spatial/temporal correlation in the multimedia-objects to estimate local irregularity in the test-object. The underlying density function based on local irregularity in the test-object is estimated in a systematic manner using a kernel density estimate (KDE) method. The *Tsallis-divergence*, a parametric divergence method, is used to quantify irregularity in the test-object. The *Tsallis-divergence* between the density function estimated from the test-object and its doubly-quantized version is used to distinguish between the cover and the stego. Simulation results presented for these message embedding parameters show that the proposed method can successfully distinguish between the quantized-cover and the QIM-stego with low false alarm rates. The proposed nonparametric steganalysis scheme in (Malik, Subbalakshami, & Chandramouli, 2007b, 2007c, Malik 2008) can also be used to detect JPEG stego-images obtained using JSteg steganographic tool.

EXISTING STEGANOGRAPHIC TOOLS

This section provides critical analysis few commonly used steganographic tools (freely available on the Web) such as GIF-Shuffle, GIF-It-Up, EzStego, S-Tools, JSteg, F5, JP-Hide-and-Seek, OutGuess, and MP3Stego.

GIF-Shuffle

GIF-Shuffle is a freeware developed by Matthew Kwan[18] that embeds messages in color GIF images by shuffling the indices of color palettes, which leaves the image visibly unchanged. It works with all GIF images, including those with transparency and animation, and provides compression and encryption of the hidden message. It has small capacity and support GIF image format only. It embeds message in spatial domain by shuffling the indices of color palette of the cover-image in GIF format based on the message bits.

- Attacking GIF-Shuffle: The color palette of the test-image in GIF format can be used to successfully attack steganographic techniques that embed message bits in palette based images by changing LBS of the cover-image palette indices. As GIF-Shuffle steganographic tool also uses LBS substitution in the color image in GIF format, therefore it is also susceptible to such visual attacks. To support this claim, a stego-image is obtained by embedding 8K bit message using GIF-Shuffle, both the stego-image and the corresponding cover-image are given in Figure 6. The color palettes of both GIF image are given in Figure 7. It can be observed from Figure 7 that color palettes of the stego-image are more irregular than the corresponding cover-image. Therefore irregularity in the palettes of the test-image can be used to distinguish between the cover and the stego image in GIF format.

GIF-It-Up

It is a freeware steganographic tool by Nelsonsoft that hides information in both color and grayscale GIF-cover images by replacing LSBs of color palette indices and generates GIF-stego images. This steganographic tool also provides message encryption option. The GUI of the steganographic tool downloaded from[19] along with stego-image obtained using GIF-It-Up steganographic tool and the corresponding cover-image are given in Figure 8.

- Attacking GIF-It-Up: The palette of the test-image in GIF format can be used to successfully attack steganographic techniques that embed message bits by replacing LBSs of palette indices of the cover-image. As GIF-It-Up steganographic tool also embeds message bits by replacing them with LSB of palette indices of the cover-image, therefore simple visual attack can be use to defeat such steganographic tools. To verify this claim, stego-image is obtained by embedding 8K bit message using GIF-It-Up steganographic tool. Palettes of both the cover- and the stego-image are given in Figure 9. It can be observed from Figure 9 that palettes of the stego-image are more irregular than the corresponding cover-image, which can be used to distinguish between the cover and the stego image in GIF format.

EzStego

This is a freeware steganographic tool developed by Romana Machado[20]. It embeds message in the color images in GIF format. EzStego copies the palette from the image. It rearranges the copy of the palette so that colors that are near to each other in the color model are near to each other in the palette. EzStego replaces the message bit with the least significant bit of the indices of pixels in the cover-image using following embedding rule:

- Find the index of the pixel's RGB color in the sorted palette.
- Get one bit from the input file. Replace the least significant bit of the index.
- Find the new RGB color that the index now points to in the sorted palette.
- Find the index of the new RGB color in the original palette.
- Change the pixel to the index of the new RGB color.

- Attacking EzStego: As EzStego steganographic tool also embeds message bits by replacing LBSs of palette indices of the cover-image, therefore simple visual attack can be used to defeat it. In addition many

Figure 6. Stego-image obtained by embedding 8K bit message using GIF-Shuffle steganographic tool (left) and the corresponding cover-image (right)

Figure 7. Color palette of the GIF Stego-image obtained by embedding 8K bit message using GIF-Shuffle steganographic tool (left) and the color palette of the GIF corresponding cover-image (right)

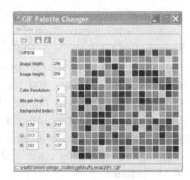 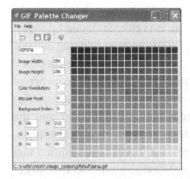

Figure 8. The GUI of steganographic tool GIF-It-Up, stego-image obtained by embedding 8K bits message (left), and the corresponding cover-image (right)

Figure 9. Palettes of the GIF stego-image obtained by embedding 8K bit message using GIF-It-Up steganographic tool (left) and the palettes of the GIF corresponding cover-image (right)

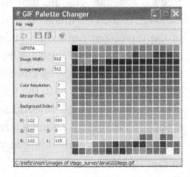 

researchers have also developed both the universal and the model based steganalysis techniques to detect GIF-stego images generated using EzStego. For example, Fridrich et al in (Fridrich, Goljan, Hogea, & Soukal, 2003) have proposed steganalysis technique to defeat EzStego. Their proposed technique uses perturbation in sequence of color pairs obtained by sorting color palettes to distinguish between the cover and the stego. Fridrich et al in (Fridrich, Goljan, Hogea, & Soukal, 2003) have claimed that natural images exhibit considerable structure due to smaller number of colors, and this natural structure is disturbed during message embedding process using *EzStego*. As a result, a sorted sequence consisting of color palette obtained from the stego-image exhibits higher entropy (or randomness) than sequence of color palette of the corresponding cover-image. Fridrich et al's steganalysis technique in (Fridrich, Goljan, Hogea, & Soukal, 2003) used measure of randomness in the sorted sequence, consisting of color palette, to detect the stego. Moreover, measure of randomness in the sorted sequence is also used to estimate length of the hidden message.

S-Tools

The S-Tools is one of the most ambitious steganographic tool available on the web by Andy Brown. S-Tools is a freeware steganographic tool that can hide information in both the images and the sound files. It can hide information in GIF and BMP images files, and WAV audio files. It can also hide information one an unallocated sectors of the disk. S-Tools uses LSB substitution to embed secret message and resulting image is saved in GIF or BMP image format.

Each of S-Tools's three programs offers encryption of the hidden message option. The S-Tools support commonly known encryption algorithms such as Data Encryption Standard (DES), International Data Encryption Algorithm (IDEA), Message Digest Cipher (MDC) or Triple-DES. The S-Tools provides nice GUI for message embedding/extraction. The Figure 10 gives snapshot of GUI of the S-Tools steganographic tool along with stego-image obtained by embedding 64K bit message and the corresponding cover-image. Similarly, Figure 11 gives GUI of the S-Tools steganographic tool along with stego-audio obtained by embedding 64K bit message and the corresponding cover-audio files both in WAV format.

- Attacking S-Tools: As S-Tools steganographic tool also embed message bits by replacing them with LSBs of the palette indices of the cover-image, therefore simple visual attack can be use to defeat it. For example, palettes of the stego-image obtained by embedding 64K bit message using S-Tools and the corresponding cover-image (see Figure 11) are given in Figure 13. It can be observed from Figure 13 that regularity in the palettes of the test-image in GIF format can be used to distinguish between the cover-image and the stego-image.

JSteg

JSteg is the first generation of steganographic tools developed by Derek Upham that embeds information in JPEG image format. JSteg is a freeware steganographic tool that hides secret message in the GIF image by replacing the LSBs of the quantized run-length coded DCT coefficients with the secret message bits, during JPEG compression process. The embedding algorithm skips all coefficients with the values '0' or '1'. It offers reasonably high embedding capacity (e.g. around 13% of the cover-image size). Pseudo-code of JSteg message embedding algorithm is given in Figure 14.

- Attacking JSteg: JSteg is robust to visual attacks as message embedding takes place in the transformed domain e.g. in DCT domain. Message embedding using JSteg, however, introduces serious statistical signature that can be used to attack JSteg. The coefficients of JPEG compression of natural images normally fall along a bell curve, but information embedding using LSB substitution in the quantized coefficients usually distorts this characteristic. More specifically, message embedding using JSteg introduces dependency between the pair of coefficient's frequency of occurrence. This is due to the fact that JSteg steganographic tool uses sequential embedding to embed message bits in the quantized AC coefficients of the cover image. This makes it susceptible to first-order statistical attacks. Westfeld et al in (Westfeld & Pfitzmann, 1999) have shown that steganographic techniques that embed message by replacing LSB of the cover-signal introduce detectable traces and so does JStego. Westfeld et al in (Westfeld & Pfitzmann, 1999) have proposed steganalysis technique, named stegodetect, based on chi-square (χ^2)-test to detect LBS steganography (further details on χ^2-test are provided in Section 6). To attack JSteg using stegdetect, a JPEG-stego image was generated using JSteg steganographic tool downloaded from[21] by embedding 1K bit message. Snapshot of the GUI of stegdetect steganalysis tool along with detection results when applied to JPEG-stego image, "LenaJstegC.jpg", generated using JSteg steganographic tool is given in Figure 15. It can be observed from Figure 15 that stegdetect has successfully detected JPEG-stego image though carrying small hidden message, e.g. 1K bits.

Many steganalysis schemes have also been developed to attack JSteg, these schemes generally by exploit traces in the JPEG-stego images introduced due to message embedding using JSteg. For example, recently Malik et al in (Malik, Subalakshami, & Chandramouli 2007, Malik 2008) have proposed nonparametric framework based on local irregularity in the JPEG-image to detect JPEG-stego image obtained using JSteg. Malik et al in (Malik, Subalakshami, & Chandramouli 2007, Malik 2008) have shown that message embedding using LSB steganography disturbs local similarity in the resulting JPEG-stego image that can be used to detect JPEG-stego images obtained using JSteg steganographic tool. Their pro-

Figure 10. Snapshot GUI of the S–Tools steganographic tool, stego-image (left) and the corresponding cover-image (right)

Figure 11. GUI of the S–Tools steganographic tool, stego-audio (left) and the corresponding cover-image (right) both in WAV format

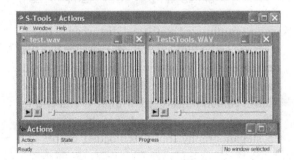

Figure 12. The signal level comparison between WAV files, cover-audio (top), stego-audio obtained by embedding 64 Kbit message using S-Tools (middle), and the embedding distortion due to message embedding (bottom)

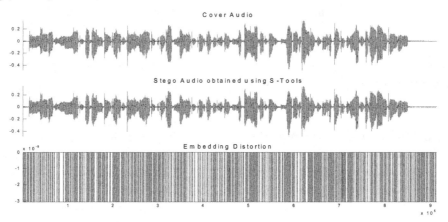

Figure 13. Palettes of the GIF stego-image obtained by embedding 64 K bit message using S-Tools steganographic tool (left) and palettes of the GIF corresponding cover-image (right)

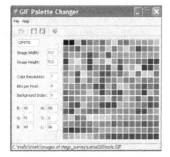 

posed schemes have successfully detected JPEG-stego images with low false rates.

F5

It is a freeware steganographic tool that is based on the F5 algorithm developed by Pfitzmann and Westfeld (Pfitzmann & Westfeld, 2001). It is an advanced version of steganographic algorithms that embed message in the JPEG images by replacing LSBs of the quantized coefficients in DCT domain with message bits e.g. F3, F4 and JSteg. As first generation of steganographic tools that

embed message in JPEG images introduce detectable traces that can be detected using first-order statistical attacks. F5 was developed to combat limitations of first generation steganographic tools for JPEG steganography. F5 steganographic algorithm embeds information in a more systematic way to minimized statistical disturbance due to message embedding. It embeds message bits that decreases absolute value of the non-zero quantized AC coefficients of the cover-image by one. Matrix embedding is used to improve embedding efficiency i.e. minimal number of changes per bit. F5 steganography tool downloaded from[22] is a

Figure 14. Pseudo-code of JSteg message embedding algorithm

Input: message bits, cover image, quality_factor
Output: stego image in JPEG format
XDCT = quantized (cover image, quality_factor, DCT)
while   data left to embed **do**
        get next quantized coefficient from the cover image
        if XDCT 0 & XDCT 1 **then**
                get next message bit
                replace LBS of XDCT with message bit
        end if
        insert XDCT into stego image
end while

Figure 15. Snapshot of stegdetect steganalysis tool when applied to JPEG-stego image (LenaJstegC.jpg) obtained using JSteg steganographic tool by embedding 1K bit message

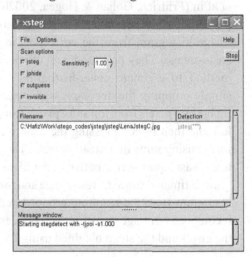

preliminary version to embed files into true color images in BMP, GIF, or JPEG format and generates JPEG stego-images. The snapshot of the GUI of F5 steganographic tools downloaded from[19] is given in Figure 16. It can be observed from the GUI that F5 algorithm accepts five parameters, e.g. 1) input image file (BMP, GIF or JPEG), 2) stego-image file name, 3) message file name, 4) quality factor of the stego-image, and 5) user password to be used as seed for PRNG.

- Embedding Algorithm: In the message embedding process, for a given message length and number of nonzero quantized AC coefficients are used to determine the best matrix embedding that introduces minimal number of modification in the cover-image due to message embedding. The F5 steganographic algorithm can be divided into the following steps:

- RGB representation of the cover-image.
- Calculate quantization table using user provided quality factor that is used for quantization.
- Compute embedding capacity without matrix embedding using following expression,

$$C = h_{AC} - \left(h_{AC}(0) + 0.51h(1) \right) \quad (5)$$

where h_{AC} is the number of quantized AC coefficients in DCT domain, $h_{AC}(0)$ is number of quantized AC coefficients equal to zero, and $h_{AC}(1)$ is number of quantized coefficients equal 1. It is important to mention that $0.51h_{AC}(1)$ is the estimated capacity loss due *shrinkage.*

- Estimated capacity, C, and message length, L, are used to determine the best matrix embedding.
- User specified password (e.g. Paraphrase: "123456" in the Figure 16) is used to generate a seed for PRNG, which is used to select random coefficients for message embedding. The PRNG is also used to generate pseudo-random bit-stream, which is used as one-time-pad to encrypt message bit stream.
- Encrypted message is divided into non-overlapping segments, each of k bits, to be embedded into a group of $2^k - 1$ nonzero quantized AC coefficients. During embedding process, if the hash of the selected group of coefficients does not match to the message bits, the absolute value of one of the selected coefficients is decreased by one to obtain a match. This embedding process may

Figure 16. Snapshot of the GUI of the F5 steg-anographic tool downloaded from[19]

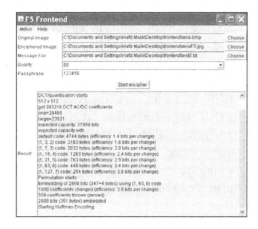

result *shrinkage*, that is, modified coefficient become zero. If shrinkage does take place, then the same *k* bit message is re-embedded into next group of $2^k - 1$ nonzero quantized AC coefficients.

- If the message length, *L*, satisfies the estimated C, i.e. $L \leq C$, message embedding will take place, otherwise an error message is displayed.

To illustrate message embedding using F5, we embedded 2808 bits message into Lena image of 512x512 pixels using F5 steganographic tool downloaded from[19]. Snapshot of the GUI for this message embedding is shown in Figure 16 and resulting stego-image and the corresponding cover-image are give in Figure 17. The Figure 17 clearly shows that the stego-image is perceptually very similar to the cover-image.

- Attacking F5: The F5 algorithm is robust to first-order statistical attacks, however it still leaves traces due to message embedding that can be exploited to defeat F5. Many steganalysis techniques have been proposed to attach F5, for example, Fridrich et al in (Fridrich, Goljan & Hogea, 2002b) have proposed steganalysis technique that successfully attacked F5 steganography algorithm. To break F5 algorithm Fridrich et al in (Fridrich, Goljan & Hogea, 2002b) proposed a simple method to estimate cover-image histogram from the corresponding stego-image. They proposed a an efficient method to estimate cover-histogram by simply cropping the decompressed stego-image by 4 pixels from top and 4 pixels from left and then re-compressing the resulting image using same quantization table. They used least square error between the histogram estimated from the test-image and the histogram from the resulting cropped and recompressed image to distinguish between the cover and the stego obtained using F5.

Figure 17. Stego-image obtained by embedding 2808 bits using F5 steganographic tool (left) and the corresponding cover-image (right)

Figure 18. The GUI of JP-Hide-and-Seek for Windows

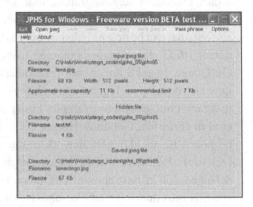

JP-Hide-and-Seek

JP-Hide-and-Seek (JPHS) is a freeware steganographic tools developed by Allan Latham that embeds a secret message in color jpeg images. The JPHS also embeds message bits by replacing LSBs of the quantized DCT coefficients during JPEG compression process. It also uses Blowfish crypto algorithm to encrypt hidden message before embedding. The JPHS steganographic tool downloaded from[23] has a nice GUI for Windows operating system. Snapshot of the GUI of JPHS for embedding 32K bit message in 512x512 pixels Lena image is given in Figure 18; and Figure 19 gives resulting stego- and the corresponding cover-image.

- Attacking JP-Hide: Like other transformed domain embedding steganographic techniques, JP-Hide is also robust to visual attacks. However, it also introduces serious statistical signature that can be used defeat it. Statistical irregularities introduces can easily be detected by applying first-order statistical attack based on χ^2-test. To verify this claim, JPEG-stego image in Figure 19 is analyzed using stegdetect steganalysis tool. Snapshot of the GUI of the stegdetect is given in Figure 20. It can be observed that stegdetect has correctly detected the steganographic tool used for message embedding.

OutGuess

Outguess is a freeware universal steganographic tool written by Nile Provos[24]. It uses LSB substitution to embed message bits in the quantized coefficients of the cover-image in DCT domain but in a careful way to ensure minimal statistical disturbance due to message embedding. To combat first-order statistical attacks based χ^2-test (Westfeld & Pfitzmann, 1999). The embedding algorithm first identifies potential information carrier coefficients but then rules out half of them to minimizing statistical disturbance due to message embedding. More specifically, embedding algorithm can be divided into two phases, that is,

Figure 19. Stego-image by embedding 32 K bit message using steganographic tool JPHS (left) and the corresponding cover-image (right)

Figure 20. Stego detection results when stegdetect steganalysis tool is applied to JPEG-stego image (lenaJPHS.jpg) obtained using JPHS stegnographic tool

1) message embedding phase, and 2) modification balancing phase. In the message-embedding phase, like JSteg, OutGuess also embed message bits along random walk using LSB substitution and skipping 1s and 0s. Whereas, during balancing phase, corrections are made to the modified coefficients to balance out changes introduced during message embedding phase. During correction phase, each time an LSB of a selected coefficient is flipped to hide information bit then algorithm searches another bit suitable coefficient to flip its LSB to maintain a balanced statistical profile. Motivation behind balanced changes during message embedding is that message embedding using LSB substitution in quantized DCT coefficients introduces first-order statistical changes in the compressed JPEG coefficients; which can be used to detect JPEG-stego images. One limitation of the OutGuess steganographic tool is that it offers embedding capacity one-half of the true available capacity. The OutGuess software can be modified to work with any data format.

- Attacking OutGuess: The OutGuess steganographic tool was developed to counter statistical attacks based on χ^2-test (Westfeld & Pfitzmann, 1999). However it still leaves traces in the stego-image that can be use to attack OutGuess steganographic tool. For example, version 13 of stegdetect steganalysis tool (that can be downloaded from[24]) can detect JPEG stego-images obtained using OutGuess. In addition, many researchers have also developed steganalysis techniques to attack OutGuess. For example, Fridrich et al in (Fridrich, Goljan & Hogea, 2002a) proposed threshold free framework to attack OutGuess. Fridrich et al in (Fridrich, Goljan & Hogea, 2002a) have shown that OutGuess actually introduces spatial *blockiness* in the resulting JPEG-stego image that can be used to attack OutGuess. Their proposed steganalysis technique used estimated *blockiness* feature along with estimated macroscopic quantity $S(L)$, which is a function of hidden message length to detect JPEG-stego image obtained using OutGuess. Simulation results presented in (Fridrich, Goljan & Hogea, 2002a) indicate that the proposed technique not only detect JPEG-stego image but also accurately estimates the length of the hidden message.

MP3Stego[25]

The MP3Stego is a freeware steganographic tool developed by Fabien Petitcolas[26] that hides information Windows WAV files during audio compression using MPEG-1 Audio Layer-III encoder. The CD quality audio WAV file is generally consists of 16 bit samples, sampled at 44.1 kHz, which results 705.7 kbits/s bit stream (in case of mono audio stream). The MP3Stego steganographic tool can also be used to compress CD quality audio using the following command,

encode *test.wav test.mp3*

Here, resulting MP3 file, test.mp3, still maintains the same sound quality with only 128 kbits/s. For a given bit rate, MEPG-1 Layer-III compression achieves the highest sound quality compared with other audio coding schemes. Popularity of MP3 file format for digital audio is probability the main driving force behind using it for steganography. The MP3Stego can embed the message (e.g. message.txt) in the MPEG-1 Layer-III stream while compressing input WAV file. Embedding algorithm first compresses the secret message, *message.txt*, using zlib[27] tool. To dilute the traces of message embedding in the resulting stego-audio, the compressed secret message is encrypted using passphrase (e.g. *malik123*) using triple-DES. Following command can be used to hide message.txt in test.wav audio file,

encode -E *hidden.txt* -P *malik123 test.wav test-stego.mp3*

Message embedding takes place during the MPEG-1 Layer-III encoding, which is a combination of two nested iterative loops, e.g. *inner-loop* used for quantization and message embedding. The inner-loop is used to fine an optimal quantization step-size (or q_factor) for a given block length (or the number of bits). If number of bits resulting from a given q_factor exceeds number of bits available budget to encode a given chunk of data then current q_factor is increased by adjusting the global gain. This process is repeated with increasing q_factor until the resulting block length is smaller than the available budget (or max_block_length).

- Message Embedding Algorithm: For message embedding, if a message-bit 0 (or 1), the inner iteration loop will repeat until an optimal q_factor is found for a given block length, which results an even (or odd) block length and if the resulting block length is not larger than the max_length. Following observation can be made from the algorithm to embed message in MPEG-1 Layer-III stream:

1. Algorithm will run into an endless loop when the block length is already 0 and hidden bit is 1. However occurrence of an endless loop during message embedding is very rare for real-world audio signals.

2. By increasing q_factor by one does not automatically flip the LSB of the block length. Generally, the block length is decreased by a value greater than one. This mean, to embed a message-bit, the LSB of the block_length might remain the same for several iterations. For example, A Westfeld in (Westfeld, A. 2002) has reported that to embed one bit they observed on average 15 (consecutive) unsuccessful iterations per track.

Like other steganographic tools MP3Stego also introduces embedding distortion due to message embedding but that embedding distortion is well below average human perceptual level and a warden probably need *golden ears* to notice it. Therefore, without the original music file, it would be difficult for a steganographer to distinguish between MP3-stego and MP3-cover. Snapshots of the GUI of the latest version of MP3Stego steganographic tool when used for message embedding in audio file is given in Figure 21.

- Attack on MP3Stego: Like every steganographic scheme, MP3Stego also leaves traces of message embedding in the resulting MP3-stego file that can be used to defeat it. For example, it can be observed from message embedding algorithm that it reduces block length in the resulting MP3 stego file, which will result smaller bit rate than the requested bit rate. More specifically, for a fixed max_length value the resulting MP3-stego would have lower bit rate than the MP3-cover (MP3 file carrying no message) both obtained using MP3Stego tool and same bit rate. To achieve requested average bit rate (say 128 kbits/s), max_length need to be adjusted for each frame by the rate control process. The MP3Stego handles this problem as follow, every time the block length is decreased due to message bit embedding, block-length of the following blocks are increased to achieve target bit rate. Therefore, both the MP3-stego and the MP3-cover obtained from the same WAV file should have equal size. This results same average block length for both the MP3-stego and the MP3-cover but different block length variance, which can be used to distinguish between the MP3-stego and the MP3-cover. Westfeld in (Westfeld, 2002) proposed steganalysis scheme to attack MP3Stego by exploiting irregularity in the variance of the block length of the MP3 file. Simulation results reported in (Westfeld, 2002) show that the proposed steganalysis scheme successfully detected MP3-stego, obtained using MP3Stego steganography tool. In addition, the proposed scheme in (Westfeld, 2002) can also detect MP3-stego

carrying very small message, e.g. 5% of the full capacity.

STEGANALYSIS SOFTWARE TOOLS

This section provides a brief overview of some of the available shareware/freeware tools used for steganalysis.

Stegdetect[28] is a freeware steganalysis tool that is can be used to detect stego-images obtained using steganographic tools that embed message using LBS substitution such as *JSteg, F5, JPHS,* and *Invisible Secrets*[29]. Stegdetect steganalysis tool uses statistical analysis based on χ^2-test to distinguish between the cover- and the stego-images. Stegdetect steganalysis technique (Westfeld & Pfitzmann, 1999) exploits the fact that message embedding using LSB substitution leaves detectable traces. Westfeld et al in (Westfeld & Pfitzmann, 1999) have observed that for a given image embedding of high entropy data (message consisting of equally probable symbols) disturbs histogram of color frequencies that can be used

Figure 21. Snapshot of the GUI of the latest version of MP3Stego (top left), message encoding (top right), and message decoding (bottom)

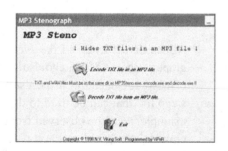
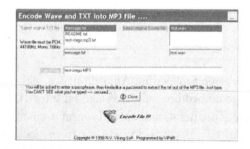
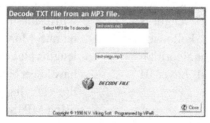

Figure 22. The signal level comparison between MP3 files; MP3-cover [MP3 file carrying no message] (top) and MP3-stego [MP3 file carrying 1K bit message embedded using MP3Stego] (bottom)

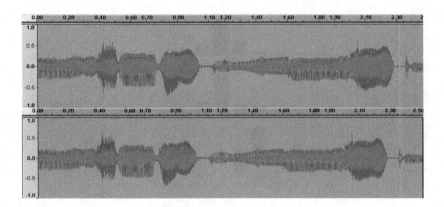

for stego detection. Their proposed algorithm in (Westfeld & Pfitzmann, 1999) assumes that embedding process changes the LSB of the colors in the cover image. Let h_i and h_i^* denote frequencies of the color indices before and after embedding respectively. Westfeld et al in (Westfeld & Pfitzmann, 1999) have observed that if $h_{2i} > h_{2i+1}$ then embedding uniformly distributed message tend to change h_{2i} to h_{2i+1} more frequently then the other way around. Based on the above assumptions the following inequality is likely hold,

$$\left| h_{2i} - h_{2i+1} \right| \geq \left| h_{2i}^* - h_{2i+1}^* \right|. \qquad (6)$$

This means embedding uniformly distributed message reduces frequency difference between adjacent colors, which is also true for JPEG images. In case of JPEG images, differences in the DCT coefficients frequency used instead of color frequencies. To illustrate this observation, histogram of DCT quantized coefficients before and after a hidden message in JPEG image and their difference is given in Figure 23. Here JPEG-stego image is obtained by embedding 10.6K bit message in grayscale Lena image of 256x256 pixels. It can be observed from Figure 23 that there is reduction in the frequency difference between coefficient −1 and coefficient −2 in DCT domain; similarly

reduction in frequency difference coefficients −3 & −4, between 2 & 3, and between 4 & 5.

Westfeld et al's stegdetect steganalysis algorithm proposed (Westfeld & Pfitzmann, 1999) used χ^2–test to determined whether observed frequency distribution, y_i, in the test-image matches expected distribution, y_i^*, estimated from the stego-image. The expected distribution y_i^* is estimated based on the assumption that the sum of adjacent DCT coefficients remains invariant during message embedding process. Let h_i denotes DCT histogram of the test-image, then expected distribution is calculated using arithmetic mean of the adjacent frequencies, i.e.

$$y_i^* = \frac{(h_{2i} + h_{2i+1})}{2}, \qquad (7)$$

And the observed distribution is determined as, $y_i = h_{2i}$.

The difference between the expected distribution and the observed distribution is used to calculate χ^2 value, that is,

$$\chi^2 = \sum_{i=1}^{n+1} \frac{\left(y_i - y_i^* \right)^2}{y_i^*} \qquad (8)$$

Figure 23. Histogram of quantized DCT coefficients without and with message embedding using JSteg and difference in the histogram difference

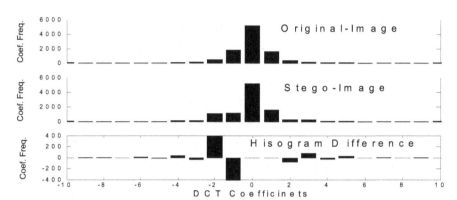

with *n* degrees of freedom, which is the number of different categories in the histogram minus one. For practical purpose, it might be required to sum adjacent values from the expected and the observed distributions to ensure sufficient count in each category. Westfeld et al in (Westfeld & Pfitzmann, 1999) have suggested that each category should have count greater than four.

Now the probability, *p*, that two distributions are equal is given by the complement of the cumulative distribution function,

$$p = \frac{1}{2^{n/2}\Gamma(n/2)} \int_{t=0}^{\chi^2} t^{(n-2)/2} e^{t/2} dt,$$

(9)

where Γ is the Euler Gamma function.

The probability of embedding is determined by calculating *p* for a sample for the DCT coefficients. Initially the sample consists the first 1% of the JPEG coefficients, then first 2%, 3%, ... and so on.

The steganalysis tool based on Westfeld et al's stegdetect algorithm can be downloaded form[30]. This steganalysis tool has a nice GUI that allows user to provide three inputs, 1) JPEG test-image, 2) image dependent *sensitivity* factor used during

steganalysis, and 3) the underlying steganographic technique used (if any) to generate the test-image. Figure 24 shows output the GUI, *xsteg*, when stegdetect tool was applied to the **Lena** image and the corresponding JPEG stego image of **Lena**. Here stego-**Lena** image was obtained by embedding a 7 KB message using *JPHS* and *Invisible Secrets* steganographic tools.

It can be observed from Figure 24 that stegdetect tool has successfully detected the cover-image (lena.jpg) and the corresponding stego-image (lenainvisible.jpg and lenaJPHS.jpg). In addition, it has also correctly detected the steganographic tool used. Detection performance of the stegdetect steganalysis tool depends on the length of the hidden message.

- **StegSpy**[31] is also a freeware steganalysis tool that can be used to detect both the presence of the hidden message and the steganographic tool used. Latest StegSpy version can be used to attack steganographic tools such as *Hiderman, JPHS, Masker*[32]*, JPegX,* and *Invisible Secrets*. Figure 25 shows an output of StegSpy GUI, when applied to gray-scale **Lena** image in GIF format and its corresponding stego-image obtained by

*Figure 24. The output from **xsteg** GUI when steganalysis tool **Stegdetect** was applied to three JPEG images of Lena: original Lena JPEG-image and corresponding JPEG-stego images obtained using JP-Hide-and-Seek, and Invisible Secrets steganographic tools*

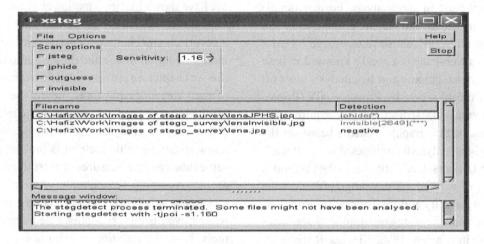

*Figure 25. The output from **StegSpy** GUI when tested for two GIF images*

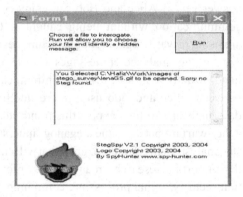 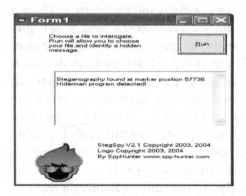

embedding a 56 K bit message using *Hiderman* steganographic tool.

It can be observed from Figure 25 that the StegSpy tool has successfully detected the cover-image (left) and the corresponding stego-image (right) along with the steganographic tool used to hide secret message. Detection performance of StegSpy depends on the hidden message length. It performs poorly when applied to stego-images carrying relatively smaller messages.

- **Stego Watch**, a commercial steganalysis software by WetStone Technologies Inc.[33] Stego Watch analyzes the test-media (e.g. video, audio, images, etc.) to detect the stego-media along with the steganographic tool used to hide the secret message in the detected stego-media. In addition, Stego Watch allows user to select various statistical tests based on the stego-signal characteristics that might be altered by different steganographic tools during message embedding.

ADDITIONAL READING

In this chapter we briefly reviewed current state-of-the-art in steganalysis. Further details on steganography and steganographic tools can be found on Neil F Johnson's web-page[34]. Neil F Johnson's web-page is a good a knowledge-base for the steganographic and steganalysis tools till 1999. A recent article by Provos et al's (Provos & Honeyman, 2003) discusses key requirements of robust steganographic systems based on the existing steganalysis techniques. Anderson et al's work in (Anderson & Petitcolas, 1998) provides analysis of existing of steganographic systems based on capacity and robustness. Information-theoretic analysis of steganographic systems can be found in (Cachin, 1998; Kiayias, Raekow, & Russell, 2005; Zollner et al., 1998) and Chanrdamouli et al's work (Chandramouli & Memon, 2003) provides analysis of steganographic systems based on a new measure of capacity. Steganography can also be used for illicit communication; Kessker in (Kessler, 2004) provides details on using steganography for illicit applications and it forensic analysis based on the current existing steganographic and list of available steganalysis tools. A book chapter by Malik et al's in (Malik, Subbalakshami & Chandramouli, 2008) provides an overview of challenges and future trends in the steganalysis community. In addition, a paper by Chanrdamouli et al (Chandramouli, Kharrazzi, & Memon, 2004) provides theoretical analysis of steganalysis attacks under practical scenarios. Review of some steganalysis techniques and steganographic algorithms can be fond in (Aura, 1997; Provos & Honeyman, 2001; Provos, 2001; Sallee, 2003; Westfeld, 2001).

CONCLUSION AND FUTURE RESEARCH DIRECTIONS

This chapter described requirements of information hiding for steganographic applications, classification of existing state-of-the-art in steganography, and countermeasure to detect/stop steganographic communication (steganalysis). We have shown that information can be hidden in almost every digital file format and can be used as a covert-channel but we focused on information hiding in digital image and digital audio files. In this we chapter we also provided through analysis of many steganography tools, most of them freely available online, and showed that due to relentless endeavor of steganalysis community almost every know steganographic method is broken. At the same time countermeasures against steganalysis are also emerging. For example, when the hidden message is small then stego detection is not very reliable even using very sophisticated steganalysis tools. Now the question is, who is wining this important 21st century cyber warfare? Steganographers or steganalysts. There is no definite answer yet, as Alice and Bob can enjoy covert communication without being caught if they are using private steganographic techniques and exchanging small secret messages. On the other hand, an active warden can deter communication between Alice and Bob using more intelligent data analysis. Authors expect this trend, that is, cyber-warfare between the steganographers and steganalysts, will continue to grow that will enrich the important research areas such as information security, signal processing, communication theory, etc. Following are the open problem in the area of digital steganography:

1. Computing steganographic capacity (Chandramouli 2003) in the presence of a steganalysis detector is still an open problem. We note that capacity as defined for a digital watermarking system is not directly applicable to steganographic systems.

2. Currently there is no benchmarking framework for both steganography and steganalysis to fairy evaluate performance of a given steganalysis or steganographic techniques. For example, there is a need to develop

cover and stego data sets, design embedding rates, message lengths etc. for unbiased performance evaluation. Therefore, future research should also focus on developing some benchmarking framework for both steganography and steganalysis.

REFERENCES

Anderson, R., & Petitcolas, F. (1998). On the limits of steganography. IEEE Journal Selected Areas in Communications: Special Issue on Copyright and Privacy, 16 (5), 474-481.

Cachin, C. (1998). Information-theoretic model for steganography. In Second int. workshop on information hiding (Vol. 1525, p. 306-318). Springer Berlin / Heidelberg.

Celik, M., Sharma, G., & Tekalp, A. (2004). Universal image steganalysis using rate-distortion curves. In Security, steganography, and watermarking of multimedia content VI (Vol. 5306, p. 467-476). IS&T/SPIE.

Chandramouli, R. (2002). Mathematical theory for steganalysis. In Security, steganography, and watermarking of multimedia contents IV (Vol. 4675, p. 14-25). IS&T/SPIE.

Chandramouli, R., & Memon, N. (2001). Analysis of lsb based image steganography techniques. In Int. conf on image processing (icip'01) (Vol. 3, p. 1019-1022).

Chandramouli, R., & Memon, N. (2003). Steganography capacity: A steganalysis perspective. In Security, steganography, and watermarking of multimedia contents V (Vol. 5020, p. 173-177). IS&T/SPIE.

Chang, C.-C., & Lin, C.-J. (2001). Libsvm: A library for support vector machines. Software Available at http://www.csie.ntu.edu.tw/~cjlin/libsvm.

Chen, B., & Wornell, G. (2000). Preprocessed and postprocessed quantization index modulation methods for digital watermarking. In Security, steganography, and watermarking of multimedia contents III (Vol. 3971). IS&T/SPIE.

Chen, B., & Wornell, G. (2001). Quantization index modulation: A class of provably good methods for digital watermarking and information embedding. IEEE Transactions on Information Theory, 47 (4).

Duda, R., & Hart, P. (1973). Pattern classification and scene analysis. New York, NY: John Wiley.

Dumitrescu, S., Wu, X., & Wang, Z. (2002). Detection of lsb steganography via sample pair analysis. In 5th int. workshop on information hiding (Vol. 2578). Springer Berlin / Heidelberg.

Farid, H. (2001). Detecting steganographic messages in digital images (Tech. Rep. No. TR2001-412). Department of Computer Science, Dartmouth College.

Fridrich, J. (2004). Feature based steganalysis for jpeg images and its implications for future design of steganographic schemes. In 6th int. workshop on information hiding (Vol. 3200). Springer Berlin / Heidelberg.

Fridrich, J., & Goljan, M. (2003). Digital image steganography using stochastic modeling. In Security, steganography, and watermarking of multimedia content V (Vol. 5020, p. 191-202).

Fridrich, J., Goljan, M., & Hogea, D. (2002a). Attacking the outguess. In ACM workshop on multimedia and security.

Fridrich, J., Goljan, M., & Hogea, D. (2002b). Steganalysis of jpeg images: Breaking the F5 algorithm. In 5th int. workshop on information hiding (Vol. 2578, p. 310-323). Springer Berlin / Heidelberg.

Fridrich, J., Holotyak, T. S., & Soukal, D. (2005). Maximum likelihood estimation of secret message length embedded using +/-k steganography in spatial domain. In Security, Steganography, and Watermarking of Multimedia Content VII (Vol. 5681, p. 595-606). IS&T/SPIE.

Harmsen, J., & Pearlman, W. (2003). Steganalysis of additive noise modelable information hiding. In Security, Steganography, and Watermarking of Multimedia Content V (Vol. 5020, p. 131-142). IS&T/SPIE.

Johnson, N., & Jajodia, S. (1998a). Exploiting steganography: Seeing the unseen. IEEE Computers, 31 (2), 26-34.

Johnson, N., & Jajodia, S. (1998b). Steganalysis of images created using current steganography software. In Second Int. Workshop on Information Hiding (Vol. 1525, p. 273-279). Springer Berlin / Heidelberg.

Kessler, G. (2004). An overview of steganography for the computer forensics examiner. Forensics Science and Communications, 6 (3).

Kiayias, A., Raekow, Y., & Russell, A. (2005). Efficient steganography with provable security guarantees. In 7th Int. Workshop on Digital Watermarking (Vol. 3727, p. 118-130). Springer Berlin / Heidelberg.

Lyu, S., & Farid, H. (2006). Steganalysis using higher-order image statistics. IEEE Transactions on Information Forensics and Security, 1 (1), 111-119.

Malik, H., Subbalakshami, K., & Chandramouli, R. (2007a). Nonparametric steganalysis of quantization index modulation based steganography using approximate entropy. IEEE Transactions on Information Forensics and Security. (submitted)

Malik, H., Subbalakshami, K., & Chandramouli, R. (2007b). Steganalysis of quantization index modulation based steganography using kernel density estimation. In 9th ACM Multimedia and Security Workshop, 2007.

Malik, H., Subbalakshami, K., & Chandramouli, R. (2007c). Nonparametric steganalysis of quantization index modulation based steganography using kernel density estimaton. IEEE Transactions on Information Forensics and Security. (submitted)

Malik, H., Subbalakshami, K., & Chandramouli, R. (2008). Nonparametric steganalysis of quantization index modulation based steganography using approximate entropy. In Security, Steganography, and Watermarking of Multimedia Contents IX. IS&T/SPIE.

Malik, H., Chandramouli, R., & Subbalakshami, K., (2008). Steganalysis: trends and challenges. In Multimedia Forensics and Security, Ed. Chang-Tsun Li, Idea Group In.

Malik, H. (2008). Steganalysis of QIM Steganography Using Irregularity Measure. In 10th ACM Multimedia and Security Workshop, 2008. (submitted)

Marvel, L., Boncelet, C., & Retter, C. (1999). Spread spectrum image steganography. IEEE Transactions on Image Processing, 8 (8), 1075-1083.

Matsuoka, H. (2006). Spread spectrum audio steganography using subband phase shifting. In Int. Conf. on Intelligent Information Hiding and Multimedia, (p. 3-6).

Provos, N. (2001). Defending against statistical steganalysis. In 10th usenix security symposium.

Provos, N., & Honeyman, P. (2001). Detecting steganographic contents on the internet (Tech. Rep. No. CITI 01-1a). University of Michigan Tech. Rep.

Provos, N., & Honeyman, P. (2003). Hide and seek: An introduction to steganography. IEEE Security and Privacy Magazine, 1 (3), 32-44.

Rowlnd, Craig H. (1997) Covert Channels in the TCP/IP Protocol. First Monday, Vol.2 No.5 - 5 May 1997.

Sallee, P. (2003). Model-based steganography. In 6th Int. Workshop on Digital Watermarking (Vol. 3929, p. 154-167). Springer Berlin / Heidelberg.

Simmons, G. J. (1984). 'Prisoners' problem and subliminal channel. In Crypto83-advances in cryptography (p. 51-67). New York, NY: Plenum Press.

Sullivan, K., Bi, Z., Madhow, U., Chandrasekaran, S., & Manjunath, B. (2004). Steganalysis of quantization index modulation data hiding. In Int. Conf. on Image Processing (icip'04) (Vol. 2, p. 1165-1168).

Torralba, A., & Olivia, A. (2003). Statistics of natural image categories. IOP Network: Computation in Neural Systems, 14, 391-412.

Trivedi, S., & Chandramouli, R. (2005). Secret key estimation in sequential steganalysis. IEEE Transactions on Signal Processing: Supplement on Secure Media, 53 (2), 746-757.

Wang, Y., & Moulin, P. (2006). Optimized feature extraction for learning-based image steganalysis. IEEE Transactions on Information Forensics and Security, 1 (2), 31-45.

Westfeld, A. (2001). F5 -a steganographic algorithm high capacity despite better steganalysis. In Fifth Information Hiding Workshop (Vol. 2137, p. 289-302). Springer Berlin / Heidelberg.

Westfeld, A. (2002). Detecting low embedding rates. In 5th information hiding workshop (Vol. 2578, p. 324-339). Springer Berlin / Heidelberg.

Westfeld, A., & Pfitzmann. (1999). Attacks on steganographic systems. In Third Information Hiding Workshop (Vol. 1768, p. 61-75). Springer Berlin / Heidelberg.

Zollner, J., Federrath, H., Klimant, H., Pfitzmann, A., Piotraschke, R., Westfeld, A., et al. (1998). Modeling the security of steganographic systems. In Second int. Workshop on Information Hiding (Vol. 1525, p. 345-355). Springer Berlin / Heidelberg.

KEY TERMS

Covert Channel: A communication channel that transfers information in a way that violates security policy.

Covert Communication: Covert communication means exchanging information using a covert (or hidden) channel.

Least Significant Bit Steganography: Message hiding by replacing least significant bits of the quantized coefficients (in transformed domain) or samples (in spatial domain) of the cover-signal with the message bits.

Quantization Index Modulation Steganography: Message hiding by quantizing the cover-signal using a set of quantizers, selected using message bits.

Steganalysis: Steganalysis refers to detection of the presence of hidden information in the stego-object.

Steganography: Steganography is a class of information hiding that deals with concealing very the existence of the hidden message.

Warden: The primary goal of warden (also known as attacker) is the detection of the presence of hidden data in the stego-object. A warden can be active or passive depending on the attack model used to disrupt covert-communication.

ENDNOTES

[1]   Software available at http://www.demcom. com/deutsch/index.htm

2   Software available at http://www.cs.bath. ac.uk/~jpc/blindside/

3   Software available at http://www.demcom. com/deutsch/index.htm

4   Software available at ftp://idea.sec.dsi. unimi.it/pub/security/crypt/code/s-tools. zip

5   Software available at http://www.ezstego. com

6   Software available at http://linux01.gwdg. de/latham/sego

7   Software available at http://www.darkside. com.au/gifshuffle/

8   Software available at http://digitalforensics. champlain.edu/download/Gif-it-up.exe

9   Software available at ftp://ftp.funet.fi

10 Software available at http://www.outguess. org

11 Software available at http://steghide.source-forge.net/download.php

12 Software available http://linux01.gwdg. de/\%7Ealatham/stego.html

13 Software available at http://www.invisibles-ecrets.com/

14 Software available at wwwwrn.inf.tu-dres-den.de/westfeld/f5

15 Software available at http:\\www.sharp-thoughts.org

16 Hydan, URL: http://www.crazyboy.com/hy-dan/

17 StegoArchive.Com, URL: http://home. earthlink.net/~emilbrandt/stego/software-windows.html

18 http://www.darkside.com.au/gifshuffle/

19 http://www.theargon.com/achilles/stegano-graphy/gif-it-up/

20 http://www.fqa.com/romana/

21 http://www.theargon.com/achilles/stegano-graphy/

22 http://www.inf.tu-dresden.de/~aw4

23 http://linux01.gwdg.de/~alatham/stego. html

24 http://www.outguess.org/detection.php

25 MP3Stego, URL: http://www.petitcolas. net/fabien/steganography/mp3stego/

26 http://www.petitcolas.net/fabien/

27 Greg Roelofs: Zlib Home Site. http://www. zlib.org

28 Software available at http://digitalforen-sics.champlain.edu/download/stegdetect-0.4.zip

29 Software available at http://www.invisibles-ecrets.com/

30 http://www.outguess.org/detection.php

31 Software available at http://www.spy-hunter. com/stegspydownload.htm

32 Software available at http://www.masker. de

33 http://www.wetstonetech.com/

34 http://www.jjtc.com/stegdoc/

Section III
Typical Applications

Chapter XX
Secure Content Distribution in Pure P2P

Esther Palomar
Carlos III University of Madrid, Spain

Juan M. E. Tapiador
Carlos III University of Madrid, Spain

Julio C. Hernandez-Castro
Carlos III University of Madrid, Spain

Arturo Ribagorda
Carlos III University of Madrid, Spain

ABSTRACT

Perhaps the most popular feature offered by Peer-to-Peer (P2P) networks is the possibility of having several replicas of the same content distributed among multiple nodes. Among the advantages of P2P networks, we emphasize the property of robust fault tolerance. Nevertheless, there are also some disadvantages (e.g. those derived from their decentralized and self-organized nature) such as the complexity of network management and the existence of new security vulnerabilities. In fact, a significant challenge for P2P file sharing systems is maintaining the correctness and consistency of their global data structures and shared contents, as peers independently and unpredictably join and leave the system. Similarly, access control to the shared resources is a noteworthy problem for users of such systems. Most of the difficulties found to apply classic security solutions (e.g. authentication and authorization services) are just related to the impossibility of deploying a public key infrastructure (PKI) in these environments, and new proposals have to deal with avoiding such a centralization by exploring alternative paradigms, which often require cooperation among peers. In this chapter, we describe the background and framework of content distribution in pure P2P networks and present the most representative schemes for providing a secure content replication.

INTRODUCTION

Advances in distributed systems with increasingly growing capabilities for efficient file transport (both wired and mobile), and their immediate consequence, i.e. the ability to rapidly replicate a content over a network, have made sharing of electronic files become a revolution in business and domestic environments. A number of emerging technologies, such as P2P and mobile ad hoc networks (MANETs), where nodes are involved in the process of sharing and collaborating without relying on central authorities, require high levels of efficiency, scalability, security and reliability. In particular, well-known file sharing systems can provide high availability of shared resources due to the fully distributed nature of pure P2P environments. However, in comparison with the classical client-server paradigm, pure P2P applications involve a number of challenges in regard to assure basic security services for content distribution.

Similarly, this increasing content availability gives rise to an attracting interest in Digital Rights Management (DRM) and, therefore, in providing "controlled" P2P computing services. In fact, several current research proposals work on facilitating the emergence of new models that maintain some control over the file-sharing process (Rubin, 1997; Tran, 2005.) Some of them address the provision of digital content protection by means of assuring the integrity of shared contents. It is necessary that some security mechanisms will be applied with the aim of avoiding attacks based on non-authorized content modifications, in order to eliminate suspicions that can generate mistrust among the community. Earlier research efforts to counter this behavior have relied on further cooperation between nodes to exchange reputation information about other nodes. On the other hand, several investigations agree with requiring the attention of a human in order to perform a task before granting access or service.

Moreover, other proposals rely on a set of peers playing the role of a certification authority (CA) since it is unrealistic to assume that appropriate trusted third parties (TTPs) can be deployed in such environments.

Another main factor attracting research attention to P2P security is to enforce appropriate access control policies, which limit the activity of legitimate users while serve as an obstacle to dishonest requesters. In such a scenario, content owners may determine if the requester attempting to download a particular content is actually authorized to access it. On the other hand, ensuring that each one of these new potential providers will behave accordingly to the owner's access policy gets more complicated (and definitely hard since a global security infrastructure is unavailable.) Many inherent characteristics of collaborative environments introduce new requirements for access control: support for mobile devices, different applications, control decentralization, and off-line working. Furthermore, authorization in such environments cannot be generally provided by means of existing models, which were developed for centralized systems. For instance, the extremely decentralized nature of a pure P2P network makes impossible to apply solutions that rely on some kind of fixed infrastructure, such as on-line decision points.

In this chapter, we first describe the background and framework of content distribution in P2P and ad hoc networks. We also elaborate on the characteristics for the provision of security services, paying special attention to authentication and access control techniques suitable for self-organized networks, and summarizing the main security solutions proposed so far. In particular, the specific purpose of the present chapter is to justify the necessity of a secure content replication in such networks. We also point out some open issues and emergent trends in this research area.

BACKGROUND: REPLICATION IN PURE P2P AND AD HOC NETWORKS

One of the main advantages of P2P systems is their capability to offer replicas of the same content at various locations. Replication is a common approach to improve performance when distributed systems need to scale in number of users and objects in the system, and/or geographical area. Faced with different locations of the same content, an application can grant priority to that which offers a less expensive path (e.g. in terms of bandwidth.) To some extent, replication also guarantees some sort of fault tolerance, since information can be available even if some parts of the network are temporarily disconnected.

However, this high degree of redundancy implies that it is necessary to apply some security mechanisms in order to avoid attacks against the suitability of content distribution, e.g. to detect whether a content has been altered, and also to verify whether it was actually sent by the person/entity claimed to be the sender.

In this section, we first present basic definitions and concepts used throughout this chapter, and discuss related work on authorization and authentication frameworks as well. In each area, there have been several previous works, which address one or more problems in P2P systems.

System and Adversary Models

P2P is often described as a type of decentralized computing paradigm where nodes communicate directly with each other. P2P applications allow users to communicate synchronously, supporting tasks such as instant messaging, working on shared documents or sharing files, among many others. As a result, the P2P paradigm provides users with the capability of integrating their platforms within a distributed environment with a broad range of possibilities.

A P2P network has neither clients nor servers; each individual node acts simultaneously as a client and as a server for the rest of the nodes in the network. Within this paradigm, any node can initiate or complete a transaction, and it can also actively play a role in the routing operations. In general, nodes will be the users' personal computers, instead of typical elements of the network infrastructure, but they can present heterogeneous characteristics regarding the local configuration, processing power, connection bandwidth, storage capacity, etc.

A particular application of such an environment that has been rather successful (and has attracted considerable attention in the last years) is file sharing. File sharing has become a common practice for Internet users to obtain, for example, software updates from public sites. However, such a practice still provokes mistrust. File corruption may occur easily by action of dishonest and malicious peers or even by mistake. Similarly, an impostor could masquerade himself as the originator of a certain file, publishing a corrupted version of the file. In fact, users of currently deployed file sharing systems are unable to verify that files they retrieve are uncorrupted, or whether the content has been truly created by the presumed owner.

Before further elaborating on the problem of distributing content in a secure manner, we first establish some generalities about P2P systems. We can identify three elements common to every P2P system:

- The user community (nodes). The user community is characterized by a highly node transience, the total ignorance of the node's intentions, and the lack of a centralized authority. These issues have been approached by different research models, protocols and systems. In particular, node identification and its relationship with anonymity is an intense research area due to the existence of potential attacks based on traffic analysis and the traceability of communications among nodes. Node identification is critical, and the lack of control on it could imply vulnerabilities in the replication process, such as ID spoofing and Denial of Service (DoS) attacks.

- The overlay architecture, which defines the logical structure of the network over the underlying communication layer(s.) Essentially, the overlay network manages the aspects related to nodes location and message routing among them. There has been a large amount of work on mapping the virtual topology to the physical network infrastructure, as well as analyzing the security vulnerabilities that P2P systems are susceptible to, depending on which overlay architecture is deployed. This is an interesting research area, which includes location and searching mechanisms among others, but lies out of the scope of this chapter. We refer the interested readers to (Zhao, 2001) for further details.

- The information (content) stored at nodes and accessible through the services offered by the network. The most commonly used content replication strategy in P2P systems simply makes replicas of objects on the requesting peer, upon a successful transaction.

Regarding the objectives of this chapter, we focus on analyzing security approaches (and their main limitations) with respect to content distribution.

Problem Statement: (In)Secure Content Distribution

The study of security issues in P2P networks becomes more difficult due to the diversity and heterogeneity of existing P2P architectures. For instance, despite the advances in P2P technology, security-related issues have remained systematically unaddressed or, at best, handled without a global perspective. Most proposals presented

so far have been focused more on the resource distribution process rather than on the provision of suitable security infrastructures to protect that resource.

The absence of a centralized server or authority makes it difficult to apply policies of authentication, authorization and fairness. Moreover, self-organization involves additional concerns. As P2P systems disperse resources and responsibilities into the network, they are also facing many security threats. Concretely, viruses and *spyware* programs are a huge problem in the P2P community. Furthermore, malicious nodes may try to spread spam or hostile content in order to tamper genuine content. Thus, the performance is sensitive to the degree of user cooperation, and it makes sense to provide incentives to users to share their resources. In particular, an adequate option would be to increase their download allocations in a manner that depends on their contributions.

Classic approaches have concentrated on specific points, such as providing anonymity to users and data (Levine, 2002), and also on establishing and managing trust relationships among users (Sandhu, 2005.) Research effort has also focused on the study of DoS attacks (Juels, 1999; Maniatis, 2004) and the abuse of multiple identities, also called Sybil attack (Douceur, 2002.) Other problems have been recently identified, such as those associated with the transience of peers (churn) and how to combat the selfish behavior exhibited by nodes that do not share their resources (denoted as free-riding.)

Moreover, new areas are being explored, such as fairness and authentication (Damiani, 2002.) Additionally, a significant part of the research on security in P2P systems intends to mitigate attacks against four main system properties: availability, authenticity, and access control. Recent work primarily focuses on addressing attacks against availability and authenticity (Daswani, 2004.) For instance, some results already exist on the provision of both security properties in traditional Gnutella-like systems (Defigueiredo,

2002.) Furthermore, current architectures for P2P networks are plagued with open (and apparently difficult to solve) issues in digital rights management and access control, e.g. (Fox, 2001) outlines some of the problems in this area. Next we discuss the two basic requirements for a secure content distribution scheme: content authentication and authorization.

Content Authentication

Among the main security properties demanded on a system, authentication has been identified as a critical issue in self-organized environments (Narasimha, 2003.) Several approaches have addressed the provision of fault tolerant authentication, most in the way of protocols relying on threshold cryptography using key sharing and agreement techniques (Desmedt, 1997). The key idea is to use a quorum of participants to create a digitally signed public key certificate (see Section below.) On the other hand, resource authentication become critical since content is replicated through different locations, and therefore the originator loses control over it. A malicious party can modify the replica according to several purposes:

- To claim ownership over the content.
- To insert malicious software into a highly demanded content. Not in vain, P2P networks are becoming an important medium to propagate recently developed viruses, spyware, etc.
- To boycott the system by offering fake contents. Eventually, this can generate distrust and bad reputation in the community.

In summary, content authentication confirms non-alteration and source identification of the content, implemented through some kind of digital evidence.

Authorization and Access Control

The decentralized and anonymous characteristics of common P2P file sharing systems enforce an inherent "open-access" policy which does not provide any mechanism to support access control decisions. However, this lack is critical in collaborative applications, especially in team-working and virtual common workplaces where community peers' privileges may not be the same, as well as the sensibility of each resource in the system.

There has been relatively little work done in controlling access to the collaboration environment and shared data (Sanchez, 2006.) Most collaborative systems give all participants the same rights to all objects and expect access to be controlled by a social protocol. They do not provide computer support for preventing mistakes, conflicting changes, or unauthorized access.

Generally, basic definitions that are commonly used in the access control community are the following (Hu, 2006):

- Object: Any kind of system resource (e.g. files, directories, registers, process, etc.) Access to an object potentially implies access to the information it contains.
- Subject: Typically, users and/or process who initiate actions or operations on objects, and therefore cause information to flow among objects.
- Operation: Active process invoked by a subject (e.g. read, write, etc.)
- Permission or privilege: Authorization to perform some operation. Generally, it refers to some combination of object and operation.

Furthermore, there are two main components in an access control system, as follows:

- The policy. The policy is a plan of action, like a high level guideline, usually a sequence of rules, that establishes how to determine the access decisions. The suitability of a given policy depends on the particular protection requirements for a given system, environment and users. On the other hand, policies are formally presented as models.

- The mechanism. Most mechanisms are based on the assumption of an authorization relation between objects and subjects. These actions are permitted or denied according to the authorization privileges established in the system, and expressed in terms of access rights (Sandhu, 1994.)

Generic access control models have been studied extensively in classic distributed domains, which provide the basic framework to describe protection systems, such as classic access matrix models (subject-object-right) (Abadi, 1993.) In particular, two main data structures have been chosen to represent the access matrix: capability lists and access control lists (ACLs.) The first stores the matrix by rows, i.e., each subject is associated with a list of pairs (object, rights) called capabilities. The second approach stores the matrix by columns, i.e., each object is associated with a list of pairs (subject, rights.) Interested readers can find further details in (Tolone, 2005.) However, access matrix-based models have several drawbacks when applied to an ad hoc environment mainly related to storage overhead, i.e. the requirement of huge contextual databases.

There are two basic types of classical access control models: discretionary and mandatory access control (DAC and MAC, respectively.) User rights and permissions are implemented differently in systems based on each of them. DAC (Sandhu, 1998) allows an object's owner to determine the access rules for that object. It is generally used to limit a user's access to a file, being the owner who controls other users' access to the file. MAC (Osborn, 2000) policy decisions are made by a central authority, and, therefore, users are not able to change or reassign access

rights. The security level related to a user, also denominated *clearance*, determines the user's trustworthiness not to disclose sensitive data to others not cleared to access it. Moreover, objects in the system are assigned a security label as well. There is, therefore, a strict relationship between the security levels associated with the two, object and subject.

A different approach is provided by Role-Based Access Control (RBAC) methods (Sandhu, 1996), wherein permissions are assigned to roles rather than to individual users; there is a need, therefore, in MANETs of an initial, centralized bootstrapping phase.

On the other hand, a number of research efforts have led to the development of Extensive Markup Language (XML)-based frameworks which unify basic access control specification (Sanchez, 2006.) Several standards are currently maintained by different corporations such as the Organization for the Advancement of Structured Information Standards (OASIS.) The three most important advances are Security Assertion Markup Language (SAML), eXtensible Access Control Markup Language (XACML), and XML Digital Signature Recommendation (XMLDSig.) These languages define the representation of authorization information, and also provide general-purpose protocols for expressing access control policies. For further details refer to (Lepro, 2003.)

SECURITY FOR CONTENT DISTRIBUTION IN P2P FILE SHARING SYSTEMS

The main concerns of securing multimedia distribution, in order to protect the distribution process against malicious actions, are twofold:

- A digital content in a P2P file sharing system is straightforwardly alterable; it can be manipulated, so that a binary stream looks like the original. The integrity of information in such a scenario may be attacked through the injection of degraded-quality content or by misrepresenting the identity of the content, for example, through falsely labeling. The confidentiality and integrity of the multimedia streaming must be protected from both passive and active attacks.

- The system must ensure that the protected content is only obtained by those users with the appropriate access level, that is, only by authorized users. Although access control is a key feature in content distribution, this has not been extensively addressed in current P2P scenarios. Traditionally, business corporations have used service-oriented collaborative tools to protect critical resources in the local communication network.

In this section, we identify content authentication and content access requirements in such environments, and propose a framework for secure content distribution.

Design Challenges and Cryptographic Primitives

The lack of message encryption has caused that exchanged messages among participant peers are sent in plain and therefore readable by anyone. Some cryptographic-based mechanisms have been suggested to solve this problem, such as Broadcast Encryption (Fiat, 1994.) This is a cryptographic technique for implementing compliant authorized domains, and can be used as a replacement for public key cryptography in certain applications. It provides mechanisms for enforcing compliance without requiring device identification or authentication, while providing a reasonable level of control to limit massive content distribution (Pestoni, 2004.)

The deployment of classic security protocols to provide services such as node authentication, content integrity or access control, presents several difficulties, most of them due to the decentralized

nature of these environments and the lack of central authorities. Nevertheless, some solutions have been already proposed based mostly on trust and reputation models, and threshold cryptography.

Particularly, there are three access control requirements which have to be carefully supported by pure P2P environments (Tran, 2005):

- No centralized control: Traditionally, a single authority, which identifies users, defines roles or groups and controls the access rights, represents a centralized decision point which simplifies the authorization decision process. However, an access control model for pure P2P networks must deal with this decentralization since such fixed access control infrastructure does not exist. Peers should have a significant level of autonomy and responsibility for storing and managing its own access control policies.

- Peer and content classification: A requester peer who wishes to download a content needs to have his clearance equal to or greater than the corresponding security label of the desired content. Content providers therefore establish a local access control policy aimed at giving requesters explicit rights to grant or deny any requests to access to the sharing files.

- Encourage file sharing: Performance efficiency may be negatively affected, since the implantation of an access control system effectively may reduce the chance that potential requesters will get their desired files. Thus, most access control proposals apply trust-based incentive mechanisms in order to reward well-behaving peers.

Problems with Conventional Approaches

Content authentication is commonly uncertain and current research efforts have adopted popularity-based ranking systems to help users discover desired contents. Traditionally, common schemes are based on *opinion polls*, which serve the requesting node to determine the suitable content provider. Similarly, a more generalized approach for preventing content alteration is to acquire several copies of a file from different sources using a voting or selection scheme. On the other hand, the confidentiality of the content can be ensured by encrypting the lookup and download transmissions.

The solutions to achieve data integrity and/or content authentication, as many other network security services offered today, mostly rely on public key cryptography. Once that a public key can be securely associated to any given party, the integrity of any content generated by her can be ensured through her signature, thus maintaining the correctness and consistency of global data structures and shared contents, even when peers independently and unpredictably join and leave the system. Nevertheless, public key certification authorities do not, traditionally, certify the behavior of the entities that possess their certificates. In classic networking paradigms, guarantees of authenticity and integrity can be provided by digital signatures. If an authenticated user, A, wishes to offer a content m, she can rely on a CA to generate and sign an associated evidence, which can be checked by the rest of the community and also ensures that m has not been modified.

The integrity of a content generated by a source A can be ensured as follows. First, the source:

- Computes a hash value $h(m)$ from m.
- Encrypts $h(m)$ with her private key, obtaining a digital signature $s_A(m)$.
- Creates a message containing m, $h(m)$, and $s_A(m)$.
- Sends this message (probably encrypted using CA's public key) to the CA.
- CA looks up author's public key and verifies her signature.
- CA signs $h(m)$ and sends this signature, $s_{CA}(m)$, to the source.

- Finally, the source can assure the integrity of the content publishing: $\langle m, s_{CA}(m) \rangle$.

Then, the receiver:

- Retrieves m and the CA's signature.
- Decrypts the digital signature enclosed by using the CA's public key certificate, thus generating a first hash value.
- Computes a second hash value from the received content.
- Compares both hash values to confirm the non-alteration of the content.

Even though the previous approach has been successfully applied in several domains (i.e. for public key authentication), it requires the existence of at least one TTP. The reasons why A cannot sign her own evidences are simple. First, because she can misbehave, offering something different of what she announces. Furthermore, her signature alone does not prevent from manipulation. Suppose that A offers m in the form of a pair: $\langle m, s_A(m) \rangle$. Once B obtains m, she can modify it and generate a new signature over the altered content. Moreover, even if B does not modify m, she can just remove $s_A(m)$ and add her own signature. As a result, several — and probably different— copies of m claimed by various parties may be circulating through the network.

Public Key Primitives and Digital Certificates

In most existing P2P file sharing systems, verifying the integrity of contents depends on a correct node authentication. Unfortunately, no infrastructure there exists for identifying peers and providing them with digital certificates. A peer can publish fake or junk files with the names or keywords of some popular files, causing normal users to frequently download wrong files. This quickly makes peers lose trust and interest in the community (Zhang, 2005.) The objective of checking content integrity is not only to verify that data is not corrupted, but also to validate that contents are really what one has requested.

A distributed access control model is addressed in (Lopez, 2004) through the idea of authentication and authorization infrastructures (AAI). An AAI is the most significative evolution of PKIs, and may be seen as the result of the union between PKI and PMI. ITU-T proposal defines four PMI models according to the application: general, control, role and delegation. An interesting point is that AAIs provide a delegation procedure by which an owner delegates authorizations to another without being involved. However, there are some problems with the application of existing delegation mechanisms in pure P2P environments. For example, the delegate could masquerade herself as the delegator, or impersonate her, since there is no control on what others can do and can not. A possible solution would be that the delegate should act in his own name, not in hers.

An advance in the provision of authorization capabilities in P2P environments is presented in (Palomar, 2007.) The proposed solution provides a content authentication scheme which allows secure content replication among peers, thus ensuring the integrity of the published contents. Non-authorized accesses are prevented by ensuring that only a user having the proper security clearance will be able to decrypt the downloaded content. Content owners can control who accesses their contents by discretionally issuing clearances in the form of authorization certificates. The clearance represents the trustworthiness of a holder not to disclose non-authorized content.

For instance, consider a common file sharing scenario wherein, for each transaction, the node P which provides the service (i.e. the content) is called the *provider*, while the node R which requests the content is called *requester*. These are the two protocol parties. To provide replication, we assume that the system always transmits and presents files encrypted using a key, K_S. This key is established by P, who maintains it in secret.

Now, we may use a *trapdoor function,* ω_m (Diffie, 1976), to supply collaborative requesters with l-bits out of the total bits of K_S. These l bits can be seen as an advantage for honest peers.

The key idea is that each owner classifies her contents according to several security classes, such as the described with a lattice-based access control policy (Sandhu, 1993.) For example, a classic set of labels is "confidential", "restricted", "secret", and "top-secret", but can also be extended to support additional usage classifications depending on the owner's desires.

On the other hand, every participant needs a certificate for accessing a desired content of a certain provider's directory. These authorization certificates are discretionally issued by the content provider. After several transactions with different providers, it is expected that a node will have a "portfolio" of authorization certificates.

The situation is analogous to people who have several admission cards for accessing libraries, museums, clubs, etc. Requesters will have an authorization certificate for each successfully contacted content provider. Nevertheless, an authorization certificate are not issued neither by the holder (the requester) nor a CA. Authorization certificates are issued by a content owner for granting access to a specific requester, with a limited validity period and a security label L_n.

Summarizing, a provider P generates a certificate C_R^P for node R, containing (see Figure 1):

Figure 1. R's authorization certificate issued by P

User authorization certificate C_R^P

Certificate C_R	
Holder:	R
Issuer:	P
Validity Period:	(ts_1, ts_2)
Clearance:	L_R, ω_m
Signatures:	
$s_P(s_R(C_B))$	

Figure 2. *Content authentication protocol (left), and Content access procedure (right)*

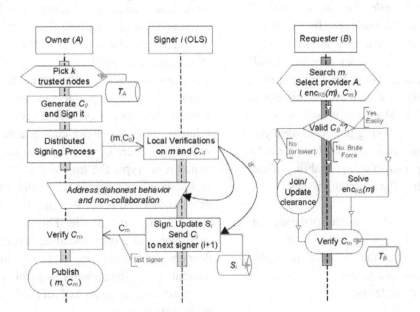

- The identity of the authorization certificate owner, also called "holder".
- The identity of the issuer, who establishes who has generated the content and is its legitimate owner.
- The validity period.
- The holder's security clearance and the corresponding trapdoor.
- Finally, the previous items are signed by the issuer and the requester.

Thus, requesters who successfully obtain this authorization certificate benefits from a trapdoor's information for a faster key recovery process, and therefore the content decryption takes less time and fewer resources. For the sake of illustration, we include Figure 2-(right) which summarizes the full operation of generating the aforementioned authorization certificate.

Threshold Cryptography

The dynamic nature of peer group membership, the changing topology, and also the lack of any

centralized authority add further complication in the provision of practical security services. Such an environment requires techniques which offer fault tolerance and resilience with respect to crashes of some of the system components since even if some nodes are unavailable, others can still perform the task.

The goal of secret sharing schemes and threshold cryptography is to distribute the provision of basic security operations (e.g. the authority to sign a file), in fully distributed environments without the existence of any fixed infrastructure, and in presence of malicious nodes (Desmedt, 1997.) Concretely, n parties share the ability of performing a cryptographic operation (e.g. creating a digital signature), and any subset of at least t out of n parties can jointly perform the operation. On the other hand, any $t-1$ (or less) parties cannot perform the operation. Moreover, any

$$t < \frac{n}{2}$$

parties cannot prevent the remaining honest parties to perform the task (Narasimha, 2003.) In particular, this work elaborates on the viability of threshold cryptography for membership control in P2P systems. Though group members handle admission procedures themselves, the approach needs that a subset of at least t (a threshold) members jointly decide to admit a new members to their group via a voting protocol based on a (t,n)-threshold signature scheme. However, a discussion is still opened on the applicability of such schemes, regarding the following issues:

- Specification and negotiation of the security policy.
- Determination of the threshold and group size, and their dynamism.
- Secret shares updating.

Byzantine Agreement

Many fault tolerant algorithms are designed under the assumption that no more than an explicit fraction of components can fail (Weatherspoon, 2002.) Byzantine Agreement protocols (Lamport, 1982) allow a set of entities to come to a unified decision, even if some of them (less than 1/3) are actively attempting to compromise the process.

Particularly, since malicious attacks and dishonest peers can cause faulty nodes to exhibit Byzantine behavior, fault-tolerant algorithms are becoming increasingly important in many environments. As an example, the work described in (Lin, 2004) proposes a mechanism based on erasure code replication for an effective replica distribution and storage. This technique is based on breaking the data into blocks and spreading them over many servers. The objects and their associated fragments are then named using a secure hash over the object contents, giving them globally unique identifiers. This provides with data integrity by ensuring that a recovered file has not been corrupted (for a corrupted file would produce a different identifier.) The authors

use a Byzantine agreement protocol to guarantee Byzantine-tolerant consistency as well. *Ocean-Store* and *Farsite*, scalable file systems, ensure the secrecy of file contents with cryptographic techniques, and maintain the integrity of file and directory data with a Byzantine-fault-tolerant protocol (Adya, 2002.) Concretely, *Farsite* assures content integrity and provides access control, as follows. When an owner creates a new file, he randomly generates a symmetric *file key* with which it encrypts the file. Moreover, this symmetric key is encrypted using the public keys of all authorized readers of the file, and then is stored along with the file. Thus, an authorized requester, with a corresponding private key, can decrypt the file key and therewith the desired content. The system maintains a global metadata structure containing an ACL of public keys of all authorized users.

Similarly, the public key authentication scheme adopted in (Pathak, 2006) depends on an honest majority of a particular subgroup of the peer community, labeled "trusted group". Concretely, honest members from trusted groups are used to provide functionality similar to that of the PKI through a consensus procedure. However, in P2P systems an authenticated peer could create multiple fake identities and act maliciously in the future. A periodic pruning of the trusted group is therefore required in order to ensure the honest majority. On the other hand, the content authentication protocol proposed in (Palomar, 2007) allows for a secure content replication among peers. This protocol is able to maintain content integrity, ensuring its authenticity and detecting if non-authorized alterations have been made on the published contents. This is achieved through the collaboration of a fraction of peers in the system. The owner of the content is responsible of generating evidence containing the most important features of the content, while a selected subset of the community signs it. Though several signers do not constitute by themselves a proper TTP, some security properties can be ensured if the group has honest majority.

An overview of the structure of a content certificate and a brief description of the scheme are provided below (see Figure 2-(left) as well.) The basic idea is that contents will be associated to a digital certificate ensuring properties such as integrity and authenticity, much in the way an X.509 public key certificate can be used to ensure these properties for a public key. According to RFC 3281 (Farrell, 2002), the attributes are digitally signed and the certificate issued by an attribute authority – an entity that pure P2P networks do not have. Instead, this scheme uses a classic challenge-response procedure among a subgroup of peers until reaching a consensus, presented in (Pathak, 2006.)

Let A be the legitimate owner of a given content m. After A joins the system and shows interest in distributing m, she must first produce two main items, as follows:

- A digest of the file, $h(m)$, using a one-way cryptographically strong hash function (such as any of the SHA-2 family.)
- A subgroup $\{n_1, n_2, ..., n_k\}$ of k cooperative nodes picked up from her group T_A of trusted nodes (previously contacted peers, not only for authentication purposes but also for access control.) These k nodes are also called signers. The way in which this selection is carried out may consider the following criteria:
    - Past transactions history. Basically, nodes use information about past transactions to make decisions regarding current interactions.
    - Availability level and reputation score level. Among the information that most commonly used P2P systems present, one can find several weighted values: the reputation of files and nodes, and the fraction of time a piece of data is accessible. These weights may serve to compute an estimation of the expected success for the current transaction.

*Figure 3. (a) Certificate for content **m**; and (b) its generation*

Content authentication certificate C_m

Certificate C	
Holder:	A
ID:	I_m
Content:	$h(m)$
OLS:	$A, n_1, ..., n_k$
Validity Period:	(ts_1, ts_2)
Signing Algorithm:	$AlgorithmDesc.$

Signatures:

$$E_k = E_{K_{n_k}^{-1}}(\cdots(E_{K_{m_1}^{-1}}(E_{K_A^{-1}}(h(C)))))$$

(a)

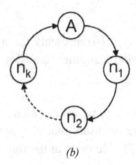

(b)

Figure 3-(a)) is structured in two parts, as follows:

- The certificate C, containing the following fields:

1. The identity of the originator, which ultimately establishes who has generated the content and is its legitimate owner.
2. The identity of the content.
3. A hash, $h(m)$, of m, assuring its integrity.
4. An ordered list of signers (*OLS*) of the certificate. It contains the identity of $k+1$ network nodes, denoted by $n_0, n_1, ..., n_k$, being $n_0 = A$ the content originator.

5. The validity period *(ts₁,ts₂)* for C_m, establishing that the certificate is valid from ts_1 until ts_2.

6. Description of the hash and signature functions which have been used.

Finally, the previous items are recursively signed by the nodes listed in the *OLS*. First, a message containing *C* is signed by *A*. The result, along with *m*, is then sent to the selected *k* participants. The resulting signature is subsequently checked and signed by n_1, and so on. In summary, at each stage, the next node in the *OLS* adds its signature to the previous ones, as follows (see

• Figure 3-(b)):

$$E_0 = E_{K_{n_0}^{-1}}(h(C)$$

$$E_{i+1} = E_{K_{n_{i+1}}^{-1}}(E_i)$$

where $E_{K_{n_0}^{-1}}(\cdot)$ represents the asymmetric encryption of any message using n_i's private key $K_{n_i}^{-1}$.

Signers have to perform a *local verification* stage in order to ensure that they are not being cheated on. This consists in the following three steps:

1. *Certificate verification.* Each participant/signer, $n_i \in OLS$, should verify the correctness of the received certificate C_{i-1}. This includes:

    1.1. Obtaining the owner's public key, and authenticating previous signers as well.

    1.2. Computing *h(m)* and comparing it with the value contained in the received certificate.

    1.3. Checking its table of signed contents, and verify that no entries exist corresponding to the same content.

2. *Signatures verification.* Each peer verifies the signatures contained in the received certificate according to the list order. If any public key is unknown, it can be acquired with an instance of Pathak and Iftode's public key authentication protocol.

3. *Local management.* If previous verifications succeed, the node adds its signatures to C_{i-1}, thus creating C_i. Furthermore, each n_i dumps the received certificate (including the signatures contained), a timestamp, and the generated signature $E_{K_{n_i}^{-1}}(E_{i-1})$ on his local table of signatures S_{n_i}. This local database keeps track of signed contents.

Finally, *A* publishes the content *m*, along with the content certificate: *(m,C_m)*.

Once downloaded the desired content, the correctness of the certificate should be verified to ensure the authenticity and integrity of *m*, so *B* must verify the correctness either of some or all of the chained signatures and their identities as well. For this, *B* performs the following steps:

• *Step 1.* B computes *h(m)* from *m* and compares the result with that included in the certificate. If both values differ, then either m has been altered or C_m is not an authentic certificate for *m*.

• *Step 2.* B should authenticate the peers listed in the *OLS*. At worst, *B* knows none of the signers' identities, having to run Pathak and Iftode's protocol, and pre-evaluating the new members' trust based, for instance, on the weighted values given by a Trust Management System (TMS) (Selcuk, 2004.)

• *Step 3.* B verifies the chain of signatures by recursively encrypting *C* with the ordered list of public keys.

Web of Trust

Since it is not realistic to assume reliance exclusively on a hierarchy of CAs in a P2P network, especially if it is the case of a MANET, some works use web-of-trust models like PGP (Zimmer, 1995) to provide, among others, authentication mechanisms. This technique has focused largely on public key authentication, digital signatures, and certificates, and creates a decentralized fault-tolerant web of confidence for all public keys. In Gnutella (Gnutella, 2008), a decentralized P2P infrastructure for sharing files, contents and peers are generally identified by their hashes and reputation value. This enables reputations to scale far beyond trust in the user and allows widely duplicated corrupt files to be recalled quickly (Schechter, 2004.) However, it is required ensuring that an attacker or a collusion of them cannot modify maliciously an honest peer's reputation information. Such information can be retrieved from other participating peers based on their prior experiences of transactions. This framework is quite close to social scenarios where people consult each other to establish the reputation of any resource. Furthermore, Gnutella protocol holds self-replication (distribution of false information), man-in-the-middle, pseudospoofing, ID stealth and shilling attacks.

Traditional P2P systems assume a high level of trust between community nodes and, as a result, cooperation plays an essential role. In (Tran, 2005), a trust-based access control framework based on DAC is proposed that uses a scoring system to differentiate peers based on their behavior. Briefly, the access control framework is characterized by the following:

- Autonomy: The system leaves the control of access rights to the discretion of the owner of the object. Moreover, the user community is unknown at the time of policy creation.
- Trust-based decisions: Access decisions are evaluated via a participation and recommendation protocol, combining four types of scores: direct trust, indirect trust, direct contribution and indirect contribution. In principle, decision rules depend on

a weighted summation of the overall trust value and the overall contribution value, and also regarding the trust thresholds for his files according to the files' quality (such as sensitivity and value of the content.)

- Cooperation: The scores make peers interdependent in term of granting access to a certain shared content. Furthermore, peers should also collaborate to isolate malicious peers.

In order to have mutual authentication among subjects, this architecture supports an authentication protocol based on SSL (TLS, 2008.)

On the other hand, the trust metric implemented in PGP is simple and can lead to counter intuitive decision being made (Eschenauer, 2004.) Concerning trust metrics, different trust models have been developed and their properties have been extensively studied. Interested readers can find further details in (Marti, 2006.)

A Note on Rationality and Fair Exchange

Originally, P2P file sharing systems are designed to share resources of each computer for the common good of everyone in the system (Ma, 2005.) As mentioned above, reputation-based incentive models seemed more promising at controlling the content distribution (Buragohain, 2003.) In such models, it is reasonable to assume that peers would not misbehave aimed at maximizing the utility (the expected payoff) that they derive from the system in each interaction. It is precisely in this context where notions such as *rationality* become particularly interesting. Informally, a rational peer, and therefore self-interested, is considered to be such that it would never behave against its own interest.

Further works focus on quantifying the cost/benefit tradeoff that will lead nodes to share theirs resources, and approach secure collaboration-based systems assuming peers' rationality

(Shneidman, 2003.) Particularly, micropayments protocols tend to meet fairness, assuring that providers are guaranteed to be paid, while requesters are discouraged to behave as freeloaders because they are refunded for each upload. Thus, system users are given an incentive to work together towards a common goal (Zhang, 2007.) Similarly, rationality is therefore forcing nodes to take specific actions; entities are *rationally* forced to follow the protocol description as they obtain a better payoff value be doing so.

On the other hand, the problem of fairness in P2P systems is an instance of the *Tragedy of the commons*, actually represented by *free-riding* problem. Almost all proposals dealing with free-riders are based on auditing mechanisms, but rely on the existence of a PKI.

FUTURE TRENDS

We have identified three different branches for future research opportunities: the use of proof-of-work mechanisms for controlling access, the provision of a secure delegation service in replication, and the emerging applications of social networks.

Proof of Work

Commercial file sharing systems have addressed different techniques to face up free-riding and authors' copyright problems. Most of the presented proposals link authorization with a "grantor" (a TTP), who produces certificates binding owners to contents, owners to requesters, and also owners to theirs providers. All verification and accounting loads fall on a unique entity, what introduces several performance and delegation inconveniences.

A common solution consists of renouncing to any form of fine-grained access controls, and simply ask each requester to invest an effort (e.g. computational, such as solving a puzzle) just to

prove that he is really interested in the file. Despite its many limitations, such a mechanism can be extremely useful to discourage non-desired behaviors in collaborative environments.

The work shown in (Rowaihy, 2005) presents an admission control system that mitigates Sybil attacks by adaptively constructing a hierarchy of cooperative admission control nodes. The admission control system, implemented by the participant nodes, vets joining nodes via client puzzles. A node wishing to join the network is serially challenged by the nodes from a leaf to the root of the hierarchy. Nodes completing the puzzles of all nodes in the chain are provided a cryptographic proof of the vetted identity.

Delegation

A particularly challenging problem in content distribution is how to carry out delegation of privileges. The use of delegation provides flexibility and scalability, as well as a reduction of the need of control. For this, a node (the delegated) will act eventually on behalf of another node (the delegating) with some of her privileges. Moreover, malicious actions may be punished by means of downgrading/revoking the misbehaved node's security label.

Unfortunately, there is a problem in the application of existing delegation mechanisms in pure P2P environments, for access control based on identity may be ineffective when the requester is unknown to the resource owner. For example, the delegated node could masquerade herself as the delegating user, or impersonate her, since there is no control on what others can do. Further works have addressed delegation services in a fully distributed environment, such as the complete framework for role-based delegation addressed in (Zhang, 2003), where all behaviors are governed by a set of explicit rules. Moreover, the work introduced in (Li, 2005) presents trust management as an approach for RBAC credential delegation in decentralized distributed systems.

Social Networks

Several works have applied rational models, such as the Prisoners' Dilemma, in order to empirically observe a networking social pattern. In principle, peers generally self-organize in social groups of similar peers, called "semantic–groups", depending on the resources they are sharing. Some works try to exploit this social phenomenon by maintaining *social networks* and using these in content discovery, content recommendation, and downloading. These social peer communities lead to challenging security concerns that seem to be more accepted by the real users. It is therefore interesting to study emergent topics related to the dynamics of cooperation and fairness, and which strategy leads to the formation of interesting social profiles, and content integrity protocols based on cooperation.

CONCLUSION

P2P networks are useful not only for relatively simple file sharing systems, in which the main goal is directly exchanging contents with others. However, large P2P distribution networks will be more robust against attacks and will consist of more sophisticated structures which self-organize into network topologies with the purpose of sharing resources such as content and CPU cycles, of maintaining secure and efficient storage, and retrieving data.

In many applications, it is crucial for a user to control who gets access to the contents he shares. This task may seem easy to be tackled by assigning permissions, and using a common access control mechanism. However, in a file sharing system contents can be soon replicated through different locations, so ensuring that each new provider will behave accordingly to another user's access policy gets more complicated (and definitely hard should a global security infrastructure be unavailable.)

In this chapter we have presented an overview of the problem of secure P2P content distribution by identifying the feature space and main requirements that an authentication and access control model for file sharing should support. Most works done in this field agree with applying schemes based on X.509 certificates and authorization attributes, and allowing users to infer the access rights locally. Thus, users should be able to specify access policies. As a result, it should allow users to take multiple security clearances simultaneously and change these credentials dynamically during different interaction phases.

However, there is not a strict classification which identifies the most suitable implementation for a certain environment, and no classification defines the space of possible distributed implementations either (Kane, 2006.) There are, however, some principles, which are built on the basic access control mechanisms, well suited for most of the distributed system environment: user group, access rules and centralized control. Fully decentralized systems must deal with these requirements, adapting them to the inherent self-organized nature of such environments.

On the other hand, P2P applications deployed over MANETs (e.g. mobile P2P) introduce a number of new issues related to naming, discovery, communication and security. In particular, these systems require a lightweight and efficient architecture due to their highly dynamic nature.

Finally, the idea of using cryptographic puzzles for decreasing spam is being extended to P2P networks. This idea could provide a form of access control and detect DoS attacks in advance.

REFERENCES

Abadi, M., Burrows, M., Manasse, M., & Wobber T. (2005). Moderately Hard, Memory-Bound Functions. *ACM Transactions on Internet Technology, 5(2),* 299-327.

Adya, A., Bolosky, W. J., Castro, M., Chaiken, R., Cermak, G., Douceur, J. R., Howell, J., Lorch, J., R., Theimer, M., & Wattenhofer, R. P.. (2002). FARSITE: Federated, Available, and Reliable Storage for an Incompletely Trusted Environment. In *Proc. of the 5th Symposium on Operating Systems Design and Implementation*.

Buragohain, C., Agrawal, D., & Suri, S. (2003). A Game Theoretic Framework for Incentives in P2P Systems. In *Proc. of the 3rd IEEE Int. Conf. on Peer-to-Peer Computing*, 48-56.

Damiani, E., De Capitani, S., Paraboschi, S., Samarati, P., & Violante, F. (2002). A Reputation-Based Approach for Choosing Reliable Resources in Peer-to-Peer Networks. In *Proc. of the 9th ACM Conf. on Computer and Communications Security*, 207-216.

Daswani, N., & García—Molina, H. (2004). Pong-Cache Poisoning in GUESS. In *Proc. of the 11th ACM Conf. on Computer and communications security*, 98-109.

Defigueiredo, D., Garcia, A., & Kramer, B. (2002). Analysis of Peer-to-Peer Network Security using Gnutella. University of California Technical Report.

Desmedt, Y. (1997). Some Recent Research Aspects of Threshold Cryptography. In *Proc. of the 1st. Int. Workshop on Information Security, LNCS 1196*, 58-173. Springer-Verlag.

Diffie, W., & Hellman, M. (1976). New Directions in Cryptography. *IEEE Trans. Info. Theory 22*(6), 644-654 .

Douceur, J. R. (2002). The Sybil Attack. In *Proc. of the 1st Int. Workshop on Peer-to-Peer Systems*, 251-260.

Eschenauer, L., Gligor, V. D., & Baras, J. (2004). On Trust Establishment in Mobile Ad-Hoc Networks. *Security Protocols, LNCS, 2845*, 47-66. Springer-Verlag.

Farrell, S., & Housley, R. (2002). *An Internet Attribute Certificate Profile for Authorization. RFC 3281*, IETF.

Fiat, A., & Naor, M. (1994). Broadcast encryption. In Proc. of the 13th Annual Int. *Cryptology Conference on Advances in Cryptology*, 480-491.

Fox, G. (2001). Peer-to-Peer Networks. *Computing in Science & Engineering, 3*(3).

Gnutella. Retrieved Jan 18, 2008 from Vanguard Gnutella Web site: http://www.gnutella.com

Hu, V.C., Ferraiolo, D. F., & Kuhn, D. R. (2006). Assessment of Access Control Systems. *NIST Technology Administration,* NIST Technical Report NISTIR 7316.

Juels, A., & Brainard, J. (1999). Client puzzles: A cryptographic defense against connection depletion attacks. In *Proc. of the Networks and Distributed Security Systems*, 151-165.

Kane, K., & Browne, J. C. (2006). On classifying access control implementations for distributed systems. In *Proc. of the 11th ACM Symposium on Access control models and technologies*, 29-38.

Lamport, L., Shostak, R., & Pease, M. (1982). The Byzantine General Problem. *ACM Transactions on Programming Languages and Systems, 4*(3), 382-401.

Lepro, R. (2003). Cardea: Dynamic access control in distributed systems. *NASA Advanced Supercomputing (NAS) Division*, NAS Technical Report NAS-03-020.

Levine, B. N., & Shields, C. (2002). Hordes: A Protocol for Anonymous Communication Over the Internet. *Computer Security, 10(*3), 213-240.

Li, N., Mitchell, J. C., & Winsborough, W. H. (2005). Beyond Proof-of-Compliance: Security Analysis in Trust Management. *Journal of the ACM, 52*(3), 474-514.

Lin, W. K., Chiu, D. M., & Lee,Y. B. (2004). Erasure Code Replication Revisited. In *Proc. of the 4th IEEE Int. Conf. on Peer-to-Peer Computing.*

Lopez, J., Oppliger, R., & Pernul, G. (2004). Authentication and Authorization Infrastructures (AAIs): A Comparative Survey. *Computer Communications, 27*(16), 1608-1616.

Ma, Y., & Wang, D. (2005). An Approach to Fair Resource Sharing in Peer-to-Peer Systems. In *Proc. of the 4th International Conference on Networking, LNCS 3421*, 643-652. Springer-Verlag.

Marti, S., & Garcia-Molina, H. (2006). Taxonomy of trust: Categorizing P2P reputation systems. *Computer Networks, 50*, 472-484.

Maniatis, P., Giuli, T. J., Roussopoulos, M., Rosenthal, D. S. H., & Baker, M. (2004). Impeding Attrition Attacks in P2P Systems. In *Proc. of the 11th ACM SIGOPS European Workshop.*

Narasimha M., Tsudik G. & Yi J.H. (2003). On the Utility of Distributed Cryptography in P2P and MANETs: The Case of Membership Control. In *Proc. of the 11th IEEE Int. Conf. on Network Protocols*, 336-345.

Osborn, S., Ravi Sandhu, R. S., & Munawer, Q. (2000). Configuring role-based access control to enforce mandatory and discretionary access control policies. *ACM Transactions on Information and System Security, 3*(2,) 85-106.

Pestoni, F., Lotspiech, J. B. & Nusser, S. (2004). xCP: Peer-to-Peer Content Protection. *IEEE Signal Processing Magazine, 21*(2), 71-81.

Palomar, E., Estevez-Tapiador, J. M., Hernandez-Castro, J. C.& Ribagorda, A. (In press, 2007). Secure content access and replication in pure P2P networks. Computer Communications.

Pathak V. & Iftode L. (2006). Byzantine Fault Tolerant Public Key Authentication in Peer-to-Peer Systems. *Computer Networks, 50(*4), 579-596. Elsevier.

Rowaihy, H., Enck, W., McDaniel, P., & La Porta, T. (2005). *Limiting Sybil Attacks in Structured Peer-to-Peer Networks.* Network and Security Research Center, Department of Computer Science and Engineering, Pennsylvania State University, USA.

Rubin, A. D. (1997). Method for the secure distribution of electronic files in a distributed environment. *Patent number, 5*, 638-446.

Sanchez, M., López, G., Cánovas, O., Juan, A. Sánchez, J. A., & Gómez-Skarmeta, A. F. (2006). An Access Control System for Multimedia Content Distribution. A.S. Atzeni and A. Lioy (Eds.): *EuroPKI, LNCS 4043*, 169-183.

Sandhu, R. S., (1993). Lattice-Based Access Control Models. *IEEE Computer, 26*(11), 9-19.

Sandhu, R. S., Coyne E.J., Feinstein H.L. & Youman C.E. (1996). *Role-based access control models. Computer, 29*(2), 38-47.

Sandhu, R.S., & Munawer, Q. (1998). How to Do Discretionary Access Control Using Roles. In *Proc. of the ACM Workshop on Role-Based Access Control*, 47-54.

Sandhu, R. S., & Samarati, P. (1994). Access Control: Principles and Practice. *IEEE Communications Magazine, 32*(9), 40-48.

Sandhu R.S. & Zhang X. (2005). Peer-to-peer access control architecture using trusted computing technology. In *Proc. of the 10th ACM Symposium on Access control models and technologies*, 147-158.

Schechter, S. E., Greenstadt, R. A., & Smith M.D. (2004). Trusted Computing, Peer-to-Peer Distribution, and The Economics of Pirated Entertainment. *Economics of Information Security, 12*, 1568-2633. Springer.

Selcuk, A. A., Uzun, E. & Pariente, M. R. (2004). A Reputation-Based Trust Management System for P2P Networks. In *Proc. of the 4th IEEE/ACM*

Int. Symposium on Cluster Computing and the Grid, 251-258.

Shneidman, J. & Parkes, D.C. (2003). Rationality and Self-Interest in Peer to Peer Networks. In *Proc. of the 2nd Int. Workshop on P2P Systems*, 139-148. Springer-Verlag.

The IETF TLS Workgroup Retrieved Jan 18, 2008 from Transport Layer Security Web site: http://www.ietf.org/html.charters/tls-charter.html

Tolone, W., Ahn, G., Pai, T. & Hong, S. (2005). Access Control in Collaborative Systems. *ACM Computing Surveys, 37*(1), 29-41.

Tran, H., Hitchens, M., Varadharajan, V., & Watters, P. (2005). A Trust based Access Control Framework for P2P File-Sharing Systems. In *Proc. of the 38th Hawaii Int. Conf. on System Sciences*.

Weatherspoon, H., Moscovitz, T. & Kubiatowicz, J. (2002). Introspective failure analysis: Avoiding correlated failures in peer-to-peer systems. In *Proc. of the Int. Workshop on Reliable Peer-to-Peer*.

Zhang, L., Ahn, G. & Chu, B. (2003). A Rule-Based Framework for Role-Based Delegation and Revocation. *ACM Transactions on Information and System Security, 6*(3), 404-441.

Zhang, X., Chen, S. & Sandhu, R. (2005). Enhancing Data Authenticity and Integrity in P2P Systems. IEEE Internet Computing, 42--49.

Zhang, Y., Lin, L. & Huai, J. (2007). Balancing Trust and Incentive in Peer-to-Peer Collaborative System. Int. Journal of Network Security, 5(1), 73-81.

Zhao, B.Y., Kubiatowicz, J.D. & Joseph A.D. (2001). Tapestry: An Infrastructure for Fault-tolerant Wide-area Location and Routing. (Tech. Rep. No.UCB/CSD-01-1141). University of California at Berkeley, CA.

Zimmermann P. (1995). The Official PGP User's Guide. MIT Press, Cambridge, Massachusetts.

KEY TERMS

Access Control System: Determines the privileges of a particular user, i.e. what a user can do. In general, it includes authentication, authorization and auditory.

Ad Hoc Environment: A self-configuring environment formed spontaneously by mobile (in MANETs) nodes, which union creates an arbitrary topology. It involves the absence of a fixed infrastructure previously established.

Content Authentication: It ensures the integrity of the shared content, and generally also the identity of its owner (or originator).

Cryptography for Distributed Networks: Cryptographic techniques and algorithms suitable for distributed environments, mainly due to the need of preventing Byzantine faults and replacing a centralized authority as well.

P2P File Sharing System: In such a system, nodes communicate directly with each other to exchange information. This provides with the capability to offer replicas of the same content at various locations.

Pure Peer-to-Peer Network: A fully decentralized network typically made up of millions of dynamic nodes involved in the process of sharing and collaboration without relying in central authorities.

Secure Content Replication: Process of sharing information provides guarantees of reliability, fault-tolerance, consistency, accessibility, and security (typically in the form of integrity, authentication and authorization services.)

Chapter XXI
Trust in the Value–Creation Chain of Multimedia Goods

Andreas U. Schmidt
CREATE-NET Research Centre, Italy

Nicolai Kuntze
Fraunhofer Institute for Secure Information Technology, Germany

ABSTRACT

Security in the value creation chain hinges on many single components and their interrelations. Trusted Platforms open ways to fulfil the pertinent requirements. This chapter gives a systematic approach to the utilisation of trusted computing platforms over the whole lifecycle of multimedia products. This spans production, aggregation, (re)distribution, consumption, and charging. Trusted Computing technology as specified by the Trusted Computing Group provides modular building blocks which can be utilized at many points in the multimedia lifecycle. We propose an according research roadmap beyond the conventional Digital Rights Management use case. Selected technical concepts illustrate the principles of Trusted Computing applications in the multimedia context.

INTRODUCTION

Major scientific efforts have gone into security issues of the value creation chain and lifecycle of digital multimedia products, see the Proceedings of the IFIP TC-6 TC-11 Conferences on Communications and Multimedia Security (1999-2007), and (Zeng, et al., 2006). Thus far these developments have been a rather traditional application of information security to the life-cycle of multimedia data. In particular, authorisation policies and meta-data for Digital Rights Management have reached a high degree of maturity (Kosch, et al., 2005). All proposed architectures for multi-media production and distribution have the common characteristic of a few-to-many association between media sources and consumers. This asymmetry is currently gradually changing. The distinction between media consumers and producers becomes less sharp in Web 2.0 communities like Flickr, YouTube and Facebook. Citizen journalism is a new buzzword. And although the mainstream of media production and distribution will still for a long time be largely resting on centralised business models, information and communication technology exhibit a trend toward convergence which treats user devices on the same technical footing as media servers, for instance.

Likewise the traditional security architectures supporting the life cycle of multimedia content are centralistic and focused on the enforcement of Digital Rights Management (DRM) policies throughout the processes. This approach has its own technical, as well as economical and societal problems (Becker, et al., 2003; Drahos, & Maher, 2004; Mulligan, et al., 2003). On the other hand, the trend toward decentralised distribution structures calls for radically new security foundations. Merabti, & Llewellyn-Jones (2006) suggest approaches to DRM which are rooted in cellular automata to establish trust between consuming and distributing nodes. The authors also mention Trusted Computing as a potential underlying technology.

The purport of this chapter is to show that Trusted Computing is a viable technology option for the security fundaments of old and new multimedia production and distribution models alike. The standardisation efforts of the Trusted Computing Group have produced what has the potential to become a universal security fundament for the information society. The distinct feature of the new technology is its inherently decentralised organisation. The consequences of this change of paradigms must not be underestimated. Though classical security systems, e.g. for access control and Public-Key Infrastructures (PKI), can easily be modelled using TC, the underlying trust models leave ample space for alternatives – already known or yet to be envisaged.

The chapter is organised as follows. Section 1.1 presents fundamental notions of Trusted Platforms which are essential for the understanding of the concepts outlined in Section 2, which structures the life-cycle of multimedia according to security requirements. Key usages of TC are highlighted in Section 2.2. Section 3 introduces TC on a more technical level, providing prerequisites for the architectural ideas sketched in Section 4. The latter presents two key concepts for TC application in multimedia content distribution, the first centred on mobile devices, the second on traditional Digital Video Broadcast (DVB) architectures. Section 5 contains a concluding discussion focused on security assessments and practical implications of this novel combination of technologies.

1.1 The Notion of Trusted Platforms

The idea of building security into open, connected systems by using computing platforms enhanced by security-relevant functionality in protected places has a long history, rooted in the often-cited study by the Rand Corporation, (1970), see also (Gasser, et al. 1989). These platforms are characterized by a few key properties.

A *hardware security anchor* is the key to the protection of the system behaviour and acts as a *root of trust* for its secure operation. Secondly, functional building blocks in a system that are assumed to be trusted, i.e., to behave in a well-defined manner for the intended purpose, form the *Trusted Computing Base (TCB)* of the system. The TCB comprises such components of a system which cannot be examined for trustworthiness during operation, but only by out-of-band processes like compliance and conformance testing, validation, and certification.

The TCB together with the hardware security anchor can be used to turn a system into a *trusted platform (TP)*, which is a very ambitious, and still today theoretical, concept. The key concept is the extension of trust in an open system from the root to other, loaded or otherwise changing components using the TCB's capabilities. This extends the *trust boundary* of a TP beyond the root and the TCB, and is commonly realized by cryptographic mechanisms of which both are capable. The establishment of the trust boundary is conceptually associated to the boot cycle of the platform. Certain functions of the hardware root and the TCB are started before other parts of the system and operate as a *root of trust for measurement*. This means that components that are started or loaded later on, are *measured*, i.e., digest values over a component's software parts, parameters and loaded programs are generated and stored protected by the root of trust. This process, if executed up to the OS loader and OS, is called *authenticated boot*.

Yet more involved is the concept of *secure boot*. It is of particular importance for devices like set-top boxes or mobile handsets that necessarily have some stand-alone and offline functional requirements. In secure boot, the device is equipped with a local verifier and enforcer supervising the boot process. They compare measurement values of new components with reference values (in a protected storage space) and decide whether they are loaded or not. Thus the system is ensured to boot into a pre-defined, secure state.

To prove trustworthiness of a TP to an external party, or *verifier*, processes called *(remote) attestation* and according protocols have been envisaged. They transport measurement values and data necessary to retrace the system state from them, so called *measurement logs*, to the verifier. The data is uniquely and verifiably bound to a particular platform, e.g. by a digital signature. Remote attestation can be supported by a PKI structure for instance to protect a platform owner's privacy by revealing the platform identity only to a trusted third party.

Today, Trusted Computing (TC) is mostly associated with the standardization efforts of the Trusted Computing Group (Trusted Computing Group, 2007a, 2007b) on which also our discussions build.

TRUST IN MULTIMEDIA PRODUCTION, DISTRIBUTION, AND CONSUMPTION

Multimedia content is in the heart of various business models today. Many web sites, journals, and television are depending on a constant flow of new or aggregated content. Also in the often referred Web 2.0 development which can be observed nowadays the quality of content is crucial. Especially in journalism the way of content production and originator are deciding for the value of the delivered content and therefore if a particular content is requested by the users or not.

2.1 The Multimedia Lifecycle

Multimedia content undergoes different stages from production to consumption. Multimedia content is created by different originators, processed or modified in postproduction or adapted for different end user scenarios (e.g. different quality and bandwidth requirements), distributed to the end user devices and there consumed by the user as depicted in Figure 1. During production content is created and aggregated by manual, semi-automatic, or automatic processes as it is for example described by Fioravanti, Spinu, & Campanai (2007). In this high level model content is feed into a distribution / consumption model as it is proposed by (Kosch, et al., 2005). Within this model users can issue a request for a certain content which is then delivered from the media storage. At some stage it is necessary to adapt the content to the receiver's requirements.

During production, distribution, and consumption charging data is created and transferred to a charging infrastructure depending on the underlying use case. The processes within the charging infrastructure and protocols there are not in the

Figure 1. High level description of the multimedia life cycle

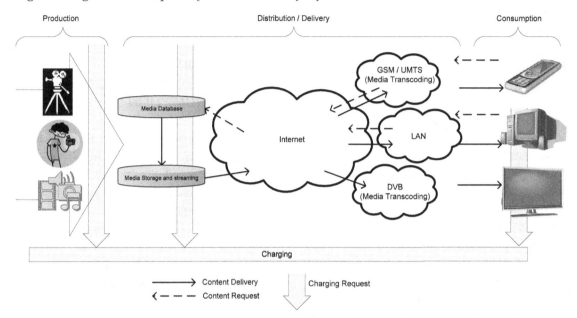

focus of this paper but it is interesting to note that the user side equipment offers very different opportunities to establish charging schemes located in the devices which are situated in the user's domain of influence. These devices do not necessarily have a bidirectional communication with the media storage as this is common for broadcast systems like television.

2.2 Trusted Platform Key Usages

Trusted Platforms as defined by the Trusted Computing Group offers distinctive features which spur certain use cases. The hardware based trust offered by the Trusted Platform Module can enable the following use cases:

- Rooted in the production process the originator can be added as additional information in the multimedia meta information. This additional data could reveal the identity of the artist or journalist who produced the content. This data helps to track a certain

content to the person or machine which created the content. Especially in the area of automated content it can be of some importance to know how and who exactly produced or aggregated a certain bit of information. Considering the importance and impact of news broadcasted by news agencies the use case here becomes obvious.

- Beside the identity of the creator it is also possible to include means to verify the integrity of the platform used to produce the actual content. In the case of mobile devices like cellular phones it is necessary to adapt the content to the abilities of the target platform. During this transformation process it is possible that certain information are suppressed or altered. Trusted Computing offers proof that the system is in the desired status.
- Device side metering of consumption is a fundamental extension of the known payment schemes in use. This change in the basic structure from a centralised authority towards a decentralised system offers high

flexibility with respect to advanced and fine granular payment schemes. It also extends the potential use of e.g. set top boxes situated by the user to consumer resale points. In case of distribution of media content or as a platform for economic usage this approach could help to spur the usage.

- Watermarks are an upcoming technology which is promoted as an alternative to Digital Rights Management tagging media content which allows determining the source it. By combining watermarks and Trusted Computing to one integrated system decentralised points of sales for digital goods can be build offering the ability to individually tag each sold bit of content. By this each sold product is bound to a certain customer. This enables to trace a file back to the latter customer. Such a point of sales could for example be located in the local music store or be part of the set top box.

- As an extension the introduced point of sales can apply certain digital rights management (DRM) functionalities upon the digital content. These restrictions can be applied by the box dependent on the contract between the partners. These restrictions can for example regulate the count of allowed copies. Depending on the rights purchased by the user different usages of the content (multiple viewing, multiple private copies, quality discrimination, commercial-free versions, etc.) can be permitted by application of DRM techniques. As every customer can buy different rights for one digital asset this restriction have to be added on customer side. It could also be intended, as an alternative to 'hard' DRM, to tag a digital asset and by this to suppress the distribution. This leads to the need to include a marking identifying the individual customer, while still preserving his/her privacy. This service can be a major reason to apply watermarking at client-side. This can be implemented with

ease within the trusted set-top box based on our concepts.

It should be noted that our applications use Trusted Computing in a way very different from Digital Rights Management, which is often considered as the sole use for Trusted Computing. All presented applications bind the economic value to a particular instantiation of the TPM. If one trust anchor breaks, only limited damage can occur as the damage is restricted in space and time, e.g., to one content stream. In contrast, if a single TPM in a DRM system breaks, the protected digital good can be converted into an unprotected version which can be freely distributed on a large scale, causing heavy monetary losses to its owner.

3. TRUSTED COMPUTING GROUP TECHNOLOGY ESSENTIALS

The Trusted Computing Group is the main industrial effort to standardize TC technology. It currently enters the mobile domain with the aim to provide a standardised security infrastructure. Trust as defined by the TCG means that an entity always behaves in the expected manner for the intended purpose. The trust anchor, called Trusted Platform Module (TPM), offers various functions related to security. Each TPM is bound to a certain environment and together they form a trusted platform from which the TPM cannot be removed.

TC as it is currently being standardized in the PC and mobile domain offers a highly flexible and reliable security infrastructure enabling various kinds of authentication, authorization, and audit schemes. A TPM provides a unique identity of the particular device, and cryptographic abilities for creation, storage such as usage of asymmetric key pairs. On top of these TPM abilities, TC offers a metric to measure the system state and to report this measurement to a third entity. A further main ability is to bind certain data cryptographically to the particular platform and its state.

Through the TPM the TP gains a cryptographic engine and a protected storage. Each physical instantiation of a TPM has a unique identity by an Endorsement Key (EK) which is created at manufacture time. This key is used as a base for secure transactions as the Endorsement Key Credential (EKC) asserts that the holder of the private portion of the EK is a TPM conforming to the TCG specification. The EKC is issued as well at production time and the private part of the key pair does not leave the TPM. There are other credentials specified by the TCG which are stating the conformance of the TPM and the platform for instance the so called platform credential. Before a TPM can be used a take ownership procedure must be performed in which the usage of the TPM is bound to a certain user. The following technical details are taken from (Trusted Computing Group 2007a, 2007b).

The TPM is equipped with a physical random number generator, and a key generation component which creates RSA key pairs. The key generator is designed as a protected capability, and the created private keys are kept in a *shielded capability* (a protected storage space *inside* the TPM). The shielded capabilities protect internal data structures by controlling their use. Three of them are essential for applications.

First, *key creation and management*, second the ability to create a *trust measurement* which can be used to assert a certain state toward a, remote party, and finally *sealing* methods to protect arbitrary data by *binding* it (in TCG nomenclature) to TP states and TPM keys.

For the TPM to issue an assertion about the system state, two *attestation* protocols are available. As the uniqueness of every TPM leads to privacy concerns, they provide pseudonymity, resp., anonymity. Both protocols rest on Attestation Identity Keys (AIKs) which are placeholders for the EK. An AIK is a 1024 bit RSA key whose private portion is sealed inside the TPM. The

simpler protocol Remote Attestation (RA) offers pseudonymity employing a trusted third party, the Privacy CA (PCA), which issues a credential stating that the respective AIK is generated by a sound TPM within a valid platform. The system state is measured by a reporting process with the TPM as central reporting authority receiving measurement values and calculating a unique representation of the state using hash values. For this, the TPM has several Platform Configuration Registers (PCR). Beginning with the system boot each component reports a measurement value, e.g., a hash value over the BIOS, to the TPM and stores it in a log file. During RA the communication partner acting as verifier receives this log file and the corresponding PCR value. The verifier can then decide if the device is in a configuration which is trustworthy from his perspective. Apart from RA, the TCG has defined Direct Anonymous Attestation. This involved protocol is based on a zero knowledge proof but due to certain constraints of the hardware it is not implemented in current TPMs.

AIKs are crucial for applications since they can not only be used, according to TCG standards, to attest the origin and authenticity of a trust measurement, but also to authenticate other keys generated by the TPM. Before an AIK can testify the authenticity of any data, a PCA has to issue a credential for it. This credential together with the AIK can therefore be used as an identity for this platform. The protocol for issuing this credential consists in three basic steps.

First, the TPM generates an RSA key pair by performing the **TPM_MakeIdentity** command. The resulting public key together with certain credentials identifying the platform is then transferred to the PCA. Second, the PCA verifies the correctness of the produced credentials and the AIK signature. If they are valid the PCA creates the AIK credential which contains an identity label, the AIK public key, and information about the TPM and the platform. A special structure containing the AIK credential is created which is

Figure 2. Remote attestation process

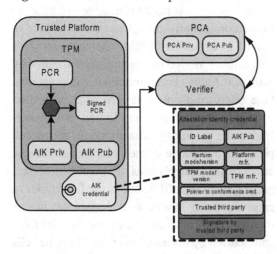

used in step three to activate the AIK by executing the **TPM_ActivateIdentity** command. So far, the TCG-specified protocol is not completely secure, since between steps two and three, some kind of handshake between PCA and platform is missing. The existing protocol could sensibly be enhanced by a challenge/response part to verify the link between the credentials offered in step one and used in step two, and the issuing TPM. The remote attestation process is shown in Figure 5.

Beside the attestation methods TC offers a concept to bind data blobs to a single instantiation and state of a TPM. The **TPM_unbind** operation takes the data blob that is the result of a **Tspi_Data_Bind** command and decrypts it for export to the user. The caller must authorise the use of the key to decrypt the incoming blob. In consequence this data blob is only accessible if the platform is in the namely state which is associated with the respective PCR value.

A mobile version of the TPM is defined by the TCG's Mobile Phone Working Group (Trusted Computing Group 2007b). This Mobile Trusted Module (MTM) differs significantly from the TPM of the PC world and is in fact more powerful in some respects. In particular, it contains a built-in verifier for attestation requests, substituting

partly for an external PCA. Both TPM and MTM are a basis for application architectures. Trusted Computing affects the world of networked PCs but also heavily impacts the mobile industry, as we have indicated in (Schmidt, & Kuntze, 2006; Schmidt, Kuntze, & Kasper, 2008).

The secure boot feature, as described in Section 1.1 is in fact a particularity of the mobile standards. The boot process is the time span from the power on to the stage when the user is able to interact with the device. Within this time span, secure boot ensures that fundamental capabilities are in place, which are critical for the reliability of the system, comprising in particular means for resource isolation and management. During secure boot, as defined in (Trusted Computing Group, 2007b), each component is measured in order of execution. These measurement values are then verified by a local verification agent using so called Reference Integrity Measurement (RIM) digital certificates. If the values match then the processing continues and the started component is registered in a log as well as in a corresponding system state register in a secure storage space. Otherwise the boot will fail and the system switches into a failed state. In case of a failed state the system may offer a Pristine Boot which as a fallback. Pristine Boot defines a device state after initial factory installation where the life cycle of a device begins.

Another use case for the Pristine Boot is an update process to rebuild the required credentials (e.g., RIM certificates) used during secure boot. If the secure boot of an MT succeeds the system on top can rely on the integrity of the system underneath. This includes all subsystems integrated in the platform including the LTE.

4. SELECTED TOPICS

As we have seen, Trusted Computing technology can be useful at several stages in the lifecycle of digital multimedia content. Here we focus on two selected topics which we think are most relevant and closest to realistic applications.

4.1 Trusted Local (Super-) Distribution of Multimedia Content

We have already pronounced the problems associated with classical DRM-based business models and the more or less futile attempts to achieve security for them. Alternative approaches to the marketing of digital media have gained importance. iTunes now offers media from major label EMI with superior quality and free of copy protection, in effect using the absence of DRM as a means of distinct quality discrimination (Chaffin, et al., 2007). Exponents of the computer and media industries issued statements raising doubts on the viability of DRM for media marketing (Jobs, 2007; Fulton 2007).

Though most approaches still rest on conventional, centralised distribution structures, some novel ideas have emerged. Network marketing emulates the distribution system of free-riders, namely peer-to-peer systems (Zerfiridis, & Karatza, 2004). It poses additional value proposition to buyers of the original (legal) version of the good by revenues or other rewards linked to resale. Important examples are Peer Impact (2007), where buyers receive rebates on subsequent acquisitions for every resale, and the Potato System (Grimm, & Nützel, 2002 and 2003), a genuine multi-level market for virtual goods. These ideas have not received the highest level of public attention, perhaps due to their similarity to illicit schemes, like pyramid and Ponzi schemes, or Peter-and-Paul scams, and the like, cf. the detailed study (Micklitz, et al., 1999). Economical research by one of the present authors (Schmidt, 2006 and 2008) shows, however, that even such fancy market models can be successful as a potential replacement of rigid DRM.

The common denominator of these models is a de-centralised content distribution structure, which calls for likewise de-centralised secu-

rity building blocks. Namely, the novel business models in any case need to be supported by some kind of protection – though not the same kind of control as centralised DRM schemes exert. This new kind of 'digital ownership', as it is called by Stini et al. (2006), can come about in many forms. One interesting option is territorial protection in mobile media super-distribution. An Owner-trader of a piece of media contained in his cell phone as a portable carrier, can for instance be entitled to exclusively resell the media in a certain geographical area (if he/she is the first trader to enter that area). In a network market this means that the trader is to some extent protected from competition by his own buyers to whom he sells the good for instance by close-range communication channels. These buyers first have to leave a certain protected zone, before they are entitled to down-line resale. This kind of protection requires enforcing authorisation decisions based on geographical position on the users' devices. We have presented a concept for this using trusted computing in (Schmidt, Kuntze, & Abendroth 2008), which we now sketch.

In order to fell authorisation decisions based on device location, an entity called location trigger must have access to location information and be able to provide this information to other entities enforcing according policies, either on the device or on the part of some service. The concept of a Trusted Location Trigger Authorisation (TLTA) we propose in the following, rests on these key ideas. First, the location trigger in TLTA operates on two separate levels: i) Handover-based localisation within a network cell and ii) GPS-based (here always meaning either full, device operated GPS or AGPS) localisation within an area circumscribed by a perimeter of cells. Second, a trusted entity on the device, called the Location Trigger Enforcer (LTE), embodying the location trigger functionality and enforcing, possibly in co-operation with a network-side counterpart, authorisation policies. The trust in the LTE rests on security properties of the device, which we assume to be a trusted computing (TC) platform for the purpose of location-based authorisation.

The network side entity establishing authorisation policies on a geographical domain, called the protected zone (pz) is the Trusted Location Trigger Authorisation Centre (TLTAC). It receives (i) the physical geometry of the protected zone and (ii) the desired policies to be enforced within this zone. Based on these data the TLTAC determines configures certain extended Nodes B (eNBs) of the MNO in Step B. After the setup TLTAC's main task is to authenticate the end users devices and to maintain a list of them for authorisation purposes. In turn, LTE (i) receives and holds the policies from TLTAC, (ii) receives and holds the protection zone geometry, (iii) determines entry and exit events to the protection zone by some high-precision location mechanism, e.g., A-GPS, and (iv) enforces the policies on the device.

The Figure 3 shows the travel of a mobile device MT through the zones consisting of an outer layer, the surveillance perimeter (sp) that serves LTE

activation, and the protected zone proper. At the point marked (1), MT enters the mobile network in a normal operational mode, with deactivated LTE and A-GPS functions. Upon crossing sp at (2), the handover between a cell marked with a 0 and the corresponding cell marked with a 1 is augmented by the activation of the LTE and the A-GPS, a remote attestation process, registration of MT with the TLTAC, and download of the authorisation policy, and the geometry of pz to MT. By attestation, the eNB of the cell marked with 1 can be convinced that MT is in a trustworthy state and has an untampered LTE present. It then sends an acknowledgement to MT, including the signal to activate the LTE for operation within the sp. From there on the device autonomously operates the location trigger to detect pz using AGPS and with the aid of an A-GPS support server. When MT enters pz at (3), LTE enforces the policy, for instance unlocks a preassigned credential for service access. During sojourn in pz, MT follows the policy and can for instance

Figure 3. Mobile station travelling through the zones and perimeers of a TLTA system

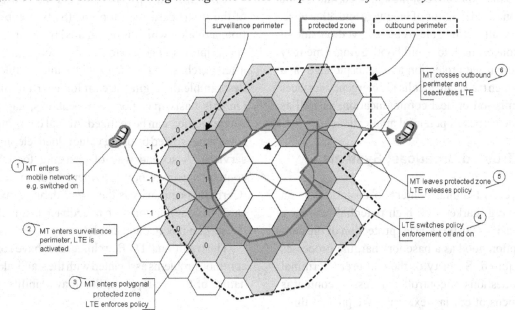

use a LBS whenever the user desires. At some points (4), MT may leave and re-enter pz and LTE switches the enforcement of the policy off and on. LTE finally releases policy enforcement at point 5, but is deactivated only at crossing of the outbound perimeter. At (6), LTE also actively de-registers MT with TLTAC. The triggering of location is cell-based only between points (1) and (2) and after (6), otherwise it relies on (assisted) GPS and MT' autonomous decision via LTE.

This basic scheme of cooperation with a trusted (software) entity on a device and a central entity which just sets policies and defers enforcement thereof to the device is typical for many TC application scenarios. Use cases for a Trusted Location Trigger abound, and DRM-like territorial protection is just one. A broadcast scenario would be situated in a Sports stadium and concert hall: The voice commentary on a sports event is broadcast encrypted to mobile devices in a stadium, which is the pz. Only TLTA-enabled devices receive the decryption keys with the Ppz data managed securely by LTE. The service provider can simply broadcast the content and has no need to operate own access control facilities. In a concert hall, the live audio broadcast should add to the experience of the audience, and can be personalised in terms of language and otherwise. This shall not be able to be received outside of the concert hall, to avoid bootlegging. One may also envisage protection against espionage on a high-tech trade fair, localised emergency services and mission-critical communication, as well as mobile games as potential applications.

4.2 Trusted Broadcast Systems

Delivery of digital content to customers is an emerging market with high potential revenues. For various business cases protection of the consumption good as a base for charging processes is required. Security of the end user's terminal and questions of controlled access to content is the focus of our last example. We present three concrete scenarios for TC application in this context, in order of increasing complexity.

Digital Video Broadcast (DVB), as the widest spread standard for digital content delivery, comprises methods for the protection of media data. DVB exists in diverse branches for special for different broadcasting techniques und formats: Satellite (DVB-S), cable (DVB-C), terrestrial (DVB-T), and mobile environment (DVB-H). The signal is encrypted with the Common-Scrambling-Algorithm (CSA) using an 8 byte seed for initialization, the so called Code Word (CW). This Code Word is provided by the Conditional Access System (CAS) (Gallery, & Tomlinson, 2007). There are many vendors like Cryptoworks or NDS offering CAS Modules to content providers, see Table 7.1 in (Leung, Yau, & Mitchell, 2007). The CAS has the essential task to bridge between the encrypted data stream and a smart card providing CWs. Due to various different CAS systems the customer needs different smart cards, often for exclusive use with different, proprietary Conditional Access Modules (CAM). CSA was kept as a secret over a couple of years, but was revealed some time ago (CSA 2007). Until now CSA is not broken (Weinmann, & Wirt 2005).

Charging and payment is another purport of the smart card – set-top box (STB) combination, a market which is dominated by smart card subscriptions. The customer registers the card after purchase with the provider and is able to descramble the digital stream for a certain time. On this basis, pay per view schemes, e.g. for single movies, can be realized. Actual charging is sometimes solved by using value added telephone services. A second way of charging for DVB content is using mobile payment solutions. One (German) peculiarity is the use of debit or credit cards in combination with a feedback channel of the set-top box (Conax 2002).

The traditional DVB architectures have some common problems associated with the stand-alone nature of the set-top box, the unavailability, respectively, costliness of an upstream channel, and the smart card-based security architecture:

1. The update of decryption algorithms and secret keys and generally the remote management of the STB, e.g., subscriber management and channel bouquet selection, are difficult and costly.
2. Accounting and charging is generally realized as an out-of-band process more or less tightly linked to smart card roll out. On-line charging solutions are scarce and of provisional nature.
3. Users selecting bouquets from a variety of subscribers have to handle a number (ever increasing as the market diversifies) of smart cards manually.
4. If bouquet selection is done via the DVB down link, sending of personalized data for this kind of access control over the DVB channel is costly and does not scale well for many subscribers.

The focus of this paper is to provide practical improvement of the existing content protection schemes used by the DVB standard providing benefits in terms of customer satisfaction and price of the individual device. Other work in this area is focused in a more general security analysis as by Gallery, & Tomlinson (2005) and Mitchell (2005). These security-theoretic approaches may be integrated in the scenarios of this paper. Nevertheless, from a economic perspective the relevance of certain protection targets like freshness and proof of origin has to be examined with respect to the practical importance.

We propose architectural concepts based on Trusted Computing (TC), to improve on this state of the matter, and present a high-level design of a trusted set-top box (TSTB) which can be reconfigured for various content protection schemes and payment methods. At the core of the concept lies a *trust-enhanced CAM*, which we describe in Section 4.2.1. In particular it realizes descram-

bling methods in software while protecting the associated access secrets of each provider. This usage of TC for STBs is rather traditional and feasible with minimal architectural changes. In a further step, we assume in Section 4.2.2 that the trusted STB has some sort of access to a communication network and use the latter for *take ownership* of it, i.e., the process of impressing a user identity and associated credential to the STB. This essentially obliterates the use of smart cards. Finally we discuss options for integration of charging functionality using a mobile device communicating with the STB in Section 4.2.3. The main benefits of deployment and usage of trusted STBs and advanced utilization options are discussed in Section 5.1.

4.2.1 Trust-Enhanced CAM

Based on the basic features of TC a soft realization (or even virtualization) of the CAS is feasible. Implementing in this way a TSTB can be implemented in many variations. An elementary implementation stores the functionality of the CAM as software protected by means of the TPM. If the user requests a scrambled channel, the TSTB uses the CAM software to create the respective CWs required by the CAS. A possible system architecture is shown in Figure 4.

Starting with the smart card on the right hand side, we observe a main conceptual change w.r.t. traditional CAS: The smart card bears merely the subscriber identity and credential. All other security-critical functionality is shifted into the trust boundary of a trust-enhanced CAM and protected by a hardware security anchor, e.g. a TPM. The TCB enables and protects upper functionality of the CAM via a secure boot process. The protected CAM functionality comprises three essentials: i) A management software and protected, non-volatile storage for *access secrets* used by the single CW generators. ii) An interface to the smart card providing a secure channel to

Figure 4. Trust-enhanced CAM in an STB

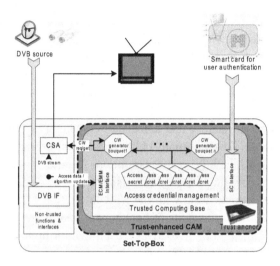

import user credentials iii) A secure interface to import algorithms and access secrets.

The access credential manager invokes soft instances of CW generators on demand, using the required access secret, e.g., a Control Word. Security of the CAS realized in this way relies on the fact that CW generation is within the trust boundary, i.e., the system state of the CW generator and access secret manager is trustworthy and tamper-resistant.

The TCB of each Set-top box is equipped with a credential which identifies it as belonging to some group or individually. This enables end-to-end (e2e) encrypted communication from the provider's headend (US Federal Standard 2000) to the Trust-enhanced CAM. This credential can be impressed at an early stage of the STB's lifecycle, e.g., by the manufacturer, the OEM, or a service provider. It can be located in the hardware trust anchor or be protected by it.

New access secrets and usage policies can be transferred to the CAM in the common Entitlement Control Messages (ECMs), Entitlement Management Messages (EMM) respectively (3GPP 2003), distilled from the DVB stream (ETSI 1996, 2005).

They are, in our scheme, e2e-encrypted for the particular CAM and enable the management software to fell authorization decisions. Comparing the subscriber identity with the policies for e.g., bouquet access in the EMMs, the manager can decide whether to import the associated Control Words which embody the access secrets for the bouquet. Algorithms can be updated for each CW generator, e.g. via IP-over-DVB (ETSI 2003).

Some key advantages of a trust-enhanced CAM are obvious. It resolves the focal problems 1. and 2. described above. The CW generators can be realized in software and implement a variety of different CW generation algorithms. These algorithms can be updated "over the air". Additionally it has the technical advantage that the frequent sending of ECMs for security reasons becomes obsolete, since the derived access control secrets, commonly today the Code Words used for initialization of the CSA, are managed inside the trust boundary and hence are not easily accessible to attackers. This helps to address problem 4.

Let us discuss algorithm updates in some more detail. CSA is designed to meet two central technical requirements. First it has to provide a secure scrambling of the data. Second it has to operate in a real-time environment. The digital stream has to be descrambled the moment it arrives. This leads to a lack of algorithm strength and the need to replace the algorithm can be foreseen (Weinmann, & Wirth, 2005; Bewick 1998), entailing a complete change of the installed infrastructure on side of the customers as well – a very costly and inconvenient effort.

The trust-enhanced CAM enables a modular system in which it is possible to replace every part of the descrambling mechanism in a trustworthy way. Using for instance Field Programmable Gate Arrays (FPGA) technology on top of TCB and root of trust enables the replacement of every part of the existing DVB architecture. For instance, algorithms can be implemented in hardware to gain speed. FPGAs are programmed (reconfigured) before they can perform the desired task. Trustworthy implementations can verify the content of the FPGA before data are transmitted between FPGA and the CAM.

In a more evolved scenario the root of trust, e.g. TPM, could be an integral element of the code word scheme replacing the smart card.

4.2.2 Online CAS

A system which emulates the actual CAS systems in software has to enforce that keys used to generate the CWs required by the CAS are kept secret. The security of the proposed system has to be guaranteed even if the algorithm is published. Beside this technical requirement online verification of the access rights is a premise for dynamical content access control. This leads to an authorization scheme where the CAS asks for permission before the CWs are created. Therefore a connection is established by a communication module granting access to a network.

A protocol solving this problem has to perform the following steps. In preparation an appropriate, controlled roll out of the STB is required. During the roll-out a *take ownership* by the provider must take place. A network operator can be used instead of the provider assigning user identities and, optionally, performing charging processes. The proposed scenario consists of four parties: customer, provider, charging provider, and network operator as depicted in Figure 5. The network operator issues the set-top boxes to the customers in the same way as they offer mobile devices. The bonding between customer and device is based e.g. on a SIM-card. An online take ownership is as well possible as described in the subsequent section.

The network operator establishes his trust in the device by a network operator issued credential which is produced by the box on request. Based on this underlying trust relation the (M)NO can assure the identity of the set-top box to a sup-

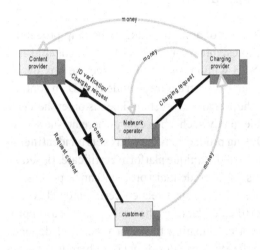

Figure 5. Online CAS scenario

plier. This second (transitive) relation (Kuntze, & Schmidt, 2006) is based on a second credential issued either by the network operator or the trusted set-top box. In either case the network operator in his role as an identity provider (ID) signs this credential which therefore is stored in the trusted set-top box. If a customer decides to consume a certain service it offers this credential to the vendor (V), for instance the content provider. V uses this credential to verify the identity against ID. V then delivers the content and requests charging by ID. In this scenario the user is unknown to V as the credential is only validated by ID. ID does not need to reveal the user identity to V.

Delivery in this context means that V transfers a secret to the TSTB and adds this secret to the list of accepted credentials as this is known by the actual process of conventional CASs. This secret is sealed in the set-top box by using the sealing functionality of the TPM. This means that it can only be used in the same trustworthy state of the box. The root of trust in this case is the ability of attestation of the integrity to a third party namely V and/or ID. An advantage is that personalized data, e.g., for bouquet access needs not to be transferred via the costly satellite downlink.

4.2.3 Online Take Ownership / Online Registration

The aim of an online take ownership procedure is to establish a user identifying credential in a TSTB without the need to issue the box over a special infrastructure provided by ID, in contrast to the previous subsection. The customer should be able to buy such a box everywhere he/she wants. During production every box gets an identifier in form of the unique platform certificate. Based on this initial credential a protocol can be performed to establish a user related certificate. This user certificate identifies the user at V. The used protocol establishing this user credential depends on the existence of a direct or only indirect communication between V and ID.

The user certificate can be created after the take ownership process of a trusted platform which binds a TPM to a certain user using a 160 bit authentication value (TPM owner authorization). AIKs are available after the take ownership to be used as credentials testifying the identity of a user. An AIK can only be created offering a valid TPM owner authorization and is a private/public key pair. The private portion is shielded inside the TPM. After this, a Privacy CA (PCA) issues a certificate to assert the relation between AIK and TPM (see Section 3). For this AIK and certificate creation process an online connection to a privacy CA is required. The pertinent protocol has to protect the origin of the key so that it is impossible to fake a TPM.

In the case of a direct communication the system is equipped with a communication device enabling the direct contact to the PCA. In this case the mentioned protocols can be used without any restrictions. If the system is not equipped with such a communication device at least a short range communication is required enabling a take ownership over a secondary communication device (SD) like a cell phone. The SD forwards the communication in the respective direction. The ensuing communication relationships are shown in Figure 6.

It is important to mention that there has to be a trust relation between the PCA and the content providers. In this use case AIKs are used as tickets which enable accounting. Therefore it could be possible that the PCA should be able to reveal the identity of a certain AIK, e.g. in case of suspected fraud (Kuntze, & Schmidt, 2007a).

After the take ownership an online registration at the respective provider is required to sign up to a certain service. In this process two goals have to be achieved. First, the identity of the mobile device (and therefore the identity of the user) has to be registered at the service provider. By issuing the AIK and the associated certificate, the identity can be proved, and by performing a handshake protocol between service provider and mobile device the origin is testified. The second aim is to negotiate the conditions of the subscription, of which the payment information is the most important part. The service provider transmits a data structure which describes the available charging models and services. The user selects from this offer, signs the selection with the private portion of the AIK and transmits this to the service provider.

Figure 6. Online take ownership via mobile device and network

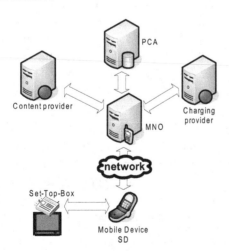

Figure 7. AIK authentication for content access

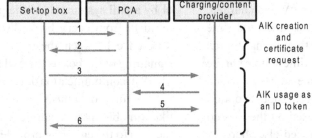

A proof of authenticity of the service provider is also required. Hence it is necessary to sign messages issued by the service provider. A verification of the authenticity can be achieved using known PKI structures or built-in root certificates. Alternatively, the MNO can vouch for the authenticity of a certain service provider replacing conventional PKI systems.

Figure 7 shows a basic scheme using AIKs as authentication tokens. The protocol is divided in two phases. Phase 1 is concerned with AIK creation and certification, phase 2 is the usage of this token. The set-top box transmits in 1) certain credentials of the platform and the public portion of the AIK to the PCA which verifies the offered credentials and then retransmits (2) a certificate stating that this AIK belongs to a an accepted platform. If the MNO works as PCA the AIK can later be used as a payment credential as the MNO can reveal the identity of the users based on the certificate. This feature is used in phase 2 where the set-top box offers the AIK and the corresponding certificate to a provider (3). This provider performs an attestation of the box in this step and then requests from the CA the validity of the offered certificate (4,5). 4 and 5 can be performed e.g. using OCSP responder. Step 6 returns the signed acceptance information of the provider. To validate the signature, an appropriate certificate must be available to the TSTB. It can be necessary to request this root certificate from a trustworthy third party. After this the TSTB

has been successfully registered with a certain provider.

Updates of TSTB algorithms can be mediated by the SD as well, in parallel to the schemes discussed in Section 4.2.1.

DISCUSSION AND CONCLUSION

5.1 Advantages of Trusted Platform Usage

New accounting and charging systems can be established using the TPM and the trusted environment. In Section 4.2.2 and 4.2.3 above the technical focus is the sealing functionality, as a replacement (or new specification) for the CAS. One box can house various CAS concurrently *without any extra hardware costs*. Charging can be transferred into the Box by adding specialized software and appropriate hardware. The trustworthy state of both can be proved in the trusted boot process and attested to an external verifier by remote or anonymous attestation. The box can handle the charging process and control the access to the charged commodity. By this, new payment infrastructures can be established, e.g., for home shopping.

TC offers the possibility for client-side payment. The main idea is that the TSTB handles charging in analogy to prepaid or pay-as-you-go scenarios. The box meters the consumption of the digital content. Either an internal deposit is decremented or the consumption data is stored and after a certain time read by V and charged. The second alternative requires a trusted time source in the device to enable time stamps for the recorded metering data. This time source can be implemented as an online time authority which offers a time-stamping service. Another option is an internal time source based on the trusted platform. This shall be discussed elsewhere. A third usage scenario is the well known distribution of keys which are descrambling a channel for a certain time.

The first alternative requires a central authority to replenish the internal deposit when it is depleted, by transmitting an increment value to the TSB. The increment value is signed by a charging service and encrypted by a key which is bound to the TSTB identity (e.g. the AIK) as explained in (Kuntze, & Schmidt, 2007b) ensuring that this packet is bound to one device. Preventing of replay attacks requires the inclusion of: (i) attestation of the particular device by the charging service testifying the integrity of the device, and (ii) integration of a Nonce issued by the charging service to prevent that the packet is used twice. The box stores these Nonces and rejects replayed packets. A basic protocol works as follows. In step (1) the box requests for an increment of the internal deposit, offering the AIK and a corresponding certificate. Step (2) performs an attestation and within this step a handshake testifying the correlation of the AIK and its certificate. At some point in these steps the charging provider has to decide if he accepts this AIK based on a contractual relation to the user or its charging provider and PCA. After step 2 the charging provider has to decide which amount is transferred to the box.

Storing the consumption in the device is the second alternative. Here it is possible to first consume the content and afterwards pay for it as it is known from e.g. cellular phones. The stored consumption data are transferred to the charging

provider either by a push system where the box is in charge for transferring the data to the provider or by a pull system where the provider requests the data from every box. The most significant difference between these two schemes is the signalling of the box as the pull solution requires a built in communication device like a GSM module. Building on a push solution, another device like a mobile phone can be utilized to transfer the data to the charging provider. Noteworthy in the second case is that the logged data require a special protection against forgery. Therefore each consumption log record needs to be time stamped by a trustworthy time source. After the transfer of the consumption log the charging provider charges the consumer belonging to the system. This relation between consumption data and user is expressed by signing the data with the respective AIK which was first registered at the charging provider. As a privacy protection, the data can be encrypted by a public key belonging to the charging provider. By this an MNO or any third party listening to the data stream cannot create usage profiles of the customers.

A third alternative is based on usage credentials which are basically descrambling keys inserted e.g. in the conventional CAS implemented in DVB and enhanced by a constraint of e.g. its usage period.. Examples for other constraints are maximum boundaries of daily usage, or time of usage. Issuing such a restricted key to a system requires (i) an attestation of the system before the key is transmitted to proof the integrity of the system, (ii) a PKI structure to enable the system to verify the origin of the data, and (iii) a charging infrastructure which maintains the keys. Based on the CAS system it can be necessary to store the key in a sealed environment as it is offered by the TPM sealing functions. A variant of this kind of content protection is exhibited in (Kuntze, & Schmidt, 2007b).

A TSTB enables the creation of a universal decoder for a broad range of different scrambling systems without the need for the user to physically change the smart card. The virtualization of the CAS hardware is also interesting for reducing the costs of a single set top box. This can sensibly be combined with either a long range communication module, e.g. GSM or UMTS, or a near range communication module like Bluetooth or NFC. This enhancement enables complex scenarios with respect to accounting and charging, some of which are presented in the following list.

- As mentioned, the communication between the trusted set-top box can be performed by an integrated long range communication device or a near range device. Using GSM/UMTS in a box enables the cooperation between a mobile network operator who can offer accounting, charging, and maintenance for the customers and box vendor/DVB provider. The MNO is also able to offer a well tested authentication system in form of the SIM-card known in the mobile domain. Based on this identifier other authentication schemes using the TPM are possible as they are shown in [24].
- Online payment using e.g. credit cards in the set-top box is one of the most important possibilities which are enabled by trusted set top boxes.
- Implementing an online CAS Module which replaces the CAS-smart card complex can eliminate the possibility of using fake smart cards as the box can control the access rights by an access control list at the side of the provider. TC provides in this scenario the authenticity and identity of the box and the attestation of its integrity (by the TC methods of remote or direct anonymous attestation). With these basic assumptions it is possible to implement a trustworthy client side CAS.
- As the set-top box can be considered as trustworthy, such a box enables easy-to-use payment schemes which have the potential to replace existing Pay-per-View schemes. By executing charging on the client side,

price schedules can depend on the consumed service or content which can be metered by the trustworthy box. It would as well be possible to recognize debit and credit cards or to prepay various contents.

- Online Algorithm updates for video decryption are an extension of the variants above, which enables on demand reconfiguration for unknown decryption schemes or the exchange of existing ones. The vendor or broadcaster can issue in a standardized configuration file the new algorithm which is to be used in the box to decrypt the incoming video stream. This also enables over the air enhancements and updates of the trusted set top box e.g. faster implementations.

Near range communication devices like Bluetooth require SDs like mobile phones as communication intermediaries to the broadcaster. As it may be cheaper than a dedicated GSM module in each set-top box this could be the better choice. This solution requires charging in the set-top box as described above. Charging and updates are performed by using SD. After this step the box works autonomous.

The presented concepts offer a high degree of co-operation of DVB service providers with mobile networks and their MNOs. This co-operation brings major benefits, though the technology DVB is not common in the mobile domain. The MNO can provide primary services to DVB operators or broadcaster:

- Management of subscribers
- Potential merging of the subscriber bases
- Charging
- Dynamical control of security features
- Enhanced CAS security
- Marketing co-operation

Furthermore the concept can complement current or development mobile content protection like OMA. In effect it enables MNOs to enter a mobile video broadcasting partial market. The underlying concept is not limited to DVB. It can enhance or substitute existing CAS systems for streaming multimedia applications. It is also possible to combine this with a bonding of the set-top box to a special mobile phone or network operator. A network operator can offer set-top boxes as part of their customer retention.

5.2 Security and Practical Issues

The application of TC should generally entail an increase in security of the supported solutions. Yet, depending on the concrete scenario, TC technology may also replace a traditional one for reasons of cost-efficiency and there may well be security trade-offs. We discuss these issues in the prototypical cases described in Section 4.

Security of the trust-enhanced CAM of Section 4.2 and the subsequent concepts hinges on the trust boundary of the platform established by a) the hardware security anchor, b) authenticated or secure boot, and c) security of the components of the TCB. On the other hand, the security of the traditional system is on the well-established level of smart cards. The main difference, which holds for most protection concepts based on TC, is that security critical data like access credentials, in particular EMMs, are held and used in the ordinary storage of the platform. Though they are protected by encryption via the hardware root of trust, they are not protected by physical separation during operations with them, as is the case with, e.g., decryption keys which are only used on a smart card and never leave it. To establish a similar protection level, the TCB must contain functionality to secure data in the memory and upon transmission to, e.g., the processor or other components. Such are known as *secure channels* and exist in several variants (ATMEL Corporation 2007; Wise, 2007; Yang et al. 2005).

If it makes practical and economical sense to raise the security of a trust-enhanced CAM to that of smart cards depends on the "commercial grade security' required in a concrete business scenario. First, the CAM is still a separate module which allows for inexpensive physical protection against tampering. Second, the maximum damage incurred by providers if a credential (e.g. an EMM) is compromised on a single platform is a new rollout of the latter. This does, however, not repair the potential for leakage of content through the compromised platform on which an attacker has found a way to obtain EMMs. This is a principal problem of the DVB architecture, which has led to costly replacements of hardware in the past. Trust-enhanced CAMs and STBs can be useful for a resolution of this problem, since their root of trust provides credentials to uniquely identify the platform, in particular in an attestation process. Thus it may be possible, using secondary communication channels like the mobile network, to disable a compromised platform and protect the DVB system as a whole.

We believe that CAMs and STBs are interesting for TC deployment and usage. Most STBs are restricted PC platforms running standard OS where a lot of TC hard- and software is available. Thus our concepts seem to be realizable in the near future.

The two-tiered architecture of TLTA naturally divides security in two levels. Security on the sp rests on the integrity of the involved B-nodes 0 and 1, which is a precondition.

Security in pz on the other hand depends on the separation of tasks between TLTAC and the LTE. The security of the LTE is enabled by the unique features of trust-enhanced MTs, namely secure boot and attestation, features which are fundamental for TLTA.

The design entails that a security assessment of TLTA must distinguish between policies for functional enforcement and access control, respectively. The former means that certain functions on all devices in pz shall be enabled or disabled. The latter allows certain content or services to be delivered or made available to the MTs registered with TLTAC. The essential difference between the two is that, in order to extend functional enforcement to all MTs in pz, LTE activation must be ensured on all of them or the policy must be enforced otherwise, e.g., by out-of-band measures and processes. Access control is less security-critical. In contrast to functional enforcement, an access control policy is effectively enforced by the TLTAC, which will yield access only to MTs with active LTE accepting the policy for pz. In this case, LTE provides the added security that proliferation of access to content or services beyond pz is effectively prevented.

Functional enforcement in TLTA is susceptible to certain attacks which do not apply to access control and whose general strategy is to subvert sp. The simplest and most effective is to cross sp and enter pz with a disabled MT, or an MT shielded against network communication. Though one could attempt to detect such rogue MTs via the network when they are activated inside pz, this might not be very efficient nor effective. A more sophisticated attacker could try to prevent the handover at the sp, e.g., using a beam antenna to tamper the MT's measurement of the base stations. In principle, this kind of attacks can only be mitigated by additional, physical access control procedures on pz's boundary.

A general caveat of architectures relying on a trusted platform built upon a hardware security anchor like an MTM is that it is more susceptible to side channel attacks than, e.g., a smart card. Applied to the TLTA concept this argument could mean to imply that, e.g., location data is tampered with while in the MT's memory or in transit between processor and memory, respectively, the wireless modem. A hardening of the MT preventing this could be achieved using secure channels as already noted above.

REFERENCES

3GPP (2003). *3GPP TSG SA WG3 Security - S3#28 S3-030257. PayTV model*. Retrieved February 29, 2008 from http://www.3gpp.org/ftp/tsg_sa/ WG3_Security/TSGS3_28_Berlin/Docs/PDF/ S3-030257.pdf

ATMEL Corporation (2007). Data sheets. Retrieved May 18, 2007 from http://www.atmel.com/ dyn/products/datasheets.asp?family_id=646

Becker, E., Buhse, W, Günnewig, D, & Rump, N. (Eds.), (2003). *Digital Rights Management — Technological, Economic, Legal and Political Aspects*. Berlin, Heidelberg: Springer-Verlag.

Bewick, S. (1998): *Descrambling DVB data according to ETSI common scrambling specification*. UK Patent Applications GB2322994A / GB2322995A

Chaffin, J., Allision K., Edgecliffe-Johnson, A., & Ibison, D. (2007). Apple sparks battle over copyright. FT.com, February 7 2007. Retrieved January 7, 2008, from http://www.ft.com/cms/s/90c03168-b6ea-11db-8bc2-0000779e2340.html

Conax (2002). Conax Newsletter 3-2002, Retrieved January 7, 2007, from http://www.conax. com/pdf/newsletter3_2002.pdf

CSA (2007). CSA – known facts and speculations. Retrieved February 29, 2008, from http://csa. irde.to/

Drahos, P., & Maher, I., (Eds.), (2004). *Information Economics and Policy. Special Issue*. Elsevier.

ETSI (1996). ETSI ETR 289: *Digital Video Broadcasting (DVB); Support for use of scrambling and Conditional Access (CA) within digital broadcasting systems*.

ETSI (2003). ETSI EN 301 192: *DVB Specification for Data Broadcasting*

ETSI (2005). ETSI TS 102 367 V1.1.1: *Digital Audio Broadcasting (DAB); Conditional access*.

Fioravanti, F., Spinu, M., & Campanai, M. (2007). AXMEDIS as the Service Oriented Architecture for the Media: Is It Feasible?. In *Axmedis* (pp. 264-269).

Fulton, S. M. III (2007). Jupiter analyst: Interoperable drm won't solve music industry dilemma. *BetaNews*, February 16, 5:58 PM 2007. Retrieved October 1, 2007, from http://www.betanews.com/article/Jupiter_Analyst_Interoperable_DRM_Wont_Solve_Music_Industry_Dilemma/1171664985/1

Gallery, E., & Tomlinson, A. (2005). Conditional Access in Mobile Systems: Securing the Application. In *The First International Conference on Distributed Frameworks for Multimedia Applications DFMA 05*, France: IEEE.

Gallery, E., & Tomlinson, A. (2007). *Secure delivery of conditional access applications to mobile receivers*. In Leung, A., Yau, P.W., & Mitchell, C.J. (2007).

Gasser, M., Goldstein, A., Kaufman, C., & Lampson, B. (1989). The Digital distributed system security architecture. In *Proceedings of the 12th National Computer Security Conference* (pp. 305-319). Baltimore: NIST/NCSC.

Grimm, R., & Nützel, J. (2002). Security and business models for virtual goods. In *Proceedings of the 2002 ACM Multimedia Security Workshp* (pp. 75–79). ACM.

Grimm, R., & Nützel, J. (2003). Potato system and signed media format — an alternative approach to online music business. In *Proceedings of the 3rd International Conference on Web Delivering of Music (WEDELMUSIC 2003)* (pp. 23–26). IEEE Press.

Jobs, S. (2007). Thoughts on music. Open Letter, February 6 2007. Retrieved December 23, 2007, from http://www.apple.com/hotnews/thoughtsonmusic/

Kosch, H., Böszörményi,L., Döller, M., Libsie, M., Schojer, P., & Kofler, A.. (2005). The Life Cycle of Multimedia Metadata. *IEEE MultiMedia*, 12(1), 80-86.

Kuntze, N., Schmidt, A. U. (2006): Transitive trust in mobile scenarios. In Günter Müller (Ed.), *Proceedings of the International Conference on Emerging Trends in Information and Communication Security (ETRICS 2006)*, Lecture Notes in Computer Science, 3995, 73-85), Berlin: Springer-Verlag.

Kuntze, N., Schmidt, A. U. (2007a): Trusted Ticket Systems and Applications. In: *Proceedings of the IFIP sec2007* (pp. 49-60), Boston: Springer.

Kuntze, N., Schmidt, A. U. (2007b): Trustworthy content push. In: *Proceedings of the Wireless Communications and Networking Conference, WCNC 2007, Hong Kong, 11-15 March 2007* (pp. 2909-2912), IEEE Press.

Leung, A., Yau, P. W., & Mitchell, C. J. (2007). Using Trusted Computing to Secure Mobile Ubiquitous Enviroments. To be published in: *Security and Privacy in Wireless Networking*. Leicester, UK: Troubador Publishing Ltd.

Merabti, M., & Llewellyn-Jones, D. (2006). Digital rights management in ubiquitous computing. *IEEE Multimedia*, 13(2), 32- 42. DOI: 10.1109/MMUL.2006.27

Micklitz, H.-W., Monazzahian, B., & Rößler, C. (1999). *Door-to-door selling — pyramid selling — multilevel marketing*. Study commissioned by the European Commission. Contract No. A0/7050/98/000156. Retrieved October 7, 2007 from http://europa.eu.int/comm/dgs/health_consumer/ library/surveys/sur10_en.html

Mitchell, C.J. (Ed.) (2005). *Trusted Computing*. IEE Press (2005)

Mulligan, D. K., Han, J., & Burstein, A. J. (2003). How DRM-based content delivery systems disrupt expectations of "personal use'. In *Proceedings of the ACM workshop on Digital Rights Management* (pp. 77–89). ACM.

Peer Impact (2007). Web Site. Retrieved June 5, 2007 from http://www.peerimpact.com/

Proceedings of the IFIP TC-6 TC-11 Conferences on Communications and Multimedia Security (1999-2007). New York : Springer-Verlag.

Rand Corporation, (1970). *Security Controls for Computer Systems. Report of Defense Science Board Task Force on Computer Security*. Retrieved December 23, 2007, from http://seclab.cs.ucdavis.edu/projects/history/papers/ware70.pdf

Schmidt, A. U. (2006). Multi-level markets and incentives for information goods. *Information Economics and Policy*, 18(2), 125–138.

Schmidt, A. U. (2008) Free riding and competition in network markets for digital goods. In: *Proceedings of the 41st Annual Hawaii International Conference on System Sciences* (HICSS-41), January 7-10.

Schmidt, A. U., & Kuntze, N. (2006). Trusted Computing in Mobile Action. In: *Peer-reviewed Proceedings of the ISSA 2006 From Insight to Foresight Conference*, Sandton, South Africa: ISSA.

Schmidt, A. U., Kuntze, N., & Abendroth, J. (2008). Trust for Location-based Authorisation. To appear in: *Proceedings of the Wireless Communications and Networking Conference WCNC 2008*, Las Vegas: IEEE.

Schmidt, A. U., Kuntze, N., & Kasper, M. (2008). On the deployment of Mobile Trusted Modules. To appear in: *Proceedings of the Wireless Communications and Networking Conference WCNC 2008*, Las Vegas: IEEE.

Stini, M., Mauve, M., & Fitzek, F.H.P. (2006). Digital Ownership: From Content Consumers to Owners and Traders. *IEEE Multimedia*, 13(4), 1- 6. DOI: 10.1109/MMUL.2006.79

Trusted Computing Group (2007a). TCG TPM Specification Version 1.2 Revision 103. Retrieved February 29, 2008, from https://www.trustedcomputinggroup.org/groups/tpm/

Trusted Computing Group (2007b). Mobile Trusted Module Specification 1.0. Retrieved February 29, 2008, from https://www.trustedcomputinggroup.org/groups/mobile/

US Federal Standard (2000). *US Federal Standard 1037C, Telecom Glossary*, Retrieved February 29, 2008, from http://www.its.bldrdoc.gov/fs-1037/dir-018/_2554.htm

Weinmann, R.-P., & Wirt, K. (2005). Analysis of the DVB Common Scrambling Algorithm. In *Proceedings of the IFIP sec2005* (pp. 195-207), Boston: Springer.

Wise, A. P. (2007). *Memory encryption for digital video*. U.S. Patent US2007140477 (A1). 2007-06-20.

Yang, J., Gao, L., & Zhang, Y. (2005). Improving Memory Encryption Performance in Secure Processors. *IEEE Transactions on Computers*, 54, 630- 640.

Zeng, W., Lan, J., & Zhuang, J. (2006).Security for multimedia adaptation: architectures and solutions. *IEEE Multimedia*, 13(2), 68- 76. DOI: 10.1109/MMUL.2006.42.

Zerfiridis, K. G., & Karatza, H. D. (2004). File distribution using a peer-to-peer network — a simulation study. *Journal of Systems and Software*, *73*, 31–44.

KEY TERMS

DVB: Digital Video Broadcasting (DVB) is the standard for the broadcast of multimedia content. Substandards are defined for satellite (-S), terrestrial (-T), and mobile (-H) broadcasting which define the physical characteristics of the signal. DVB is based on the MPEG-2 coding of content and published by a Joint Technical Committee (JTC) of European Telecommunications Standards Institute (ETSI), European Committee for Electrotechnical Standardization (CENELEC) and European Broadcasting Union (EBU).

Mobile Trusted Module (MTM): The Mobile Phone Working Group (MPWG) derived from the specification of the TPM a mobile version which is adapted to the special technical and organisational requirements in this environment. The MTM defines isolated compartments providing secured and trustworthy environments for different stakeholders in the mobile economic chain.

Privacy CA: One of the first protocols developed by the TCG the privacy certification authority (Privacy CA) offers as third party service pseudonyms which are used within all authentication protocols later on. Only the Privacy CA can later on bring together the identity of a certain user with the identity issued by the Privacy CA.

Secure Boot: In contrast to the trusted boot where all components are only measured and reported secure boot requires an internal verifier which decides on every step of boot if the boot will continue or not. At the end of the boot process the system is in a fully checked status.

Trusted Boot: During boot each component is verified and the measurements are stored in a special log. Using the log together with the TPM produced reference an external verifier is able to judge if a certain platform is in a trustworthy state according to the verifier's policies.

Trusted Platform Module (TPM): (From the TCG's FAQ) The TPM is a microcontroller that stores keys, passwords and digital certificates. It typically is affixed to the motherboard of a PC. It potentially can be used in any computing device that requires these functions. The nature of this silicon ensures that the information stored there is made more secure from external software attack and physical theft. Security processes, such as digital signature and key exchange, are protected through the secure TCG subsystem. Access to data and secrets in a platform could be denied if the boot sequence is not as expected. Critical applications and capabilities such as secure email, secure web access and local protection of data are thereby made much more secure. TPM capabilities also can be integrated into other components in a system.

Chapter XXII
Copyright Protection of A/V Codec for Mobile Multimedia Devices

Goo-Rak Kwon
Chosun University, Korea

Sung-Jea Ko
Korea University, Korea

ABSTRACT

The objective of this chapter introduces an advanced encryption of MP3 and MPEG-4 coder with a quality degradation-based security model. For the MP3 audio, the magnitude, and phase information of modified discrete cosine transform (MDCT) coefficients is encrypted. DCT coefficients and motion vectors (MVs) are used for the scrambling of the MPEG-4 video. This encryption scheme has a level of security, secures in perception, keeps format compliance, and obtains high time efficiency though reducing the encrypted the volumes of multimedia contents. These properties make it practical to incorporate encryption and decryption process into compression and decompression process, and thus suitable for secure A/V transmission or sharing.

INTRODUCTION

With the advance of multimedia technology, multimedia sharing among multiple devices has become the main issue. This allows users to expect the peer-to-peer distribution of unprotected and protected contents over public network. Many audio and video (A/V) processing software including DVD players, CD rippers, MP3 encoders, and A/V players have been posted for free on the Web allowing users to build their own A/V record collections from their own CD and DVD. Inevitably, this situation has caused an incredible piracy activity and some Web sites have begun to provide copyrighted A/V data for free. In order to protect the contents from illegal attacks, digital rights management (DRM) is required as shown in Fig. 1.

Figure 1. Application of DRM technique

The DRM system generally provides two essential functions: management of digital rights by identifying, describing, and setting the rules of the content usage, and digital management of right by securing the contents and enforcing usage rules. The basic principle of the DRM model (Schneier, 1996; Piva, 2002; Petitcloas, 1999) is to separate and identify three core entities: Users, Content, and Rights. Users can be any type of users from a rights holder to an end-consumer. Content is any type of contents at any level of aggregation. A right is an expression of permissions, constraints, and obligations between Users and Content. This model provides the greatest flexibility when assigning rights to any combination or layering of Users and Content. Fig. 2 shows the example of contents distribution service using DRM. In Fig. 2, a user A requests image, audio, or video in the network and goes through payment. Billing system informs payment approval, and then CP delivers encrypted contents to only an authorized user through the network.

Various encryption techniques for DRM have been researched. These techniques are classified into two approaches: scrambling and watermarking. Scrambling that is generally based on old and proven cryptographic tools, efficiently ensures confidentiality, authenticity, and integrity of messages. However, it does not protect against unauthorized copying after the message has been successfully transmitted and descrambled (Matsunaga, et al., 1989; Schneier, 1996; Spanos, et al., 1995). This kind of protection can be handled by watermarking (Piva, 2002; Aeng, 2003), which is a more recent topic that has attracted a large amount of research and is perceived as a complementary aid in encryption. A digital watermark is a piece of information inserted and hidden in the media content (Bassia, 2001; Borujeni, 2000; Cox, 2000; Li, et al., 2004; Neubauer, et al., 1998; Yeh & Kuo, 1999). This information is imperceptible to a human observer but can be easily detected by a computer. Moreover, the main advantage of this technique is to provide the nonseparability of the hidden information and the content.

A watermarking system consists of an embedding algorithm and a detecting function. The embedding algorithm inserts a message into a media and the detecting function is then used to verify the authenticity of the media by detecting the message. The most important properties of a watermarking scheme include robustness, fidelity,

Figure 2. Example of the contents distribution service using DRM

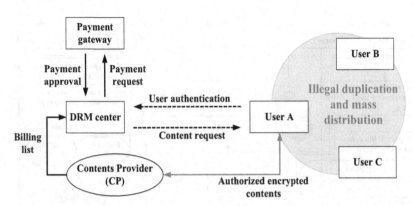

tamper resistance, and data payload (Petitcolas, 1999; Zeng, 2003).

The rest of the paper is organized as follows. Section 0 briefly describes the Background such as DRM architecture, MP3, and MPEG-4. In Section 0, the joint and partial encryption techniques are presented using MPEG-1 audio coder and MPEG-4 video coder.

BACKGROUND

2.1 DRM Architecture

This section describes the common components in DRM systems, the working process of DRM models and the role taken by client-side applications in DRM. Each DRM vendor supports different DRM implementation, names and ways to specify the content usage rules, however, the basic DRM process is the same, which usually involves four parties: the content provider, the distributor, the clearinghouse, and the consumer. Usually a DRM system is integrated with an e-commerce system that handles financial payments and triggers the function of the clearinghouse, however, due to space considerations we does not describe the details. Fig. 3 displays the common components of a DRM system based on most existing com-

mercial systems. Following the explanation of these common elements, a typical model used by current DRM implementations is presented.

- Content Provider such as a music record label or a movie studio holds the digital rights of the content and wants to protect these rights.
- Distributor provides distribution channels, such as an online shop or a web retailer. The distributor receives the digital content from the content provider and creates a web catalogue presenting the content and rights metadata for the content promotion.
- Consumer uses the system to consume the digital content by retrieving downloadable or streaming content through the distribution channel and then paying for the digital license. The player/viewer application used by the consumer takes charge of initiating license request to the clearinghouse and enforcing the content usage rights.
- Clearinghouse handles the financial transaction for issuing the digital license to the consumer and pays royalty fees to the content provider and distribution fees to the distributor accordingly. The clearinghouse is also responsible for logging license consumptions for every consumer.

Figure 3. Architecture of the proposed DRM system

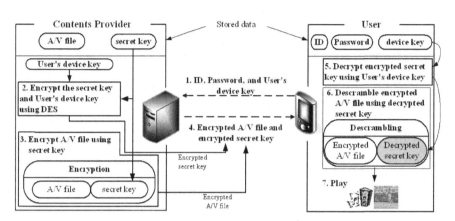

A typical DRM model used by current DRM implementations works as follows: Firstly, the content provider encodes the digital content into the format supported by the DRM system. Different DRM systems provided by different DRM vendors may support different content formats. The digital content is then encrypted and packaged for the preparation of distribution. The content provider may use watermarking technology to embed digital codes into the digital content that can identify the ownership of the content and the usage rules. Next, the protected content is transferred to the appropriate content distribution server, web server or steaming server, for on-line distribution.

The digital license containing content decryption keys and usage rules is sent to the clearinghouse. The usage rules specify how the content should be used, such as copy permit, pay-per-view, a one-week rental, etc. At the other end of the process, the consumer downloads the digital content from the web server or requests streaming content from the streaming server. To be able to consume the protected content, the user has to request a valid license from the clearinghouse. After receiving the license request, the clearinghouse verifies the user's identity for example by having the user present a valid digital certificate,

charges his account based on the content usage rules, and generates transaction reports to the content provider. Finally, the license is delivered to the consumer's device after the consumer has paid through the e-commerce system, and the protected content can be decrypted and used according to the usage rights in the license.

In DRM system, consumers can login along received digital content to other people through super-distribution, which lets vendors market their digital content to a vast amount of potential customers without direct involvement. Although digital content can be freely distributed, to utilize the content, the recipient has to contact the clearinghouse and provide whatever information or payment required for the license.

2.2 MPEG-1 Layer III (MP3) Audio Coder

MP3 compression (Pan, 1995) is composed of psychoacoustic analysis, subband filtering, MDCT transform, quantization and Huffman encoding. The polyphase filter bank and windowed MDCT are employed for subband filtering, which is used to translate time domain into the frequency domain. After this translation, the original 576 music signals will be divided into 576 MDCT coefficients.

The value of MDCT coefficients represents band energy for 576 subbands. Human psychoacoustic model is used to shape the quantization noise. One quantization step size (specified by scale factor) is applied for coefficients in one scale factor band. The quantization procedure is composed of two loops - inner loop for bit rate control and outer loop for distortion control. In the inner loop, the MDCT coefficients are nonlinearly quantized and Huffman coded. If the bit budget is larger than the bits available, the step size is increased until the bit consumption is acceptable. Outer loop calculates the quantization distortion in every scale factor band and compares it with the allowed distortion obtained from the psychoacoustic analysis. If it is larger than the allowed distortion, the step size is decreased to reduce the artifact audibility. In the Huffman encoding procedure, the sign and amplitude of coefficients is coded separately. The total MDCT coefficients are divided into 3 regions: big-value region, small-value region and zero region. The big value region (usually at low frequency end) is further divided into 3 sub-regions where different Huffman tables are used. The small-value region is composed of coefficient values of +1, -1, or 0. Each codeword represents a pairs of contiguous coefficients in the big-value region or 4 coefficients (quadruple) in the small-value region. The remaining coefficients are implicitly set to zeros. MP3 encoder deletes the subbands, unsusceptible to human ears and masked by other signals, to achieve the goal of reducing bit rate. Then it further compresses the signals by using Huffman encoding to reduce bit rate and carry out the goal of a large number compression.

In the MP3 decoder, the bitstream is unpacked and the relative information of bitstream performed by Huffman decoding. We can obtain 576 MDCT lines of data, which have been reconstructed. Then 32 subbands are obtained by using Inverse MDCT (IMDCT) to deal with the lines of data. Finally, audio data of time-domain are obtained by using synthesis filterbank to deal with the subbands.

2.3 MPEG-4 Simple Profile Video Coder

The MPEG-4 standard (Khan & Das, 2002) is designed to play the role of a global multimedia language. Within its source coding parts, MPEG-4 embraces a multitude of natural and synthetic audio and video coding schemes and representations, providing a generic tool set for numerous applications for the transmission and storage of audiovisual signals. In addition, MPEG-4 introduces and supports completely new concepts of object-based user interactivity as well as a rich feature set to maintain a useful quality of service within error-prone channels.

2.3.1 Coding Scheme

The basis of MPEG-4 video coding is a block-based predictive differential video coding scheme. The main techniques for compression are:

- Division of the picture in 8x8-blocks or 16x16-macroblocks (MB)
- Motion compensated prediction
- Transform coding with discrete cosine transform (DCT)
- Quantization
- Run length and huffman coding for variable length codes (VLC)

There are two basic coding modes available as follows:

In the Intra-Mode, both the spatial redundancy and irrelevancy are exploited with block based DCT coding, quantization, run length and huffman coding. Only information from the picture itself is used and thus every frame can be decoded independently.

In the Inter-Mode, additionally, the temporal redundancy between the pictures in a video sequence is taken into account. An MB-based motion estimation between two successive images is done allowing a motion compensated prediction of the current picture. Afterwards the predicted image is subtracted from the original image. The resulting difference picture is DCT coded, quantized and VLC coded. The motion vectors describing the motion of the blocks in the picture are necessary side information for the decoder and are also encoded with VLC. Interframe coding usually requires much lower bitrate in comparison to intraframe coding (only about 10 to 20%) because there is less information in the difference picture than in the original picture.

2.3.2 Coding Options

The ISO/IEC standard MPEG-4 offers a great toolbox for coding natural and synthetic audiovisual objects. Part 2 of the standard specifies the coded representation of natural or synthetic visual objects. It describes all tools for coding visual objects, including video coding of natural objects. Profiles are defined within the standard to allow the implementation of some well defined subsets of the complete toolbox. For the Simple Profile (SP) of MPEG-4 the basic coding techniques described in the last chapter are used together with the following additional techniques:

- Advanced Intra Coding (mandatory): Intraframe prediction for the DCT coefficients (AC/DC-Prediction) and other VLC-tables are used.
- 4-vectors per MB (optional): Four motion vectors are used for one MB (one vector for each 8x8 block).
- Unrestricted motion vectors and long vectors (optional): A greater search area for motion estimation is used and the vectors may point outside the picture area; vectors may be longer than 16 pixels.

The Advanced Simple Profile (ASP) provides the following additional (to the Simple Profile) coding tools:

- Quarter-Pel Motion Compensation (optional): The spatial resolution of the motion compensation is increased to 1/4 pixel.
- B VOP (optional): Bidirectional Video Object Planes (B VOPs) are bidirectionally predicted from a past and a future reference Video Object Plane (VOP).
- Global Motion Compensation (optional): Special motion compensation technique for movements of the entire VOP.
- Interlace (optional): Coding of interlace material. Only allowed for level 4 and higher. Not supported by this encoder yet. Furthermore MPEG-4 provides a wide flexibility for the following parameters of the source material:
- Picture format (the library supports width and height in steps of 16 pixel according to the macroblock size).
- Video format (PAL, NTSC).
- Pixel aspect ratio (e.g. 1:1, 12:11 for 4:3 PAL, 10:11 for 4:3 NTSC).
- Source framerate (e.g. 25fps, 29.97fps, 30fps).

JOINT AND PARTIAL ENCRYPTION TECHNIQUE IN A/V CODEC

Before explaining the A/V scrambling technique in detail, we first introduce the concept of the joint and partial scrambling. The joint scrambling method can provide levels of security for contents encryption. The security level can be determined by the number of independent encryption methods combined. The partial encryption method obtains the higher security by simply encrypting only significant parts of the compressed data. Next, we provide a detailed explanation on the A/V encryption technique.

In order to protect the contents against eavesdropping and moreover against illegal mass distribution after descrambling, we propose an A/V watermarking and scrambling (WS) method based on our previous research results (Kwon, 2005).

Fig. 4 shows the block diagram of the WS method for the audio data. Fig. 4(a) shows the MP3 encoder with watermark embedding and scrambling. The original PCM data is decomposed into 32 subbands using the polyphase quadrature filterbank. Each decomposed signal is transformed using MDCT to increase the resolution of frequency. The watermark is embedded into MDCT coefficients. The watermarked MDCT coefficients are synchronously scrambled using both the watermark sequence and the secret key and quantized into watermarked/scrambled MP3 bitstream. Fig. 4(b) shows the MP3 decoder with watermark extraction and descrambling. The watermarked/scarambled MP3 bitstream is quantized. The watermark sequence is extracted from the dequantized signal. Then, the dequantized signal is descrambled using the extracted watermark sequence and the secret key. The descrambled signal is inversely transformed using

inverse MDCT and passed through the synthesis filterbank to produce the restored audio data.

Fig. 5 shows the block diagram of the scrambling/descrambling algorithms for the video data. At the encoder, in the case of intraframe, the original frame is transformed and encrypted using the secret key. Then, the scrambled DCT coefficients are quanitzed and fed to the entropy encoder. In the case of interframe, MVs obtained by motion estimation are scrambled using the secret key and fed to the entropy encoder while DCT coefficients are quantized and fed to an entropy encoder without scrambling. At the decoder, the compressed video bitstream is decompressed by the entropy decoder and the dequantizer. Prior to IDCT and motion compensation, the decompressed DCT coefficients of interframe and MVs of intraframe are descrambled using the secret key provided only for the authorized devices.

Figure 4. Proposed audio encryption using watermarking and scrambling. (a) Encoder with watermark embedding and scrambling. (b) Decoder with watermark extracting and descrambling.

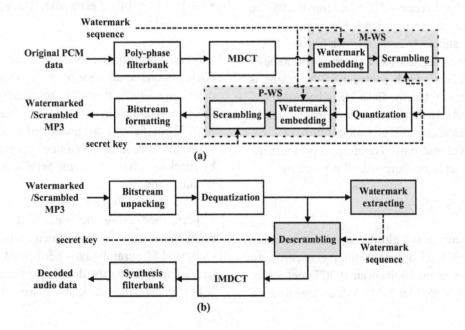

Figure 5. Proposed video encryption using scrambling. (a) Scrambler. (b) Descrambler.

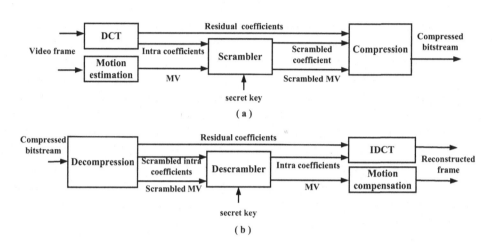

3.1 Audio Encryption Technique

3.1.1 Magnitude-Based Watermarking and Scrambling (M-WS)

The WS technique encrypts MDCT coefficients in the MP3 audio. The MP3 bitstream is a concatenation of a sequence of channels. Each channel corresponds to two granules, where each granule is defined as precisely 576 consecutive samples. Therefore, each channel has 1152 samples consisting of 32 subbands each of which has 36 MDCT coefficients. Fig. 6 shows an example of the MP3 audio channel. Each subband of the frame is divided into 6 blocks. Each block has 6 MDCT coefficients. In the watermarking technique, the watermark sequence is embedded into MDCT coefficients of subband 0. The binary representation of the watermark sequence, W, is given by

$$W = b_1 b_2 b_3 \cdots b_N , \qquad (1)$$

where b_i represents the ith digit and N is the number of bits in W. Let P denote the number of zeros in a row after a decimal point of an MDCT coefficient. For example, P=2 for 2.003. In the watermarking

technique, the first MDCT coefficient of each block except the 6th block is watermarked using value P of the MDCT coefficients and b_i's of W. The watermarked MDCT coefficients are replaced by original MDCT coefficients if the following conditions are satisfied:

- $b_i = 1$ and P of each MDCT coefficient is odd.
- $b_i = 0$ and P of each MDCT coefficient is even.

On the other hands, the watermarked MDCT coefficients is equal to $5 \times 10^{(-p+1)}$. As the remainder is equal to 5, P has the robustness against the quantization error after the watermarked MDCT coefficients are quantized and dequantized. In the decoder, W can be easily extracted by checking whether P of the MDCT coefficient is odd or not.

After embedding the watermark, scrambling is performed using the watermark sequence. Since the energy is concentrated on [subband 1 - subband 6], scrambling is performed for these bands. Fig. 7 shows the flowchart of scrambling. If bi = 0, subbands 2, 4, and 6 are selected for

Figure 6. Scrambling region in MDCT sub-bands

Subband 0						
Subband 1	1		3		5	
Subband 2		2		4		6
Subband 3	1		3		5	
Subband 4		2		4		6
Subband 5	1		3		5	
Subband 6		2		4		6
Subband 7						
Subband 8						
⋮			⋮			
Subband 31						

scrambling. Otherwise, subbands 1, 3, and 5 are selected. The secret key determines which block of the selected bands is scrambled. Fig. 3 shows the blocks selected by the secret key. Scrambling can be performed by simply amplifying the selected coefficients.

3.1.2 Phase-Based Watermarking-Scrambling (P-WS)

In the P-WS technique, the watermark sequence is applied to some frequency bands which are insensitive parts to hear in Human Auditory System (HAS). Fig. 8 shows the watermarking process using phase modification. In order to select some frequency bands for watermarking while preventing the permanent degradation of the music, we use the psycho-acoustic model.

In MP3 coding, MDCT coefficients of bands selected by the psycho-acoustic model are modified in watermarking. To minimize permanent damages of the MP3 audio, the watermark is inserted to the phase parts of selected MDCT coefficients. Thus, the phase information of the watermark sequence and MDCT coefficients is first obtained. Then, the phases of MDCT coefficients are replaced by that of the watermark sequence. It is possible since the phases of MDCT coefficients selected by the psycho-acoustic model can be negligible when hearing.

After embedding the watermark, scrambling is performed. As shown in Fig. 9, the watermarked MDCT coefficients of subbands 7 and 8 are selected to scramble. Then, the phase sign of selected coefficients is reversed using the secret key. This method has little effect on the total number of bits of the MP3 bitstream because of changing only the sign bit.

3.1.3 M-WS Plus P-WS (M-WS/P-WS)

M-WS/P-WS is a combined encryption of M-WS and P-WS. According to the MP3 encoding procedure, M-WS is performed in the process of MDCT at first. Next, P-WS is applied after the MDCT coefficients are quantized.

Figure 7. Scrambling process of M-WS

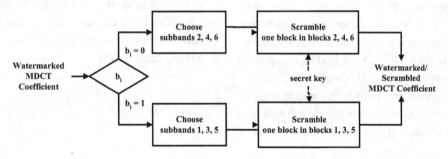

Figure 8. Watermarking process of P-WS

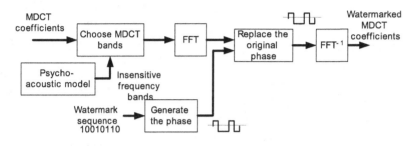

Figure 9. Scrambling process of P-WS

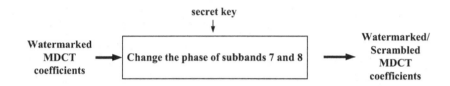

3.2 Video Encryption Technique

3.2.1 Segment-Based DCT Coefficient Scrambling (S-DCTCS) for Intraframes

To scramble intraframes in MPEG-4, the S-DCTCS is applied to each MB in intraframes. The conventional approaches for scrambling change the sign bit of each coefficient in the 8×8 DCT based frames (Cox, 1997; Tang, 1996). This sign scrambling efficiently provides an impact on distortion. However, in this method, high computational complexity is required to encrypt all coefficients for each MB. In addition, the scrambling can be easily cracked since the scrambling scheme is very simple. To solve these problems, we propose the S-DCTCS method that scrambles the sign bits of DC and AC coefficients.

In this algorithm, in order to reduce computational complexity, we first divide a frame into segments consisting of several MBs. Instead of encrypting all the coefficients, we scramble the largest DC coefficient among the DC coefficients of MBs in the segment and the largest AC coefficient of each MB. Changing the sign bits of DC coefficients and AC coefficients heavily depends on the number of MBs in Table I. As a result, Fig. 10 shows the effectiveness on efficient distortion for the sign-scrambling of each DC and AC coefficients in intraframes. Each scrambling mode is defined as shown in Table I. The mode in Table I is encrypted with the device key at a contents provider and transmitted to a user. Note that the scrambled mode set is considered as the secret key in the DRM system in Fig. 3. Therefore, a user who does not have the same key for decryption cannot access the original contents without visual quality degradation.

Table 1. Video encryption mode set based as secret key

The number of MBs	Intraframe	Interframe
0	$DC' = -DC$	$MV' = MV + \Delta\alpha$
1	$AC' = -AC$	$MV' = -MV$
⋮	⋮	⋮
k	DCT sign encryption	MV sign/phase angle encryption

Figure 10. Picture after encrypting DCT coefficients. (a) DC sign scrambling. (b) AC sign scrambling.

(a)   (b)

3.2.2 MV Scrambling (MVS) for Interframes

Since encoded DCT coefficients of interframes (i.e., P or B frames) represent residual errors, DCT coefficients have typically small values. Thus, it is not good enough to apply the S-DCTCS for interframes. That is, for unauthorized users, the S-DCTCS cannot guarantee original visual quality caused by video encryption (Agi, 1996; Qiao, 1998; Farkash, 1991; Tang, 1996). In order to solve this problem, we propose two video encryption methods for scrambling MVs in interframes of MPEG-4 video: phase angle and sign scrambling.

The phase angle, θ, is calculated as

$$\theta = \arctan\left[\frac{MV_v}{MV_h}\right], \qquad (2)$$

where MV_v and MV_h, respectively, are the vertical and horizontal components of the MV. θ can be changed by adding weighting factors to each component. If the vertical and horizontal components of an MV are changed, the phase angle of the MV is modified as:

$$MV_v' = MV_v + \Delta v,$$
$$MV_h' = MV_h + \Delta h, \qquad (3)$$

where MV_v' and MV_h' represent the modified MV. The MV sign encryption scheme is very simple to implement. The direction of the MV is reversed as follows:

$$MV_v' = -MV_v,$$
$$MV_h' = -MV_h. \qquad (4)$$

Fig. 11 shows the result of MV encryption. Results of MV phase and MV sign scrambling are shown in Fig. 11 (a) and (b), respectively. Fig. 11 shows the results of differential encrypting methods. Fig. 12 (a) and (b) show the results of DC sign and MV phase angle scrambling and AC sign and MV sign encryption. These methods provide

Figure 11: Picture after encrypting MVs. (a) MV phase angle encryption. (b) MV sign encryption.

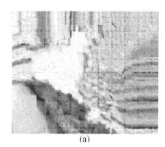
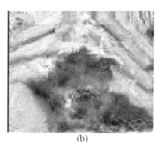

Figure 12. Hybrid encryption. (a) DC sign plus MV phase angle encryption. (b) AC sign plus MV sign encryption.

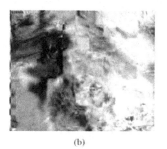

a very good compromise between compression ratio and coding efficiency since they produce a little bit overhead while scrambling DCT coefficients and MVs.

CONCLUSION

A new encryption method for copyright protection of MP3 and MPEG-4 Codec is shown. The magnitude and phase information of MDCT coefficients is scrambled for audio encryption. DCT coefficients and MVs in MPEG-4 coder are used for video scrambling. With watermarking-scrambling technique, only users who have the secret key can access the watermarked-scrambled MP3/MPEG-4 contents and moreover protect illegal copies of descrambled contents.

In addition, the minimal cost encryption scheme for securing the copyrighted MP3/MPEG-4 A/V data is presented. The scrambling and watermarking techniques achieve a very good compromise between several desirable properties such as speed, security, and file size.

REFERENCES

Agi, I., & Gong, L.. (1996). An Empirical study of mpeg video transmissions. In *Proceedings of the Internet Society Symposium on Network and Distributed System Security*. San Diego. 137–144.

Bassia, P., & Pitas, I., & Nikolaidis, N. (2001). Robust audio watermarking in the time domain. *IEEE Trans. on Multimedia, 3*(2) 232–241.

Borujeni, S.E. (2000). Speech encryption based on fast Fourier transform permutation. *Proc. of The 7th IEEE International Conference on Electronics, Circuits and Systems, 1*, 290–293.

Cox, I., Kilian, J., Leighton, F., & Shamoon, T. (1997). Secure spread spectrum watermarking for multimedia. *IEEE Trans. on Image Processing, 6*(12), 1673–1687.

Cox, I. J., Miller, M. L., & Bloom, J. A.. (2000) watermakrking applications and their properties. *Proc. IEEE International Conference on Information Technology, Coding and Computing.* Las Vegas, Nev, USA. 6–10.

Farkash, S., Raz, S., & Malah, D. (1991). Analog speech scrambling via the Gabor representation. *Proc. of the 17th Convention of Electrical and Electronics Engineers in Israel.* 365–368.

Khan, J. Y., & Das, P. (2002). MPEG-4 video over packet switched connection of the WCDMA air Interface. *Proc. of the 13th IEEE International Symposium on Personal Indoor and Mobile Radio Communications, 5.* 2189–2193.

Kwon, G. R., Lee, T. Y., Kim, K. H., Jin, J. D., & Ko, S. J. (2005). Multimedia digital right management using selective scrambling for mobile handset. *LNAI, 3802,* 1098-1103.

Li, W., Hu, X., & Leung, H. (2004). Performance evaluation of digital audio watermarking algorithms. *IEEE Trans. on Aerospace and Electronic Systems, 40,* 12–26.

Matsunaga, A., Koga, K., & Ohkawa, M. (1989). An analog speech scrambling system using the FFT technique with high level security. *IEEE Trans. on Selected Areas in Communications, 7*(4), 540–547.

Neubauer, C., Herre, J., & Brandenburg, K. (1998). Continuous steganographic data transmission using uncompressed audio. *Proc. Information HidingWorkshop.* Portland, OR, pp. 208–217, 1998.

Pan, D.. (1995). A Tutorial on MPEG/Audio Compression. *IEEE Multimedia,* Summer, pp. 60-74.

Petitcolas, F. A., Anderson, R. J., & Kuhn, M. G.. (1999). Information hiding: a survey. *Proceedings of the IEEE, 87*(7). 1062–1078.

Piva, A., Bartolini, F, & Barni, M. (2002). Managing copyright in open networks. *IEEE Internet Computing, 6*(3). 18–26.

Qiao, L., & Nahrstedt, K. (1998). Comparison of MPEG encryption algorithms. *Computers and Graphics, 22*(4), 437–448.

Schneier, B. (1996). *Applied cryptography.* (2nd ed.) New York: Wiley and Sons.

Spanos, G., & Maples, T. (1995). Performance study of a selective encryption scheme for the security of networked, real-time video. *Proc. of 4th International Conference on Computer Communications and Networks.* Las Vegas. Nevada.

Tang, L. (1996). Methods for encrypting and decrypting MPEG video data efficiently. *Proc. ACM Multimedia, 96.* Boston. 219–230.

Yeh, C., & Kuo, C. (1999). Digital watermarking through quasi m-arrays. *Proc. IEEE Workshop on Signal Processing Systems.* Taipei, Taiwan. 456–461.

Zeng, W., & Lei, S. (2003). Efficient frequency domain selective scrambling of digital video. *IEEE Trans. on Multimedia, 5,* 118–129.

KEY TERMS

A/V Encryption: This algorithm can be used as one of access content system. The access content system (ACS) is a standard for content distribution and digital rights management, intended to restrict access to and copying of the next generation of optical discs and DVDs. The specification was publicly released in Apr. 2005 and the standard has been adopted as the access restriction scheme for HD DVD and Blu-ray Disc (BD).

A/V Scrambling: This technology and contents scrambling system are the same. The purpose of contents scrambling system is two-fold. First and foremost, it prevents byte-for-byte copies of an MPEG stream from being playable since such copies will not include the keys that are hidden on the lead-in area of the protected DVD disk. Second, it provides a reason for manufacturers to make compliant devices, since contents scrambling system scrambled disks will not play on noncompliant devices. Anyone wishing to build compliant devices must obtain a license, which contains the requirement that the rest of the copy-protection system be implemented

Authorized Device: The technology may be a physical device that an authorized user of computer services is given to aid in authentication. An authorization is the concept of allowing access to resources only to those permitted to use them. More formally, authorization is a process (often part of the operating system) that protects computer resources by only allowing those resources to be used by resource consumers that have been granted authority to use them. Resources include individual files' or items' data, computer programs, computer devices and functionality provided by computer applications.

Copyright Protection: The mechanisms that prevent data, usually digital data, from being copied. The term "copyright protection" is occasionally seen in this usage, but is an error; copy protection is the usual term. Permission is not granted to use these images, which are protected by copyright.

Joint Encryption: This technology is the joint of each encryption which is independently the difference process for encryption. It has ability that is a level of security against accessing the unauthorized device or users.

Partial Encryption: It is similar to the joint encryption. However, this technology is how to degree the robustness of the encryption. And it provides some information of unauthorized consumer in advertizing the contents.

Watermarking and Scrambling: A watermarking system consists of an embedding algorithm and a detecting function. And scrambling is generally based on old and proven cryptographic tools, efficiently ensures confidentiality, authenticity, and integrity of messages. This mechanism is the combination ones.

Chapter XXIII
Digital Steganography Based on Genetic Algorithm

Frank Y. Shih
New Jersey Institute of Technology, USA

Yi-Ta Wu
Industrial Technology Research Institute, Taiwan

ABSTRACT

*Steganography is the art of hiding secret data inside other innocent media file. **Steganalysis** is the process of detecting hidden data which are crested using **steganography**. **Steganalysis** detects stego-images by analyzing various image features between stego-images and cover-images. Therefore, we need to have a system that develops more critical stego-images from which **steganalysis** cannot detect them. In this chapter, we present a **Genetic algorithm**-(GA) based method for breaking steganalytic systems. The emphasis is shifted from traditionally avoiding the change of statistic features to artificially counterfeiting the statistic features. Our idea is based on the following: in order to manipulate the statistic features for breaking the inspection of steganalytic systems, the GA-based approach is adopted to counterfeit several stego-images (candidates) until one of them can break the inspection of steganalytic systems.*

INTRODUCTION

As digital information and data are transmitted more often than ever over the Internet, the technology of protecting and securing the sensitive messages needs to be discovered and developed. Digital **steganography** is the art and science of hiding information into covert channels, so as to conceal the information and prevent the detection of the hidden message. Covert channel is a genre of information security research, which generally is not a major player, but has been an extremely active topic in the academia, industry and government domains for the past 30 years.

The data hiding in **steganography** is intended in such a way that only the receiver knows the existence of the secret data. It is different from cryptography which encodes messages by scrambling, so nobody can read it without the specific key. Another technique, **digital watermarking**, is concerned with issues related to copyright protection and intellectual property (Shih, 2007; Cox, 2001; Wu, 2004); therefore, a watermark usually contains the information pertaining to the carrier and the owner. The well-known steganographic methods include covert channel, invisible ink, microdot, and spread-spectrum communication (Kahn, 1996; Norman, 1973).

There is a classic example to explain **steganography** illustrated by Simmons in1983, which is called the prisoners' problem (Simmons, 1984). There are two prisoners, called Alice and Bob, who are planning to escape from jail. All the communications between them are monitored by a warden, called Wendy. So to escape from the eyes of Wendy, the two prisoners must communicate with each other by a cover on their messages. They create a stego-object, which is sent through the public channel to be observed by Wendy who can freely inspect it. Wendy's observation is classified into two types, called *active* and *passive*. In an active state, Wendy can modify the message by a little thwart any hidden communication, but the hidden message may be survived under Wendy's modification. In a passive state, Wendy can examine all the messages between Alice and Bob and does not change any message but finds whether the message contains any hidden message. In most of the cases, the warden is considered as passive, and it is highly possible that Wendy cannot find the hidden message from the stego-object.

For steganographic systems, the fundamental requirement is that the stego-object should be perceptually indistinguishable to the degree that it does not raise suspicion. In other words, the hidden information introduces only slight modification to the cover-object. Most passive warden distinguishes the stego-images by analyzing their statistic features. Since hiding information within an image causes some form of image degradation or unusual characteristics, *steganalysis* intends to identify suspected information streams and determine whether they have hidden messages encoded into them. Figure 1 shows an example of **steganography**, where (a) is a cover-image, (b) is the secret image containing NJIT logo, and (c) is the stego-image after the *least-significant-bit* (LSB) embedding of the secret image into the cover-image.

Modern techniques in **steganography** have far-more-powerful tools. Many software tools allow a paranoid sender to embed messages in digitized information, typically audio, video or still image files that were sent to a recipient. Although **steganography** has attracted great interests from the military and governmental organizations, there is even a big interest shown from commercial companies to safeguard their information from piracy. Today, **steganography**

Figure 1. (a) A Lena cover-image, (b) the NJIT logo, (c) the stego-image after embedding the NJIT logo into the Lena image

is often used to transmit information safely and embed trademarks securely in images and music files to assure copyright.

This chapter presents a GA based steganographic technique for breaking the inspection of steganalytic systems. The overview of steganographic and steganalytic techniques is respectively described in sections 2 and 3. The GA based breaking methodology is presented in section 4. Then the GA based breaking algorithm is applied on the spatial-domain steganalytic system given in section 5, and is applied on the frequency-domain steganalytic system given in section 6. Experimental results are provided in section 7. Finally, we draw conclusions in section 8.

STEGANOGRAPHIC TECHNIQUES

Steganographic techniques can be divided into three types: technical **steganography**, linguistic **steganography**, and digital **steganography**. Technical **steganography** applies scientific methods to conceal a secret message, such as the use of invisible ink, microdots, and shaved heads. The invisible ink is the simplest method to write secret information on a piece of paper, so when it dries, the written information disappears. The paper looks the same just as the original blank piece of paper. With the advent of photography, microfilm was created as a medium of recording a great amount of information in a very small piece. In World War II, the Germans used 'microdots' to convey secret information.

Linguistic **steganography** utilizes written natural language to hide information. It can be categorized into semagrams and open codes. Semagrams hide secret messages using visual symbols or signs. Modern updates to this method use computers to hide the secret message even less noticeable. Another secret method is used when spies want to set up meetings or pass information to their networks. This includes hiding information

in everyday matters, such as newspapers, dates, clothing or conversation. Sometimes meeting times can be hidden in reading materials. Open codes hide the secret messages in a specifically designed pattern on the document that is not obvious to the average reader.

Computer technology has made **steganography** a lot easier to hide messages and more difficult to discover the messages. Digital **steganography** is the science to hide secret messages within digital media, such as digital images, audio files or video files. There are many different methods for digital **steganography** including least significant bit substitution, message scattering, masking and filtering, and image processing functions. Secret information or images can be hidden in image files because image files are often very large. When a picture is scanned, a sampling process is conducted to quantize the picture into a discrete set of real numbers. These samples are the gray levels at an equally spaced array of pixels. The pixels are quantized to a set of discrete gray level values, which are also taken to be equally spaced. The result of sampling and quantizing produces a digital image.

Steganography embeds secret messages into innocuous files. Its goal is not only to hide the message, but also let the stego-object pass without causing any suspicion. There are many **steganography** tools available for hiding messages in images, audio files and video, for example, S-Tools, StegoDos, EzStego, and JSteg-Jpeg. The S-Tools (Brown, 1994), standing for **Steganography** Tools, was written by Andy Brown to hide the secret messages in BMP, GIF, and WAV files. It is a combined steganographic and cryptographic product since the messages to be hidden are encrypted using symmetric keys. It uses the least significant bit (LSB) substitution in files that employ lossless compression, such as 8- or 24-bit color and pulse code modulation. It also applies a pseudo random number generator to make the extraction of secret messages more difficult. It also provides the encryption and decryption of hidden files with several different encryption algorithms.

StegoDos (Wolf, 2007), also known as Black Wolf's Picture Encoder, consists of a set of programs that allow us to capture an image, encode a secret message and display the stego-image. This stego-image may also be captured again into another format using a third-party program. Then we can recapture it and decode the hidden message. It only works with 320×200 images with 256 colors. It also uses the LSB substitution to hide messages.

EzStego, developed by Romana Machado, simulates the invisible ink for Internet communication. It hides an encrypted message in a GIF format image file by modulating the least significant bits. It begins by sorting the colors in the palette, so closest colors fall next to each other. Then similar colors are paired up, and for each pair one color will represent 1 while the other will represent 0. It encodes the encrypted message by replacing the LSB.

Jsteg-Jpeg (Korejwa, 2007), developed by Derek Upham, can read multiple format images and embed the secret messages to be saved as the JPEG format images. It utilizes the splitting of the JPEG encoding into lossy and lossless stages. The lossy stages use DCT and a quantization step to compress the image data, and the lossless stage uses Huffmann coding to further compress the image data. It therefore inserts the secret message into the image data between these two steps. It also modulates the rounding processes in the quantized DCT coefficients.

STEGANALYTIC TECHNIQUES

In general, the steganalytic systems can be categorized into two classes: *spatial-domain steganalytic system* (SDSS) and *frequency-domain steganalytic system* (FDSS). The SDSS (Westfeld, 1999; Avcibas, 2003) is adopted for checking the lossless compressed images by analyzing the spatial-domain statistic features. For the lossy compression images such as JPEG, the FDSS (Fridrich, 2003; Farid, 2001) is used to analyze the frequency-domain statistic features. Westfeld and Pfitzmann (1999) presented two SDSSs based on visual and chi-square attacks. The visual attack uses utilizes human eyes to inspect stego-images by checking their lower bit-planes. The chi-square attack can automatically detect the specific characteristic generated by the LSB steganographic technique. Avcibas et al. (2003) proposed *image quality measure* (IQM) which is based on a hypothesis that the steganographic systems leave statistic evidences that can be exploited for detection using IQM and multivariate regression analysis. Fridrich et al. (2003) presented a FDSS for detecting the JPEG stego-images by analyzing their *discrete cosine transformation* (DCT) with cropped images. The above steganalytic systems are used in our experiments to test the correctness of our GA-based methodology.

Since the steganalytic system analyzes certain statistic features of an image, the idea of developing a robust steganographic system is to generate the stego-image by avoiding changing the statistic features of the cover-image. In literature, several papers have presented the algorithms for steganographic and steganalytic systems. Very few papers have discussed the algorithms for breaking the steganalytic systems. Chu et al. (2004) presented a DCT-based steganographic system by utilizing the similarities of DCT coefficients between the adjacent image blocks where the embedding distortion is spread. Their algorithm can allow random selection of DCT coefficients in order to maintain key statistic features. However, the drawback of their approach is that the capacity of the embedded message is limited, i.e., only 2 bits for an 8×8 DCT block.

GA-BASED BREAKING METHODOLOGY

The **genetic algorithm** (GA), introduced by Holland (1975) in his seminal work, is commonly used as an adaptive approach that provides a randomized, parallel, and global search based on the mechanics of natural selection and genetics in order to find solutions of a problem. Every organism has a set of rules describing how it is built up from the tiny building blocks of life. These rules are encoded in the *genes* of an organism, which in turn are connected together into long strings called *chromosomes*. Each gene represents a specific trait of an organism like eye color to hair color. These genes and their settings are usually referred to as *an organism's genotype*. When two organism mates, they share their genes and the resultant offspring may end up having a half of the genes from one parent and the other half from the others. This process is called *recombination*. The *crossover* is a genetic operator used to vary the programming of a chromosome or chromosomes from one generation to the next. It is analogous to reproduction and biological crossover, upon which **genetic algorithm**s are based.

The procedure of **genetic algorithm** is given as follows. At the beginning of the **genetic algorithm** a large population of random chromosomes is created.

Assume that there are N chromosomes in the initial population. The following steps are repeated until we obtain the required output:

(1) Test each chromosome to see how good it is at solving the problem at hand and assigning a fitness score.

(2) Select two members from the current population. The chance of being selected is proportional to the chromosome fitness.

(3) Depend on the crossover rate to cross over the bits from each chosen chromosome pair at randomly chosen point.

(4) Flip on the mutation rate through the chosen chromosomes bits. Repeat steps 2-4 until

a new population of N members has been created.

In general, the **genetic algorithm** defines an objective, called *fitness function*, to evaluate the quality of each chromosome. The chromosomes of high quality will survive and form a new population of the next generation. Using the three operators — reproduction, crossover, and mutation, we recombine a new generation to find the best solution. The process is repeated until a predefined condition is satisfied or a constant number of iterations are reached. The predefined condition is the situation when we can correctly extract the desired hidden message.

In order to apply the **genetic algorithm** for embedding messages into the frequency domain of a cover-image to obtain the stego-image, we use the chromosome, ξ, consisting of n genes as $\hat{1} = g_0, g_1, g_2, \cdots, g_n$. Figure 2 gives an example of a chromosome ($\xi \in Z^{64}$) containing 64 genes ($g_i \in Z$ (integers)). Figure 2(a) shows the distribution order of a chromosome in an 8×8 block, and (b) shows an example of the corresponding chromosome.

The chromosome is used to adjust the pixel values of a cover-image to generate a stego-image, so the embedded message can be correctly extracted and at the same time the statistic features can be remained in order to break steganalytic systems. A fitness function is used to evaluate the embedded message and statistic features. Let C and S respectively denote the cover- and the stego-images of size 8×8. We generate the stego-images by adding the cover-image and the chromosome as

$$S = \{s_i \mid s_i = c_i + g_i, \quad \text{where} \quad 0 \le i \le 63\}. \tag{1}$$

Fitness Function.

In order to embed messages into DCT-based co-efficients and avoid the detection of steganalytic systems, we develop a fitness function to evaluate the following two terms:

Figure 2. The numbering positions corresponding to 64 genes

g_0	g_1	g_2	g_3	g_4	g_5	g_6	g_7
g_8	g_9	g_{10}	g_{11}	g_{12}	g_{13}	g_{14}	g_{15}
g_{16}	g_{17}	g_{18}	g_{19}	g_{20}	g_{21}	g_{22}	g_{23}
g_{24}	g_{25}	g_{26}	g_{27}	g_{28}	g_{29}	g_{30}	g_{31}
g_{32}	g_{33}	g_{34}	g_{35}	g_{36}	g_{37}	g_{38}	g_{39}
g_{40}	g_{41}	g_{42}	g_{43}	g_{44}	g_{45}	g_{46}	g_{47}
g_{48}	g_{49}	g_{50}	g_{51}	g_{52}	g_{53}	g_{54}	g_{55}
g_{56}	g_{57}	g_{58}	g_{59}	g_{60}	g_{61}	g_{62}	g_{63}

(a)

0	0	1	0	0	2	0	1
1	2	0	0	1	1	0	1
2	1	1	0	0	-2	0	1
3	1	2	5	0	0	0	0
0	2	0	0	0	1	0	0
0	-1	0	2	1	1	4	2
1	1	1	0	0	0	0	0
0	0	0	0	1	-2	1	3

(b)

(1)　$Analysis(\xi, C)$: The analysis function evaluates the difference between the cover-image and the stego-image in order to maintain the statistic features. It is related to the type of the steganalytic systems used.

(2)　$BER(\xi, C)$: The *bit error rate* (BER) sums up the bit differences between the embedded and the extracted messages. It is defined as

$$BER(\xi,C) = \frac{1}{|Message^H|} \sum_{i=0}^{all\ pixels} \left| Message_i^H - Message_i^E \right|$$

(2)

where $Message^H$ and $Message^E$ denote respectively the embedded and the extracted binary messages, and $|Message^H|$ denotes the length of the message.

We use a linear combination of the analysis and the bit error rate to be the fitness function as

$$Evaluation\ (\xi,C) = \alpha_1 \times Analysis(\xi,C) + \alpha_2 \times BER(\xi,C)$$

(3)

where α_1 and α_2 denote weights. The weights can be adjusted according to the user's demand on the degree of distortion to the stego-image or the extracted message.

Reproduction.

$$Reproduction(\Psi,k) = \{\xi_i \mid Evaluation(\xi_i, C) \leq \Omega \text{ for } \xi_i \in \Psi\}$$

where Ω is a threshold for sieving chromosomes, and $\Psi = \{\xi_1, \xi_2, \cdots, \xi_n\}$. It is used to reproduce k better chromosomes from the original population for higher qualities.

Crossover.

$$Crossover(\Psi,l) = \{\xi_i\ \Theta\ \xi_j \mid \xi_i, \xi_j \in \Psi\}$$

(5)

where Θ denotes the operation to generate chromosomes by exchanging genes from their parents: ξ_i and ξ_j. It is used to gestate l better offsprings by inheriting well genes (i.e. higher qualities in the fitness evaluation) from their parents. The often-used crossovers are one-point, two-point, and multi-point crossovers. The criteria of selecting a suitable crossover depend on the length and structure of chromosomes. We adopt the one- and two-point crossovers as shown in (Shih, 2005).

Mutation.

$$Mutation(\Psi,m) = \{\xi_i \circ j \mid$$
$$0 \leq j \leq |\xi_i| \text{ and } \xi_i \in \Psi\},$$

(6)

where ∘ denotes the operation to randomly select a chromosome ξ_i from Ψ and change the j-th bit from ξ_i. It is used to generate m new chromosomes. The mutation is usually performed with a probability p ($0 < p \leq 1$), meaning only p portion of the genes in a chromosome will be selected to be mutated.

Note that in each generation, the new population is generated by the above three operations. The new population is actually the same size of $k + l + m$ as the original population. Note that, to break the inspection of the steganalytic systems, we use a straightforward GA selection method that the new generation is generated based on the chromosomes having superior evaluation values in the current generation. For example, only top 10% of the current chromosomes will be considered for the GA operations, such as reproduction, crossover, and mutation.

The mutation tends to be more efficient than the crossover if a candidate solution is close to the real optimum solution. In order to enhance the performance of our GA-based methodology, we generate a new chromosome with desired minor adjustment when the previous generation is close to the goal. Therefore, the strategy of dynamically determining the ratio of three GA operations is utilized. Let R_P, R_M, and R_C respectively denote the ratios of production, mutation, and crossover. In the beginning, we select a small R_P and R_M and a large R_C to enable the global search. After certain iterations, we will decrease R_C and increase R_M and R_P to shift focuses on local search if the current generation is better than the old one; otherwise, we will increase R_C and decrease R_M and R_P to enlarge the range of global search. Note that, this property must be satisfied: $R_P + R_M + R_C = 100\%$.

The recombination strategy of our GA-based algorithm is presented below. We apply the same strategy in recombining the chromosome except that the fitness function is differently defined with respect to the properties of individual problem.

The Algorithm for Recombining the Chromosomes (Wu, 2006).

1. Initialize the base population of chromosomes, R_P, R_M, and R_C.
2. Generate candidates by adjusting pixel values of the original image.
3. Determine the fitness value of each chromosome.
4. If a predefined condition is satisfied or a constant number of iterations are reached, the algorithm will stop and output the best chromosome to be the solution; otherwise, go to the following steps to recombine the chromosomes.
5. If a certain number of iterations are reached, go to step 6 to adjust R_P, R_M, and R_C; otherwise, go to step 7 to recombine the new chromosomes.
6. If 20% of the new generation are better than the best chromosome in the preceding generation, then $R_C = R_C - 10\%$, $R_M = R_M + 5\%$ and $R_P = R_P + 5\%$; otherwise, $R_C = R_C + 10\%$, $R_M = R_M - 5\%$ and $R_P = R_P - 5\%$.
7. Obtain the new generation by recombining the preceding chromosomes using production, mutation, and crossover.
8. Go to step 2.

THE GA-BASED BREAKING ALGORITHM ON SDSS

As aforementioned, in order to generate a stego-image to pass though the inspection of *spatial-domain steganalytic system* (SDSS), the messages should be embedded into the specific positions for maintaining the statistic features of a cover-image. In the spatial-domain embedding approach, it is difficult to select such positions since the messages are distributed regularly. On the other hand, if the messages are embedded into specific positions of coefficients of a transformed image, the changes in the spatial domain are difficult to predict. In this section, we intend to find the desired positions on the frequency domain that produce minimum statistic features disturbance on the spatial domain. We apply the **genetic algorithm** to generate the stego-image by adjusting the pixel values on the spatial domain using the following two criteria:

(1) Evaluate the extracted messages obtained from the specific coefficients of a stego-image to be as close as to the embedded messages.

(2) Evaluate the statistic features of the stego-image and compare them with those of the cover-image such that the differences should be as small as possible.

Generating the Stego-Image on the Visual Steganalytic System (VSS)

Westfeld and Pfitzmann (1999) presented a *visual steganalytic system* (VSS) that uses an assignment function of color replacement, called the *visual filter*, to efficiently detect a stego-image by translating a gray-scale image into binary. Therefore, in order to break the VSS, the two results, VF^C and VF^S, of applying the visual filter on the cover- and the stego-images respectively should be as identical as possible. The VSS was originally designed to detect the GIF format images by reassigning the color in the color palette of an image. We extend their method to detect the BMP format images as well by setting the odd- and even-numbered gray scales to black and white, respectively. The *Analysis*(ξ, C) to VSS indicating the sum of difference between LSB^C and LSB^S is defined as

$$Analysis(\xi, C) = \frac{1}{|C|} \sum_{i=0}^{all\ pixels} (VF_i^C \oplus VF_i^S),$$

(7)

where $\oplus$ denotes the Exclusive-OR (XOR) operator. Our algorithm is described below.

The Algorithm for Generating a Stego-Image on VSS.

1. Divide a cover-image into a set of cover-images of size 8×8.

2. For each 8×8 cover-image, we generate a stego-image based on the GA to perform the embedding procedure as well as to ensure that LSB^C and LSB^S are as identical as possible.

3. Combine all the 8×8 stego-images together to form a complete stego-image.

Generating the Stego-Image on the IQM-Based Steganalytic System (IQM-SDSS)

Avcibas et al. (2002) proposed a steganalytic system by analyzing the *image quality measures* (IQMs) of the cover- and the stego-images. The IQM-SDSS consists of two phases: training and testing. In the training phase, the IQM is calculated between an image and its filtered image using a low-pass filter based on the Gaussian kernel. Suppose there are N images and q IQMs in the training set. Let x_{ij} denote the score in the ith image and the jth IQM, where $1 \le i \le N$, $1 \le j \le q$. Let y_i be the value of -1 or 1 indicating the cover- or stego-image, respectively. We can represent all the images in the training set as

$$y_1 = \beta_1 x_{11} + \beta_2 x_{12} + \cdots + \beta_q x_{1q} + \varepsilon_1$$
$$y_2 = \beta_1 x_{21} + \beta_2 x_{22} + \cdots + \beta_q x_{2q} + \varepsilon_2$$
$$\vdots$$
$$y_N = \beta_1 x_{N1} + \beta_2 x_{N2} + \cdots + \beta_q x_{Nq} + \varepsilon_N$$

(8)

where $\varepsilon_1, \varepsilon_2, \cdots, \varepsilon_N$ denote random errors in the linear regression model (Rencher, 1995). Then the linear predictor $\beta = [\beta_1, \beta_2, \cdots, \beta_q]$ can be obtained from all the training images.

In the testing phase, we use the q IQMs to compute y_i to determine whether it is a stego-image. If y_i is positive, the test image is a stego-image; otherwise, it is a cover-image. We first train the IQM-SDSS in order to obtain the linear predictor, i.e., $\beta = [\beta_1, \beta_2, \cdots, \beta_q]$, from our database. Then, we use β to generate the stego-image by our GA-based algorithm, so that it can pass through the inspection of IQM-SDSS. Note that the GA procedure is not used in the training phase. The $Analysis(\xi, C)$ to the IQM-SDSS is defined as

$$Analysis(\xi, C) = \beta_1 x_1 + \beta_2 x_2 + \cdots + \beta_q x_q \tag{9}$$

The Algorithm for Generating a Stego-image on IQM-SDSS.

1. Divide a cover-image into a set of cover-images of size 8×8.
2. Adjust the pixel values in each 8×8 cover-image based on GA to embed messages into the frequency domain and ensure that the stego-image can pass through the inspection of the IQM-SDSS. The procedures for generating the 8×8 stego-image are presented next after this algorithm.
3. Combine all the 8×8 embedded-images together to form a completely embedded image.
4. Test the embedded-image on IQM-SDSS. If it passes, it is the desired stego-image; otherwise, repeat steps 2 to 4.

The Procedure for Generating an 8×8 Embedded-image on IQM-SDSS.

1. Define the fitness function, the number of genes, the size of population, the crossover rate, the critical value, and the mutation rate.

2. Generate the first generation by a random selection.
3. Generate an 8×8 embedded-image based on each chromosome.
4. Evaluate the fitness value for each chromosome by analyzing the 8×8 embedded-image.
5. Obtain the better chromosome based on the fitness value.
6. Recombine new chromosomes by crossover.
7. Recombine new chromosomes by mutation.
8. Repeat steps 3 to 8 until a predefined condition is satisfied or a constant number of iterations are reached.

THE GA-BASED BREAKING ALGORITHM ON FDSS

Fridrich et al. (2003) presented a steganalytic system for detecting JPEG stego-images based on the assumption that the histogram distributions of some specific AC DCT coefficients of a cover-image and its cropped image should be similar. Note that, in the DCT coefficients, only the zero frequency (0,0) is the DC component, and the remaining frequencies are the AC components. Let $h_k(d)$ and $\bar{h}_k(d)$ respectively denote the total number of AC DCT coefficients in the 8×8 cover and its corresponding 8×8 cropped images with the absolute value equal to d at location (k, l), where $0 \leq k, l \leq 7$. Note that, the 8×8 cropped images, defined in Fridrich et al. (2003), are obtained using the same way as the 8×8 cover images with a horizontal shift by 4 pixels.

The probability, ρ_{kl}, of the modification of a non-zero AC coefficient at (k, l) can be obtained by

$$\rho_{kl} = \frac{\bar{h}_{kl}(1)[h_{kl}(0) - \bar{h}_{kl}(0)] + [h_{kl}(1) - \bar{h}_{kl}(1)][\bar{h}_{kl}(2) - \bar{h}_{kl}(1)]}{[\bar{h}_{kl}(1)]^2 + [\bar{h}_{kl}(2) - \bar{h}_{kl}(1)]^2} \tag{10}$$

Note that, the final value of the parameter ρ is calculated as an average over the selected low-frequency DCT coefficients $(k, l) \in \{(1,2),(2,1),(2,2)\}$, and only 0, 1, and 2 are considered when checking the coefficient values of the specific frequencies between a cover and its corresponding cropped image.

Our GA-based breaking algorithm on the JFDSS is intended to minimize the differences between the two histograms of a stego-image and its cropped-image. It is presented below.

Algorithm for Generating a Stego-image on JFDSS.

1. Compress a cover-image by JPEG and divide it into a set of small cover-images of size 8×8. Each is performed by DCT.

2. Embed the messages into the specific DCT coefficients and decompress the embedded image by IDCT.

3. We select a 12×8 working window and generate an 8×8 cropped-image for each 8×8 embedded-image.

4. Determine the overlapping area between each 8×8 embedded-image and its cropped-image.

5. Adjust the overlapping pixel values by making that the coefficients of some specific frequencies (k,l) of the stego-image and its cropped-image are as identical as possible and the embedded messages are not altered.

6. Repeat steps 3 to 5 until all the 8×8 embedded-images are generated.

Let $Coef^{Stego}$ and $Coef^{Crop}$ denote the coefficients of each 8×8 stego-image and its cropped-image. The $Analysis(\xi, C)$ to the JFDSS is defined as

$$Analysis(\xi, C) = \frac{1}{|C|} \sum_{i=0}^{all\ pixels} (Coef_i^{Stego} \otimes Coef_i^{Crop}),$$

$$(11)$$

Figure 3. An example of our GA-based algorithm on the JFDSS

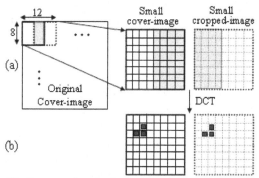

The frequency domain of cover image and cropped images

where $\otimes$ denotes the operator defined by

$$\begin{cases} Coef_i^{Stego} \otimes Coef_i^{Crop} = 1 & \text{if } (Coef_i^{Stego} = 0 \text{ and } Coef_i^{Crop} \neq 0) \text{ or} \\ & (Coef_i^{Stego} = 1 \text{ and } Coef_i^{Crop} \neq 1) \text{ or} \\ & (Coef_i^{Stego} = 2 \text{ and } Coef_i^{Crop} \neq 2) \text{ or} \\ & (Coef_i^{Stego} \neq 0,1,2 \text{ and } Coef_i^{Crop} = 0,1,2) \\ Coef_i^{Stego} \otimes Coef_i^{Crop} = 0 & \text{otherwise} \end{cases}$$

$$(12)$$

Note that, 0, 1, and 2 denote the values in the specific frequencies obtained by dividing the quantization table. We only consider the values of the desired frequencies to be 0, 1, 2, or some values in equation (12) because of the strategy of JFDSS in equation (10).

Figure 3 shows an example of our GA-based algorithm on the JFDSS. In Figure 3(a), we select a 12×8 working window for each 8×8 stego-image, and generate its 8×8 cropped-image. Note that, the shaded pixels indicate their overlapping area, and the three black boxes in Figure 3(b) are the desired locations.

EXPERIMENTAL RESULTS

In this section, we provide experimental results to show that our GA-based steganographic system can successfully break the inspection of stegana-

Figure 4. A stego-image generated by our GA-based algorithm and its 8 bit-planes

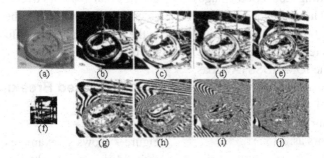

lytic systems. For testing our algorithm, we use a database of 200 gray-scale images of size 256 ×256. All the images were originally stored in the BMP format.

The GA-Based Breaking Algorithm on VSS

We test our algorithm on VSS. Figures 4(a) and (f) show a stego-image and a message-image of sizes 256×256 and 64×64, respectively. We embed 4 bits into the 8×8 DCT coefficients on frequencies (0,2), (1,1), (2,0), and (3,0) for avoiding distortion. Note that, the stego-image in Figure 4(a) is generated by embedding Figure 4(f) into the DCT coefficients of the cover-image using our GA-based algorithm. In Figure 4, (b) to (j) respectively display the bit-planes from 7 to 0. Figure 5 shows the stego-image and its visual filtered result. It is difficult to determine that Figure 5(a) is a stego-image.

Figure 6 shows the relationship of the average iteration for adjusting an 8×8 cover-image vs. the correct rate of the visual filter. The correct rate is the percentage of similarity between the transformed results of the cover- and the stego-images using the visual filter. Note that, the BERs in Figure 6 are all 0%.

Figure 5. A stego-image and its visual filtered result

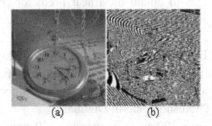

Figure 6. The relationship of the average iteration vs. the correct rate of the visual filter

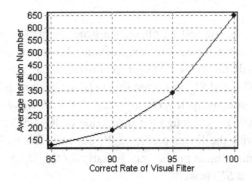

The GA-Based Breaking Algorithm on IQM-SDSS

We generate 3 stego-images as the training samples for each cover-image by Photoshop plug-in Digimarc (PictureMarc, 2007), Cox's technique (Cox, 1997), and S-tools (Brown,

1994). Therefore, there are totally 800 images of size 256×256, including 200 cover-images and 600 stego-images. The embedded message size were 1/10, 1/24, and 1/40 of the cover image size for Digimarc, Cox's technique, and S-tools, respectively. Note that the IQM-SDSS (Avcibas, 2003) can detect the stego-images containing the message size of 1/100 of the cover image. We develop the following four training strategies to obtain the linear predictors as:

(A) Train all the images in our database to obtain the linear predictor β^A.

(B) Train 100 cover-images and 100 stego-images to obtain the linear predictor β^B, in which the stego-images are obtained by Cox's technique.

(C) Train 100 cover-images and 100 stego-images to obtain the linear predictor β^C, in which the stego-images are obtained by Photoshop plug-in Digimarc.

(D) Train 100 cover-images and 100 stego-images to obtain the linear predictor β^D, in which the stego-images are obtained by S-tools.

In the testing phase, we generate 50 stego-images for each linear predictor. Therefore, we will obtain 4 types of stego-images SI_A, SI_B, SI_C, and SI_D corresponding to β^A, β^B, β^C, and β^D, respectively. It is obvious that all the SI_A images will pass through the inspection of IQM-SDSS with the linear predictor β^A, but may fail with other linear predictors; similarly for the SI_B, SI_C, and SI_D as well.

Table 1 shows the false negative (Type I Error) and false positive (Type II Error) rates of testing each type of stego- and cover-images under different linear predictors. For example, the false negative (FN) rate of testing 50 SI_A stego-images under β^B is 94% indicating that the β^B-IQMSS falsely decides that 94% of our stego-images belong to the cover-image. On the other hand, the false positive (FP) rate of testing 50 cover-images

under β^B is 10% indicating that the β^B-IQMSS decides that 10% of cover-images belong to the stego-images. Note that the cover-images used in the testing phase are different to those used in the training phase.

The GA-Based Breaking Algorithm on JFDSS

Figure 7 shows an example of adjusting an 8×8 embedded-image to obtain an 8×8 stego-image for breaking the JEDSS. Figure 7(a) shows a 12×8 working window, where the enclosed is the overlapping area. Figures 7(b) and (c) show the original 8×8 embedded- and cropped-images, respectively. We embed "1" on (1,2), (2,1), and (2,2) by compressing Figure 7(b) using JPEG under 70% compression quality to obtain Figure 7(d). Note that, the top-left pixel is (0,0) and the messages can be embedded into any frequency of the transformed domain, so that the embedding capacity could be sufficiently high. Due to that the JFDSS only checks frequencies (1,2), (2,1), and (2,2), we show an example of embedding 3 bits into these 3 frequencies. Similarly, Figure 7(e) is obtained by compressing Figure 7(c) using JPEG under the same compression quality. By evaluating the frequencies (1,2), (2,1), and (2,2), the JFDSS can determine whether the embedded-image is a stego-image. Therefore, in order to break the JFDSS, we obtain the stego-image as in Figure 7(f). Figures 7(g) and (h) respectively show the new embedded- and cropped-images. Similarly, we obtain Figures 7(i) and (j) by compressing Figures 7(g) and (h) respectively using JPEG under 70% compression quality. Therefore, the JFDSS cannot distinguish from the frequencies (1,2), (2,1), and (2,2).

Let $QTable(i, j)$ denote the standard quantization table, where $0 \leq i, j \leq 7$. The new quantization table, $NewTable(i, j)$, with $x\%$ compression quality can be obtained by

Table 1. Experimental results of GA-based agorithm on IQM-SDSS

		β^A	β^B	β^C	β^D	Average
50 SI_A images	FN		94 %	94 %	100 %	96 %
50 SI_B images	FN	84 %		84%	80 %	83 %
50 SI_C images	FN	82 %	86 %		88 %	85 %
50 SI_D images	FN	82 %	86 %	82 %		83 %
50 cover images	FP	6 %	10 %	16 %	16 %	12 %

Figure 7. An example of adjusting an 8x8 embedded-image

169	166	162	158	157	158	161	163	157	158	161	163
166	164	162	159	159	159	161	162	159	159	161	162
162	162	161	161	161	161	161	161	161	161	161	161
158	159	161	162	162	162	160	160	162	162	160	160
157	159	161	163	163	161	160	158	163	161	160	158
158	159	161	162	162	160	158	157	162	160	158	157
160	161	161	160	160	158	157	156	160	158	157	156
162	162	161	159	158	157	156	156	158	157	156	156

(a)

169	166	162	158	164	163	164	159	157	158	161	163
166	164	162	159	162	162	162	161	159	159	161	162
162	162	161	161	162	162	161	161	161	161	161	161
158	159	161	162	160	162	161	161	162	162	160	160
157	159	161	163	160	158	159	160	163	161	160	158
158	159	161	162	160	160	157	159	162	160	158	157
160	161	161	160	161	159	161	158	160	158	157	156
162	162	161	159	161	161	158	159	158	157	156	156

(f)

169	166	162	158	157	158	161	163
166	164	162	159	159	159	161	162
162	162	161	161	161	161	161	161
158	159	161	162	162	162	160	160
157	159	161	163	163	161	160	158
158	159	161	162	162	160	158	157
160	161	161	160	160	158	157	156
162	162	161	159	158	157	156	156

(b)

127	1	0	0	0	0	0	0
1	0	1	0	0	0	0	0
0	1	1	0	0	0	0	0
0	0	0	0	0	0	0	0
0	0	0	0	0	0	0	0
0	0	0	0	0	0	0	0
0	0	0	0	0	0	0	0
0	0	0	0	0	0	0	0

(d)

169	166	162	158	164	163	164	159
166	164	162	159	162	162	162	161
162	162	161	161	162	162	161	161
158	159	161	162	160	162	161	161
157	159	161	163	160	158	159	160
158	159	161	162	160	160	157	159
160	161	161	160	161	159	161	158
162	162	161	159	161	161	158	159

(g)

127	1	0	0	0	0	0	0
1	0	1	0	0	0	0	0
1	1	1	0	0	0	0	0
0	0	0	0	0	0	0	0
0	0	0	0	0	0	0	0
0	0	0	0	0	0	0	0
0	0	0	0	0	0	0	0
0	0	0	0	0	0	0	0

(i)

157	158	161	163	157	158	161	163
159	159	161	162	159	159	161	162
161	161	161	161	161	161	161	161
162	162	160	160	162	162	160	160
163	161	160	158	163	161	160	158
162	160	158	157	162	160	158	157
160	158	157	156	160	158	157	156
158	157	156	156	158	157	156	156

(c)

126	0	0	0	0	0	0	0
1	-1	0	-1	0	0	0	0
-1	0	0	0	0	0	0	0
0	0	0	0	0	0	0	0
0	0	0	0	0	0	0	0
0	0	0	0	0	0	0	0
0	0	0	0	0	0	0	0
0	0	0	0	0	0	0	0

(e)

164	163	164	159	157	158	161	163
162	162	162	161	159	159	161	162
162	162	161	161	161	161	161	161
160	162	161	161	162	162	160	160
160	158	159	160	163	161	160	158
160	160	157	159	162	160	158	157
161	159	161	158	160	158	157	156
161	161	158	159	158	157	156	156

(h)

127	1	0	0	0	0	0	0
1	0	1	0	0	0	0	0
0	1	1	0	0	0	0	0
0	0	0	0	0	0	0	0
0	0	0	0	0	0	0	0
0	0	0	0	0	0	0	0
0	0	0	0	0	0	0	0
0	0	0	0	0	0	0	0

(j)

$$NewTable(i,j) = \frac{QTable(i,j) \times factor + 50}{100}, \tag{13}$$

where the factor is determined by

$$\begin{cases} factor = \dfrac{5000}{x} & \text{if } x \leq 50 \\ factor = 200 - 2x & \text{otherwise} \end{cases} \tag{14}$$

In Figure 8, (a) and (b) show the quantization tables of the standard and 70% compression quality, respectively.

CONCLUSION

In this chapter, we have presented a GA-based algorithm of generating a stego-image to break

Figure 8. The quantization table of JPEG

16	11	10	16	24	40	51	61
12	12	14	19	26	58	60	55
14	13	16	24	40	57	69	56
14	17	22	29	51	87	80	62
18	22	37	56	68	109	103	77
24	35	55	64	81	104	113	92
49	64	78	87	103	121	120	101
72	92	95	98	112	100	103	99

(a)

10.1	7.1	6.5	10.1	14.9	24.5	31.1	37.1
7.7	7.7	8.9	11.9	16.1	35.3	36.5	33.5
8.9	8.3	10.1	14.9	24.5	34.7	41.9	34.1
8.9	10.7	13.7	17.9	31.1	52.7	48.5	37.7
11.3	13.7	22.7	34.1	41.3	65.9	62.3	46.7
14.9	21.5	33.5	38.9	49.1	62.9	68.3	55.7
29.9	38.9	47.3	52.7	62.3	73.1	72.5	61.1
43.7	55.7	57.5	59.3	67.7	60.5	62.3	59.9

(b)

the detection of the spatial-domain and the frequency-domain steganalytic systems by artificially counterfeiting statistic features. We design a fitness function to evaluate the quality of each chromosome in order to generate the stego-image that can pass through the inspection of steganalytic systems. Experimental results show that our GA-based algorithm can not only successfully break the detection of the current steganalytic systems, but also correctly embed messages into the frequency domain of a cover-image. Moreover, our GA-based algorithm can be used to enhance the quality of stego-images.

REFERENCES

Avcibas, I., Memon, N., & Sankur, B. (2003). Steganalysis using image quality metrics. *IEEE Trans. Image Processing, 12*(2), 221-229.

Avcibas, I., & Sankur, B. (2002). Statistical analysis of image quality measures. *Journal Electron. Imag., 11*, 206-223.

Brown, A. (1994). *S-Tools for Windows*. Shareware. ftp://idea.sec.dsi.unimi.it/pub/security/crypt/code/s-tools4.zip.

Chu, R., You, X., Kong, X., & Ba, X. (2004). A DCT-based image steganographic method resisting statistical attacks. In *Proc. International Conference on Acoustics, Speech, and Signal Processing*, Montereal, Quebec, Canada.

Cox, I. J., Bloom, J., Miller, M., & Cox, I. (2001). *Digital watermarking: Principles & Practice*. Morgan Kaufmann.

Cox, I. J., KIlian, J., Leighton, T., & Shamoon, T. (1997). Secure spread spectrum watermarking for multimedia. *IEEE Trans. Image Processing, 6*, 1673-1686.

Farid, H. (2001). *Detecting steganographic message in digital images*. Technical Report, TR2001-412, Computer Science, Dartmouth College.

Fridrich, J., Goljan, M., & Hogea, D. (2003). New methodology for breaking steganographic techniques for JPEGs. In *Proc. EI SPIE*, Santa Clara, CA, 143-155.

Holland, J. H. (1975). *Adaptation in Natural and Artificial Systems*. The University of Michigan Press.

Kahn, D. (1996). *The Codebreakers*. 2nd edition, New York: Macmillan.

Korejwa, J. (2007). *Jsteg shell 2.0*. http://www.tiac.net/users/korejwa/steg.htm.

Norman, B. (1973). *Secret Warfare*. Washington, DC: Acropolis Books.

PictureMarc. (2007). *Embed Watermark*. v 1.00.45, Digimarc Corporation.

Rencher, A. C. (1995). *Methods of Multivariate Analysis*. New York: John Wiley, ch. 6, 10.

Shih, F. Y. (2007). *Digital watermarking and Steganography: Fundamentals and Techniques*, CRC Press, Boca Raton, FL.

Shih, F. Y., & Wu, Y.-T. (2005). Enhancement of image watermark retrieval based on genetic algorithm. *Journal of Visual Commu. and Image Repre., 16*, 115-133.

Simmons, G. J. (1984). Prisoners' problem and the subliminal channel. In *Proc. International Conf. on Advances in Cryptology*, 51-67.

Westfeld, A., & Pfitzmann, A. (1999). Attacks on steganographic systems breaking the steganographic utilities EzStego, Jsteg, Steganos, and S-Tools and some lessons learned. In *Proc. 3ʳᵈ International Workshop on Information Hiding*, Dresden, Germany, 61-76.

Wolf, B. (2007). StegoDos - Black Wolf's Picture Encoder v0.90B, Public Domain. ftp://ftp.csua. berkeley.edu/ pub/ cypherpunks/ steganography/ stegodos.zip.

Wu, Y., & Shih F. Y. (2004). An adjusted-purpose digital watermarking technique. Pattern Recognition, 37(12), 2349-2359.

Wu, Y., & Shih F. Y. (2006). Genetic algorithm based methodology for breaking the steganalytic systems. *IEEE Trans. SMC, Part B, 36*(1), 24-31.

KEY TERMS

Digital Steganography: The science to hide secret messages within digital media, such as digital images, audio files or video files.

EzStego: The tool simulates the invisible ink for Internet communication.

Genetic Algorithm: An adaptive approach that provides a randomized, parallel, and global search based on the mechanics of natural selection and genetics in order to find solutions of a problem.

Jsteg-Jpeg: The tool can read multiple format images and embed the secret messages to be saved as the JPEG format images.

Linguistic Steganography: The technique utilizes written natural language to hide information. It can be categorized into semagrams and open codes.

S-Tools or **Steganography Tools:** The tools to hide the secret messages in BMP, GIF, and WAV files.

Steganalysis: The process of detecting the hidden data which are crested using steganography.

Steganography: The art of hiding secret data inside other innocent media file.

StegoDos: The tools consists of a set of programs that allow us to capture an image, encode a secret message and display the stego-image.

Technical Steganography: The scientific methods to conceal a secret message, such as the use of invisible ink, microdots, and shaved heads.

Chapter XXIV
Adaptive Image Steganography Based on Structural Similarity Metric

Guangjie Liu
Nanjing University of Science and Technology, China

Shiguo Lian
France Telecom R&D (Orange Labs) Beijing, China

Yuewei Dai
Nanjing University of Science and Technology, China

Zhiquan Wang
Nanjing University of Science and Technology, China

ABSTRACT

Image steganography is a common form of information hiding which embeds as many message bits into images and keep the introduced distortion imperceptible. How to balance the trade-off between the capacity and imperceptibility has become a very important issue in the researches of steganography. In this chapter, we discuss one kind of the solution for disposing the trade-off, named adaptive image steganography. After a brief review, we present two methods based on structural similarity metric. The first one is based on the generalized LSB, in which the substitution depth vector is obtained via the dynamic programming under the constraint of an allowable distortion. The second method is proposed to use adaptive quantization-embedder to carry message bits. Different from the first method, the distortion index is constructed by contrast-correlation distortion. The other difference is that the parameters of the adaptive quantization embedder are embedded into the image containing message bits by the reversible data hiding method. Beside that, we also bring forward some attractive directions worthy of being studied in the future. Furthermore, we find that the existing methods do not have a good way to control the amount of information and the distortion as an extract manner, and most schemes are designed just according to the experiences and experiments.

INTRODUCTION

Steganography is the art of covered or hidden writing. The practice of steganography has quite a history. The earliest example can be dated to the Greek historian Herodotus, who describes how one of his cunning countrymen sent a secret message warning of an invasion by scrawling it on the wood underneath a wax table. To casual observers, the tablet appeared blank. Roman empires would hide secret message in ordinary message that only a certain formula when applied could reveal the real message. This was of course to prevent the real message from falling into the wrong hands. Both Axis and Allied spies during World War II used such measure as invisible inks as tiny punctures above key characters in a document that form a message when combined or 'invisible inks' that could only be read when heat was applied.

The earliest study concerning modern steganography was presented by G. J. Simmons (Simmons, 1983). In (Simmons, 1983), the famous story of Prisoners' problem explains what capabilities and merits steganography has to offer when public communication channel is insecure. The story is about two prisoners Alice and Bob who are put to different cells in a jail and what to plan to escape form the prison together as Fig.1 illustrates.

However, any communications between them have to pass though the warden Eve, so only plaintext (i.e. content that have clear meanings) can be handed on by Eve, while anything in the form of ciphertext(i.e. contents that seems meaningless) will not be allowed. Bob and Alice want to conspire to escape, but they can not send a clear message to each other showing the intention of escaping, and neither can they encrypt the secret message about their plan of escape into a cipher text in an attempt to hide their intention before the message comes to Eve. To solve this problem, Alice can use a picture (like illustrated in Fig.1) as the cover to conceal the very existence of the secret message from Eve.

It is worthy to be noticed that often dictionaries have defined steganography the same as cryptography, however there is a clear difference between the two. The purpose of steganography is covert communication to hide the existence of a message from a third party, which differs from cryptography, the art of secret writing, which is intended to make a message unreadable by a third party but does not hide the existence of the secret communication. The steganographic process generally involves placing a hidden message in some transport medium, called the carrier or the cover medium. The secret message is embedded in the cover medium to form the stego medium. The use

Figure 1. Prisoners' problem

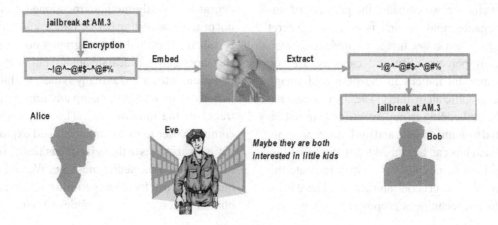

Figure 2. Steganographic process

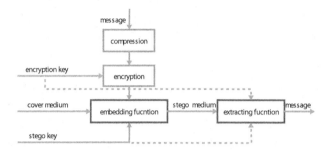

of a stego key may be employed for encryption of the hidden message or for randomization of the embedding locations in the steganographic scheme. The whole process to embedding message bits into images can be depicted by Fig.2.

Nowadays, digital steganography has been a specialized field to research the art and science of how to conceal a secret message in various kinds of media, such as image, audio, video and so on. Steganography essentially is a multidisciplinary field combining use of image and signal processing techniques with cryptography, communication theory, coding theory, signal compression theory of visual perception, etc(Fridrich, 1999).

CURRENT ARTS ON ADAPTIVE STEGANOGRAPHY IN IMAGES

In this chapter, we consider the problem of image steganography, which is to hide a secret message into a *cover* image to produce a *stego* image. Imperceptibility and capacity are the two important indices in the design of image steganographic algorithms. The former ensures that the embedding is imperceptible (can not be detected by human eyes), and the latter represents how much bits can be embedded in the cover image without being "*visible*", which indicate the efficiency of covert communication. There have been lots of techniques proposed to balance the trade-off between the two. Wang et al.(Wang, 2001) developed a technique to hide secret data by LSB substitution and a genetic algorithm (GA). The key idea of Wang is to use GA to find the optimal matching between the message bits and the cover image LSBs. Based on the same consideration like Wang, Chang et al. (Chang C. C. et al., 2003) using dynamic programming strategy to replace GA. In (Chan, 2004), Chan et al. proposed a simple LSB substitution with an optimal pixel adjustment process(OPAP). OPAP is to achieve good imperceptibility though adjust the modified pixel value to let them closer to the original value, while keep the receiver can extract the message bits correctly. These techniques mentioned above can all be concluded as LSB-like methods, which realized optimal data embedding in meanings of mean square error (MSE). But, it is known that MSE is not a good metric for measuring the image degradation, so the methods mentioned above can not provide satisfying performance, and can only be taken as optimal steganography not adaptive steganography. An ideal steganographic technique must be able to embed as many as message bits into images while without causing any imperceptible tracks of the modification. The steganography coming closer to this demand should exploit the natural variations in the pixel intensities of a cover image to hide the secret message. We call those methods to use local image information (or said human vision system) to achieve high capacity and less distortion as *adaptive steganography*. The principle of adaptive steganography can be illustrated by Fig.3. In Fig.3, the current pixel or region containing some pixels (such as an image block) waiting for being embedded data is firstly input the HVS analysis module along with the cover image I to determine how many bits can be embedded in it. Then the chosen bits are embedded into X to generate the stego pixel or region X'. The adaptation of steganography is just to denote choosing the message bits amount adaptively.

Till now, there have been lost of endeavors proposed for realize the adaptive steganography and improve the performance of capacity and imperceptibility. Wu(Wu, 2003) proposed a steganography method for images by pixel-value differencing(PVD), which divided the image into two-pixel block ,and embedded information into the difference value of each two pixel. Wu maybe is the first person to propose to use non-uniform quantization method to embed different amount bits in the cover signals. But the shortcoming of Wu's method is the amount of bits embedded in different PVD is determined just by authors' subject experience, which cause the performance can not achieve the optimal level. In(Wang, 2008), Ming et al. improved Wu's method by using modulation function to realize the optimal alteration. Comparing with Wu's method, Wang's method is to accomplish data hiding be modify the remainder of the sum of two pixel to make it

equal to the decimal value of message bits. As a general case of using some adjacent pixels to reflect the smoothness of image regions, Chang and Tseng(Chang, 2004) proposed a steganographic method using side match. In(Chang C. C. & Tseng H. W. , 2004), two, three and four pixels are used to determine how many bits can be embedded in the target pixel, respectively. In(Liu, 2006), we also gave an alike implement in neural network prediction errors. Different from Wu's, Wang's and Chang's method, the data hiding in neural network prediction errors can achieve better image quality performance. Another methods being valuable of mentioned is BPCS-based algorithm. In(Eason, 2003), the authors proposed to divide the image into regions and perform complexity measurement using a binary complexity measure on the individual bit planes to embed data in these regions. BPCS can embed message bits adaptively according to the binary complexity measure of local image region, which make it easy to be applied in other domains, (Spaulding, 2002)give an example of extending to EZW lossy compressed images.

In (Park, 2005) Park et al. proposed to use the different value between two pixels adjacent to the target pixel to decide the number of insertion bits. Based on the same idea, in(Park, 2005, pp. 962-967), Park et al. proposed to use the difference between the maximum and minimum value of the neighboring pixels of the target pixel. But, both (Park, 2005) and (Park, 2005, pp. 962-967) can

Figure 3. Principle of adaptive steganography

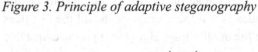
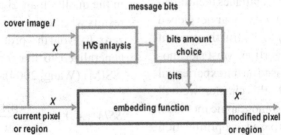

be taken as the special or little modified case of (Chang, 2004) or (Wang, 2008). Having a little difference, Zhang and Wang(Zhang, 2005) proposed to convert data into a series of symbols in a notation system with multiple bases, and the specific bases were obtained by the degree of local variations of the neighboring pixels in the stego image. In fact, Zhang's MBS method provided a smart method which can embed message bits with non 2-power length. Yang and Lin(Yang, 2006) proposed a base-oriented hiding algorithm(named BOA), which classified each block of the host image according to the based value, and make data embedding according to the base value, and make data embedding according to some predeterminative parameters. Comparing with Zhang's method, the difficulty of Yang's method is to have to make lots of checks in data hiding process to guarantee the base not changing after data hiding, but Yang's method maybe the best embedding algorithm so far under PSNR distortion meanings. In(Kang, 2007), Kang et al. firstly divided an image into blocks, and decomposed them into one-level wavelet, then decided how many bits can be embedded according to the number of wavelet coefficients of larger magnitude, at last embedded the secret information based on the modulus function. In(Santosh, 2006), the authors proposed to utilize the sensitivity of the HVS to adaptively modify the pixels in a high frequency components spatial(HFIS) image of the cover image. The modification of pixel depended on the magnitude of the pixel in HFSI and also the local features of the cover image. In (Dulce, 2007), the authors proposed to use the regions without homogeneous texture to carry message bits.

Reviewing the existing techniques mentioned above, we can find the methods so far developed do not seem to have a way to control the amount of information and the distortion. Most steganographic schemes are just based on the experiential or experimental designs. In this chapter, we will introduce two adaptive steganographic methods. Both of them are designed based on optimization

idea and have exact control of the capacity and distortion. Different from the existing methods, we use the structural-similarity metric derived from SSIM(Wang, 2004) to depict the distortion, and take the distortion index as restriction to optimally maximize the steganographic capacity.

STEGANGORAPHY BASED ON NON-UNIFORM GENERALIZED LSB AND DYNAMIC PROGRAMMING

Structural Similarity Metric

In(Wang, 2002), Wang et al. present a new numerical measure for gray scale images, called the universal image quality index, Q, which is defined as

$$Q = \frac{4\sigma_{xy}\,\mu_x\mu_y}{(\sigma_x^2 + \sigma_y^2)(\mu_x^2 + \mu_y^2)} \qquad (1)$$

where x_i, y_i, $i=1,\dots,n$ represent the original and distorted signals respectively, $\mu_x = \frac{1}{n}\Sigma_{i=1}^n x_i$, $\mu_y = \frac{1}{n}\Sigma_{i=1}^n y_i$, $\sigma_x^2 = \frac{1}{n-1}\Sigma_{i=1}^n (x_i - \mu_x)^2$, $\sigma_y^2 = \frac{1}{n-1}\Sigma_{i=1}^n (y_i - \mu_y)^2$, and $\sigma_{xy} = \frac{1}{n-1}\Sigma_{i=1}^n (x_i - \mu_x)(y_i - \mu_y)$. As described in(Wang., 2004), Q models any distortion as a combination of three factors: loss of correlation $\frac{\sigma_{xy}}{\sigma_x\sigma_y}$, mean distortion $\frac{2\mu_x\mu_y}{\mu_x^2+\mu_y^2}$ and variance distortion $\frac{2\sigma_x\sigma_y}{\sigma_x^2+\sigma_y^2}$. Q can be applied to a gray level image using a sliding window with size of 8×8, then the index is computed for each window, leading to a quality map of the image, the overall quality index is just the average of the all the Q values in the quality map. But Q will produce unstable results when either $\mu_x^2 + \mu_y^2$ or $\sigma_x^2 + \sigma_y^2$ is close to zero. To avoid this problem, the measure has been generalized to the Structural Similarity Index (SSIM) (Wang, 2004):

$$SSIM(X,Y) = \frac{(2\mu_x\mu_y + C_1)(2\sigma_{xy} + C_2)}{(\mu_x^2 + \mu_y^2 + C_1)(\sigma_x^2 + \sigma_y^2 + C_2)}$$

$$(2)$$

Here, the constants $C_1=(K_1R)^2$, $C_2=(K_2R)^2$ and R is the dynamic range of the pixel value (255 for 8-bit gray images), and $K_1 \ll 1, K_2 \ll 1$. The author also uses the circular-symmetric Gaussian weighting function with standard deviation of 1.5 to avoid the undesirable "blocking" artifacts. The dynamic range of SSIM is [-1,1], with the best value 1 achieved when $y_i = x_i, i = 1, 2, ..., n$. So we define the distortion based on SSIM metric as

$$D(X,Y) = \tfrac{1}{2}\big(1 - SSIM(X,Y)\big) \qquad (3)$$

In this chapter, different from the computation in (Wang, 2004) that the square block is moved pixel-by-pixel over the entire image, the computation based on non-overlapping 8×8 square blocks is used. It does not also speed and simplify the computation but facilitate the distortion estimation caused by data hiding.

Non-Uniformation Generalized LSB Substitution

A. Embedding Method

In the simple LSB substitution, the least significant bit of each signal sample is replaced by a payload data bit. If additional capacity is required, two or more LSBs may be over written on per sample, while during extraction, these bits are read in the same scanning order, which may be controlled under some key to enhance the security of the algorithm. If the host signal is represented by a vector x, the non-uniform generalized LSB embedding and extraction process can be represented as:

$$y = Q_L(x) + s$$
$$s = y - Q_L(y) = y - Q_L(x) \qquad (4)$$

Here, y represents the stegosignal containing the embedded information s, and

$$Q_L(x) = q_i \left\lfloor \frac{x_i}{q_i} \right\rfloor, i = 1,...,N, q_i = 2^{l_i} \qquad (5)$$

It is a non-uniform scalar quantization function, and $\lfloor \cdot \rfloor$ represents the operation of truncation to the integer part. The vector $L = \{l_i, i = 1,...,N\}$ is called the substitution depth vector (SDV). During hiding, the lowest l_i bits of signal samples are replaced by the data bits. During extraction, the message is read from the lowest l_i bits of the stego pixel. The traditional LSB modification can be considered as the special case when $L = \{l_i = 2, i = 1,...,N\}$.

But, it is unnecessary to use the different l_i for each pixel because the pixels in a local region may have approximately equal gray value and the same HVS characters, such as the texture, edges and so on. We can divide the image into some local blocks and use the same l_i for pixels in a block and the different l_i for the different block. So the SDV L can be written as

$$L = [\underbrace{k_1,...,k_1}_{m_1},...,\underbrace{k_i,...,k_i}_{m_i},...,\underbrace{k_M,...,k_M}_{m_M}], m_1 + ... + m_M = N$$

In the proposed scheme, the whole image is divided into amounts of square 8×8 non-overlapped blocks, which consistent with the computation of SSIM. It means m_i=64, i=1,…,N/64. For simplicity, L is written as $L = [k_1, k_2,...,k_M]$ to block-based non-uniform case.

B. Capacity

The embedding capacity can be denoted by the average payload of all image pixels. Considering the block-based non-uniform scheme, so the capacity can be written as

$$C(L) = \frac{1}{N}\sum_{i=1}^{N} l_i = \frac{1}{N}\sum_{i=1}^{M} 64k_i \qquad (6)$$

In the practical application, before the extraction of the message, the decoder should know the additional information about the SDV in advance. To realize the blind extraction, i.e. without the aid of the extra side information, L must be embedded into the image. Because the possible maximum substation depth is 7, we can use three bits of one block to carry the substitution depth k_i. The three bits can be chosen from 64 LSBs of block pixels controlled by some key to ensure the security of the whole system, and these bits to carry the SVD should be skipped during data hiding. Therefore, the available capacity is $\frac{1}{N}\Sigma_{i=1}^{M}(64k_i - 3)$.

C. Distortion

Suppose the cover image X is embedded by the binary message S using the SDV L, the structural similarity measurement of the cover image and stego image is $SSIM(X,L,S)$. According to Equation (3), the distortion is

$$D(X,L,S) = \tfrac{1}{2}\big(1 - SSIM(X,L,S)\big) \quad (7)$$

It is obvious that the distortion is the function of L and binary message S. But in the practical application, the message bits to be hidden are not determined beforehand. Therefore, the expected distortion of different S is used to evaluate quality loss because of data hiding, which is shown in Equation (8).

$$E_S(D(X,L,S)) = \tfrac{1}{2} - \tfrac{1}{2}E_S(SSIM(X,L,S)) \quad (8)$$

According to the description above, $D(X, L)$ can be computed block-by-block. Suppose, in a local block B, the corresponding substitution depth is k, $Q_k(B)$ is $\bar{B}$ and the embedded message is s, then

$$E_s(SSIM(B,B(k,s)) =$$
$$E\left[\frac{2\mu_B\mu_{\bar{B}+s} + C_1)(\sigma^2_{B(\bar{B}+s)} + C_2)}{(\mu^2_B + \mu_{\bar{B}+s} + C_1)(\sigma^2_B + \sigma^2_{\bar{B}+s} + C_2)}\right] \quad (9)$$

Because s is irrelevant to B and $\bar{B}$, so Equation (9) can be written as

$$E_s(SSIM(B,B(k,s)) =$$
$$E\left[\frac{(2\mu_B\mu_{\bar{B}} + 2\mu_B\mu_s + C_1)(2\sigma_{B\bar{B}} + C_2)}{(\mu^2_B + (\mu_{\bar{B}} + \mu_s)^2 + C_1)(\sigma^2_{\bar{B}} + \sigma^2_{\bar{B}} + \sigma^2_s + C_2)}\right] \quad (10)$$

It is appropriate to suppose the embedded binary bit obeys uniform distribution on $\{0,1\}$, because the message is usually compressed and encrypted before being embedded. When using the binary message substitute the k least significant bits of the local block pixels, the means $\mu_s = (2^k - 1)/2$ and $\sigma_s = \sqrt{(2^k - 1)^2/12}$. Therefore, Equation (10) is finally equal to

$$E_s(SSIM(B,B(k,s)) =$$
$$\frac{(2\mu_B\mu_{\bar{B}} + 2\mu_B(2^k - 1) + C_1)(2\sigma_{B\bar{B}} + C_2)}{(\mu^2_B + (\mu_{\bar{B}} + (2^k - 1)/2)^2 + C_1)(\sigma^2_B + \sigma^2_{\bar{B}} + (2^{k_i} - 1)^2/12 + C_2)} \quad (11)$$

Optimal Steganography Based on the Dynamic Programming

According to Equation (11), the distortion is the function of the SDV. Suppose $D(X,L) \le \varepsilon, \varepsilon$ must be very small value to keep the visual quality of image not being destroyed by the data hiding. To get the maximum embedding capacity under the given maximum allowable distortion is equal to resolve the following optimization problem

$$\max_L C(L) = \frac{1}{N}\sum_{i=1}^{N}l_i = \frac{1}{N}\sum_{i=1}^{M}(64k_i - 3)$$
$$s.t.\ D(X,L) = 1 - E(SSIM(X,L,S)) \le \varepsilon \quad (12)$$

To resolve the optimization problem (12), we firstly use the penalty function to convert the constrained optimization problem to unconstrained one. After addition of the penalty function to the optimization object, the problem (12) changes to

$$\max_L f(X,L) = C(L) + P \cdot \max[0, D(X,L) - \varepsilon]$$

$$(13)$$

Here, P is a large negative value. Let P is equal to -10000 to make the penalty when the distortion caused by embedding using L exceeds the allowable ε. The problem (13) can be resolved by dynamic programming.

At the beginning, the optimization process is partitioned into successive stages. In each stage, the decision is to choose the optimum k_i of L to increase one, and the state of each stage is the corresponding L. The process to find the optimum L can be described as follows.

Step 1. Input the cover image X and initiate the substitution depth vector $L^0 = [0,...,0]^M$, the dimension M of L is determined by the image size and the size of square block. For a m×n gray image and the 8×8 square block, the dimension $M = mn/64$.

Step 2. For the ith stage, Let $L' = L^i + [1,...,1]^M$, according to equation (8), compute the local distortion change,

$$dD_j = D_j(X,L') - D_j(X,L^i), j = 1,...,M$$

$$(14)$$

Then, choose the optimum position j^* according to the below equation

$$j^* = \min_j \frac{\left| dD_j(X,L',L^i) \right|}{D_j(X,L^i)^a}, j = 1,...,M \quad (15)$$

It means to find the least distortion change block to increase the substitution depth, i.e. the capacity. The dominator of the above equation is to avoid excessive destroys in one local block. In

the paper, we choose α equal to 2. Then L'' can be obtained by $L'' = [k_1^i,...,k_{j^*}^i + 1,...,k_N^i]$

Step 3. Compute the values $f(X,L'')$ and $f(X,L^i)$. If $f(X,L'') > f(X,L^i)$, let L^{i+1} be L'' and go to STEP 2, else stop the finding and output the optimal SDV L.

According to the above description of the details of the adaptive steganography, we can give the whole flow of the propose scheme as Fig.4 shows. In Fig.4, the cover image is firstly input the module of finding optimal SDV by DP to generate the optimal SDV L^*, then L^* is input to the module of simple LSB and non-uniform generalized LSB respectively. Through simple LSB, the information of L^* is embedded into part pixels U chosen by sub-key K_1 from the image I. Through the non-uniform generalized LSB, the encrypted message bits are embedded into V. The ultimate stego image is combined by U' and V'. To extract the message bits, the receiver needs to extract the SVD beforehand and use it to decode the encrypted message bits, at last decrypted those bits to get the original message.

STEGANOGRAPHY BASED ON ADAPTIVE QUANTIZATION EMBEDDER AND REVERSIBLE DATA HIDING

In this section, we will propose the other new steganographic method via adaptive quantization embedder(AQE). There are three different points comparing with the method proposed in the above section, Firstly, the AQE method can embedded bits with any system integers; Secondly, the parameter of the AQE is embedded into the cover image by reversible data hiding method, which does not occupy the steganographic space, while will introduce additional distortion. Thirdly, the distortion index is modified to contrast-correlation distortion (CCD), the mean distortion component is discarded. Now let's describe the details of the method.

Figure 4. The DP-based steganography scheme

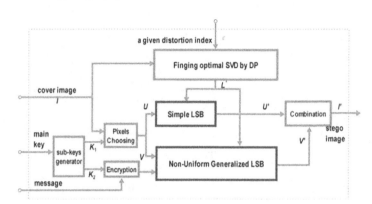

Adaptive Quantization Embedder

Suppose the cover image X to be composed of pixel such as $x_1, x_2, ..., x_L$, we can write the quantization embedder(QE) with integer step being q as:

$$\Phi(x,q) = x - \mathrm{mod}(x,q)$$
$$x' = \Phi(x,q) + m;$$
$$\Omega = \{x', x'+q, x'-q\}$$
$$y = \arg\min_{z \in \Omega}(|z - x|) \qquad (16)$$

Here x belongs to $\{x_1, x_2, ..., x_L\}$, $\Phi(x,q)$ is the quantization function, $\mathrm{mod}(x,q)$ denotes to calculate the residue of x divided by q, and m represents the integer between $[0, q-1]$ which may be converted form the message bits. The latter two equations is used to find the optimal value which has the residue after dividing q is equal to m. We can rewrite the whole process as $y = \Upsilon(x,q,m)$.

When the quantization step q is fixed and independent on different pixels, we call the quantization embedder as fixed one. While, if q changes with the corresponding pixel, the quantization embedder are called adaptive one. In pixel-wised adaptive quantization embedders, the step q_i for each pixel is different, which means that the most

meticulous parameters choosing manner. But in most case, it is unnecessary to chose different q for different pixel. The more practical and efficient fashion is to choose one quantization step for a set of neighboring pixels, i.e. one block, because the pixels in one block may have the same HVS characteristics. Comparing with the pixel-wise AQE such as(Zhang, 2005), block-wise one does not only hold less computation complexity, but also has the advantage to dispose quantization parameters, because the quantization step vector Q has less dimension that that of pixel-wised one. In this chapter, we concentrate our attention on the block-wise AQE. Suppose that the cover image pixels are divided into blocks $b_1, b_2, ..., b_i, ..., b_N$, which have the same size $n \times n$, the quantization step vector Q is defined as $\mathrm{m}[q_1, q_2, ..., q_N]$. The steganographic process can be described as:

$$Y = \Upsilon(X, Q, M) \qquad (17)$$

Here, $M = [\mu_1, \mu_2, ... \mu_N], \mu_i = [m_{i1}, m_{i2}, ..., m_{in^2}]$ and m_{ij} is the integer falling in $[0, q_i - 1]$. The data extracting process can be described as:

$$M = Y - \Phi(Y, Q) \qquad (18)$$

The embedded message can be converted form the extracted M according to the step vector Q.

If we define the capacity of steganography as the ratio between the bit numbers of embedded message and the host image, then the capacity can be depicted as Equation (19).

$$C = \sum_{i=1}^{N} \left\lfloor \log_2(q_i) \cdot n^2 \right\rfloor \tag{19}$$

where, $\lfloor \cdot \rfloor$ is the function to get the largest integer that is less than ' $\cdot$ '. In data embedding process, for block b_i, if the embedder known the quantization step q_i, he can read $\left\lfloor \log_2(q_i) \cdot n^2 \right\rfloor$ from the message bit sequence, and convert them into n^2 integers between $[0, q_i - 1]$ from binary system to q_i-system. The data extracting is the adverse manipulation.

Obviously, the capacity is the function of Q, so the capacity can be written as $C(Q)$. And the larger the components of Q are, the higher the achievable capacity is. While increase the larger quantization q_i will also cause the corresponding distortion enlarged. So we need choose Q through a optimal manner to guarantee higher capacity and lower distortion.

Contrast-Correlation Distortion

Considering the distortion measurement between the cover image block and stego block after AQE steganography, when the embedded message bits are encrypted or compressed before hiding, the binary message bits obey uniform distortion on $\{0,1\}$. For an arbitrary block b, suppose the used quantization step to be q, the converted integer m must obey the uniform distribution on $\{0,1,...,q-1\}$. Reviewing Equation (16), it is also true that the residues m obey uniform distribution on $\{0,1,...,q-1\}$ for natural images when q is not too large. Based on the above analysis, the luminance comparison of the AQE is not important, and only the contrast and cor-

relation comparison are taken into consideration in this section.

Between the contrast and correlation comparison, the former give the whole measurement of noise introduce by data embedding, and the latter summarized the correlation distortion on each pixel. For evaluate the distortion of data embedding subtly, we prefer to emphasize the correlation comparison and combine the two by the below equation.

$$\varphi(x,y) = \left(1 - \frac{2\sigma_x \sigma_y + C}{\sigma_x^2 + \sigma_y^2 + C} \right) \cdot \left(\frac{1 + \frac{\sigma_{xy} + C}{\sigma_{xy} + C}}{2} \right)^2 \tag{20}$$

Where, x, y denotes the cover and stego image block, and C is the constants equal to $(KR)^2$ with R the dynamic range of the pixel value (255 for 8-bit gray images) and $K \ll 1$. The first term of Equation (20) is contrast distortion, while falls into the range [0,1] with 0 stands for no distortion and 1 standing for largest distortion. Because $\frac{\sigma_{xy}}{\sigma_x \sigma_y}$ belongs to the set $[-1,1]$, so the transform from correlation comparison to distortion is different from correlation comparison to distortion is different from the contrast one, and we assign 2 for the exponent of correlation distortion to emphasize its significance. We name the combined distortion defined by Equation (20) as contrast-correlation distortion (CCD), which always falls in the range [0,1]. The smaller the value of CCD is, the less distortion introduced by data embedding is.

AQE Parameters Embedding Based on Reversible Data Hiding Method

For extracting the embedded message, Q must be known by the extractor beforehand, which is greatly different from the conditional method with fixed quantization steps. So it becomes a key point to transmit the information of Q from the embedder to the extractor.

There might be two kinds of method competent for the mission. In the first one, the adaptive quantization step are constructed according to the stego image itself like (Zhang, 2005) and (Yang, 2006). The second method is to directly embed the parameters into the image with the message bits, and extract these parameters at receiver side before the message extracting. The method of the above section is just to use part of the cover image pixels to carry the SDV information. The other choice is to embed parameter to images by reversible data hiding manner after the true message hiding. Of course, the former will cause the efficient capacity decreased, the latter will introduce the supererogatory distortion. But if the size of blocks is chosen appropriately, and some efficient compression algorithm aiming at parameters of AQE is employed, the payload of parameters will be economized markedly. So the capacity or distortion influence introduce by parameters embedding will be controlled to acceptable extent. In this section, we adopt the reversible data hiding (Tian J., 2003) to embed the parameters of the AQE.

Assuming that the size of block is equal to $n \times n$, the size of cover is equal to $W \times H$, and the maximum value of quantization step does not exceed q_{max}, we can obtain the length of the parameters Π is nearly equal to $\left\lfloor \frac{W}{n} \right\rfloor \cdot \left\lfloor \frac{H}{n} \right\rfloor \cdot \left\lceil \log_2(q_{max}) \right\rceil$. Our experiments show that through the compression algorithm ZLIB, provided by Java.Util.Zip. DeflaterOutputStream, this data length can be reduced to about 40%. i.e. the actual length is about $40\% \left\lfloor \frac{W}{n} \right\rfloor \cdot \left\lfloor \frac{H}{n} \right\rfloor \cdot \left\lceil \log_2(q_{max}) \right\rceil$. For example, if the block size if equal to 5×5, the image size is equal to 512×512, the max allowed quantization step is equal to 32, the length of Π is about 20808. So we need a high capacity reversible data hiding method which can provide at least 0.079bpp (bits per pixel). For a general case, if we suppose the compression ratio is ρ, the demand capacity χ provided by the reversible data hiding algorithm can be expressed as

$$\chi \approx (1 - \rho) \frac{\log_2(q_{max})}{n^2} \tag{21}$$

Fortunately, Tian presented a promising high capacity reversible data embedding method in (J. Tian, 2003). In the algorithm, two techniques are employed, i.e. difference expansion and generalized least significant bit embedding, to achieve a very high embedding capacity, while keep the distortion low. The main idea of this technique is described.

For a pair of pixel value x and y, the algorithm first computes the integer average l and difference h of x and y, where $h = x - y$. The h is modified to $h' = 2 \times h + b$, where h' denotes the expanded difference which explains the term of Difference Expansion. Finally, the new x and y, denoted by x' and y', respectively, are calculated based on the new difference value h' and the original integer average value l. In this way, the stego image is obtained. To avoid over/underflow, the algorithm only embeds data into the pixel pairs that shall not lead to over/underflow. Therefore, a two-dimensional location map is compressed by JBIG2 and embedded as overhead.

In difference expansion method, Tian create four disjoint sets of difference values, EZ, EN, CN and NC:

- EZ: contains all expandable $h = 0$ and expandable $h = -1$.
- EN: contains all expandable $h \notin EZ$.
- CN: contains all changeable $h \notin EZ \cup EN$.
- NC: contains all nonchangeable h.

And, the set EN are partitioned by a threshold T according to:

$$\begin{aligned} EN1 &= \{h \in EN : |h| \le T\} \\ EN2 &= \{h \in EN : |h| > T\} \end{aligned} \tag{22}$$

Assuming the total number of '1' and '-2' in $EN2 \cup CN$ is Z_1, then the capacity of Tian's method is about:

$$C_{DE} = \frac{|EZ| + |EN| + Z_1 - Z_2}{WH} \tag{23}$$

Here, $|\cdot|$ is the cardinality of a set, Z_2 is the length of compressed binary location map. According to Equation (21), we can control the threshold T to satisfy the below equation.

$$(1-\rho)\frac{\log_2(q_{max})}{n^2} \le \frac{|EZ|+|EN1|+Z_1-Z_2}{WH} \quad (24)$$

Steganography Based on AQE

A. Embedding method

Initialization: Read a finite binary message bit sequence M, divide the $W \times H$ cover image into $V(V=\frac{WH}{n^2})$ non-overlapping blocks $\{b_1, b_2, ..., b_V\}$, each with size $n \times n$ m set the allowed distortion index be ε, let $k = 0, Q = []$, set the block reading order using the stego-key K.

Message Embedding: Deal with block according to the assigned order. For the current block b_i, allocate the quantization step candidate range Ξ according to the below equation. $\langle A, B \rangle$ denotes all integers falling in the range $[A, B]$.

$$\Xi = \langle \min(\alpha\,\sigma_{b_i}, 30)+2, \max(\beta\sigma_{b_i}, 2)\rangle \quad (25)$$

Here, σ_{b_i} is the standard deviation of block b_i, α and β are two parameters to tuning the size of candidate range, we choose $\alpha=1.5$ and $\beta=0.2$ in the proposed algorithm. Obtain the optimal quantization step q^* via the below steps.

Step 1. Let $q = \min(\Xi)$

Step 2. Compute the below two equations:

$$\mu = \Psi(M(\kappa, \kappa + \lfloor n^2 \log_2(q) \rfloor), q) \quad (26)$$

$$b_i' = \Upsilon(b_i, q, \mu) \quad (27)$$

$$J = \varphi(b_i', b_i) \quad (28)$$

Step 3. if $J \le \varepsilon$, then let $q_{temp} = q+1$. If $q_{temp} > \max(\Xi)$, then $q^* = q$, goto **Step 5**, else

let $q = q_{temp}$, goto **Step 2**.

Step 4. If $q = \min(\Xi)$, $q^* = q$, else $q^* = q-1$ goto **Step 5**.

Step 5. Output q^*.

Embed message bits in block b_i by the AQE with quantization step equal to q^*, update κ by $\kappa \leftarrow \kappa + \lfloor n^2 \log_2(q^*) \rfloor$, then add q^* to the end of vector Q, move to the next block, and repeat the same embedding process until all blocks are occupied or message bits are embedded completely. In the chapter, we always think about full-embedding, i.e. all pixels are used to carry message bits.

Parameter Embedding: Before embedding parameters, we first use DPCM to encode Q and make further compression by ZLIB(java. util.zip.DeflaterOutputStream) to get the ultimate compressed parameters G with size equal to U bits. According to U and Equation (24) to choose proper threshold and make reversible data hiding based on difference expanding.

B. Extracting Method

The decoding part is much simpler than the encoding part. The extractor just need extract AQE parameters G, and perform corresponding decoding to get the true quantization step vector Q. Once Q is obtained, the decoding of message bits is very simple according to Equation (18). Through being converted from q_i-system to binary system, all message bits can be resumed immediately.

According to the above description, the scheme of AQE-based steganography can be described as Fig.5. In Fig.5, the cover image is firstly input the module of block picking to get the current block b_i for data hiding, then the optimal q^* is compute. q^* is input to message bits conversion module to generate the data to be embedding. AQE module is used to complete the data hiding in block b_i.

Figure 5. The AQE-based steganography scheme

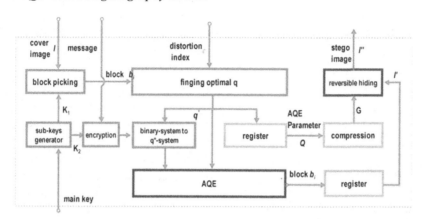

After all block being embedded. The registered Q is compressed and embedded into I' by reversible hiding algorithm to form the stego image I''.

EXPERIMENTS

In our experiments, four standard test images 'Lena', 'Baboon', 'Peppers' and 'Boat' are used, each with size 512×512. The first experiment is performed to evaluate the performance of the first method, for speaking simply, we call it Method A; the second one is alike to the first to evaluate the performance of the second method, we call it Method B. In the two experiments, the message bits for hiding are generated by a pseudo-random number generator based on a pre-chosen seed. In all steganographic experiments, the full-embedding strategy is adopted in order to evaluate the possible largest capacity and distortion. The capacity index is redefined as the number of bits per bit of the cover image, as listed in Table 1 and Table 2. For evaluating the distortion level under full-embedding, three HVS-based quality metrics are used to measure the distortion induced by data embedding: wPNSR, the Watson metric, and mssim. The wPNSR and Watson metric are all designed in (Voloshynovshiy, 2001) by using

characteristics of HVS and measure the total perceptual error, mssim is defined in (Wang, 2004).

Experimental Results of Method A

This first experiment is performed with the maximum allowable distortion equal to 0.02. Two of the four stego images and the corresponding SDV map are shown in Fig. 6 and Fig.7 (In Fig.6(b) and Fig.7(b), the SDV map is enhanced 50 times for showing). From Fig.6 and Fig.7, we can see that the larger substitution depth is assigned on the edged and textured regions of the cover image through the process of dynamic programming.

Let $\varepsilon = 0.01$ and 0.03 respectively, the second experiment is done to generate the results as Table 1 shows. It is indicated in Table 1 that the images with ore edges and textures can carry more information that the flat one.

The third experiment is used to evaluate the relationship between the allowable distortion and the achieve capacity, which is performed with e changing from 0.001 to 0.03. Fig. 8 reflects that with the increase of the allowable distortion, the capacity increases correspondingly, while the increase speed becomes low.

Figure 6. Method A results of Lena under ε = 0.02

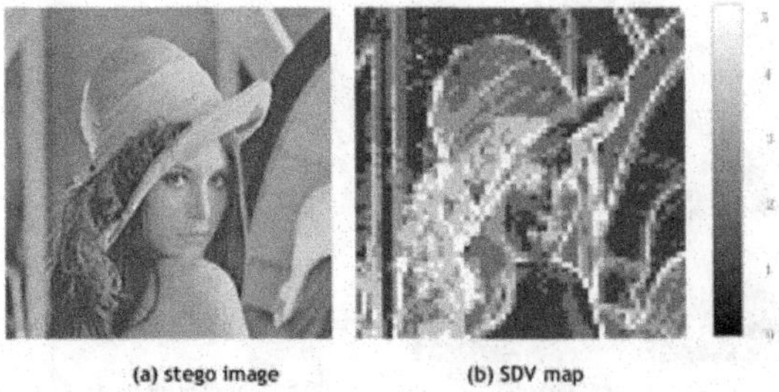

Figure 7. Method A results of Baboon under ε = 0.02

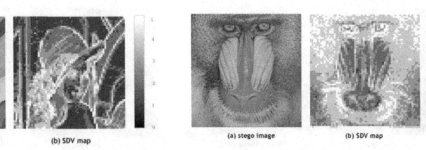

Table 1. Experimental results of four standard test images

Cover image	Capacity		wPSNR(dB)		Waston Metrics		SSIM	
	ε = 0.01	ε = 0.03	ε = 0.01	ε = 0.03	ε = 0.01	ε = 0.03	ε = 0.01	ε = 0.03
Lena	0.2532	0.3396	41.5	36.4	0.0421	0.0752	0.9756	0.9310
Baboon	0.3916	0.4888	41.8	36.7	0.0774	0.1380	0.9748	0.9268
Peppers	0.2871	0.3792	39.2	34.4	0.0528	0.0909	0.9650	0.9144
Boat	0.3242	0.4199	39.8	35.1	0.0597	0.1054	0.9687	0.9153

Figure 8. The relationship between the allowable distortion and the achieved capacity

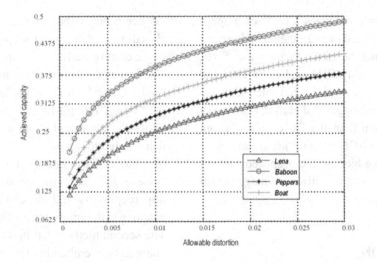

Experimental Results of Method B

Using 512×512 8-bit gray image 'Lena' as the cover image and choosing $ε = 0.02$, $n = 5$, a total of 5.57×10^5 secret bits are embedded, so the capacity is equal to 0.25. The stego images are shown in Fig.9 (a). Also shown is the error image, which has been enhanced by a 35-time gray-level stretch for the purpose of display. The similar experimental results are shown in Fig.10 for the cover image baboon. We can see that the modification were mainly in busy areas and on edges, which means less perceptual distortion is achieved.

Figure 9. Method B results of Lena under ε = 0.02

Figure 10. Method B results of Baboon under ε = 0.02

(a) stego image   (b) Enhanced error image

(a) stego image   (b) Enhanced error image

Table 2. Experimental results of four standard test images

Cover image	Capacity		w PSNR(dB)		Waston Metrics		SSIM	
	ε = 0 01	ε = 0 03	ε = 0 01	ε = 0 03	ε = 0 01	ε = 0 03	ε = 0 01	ε = 0 03
Lena	0.198	0.302	44.3	40.1	0.0490	0.0677	0.9713	0.9511
Baboon	0.313	0.427	43.7	40.6	0.0612	0.0936	0.9704	0.9545
Peppers	0.199	0.311	43.5	39.8	0.0530	0.0751	0.9685	0.9518
Boat	0.239	0.344	43.6	39.1	0.0507	0.0820	0.9719	0.9513

Four standard test images, lena, baboon, peppers and boat are used to make the second experiment. Table 2 lists the value of capcity, wPSNR, Waston metrics and SSIM under ε = 0.01 and ε = 0.03. It can be seen from Table.1 that the images with more edges and textures can carry more information than the flat one, and given the larger ε, the AQE can provides more space to carry message bits. So the proposed method can be adaptive with the different image region and different image.

CONCLUSION

In this chapter, we discussed the mechanism of adaptive image steganography used to balance the trade-off between imperceptibility and capacity. Through a brief review, we find the existing adaptive mage steganographic methods have not a good way to control the amount of information and the distortion as an extract manner, and most schemes are designed to choose the parameters just according to the experiences or experiments. Based on the observation, we present two methods that are both based on structural similarity metric. The first method is based on the generalized LSB method, in which the substitution depth vector is obtained though the dynamic programming under the constraint of an allowable distortion defined based on structural similarity metric of a block. Experiments show the method can achieve good combination of the capacity and imperceptibility and the embedding process is adaptive to the smoothness of blocks and images. The second method is proposed to use adaptive quantization embedder to carry out message bits embedding. Different from the first method, we modify the structural similarity metric to construct a contrast-correlation distortion index, and the quantizer parameters are embedded into the image containing secret bits by the reversible data hiding method. Through the corresponding experiments, we can see the second method have better performance than the first one. We also make some experiments for comparing with the current better methods, the detailed experimental data are not list in the chapter, but the conclusion is that comparing with Zhang's MBS method and Yang's BOA method mentioned above, at the same distortion level (PSNR), the capacity of our method(the second one) is less than MBS about 25%, less than BOA about 40%, while when taking mssim as the distortion metric, MBS is a little better than BOA, our method are still on patch on the other two. It is because that our method must deal with the parameters by embedding them into image along with message bits or after message bits embedding via reversible fashion. These techniques to dispose the parameters may cause the loss of capacity or introduce additional distortion. The other reason may be that the structural-similarity-based distortion metric is not very fit to measure the loss of image quality caused by data hiding. So in the future work, we will find a better way to dispose the parameters of the embedder, of course, it is better to make these parameters can be obtained directly from the stego image through the HVS analysis not through extracting. The other direction is to find the simpler and more fitful distortion metric for image pixel or block.

FUTURE TRENDS

The works to balance the trade-off between imperceptibility and capacity will be a not-ending story to attract more researchers to contribute their brightness. It is because, from the viewpoint of steganography benchmarking, there still has not been a better distortion metric, and it should be noticed that the current distortion metric such as PSNR, wPSNR, Waston matric and mssim are all designed for image compression, restoration and so on, but not for data hiding or steganography. To resolve the problem to describe the distortion has become the bottleneck of the development of steganography. One feasible idea to considering

the particularity of different data hiding fashions adequately.

The other problem is that the current developed methods are mostly based on gray images and for spatial domain. The emergence of the situation is partly because it is easy to make HVS analysis from spatial domain data and it is easy to depict the distortion of gray images. While, we must be clear that most of images around us are all colored and stored as JPEG format. How to design adaptive stegangoraphy for colored JPEG image is more applied subject, which must come down to the question that how to depict the distortion from JPEG coefficients with three color channels, and how to make more powerful modification on those coefficients to avoid introduce distortion.

Another direction that can be make efforts is to replace the kernel of the embedders which based on the quantization or modulation function by the more powerful kernel. While, does more efficient embedding method exist? The answer is positive. There have been lots of papers(Fridrich, 2007; Fridrich, 2006; Galand, 2003; Zhang, 2006) reported having high embedding efficiency that means to embed more bits with less modification of cover signals. If using this kind of stego coding as the kernel of adaptive steganography, i.e. choosing the coding modes according to the HVS analysis, one can expect to get more efficient steganographic schemes.

REFERENCES

Chan, C. K., & Cheng, L. M. (2004). Hiding data in images by simple LSB substitution. *Pattern Recognition, 37*(3), 469-474.

Chang, C. C., Hsiao, J. Y., & Chan, C. S. (2003). Finding optiaml least-significant-bit substitution in image hiding by dynamic programming strategy. *Pattern Recognition, 36*(7), 1583-1595

Chang, C. C., & Tseng, H. W. . (2004). A steganographic method for digital images using side match. *Pattern Recognition, 25*(12), 1431-1437.

Dulce, R. H.-M., Raul, R.-C., & Claudia, F.-U. (2007). *Adaptive steganography based on textures*. Paper presented at the Proceedings of the 17th International Conference on Electronics, Communications and Computers, Washington, DC, USA.

Eason, R. (2003). A tutorial on BPCS steganography and its applications. *Proceedings of IEEE Pacific-Rim Workshop on Digital Steganography*, 18-31

Fridrich, J. (1999). Applications of data hiding in digital images. *Proceeding of ISSPA'99*, 22-25.

Fridrich, J., & Lisoněk, P. (2007). Grid Coloring in Steganography. *IEEE Transactions on Information Theory, 53*(4), 1547-1549.

Fridrich, J., & Soukal, D. (2006). Matrix embedding for large payloads. *IEEE Transactions on Information Security and Forensics, 1*(3), 390-394.

Galand, F., & Kabatiansky, G. (2003). Information hiding by coverings. *Proceedings of 2003 IEEE Information Theory Workshop*, 151-514.

Kang, Z. W., Liu, J., & Yi, Y. G. (2007). Steganography based on wavelet transform and modulus function. *Journal of Systems Engineering and Electronics, 18*(3), 628-632.

Liu, G. J., Wang, J. W., Lian, S. G., Dai, Y. W., & Wang, Z. Q. (2006). Data hiding in neural network predictioni errors. *Lecture Notes in Computer Scence: ISNN2006, 3973*, 273-278.

Park, Y.-R., Kang, H.-H., Shin, S.-U., & Kwon, K.-R. (2005). An image steganography using pixel characteristics. *Lecture Notes in Artificial Intelligence: CIS2005*, 581-588.

Park, Y.-R., Kang, H.-H., Shin, S.-U., & Kwon, K.-R. (2005). A steganographic scheme in digital images using information of neighboring pixels. *Lecture Notes in Computer Scence: ICNC2005, 3612*, 962-967.

Santosh, A. N., & Atul, N. (2006). A filtering based approach to adaptive steganography. *Proceedings of 2006 IEEE Region 10 Conference*, 1-4.

Simmons, G. J. (1983). The prisoner's problem and the subliminal channel. *Proceedings of Crypto'83*, 51-67.

Spaulding, J., Noda, H., Shirazi, M. N., & Kawaguchi, E. (2002). BPCS steganography using EZW lossy compressed images. *Pattern Recognition Letters, 23*(13), 1579-1587.

Tian, J. (2003). Reversible data embedding using a difference expansion. *IEEE Transaction on Circuits and Systems for Video Technology, 13*(8), 890-896.

Voloshynovshiy, S., Pereira, S., Iquise, V., & Pun, T. (2001). Attacking modelling: towards a second generation watermarking benckmark. *Signal Processing, 81*(6), 1177-1214.

Wang, C.-M., Wu, N.-I., Tsai, C.-S., & Hwang, M.-S. (2008). A high quality steganographic method with pixel-value differencing and modulus function. *Journal of Systems and Software, 81*(1), 150-158.

Wang, R. Z., Lin, C. F., & Lin, J. C. (2001). Image hiding by optimal LSB substitution and genetic algorithm. *Pattern Recognition, 34*(3), 671-683.

Wang, Z., & Bovik, A. C. (2002). A universal image quanlity index. *IEEE Signal Processing Letters, 9*(3), 81-84.

Wang, Z., Bovik, A. C., Sheikh, H. R., & Simoncelli, E. P. (2004). Image quality assessment: From error visibility to structural similarity. *IEEE Transaction on Image Processing, 13*(4), 600-612.

Wu, D. C., & Tsai, W. H. (2003). A steganographic method for images by pixel-value differencing. *Pattern Recognition Letters, 24*(9-10), 1613-1626.

Yang, C. Y., & Lin, J. C. (2006). Image hiding by base-oriented algorithm. *Optical Engeering, 45*(11), 117001_117001-117001_117010.

Zhang, X. P., & Wang, S. Z. (2005). Steganography using multiple-base notational system and human vision sensitivity. *IEEE Signal Processing Letters, 12*(1), 67-70.

Zhang, X. P., & Wang, S. Z. (2006). Efficient Steganographic Embedding by Exploiting Modification Direction. *IEEE Communication Letters, 10*(11), 781-783.

KEY TERMS

Adaptive Steganography: In the chapter, the adaptive steganography is defined as the mechanism to choose the amount of the bits for hiding according to the HVS characteristics of the target pixel of a group of pixels.

AQE (Adaptive Quantization Embedder): The AQE is the embedding function that can be used to make adaptive steganography. With the changes of the sizes of the quantizers of AQE, the amount of message bits that can be embedded changes.

Capactity: The capacity denotes the amount of the message bits that can be embedded into the cover object under the given constraints such as imperceptibility, security and robustness etc.

Contrast-Correlation Distortion: The constrast-correlation distortion is defined as the combination of the constrast distortion and correlation distortion, which are both borrowed from the structural similarity metrics.

Imperceptibility: The imperceptibility is defined as the perceptual quality distortion between the cover media and the stego one. For image, the PSNR, wPSNR, Waston Metric and SSIM are usually used to depict the distortion cause by the steganography.

SDV (Substitution Depth Vector): The SDV is defined in the part of generalized-LSB-based adaptive steganography in the chapter, which denotes the substitution depths assigned for all image blocks. Under the given allowance distortion, SDV can be calculated according to the proposed algorithm in the chapter.

Steganography: The technique to hide the secret message into the cover object to realized the covert communication without being found by the third part, which can conceal the existence of the communication itself.

Structural Similarity Metric: The structural similarity metric is the image quality index proposed by Wang and Bovik at about 2000, which models any distortion as a combination of the loss of correlation, mean distortion and variance distortion. The Q index and SSIM are two realization of the structural similarity metric.

Chapter XXV
A Survey on
Video Watermarking

Shiguo Lian
France Telecom R&D (Orange Labs) Beijing, China

ABSTRACT

Video watermarking technique embeds some information into videos by modifying video content slightly. The embedded information, named watermark, may be ownership information, customer information, integrity information, redundancy information, and so forth. Thus, this technique can be used for copyright protection, piracy tracing, content authentication, advertisement surveillance, error resilience, and so forth. In this chapter, we give an overview on video watermarking technology, including its architecture, performance requirement, typical algorithms, hot topics, and open issues.

INTRODUCTION

Watermarking is a technology with the aim of embedding information into carrier (image, video, audio, text, program, web, database, etc.), and related early work can be traced back as far as 1954. The last 10 years has seen considerable interest in digital video watermarking, due in large part to ever growing of digital video content everywhere and concerns on spreading of pirate programs.

A general video watermarking system, shown in Fig. 1, is composed of three parts: watermarking embedding, attack channel and watermark detection. According to the structure, the message (watermarking) is embedded into the original signal under the control of the embedding key, which produces the watermarked signal. In transmission channel, the watermarked signal may be attacked or distorted. The attacks include cutting, rotation, scaling or translation, and so on. The distortion includes such signal processing operations as compression, filtering, adding noise, A/D, D/A,

Figure 1. General watermarking system

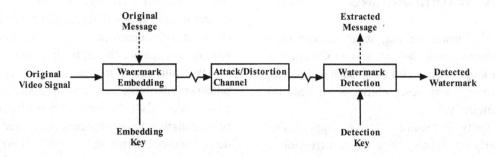

etc. Then, the test signal, including the attacked or distorted signal or an arbitrary signal, is detected under the control of detection key, which tells the detected watermark or the existence of the watermark.

Since it is still a technology in development, summarizing all its aspects is quite hard. In this chapter, we try to give an overview on video watermarking, briefly summarize its development, present its potential applications, give some performances requirements, present its research progress, and give the hot topics and open issues in research.

The rest of the chapter is arranged as follows. First, the brief history will be introduced in Section 2. The requirements and applications will be described in Section 3 and Section 4 respectively. In Section 5, the research achievements, including patent and paper publications, will be summarized. The typical attacks to video watermarking are given in Section 6. In Section 7, the ongoing work is presented. Hot topics and open issues are given in Section 8. Finally, some conclusions are drawn in Section 9.

BRIEF HISTORY OF VIDEO WATERMARKING

The earliest watermarking related activity is regarded as happening thousands of years ago.

Around 480 B.C., Histiaeus sent secret message to Greek city through an ingenious method (Moulin & Koetter, 2005): shave the head of a slave, tattoo the message on his skull, allow the hair to grow back, and finally dispatch the slave. And the slave was shaved again to reveal the secret message.

In 1954, Emil Hembrooke of the Muzac Corporation filed a patent entitled "Identification of sound and like signals" (Hembrooke, 1961) in which is described a method for imperceptibly embedding an identification code into music for the purpose of proving ownership. This might be the first application of watermarking in digital form.

Digital watermarking (Cox, & Miller, 2001) was firstly introduced by Tanaka in 1990 and Caronni & Tirkel in 1993. In these schemes, the technology of embedding mark information in digital work is presented. The word "Water Mark" is firstly used in their papers. Electronic watermarking had been invented. From 1990s on, digital watermarking has received substantial interest as a research topic (Swanson, et al., 1998a).

Video watermarking was first introduced in 1996 when the video compression standard MPEG2 (Woolley, 2007) is published and widely applied. From then on, the related theoretical and technical work attracts more and more researchers. Besides academic perspective, its commercial implementations are also emphasized together with economic and engineering constraints.

PERFORMANCE REQUIREMENT OF VIDEO WATERMARKING

For video watermarking, some performances are required, both the ones same to image watermarking and its extra ones, such as security, robustness, transparency, oblivious, vindicability and efficiency.

Security is required in some applications. Similarly to cryptosystem, the construction of watermarking system should consider the security against various attacks (Petitcolas, et al., 1999; Linnartz & Dijk, 1998). According to the attacker's ability, the attacks can be classified into several types: attack under the condition of knowing nothing about the watermarking system, attack knowing some watermarked copies, attack knowing the embedding algorithm, and the attack knowing the watermark detector.

Robustness is an important performance for video watermarking. The media data are often processed during transmission process, and some of the processing operations are accepted. Thus, the watermarking should still be detected after these operations. Such operations (Moulin & Koetter, 2005; Johnson, et al., 2001) include general signal processing operations (filtering, noising, A/D, D/A, re-sampling, etc.) and geometric attacks (rotation, scaling, shifting, transformation, etc.). For videos, temporal attacks are more practical than spatial ones, such as removing frames, inserting frames, collusion between frames (averaging frames), etc. Against these attacks, some image-based algorithms may be no longer secure.

Transparency means that the watermarked media data have no difference with the original ones in perception. It is also named imperceptibility or fidelity. This make sure that the watermarked copy is still of high quality and suitable for practical applications, such as HDTV.

Capacity means the maximal data volumes that can be embedded in carrier. Considering of transparency, the capacity of each approach is not infinite, which is in relation with the carrier. For different applications, the capacity requirement is different. Thus, before practical application, each approach's capacity should be analyzed.

Oblivious detection means that the detection process needs not the original copy. It is also named blind detection. On the contrary, non-blind detection means that the original copy is required by the detection process. In practical applications, blind or oblivious detection is preferred. Considering of the large volumes of videos, the original copy should not be necessary to recover the watermarking. That is, for videos, blind detection is preferred, which saves much storage space.

Vindicability means that the detected watermark can be used as a proof in court. In practical applications, if watermarking is used in ownership protection, it should have the property of vindicability.

Efficiency means that watermarking algorithm should be of low complexity, which makes it suitable for practical applications. Different from images, videos are often involved in real time applications, such as video-on-demand, online news, video conference, etc. In these applications, embedding or detection should be of low complexity.

APPLICATIONS OF VIDEO WATERMARKING

According to the properties of video watermarking technology, its general applications can be classified into the following categories:

Copyright Protection Watermarking is used to prove the ownership of the media data, which includes ownership identification and proof of ownership (Bloom, et al., 1999). In the first case, the embedded watermarking represents the information of ownership, such as the author name, the serial number or the pseudorandom sequence. In the second case, the watermarking is generated or embedded under the control of user key, which makes it suitable for proof of ownership.

Integrity Authentication Watermarking can be used to authenticate the integrity of media data (Bartolini, et al., 2001). Media data's features are embedded into the media data. The watermark is often robust to some accepted operations (compression or adding noise), but fragile to some malicious operations (cut-copy-paste). Suitably designed, this technology can detect not only the media data tampered maliciously but also the tampered positions.

Product Tracking Fingerprinting consists of uniquely marking and registering each copy of the data. This marking allows a distributor to detect any unauthorized copy and trace it back to the user. This threat of detection will deter users from releasing unauthorized copies (Boneh & Shaw, 1998).

Copy Protection Watermarking is used to control the copy operations, such as copy prevention or copy time limitation (Cox & Linnartz, 1998). This application often depends on the hardware. For example, if a recording device contains a watermark detector, then the detected watermark can be used to prevent copying of copyrighted material. Moreover, if the watermark represents the permitted copy time, and the watermark can

be modified during each copy, then the copy time can be controlled.

Broadcast Monitoring Watermark can be embedded into the broadcast or TV program, which is used to monitor whether the program is legal or not and whether the program is played corresponding to the contract (Kalker, et al., 1999). In this case, watermark detector is included in the broadcast player or TV set.

Error Concealment The redundancy information can be embedded into video data as watermark, which is used to compensate the lost data blocks or modify the error blocks (Chen, et al., 2003).

RESEARCH ACHIEVEMENTS

Till now, more than 200 patents about video watermarking have been registered all over the world. Fig. 2 shows the patents indexed by European Patent Office in each year (from 1997 to 2007). As can be seen, the application increases greatly after 2003.

From 1996 on, video watermarking attracts more and more researchers. The high increasing is shown both in paper publication and research group construction. The paper publication (Ei Compendex indexed) in video watermarking is shown in Fig. 3. As can be seen, the publication increases with time. After 2004, video watermarking becomes a hot topic. The well-known research

Figure 2. Patent publication related to video watermarking

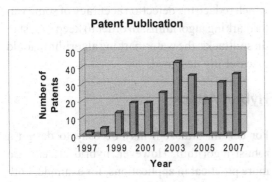

Figure 3. Video watermarking related publications

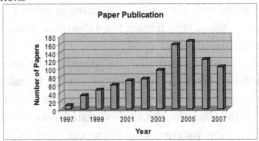

organizes include Multimedia Lab in MIT, Multimedia Lab in Cambridge University, Digital Lab in IBM, National Information Research Center of German, and NEC Research Center, etc. Over Internet, Martin Kutter constructed a non-official e-mail list for watermarking researchers. This public list strengthens the exchange among researchers, and thus fastens the research progress. It was reported that the population was over 2500 till 2005. Now, the users are many more than before.

TYPICAL ATTACKS AGAINST VIDEO WATERMARKING

For image watermarking, the typical attacks include cutting, copying, RST (rotation, scaling, translation), etc., which are called spatial attacks (Johnson, et al., 2001). Different from image or audio data, video data are often of large volume with real time interaction in practical applications. Furthermore, video data are composed of both temporal and spatial information. Therefore, video watermarking faces more attacks than image or audio watermarking. Among these attacks, collusion and de-synchronization are the most important ones, which are called temporal attacks (Lin, 2005).

Collusion Attack

In video sequence, the adjacent frames are similar in content. Thus, attackers may substitute one frame with another frame. Furthermore, they can estimate a new frame by use of the existing two frames, and then use the new frame to substitute one of the existing frames. Fig. 4 shows the general collusion process.

For the former collusion operation, the substitution between two adjacent frames may make the watermarking detection lose synchronization. For the later one, the new estimated frame may make the watermarking disappear. Therefore,

Figure 4. Collusion process in video sequence

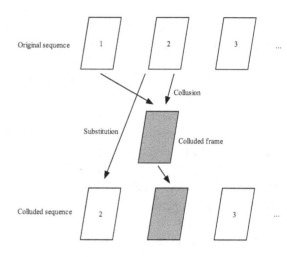

some means should be adopted in order to resist these collusion attacks.

De-Synchronization Attack

Due to the property in temporal axis, de-synchronization attack to video watermarking is easy to be applied. The attacks include removing frames, inserting frames and frame exchange, etc. Fig. 5 shows some of the de-synchronization attacks. Considered that video data are often compressed with such codec as MPEG1/2/4 or H.261/3/4 (Woolley, 2007), another de-synchronization attack is also practical. That is, to change the GOP length. GOP regrouping changes the encoding mode and thus produces the different data stream, which reduce the detection accuracy of some watermarking algorithms. In order to keep robust to these attacks, the watermarking algorithm should be carefully designed.

Hybrid Attack

For certain attack, it may be easy to design a robust algorithm. However, hybrid attacks are more practical in applications, for example, both

Figure 5. De-synchronization process in video sequence

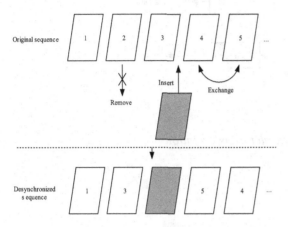

collusion attack and de-synchronization attack, both collusion attack and RST (rotation, scaling, translation) attack, both de-synchronization and RST, or both temporal attack and spatial attack. For practical applications, these attacks should be considered when designing watermarking algorithms.

RESEARCH PROGRESS

Video watermarking embeds identification information or authentication information into video data in order to protect ownership or integrity. For videos are composed of image frames, some image watermarking algorithms can be used in videos directly. However, for videos contain temporal information compared with images, video watermarking has some extra requirements. This property encourages the research in video watermarking algorithms. According to the applications, video watermarking can be classified into three types, i.e., robust video watermarking, authentication watermarking and video fingerprinting. Among them, robust video watermarking is used for ownership protection, authentication watermarking is used for content integrity protection, and video fingerprinting is used for copy tracing. In the following content, they will be reviewed in detail.

Robust Video Watermarking

Watermarking Embedding and Compression

For videos are often compressed before storing or transmission, videos can be watermarked during different process: embed before compression, embed during compression or embed after compression. The three schemes are shown in Fig. 6, i.e., the first one embeds watermarking in raw data, the second one during compression and the third one in the compressed data stream. The detection process is symmetric to the embedding process.

Embed before compression Watermarking is embedded in raw videos. This kind of watermarking algorithm can be constructed based on image watermarking. For example, LSB algorithm embeds information in the least significant bits of pixels (Mobasseri, 1998). In order to improve the robustness to attacks, some algorithms (Li, et al., 2003) are proposed, which employ the temporal properties. For example, temporal wavelet transformation is applied to video sequence before embedding watermarking, as shown in Fig. 7. In this example, video sequence is segmented into scenes, temporal wavelet transform is applied to each scenes, yielding temporal low-pass and high-pass frames, watermarking is embedded into each of the temporal components (low-frequency, LLL_2), and inverse-transform the watermarked components to get the watermarked video. This watermarking has some components that change over time, since they are embedded in low frequency coefficient. This allows robustness against frame averaging or dropping in some extent. However, it is often of high complexity and low efficiency.

Figure 6. Watermarking embedding in video data

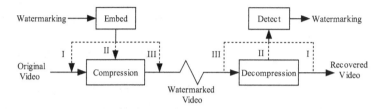

Figure 7. Embed watermarking based on temporal wavelet transformation

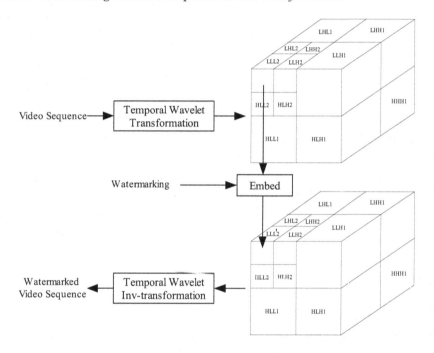

Embed during compression Watermarking is embedded during transformation-based encoding and motion estimation/compensation. And the information is embedded in DCT/wavelet coefficients (Liu, et al., 2002) or motion vectors (Kung, et al., 2003). This kind of algorithm is incorporated into compression process, and is often time-efficient. However, the encoder or decoder should be modified, and errors often accumulate in GOP. These algorithms will be further described in the next section.

Embed after compression Watermarking is embedded in the compressed bit-stream. For example, the algorithms based on (variable length code) VLC (Langelaar, et al., 1997) hide information through modifying the VLC code words. The watermarking can be added directly in the MPEG bit stream by replacing variable length codes of DCT coefficients. The key problem is to select the suitable VLC codes. In MPEG2 code tables there are pairs of code which represent the same run and levels that deviate only by one from each other. Thus, one code can be chosen as bit "1" the other as "0". Fig. 8 gives an example based on VLC modification.

Figure 8. VLC based video watermarking

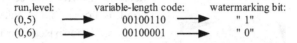

In this scheme, it is not necessary to decode and re-encode the videos, which saves much cost and keeps efficient. However, the embedding method depends on the compression standard, the low redundancy of the bit-stream limits the embedding capacity, and the detection is sensitive to channel interference or video signal processing.

The Domain of Watermarking Embedding

Videos are often transformed from spatial domain to frequency domain, and they are composed of texture information and motion information. Some algorithms have been presented, which embed information in different parts.

Embed in coefficients In frequency domain, DCT or wavelet coefficients contain much more information than motion vectors, which can obtain higher capacity. Some algorithms used in images can be extended to videos. And HVS or JND (Swanson, et al., 1998b; Watson, 1993) in DCT or wavelet domain can be used to get tradeoff between imperceptibility and robustness. This kind of algorithms aims at improving the robustness to recompression or interpolation. Alternatively, the watermarking can be embedded by modifying some DCT coefficients, similar to Patchwork. Here, the image is partitioned into a set of 8*8-blocks that are then divided into two subsets of equal size. For each subset, the energy of the high-freq DCT coefficient is measured. In order to embed the bit, the energy of the high-freq coefficient in one or the other subset is reduced by removing high frequency coefficients.

Embed in motion vector As is reported that human's eyes are more sensitive to texture information than to motion information. Additionally, motion vector is often more robust to signal processing or attacks. Thus, embedding information in motion vector is selected to obtain high robustness. For example, Jordan (Jordan, et al., 1997) proposed the algorithm that embeds information in the vertical or horizontal component of motion vector. Set Vx and Vy as the horizontal and vertical vector respectively. A watermarking embedding process is shown as below (suppose the prediction is half-pixel):

Embed "1":

$Vx=Vx+0.5$ if $Vx/0.5$ is odd and $Vy/0.5$ is even
$Vy=Vy+0.5$ if $Vx/0.5$ is even and $Vy/0.5$ is odd
$Vy=Vy+0.5$ if $Vx/0.5$ is even and $Vy/0.5$ is even

Embed "0":

$Vx=Vx+0.5$ if $Vx/0.5$ is odd and $Vy/0.5$ is even
$Vy=Vy+0.5$ if $Vx/0.5$ is even and $Vy/0.5$ is odd
$Vx=Vx+0.5$ if $Vx/0.5$ is even and $Vy/0.5$ is even

The detection process is

Extract "1": if $Vx/0.5$ is even and $Vy/0.5$ is odd

Extract "0": if $Vx/0.5$ is odd and $Vy/0.5$ is even

This kind of watermarking faces some problems: high degradation to video quality, error accumulation and error floating. For the first one, some schemes (Dai, et al., 2003) are presented to select only the vectors bigger than the threshold. For the second and third ones, some schemes (Bodo, et al., 2003) are presented to compensate the errors caused by vector modification. This kind of algorithms aims at decreasing the effect on video quality.

Figure 9. Direction emendation based on ellipse

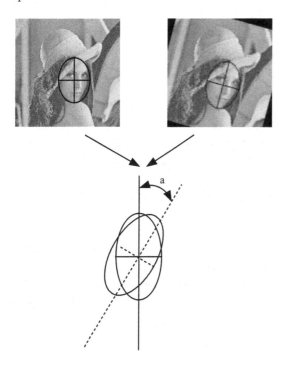

Robust Embedding Against Attacks

Embedding against Spatial Attacks

Spatial attacks include cutting, rotation, scaling, translation, warping, etc. Till now, some algorithms have been reported to obtain robustness to these attacks, which can be classified into several types: spread spectrum based algorithm, template based algorithm, emendation based algorithm, invariant-feature based algorithm, tiled watermarking algorithm and Synchronization-insensitive algorithm.

The spread spectrum based embedding algorithm (Ruanaidh & Pun, 1998) is robust to cutting, which benefits from the pseudorandom sequence's high auto-correlation, but not to other attacks.

The template based algorithm (Hartung, 1999; Hartung & Girod, 1998) embeds template together with the watermark. Through detecting the template, the watermark can be synchronized.

However, the template is also a watermark whose detection is often time cost and difficult under the condition of spatial attacks.

Emendation based algorithm (Guo & Shi, 2002) first detects the desynchronization, then amends the watermarked media, and finally extracts the watermark. In this kind of scheme, to detect the desynchronization is important but also difficult. For person-based images or videos, the ellipse curve of the face edge can be used to detect the rotation angle, as shown in Fig. 9.

Some algorithms adopt the invariant features to improve the robustness against spatial desynchronization. For example, the algorithms (Langelaar, et al., 1998; Zheng, et al., 2003) make use of Fourier-Mellin Transform's invariance to uniform scaling, translation and rotation to insert watermarks. Additionally, some algorithms (Qi & Qi, 2005; Nikolaidis & Pitas, 2000) use the edges, shapes or corner points to help watermark embedding and detection, for these features of media data are often invariant to attacks. However, the computing of the features is often of high time cost, and some of the features are not robust to such general attacks as adding noise or filtering, which restrict their applications.

Some other algorithms (Kalker, et al., 1999; Deguillaume, et al., 2002) consider synchronization by using the autocorrelation or constructing a tiled watermark structure. For tiled watermark algorithm, the related watermarks are embedded repeatedly in order to obtain robustness with the sacrifice of security. For example, the algorithm (Kalker, et al., 1999) uses a log-polar mapping of the autocorrelation to estimate the watermark rotation and scale under the help of tiled watermark structure, the algorithm (Deguillaume, et al., 2002) uses Hough Transform to estimate the affine coordinate transformation combining with tile watermark, and the algorithm (Lin, 2005) uses the correlation peaks to resembling the grids and estimates the rotation. Fig. 10 shows the tiled watermark proposed in (Lin, 2005). In this algorithm, the image is partitioned into macroblocks

Figure 10. Tiled watermarking robust to rotation and scaling

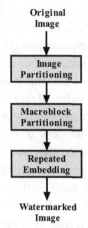

Original
Image

Image
Partitioning

Macroblock
Partitioning

Repeated
Embedding

Watermarked
Image

(a) Watermark embedding

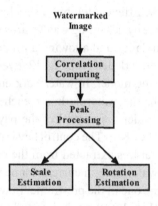

Watermarked
Image

Correlation
Computing

Peak
Processing

Scale
Estimation

Rotation
Estimation

(b) Watermark extraction

and further into blocks, and the watermark is embedded into each block repeatedly, as shown in Fig. 10(a). In watermark detection, the watermarked image is filtered with decorrelating filter, and then the autocorrelation peak is computed and used to estimate the scaling or rotation strength. This algorithm is only robust to scaling or rotation attack in some extent.

Synchronization-insensitive algorithm (Setyawan, et al., 2002) does not use invariant transformation or features. This technique creates a watermark using patches of colored noise such that the watermark detector does not require precise (sample-to-sample) correspondence to successfully detect the watermark. The technique is promising in that some degree of robustness against synchronization attack is observed, however much more development and evaluation is needed.

Embedding Against Temporal Attacks

Different from image watermarking, video watermarking is often attacked by such temporal attack as removing frames, inserting frames or collusion attack. Temporal synchronization for video watermarking is a relatively unexplored area. Till now, some algorithms have been designed to improve video watermarking algorithms' robustness against these attacks, which can be classified into several types: time-stamp based algorithm, template based algorithm, invariant-feature based algorithm and tiled watermarking algorithm.

Time-stamp based algorithms generally embed an "address" or index into the watermarked video frames (Niu, et al., 2002; Hauer & Thiemert, 2004). The embedded addresses allow the watermark detector to detect dropped or transposed frames. In (Hauer & Thiemert, 2004), only the intra-frames of compressed video are watermarked and the performance was found to be dependent on the degree of motion in the video. In (Niu, et al., 2002), orthogonal sequences are embedded into each video frame which encodes the frame's temporal index relative to the video sequence. A correlation based technique is used to recover the index. This kind of algorithm is not secure against the attacks that wipe up the "address" or index information.

Template based algorithms insert an auxiliary synchronization signal into the watermarked video. In this kind of method, the synchronizer is able to estimate of the position of the watermark by examining where the template resides in the attacked signal. Video watermarking techniques using explicit template embedding include, as well as the "helper watermarks" and the orthogonal sequences used for temporal synchronization in (Lancini, et al., 2002). Unlike the embedded watermark (which is often noise-like), the synchronization signal is designed to be easily detected or identified by the synchronizer but generally invisible in the spatial domain. For the synchronization signal acts as a watermark, the robustness is pending.

Invariant-feature based algorithms embed watermarks into the features invariant with attacks or realize synchronization based on the features. For example, the algorithm based on Insignificant Component Analysis (ICA) (Joumaa & Davoine, 2005) transforms videos into motion component and static component with Independent Component Analysis, and embeds information in motion component that is not sensitive to human's eyes but robust to attacks. Another algorithm is content-dependent (Dittmann, et al., 2000), in which, watermarking pattern changes with video content and the detection is robust to collusion or interpolation attacks in some extent. Considered that these attacks have not been suitably defined, the watermarking algorithms resisting these attacks should be further studied. Fig. 11 shows an ICA-based watermarking scheme. First, the video sequence is transformed with ICA, and the produced motion component is further transformed with wavelet. Then, the watermarking is embedded into the low frequency, and the motion component is recovered with wavelet inv-transformation. Finally, the static

component together with the motion component is transformed with inv-ICA that produces the watermarked video sequence. This scheme is robust to some de-synchronization attacks but is also of high computational complexity for the ICA or wavelet transformation is time cost. Some other schemes have also this property.

Tiled watermarking algorithms embed non-orthogonal watermarks into video frames. The watermarks may be same to each other, or just in relation with each other. A framework is developed for temporal synchronization in blind symmetric video watermarking (Lin & Delp, 2004). New models are proposed for watermark embedding and detection that apply to a large class of video watermarking techniques. The models demonstrate that temporal synchronization is challenging for video watermarks lacking temporal redundancy. Efficient temporal synchronization is achievable by designing watermarks with temporal redundancy and allowing a limited search by the watermark detector. Fig. 12 gives the tiled watermarking model. In watermark embedding (Fig. 12(a)), the watermark for each frame is generated under the control of the payload and the control key K(t). The control key is computed from the features extracted from the pre-frame. Thus, the watermark in current frame is in relation with the one in the pre-frame. In watermark detection (Fig. 12(b)), each detected watermark is compared with the one predicted by state predictor under the control of the features extracted from the watermarked frame. The detector control determines whether the detected watermark is effective, and it can dismiss such watermark

Figure 11. ICA-based video watermarking

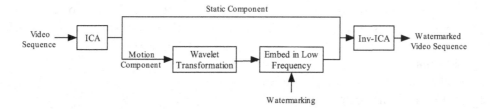

Figure 12. Tiled watermarking model

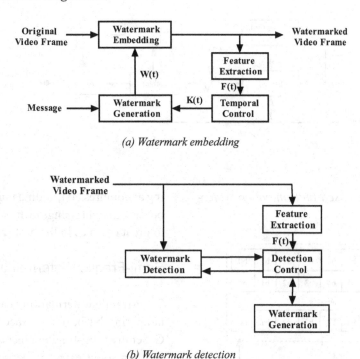

(a) Watermark embedding

(b) Watermark detection

extracted from the repeated frame or colluded frame. This model explains the relationship between security and robustness. As is known, the relationship between adjacent watermarks reduces the system's security. For example, if different frame is marked with the same watermark, then the watermark is much easier to be estimated. By reducing the relation between the watermarks, the security is improved, while the robustness is reduced too. Thus, the tradeoff should be carefully determined when the algorithm is constructed based on this model.

Authentication Watermarking

Authentication watermarking (Fridrich, 2002) is presented to protect multimedia data's integrity. A general authentication watermarking system is shown in Fig. 13. In the sender end, the cover work's feature (watermarking) is embedded into

the cover work itself, which is robust to accepted operations but sensitive to unacceptable operations that are defined in practical applications. In the receiver end, the embedded feature is extracted, which is compared with the one generated from the cover work. If the difference is below the threshold, then the cover work is not changed. Otherwise, the cover work is changed. According to the functionality, authentication watermarking can be classified into two categories, i.e., fragile watermarking and semi-fragile watermarking.

Fragile Watermarking

Fragile watermarking, also named complete authentication, is sensitive to any operation. That is, a bit's change can be detected by this kind of watermarking. A straightforward method is to authenticate the data with Hash-based digital signature algorithms (Lin & Chang, 2002; Iwan &

Figure 13. General architecture of authentication watermarking

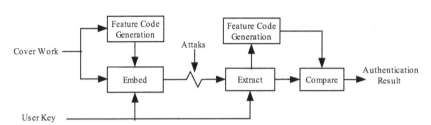

Figure 14. A hash-based authentication water-marking

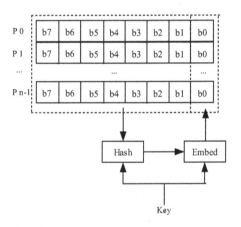

Lagendijk, 2001). Alternatively, some algorithms (Wong & Memon, 2000; Yeung & Mintzer, 1997) adopt LSB method to embed information in spatial domain, temporal domain or frequency domain (DCT or wavelet). For example, Wong (Wong & Memon, 2000) proposed the algorithm that compute the hash value of the 7 most significant bits and then embed it in the LSB, while Yeung-Mintzer (Yeung & Mintzer, 1997) proposed the one that adopted a map to generate binary sequence and then embedded them in the cover. Fig. 14 shows an authentication watermarking that embeds the hash value of the 7 most significant bits into the LSB. This kind of authentication watermarking has large capacity and locates the tampered region accurately. It is sensitive to such signal process-

ing as compression, adding noise or re-sampling, because a slight change in the significant bits leads to great changes in the hash value.

Semi-Fragile Watermarking

Semi-fragile watermarking can detect malicious tampering, but be robust to acceptable operations. Generally, semi-fragile authentication watermarking has some extra properties compared with traditional watermarking.

Sensitivity Authentication system is sensitive to such tampering operations as cutting, shifting, replacement, etc.

Robustness Authentication system is robust to such acceptable operations as compression, adding noise, A/D, D/A, etc.

Localization Authentication system can not only detect whether the data are tempered or not but also detect the location of the tempered region.

The key problem in semi-fragile watermarking is how to generate authentication code that is robust to some acceptable operations but sensitive to malicious ones. For example, Lin (Lin & Chang, 1999) found that the relationship between DCT coefficients keeps unchanged with MPEG1/2 or JPEG compression, and he adopted the relationship to generate authentication code. Thus, this algorithm is robust to compression or slight noise. Dai (Dai, et al., 2004) extended Lin's scheme

Figure 15. A semi-fragile authentication watermarking scheme

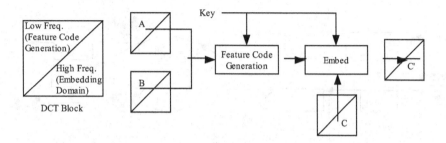

by adopting the relationship of energy between DCT blocks, which is of higher robustness to some accepted operations. This watermarking scheme is shown in Fig. 15. Each DCT block is partitioned into two parts: low frequency is used to generate feature code, and high frequency is used to embed feature code. By comparing the coefficients in two DCT blocks, the authentication code is generated, which is embedded into the selected block's high frequency. The authentication process is straightforward. Some other features can also be used to generate authentication code, such as edges or motion objects. The definition of acceptable or malicious operations depends on practical applications, and it encourages the research of semi-fragile watermarking.

Video Fingerprinting

Fingerprinting is a technology used to trace traitors. The earliest fingerprinting scheme is used in broadcast encryption. In this scheme, the broadcast program is partitioned into blocks, with each block encrypted by two sub-keys. Thus, each user is assigned a unique string of sub-keys. This scheme requires twice the storage space, which has been improved by the following works. However, this kind of schemes requires the keys transmitted over extra channel, and it cannot solve the problem of super distribution. As a substitution, watermarking-based scheme can solve these problems, which embeds us-

ers' identification information in the broadcast program before transmitting it. Thus, different users receive the broadcast programs containing different identification information, which realizes traitor tracing. Fig. 16 shows a general fingerprinting system, in which, fingerprinting is generated and embedded into the cover work, the fingerprinted copies are distributed to customers, and the copies redistributed or colluded by customers can be detected.

This system is composed of five components: fingerprinting generation, fingerprinting embedding, content distribution, collusion attack and fingerprinting detection. Among them, fingerprinting embedding/detection is similar to watermarking embedding/detection. Thus, we emphasize on fingerprinting generation, collusion attack and content distribution.

Inter-Video Collusion Attack

The biggest threat to watermarking-based fingerprinting is collusion attack. That is, several attackers fabricate a new copy through combining their unique copies in order to avoid the tracing. They intend to remove the embedded fingerprinting by use of the slight difference between different copies. This kind of attack is often classified into two categories (Wu, et al., 2004), i.e., linear collusion and nonlinear collusion. Among them, linear collusion means to average, filter or cut-and-paste the copies, while

Figure 16. General watermarking-based fingerprinting system

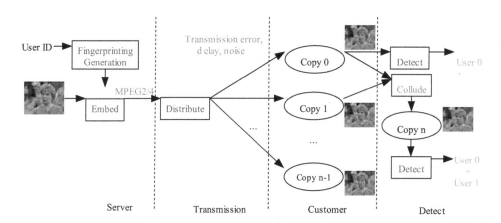

nonlinear collusion means to take the minimal, maximal or median pixels in the copies. Generally, four kinds of collusion attacks are considered. They are averaging attack, min-max attack, negative-correlation attack and zero-correlation attack.

A secure fingerprinting scheme is able to detect collusion attacks and detect the colluders. Some solutions have been proposed, for example, orthogonal fingerprinting, coded fingerprinting and warp-based fingerprinting, etc. They are described in detail as below.

Fingerprinting Generation

Some fingerprinting generation approaches have been presented to resist collusion attacks, which can be classified into three categories: orthogonal fingerprinting, coded fingerprinting and warp-based fingerprinting.

Orthogonal fingerprinting Each fingerprinting is orthogonal to another (Trappe, et al., 2003; Herrigel, et al., 1998), which keeps the colluded copy still detectable. According to the property of orthogonal sequence, such detection method as correlation detection is still practical although there is some degradation caused by collusion

attacks. For example, the algorithm (Herrigel, et al., 1998) produces orthogonal fingerprinting for each customer, the fingerprinting is then modulated by the cover video, and correlation detection is used to determine the ownership or colluders. Fig. 23 shows a typical orthogonal fingerprinting system. In this system, orthogonal fingerprinting is generated from pseudorandom sequence generator and then embedded into the video to be transmitted, which produces different video copies. For each copy, correlation detection obtains a big correlation value that determines the customer who receives the copy. For the colluded copy (averaging two copies), correlation detection obtains a relative small correlation value that is still bigger than the threshold. Thus, the colluders can still be traced.

In collusion attacks, the correlation value decreases with the rise of colluders. That is because the fingerprinting is cross-affected by other ones. In order to improve the detection efficiency, some detection methods are proposed, such as recursive detection (tree-based, correlation based) (Wu, et al., 2004). However, another disadvantage limits its applications: the supported customer population is limited by the dimension of the orthogonal vector.

Coded fingerprinting Fingerprinting can be carefully designed in codeword that can detect the colluders partially or completely. Till now, two kinds of encoding methods are often referenced. They are the Boneh-Shaw scheme (Boneh & Shaw, 1998) and the combinatorial design based code (Wang, et al., 2005). Boneh-Shaw scheme is based on the Marking assumption: only the different bits are changed by colluders, while the same bits can not be changed. By designing the primitive binary code, at least one colluder can be captured out of up to c colluders. And it can support more customers if it is extended to outer code. Differently, in combinatorial design based anti-collusion scheme, the fingerprinting acts as a combinatorial codeword. The combinatorial codes have such property as: each group of colluders' fingerprinting produces unique codeword that determines all the colluders in the group. The codeword is constructed based on combinatorial theory, such as AND-ACC (anti-collusion codes) or BIBD (Dinitz & Stinson, 1992).

Warp-based fingerprinting This kind of fingerprinting aims to make collusion impractical under the condition of imperceptibility (Celik, et al., 2005; Mao & Mihcak, 2005). That is, to de-synchronize the carrier. Thus, the colluded copy is perceptible (generates perceptual artifacts). These de-synchronization operations include random temporal sampling (video frame interpolation, temporal re-sampling, etc.), random spatial sampling (RST operations, random bending, luminance filtering or parameter smoothing) or random warping. Fig. 24 shows an example of warp-based fingerprinting. Here, the original video copy is warped under the control of customer ID, which produces different copies with slight degradation. In collusion attacks, the colluded copy is degraded so greatly that it can not be used in high definitional applications. Additionally, the more the colluders, the greater the degradation. According to this case, warp-based fingerprinting makes collusion attacks unpractical, and thus is secure against collusion attacks. However, in this scheme, the compression ratio is often changed because of the pre-warping operations. And the transmission cost is increased especially in multicast channels because multi-copies should be produced for multi-customers.

Fingerprinting Distribution

In watermarking-based fingerprinting, distribution efficiency (Wu, et al., 2004) is a problem. That is, each customer should be assigned a unique copy, which costs much in broadcast or multicast channel. Generally, the cost depends on the embedding point. For example, if the fingerprinting is embedded at the server side, then the server must deal with many copies before transmission, and much time or storage space will be cost. As a substitution, embedding at customer side (Parviainen & Parnes, 2001) is proposed, which deals with only one copy at each side. However, this kind of embedding is not secure for some one may feign the server to sending copies. As a tradeoff, an algorithm embeds fingerprinting in the middle of the server side and customer side, which strengthens the system while increasing its complexity. Thus, suitable distribution system needs to be studied.

HOT TOPICS AND OPEN ISSUES IN VIDEO WATERMARKING

Robust to interpolation or collusion attacks Such interpolation or collusion attacks as frame average, frame insertion or frame removing threaten video watermarking greatly. Although some work has been done to design robust algorithms, the obtained result is still not acceptable. The algorithm combining videos' temporal property and spatial property is further studied.

Real time realization In video-related applications, real time operation is necessary. Thus, embedding during compression or after compression is prior to embedding before compression. However, the problems in embedding during compression or after compression should be solved. For example, embedding during compression needs to change encoder or decoder and causes error accumulation in GOP, while embedding after compression limits the embedding capacity and causes low robustness to signal processing or attacks.

Low bit-rate applications. In nowadays, low bit-rate applications become more and more popular, such as mobile terminal based videos or H.264 compressed videos. For these applications, the capacity is greatly decreased, and the robustness should be re-defined. Thus, novel algorithms need to be studied.

Functional watermarking. In different applications, watermarking algorithm has different functionality, such as ownership protection, product tracking, tampering detection, etc. Among them, product tracking (video fingerprinting) and tampering detection (video authentication) attract more and more researchers, which will be summarized in the following content.

CONCLUSION

This chapter gives a brief overview to video watermarking technology, including the applications, performance requirements, state of the art progress, hot topics and open issues. As is known, watermarking technology is not mature and still in development although it has attracted many researchers and companies during the past decade. The most important problem is how to assure its robustness against de-synchronization attacks. The typical application is to prevent the pirates from camera-recording the films. To solve this problem, it requires more research work, and needs to borrow some other tools from computer vision, geometry or pattern recognize, etc. Due to the urgent requirement in video protection, it is expected to have a bright future.

REFERENCES

Bartolini, F., Tefas, A., Barni, M., & Pitas, I. (2001, October). Image Authentication Techniques for Surveillance Applications. *Proc. IEEE, 89*(10), 1403-1418.

Bloom, J. A., Cox, I. J., Kalker, T., Linnartz, J. P., Miller, M. L., & Traw, C. B. (1999, July). Copy Protection for Digital Video. *Proceedings IEEE, Special Issue on Identification and Protection of Multimedia Information, 87*(7), 1267-1276.

Bodo, Y., Laurent, N., & Dugelay, J. (2003). Watermarking video, hierarchical embedding in motion vectors. In *IEEE International Conference on Image Processing*, Spain.

Boneh, D., & Shaw, J. (1998). Collusion-Secure Fingerprinting for Digital Data. *IEEE Trans. Information Theory, 44*(5), 1897-1905.

Chen, M., He, Y., & Lagendijk, R. L. (2003, August). A Fragile Watermark Error Detection Scheme for Wireless Video Communications. *IEEE Transactions on Multimedia.*

Cox, I. J., & Linnartz, J.-P. (1998). Some general methods for tempering with watermarks. *IEEE Journal of Selected Areas in Communication, 16*(4), 587-593.

Cox, I. J., & Miller, M. L. (2001). Electronic watermarking: the first 50 years. In *Proc. IEEE Fourth Workshop on Multimedia Signal Processing*, pp. 225-230.

Dai, Y., Thiemert, S., & Steinebach, M. (2004). Feature-based watermarking scheme for MPEG-I/II video authentication. In *Proc. SPIE, Security and Watermarking of Multimedia Contents VI, San Jose, 5306*, 325-335.

Dai, Y., Zhang, L., & Yang, Y. (2003). A new method of MPEG video watermarking technology. In *Proceedings of ICCT*, 1845-1847.

Deguillaume, F., Voloshynovskiy, S., & Pun, T. (2002). A method for the estimation and recovering from general affine transforms in digital watermarking applications. *Proceedings of the SPIE Security and Watermarking of Multimedia Contents IV, 4675*, 313-322.

Dinitz, J. H., & Stinson, D. R. (1992). Contemporary Design Theory: A Collection of Surveys, New York: Wiley, 1992.

Dittmann, J., Fiebig, T., Steinmetz, R., et al. (2000). Combined video and audio watermarking: Embedding content information in multimedia data. In *Proc. SPIE Electronic Imaging'00, Security and Watermarking of Multimedia Content II*, San Jose, 2000, pp. 397-408.

Celik, M. U., Sharma, G., & Tekalp, A. M. (2005). Collusion-resilient fingerprinting by random pre-warping. *IEEE Signal Processing Letters*, Preprint.

Fridrich, J. (2002). Security of fragile authentication watermarks with localization. In *Proc. SPIE Photonic West, 4675,* Electronic Imaging 2002. Security and Watermarking of Multimedia Contents IV. San Jose, 2002, pp. 691-700.

Guo, J., & Shi, P. F. (2002, December). Object-based watermarking scheme robust to object manipulations. *Electronics Letter, 38*(25), 1656 –1657.

Hartung, F. (1999*). Digital watermarking and fingerprinting of uncompressed and compressed video.* Ph.D. dissertation, University Erlangen-Nurnberg.

Hartung, F., & Girod, B. (1998). Watermarking of uncompressed and compressed video. *Signal Processing, 66*(3), 283-301, May 1998.

Hauer, E., & Thiemert, S. (2004). Synchronization techniques to detect MPEG video frames for watermarking retrieval. *Proceedings of the SPIE Security and Watermarking of Multimedia Contents IV, 5306*, pp. 315-324.

Hembrooke, E. F. (1961). Identification of sound and like signals. United State Patent, 3004104, 1961.

Herrigel, A., Oruanaidh, J., Petersen, H., Pereira, S., & Pun, T. (1998). Secure copyright protection techniques for digital images. In second Information Hiding Workshop (IHW), LNCS 1525, Springer-Verlag, 1998.

Iwan, S., & Lagendijk, R. L. (2001). Low bit-rate video watermarking using temporally extended differential energy watermarking (DEW) algorithm. In *Proc. SPIE, Security and Watermarking of Multimedia Contents III. San Jose, 2001, 4314*, pp. 73-84.

Johnson, N. F., Duric, Z., & Jajodia, S. (2001). Information Hiding, Steganography and Watermarking – Attacks and Countermeasures, Kluwer, Boston.

Jordan, F., Martin, K., & Touradj, E. (1997). Proposal of a watermarking technique for hiding/retrieving data in compressed and decompressed video. ISO/IEC JTC1/SC29/WG11 MPEG97/M2281, 1997.

Joumaa, H., & Davoine, F. (2005). An ICA based algorithm for video watermarking. In Proc. ICASSP 2005, II, 805-808.

Kalker, T., Depovere, G., Haitsma, J., & Maes, M. (1999, January). A video watermarking system for broadcast monitoring. Proceedings of the SPIE Security and Watermarking of Multimedia Contents, 3657, 103-112.

Kung, C. H., et al. (2003). Video watermarking using motion vector. The 16th IPPR Conference on Computer Vision, Graphics and Image Processing, 2003, pp. 547-551.

Lancini, R., Mapelli, F., & Tubaro, S. (2002). A robust video watermarking technique in the spatial domain. IEEE Symposium on Video/Image Processing and Multimedia Communications, pp. 251-256.

Langelaar, G. C., Lagendijk, R. L., & Biemond, J. (1997). Real-time labelling methods for MPEG compressed videos. In *Proceedings of the Eighteenth Symposium on Information Theory in the Benelux*, pp. 25-32.

Langelaar, G. C., Lagendijk, R. L., & Biemond, J. (1998, December). Real-time labelling of MPEG-2 compressed video. *Journal of Visual Communication and Image Representation, 9*(4), 256-270.

Li, Y., Gao, X., & Ji, H. (2003). A 3D Wavelet Based Spatial-Temporal Approach for Video Watermarking. In Proc. 8th International Conference on Computational Intelligence and Multimedia Applications, 2003.

Lin, C. Y., & Chang, S. F. (1999). Issues and solutions for authenticating MPEG video. In Proc. SPIE Photonic West, 3657, Security and Watermarking of Multimedia Contents IV. San Jose, 1999, pp. 54-65.

Lin, C. Y., & Chang, S. F. (2002). Semi-fragile watermarking for authenticating JPEG visual content. In *Proc. SPIE Photonic West, 4675*, Electronic Imaging 2002. Security and Watermarking of Multimedia Contents IV. San Jose, 2002, pp. 140-151.

Lin, E. T., & Delp, E. J. (2004, October). Temporal synchronization in video watermarking. IEEE Transactions on Signal Processing: Supplement on Secure Media, 52(10), 3007-3022.

Lin, E. (2005). Video and Image Watermark Synchronization. CERIAS Tech Report 2005-56.

Linnartz, J. P., & Dijk, M. V. (1998). Analysis of the sensitivity attack against electronic watermarks in images. In *Workshop on Information Hiding*, Portland, 15-17 April, 1998.

Liu, H., Chen, N., Huang, J., et al. (2002). A robust DWT-based video watermarking algorithm. *IEEE International Symposium on Circuits and Systems, 3*(26-29), 631-634.

Mao, Y., & Mihcak, M. K. (2005). Collusion-resistant international de-synchronization for digital video fingerprinting. *IEEE Conference on Image Processing.*

Mobasseri, B. (1998). Direct sequence watermarking of digital video using m-frames. In International Conference on Image Processing, ICIP'98, 1998.

Moulin, P., & Koetter, R. (2005). Data-Hiding Codes. *Proceedings of IEEE, 93*(12), 2083--2126, December 2005.

Nikolaidis, A., & Pitas, I. (2000). Robust watermarking of facial images based on salient geometric pattern matching. *IEEE Trans. Multimedia, 2*, 172-184, Sept. 2000.

Niu, X., Schmucker, M., & Bush, C. (2002). Video watermarking resisting to rotation, scale and translation. *Proceedings of the SPIE Security and Watermarking of Multimedia Contents IV, 4675*, 512-519.

Parviainen, R., & Parnes, P. (2001). Large scale distributed watermarking of multicast media through encryption. In Proceedings of IFIP Communications and Multimedia Security 2001. Norwell MA: Kluwer Academic Publishers, pp.149-158, 2001.

Petitcolas, F. A. P., Anderson, R. J., & Kuhn, M. G. (1999). Information Hiding - A Survey,.Proc. IEEE, July 1999, pp. 1062-1078.

Qi, X., & Qi, J. (2005). *A feature-point-based RST resistant watermarking scheme.* Signal and Image Processing 2005, pp. 255-258.

Ruanaidh, J., & Pun, T. (1998). Rotation, scale and translation invariant spread spectrum digital image watermarking. *Signal Processing, 66*(3), 303-317, 1998.

Setyawan, I., Kakes, G., & Lagendijk, R. L. (2002). Synchronization-insensitive video watermarking using structured noise pattern. *Proceedings of the*

SPIE Security and Watermarking of Multimedia Contents IV, 4675, 520-530.

Swanson, M. D., Kobayashi, M., & Tewfik, A. H. (1998a, June). Multimedia Data-Embedding and Watermarking Technologies. *Proc. IEEE, 86*(6), 1064-1087.

Swanson, M. D., Zhu, B., Tewfik, A. H., & Boney, L. (1998b). Robust audio watermarking using perceptual masking. *Signal Processing, 66*(3), 337-355.

Trappe, W., Wu, M., Wang, Z. J., & Liu, K. J. R. (2003). Anti-collusion fingerprinting for multimedia. *IEEE Trans. Signal Processing, 51*, 1069-1087.

Wang, Z. J., Wu, M., Trappe, W., Liu, K. J. R. (2005). Group-oriented fingerprinting for multimedia forensics. Preprint, 2005.

Watson, A. B. (1993). DCT quantization matrices optimized for individual image. Human Vision Visual Processing, and Digital Display IV, 1993, SPIE 1913, 202-216.

Wong, P. W., & Memon, N. (2000). Secret and public key authentication watermarking schemes that resist vector quantization attack. In *Proc. SPIE, Security and Watermarking of Multimedia Contents II*. San Jose, 2000, pp. 417-427.

Woolley, S. (2007). Introduction to Multimedia Coding. John Wiley & Sons Inc, 2007.

Wu, M., Trappe, W., Wang, Z. J., & Liu, R. (2004). Collusion-resistant fingerprinting for multimedia. *IEEE Signal Processing Magazine*, March 2004, pp. 15-27.

Yeung, M. M., & Mintzer, F. (1997). An invisible watermarking technique for image verification. In Proc. of ICIP, 1997.

Zheng, D., Zhao, J., & Saddik, A. E. (2003, August). RST-Invariant digital image watermarking based on log-polar mapping and phase correlation. IEEE Transactions on Circuits and Systems for Video Technology, 13(8), 753-765.

KEY TERMS

Authentication Watermarking: The watermarking technology that embeds the integrity information into multimedia content. By detecting the embedded information, whether the media content is tampered and even where it is tampered can be told.

Collusion Attack: The operations that combine several media copies together to produce a new copy. The operations include averaging, replacement, linear combination, etc. They are often used to break a video fingerprinting technology.

Desynchronization Attack: The operations that change the media content in spatial domain, temporal domain or transformation domain while still keeping its usability. The operations include frame removing, frame insertion, frame replacement, picture rotation, picture shifting, etc. This technology is often used to break a watermarking technology.

Fragile Watermarking: The watermarking technology that makes the embedded information sensitive to any operations. This technology is suitable for content authentication.

Robust Watermarking: The watermarking technology that makes the embedded information survive such operations as compression, adding noise, filtering, A/D or D/A conversion, cutting, rotation, resizing, etc. This technology is suitable for ownership protection.

Semi-Fragile Watermarking: The watermarking technology that makes the embedded information survive such acceptable operations as compression, slight noising, filtering, A/D or D/A conversion, etc., while be sensitive to such tampering operations as cutting, rotation, shifting, etc. This technology is suitable for content authentication.

Video Fingerprinting: The technology to embed unique information into video content with watermarking technology. The produced copy contains the unique information that can be used to trace the distributor.

Video Watermarking: The technology to embed information into video content by modifying parts of video data. The produced video data are still usable, from which, the information can be detected or extracted.

Chapter XXVI
Multiple Description Coding with Application in Multimedia Watermarking

Minglei Liu
Nanyang Technological University, Singapore

Ce Zhu
Nanyang Technological University, Singapore

ABSTRACT

Digital watermarking is a useful and powerful tool for multimedia security such as copyright protection, tamper proofing and assessment, broadcast monitoring, and fingerprinting. Many multimedia services are provided through wire/wireless communications, where transmission errors are present. Robustness of watermarking is a major concern during the transmission of watermarked multimedia messages. Multiple description coding (MDC) is a promising method for robust transmission of information over non-prioritized and unpredictable networks. As a source coding scheme, multiple description coding has been extensively studied and applied in audio, image, and video sources. It is also interesting to find that multiple description coding can be applied in multimedia watermarking. Recently several multiple description watermarking schemes have been developed which have exhibited some advantages. In this chapter, the concept, design algorithms, and some applications of multiple description coding are reviewed. Particularly, the application of MDC in watermarking, known as multiple description watermarking, is elaborated based on recent research results.

Figure 1. Block diagram for MD codec with two channels and three receivers

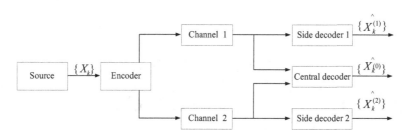

INTRODUCTION

Digital multimedia information (text, audio, image and video) and applications have widely penetrated into our every-day lives in last decades. Advances in wireless communication, mobile computing and networking are providing us with business demands and opportunities for multimedia services. This has given rise to the urgent need for the creation and application of new methods for multimedia security. Digital watermarking is a useful and powerful tool for multimedia security applications such as copyright protection, tamper proofing and assessment, broadcast monitoring and fingerprinting (Kundur, 2001). However, the watermark could be damaged by incidental/intentional attacks during transmission. The robustness of the extracted watermark is a major challenge in the watermarking application. On the other hand, as one of the efficient error resilient encoding techniques, multiple description coding attempts to overcome transmission loss in applications where transmission channels are imperfect. Many audio, image and video applications using multiple description coding have been developed. In view of the strong error resilience of MDC, it is reasonable to applying multiple description coding in watermarking to improve the robustness of the extracted watermark. In this chapter, recent research results on the multiple description watermarking are surveyed.

This chapter is organized as follows. Section 2 introduces the concept, design algorithms, and some applications of multiple description coding. In Section 3, multiple description watermarking frameworks are categorized and discussed based on recent research results. Concluding remarks are given in Section 4.

MULTIPLE DESCRIPTION CODING

Basic Concepts

Among error resilient encoding techniques, multiple description coding (MDC) (Wolf, Wyner, & Ziv 1980; El-Gamal & Cover, 1982) attempts to overcome retransmission problem in applications where some transmission channels may fail to work. MDC generates multiple (two or more) independent descriptions of the source such that each description independently describes the source with a certain desired fidelity. When more than one description is received, they can be synergistically combined to enhance the quality. Therefore, distortion in the reconstructed signal decreases upon the reception of any additional description, which is lower bounded by the distortion attainable by single description coding. In MDC, side distortion and central distortion are defined to measure reconstruction quality when part and all descriptions are received, respectively. In contrast with the traditional single description coding which aims to achieve optimal rate-distortion performance, MDC needs to consider both central and side distortions given a total bit rate budget. However, it is known that the minimizations of central and side distortions are conflicting each other, and the trade-off is controlled by redundancy among different descriptions. Generally speaking, more redundancy will favor side distortion but result in less improvement of central distortion over side distortion. Therefore, MDC attempts to strike a balance between minimizing the central and side distortions for a given rate.

In a typical MDC, an MD encoder generates two descriptions or streams for one source. The two streams are transmitted over two separate channels respectively, where each channel has its own rate constraint. Figure 1 shows the block diagram of MDC with two channels and three receivers. At the encoder, a sequence of source symbols $\{X_k\}_{k=1}^{N}$ is encoded and then transmitted three receivers over two noisy channels. At the decoder, depending on the number of descriptions received correctly, different reconstruction quality will be obtained. The reconstruction sequence produced by decoder i is denoted by $\{\hat{X}_k^{(i)}\}_{k=1}^{N}$, and distortions attained by these reconstructions are denoted by D_i ($i=0, 1, 2$). That is, if only one stream is received, the reconstruction quality corresponding to a side distortion (D_i, $i=1$ or 2) is expected to be acceptable, and an incremental improvement will be achieved associated with a smaller central distortion D_0 if both streams are received. The central decoder receives information sent over both channels while the remaining two side decoders receive information only over their respective channels. The transmission rate over Channel i is denoted by $R_i (i=1, 2)$. The MDC design attempts to achieve the best trade-off between the central and side distortions given a rate budget R_i for each channel. Making descriptions individually good, yet not too similar, is the fundamental trade-off of MDC (Goyal, 2001). In the 2-channel MDC analysis, there are two noisy channel models. In the early work, each description of source symbols $\{X_k\}_{k=1}^{N}$ is assumed totally lost or intact, which is referred to as MD channel model

I in this chapter. Later on, a more general model termed MD channel model II will be considered, in which both descriptions can be received, but each description may contain errors.

MDC Design Algorithms

A variety of practical MDC algorithms have been proposed during recent years, which typically include multiple description quantization (MDQ) (Vaishampayan, 1993; Vaishampayan, Sloane & Servetto, 2001; Gortz & Leelapornchai, 2003), multiple description transform coding (MDTC) (Wang, Orchard, Vaishampayan & Reibman, 2001), subsampling based MDC (Wang et al., 2004; Apostolopoulos, 2000; Zhang & Stevenson, 2004; Bajic & Woods, 2003; van der Schaar & Turaga, 2003; Akyol et al., 2005) (in the spatial, frequency or temporal domain) and forward error correction (FEC) based MDC (Puri & Ramchandran, 1999) . Goyal (2001) and Wang, Reibman & Lin (2005) presented a comprehensive review of these methods. There are three commonly used MD quantization algorithms, one being MD scalar quantizer (MDSQ) (Vaishampayan, 1993) and the other two being MD lattice vector quantization (MDLVQ) (Vaishampayan, Sloane & Servetto, 2001) and MD vector quantization (MDVQ) (Gortz & Leelapornchai, 2003). In these MD quantization algorithms, an index assignment function is used to create two or more representations for a symbol. In MD transform coding a pairwise correlating transform or generalized transforms are applied on the source symbols and introduces a controlled amount of redundancy directly at the source level. Within each description, coefficients should be uncorrelated for maximum coding efficiency. At the decoder, missing coefficients can be estimated from the received description. MD subsampling decomposes the original signal into subsets, either in the spatial, frequency or temporal domain, where each subset produces one description. In the FEC-based multiple description coding, maximum distance

Figure 2. Three different stages in the encoder to generate multiple coded descriptions. Reproduced from Zhu & Liu (2008).

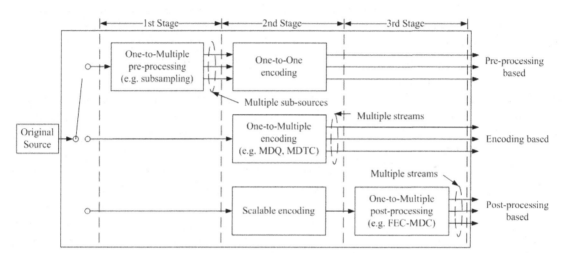

separable (MDS) (n, k) erasure codes are used to construct multiple independent bitstreams under a joint source-channel coding framework. The information symbols can be recovered if any k description symbols are correctly received.

To gain a better understanding of these different algorithms, MDC methods can be classified in the following way. The source may be split into multiple streams (descriptions) in different stages at the encoder side, which include the pre-processing stage, encoding stage and post-processing stage. Accordingly, all the MDC methods can be classified according to which stage the one-to-multiple mapping occurs (Zhu & Liu, 2008). In pre-processing based MDC, the original source is split into multiple subsources before encoding and then these subsources are encoded separately to generate multiple descriptions. Typical examples are MDC based on subsampling in temporal and spatial domain. For encoding based MDC, the one-to-multiple mapping is performed by adopting coding techniques such as the above mentioned MDSQ/MDLVQ/MDVQ and MDTC. The post-processing based MDC realizes the one-to-multiple mapping by transforming the encoded

bit stream to multiple streams in the compressed domain. The FEC-based MDC for embedded bitstream (Puri & Ramchandran, 1999) is an example. Figure 2 illustrates these three classes of MDC schemes. More sophisticated MDC structure can be achieved with any combination of these three basic types. In this chapter, only 2-channel MDC is considered. In the following, a few 2-channel MDC design algorithms are briefly reviewed.

Multiple Description Scalar Quantization

V. A. Vaishampayan (1993) developed the MDSQ technique for communication systems that uses diversity to overcome channel impairments. Given a fixed rate, 2-channel MDSQ is comprised of an encoder α_0 and three decoders. The encoder α_0 generates from each scalar sample x a pair of quantization indices (i_1, i_2), and three decoders reconstruct from (i_1, i_2), i_1 and i_2, respectively. In MDSQ, α_0 is decomposed in two steps: $\alpha_0 = \alpha(Q(x))$, where Q is a regular quantizer and the index assignment function α maps the index

Figure 3. An example of MDSQ index assignment matrix

	1	2	3	4	5	6	7	8
1	1	3						
2	2	4	5					
3		6	7	9				
4			8	10	11			
5				12	13	15		
6					14	16	17	
7						18	19	21
8							20	22

Figure 4. An example of 2DLVQ index assignment using A_2 lattice and its sublattice with index number 13. Fine lattice points are marked by '×' and sublattice points are marked by ''. Seven sublattice points used in the index assignment are labeled by 'O' and 'A' to 'F', respectively. Thirteen fine lattice points, which lie in the Voronoi cell of the sublattice point 'O', are labeled by 'o' and 'a' to 'l', respectively.*

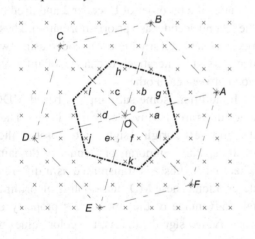

generated by Q to a pair of indices (i_1, i_2). α must be invertible so that the central decoder can recover the output of Q. The index assignment matrix can represent α^{-1} visually. Figure 3 shows an example of the index assignment matrix. In this matrix, the cells of the quantizer Q, taken in increasing values of x, are numbered from 1 to 22. One number corresponds to a pair of indices. For

instance, the number 11 in the table corresponds to the index pair (4, 5). The quality of the side distortions is represented by the ranges of values in any row or column.

Multiple Description Lattice Vector Quantization

MDLVQ is an effective technique to generate two representations for a symbol. Symmetric two-description LVQ (2DLVQ) was developed by Servetto, Vaishampayan, and Sloane (1999) (known as the SVS technique) for two balanced (symmetric) channels, whereas asymmetric multiple description lattice vector quantization (AMDLVQ) was developed for possibly unbalanced (asymmetric) channels (Diggavi, Sloane & Vaishampayan, 2002). For a given fine lattice and sublattice, the SVS technique maps each point in the fine lattice to a pair of sublattice points, where the key is to design such a mapping (also known as labeling function or index assignment) α to minimize the side distortion. In particular, to generate two descriptions in the SVS algorithm, one clean similar sublattice Λ' is predefined. For each given input vector x, it is firstly mapped to a lattice point λ, where $\lambda = Q(x) = \arg\min_{z \in \Lambda} \|x - z\|$.

An index assignment mapping $\alpha : \Lambda \rightarrow \Lambda' \times \Lambda'$ is designed to minimize the side distortions. Then an ordered pair of vectors is generated: $(\lambda'_1, \lambda'_2) = (\alpha_1(\lambda), \alpha_2(\lambda)) = \alpha(\lambda)$. This ordered pair is also known as an edge with two endpoints λ'_1 and λ'_2 ($\lambda'_1, \lambda'_2 \in \Lambda'$). Given an index N of Λ', we need to determine the discrete Voronoi cell $V_0(0)$ of Λ' and map each point $\lambda \in \Lambda$ in $V_0(0)$ to two ordered sublattice points in Λ'. Finally the assignment is extended to the entire lattice using shift property. The guiding principle for the SVS assignment is to choose the shortest possible edge (λ'_1, λ'_2) with midpoint as close as possible to the fine lattice point λ. In Figure 4, an example of the 2DLVQ index assignment is given based on A_2 lattice and its sublattice with index number 13. The index

Table 1. 2DLVQ index assignment table for A_2 lattice and its sublattice with index number 13

Lattice Point λ	Ordered Index Pair	Lattice Point λ	Ordered Index Pair
o	(O, O)	--	--
a	(O, A)	d	(O, D)
b	(O, B)	e	(O, E)
c	(O, F)	f	(O, C)
g	(B, F)	j	(E, C)
h	(C, A)	k	(F, D)
i	(D, B)	l	(A, E)

assignment table (or labeling function table) for Figure 4 is shown in Table I. Three or more description LVQ design is more complex, which were studied by Huang & Wu (2006), Ostergaard, Jensen & Heusdens (2006) and Liu, Zhu & Wu (2006). At the decoder, if only $\lambda_i^{'}$ (i=1 or 2) is available, the reconstruction vector is directly mapped to $\lambda_i^{'}$ by a side decoder. If both $\lambda_1^{'}$ and $\lambda_2^{'}$ are received, the reconstruction vector is mapped to λ by the central decoder.

Iterative Coding of Multiple Descriptions

Iterative coding of multiple description (ICMD) scheme (Srinivasan, 1999) is a complicated MD scheme, which is mainly designed to overcome channel impairments by using the correlation between descriptions. Block diagrams of the ICMD encoder and decoder are illustrated in Figure 5 and Figure 6, respectively. An MDC algorithm, such as multiple description scalar quantization, is applied on the source to generate two descriptions. The actually transmitted codeword is obtained in the following way. The first codeword is obtained by encoding the data of description 1, while the second codeword is obtained by encoding an interleaved version of description 2. At the receiver, each decoder generates soft infor-

mation for corresponding information bits. Soft information usually takes the form of a posteriori log-likelihood ratios and can be derived using a symbol-by-symbol maximum a posteriori (MAP) algorithm (Jelinek, Bahl, Cocke & Raviv, 1974). This information from Decoder 1 is interleaved to match the bit order of Decoder 2 and used by the second decoder as a priori information. These two correlated bit streams are decoded using two decoders which iteratively exchange soft information between each other.

In addition, some subsampling based MDC algorithms are also involved in this chapter. They decompose the original signal into subsets, either in the spatial, temporal, or frequency domain, where each subset is transmitted as a different description. These MD subsampling algorithms take advantage of the smoothness property of image/video signals, that is, the color values of spatially or temporally adjacent pixels are correlated or vary smoothly, except in regions of edges. Thus, one description can be estimated from the other.

Applications

The optimized multiple description scalar quantization image coding was proposed in

Figure 5. Block diagram of the ICMD encoder. Reproduced from Hsia, Chang & Liao (2004). ©2004 IEEE. Used with permission.

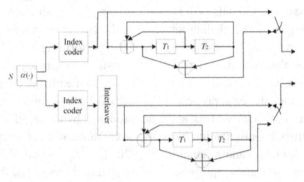

Figure 6 Block diagram of the ICMD decoder. Reproduced from Hsia, Chang & Liao (2004). ©2004 IEEE. Used with permission.

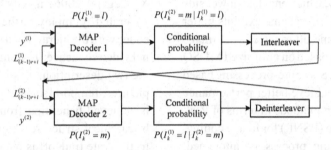

Figure 7. Block diagram of the optimized MDLVQ for wavelet image coding (Bai, Zhu & Zhao, 2007). Reproduced from Bai, Zhu & Zhao (2007). ©2007 IEEE. Used with permission.

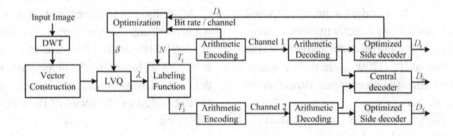

Servetto, Ramchandran, Vaishampayan & Nahrstedt (2000). The scheme combines MDSQ with techniques efficiently applied to the construction of the wavelet-based image coders and achieves very good performance. Tian & Hemami (2005) proposed a modified MDSQ (MMDSQ) in two stages. The first stage is a basic MDSQ stage, whereas the second stage is a finer central quantizer to quantize the residuals from the first one. MMDSQ is applied to the Tarp filter image coder with classification for embedding (TCE) (Tian & Hemami, 2004), which was reported to achieve better rate-distortion performance than MDSQ for image coding. Some image coding schemes based on multiple description lattice vector quantization can be found in Bai, Zhao

& Zhu (2005) and Bai, Zhao & Zhu (2006). Bai, Zhu & Zhao (2007) developed an effective MD image coding scheme based on the MDLVQ for wavelet transformed images. The block diagram for this scheme is shown in Figure 7. Considering the characteristics of wavelet coefficients in different frequency subbands, MDLVQ is applied in an optimized way which includes an appropriate construction of wavelet coefficient vectors and MDLVQ encoding parameters optimization like the choice of sublattice index values and the quantization accuracy for different subbands. Optimized side decoding is used to estimate lost information based on inter-vector correlation and an alternative transmission way, which enables a lower side distortion. This MDLVQ scheme exhibits better performance than some other tested MD image codecs including that based on optimized MDSQ (Servetto et al., 2000). Some pre-processing based MDC methods also achieve better performance than MD quantization methods in terms of Peak Signal-to-Noise Ratio (PSNR) for image coding, in which the encoding process is untouched, thus facilitating all the existing standard codecs of high efficiency to be conveniently applied in coding each description without any change. For example, the MD coding scheme proposed by (Tilo & Olmo, 2004) directly utilizes streams produced by a JPEG2000 encoder and exploits the rate-allocation of JPEG2000 streams to produce MD streams without using any special transforms and MD quantizers.

In multiple description video coding (MDVC), many algorithms are based on the pre-processing scheme, e.g., subsampling in spatial or temporal domain. These subsampling based MDVC algorithms take advantage of the assumption that spatially or temporally adjacent video data samples are highly correlated. Thus, one description can be estimated from the others. Van der Schaar & Turaga (2003) developed the multiple description scalable video coding (MDSVC) scheme based on the motion compensated temporal filtering

(MCTF) (Ohm, 1994), where high frequency frames are grouped into two descriptions and missing frames are estimated using motion vectors in the two descriptions. In Akyol et al. (2005), after performing MCTF, a 2-D spatial wavelet transform is employed to achieve spatial scalability and embedded bitplane coding is used to achieve SNR scalability. Different descriptions are produced by coding different codeblocks in different rates. Wang, Canagarajah, Redmill & Bull (2004) designed MDVC based on subsampling in spatial domain. Liu & Zhu (2007) developed a generalized multiple description video coding based on hierarchical B pictures (Schwarz, Marpe & Wiegand, 2006), in which two descriptions are generated by employing the H.264/MPEG4-AVC codec with the hierarchical structure on the original video sequence. The only difference between the two descriptions lies in the selection of key pictures. Temporal scalability for each description is achieved benefiting from the high-efficiency hierarchical structure. A good central-side-distortion-rate tradeoff is obtained by this scheme. For the post-processing based MDVC, Puri, Lee & Bharghavan (2001) extended FEC-based MD image coding to MD video coding.

MDC has found its application in multimedia watermarking. Researchers (Chandramouli et al., 2001; Hsia et al., 2004; Chu et al., 2005; Day et al., 2007) have also developed many multiple description watermarking schemes, which will be elaborated as the focus of the chapter in the following.

MULTIPLE DESCRIPTION WATERMARKING FRAMEWORK

Introduction

A digital watermark is a message which is embedded into the digital content (such as text, audio, image or video) that can be detected or extracted if necessary. Such messages mostly carry

Figure 8. Block diagram for the watermarking system

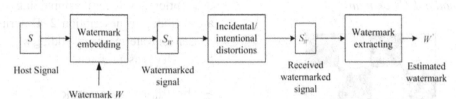

copyright information of the content. In digital watermarking, the message is assumed not to be visible or not interfering with the user experience of the content. Such a watermark is supposed to be robust against typical transformation of the content. Therefore the watermark needs to be reliably detectable, even if the content (e.g. the image) is cropped, rotated, compressed, etc. These incidental or unintentional processes on the watermarked media during transmission or delivery are called *attacks*. Figure 8 shows a general watermarking system. The host signal S is embedded (or inserted) by the watermark signal W to generate watermarked signal S_W. The watermarked signal is attacked by incidental or intentional distortions and transmitted to the receiver. At the receiver, the watermark extraction or detection process is applied to the received watermarked signal S'_W to obtain the estimated watermark signal W'.

Most research (Cox et al., 1997; Lu, Huang, Sze & Liao, 2000; Malvar & Florencio, 2003) on robust and imperceptible watermarking is based on spread-spectrum principles. In spread-spectrum watermarking, the embedded signal is a pseudo-randomly generated white-noise sequence with low-energy (Kundur, 2001). However the capacity of spread-spectrum watermarking is lower than quantization-based watermarking (Day, Lee & Jou, 2007). In quantization-based watermarking, watermark information is used as an index to select a dither signal. This dither signal is embedded to the host signal.

Detecting the presence/absence of a watermark in a given digital content without using the original host signal S is called oblivious (or public) watermark detection and the watermarking process is oblivious watermarking. However, if the host signal S is used for the detection, the watermarking process is called private watermarking.

As one of the solutions for multimedia security, digital watermarking implementations can provide multimedia security applications with copyright protection, tamper proofing and assessment, broadcast monitoring and fingerprinting, etc.. Many multimedia services are provided in wireless communication networking, thus error resilience of watermark over wireless channels should be considered. In this regard, multiple description coding is a good choice among error resilient encoding techniques, and may protect the embedded watermark or watermarked signal against different attacks. It is natural to combine these two techniques into one framework—multiple description watermarking (MDWM) framework (Chandramouli et al., 2001; Hsia et al., 2004; Chu et al., 2005; Day et al., 2007). It can be seen from Figure 8 that there are three different signals before transmission, named host signal, watermark, and watermarked signal, respectively. Depending on what signal will use MD coding, various multiple description watermarking frameworks can be classified in the following way: MDC for host signal, MDC for watermark, and MDC for watermarked signal. In the following, three

Figure 9. A simple multiple description subsampling method in DCT domain

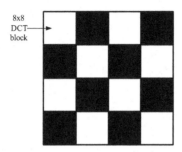

types of MDWM schemes are studied based on the literatures published in the recent years.

MDWM Framework I: MDC for Host Signal

Chandramouli, Graubard & Richmond (2001) developed a multiple description framework for watermarking. In this framework, the MD encoder is used on the host signal. Depending on the host signal characteristics, application, and the watermarking procedure, only partial descriptions are selected for watermark embedding. After inserting the watermark, MD decoder is applied to all the descriptions to obtain the watermarked signal. A two-description image watermarking example using discrete cosine transform (DCT) is given below to show how the framework works.

Algorithm Description

Applying MDC to the Host Image

The two-dimensional DCT of 8×8 blocks are computed for the host image. A very simple subsampling based multiple description algorithm is used on DCT coefficients to generate two descriptions. That is, as shown in Figure 9, all the odd-indexed DCT coefficients, i.e., $AC_1, AC_3, \ldots$, in each white block and all the even-indexed coefficients (i.e.,

$AC_2, AC_4, \ldots$) in each black block contribute to description 1, whereas the remaining coefficients are included in description 2. Description 2 is chosen for watermark embedding whilst description 1 serves as a reference.

Embedding Watermark

Figure 10 shows the watermark embedding procedure of this MDWM scheme. A relationship between the watermarked coefficients in description 2 and the corresponding non-watermarked coefficients in description 1 is computed. This relationship will be recorded as a watermark key and used in the watermark extraction process. After embedding the watermark, the DCT coefficients of both the descriptions are arranged in their original positions and the inverse DCT is taken for each block to obtain the watermarked image.

The watermark embedding process is as follows. Firstly, for each DCT block in description 2, the first few high magnitude coefficients (after zig-zag scanning) are selected and replaced by corresponding coefficients (belonging to description 1) from one of neighboring blocks. Given a DCT block, for example any one of white blocks shown in Figure 9, there are at most 4 black neighboring blocks and at most 4 white blocks around it. Further concentrate on an odd-indexed high magnitude coefficient (belonging to description 1) in this white block. Only those black neighboring blocks contain the corresponding odd-indexed coefficients (belonging to description 2), according to the subsampling algorithm. Since the corresponding candidate coefficient may not be unique, a decision criterion has to be considered. This criterion is to find the coefficient s_1 in description 1 which can minimize the value of $|s_2 - s_1|$, where s_2 is the coefficient to be replaced in description 2 by s_1. High magnitude coefficients are more resilient to attacks, therefore they are used here for embedding. The reason

Figure 10. DCT based watermark embedding process of the MDWM scheme proposed by Chandra-mouli, Graubard & Richmond (2001). Reproduced from Channdramouli (2001). ©2001 Rajarathnam Chandramouli. Used with permission.

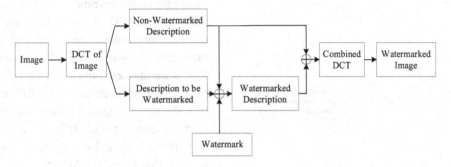

Figure 11. DCT based watermark extraction process of the MDWM scheme proposed by Chandramouli, Graubard, & Richmond (2001). Reproduced from Channdramouli (2001). ©2001 Rajarathnam Chandramouli. Used with permission.

using coefficients in description 1 to replace the coefficients in description 2 is that description 1 serves as the reference for watermark extraction. This coefficient replacement does not cause much visible distortion due to the high amount correlation among neighboring blocks in natural images. Secondly, the watermark is embedded by using $s' = s_1(1 + \beta w)$, where s' is the watermarked coefficient, β is a constant and w is the watermark symbol. Finally, the locations of s_1 and s_2 (or s') are recorded and placed into the watermark key for further use. Each location in the key is unique. The recorded coefficients s_1 and s_2 can no longer be used in the embedding process for other watermark symbols.

Extracting and Detecting Watermark

Figure 11 shows the extraction and detection process of the watermark. Given a watermarked image and the watermark key, one can easily extract the watermark. For each watermarked DCT coefficient, the extracted watermark is

$$w' = \begin{cases} (s'/s_1 - 1)/\beta \ , & s_1 \neq 0 \\ 0 \ , & s_1 = 0 \end{cases}.$$

Experimental Results

Chandramouli, Graubard, & Richmond (2001) reported the performance of the above MDWM

503

Figure 12. Robustness of the extracted watermark under both compression and random channel bit-error attacks. The data are from Channdramouli (2001).

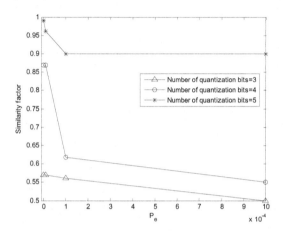

under different attacks including additive white Gaussian noise, JPEG compression, and bit error channels. The spread spectrum watermark is generated by a Gaussian (zero mean, unit variance) distributed watermark of length 100. β in the embedding equation is equal to 0.1. 'Lena' image with 256 gray levels is used for testing.

The experimental results show that the framework produces reasonable performance by adding Gaussian noise either in DCT domain or in spatial domain. For example, when the noise is added in DCT domain, the similarity factor *sim* varies from 0.87 to 0.52 when the Gaussian noise variance changes from 0 to 500. *sim* is defined as

$$sim = \sum_{i=1}^{n} \frac{w_i' w_i}{\sqrt{w_i' w_i'}},$$

where w_i' is the extracted watermark and w_i is the original watermark.

When JPEG compression is used on the water-marked 'Lena' image, the similarity factor *sim* is larger than 0.6 as the quality factor in JPEG coder is above 10. When the quality factor is smaller than 10, the value of *sim* rapidly drops.

Consider bit-error attack together with compression attack. Bit-error attack is to simulate wireless transmission since in wireless environments bit errors commonly occur. After watermark insertion, DCT coefficients are quantized using a uniform quantizer with quantization factor ranging from 8 to 32 (3-bit to 5-bit quantizers). The watermarked image is transmitted over a binary symmetric channel with different bit error probabilities P_e. Figure 12 shows the performance of the framework with different P_e values (10^{-3}, 10^{-4}, 10^{-5} and 0) and quantization levels. It can be seen that the MDWM algorithm is resistant to bit errors when the quantization factor is 16 (4 bits) or 32 (5 bits) with small P_e values, whereas it performs poorly as the quantization factor is 8 (3 bits) or with larger P_e values.

Conclusion

This MDWM scheme is not a completely oblivious technique, since the watermark key is needed during the watermark detection process, which depicts the relationship between the watermarked coefficients in one description and the corresponding coefficients in the referential one. In view of the fact that the embedded watermark can not be extracted unless both descriptions are received, it does not serve as a good choice for error-prone packet transmission network applications.

MDWM FRAMEWORK II: MDC FOR WATERMARK

In view that watermarking is a communication problem (Cox, Miller, Leighton, & Mckellips, 1999) regarding the host signal as a communication channel, MDC finds another way to work on watermarking. To increase reliability of a communication channel, error correcting codes can be applied. Hsia et al. (2004) divided the applications of error correcting codes in watermarking into three types, which are signal repetition,

Figure 13. The process of watermark embedding and extracting with ICMD coding proposed by Hsia et al. (2004).

Figure 14. Watermark embedding process using fast frequency hopping spread spectrum (FFHSS)

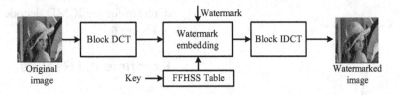

Figure 15. An example of embedding 5 bits with a spreading factor of 3 by using FFHSS. Reproduced from Hsia et al. (2004). ©2004 IEEE. Used with permission.

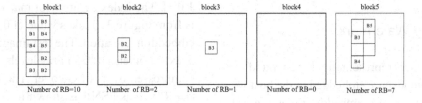

sophisticated error correcting codes such as block codes (Perez-Gonzalez et al., 2001) and turbo codes (Ambroze et al., 2001), and the combination of both signal repetition and channel coding (Desset et al., 2002). Signal repetition could also be considered as a means of increasing diversity and is more effective in combating channel fading (Hsia et al., 2004). However, signal repetition needs double bandwidth, which further limits the transmission capacity. Multiple description coding achieves a good trade-off between the transmission bandwidth and bit error rate, which increases diversity without requiring as much bandwidth as signal repetition. Hsia et al. (2004) proposed such an MDMW framework by applying the MDC algorithm to watermark. In order to better combat with the transmission errors in noisy channels, iterative coding of multiple descriptions

(ICMD) (Srinivasan, 1999) was used. Figure 13 shows the process of the watermark embedding and extraction in this scheme.

Algorithm Description

Applying MDC to the Watermark

The watermark signal is encoded by MDSQ. Two generated descriptions are further iterative encoded (referring to Figure 5). The first codeword is obtained by encoding the data of the first description, while the second codeword is obtained by encoding an interleaved version of the second description. This two-stage encoder is a typical iterative encoder of multiple descriptions.

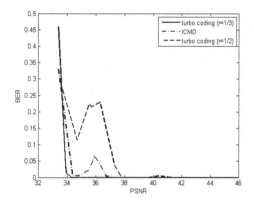

Embedding Watermark

Two watermark representations generated by the ICMD encoder are embedded in the host image. Many watermark embedding methods can be applied here. Hsia et al. (2004) adopted the watermark insertion method shown in Figure 14. In DCT domain of the host image, watermarks are inserted by "fast frequency hopping spread spectrum" (FFHSS) technique. That is, a number of middle frequency bands from each DCT block are selected as candidates to insert watermark bits. Each watermark bit w is then embedded by randomly selecting some candidates from all the blocks. For example, if five bits with a spreading factor of three should be embedded, all the candidate positions are shown in Figure 15 and watermark bits are embedded only in some positions. The formula for data embedding is $s' = s(1 + \beta)$.

Extracting and Detecting Watermark

At the receiver, the embedded bit stream is extracted by the majority-vote rule. The extracted

bit stream is then decoded using ICMD decoder. In particular, each decoder generates soft information for corresponding information bits. The information from one decoder is interleaved to match the bit order of the other decoder and used as a priori information for the other decoder. Thus two correlated bit streams are decoded using these two decoders by iteratively exchanging soft information between each other. The block diagram for the ICMD decoder has been shown in Figure 6.

Experimental Results

The MDWM using ICMD algorithm is tested by the JPEG compression attack. Turbo codes are applied to two descriptions independently with the generator matrix for turbo codes being [1 1 1; 1 0 1]. The index assignment matrix for MDSQ is from Figure 3. β takes value of 0.3 in the data embedding equation. The test image is 'Lena' of 512x512 pixels and 256 gray levels. Lena is then compressed by a JPEG coder. The bit error rate (BER) versus PSNR is shown in Figure 16. For independent turbo coding at coding rate=1/3, the BER is zero up to the point where PSNR equals 33.95 dB with compression ratio 12.7%. However the BER is much worse when turbo coding rate equals 1/2. Compared with the capacity in the uncoded case, the capacity of the embedded information is 2/9 and 1/3, respectively, for coding rate 1/3 and 1/2. The ICMD system can achieve a larger capacity of 1/3 (for independent turbo coding at rate 1/2) and resist compression attack much better.

Conclusion

The ICMD based MDWM scheme is robust to JPEG compression attacks even at higher capacity. In addition, the ICMD decoder consists of two MAP decoders and one interleaver, whereas independent turbo coding needs four MAP decoders and two interleavers. Therefore ICMD is

Figure 17. Structure of Chu's scheme (Chu et al., 2005)

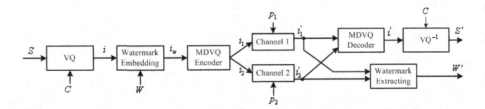

simpler than independent turbo coding in terms of system complexity. The results show that a well designed MDWM framework II can achieve reasonable results for protecting the watermark during transmission.

MDWM FRAMEWORK III: MDC FOR WATERMARKED SIGNAL

If an MD algorithm is applied to the watermarked signal before transmission, the MDWM framework is more likely to utilize the error-resilience of MDC for watermarked signals over noisy channels. This kind of MDWM framework can be considered as an MD coding with the input source signal being the watermarked signal. In this framework, the noisy transmission channel is just an MD transmission channel. Although the watermarked signal is protected by MDC, the robustness of extracted watermark is still a problem to be concerned. For watermark signals, MD channel can be considered as one kind of attacks, i.e., MD attack. Chu et al. (2005) and Day et al. (2007) studied the robustness of extracted watermark over MD transmission channels, or under the MD attack. It has been mentioned previously that MD transmission channel may be included in two channel models. In MD channel model I, each description either fails or is received correctly. In channel model II, all the descriptions are received, but each description may contain

errors. Channel model I is a special case of model II. Chu et al. (2005) tested the robustness of the watermark using both channel models, and Day et al. (2007) considered the first channel model. Both schemes reviewed here are vector quantization based schemes.

Chu's Scheme

The overall process of the watermarked-signal-based scheme proposed by Chu et al. (2005) is shown in Figure 17.

Algorithm Description

Embedding Watermark

Firstly, the VQ operation (Linde, Buzo & Gray, 1980) is applied on the host image S. A VQ codebook C with length L is obtained by training. Each index in C is represented by a $\lceil \log_2 L \rceil$-bit binary string. S is divided into non-overlapping blocks and the size of each block b_S is equal to the number of watermark bits. Then each b_S finds its nearest codeword c_i in the codebook C, and the index i is assigned to b_S. Secondly, embed each binary element w_i of W into the corresponding index of b_S. It is a one bit to one block insertion. The new index i_w for representing b_S is generated by first shifting the original index i to the left by one bit, and then tagging watermark bit w_i to the end of the shifted index. That is, $i_w = (i << 1) + w_i$.

Figure 18. Robustness of the watermarked image and extracted watermark over erasure channel attack. (a) Watermarked image quality. (b) Detection ratio of the extracted watermark. Data in the figure are from Chu et al. (2005).

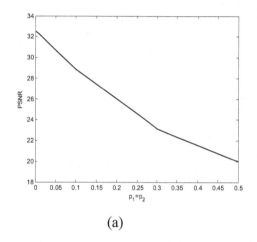
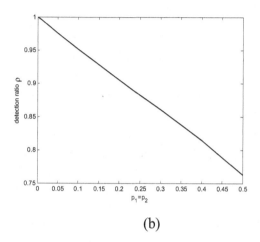

(a)   (b)

Applying MDC to the Watermarked Image

The MDVQ algorithm is applied to the watermarked index i_w to generate two descriptions i_1 and i_2, which are transmitted over two channels, respectively. The index assignment table generated by MDVQ is similar to the table by MDSQ, but the computational complexity is higher for optimization.

Extracting and Detecting Watermark

At the decoder, for one block b_s, if both descriptions for this block are available, the resulting index decoded by MDVQ can be uniquely determined, and the watermark bit is extracted by taking out the last bit. When only one description is received, several possible indices assigned in MDVQ are pending. An estimation criterion is needed from possible indices to determine the value of the watermark bit w'. The majority-vote rule is used here to determine the watermark bit '0' or '1'. If the majority-vote rule does not work or no description is received, the watermark bit w' is randomly assigned. In addition, the reconstructed host image can be obtained as follows.

The received binary indices i_1' and i_2' are firstly shifted to the right by one bit to smooth away the effects from watermark embedding. The outcome i' is output by the MDVQ decoder after decoding i_1' and i_2'. Next, it performs a table look-up process on the determined i' with codebook C to the reconstruct block b_s'. After all the watermark bits are extracted from blocks, the host image S' is reconstructed.

Experimental Results

The gray image 'Lena' with size 512×512 is tested as the host image. The watermark signal used here is the binary 'rose' image with the size of 128×128. The original source is divided into 4×4 blocks for VQ compression, which also meets the requirement for the number of bits for watermark embedding. The codebook size L equals 512. The detection ratio ρ is used to measure the robustness of the extracted watermark, where ρ is defined by

Figure 19. A watermark embedding example using multirate lattice quantization index modulation (MRL-QIM)

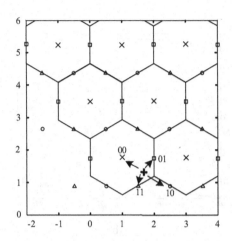

$$\rho = \frac{\text{number of correctly detected bits}}{\text{number of embedded bits}}\ .$$

Two channels have different erasure probabilities with p_1 for Channel 1 and p_2 for Channel 2, respectively.

Now consider MD channel model I. For $p_1 = 0$ and $p_2 = 1$, which means that only description 1 is available, the extracted watermark is recognizable with $\rho = 73.34\%$. The reconstruction quality of the watermarked 'Lena' is about 26.2 dB. On the other hand, when $p_1 = 1$ and $p_2 = 0$, the extracted watermark is recognizable with detection ratio of 80.55% and the resulting watermarked reconstruction of 'Lena' is 26.1 dB.

Consider MD channel model II. Assume $p_1 = p_2$ and each changes from 0 to 0.5. When p_1 and p_2 are not zero, both channels contain errors. As p_1 (or p_2) increases, both the PSNR value of the watermarked image and detection ratio of the extracted watermark decreases, which have been shown in Figure 18. The reconstruction quality of the watermarked image is still acceptable even under severely erased channel conditions (e.g. as $p_1 = p_2 = 0.25$, PSNR is a little worse

than 25 dB), due to the excellent error-resilience of MDC. Moreover, the extracted watermark is still recognizable.

Conclusion

Chu's MDWM scheme for image coding provides both better robustness for the extracted watermark and more resilience to combat with channel noises over erased channels. In addition, capabilities for watermarking are also assured.

Day's Scheme

Day, Lee & Jou (2007) developed another watermarked-signal-based scheme for image coding. The main difference between Chu's and Day's scheme lies in the watermark embedding and detecting process. Another one is that in Chu's scheme VQ is directly used in spatial domain of the host image, whilst in Day's scheme the lattice VQ is applied in DCT domain of the host image.

A multirate lattice quantization index modulation (MRL-QIM) is used for multi-rate watermark embedding in Day, Lee & Jou (2007), since it can increase the robustness for error-prone transmission over unreliable networks. MRL-QIM can also increase the watermark capacity while preserving the perceiving transparency (Day et al., 2007), which is achieved by modulating the selected coefficient pair appropriately so that the two bits of information can be embedded. At each time, two DCT coefficients are selected to form a vector, which is considered as the original input of the MRL-QIM quantizer. As shown in Figure 19, if two watermark bits '00' are embedded, then the original input (marked by "+") should be quantized to the nearest lattice point marked by "×". Similarly, if embedded watermark bits are '01', the original point should be quantized to the nearest lattice point marked by "□". In the same way, '10' corresponds to the nearest lattice point marked by "○", and '11' corresponds to the nearest lattice point marked by "Δ".

Figure 20. Comparison in terms of detection ratio between the MDWM scheme using MRL-QIM (i.e. Day's scheme) and the scheme using QIM. 'Lena' image is used for testing. (a) Under MD attack. (b) Under JPEG compression attack. The data in the figure are from Day et al. (2007). ©2007 Miin-Luen Day. Used with permission.

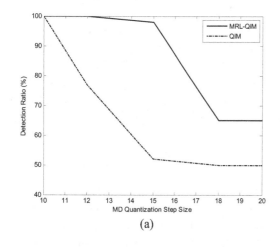
(a)

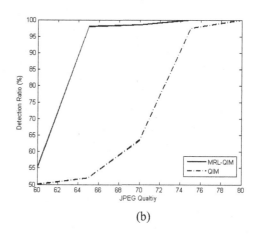
(b)

Algorithm Description

Embedding Watermark

To embed the bits of watermark message W, we proceed as follows. First apply 8×8 block DCT to the original image S. DCT coefficients are grouped into 64 feature bands $F(i, j) = (f_1, f_2, \cdots f_c)$, where i=1 to 8, j=1 to 8, and c is the total number of coefficients for each band. Then apply the embedding process of MRL-QIM to F and embed the watermark W, depending on the key K. Thus, watermarked coefficients $F_W(i, j)$ are obtained.

Applying MDC to the Watermarked Image

Each of the watermarked coefficients F_W is quantized by the MDSQ encoder to generate two indexes denoted as Y_1 and Y_2. Y_1 and Y_2 are transmitted to the receiver via two different channels separately.

Extracting and Detecting Watermark

To extract the bits of estimated watermark W' at the receiver, the algorithm is described as follows.

The received indexes Y_1' and Y_2' are decoded by the MDSQ decoder. The reconstructed Y' (which may be from the MD side decoder or MD central decoder) is fed into the MRL-QIM coder again. Through the help of the key K, the estimated watermark W' can be extracted.

Experimental Results

Simulations on the 'Lena' image (256×256 with 256 gray levels) are performed by using Day's scheme and the traditional vector watermark technique QIM (Chen & Wornell, 2001). In Day's scheme, totally 1024 coefficients are used to embed 1024 bits of watermark information. For the traditional vector QIM scheme, two DCT transformed coefficients are formed as a vector to embed one bit of watermark information, and 2048 coefficients in total are used to embed 1024 bits of watermark information. It was reported (Day et al., 2007) that for the watermarked image, the PSNR dropping depends on the embedding quantization step size. A larger quantization step size results in more robustness, but introduces more distortions. The performance of the extracted watermark under MD attacks is shown in Figure 20 (a), using the MD channel model I. It is clear that MRL-QIM (in Day's scheme) outperforms the traditional vector QIM for all transmission rates. As for the JPEG compression attack, the detection ratio of the extracted watermark is shown in Figure 20 (b). MRL-QIM still outperforms the traditional vector QIM.

Conclusion

Day's scheme is robust to MD attacks. Considering MD channel model I, the embedded watermark can be extracted with the reception of either one or two descriptions. In the case of JPEG compression attack, the scheme still gives rise to good detection ratios. Day et al. (2007) also suggested that other transforms and statistic models could be found to further enhance the robustness and increase the watermark payload while preserving the visual quality of the transmitted image. Statistical steganalysis attack is also a valuable question for further research.

CONCLUDING REMARKS

In this chapter, multiple description coding and its applications towards on multimedia watermarking have been discussed. In recent years, MD image/video source coding has been extensively studied to combat channel errors. Due to its strong error-resilience characteristic, many MDC based watermarking systems have been developed. Since MDC can be applied to three different signals in the watermarking process, the multiple description watermarking is classified accordingly, namely host-signal-based MDWM, watermark-based MDWM and watermarked-signal-based MDWM. The advantages and disadvantages for each type of multiple description watermarking have been discussed. All the MDWM frameworks have shown that the robustness of the extracted watermark can

benefit from multiple description coding more or less under different attacks, including transmission over lossy channels. The MDWM schemes discussed in the chapter mainly deal with image sources. The MDMW study for video sources is another interesting topic to be considered.

REFERENCES

Akyol, E., Tekalp, A., & Civanlar, M. (2005, September). Scalable multiple description video coding with flexible number of descriptions. *IEEE International Conference on Image Processing 2005, 3*, Genoa, Italy, 712-715.

Ambroze, A., Wade, G., Serdean, C., Tomlinson, M., Stander, J., & Borda, M. (2001). Turbo code protection of video watermark channel. *IEEE Proc. Vis. Image Signal Process.148*, 54-58.

Apostolopoulos, J. (2000, September). Error-resilient video compression through the use of multiple states. *IEEE International Conference on Image Processing 2000, 3*, Vancouver, Canada, 352-355.

Bai, H., Zhao, Y., & Zhu, C. (2005, May). Optimized multiple description image coding using lattice vector quantization. *IEEE International Symposium on Circuits and Systems, 4*, Kobe, Japan, 4038-4041.

Bai, H., Zhao, Y., & Zhu, C. (2006, October). Multiple Description Shifted Lattice Vector Quantization for Progressive Wavelet Image Coding. *IEEE International Conference on Image Processing 2006*, Atlanta, GA, USA, 797-800.

Bai, H., Zhu, C., & Zhao, Y. (2007, July). Optimized Multiple Description Lattice Vector Quantization for Wavelet Image Coding. *IEEE Transactions on Circuits and Systems for Video Technology, 17*(7), 912-917.

Bai, I., & Woods, J. (2003, October). Domain-based multiple description coding of images and video. *IEEE Transactions on Image Processing, 12*, 1211-1225.

Chandramouli, R., Graubard, B., & Richmond, C. (2001). A multiple description framework for oblibious watermarking. *SPIE Security and Watermarking for Multimedia Contents, 3*, 585-593.

Chen, B., & Wornell, G. (2001). Quantization index modulation: A class of provably good methods for digital watermarking and information embedding. *IEEE Transactions on Information Theory, 47*(4), 1423-1443.

Chu, S., Hsin, Y., Huang, H., Huang, K., & Pan, J. (2005, May). Multiple description watermarking for lossy network. *IEEE International Symposium on Circuits and Systems,* 3990-3993.

Cox, I., Kilian, J., Leighton, T., & Shamoon, T. (1997, December). Secure spread spectrum watermarking for multimedia. *IEEE Transactions on Image Processing, 6*, 1673-1687.

Cox, I., Miller, M., Leighton, T., & Mckellips, A. (1999). Watermarking as communications with side information. *Proceedings of the IEEE, 87*, 1127-1141.

Day, M., Lee, S., & Jou, I. (2007). Robust multirate lattice quantization index modulation watermarking resilient to multiple description transmission channel. *SPIE Optical Engineering, 46*(3), 037005.

Desset, C., Macq, B., & Vandendorpe, L. (2002). Block error-correcting codes for systems with a very high BER: Theoretical analysis and application to the protection of watermarks. *Signal Processing: Image Communication, 17*, 409-421.

Diggavi, S. N., Sloane, N. J. A., & Vaishampayan, V. A. (2002, May). Asymmetric multiple description lattice vector quantizers. *IEEE Transactions on Information Theory, 48*(1), 174-191.

El-Gamal, A., & Cover, T. (1982, November). Achievable rates for multiple descriptions. *IEEE Transactions on Information Theory, 28*, 851-857.

Gortz, N., & Leelapornchai, P. (2003, March). Optimization of the Index Assignment for Multiple Description Vector Quantizers. *IEEE Transactions on Communications, 51*(3), 336-340.

Goyal, V. (2001, September). Multiple description coding: Compression meets the network. *IEEE Transactions on Signal Processing, 18*, 74-93.

Hsia, Y., Chang, C., & Liao, J. (2004, October). Multiple-description coding for robust image watermarking. *International Conference on Image Processing, 4*, 2163-2166.

Huang, X., & Wu, X. (2006, March). Optimal index assignment for multiple description lattice vector quantization. *IEEE Proceedings Data Compression Conference,* 272-281.

Jelinek, F., Bahl, L., Cocke, J., & Raviv, J. (1974). Optimal decoding of linear codes for minimizing symbol error rate. *IEEE Transactions on Information Theory, IT-20, no. 2,* 284-287.

Kundur, D. (2001). Watermarking with diversity: Insights and implications. *IEEE multimedia, 8*(4), 46-52.

Linde, Y., Buzo, A., & Gray, R. (1980, January). An Algorithm for Vector Quantizer Design. *IEEE Trans. Communication, 28*(1), 84-95.

Liu, M., & Zhu, C. (2007, July). Multiple description video coding using hierarchical B pictures. *2007 IEEE International Conference on Multimedia & Expo,* Beijing, China, 1367-1370.

Liu, M., Zhu, C., & Wu, X. (2006, May). Index assignment design for three-description lattice vector quantization. *IEEE International Symposium on Circuits and Systems,* 3101-3104.

Lu, C. S., Huang, S. K., Sze, C. J., & Liao, H. Y. M. (2000, December). Cocktail watermarking for digital image protection. *IEEE Transactions on Multimedia, 2*(4), 209-224.

Malvar, H. S., & Florencio, D. A. F. (2003, April). Improved spread spectrum: A new modulation technique for robust watermarking Improved spread spectrum: A new modulation technique for robust watermarking. *IEEE Transactions on Signal Processing, 51*(4), 898-905.

Ohm, J.-R. (1994, September). Three-dimensional subband coding with motion compensation. *IEEE Transactions on Image Processing, 3*, 559-571.

Ostergaard, J., Jensen, J., & Heusdens, R. (2006, May). N-channel entropy-constrained multiple-description lattice vector quantization. *IEEE Transactions on Information Theory, 52*(5), 1956-1973.

Perez-Gonzalez, F., Hernandez, J., & Balado, F. (2001). Approaching the capacity limit in image watermarking: A perspective on coding techniques for data hiding applications. *Signal Processing, 81*, 1215-1238.

Puri, R., Lee, K.W., & Bharghavan, V. (2001, May). Forward error correction (FEC) codes based multiple description coding for internet video streaming and multicast. *Signal Processing: Image Communication, 16*(8), 745-762(18).

Puri, R., & Ramchandran, K. (1999, October). Multiple description source coding using forward error correction codes. *33rd Asilomar Conf. on Signals, Systems and Computers 1999, 1*, Pacific Grove, CA, 342-346.

Schwarz, H., Marpe, D., & Wiegand, T. (2006, July). Analysis of hierarchical B pictures and MCTF. *2006 IEEE International Conference on Multimedia & Expo,* Toronto, Canada, 1929-1932.

Servetto, S. D., Ramchandran, K., Vaishampayan, V. A., & Nahrstedt, K. (2000, May). Multiple description wavelet based image coding. *IEEE Transactions on Image Processing, 9*(5), 813-826.

Servetto, S. D., Vaishampayan, V. A., & Sloane, N. J. A. (1999, March). Multiple description lattice vector quantization. *Proc. Data Compression Conference, 29*(31), 13-22.

Srinivasan, M. (1999). Iterative Decoding of Multiple Descriptions. *Data Compression Conference, 463-472.*

Tian, C., & Hemami, S. S. (2005, April). A new class of multiple description scalar quantizer and its application to image coding. *IEEE Signal Processing Letters, 12*, 329-332.

Tian, C., & Hemami, S.S. (2004, May). An embedded image coding system based on Tarp filter with classification. *Proc. Int. Conf. Acoustics, Speech, Signal Process, 3*, 49-52, Montreal, QC, Canada.

Tilo, T., & Olmo, G. (2004, November). A novel multiple description coding scheme compatible with the JPEG2000 decoder. *IEEE Signal Processing Letters, 11*(11), 908-911.

Vaishampayan, V. A. (1993, May). Design of multiple description scalar quantizers. *IEEE Transactions on Information Theory, 39*, 821-834.

Vaishampayan, V. A., Sloane, N., & Servetto, S. (2001, July). Multiple-description vector quantization with lattice codebooks: Design and analysis. *IEEE Transactions on Information Theory, 47*, 1718-1734.

van der Schaar, M., & Turaga, D. (2003, September). Multiple description scalable coding using wavelet-based motion compensated temporal filtering. *IEEE International Conference on Image Processing 2003, 2*, Barcelona, 489-492.

Wang, D., Canagarajah, N., Redmill, D., & Bull, D. (2004, May). Multiple description video coding based on zero padding. *IEEE 2004 International*

Symposium on Circuits and Systems, 2, Vancouver, Canada, 205-208.

Wang, Y., Orchard, M., Vaishampayan, V. A., & Reibman, A. (2001, March). Multiple description coding using pairwise correlating transforms. *IEEE Transactions on Image Processing, 10,* 351-366.

Wang, Y., Reibman, A., & Lin, S. (2005, January). Multiple description coding for video delivery. *Proceedings of the IEEE, 93,* 57-70.

Wolf, J. K., Wyner, A. D., & Ziv, J. (1980, October). Source coding for multiple descriptions. *Bell System Technical Journal, 59,* 1417-1426.

Zhang, G., & Stevenson, R. (2004, October). Efficient error recovery for multiple description video coding. *IEEE International Conference on Image Processing 2004, 2,* Singapore, 829-832.

Zhu, C., & Liu, M. (2008). Multiple description video coding based on Hierarchical B pictures. *IEEE Transactions on Circuits and Systems for Video Technology,* to be published.

KEY TERMS

Iterative Coding of Multiple Description: Iterative coding of multiple description (ICMD) is a complicated MD algorithm, which is mainly designed to overcome channel impairments by using the correlation between the descriptions. Two correlated bit streams are decoded using two decoders which iteratively exchange soft information between each other.

Multimedia Security: Multimedia communication plays an important role in multiple areas in today's society including politics, economics, industries, militaries, entertainment, etc. It is of ultimost importance to secure multimedia data by providing confidentiality, integrity, and identity or ownership. Multimedia security addresses the problems of digital watermarking, data encryption, multimedia authentication, digital rights management, etc.

Multiple Description Coding: As one of error resilient encoding techniques, multiple description coding (MDC) attempts to overcome the retransmission problem in applications where transmission channels may not be perfect. A multiple description encoder generates two or more streams (known as descriptions) for one source. These streams are transmitted over separate channels respectively, and each can be individually decoded with a certain level of fidelity. Since these streams are also designed to complement each other, the incremental reconstruction quality is achievable with more received descriptions.

Multiple Description Quantization: Multiple description quantization (MDQ) is one kind of multiple description algorithms. MDQ generally uses an index assignment function to create two or more representations for a symbol. Typical MD quantization algorithms include MD scalar quantization, MD lattice vector quantization, etc.

Multiple Description Watermarking Framework: It is a framework that applies multiple description algorithms to watermarking systems.

Watermarking: Watermarking is a well-known technique used to hide data or information imperceptibly within image, audio, or video so that valuable contents can be protected.

Watermarking Attacks: Incidental or unintentional processes during transmission or delivery of the watermarked media are called *attacks*.

Chapter XXVII
Fractal–Based Secured Multiple–Image Compression and Distribution

Hsuan T. Chang
National Yunlin University of Science and Technology, Taiwan, ROC

Chih-Chung Hsu
National Yunlin University of Science and Technology, Taiwan, ROC
National Tsing Hua University, Taiwan, ROC

ABSTRACT

This chapter introduces a pioneer concept in which multiple images are simultaneously considered in the compression and secured distribution frameworks. We have proposed the so-called fractal mating coding scheme to successfully implement the joint image compression and encryption concept through a novel design in the domain pool construction. With the exploration of the intra- and inter-image similarity among multiple images, not only the coding performance can be improved, but also the secured image distribution purpose can be achieved. The authors hope that the revealed fractal-based ideas in this chapter will provide a different perspective for the image compression and distribution framework.

INTRODUCTION

Recently, the algorithms for multimedia content compression, protection, and transmission through the Internet have been drastically developed. For secured data transformation, cryptography such as Data Encryption Standard (DES) or Advanced Encryption Standard (AES) is very commonly used to prevent from illegal steals. For multimedia contents such as images and videos, watermarking (Cox, 1997; Hsu, 1999; Lin, 2005; Podilchuk, 2001), secure image coding/encryption (Dang, 2000; Yeo, 2000), and/or image secret sharing schemes (Naor, 1995) are used. By using watermarking schemes one can claim the data authority via the insertion of visible or invisible marks. Image encryption schemes (Imaizumi, 2005; Lian, 2004; Lukac, 2005a; Martin, 2005; Sinha, 2005) shuffle the original content into noise-like data, which cannot be correctly reconstructed without the secret keys used in the encryption stage. On the other hand, modern image secret sharing schemes (Guo, 2003; Lin, 2005; Lukac, 2004; Lukac, 2005b; Lukac, 2005c; Lukac, 2005d; Sudharsan, 2005) are based on visual cryptography (Hou, 2003; Jin, 2005) and human visual system characteristics (Tsai, 2004). Since a secret image can be recovered without any computation, the disadvantage of complex computation required in traditional cryptography can be released.

In general, the encryption and watermarking techniques are solely utilized to secure images or video clips. However, most image and video data are transmitted or stored in compressed forms in order to save the network bandwidth or memory requirement, respectively. Therefore, many approaches (Cheng, 2000; Salama, 2005; Wu, 2005; Wen, 2002; Zeng, 2003), which combine both the compression and encryption techniques, were proposed such that the compressed data can be transmitted or stored with more efficient and highly-secured ways. For example, the modifications of discrete-cosine-transform (DCT) and wavelet coefficients in the JPEG (Wallace, 1991) and JPEG-2000 (Christopoulos, 2000) codecs, respectively, constitute a popular choice in various secure coding schemes. Without properly decryption of the transform coefficients, the images cannot be correctly reconstructed. On the other hand, the selective or partial encryption solutions (Lookabaugh, 2004; Sadourny, 2003) for the compressed data were also proposed. These solutions reduce the key size in the encryption system and the massive computational complexity required in overall encryption. The integrated compression and encryption systems for video, audio, and multimedia also have been investigated for content protection purposes (Lin, 2005; Wen, 2002; Wu, 2005). Obviously, the research on joint compression and encryption/watermark-

ing has been received a great attention and has become a significant issue in current multimedia applications.

Images are considered as independent and separate data sources in conventional still-image coding framework. For example, images is transformed to the frequency domain and then the corresponding spectral coefficients are quantized, encoded, and recorded as the compressed data in current coding standards such as JPEG and JPEG-2000. Then the encryption/security schemes are applied on the image/video data. Different from applying the encryption/security schemes on the independent image data, certain novel methods, which implements inter-secured multiple image compression together with image encryption using an adapted fractal coding scheme, have been proposed (Chang, 2003; Chang, 2004; Chang, 2005; Chang, 2007). The major difference between the proposed method and above-mentioned work is that both the encoding and decoding processes of certain group images are no longer independent. Instead of using conventional encryption/security schemes to protect images, two or more jointly coded images can protect each other with negligible extra information. For any one of the group images, this can be achieved by accessing the content in other image(s) during both the encoding and decoding process.

In this chapter, the fractal mating coding (FMC) scheme and the adapted fast version of FMC scheme, called the iteration-free FMC (IFMC) scheme, are presented. Both schemes can increase the diversity of the domain pool and benefit the security property. In addition to extracting the self-similarity in a single image in conventional fractal block coding (FBC) scheme (Jacquin, 1993), the inter-similarity between the selected pairwise images is also explored. The key idea is to construct the domain pools using the domain blocks selected from both the pairwise images. Consequently, the best matching domain block of the range block in the current image may be found in the other image. In decoding, two images must be iteratively reconstructed with an interlacing order. Otherwise, the self-decoded images will be seriously distorted. For the images with strong inter-similarities in a block-based perspective, the proposed FMC scheme can improve the rate-distortion performance. Even two dissimilar images are jointly encoded; the rate-distortion performance can be preserved as well because the mating ratio can be selected as zero.

The proposed FMC and IFMC schemes also provides secured transmission/storage for the jointly coded multiple images. Without the pairwise or group relation, the decoded images will be degraded because the range blocks coded by the domain blocks located in the other image(s) cannot be correctly reconstructed. Furthermore, two encryption schemes are used to protect the coded result. First, a secret key is used to scramble the block means in the encoding stage. The block-mean permutation can be obtained by performing exclusive OR (XOR) operations on a secret key and the pixel addresses. Second, the fractal codes of jointly coded images can be shuffled by the use of a mating table. Only a noise-like image is reconstructed without having the correct keys and the mating tables.

The rest of this chapter is organized as follows: Section 2 briefly reviews the FMC and IFMC schemes. Further encryption methods based on the FMC and IFMC schemes are also discussed. The joint multiple-image compression and distribution and related security aspects are presented in Section 3. Section 4 deals with the discussions on potential future work. Conclusions are finally drawn in Section 5.

BACKGROUND: FRACTAL MATING CODING SCHEMES

Conventional fractal coding techniques are based on the self-similarity in images (Barnsley, 1988). The parameters, which denote the contractive af-

fine transformation (CAT) between two similar blocks, are called the fractal code (Jacquin, 1993). In general, the size of domain block is four times the size of range block. The coding performances of conventional FBC schemes are significantly dominated by the domain pool design. Efficient domain pool design greatly improves the coding performance. General design methods are summarized as follows:

1. Full search – select all the possible domain blocks in the whole image;
2. Neighboring search – select the domain blocks at the neighboring region of the current range block;
3. Subsampling search – select the domain blocks that are uniformly subsampled from the whole image;
4. Others – hierarchical (pyramid or quadratic) searching, block averaging, block-mean image, combinations of two or more methods, etc.

For the methods above, the domain blocks are all selected from the image itself and thus only the intra-image similarity is explored.

The FMC scheme explores both the intra- and inter-image similarities such that better coding performance is expected. Consider to encode the image f_A in the FMC scheme. In addition to explore the intra-image similarity via selecting N_A domain blocks in the image f_A, the inter-image similarity is explored via selecting N_B domain blocks $D_{N_B}^{(inter)}$ from the other jointly coded image f_B. The domain blocks selected from the two different images could provide larger diversity than that only from a single image. That is, the domain pool DP is composed of the domain blocks from two images, i.e. $DP = \{D_{N_A}^{(intra)}, D_{N_B}^{(inter)}\}$. The FMC scheme explores both the intra-image and inter-image similarities and encodes or decodes multiple images simultaneously. Here the mating ratio r is used to control the number of domain

Figure 1. The neighboring blocks in the currently coded image and the subsampled blocks in the other image

Current range block

Neighboring domain blocks   Subsampled domain blocks

blocks selected from the other image. It is determined by

$$r_{AB} = \frac{N_B}{N_A + N_B},\qquad(1)$$

where r_{AB} denotes the mating ratio for the current image f_A and the other image f_B, N_A and N_B denote the number of domain blocks selected from the current and the other images, respectively. The mating ratio r_{BA} for the current image f_B and the other image f_A can be determined in a similar manner.

Figures 1(a) and 1(b) show the block diagrams of the encoder and decoder of the FMC scheme for the jointly coded pairwise images. The procedures of the encoder and decoder in the FMC scheme are summarized as follows:

Encoder:

1. Input two images and partition into range blocks.
2. Determine the variance value V_{th} of each range block. If the variance value is less then a threshold value E_{th}, the block is coded by mean, otherwise go to Step 3.
3. Construct the domain pool with a given mating ratio for the two images. The domain blocks from the currently coded image can be obtained by using the neighboring method. The domain blocks from the other image can be obtained by using the subsampling method. Then, the domain pool is composed on the domain blocks obtained from the two images.
4. For each range block, the CAT is applied to the domain blocks in the domain pool to find the best matching one and then the transformation parameters are recorded.
5. Repeat Steps 2~4 for the other image. Note that a different mating ratio can be used and another domain pool is constructed.
6. Output the fractal codes of both images.

Decoder:

1. Input two fractal codes and arbitrarily given two initial images.
2. If a range block is coded by mean, it is filled with the mean value. Otherwise go to Step 3.
3. Use the fractal code to decode the range blocks using the CAT.
4. If two iterated images converge, then stop and output the reconstructed images. Otherwise, the decoded images replace the previously iterated images and repeat Steps 2 and 3.
5. Output two reconstructed images.

The FMC scheme must utilize larger memory than that in conventional FBC schemes because two images are jointly encoded and decoded. Also the iteratively decoding process of two images is longer than decoding only one image. Therefore, it is desirable to reduce the required memory size and accelerate the decoding processing in the FMC scheme. Iteration-free FBC algorithm was first proposed by Chang and Kuo (2000; 2001) and it can accelerate the decoding process because the iterative operation can be discarded. In the encoder, the means and variances of all range blocks are measured and then we used to establish the

Figure 2. (a) Encoder and (b) decoder of the FMC scheme for two images

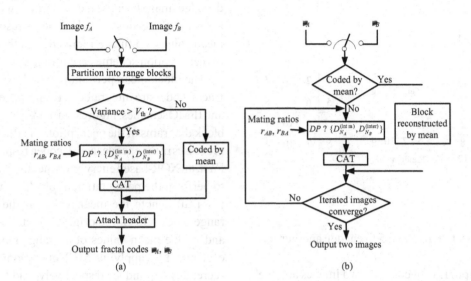

(a)　　　　　　　　　　　　　(b)

mean image as the domain pool. In the decoder, the mean image can be reconstructed only from the fractal codes and it will provide all the information required for the domain pool. Thus, the decoding process can be accelerated. On the other hand, a refined FBC scheme was also proposed to improve the coding performance furthermore (Chang, 2002). Therefore, we proposed the IFMC scheme which combines the FMC and iteration-free FBC schemes to solve the problems described above (Chang, 2006). Instead of iteratively decoding two images in the FMC scheme, the IFMC scheme only need to access the block mean information in the fractal code of the other image. Therefore, the memory usage can be significantly reduced because the domain pool can be easily constructed from the two mean images, which are accessible from the fractal codes only. Moreover, both the same sizes of the range and domain blocks and the discarded iteration process lead to speed up the decoding process.

The block diagrams of the IFMC scheme are similar to that shown in Fig. 2 except that the domain pools are constructed from two mean images. Figure 3 shows that the domain blocks from

the currently coded image can be obtained using the neighboring search, while the domain blocks from another image can be obtained by using a random table. The random table is created by the use of random seed and the values are all different. The procedures of the encoder and decoder in the IFMC scheme are summarized as follows:

Encoder:

1. Input two images and calculate the mean and variance values of each range block.

2. Construct two mean images of the two original images. The sizes of range block are 8×8 and 4×4 and thus the sizes of mean images are 64×64 and 128×128, respectively.

3. If the variance value V_{th} of the range block is less than a threshold value, it is coded by the mean value, otherwise go to Step 4.

4. Construct the domain pools from two images according to the given mating ratios.

5. Search for the best matching domain block by the use of CAT and record the transformation parameters.

Figure 3. Domain pool construction in the IFMC scheme

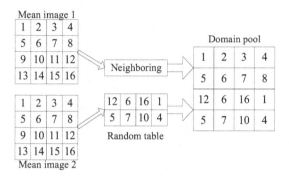

6. Repeat Steps 3 and 5 to encode another image.

7. Output fractal codes of two images and the random seed used in the encoding stage.

Decoder:

1. Input two fractal codes and reconstruct two mean images from the mean values denoted in the fractal codes.

2. Use the same random seed to reconstruct the random table and then the domain pools of the two images.

3. Perform the non-contractive affine transformation to reconstruct the range blocks which are not coded by the mean values.

4. Repeat step 3 until two images are completely reconstructed.

In conventional FBC schemes, the range blocks in an image are classified as two types: (1) the uniform blocks that are coded by their block means; (2) the other blocks that are coded by the fractal code representing the CATs between the domain and range blocks. Generally the number of blocks belonging to the first type is larger than that of the second type, especially when the block size is small (for example, 4×4). In the FMC and IFMC schemes, the range blocks of the second type will be seriously distorted if only one image is decoded

independently. However, it is easy to recognize the decoded image because the uniform range blocks are correctly reconstructed by the corresponding mean values. To furthermore encrypt the image, two encryption schemes are utilized.

The block mean permutation and mating the fractal codes are integrated in the proposed FMC and IFMC schemes. Figures 4(a) and 4(b) show the block diagrams of the encryption and decryption processes in the encoder and decoder, respectively. First, an XOR-based encryption method is applied to perform the permutation of block means. Let $\mu_R(m, n)$ denote the mean value of the $(m,n)^{th}$ range block. Given the original fractal codes τ_A and τ_B, the mean values of all range blocks are exchanged by applying XOR operations on the secret keys s_A and s_B, respectively, and their addresses, m and n. That is,

$$\mu_R (m', n') = \mu_R (m \oplus s, n \oplus s), \qquad (2)$$

where the symbol '$\oplus$' denotes the XOR operation. Therefore, the mean value $\mu_R(m, n)$ of the range block $R(m, n)$ becomes to $\mu_R (m', n')$ of another range block $R(m', n')$. Without the secret key, the decoded result can hardly be recognized because the mean values have been scrambled. To correctly reconstruct the range block $R(m, n)$ in the decoding stage, the addresses of the original mean value $\mu_R(m, n)$ must be retrieved by performing the XOR operation using the same secret key. That is,

$$\mu_R (m' \oplus s, n' \oplus s) = \mu_R(m, n). \qquad (3)$$

Note that the images f_A and f_B can use different secret keys s_A and s_B during the block mean permutation. In addition to the pairwise information and mating ratios (r_{AB} and r_{BA}), both the secret keys (s_A and s_B) can also contribute to the security in the proposed FMC and IFMC schemes.

Since the lengths of secret keys may be not enough to resist brute-force attacks, here the second encryption scheme, which applies the similar idea of the domain pool design, is proposed. The fractal codes τ_A and τ_B of the range blocks in two jointly coded images f_A and f_B are exchanged according to a mating table M_{AB}, which is an array of binary digits and whose size is the same as the number of range blocks. In the mating table, the binary digit `1' denotes that the fractal codes of two range blocks are exchanged, while the digit `0' means not. After applying the mating table on the two original fractal codes τ_A and τ_B, the encrypted fractal codes $\hat{\tau}_A$ and $\hat{\tau}_B$ are obtained as the final compressed data for images f_A and f_B.

The mathematical expressions for fractal code encryption and decryption using the mating table can be expressed as $[\tau_A, \tau_B] \oslash M_{AB} = [\hat{\tau}_A, \hat{\tau}_B]$ and $[\hat{\tau}_A, \hat{\tau}_B] \oslash M_{AB} = [\tau_A, \tau_B]$, respectively, where the symbol '$\oslash$' denotes the operation of exchanging the fractal codes of two corresponding blocks if the entry value in the matrix M_{AB} is unity. The binary digits in the mating table can be randomly generated and its size is large enough to prevent the brute-force attack. For example, the size of the mating table is 64×64 when a 512×512 image

Figure 4. Block mean permutation and fractal code mating in (a) the encoder and (b) the decoder

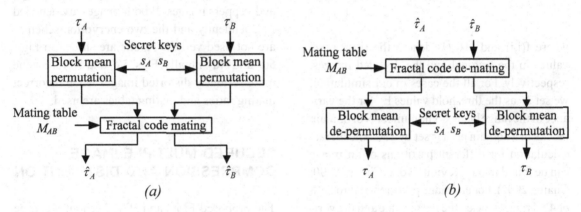

Table 1. Comparison of rate-PSNR performance (in bpp and dB) for the cases of single range block sizes 8×8 and 4×4 under various mating ratios r

8×8

r	0	0.25	0.5	0.75	1
Lena, 0.222 bpp	29.09	30.06	30.16	30.2	29.89
Peppers, 0.251 bpp	28.00	28.43	28.59	28.60	27.81

4×4

r	0	0.25	0.5	0.75	1
Lena, 0.706 bpp	33.30	33.51	34.04	33.86	33.10
Peppers, 0.771 bpp	31.20	31.31	31.23	31.03	30.69

is partitioned into the range blocks of size 8×8. The possible combinations in the mating table will become $2^{64\times64}=2^{4096}$, which is a huge number. In the decoder shown in Fig. 3(b), the encrypted fractal codes $\hat{\tau}_A$ and $\hat{\tau}_B$ must be correctly decrypted with the same secret keys and mating table.

The coding performance of the decoded image is evaluated by the peak signal-to-noise ratio (PSNR) and the bit rate. The PSNR of the decoded image is defined as

$$PSNR = 10\log_{10}\frac{255^2\cdot512^2}{\sum_{i,j=1}^{512}[f(i,j)-\hat{f}(i,j)]^2}\ dB,$$

(4)

where $f(i,j)$ and $\hat{f}(i,j)$ denote the $(i,j)^{th}$ pixel values in the original and the decoded images, respectively. For all the cases in our simulation, we set 25 as the threshold values E_{th} for the variance of the range blocks. The number N of domain blocks in a domain pool is set by 256. The bit rate calculation for different partitions of an image can be found in our previous work (Chang, 2000; Chang, 2002). For an image partitioned into 8×8 or 4×4 range blocks, the mean value and the variance of every range block are determined at first. If the block variance V_{th} is less than the threshold value $E_{th}=25$, the range block is coded by its mean value. Otherwise, the range block is coded by the proposed FMC or IFMC scheme.

First, two 512×512 images (Lena and Peppers) with the eight-bit grayscale resolution are used to test the proposed FMC scheme. The coding performance is evaluated by the PSNR and the bit rate. In our simulation, an image is partitioned into range blocks of a single size, either 8×8 or 4×4; or an image is partitioned into two-level block sizes: 8×8 and 4×4. The number of domain blocks is 256. Table 1 shows the rate-PSNR comparisons of the proposed FMC scheme for the Lena and Peppers images under different mating ratios. Obviously the proposed FMC scheme can significantly improve the image quality for the Lena image. For the Peppers image, however, the improvement is not so significant. The PSNR even decreases for some mating ratios. Figures 5(a) and 5(b) show the correctly decoded Lena and Peppers images. If both images are decoded independently and the two encryption schemes are not used yet, the results are shown in Figs. 5(c) and 5(d). Finally, Figs. 5(e) and 5(f) show the more seriously distorted images when incorrect mating ratios and mating tables are used.

SECURED MULTIPLE-IMAGE COMPRESSION AND DISTRIBUTION

The proposed FMC and IFMC schemes can be extended in order to deal with more than two images. For example, a specific group of images in a database can be jointly compressed and encrypted for secured image distribution or multiplexing purpose, in which different implementation strategies can be applied. Figures 6 and 7 show the block diagrams of the encoder and decoder of the

Figure 5. Decoded Lena and Peppers images: (a) and (b) are obtained from using correct keys; (c) and (d) are obtained from independently decoding; (b) and (d) are obtained from using incorrect keys

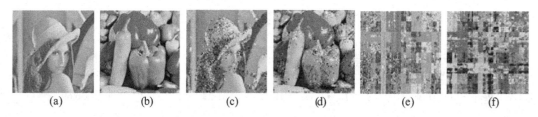

| (a) | (b) | (c) | (d) | (e) | (f) |

proposed FMC scheme adapted for multiple-image joint compression and encryption. Suppose that a user acquires a group of n images {$f_1, f_2, \ldots, f_n$} from an image database. The joint compression of multiple images is performed by the FMC scheme (Chang, 2004) in our previous work. In the encoding stage shown in Fig. 4, there are n images {$f_1, f_2, \ldots, f_n$} simultaneously considered in designing the domain pool. To construct the domain pool for a specific image, for example the image f_1, the domain blocks can be selected from itself and the other images. Basically, the construction the domain pool for the image f_1 can be divided into two parts: First, the domain blocks are selected from the image f_1 itself. Here the n_1 neighboring blocks located in the neighboring region of the current block are selected. Next, the n_2, n_3, ..., and n_n domain blocks are selected by uniformly subsampling the other images f_2, f_3, ... , and f_n, respectively. The total number of the domain blocks in the domain pool is thus the sum of $N_1 + N_2 + \ldots + N_n$. For a given size N of the domain pool, the mating ratio $r_{i,j}$ between different two images f_i and f_j can be defined as

$$r_{i,j} = \frac{N_j}{\sum_{k=1}^{n} N_k}, \quad i = 1, \ldots, N. \tag{5}$$

Note that the range of $r_{i,j}$ is within the range [0,1]. Once the domain pool has been determined, the rest procedures are similar to that in conventional FBC schemes (Jacquin, 1993; Chang, 2000; Chang, 2002). After the encoding of the image f_1 is completed, the similar procedures can be applied to other images $f_2, \ldots, f_n$. The mating ratio array **R**, which composes of the mating ratios between every two images in the same group, thus can be constructed. That is, $R = \{r_{i,j} \mid 1 \le i \le n, 1 \le j \le n\}$. Both the group information and the mating ratio array that denotes the information about the domain pool construction are critical in the encoding stage. Consequently, the original fractal codes τ_1,

τ_2, ... , τ_n corresponding to the group images f_1, f_2, ... , f_n are obtained.

To further encrypt the group of images, the mating tables used to exchange the original fractal codes of any two images are employed. For example, the size of the mating table is 64×64 when a 512×512 image is partitioned into the range blocks of size 8×8. The fractal codes τ_i and τ_j of two jointly coded images f_i and f_j are exchanged according to the mating table T_{ij}. After applying the mating table on two original fractal codes τ_i and τ_j, the encrypted fractal codes $\hat{\tau}_i$ and $\hat{\tau}_j$ are obtained as the final compressed data for images f_i and f_j. Since a mating table can only be applied to two images for encryption purpose, multiple mating tables can be used for different pairs of two jointly coded images. On the other hand, the exchanged fractal codes can be mated again with another fractal code by the use of another mating table. Finally, the encrypted fractal codes will be denotes by $\hat{t}_1, \hat{t}_2, \ldots, \hat{t}_n$, which have been very different from original fractal codes $t_1, t_2, \ldots, t_n$. Therefore, the dependency of the encrypted fractal code to the original image is greatly reduced because all the fractal codes have been mixed and re-shuffled. When the mating tables are not used in the decoding stage, the decoded results will become noise-like images.

Figure 7 shows the block diagram of the decoding stage in the proposed method. The decoding processes for n images should proceed together in order to correctly reconstruct all images. First of all, the encrypted fractal codes {$\hat{\tau}_1, \hat{\tau}_2, \ldots, \hat{\tau}_n$} should be decrypted as to the original fractal codes {$\tau_1, \tau_2, \ldots, \tau_n$} according to the same mating tables used in the encoding stage. Without the correct mating tables used in the encoding process, the original fractal codes cannot be recovered. During the decoding process, all the images are iteratively reconstructed with a progressive order. Note that the contractive affine transformations are used for all the range blocks that are not coded by the block mean. The mating ratio array denoting the construction of all the domain pools of all im-

Figure 6. The block diagram of the encoder in the FMC scheme for multiple images

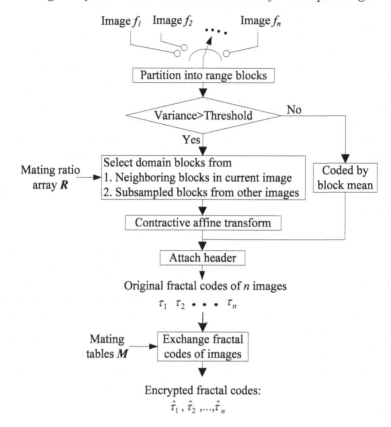

ages should be employed accordingly. If each of the group images is independently decoded, the domain blocks located in other images will not be available such that the range blocks cannot be corrected decoded. This provides a secured decoding process, in which only the mutually encoded images can be correctly decoded.

The block diagrams of the encoder and decoder for the IFMC scheme are similar to that shown in Figs. 6 and 7. There are three major different parts: First, the domain blocks are selected from the mean images rather than the original images. Second, the CAT in the FMC scheme is replaced by the non-contractive affine transformation because the sizes of domain and range blocks are the same. Finally, there is no iteration process required in the decoder. Thus the decoding speed

in the IFMC scheme is much faster than that in the FMC scheme.

The proposed method can be applied to the secured image distribution in electronic commerce. Suppose that two different users A and B request the two different groups of images, $\{f_1, f_2, \dots, f_n\}$ and $\{f_{n+1}, f_{n+2}, \dots, f_{2n}\}$ in the database or from an image server over the Internet. Two different mating ratio arrays $\mathbf{R}_1$ and $\mathbf{R}_2$ can be employed when the n images in each group are jointly coded. Thus two sets of fractal codes $\{t_1^A, t_2^A, \dots, t_n^A\}$ and $\{t_{n+1}^B, t_{n+2}^B, \dots, t_{2n}^B\}$ can be obtained. Moreover, two sets of mating tables can be applied to the two groups of fractal codes, which are the two sets of compressed data of the original images. That is, the final encrypted fractal codes of two groups of images for the users A and B are $\{\hat{t}_1^A, \hat{t}_2^A, \dots, \hat{t}_n^A\}$ and $\{\hat{t}_{n+1}^B, \hat{t}_{n+2}^B, \dots, \hat{t}_{2n}^B\}$, respectively.

Figure 7. The block diagram of the decoder in the FMC scheme for multiple images

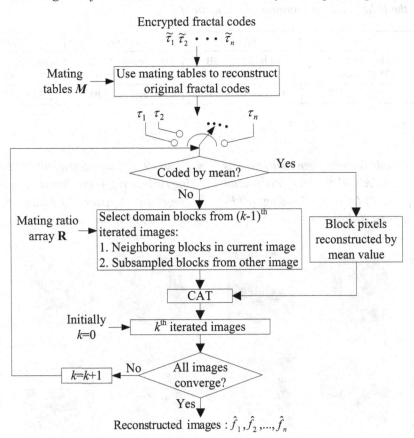

The mating ratio array and mating tables for two different groups of images are all different in jointly compressing two groups of images. Therefore, the user A cannot reconstruct the images $\{f_{n+1}, f_{n+2}, \ldots, f_{2n}\}$ without the mating ratio array $\mathbf{R}_2$ and the corresponding mating tables, even he/she owns the encrypted fractal codes $\{t^B_{n+1}, t^B_{n+2}, \ldots, t^B_{2n}\}$. Similarly, the user B cannot reconstruct the images $\{f_1, f_2, \ldots, f_n\}$ without the mating ratio array $\mathbf{R}_1$ and the corresponding mating tables, even he/she owns the encrypted fractal codes $\{t^A_1, t^A_2, \ldots, t^A_n\}$. Thus the compressed data of the distributed images are secured and cannot be easily copied without the secret information used during the encoding stage. The security level would be high enough because the number of possible combinations of

the mating ratios in the mating ratio array and the mating tables is huge and thus safe enough.

In the computer simulation, six images (n=4) of size 512×512 and 8-bit grayscale resolution are mutually coded based on the proposed IFMC method. Table 2 shows the rate-PSNR performance of the proposed method for four images under a given mating ratio array. Here the numbers of the domain blocks for the 8×8 and 4×4 range blocks are 1024 and 256, respectively. The image name appearing behind the mating ratio is the pairwise image. Obviously, the proposed IFMC scheme outperforms the conventional IFBC method when the best mating ratio is chosen. On the other hand, consider the cases of independently decoding of each image. Figures

Table 2. The comparison of the rate-PSNR performance (in bpp and dB) of the four mutually coded images using the IFMC and conventional IFBC methods

Image	Lena	Baboon	Building	Goldhill
IFMC	0.512 bpp/35.33 dB r =0.75 (Baboon)	1.184 bpp/27.56 dB r =0.25 (Building)	0.935 bpp/31.32 dB r =0.25 (Goldhill)	0.960 bpp/33.42 dB r =0.25 (Building)
IFBC	0.508 bpp/35.12dB	1.169 bpp/26.76dB	0.919 bpp/30.81dB	0.932 bpp/33.08 dB

Figure 8. The decoded results when each image is independently decoded with the encrypted fractal code: (a) Peppers, (b) Lena, (c) Building, (d) F-16, (e) Harbour, and (f) Baboon

Figure 9. The decoded results when a wrong mating ratio array is employed during the decoding stage: (a) Peppers, (b) Lena, (c) Building, (d) F-16, (e) Harbour, and (f) Baboon

(a)   (b)   (c)

(d)   (e)   (f)

(a)   (b)   (c)

(d)   (e)   (f)

8(a)-8(f) show the reconstructed images, which are independently decoded only with their own fractal codes. The major distortions occur at the range blocks whose domain blocks are selected from the other image and thus those blocks cannot be correctly reconstructed by the use of CAT. Figures 9(a)-9(f) show the reconstructed images when the wrong mating ratio array is employed during the decoding process. The major distortions also occur at the range blocks reconstructed by the use of CAT because the wrong domain blocks are selected.

Finally, consider three original images f_a, f_b, and f_c, which are shown in Figs. 10(a), 10(b), and 10(c), respectively. Figures 10(d)-10(l) show the

decoded results when different kinds of combinations of the mating tables are used in the encoding stage but are unavailable in the decoding stage. Suppose that in the encoding stage, three mating tables are randomly generated and are applied to three pairs of the original fractal codes. First of all, the fractal codes of the images f_a and f_b, τ_A and τ_B, are exchanged according to a mating table T_{ab} and become the encrypted fractal codes $\hat{t}_a$ and $\hat{t}_b$. Then the similar procedures are applied to the fractal codes τ_c and $\hat{t}_b$, and then the fractal codes $\hat{t}_c$ and $\hat{t}_b$ are obtained. Finally, the encrypted fractal codes $\hat{t}_c$ and $\hat{t}_a$ will become the further encrypted fractal codes $\hat{\hat{t}}_c$ and $\hat{\hat{t}}_a$. As shown in Figs. 10(d) and 10(e), the decoded

Figure 10. The decoded results under different numbers of mating tables are employed in the encoding stage but not used in the decoding stage. (a) The Harbour image; (b) The Building image; (c) The Baboon image; (d)-(f) a mating table is used for the fractal codes τ_a and τ_b, the fractal code τ_c is unchanged; (g)-(i) a second mating table is used for the fractal codes τ_c and $\hat{t}_b$; (j)-(l) a third mating table is used for the fractal codes $\hat{t}_c$ and $\hat{t}_a$.

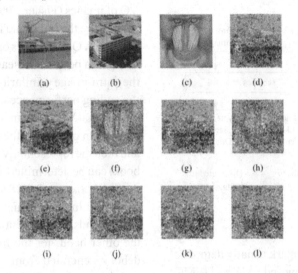

results are similar to the original images. However, when the fractal codes are exchanged in twice, it is impossible to recognize the decoded results from the results shown in Figs. 10(f) and 10(l). Therefore, higher security level can be achieved when more mating tables are employed.

In practical applications, two different implementations of the proposed joint image compression and encryption for a specific group of images are given here. First, the secret key information such as the pairwise relations, the mating ratios, and the mating table of every two pairwise images are embedded in the specific decoder. The entire group images can only be decoded by the specifically designed decoder. Seriously distorted images will be obtained if an incorrect decoder is utilized. Next, the secret key information of each image is stored in an extra file. A general purpose decoder can be used to decode each of the group images. To successfully decode a specific image, however, the user must provide the corresponding key information. This concept shows the potential on the secured image distribution for specific group of users. Figure 11 shows an example, in which three group images distributed to three corresponding group users are selected from an image database. First, each group images are jointly encoded by the proposed FMC or IFMC scheme to generate the specific fractal codes, secret keys, and the decoder, which can be the same for all the three groups or is different from each other. For the group users, their decoder can only successfully decode the corresponding group images with the correct secret keys. If the decoder tries to decode the fractal codes of other group images, only the seriously distorted images can be obtained.

FUTURE TRENDS

Recently, fractal-based watermarking methods have been proposed for image authorization (Bas, 1998; Roche, 1998; Wu, 2003; Pi, 2006). However,

Figure 11. An example for the application of secured image distribution using the proposed FMC/IFMC schemes

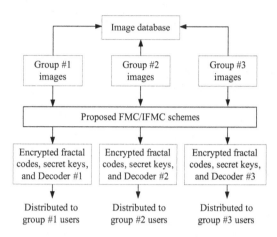

the embedding of a watermark usually degrades the image quality. The proposed FMC and IFMC schemes provide alternatives to protect the image in the compression domain, which is more practical because images are stored or transmitted in the compressed form. Consider a set of images or an image database. Let an image be selected as the key image. Each of the other images can be pairwisely coded with the key image based on the proposed FMC and IFMC schemes. Thus the compressed images are protected by the key image because they cannot be correctly decoded without the information of the secret key image. The proposed FMC and IFMC schemes show a promising application for securing storage and distribution of the coded images.

As shown in the simulation results, the coding performance depends on the mating ratio and the selection of pairwise images. Given a set of images, all the possible mating ratios and selections of the pairwise images can be tested to find the optimal one. However, it requires massive computation and seems unrealistic in practical applications. In addition to the determination of the optimal mating ratio, it is also desirable to measure the

inter-image similarity between every two images and then to select the pairwise images with the highest similarity as the input of the proposed FMC and IFMC schemes.

Since the FBC scheme is also called the self-VQ of images (Fisher, 1994), a possible approach to measure the intra- and inter-image similarities based on VQ techniques of images (Gersho, 1992) could be a potential research topic. For example, the intra-image similarity can be measured by the coding performance determined by applying the original VQ on the image. The mean-removed blocks can be used as the training vectors in VQ and then the representative codewords (i.e., codebook) can be determined. For the image coded by the codebook generated from using the same image as the training image, higher coding performance corresponds to higher intra-image similarity. On the other hand, for the image coded by the codebook generated from using another image as the training image, higher coding performance corresponds to higher inter-image similarity. Therefore, the intra- and inter-image similarities can be estimated.

Since more than two images can be processed to extend the capability of the proposed FMC and IFMC schemes, an intuitive and useful usage of the extended schemes is the application on the color image compression and encryption framework. Three spectral components (R, G, B) of a color image are expected to be with high inter-image similarities because strong local similarities could exist among the three monochrome images. The selection of domain blocks from three images shall be somewhat different from that in the current FMC or IFMC scheme. For each monochrome image, two mating ratios will be used to describe how the domain blocks are selected in three images. If the three monochrome images are jointly coded by the use of the proposed FMC or IFMC scheme, the coding performance higher than that obtained by the use of independently coding each monochrome image based on conventional FBC schemes can be expected.

Finally, other image coding techniques can be considered to implement the aspect of the proposed inter-secured pairwise image compression and encryption. For example, the inter-image similarities can be sought by examining the DCT and wavelet coefficients between the pairwise images in JPEG and JPEG-2000 standards, respectively. However, how to efficiently search for the inter-image similarity between the transform-domain coefficients of the pairwise images will be a critical issue.

CONCLUSION

In this study, the joint multiple-image compression and encryption frameworks for secured image distribution based on the FMC and IFMC schemes are proposed. The secret information includes the group information of images, mating ratio array, and mating tables for the original fractal codes such that it can successfully protect a specific group of images from illegal access. This is a different encryption concept from the public key cryptography or secret key cryptography such as DES and AES schemes. In the future work, in addition to the FBC techniques, other image coding techniques can be considered to implement the aspect of inter-secured joint image compression and encryption, which has been revealed in this chapter.

REFERENCES

Barnsley, M. (1988). A better way to compress images, Byte, 13(1), 215-223.

Bas, P., Chassery, J.-M., & Davoine, F. (1998). Using the fractal code to watermark images. 1998 IEEE International Conference on Image Processing, 1, 469-473.

Beaumont, J. M. (1990). Advances in block based fractal coding of still images. IEE Colloquium on 'Application of Fractal Techniques in Image Processing,' 3/1-3/5.

Chang, H. T., & Kuo, C. J. (1999). Adaptive schemes for improving fractal block coding of images. Journal of Information Science and Engineering, 15(1), 11-25.

Chang, H. T., & Kuo, C. J. (2000). Iteration-free fractal image coding based on efficient domain pool design. IEEE Transactions on Image Processing, 9(3), 329-339.

Chang, H. T., & Kuo, C. J. (2001). A novel non-iterative scheme for fractal image coding. Journal of Information Science and Engineering, 17(3), 429-443.

Chang, H. T. (2002). Gradient match and side match fractal vector quantizers for images. IEEE Transactions on Image Processing, 11(1), 1-9

Chang, H. T., & Lin, C. C. (2003). Fractal-based mating coding of secured joint compression of images. The Chinese IPPR Conference on Computer Vision, Graphics, and Image Processing, (pp. 802-809), Kingmeng, Taiwan.

Chang, H. T., & Lin, C. C. (2004). Mutual image compression based on fractal mating coding. Proceedings of IEEE International Conference on Multimedia and Expo (ICME 2004), (pp. 1087-1090) Taipei, Taiwan.

Chang, H. T., Lin, C. C., & Shen, D.-F. (2005). Joint multiple-image compression and encryption based on fractal mating coding for secured image distribution. Proceedings of The Seventh IASTED International Conference on Signal and Image Processing (SIP 2005), (pp. 77-82), Hawaii, USA.

Chang, H. T., & Lin, C. C. (2007). Inter-secured joint image compression with encryption purpose based on fractal mating coding. Optical Engineering, 46(3), 037002.

Cheng, H. T., & Li, X. (2000). Partial encryption of compressed images and videos. IEEE Transactions on Signal Processing, 48(8), 2439-2451.

Christopoulos, C., Skodras, A., & Ebrahimi, T. (2000). The JPEG2000 still image coding system: an overview. IEEE Transactions on Consumer Electronics, 46(4), 1103-1127.

Cox, I. J., Kilian, J., Leighton, F. T., & Shamoon, T. (1997). Secure spread spectrum watermarking for multimedia. IEEE Transactions on Image Processing, 6(12), 1673-1687 .

Dang, P. P., & Chau, P. M. (2000). Image encryption for secure Internet multimedia applications. IEEE Transactions on Consumer Electronics, 46(3), 395-403.

Fisher, Y., Rogovin, D., & Shen, T. P. (1994). Fractal (self-VQ) encoding of video sequences. Proceedings of SPIE, Vol. 2308, pp. 1359-1370.

Fisher, Y. (Ed.). (1995). Fractal Image Compression: Theory and Applications, New York: Springer Verlag.

Gersho, A., & Grey, R. M. (1992). Vector Quantization and Signal Compression, Boston, MA: Kluwer.

Guo, H., & Georganas, N. D. (2003). A novel approach to digital image watermarking based on a generalized secret sharing schemes. Multimedia Systems, 9, 249-260.

Hsu, C.-T., & Wu, J.-L. (1999). Hidden digital watermarks in images. IEEE Transactions on Image Processing, 8(1), 58-68.

Hou, J.C. (2003) Visual cryptography for color images. Pattern Recognition, 36(7), 1619-1629

Imaizumi, S., Watanabe, G., Fujiyoshi, M., & Kiya, H. (2005). Generalized hierarchical encryption of JPEG 2000 codestreams for access control. Proc. IEEE International Conference on Image Processing, 2, 1094-1097.

Jacquin, A. E. (1993). Fractal image coding: a review. Proceedings of IEEE, 81(10), 1451-1465.

Jin, D., Yan, W. Q., & Kankanhalli, M. S. (2005). Progressive color visual cryptography. Journal of Electronic Imaging, 14(3), 033019.

Lian, S., Sun, J., Zhang, D., & Wang, Z. (2004). A selective image encryption scheme based on JPEG2000 codec, Lecture Notes in Computer Science, 3332, 65-72.

Lepsoy, S., Carlini, P., & Oien, G.E. (1998). On fractal compression and vector quantization, in Y. Fisher (ed.), Fractal Image Encoding and Analysis: A NATO ASI Series Book, Chapter 2, Springer Verlag

Lin C. C., & Tsai, W. H. (2005). Secret image sharing with capability of share data reduction. Optical Engineering, 42(8), 2340-2345

Lin, E.T., Eskicioglu, A. M., Lagendijk, R. L., & Delp, E. J. (2005). Advances in digital video content protection. Proceedings of IEEE, 93(1), 171-183

Lookabaugh, T., & Sicker, D. C. (2004). Selective encryption for consumer applications. IEEE Communication Magazine, 42(5), 124-129

Lukac, R., & Plataniotis, K. N. (2004). Colour image secret sharing. IEE Electronics Letters, 40(9), 529-530

Lukac, R., & Plataniotis, K. N. (2005a). A cost-effective encryption scheme for color images, Real-Time Imaging. Special Issue on Multi-Dimensional Image Processing, 11(5-6), 454-464

Lukac, R., & Plataniotis, K. N. (2005b). Bit-level based secret sharing for image encryption. Pattern Recognition, 38(5), 767-772

Lukac, R., & Plataniotis, K. N. (2005c). Digital image indexing using secret sharing schemes: A unified framework for single-sensor consumer electronics. IEEE Transactions on Consumer Electronics, 51(3), 908-916

Lukac, R., & Plataniotis, K. N. (2005d). Image representation based secret sharing, Communications of the CCISA. Special Issue on Visual Secret Sharing, 11(2), 103-114

Martin, K., Lukac, R., & Plataniotis, K. N. (2005). Efficient encryption of wavelet-based coded color images. Pattern Recognition, 38(7), 1111-1115

Naor, N., & Shamir, A. (1995). Visual Cryptography. Advances in Cryptography: Eurocrypt'94, Lecture Notes in Computer Science, Vol. 950 (pp. 1-12)

Roche, S., & Dugelay, J.-L. (1998). Image watermarking based on the fractal transform: a draft demonstration. 1998 IEEE Second Workshop on Multimedia Signal Processing, pp. 358-363

Sadourny, Y., & Conan, V. (2003). A proposal for supporting selective encryption in JPSEC. IEEE Transactions on Consumer Electronics, 49(4), 864-849

Salama, P., & King, B. (2005). Efficient secure image transmission: compression integrated with encryption, Proceedings of SPIE, 5681, 47-58

Sinha, A., & Singh, K. (2005). Image encryption by using fractional Fourier transform and jigsaw transform in image bit planes. Optical Engineering, 44(5), 057001

Sudharsan, S. (2005). Shared key encryption of JPEG color images. IEEE Transactions on Consumer Electronics, 51(4), 1204-1211

Tsai, C. S., & Chang, C. C. (2004). A new repeating color watermarking scheme based on human visual model. Eurasip Journal on Applied Signal Processing, 2004(13), 1965-1972

Pi, M. H., Li, C. H., & Li, H. (2006). A novel fractal image watermarking. IEEE Transactions on Multimedia, 8(3), 488-499

Podilchuk, C. I., & Delp, E. J. (2001). Digital watermarking: algorithms and application. IEEE Signal Processing Magazine, 18(4), 33-46

Wallace, G. K. (1991). The JPEG still picture compression standard. Communications of the ACM, 34(4), 31-44

Wen, J., Severa, M., Zeng, W. J., Luttrell, M. H., & Jin, W. (2002). A format-compliant configurable encryption framework for access control of video. IEEE Transactions on Circuits and Systems for Video Technology, 12(6), 545-557

Wu, H. C., & Chang, C. C. (2003). Hiding digital watermarks using fractal compression technique. Fundamenta Informaticae, 58(2), 189-202

Wu, C.P. & Kuo, C.-C.J. (2005). Design of Integrated Multimedia Compression and Encryption Systems. IEEE Transactions on Multimedia, 7(5), 828-839

Yeo, J.-C., & Guo, J.-I. (2000). Efficient hierarchical chaotic image encryption algorithm and its VLSI realisation. IEE Proceedings on Vision, Image and Signal Processing, 147(2), 167-175

Zeng, W., & Lei, S. (2003). Efficient frequency domain selective scrambling of digital video. IEEE Transactions on Multimedia, 5(3), 118-129

KEY TERMS

Domain Pool: Constructed by the domain blocks, which are used for searching the similarity in images.

Fractal Image Coding: Search for the self similarity in an image and then the parameters denoting the contractive affine transformation between the domain and range blocks are recorded to perform image compression.

Image Encryption: To protect the image content from illegal users, some schemes are used to make the original plain image become unrecognizable.

Inter-Image Similarity: (1) Self-similarity; the similarity exists within an image; (2) The similarity of the contents among different images.

Joint Compression and Encryption: Image encryption is simultaneously performed in the compression stage.

Mating Coding: Consider the compression of two or more images. While compressing one of images, the information in other images is also utilized. In decoding, therefore, the information from other images is required.

Mating Ratio: The percentage of the domain blocks selected from a specific image.

Mating Table: A binary array which is used to shuffle the fractal codes of two or more images.

Compilation of References

3GPP (2003). *3GPP TSG SA WG3 Security - S3#28 S3-030257. PayTV model*. Retrieved February 29, 2008 from http://www.3gpp.org/ftp/tsg_sa/WG3_Security/TSGS3_28_Berlin/Docs/PDF/S3-030257.pdf

Abadi, M., Burrows, M., Manasse, M., & Wobber T. (2005). Moderately Hard, Memory-Bound Functions. *ACM Transactions on Internet Technology, 5(2)*, 299-327.

Ackerman, E. (2003). *Student skirts CD's piracy guard*, http://www.newmediamusings.com/blog/2003/10/student_skirts_.html

Adobe® LiveCycle® ES Rights Management for multiformat enterprise rights management. (2006, September). Adobe. Retrieved from http://www.adobe.com/products/livecycle/pdfs/95009150_lc_es_rts_mngmt_multi_sb_ue.pdf.

Adya, A., Bolosky, W. J., Castro, M., Chaiken, R., Cermak, G., Douceur, J. R., Howell, J., Lorch, J., R., Theimer, M., & Wattenhofer, R. P.. (2002). FARSITE: Federated, Available, and Reliable Storage for an Incompletely Trusted Environment. In *Proc. of the 5th Symposium on Operating Systems Design and Implementation.*

AES. (2006). Advanced Encryption Standard. Retrieved March 2006 from http://csrc.nist.gov/CryptoToolkit/aes/

Agi, I., & Gong, L.. (1996). An Empirical study of mpeg video transmissions. In *Proceedings of the Internet Society Symposium on Network and Distributed System Security*. San Diego. 137–144.

Agrawal, R., Kiernan, J., Srikant, R., & Xu, Y. (2002). Hippocratic Databases. *Int. Conf. on Very Large Data Bases.*

Akl, S., & Taylor, P. (1983). Cryptographic solution to a problem of access-control in a hierarchy. *ACM Transactions on Computer Systems, 1*(3), 239-248.

Akyol, E., Tekalp, A., & Civanlar, M. (2005, September). Scalable multiple description video coding with flexible number of descriptions. *IEEE International Conference on Image Processing 2005, 3*, Genoa, Italy, 712-715.

Alattar, A. M., & Alattar, O. M. (2004). Watermarking electronic text documents containing justified paragraphs and irregular line spacing. *Proceedings of SPIE, vol. 5306, Security, Steganography, and Watermarking of Multimedia Contents VI*, 685-695.

Al-Karaki, J. N., & Kamal, A. E. (2004). Routing techniques in wireless sensor networks: A survey. *IEEE Wireless Communications, 11*(6), 6-28.

Ambroze, A., Wade, G., Serdean, C., Tomlinson, M., Stander, J., & Borda, M. (2001). Turbo code protection of video watermark channel. *IEEE Proc. Vis. Image Signal Process.148*, 54-58.

Amoroso, A., & Masotti, M. (2006). Lightweight Steganography on Smartphones. *Proceedings of the 2nd IEEE International Workshop on Networking Issues in Multimedia Entertainment - Consumer Communications and Networking Conference 2006 Satellite Workshop, vol. 2*, (pp. 1158-1162), Las Vegas, Nevada.

Anciaux N. (2004). *Database Systems on Chip*. Unpublished doctoral dissertation, University of Versailles, France.

Anciaux, N., Benzine, M., Bouganim, L., Jacquemin, K., Pucheral, P., & Shaoyi Yin. (2008) Restoring the Patient Control over her Medical History. *IEEE Int. Symposium on Computer-Based Medical Systems.*

Anciaux, N., Benzine, M., Bouganim, L., Pucheral, P., & Shasha, D. (2007). GhostDB: Querying visible and hidden data without leaks. *ACM SIGMOD Int. Conf. on Management of Data.*

Anciaux, N., Bobineau, C., Bouganim, L., Pucheral, P., & Valduriez, P. (2001). PicoDBMS: Validation and Experience. *Int. Conf. on Very Large Data Bases.*

Anciaux, N., Bouganim, L., & Pucheral, P. (2003). Memory Requirements for Query Execution in Highly Constrained Devices. *Int. Conf. on Very Large Data Bases.*

Anciaux, N., Bouganim, L., & Pucheral, P. (2006). Data Confidentiality: to which extent cryptography and secured hardware can help. *Annals of Télécommunications, 61*(3-4).

Anciaux, N., Bouganim, L., Pucheral, P., & Valduriez, P. (in press). DiSC: Benchmarking Secure Chip DBMS. *IEEE Transactions on Knowledge and Data Engineering.*

Anderson, R. (2001). *Security Engineering: A Guide to Build Dependable Distributed Systems*, John Wiley & Sons, Inc. http://www.cl.cam.ac.uk/~rja14/book.html

Anderson, R., & Manifavas, C. (1997, January). Chameleon - A new kind of stream cipher. In *Proceedings of the Fourth International Workshop on Fast Software Encryption FSE'97* (pp. 107–113).

Anderson, R., & Petitcolas, F. (1998). On the limits of steganography. IEEE Journal Selected Areas in Communications: Special Issue on Copyright and Privacy, 16 (5), 474-481.

Androutsellis-Theotokis, S. (2004). A survey of peer-to-peer content distribution technologies. ACM Computing Surveys, *36*, 335–371.

Anonymous. (2006). Hymn Manual, Retrieved on August 30, 2006 at http://hymn-project.org/documentation.php.

Aoki, Y. (2001). Fresnel Transform of Images for Applications to Watermarking. *Electronics and Communications, Japan, 82*, 1612-1622.

Apostolopoulos, J. (2000, September). Error-resilient video compression through the use of multiple states. *IEEE International Conference on Image Processing 2000, 3*, Vancouver, Canada, 352-355.

Apple Computers, Inc. (2006). MPEG-4: The container for digital media, Retrieved on August 21, 2006 at http://www.apple.com/quicktime/technologies/mpeg4/.

Aramvith, S., & Hantanong, W. (Dec. 2006). Joint Flexible Macroblock Ordering and FEC for H.264 Wireless Video Transmission. *Paper presented at the IEEE Symposium on Intelligent Signal Processing and Communications (ISPACS).*

Aramvith, S., Lin, C.-W., Roy, S., & Sun, M.-T. (June 2002). Wireless Video Transport using Conditional Retransmission and Low-Delay Interleaving. *IEEE Trans. on Ckts. and Sys. for Video Tech, 12*(6), 558-565.

Aramvith, S., Pao, I.-M., & Sun, M.-T. (May 2001). A Rate-Control Scheme for Video Transport over Wireless. *IEEE Trans. on Ckts. and Sys. for Video Tech, 11*(5), 569-580.

Arefin F. (2004). *Information hiding in images: Implementing a steganographic application for hiding information in images*, B.S. Thesis, Computing and Information Systems, University of London, London, England.

Arnab, A., & Hutchison, A. (2005, July). *Extending ODRL to Enable Bi-Directional Communication.* In Proceedings of the Second International ODRL Workshop, Lisbon, Portugal.

Arnab, A., & Hutchison, A. (2005, November). *Fairer usage contracts for DRM.* In Proceedings of the Fifth ACM Workshop on Digital Rights Management, pp. 1–7, Alexandria, VA, USA.

Arnab, A., & Hutchison, A. (2007, October). *Persistent Access Control: A Formal Model for DRM.* In DRM '07: Proceedings of the 2007 ACM workshop on Digital Rights Management, pp. 41–53, New York, NY, USA.

Arnold, M., & Schmucker, M. (2003). *Techniques and Applications of Digital Watermarking and Content Protection.* Artech House.

Ates, H. F., & Altunbasak, Y. (February 2008). Rate-Distortion and Complexity Optimized Motion Estimation for H.264 Video Coding. *IEEE Trans. on Ckts. and Sys. for Video Tech, 18*(2).

ATMEL Corporation (2007). Data sheets. Retrieved May 18, 2007 from http://www.atmel.com/dyn/products/data-sheets.asp?family_id=646

Atrey, P. K., Yan, W.-Q., & Kankanhalli, M. (2007). A scalable signature scheme for video authentication. *Springer Journal of Multimedia Tools and Applications*, 34(1), 107–135.

Aubrey de Sélincourt. (1954). *The Histories of Herodotus*. London, Penguin Books.

Audiodriver (2007). http://community.qnx.com/sf/wiki/do/viewPage/projects.bsp/wiki/Audiodriver

Avcibas, I., & Sankur, B. (2002). Statistical analysis of image quality measures. *Journal Electron. Imag., 11*, 206-223.

Avcibas, I., Memon, N., & Sankur, B. (2003). Steganalysis using image quality metrics. *IEEE Trans. Image Processing, 12*(2), 221-229.

Axalto Simagine. (2005). Worldwide Mobile Communication and Java CardTM developer contest. 6th ed. held at 3GSM, Cannes, France. http://www.simagine.axalto.com.

Bai, H., Zhao, Y., & Zhu, C. (2005, May). Optimized multiple description image coding using lattice vector quantization. *IEEE International Symposium on Circuits and Systems, 4*, Kobe, Japan, 4038-4041.

Bai, H., Zhao, Y., & Zhu, C. (2006, October). Multiple Description Shifted Lattice Vector Quantization for Progressive Wavelet Image Coding. *IEEE International Conference on Image Processing 2006*, Atlanta, GA, USA, 797-800.

Bai, H., Zhu, C., & Zhao, Y. (2007, July). Optimized Multiple Description Lattice Vector Quantization for Wavelet Image Coding. *IEEE Transactions on Circuits and Systems for Video Technology, 17*(7), 912-917.

Bailes and Templeton. (2004). Managing P2P security. *Communications of the ACM, 47*, 95–98.

Bajic, I., & Woods, J. (2003, October). Domain-based multiple description coding of images and video. *IEEE Transactions on Image Processing, 12*, 1211-1225.

Balepin, I. (2003). *Superworms and crpytovirology: A deadly combination*, http://wwwcsif.cs.ucdavis.edu/~balepin/new_pubs/worms-cryptovirology.pdf

Banks, W., Friedlander, J., Konyagin, S., and Shparlinski, I. (2006). Incomplete exponential sums and Diffie-Hellman triples. *Math. Proc. Cambridge Philos. Soc. 140*, 193–206.

Bao, F., & Wang, X. (2002). Steganography of Short Messages through Accessories. *Proceedings of Pacific Rim Workshop on Digital Steganography 2002 (STEG'02)*, (pp. 142-147), Kitakyushu, Japan.

Barlas, C. (2006, May). *Digital Rights Expression Languages*. Rightscom Ltd. Retrieved from www.jisc.ac.uk/uploaded_documents/TSW0603.pdf.

Barlas, C., Coyle, K., Daz, T., Erickson, J., Gandee, B., Iannella, R., Kimmel, A., Mathews, R., McCoyd, E., Mooney, S., Parrott, D., Sajka, J., Samtani, R., Shaw, W., & Yaacovi, Y. (2003, March). *OeBF Rights Grammar Requirements*. OeBF. Retrieved from www.idpf.org/specifications/coodinatedfiles/OeBF%20Rights%20Grammar%20Requirements. doc

Barni, M., Bartolini, F., & Piva, A. (2001). Improved Wavelet Based Watermarking Through Pixel-Wise Masking, *IEEE Trans. on Image Processing, 10*, 783-791.

Barni, M., Bartolini, F., De Rosa, A., & Piva, A. (1999). Capacity of the watermarking-channel: how many bits can be hidden within a digital image. In *Security and Watermarking of Multimedia Contents, Proceedings of SPIE, 3657*, 437–448. USA: SPIE Press.

Barni, M., Bartolini, F., De Rosa, A., & Piva, A. (2000). Capacity of full frame DCT image watermarks. *IEEE Transactions on Image Processing, 9*(8), 1450–1455.

Barnsley, M. (1988). A better way to compress images, Byte, 13(1), 215-223.

Bartolini, F., Tefas, A., Barni, M., & Pitas, I. (2001, October). Image Authentication Techniques for Surveillance Applications. *Proc. IEEE, 89*(10), 1403-1418.

Bas, P., Chassery, J.-M., & Davoine, F. (1998). Using the fractal code to watermark images. 1998 IEEE International Conference on Image Processing, 1, 469-473.

Bassia, P., & Pitas, I., & Nikolaidis, N. (2001). Robust audio watermarking in the time domain. *IEEE Trans. on Multimedia, 3*(2) 232–241.

Baugher, M., et al. (2004). The Secure Real Time Transport Protocol, *RFC 3711* http://www.ietf.org/rfc/rfc3711.txt

"Beale Screamer". (2001). *Microsoft's digital rights management scheme—technical details*, http://cryptome.org/ms-drm.htm

Beaumont, J. M. (1990). Advances in block based fractal coding of still images. IEE Colloquium on 'Application of Fractal Techniques in Image Processing,' 3/1-3/5.

Becker, E., Buhse, W, Günnewig, D, & Rump, N. (Eds.), (2003). *Digital Rights Management — Technological, Economic, Legal and Political Aspects*. Berlin, Heidelberg: Springer-Verlag.

Bell, D. E., & LaPadula, L. J. (1976). *Secure computer systems: Unified exposition and multics interpretation (Technical Report ESD-TR-73-306)*. The MITRE Corporation.

Bender, W., Gruhl, D., Morimoto, N., & Lu, A. (1996). Techniques for data hiding. *IBM Systems Journal, 35*(3-4), 313-336.

Bennett, K. (2004). *Linguistic Steganography: Survey, Analysis, and Robustness Concerns for Hiding Information in Text* (CERIAS Technical Report 2004-13). Purdue University.

Berket, K., Essiari, A., & Muratas, A. (2004). PKI-based security for peer-to-peer information sharing. *Proceedings of the Fourth International Conference on Peer-to-Peer Computing.*

Berstel, J., & Boasson, L. (2002). *Formal Properties of XML Grammars and Languages.* Acta Informatica, 38(9), 649–671.

Bertino E., Castano S., & Ferrari E. (2001). Securing XML documents with Author-X. *IEEE Internet Computing, 5*(3).

Bertino, E., & Ferrari, E. (2002). Secure and Selective Dissemination of XML Documents. *ACM Transactions on Information and System Security, 5*(2).

Bertino, E., Castano, S., Ferrari, E., & Mesiti, M. (2000). Specifying and Enforcing Access Control Policies for XML Document Sources. *WWW Journal, 3*(3).

Betamax. (1984). *Sony Corp. of America v. Universal City Studios, Inc.*, 464 U.S. 417, January 17, 1984.

Bewick, S. (1998): *Descrambling DVB data according to ETSI common scrambling specification.* UK Patent Applications GB2322994A / GB2322995A

Biddel, P., England, P., Peinado, M., & Willman, B. (2002). The Darknet and the Future of Content Distribution. Microsoft Corporation. *Digital Rights Management Conference.*

Birget, J., Zou, X., Noubir, G., & Ramamurthy, B. (2001). Hierarchy-Based Access Control in Distributed Environments. *IEEE International Conference on Communications.*

Blakley, G. R. (1979). Safeguarding Cryptographic Keys. Proceedings of AFIPS 1979 National Computer Conference, 48, 313-317.

Bloom, J. A., Cox, I. J., Kalker, T., Linnartz, J. P., Miller, M. L., & Traw, C. B. (1999, July). Copy Protection for Digital Video. *Proceedings IEEE, Special Issue on Identification and Protection of Multimedia Information, 87*(7), 1267-1276.

Bodo, Y., Laurent, N., & Dugelay, J. (2003). Watermarking video, hierarchical embedding in motion vectors. In *IEEE International Conference on Image Processing*, Spain.

Bolchini, C., Salice, F., Schreiber, F. A., & Tanca, L. (2003). Logical and physical design issues for smart card databases. *ACM Transactions on Information Systems, 21*(3).

Boneh, D. (1998). The Decision Diffie-Hellman problem. *Lecture Notes in Computer Science 1423*, 48–63.

Boneh, D., & Lipton, R. J. (1996). Algorithms for black-box fields and their application to cryptography (extended abstract). In *CRYPTO '96: Proceedings of the 16th Annual International Cryptology Conference on Advances in Cryptology*, London, UK, pp. 283–297. Springer-Verlag.

Boneh, D., & Shaw, J. (1998). Collusion-Secure Fingerprinting for Digital Data. *IEEE Trans. Information Theory, 44*(5), 1897-1905.

Boneh, D., Gentry, C., Lynn, B., & Shacham, H. (2003). Aggregate and Verifiably Encrypted Signatures from

Bilinear Maps. In Eli Biham (Ed.): *Advances in Cryptology - EUROCRYPT 2003*.

Bornstein, N. (2007). *Hacking iTunes*, Retrieved on April 5, 2007 at http://www.xml.com/pub/a/2004/11/03/itunes.html.

Borujeni, S.E. (2000). Speech encryption based on fast Fourier transform permutation. *Proc. of The 7th IEEE International Conference on Electronics, Circuits and Systems, 1*, 290–293.

Bouganim, L., & Pucheral, P. (2002). Chip-Secured Data Access: Confidential Data on Untrusted Servers. *Int. Conf. on Very Large Data Bases*.

Bouganim, L., & Pucheral, P. (2007). Fairness concerns in digital right management models. *Int. Journal of Internet and Enterprise Management, 5*(1).

Bouganim, L., Dang-Ngoc, F., & Pucheral, P. (2004). Client-Based Access Control Management for XML Documents. *Int. Conf. on Very Large Data Bases*.

Bouganim, L., Pucheral, P., & Dang-Ngoc, F. (2007). Dynamic Access-Control Policies on XML Encrypted Data. *ACM Transactions on Information and System Security, 10*(4).

Bramberger, M., Doblander, A., Maier, A., Rinner, B., & Schwabach, H. (2006). Distributed embedded smart cameras for surveillance applications. *IEEE Computer, 39*(2), 68–75.

Briscoe, B., & Fairman, I. (1999). Nark: Receiver-based multicast nonrepudiation and key management. In *Proceedings of the First ACM conference on Electronic commerce* (pp. 22–30).

Britannica. (2007). *Encyclopedia Brittanica Online*, Retrieved December 12, 2008 from http://www.britannica.com.

Brown, A. (1994). *S-Tools for Windows*. Shareware. ftp://idea.sec.dsi.unimi.it/pub/security/crypt/code/s-tools4.zip.

Brown, I., Perkins, C., & Crowcroft, J. (1999, November). Watercasting: Distributed watermarking of multicast media. In *Proceedings of the First International COST264 Workshop on Networked Group Communication* NGC'99, (pp. 286–300).

Buragohain, C., Agrawal, D., & Suri, S. (2003). A Game Theoretic Framework for Incentives in P2P Systems. In *Proc. of the 3rd IEEE Int. Conf. on Peer-to-Peer Computing*, 48-56.

Cachin, C. (1998). Information-theoretic model for steganography. In Second int. workshop on information hiding (Vol. 1525, p. 306-318). Springer Berlin / Heidelberg.

Cai, X., Ali, F. H., & Stipidis, E. (2003). MPEG-4 over local area mobile surveillance system. In *Proceedings of the IEE Symposium on Intelligence Distributed Surveillance Systems, 15*(3), 1-15.

Cajote, R. D., Aramvith, S., Guevara, R. C. L., & Miyanaga, Y. (May 2007, May 2007). *FMO Slice Group Maps Using Spatial and Temporal Indicators for H.264 Wireless Video Transmission*. Paper presented at the Int'l Symposium in Ckts. and Systems (ISCAS), Seatle, Washington.

Calbet, X. (2006). *Writing device drivers in Linux: a brief tutorial*. http://www.freesoftwaremagazine.com/articles/drivers_linux

Camouflage (2008), CamouflageSoftware, http://camouflage.unfiction.com, last visited: January 23, 2008.

Canetti, R., Friedlander, J., Konyagin, S., Larsen, M., Lieman, D, & Shparlinski, I. (2000). On the statistical properties of Diffie-Hellman distributions. *Israel Journal of Mathematics 120*(part A), 23–46.

Canetti, R., Friedlander, J., & Shparlinski, I. (1999). On certain exponential sums and the distribution of Diffie-Hellman triples. *J. London Math. Soc. 59*, 799–812.

Caronni, G., & Schuba, C. (2001, December). Enabling hierarchical and bulk-distribution for watermarked content. In *Proceedings 17th Annual Computer Security Applications Conference ACSAC'01*, (pp. 277-285).

Carrasco, L. C. (1999). RDBMS's for Java Cards ? What a Senseless Idea !. http://www.sqlmachine.com

CDFreaks. (2002). *Easy solution to bypass latest CD-audio protection*, 2002, http://www.cdfreaks.com/news/4068

Celik, M. U., Sharma, G., & Tekalp, A. M. (2005). Collusion-resilient fingerprinting by random pre-warping. *IEEE Signal Processing Letters*, Preprint.

Celik, M. U., Sharma, G., Tekalp, A. M., & Saber, E. S. (2002). Video authentication with self-recovery. In *SPIE Security and Watermarking of Multimedia Contents IV, Vol. 4675.* (pp 531–541), San Jose, CA, USA.

Celik, M. U., Sharma, G., Tekalp, A. M., & Saber, E. S. (2003). Localized lossless authentication watermark. In *SPIE Security and Watermarking of Multimedia Content V 2003,* Santa Clara, CA, USA.

Celik, M., Sharma, G., & Tekalp, A. (2004). Universal image steganalysis using rate-distortion curves. In Security, steganography, and watermarking of multimedia content VI (Vol. 5306, p. 467-476). IS&T/SPIE.

Cerven, P. (2002). *Crackproof Your Software*, No Starch Press

Chaffin, J., Allision K., Edgecliffe-Johnson, A., & Ibison, D. (2007). Apple sparks battle over copyright. FT.com, February 7 2007. Retrieved January 7, 2008, from http://www.ft.com/cms/s/90c03168-b6ea-11db-8bc2-0000779e2340.html

Champeau, G. (2004). Fnacmusic.com: Le test complet sur Ratiatum.com - Le Peer-to-Peer (P2P) au delà du téléchargement. (In French). http://www.ratiatum.com/p2p.php?id_dossier=1708&page=1.

Chan, C. K., & Cheng, L. M. (2004). Hiding data in images by simple LSB substitution. *Pattern Recognition, 37*(3), 469-474.

Chan, C., Felber, P., Garofalakis, M., & Rastogi, R. (2002). Efficient filtering of XML documents with XPath expressions. *Int. Conf. on Data Engineering.*

Chandak, G. (2005). Can iTunes be weTunes? — Is FairPlay playing fair? 20th BILETA Annual Conference, 2005.

Chandramouli, R. (2002). Mathematical theory for steganalysis. In Security, steganography, and watermarking of multimedia contents IV (Vol. 4675, p. 14-25). IS&T/SPIE.

Chandramouli, R., & Memon, N. (2001). Analysis of LSB based image steganography techniques. *Proceedings of the International Conference on Image Processing, 3,* 1019-1022.

Chandramouli, R., & Memon, N. (2003). Steganography capacity: A steganalysis perspective. In Security, steganography, and watermarking of multimedia contents V (Vol. 5020, p. 173-177). IS&T/SPIE.

Chandramouli, R., Graubard, B., & Richmond, C. (2001). A multiple description framework for oblibious watermarking. *SPIE Security and Watermarking for Multimedia Contents, 3,* 585-593.

Chang, C. C., & Tseng, H. W. (2004). A steganographic method for digital images using side match. *Pattern Recognition, 25*(12), 1431-1437.

Chang, C. C., Hsiao, J. Y., & Chan, C. S. (2003). Finding optiaml least-significant-bit substitution in image hiding by dynamic programming strategy. *Pattern Recognition, 36*(7), 1583-1595

Chang, C.-C., & Lin, C.-J. (2001). Libsvm: A library for support vector machines. Software Available at http://www.csie.ntu.edu.tw/~cjlin/libsvm.

Chang, H. T. (2002). Gradient match and side match fractal vector quantizers for images. IEEE Transactions on Image Processing, 11(1), 1-9

Chang, H. T., & Kuo, C. J. (1999). Adaptive schemes for improving fractal block coding of images. Journal of Information Science and Engineering, 15(1), 11-25.

Chang, H. T., & Kuo, C. J. (2000). Iteration-free fractal image coding based on efficient domain pool design. IEEE Transactions on Image Processing, 9(3), 329-339.

Chang, H. T., & Kuo, C. J. (2001). A novel non-iterative scheme for fractal image coding. Journal of Information Science and Engineering, 17(3), 429-443.

Chang, H. T., & Lin, C. C. (2003). Fractal-based mating coding of secured joint compression of images. The Chinese IPPR Conference on Computer Vision, Graphics, and Image Processing, (pp. 802-809), Kingmeng, Taiwan.

Chang, H. T., & Lin, C. C. (2004). Mutual image compression based on fractal mating coding. Proceedings of IEEE International Conference on Multimedia and Expo (ICME 2004), (pp. 1087-1090) Taipei, Taiwan.

Chang, H. T., & Lin, C. C. (2007). Inter-secured joint image compression with encryption purpose based on fractal mating coding. Optical Engineering, 46(3), 037002.

Chang, H. T., Lin, C. C., & Shen, D.-F. (2005). Joint multiple-image compression and encryption based on fractal mating coding for secured image distribution. Proceedings of The Seventh IASTED International Conference on Signal and Image Processing (SIP 2005), (pp. 77-82), Hawaii, USA.

Chang, H., & Atallah, M. J. (2002). Protecting software code by guards. In *Security and Privacy in Digital Rights Management, LNCS 2320*, 150-175. Springer.

Chang, Y. H., & Tsai, W. H. (2003). A steganographic method for copyright protection of HTML documents. *Proceedings of National Computer Symposium 2003*, Taichung, Taiwan.

Chaum, D., & van Antwerpen, H. (1989). Undeniable signatures. In *CRYPTO '89: Proceedings on Advances in cryptology*, New York, NY, USA, pp. 212–216. Springer-Verlag New York, Inc.

Chen, B., & Wornell, G. (2000). Preprocessed and post-processed quantization index modulation methods for digital watermarking. In Security, steganography, and watermarking of multimedia contents III (Vol. 3971). IS&T/SPIE.

Chen, B., & Wornell, G. (2001). Quantization index modulation: A class of provably good methods for digital watermarking and information embedding. *IEEE Transactions on Information Theory, 47*(4), 1423-1443.

Chen, C. (Sept. 1995). Error Detection and Concealment with Unsupervised MPEG2 Video Decoder. *Journal of Visual Communication and Image Representation, 6*(3), 265-278.

Chen, M., He, Y., & Lagendijk, R. L. (2003, August). A Fragile Watermark Error Detection Scheme for Wireless Video Communications. *IEEE Transactions on Multimedia.*

Chen, T.-C., Chang, L.-F., Wong, A. H., Sun, M.-T., & Hsing, T. R. (April 1995). Real-time software-based end-to-end wireless visual communications simulation platform. *Paper presented at the Proc. of SPIE: Visual Comms and Image Processing.*

Chen, Y. Y., Pan, H. K., & Tseng, Y. C. (2000). A Secure Data Hiding Scheme for Two-Color Images. *Proceedings of the Fifth IEEE Symposium on Computers and Communications (ISCC 2000)*, (pp. 750-755), Antibes, France.

Cheng, H. T., & Li, X. (2000). Partial encryption of compressed images and videos. IEEE Transactions on Signal Processing, 48(8), 2439-2451.

Cherriman, P., & Hanzo, L. (June 1998). Programmable H,263-based video transceivers for interference-limited environments. *IEEE Trans. on Ckts. and Sys. for Video Tech, 8*(3), 275-286.

Chiang, T., & Zhang, Y.-Q. (1997). A new rate control scheme using quadratic rate distortion model. *IEEE Trans. on Ckts. and Sys. for Video Tech, 7*(1), 246-250.

Cho, S., Amer-Yahia, S., Lakshmanan, L., & Srivastava, D. (2002). Optimizing the secure evaluation of twig queries. *Int. Conf. on Very Large Data Bases.*

Chong, C. N., Corin, R., Etalle, S., Hartel, P., Jonker, W., & Law, Y. W. (2003, September). *LicenseScript: A Novel Digital Rights Language and its Semantics.* In proceedings of the Third International Conference on the Web Delivery of Music, pages 122–129, Los Alamitos, CA USA.

Christian, R., & Dugelay, J. L. (2002). A survey of watermarking algorithms for image authentication. *Journal of Applied Signal Processing,* (6), 613–621.

Christopoulos, C., Skodras, A., & Ebrahimi, T. (2000). The JPEG2000 still image coding system: an overview. IEEE Transactions on Consumer Electronics, 46(4), 1103-1127.

Chu, H. H., Qiao, L., & Nahrstedt, K. (2002, April). A secure multicast protocol with

Chu, R., You, X., Kong, X., & Ba, X. (2004). A DCT-based image steganographic method resisting statistical attacks. In *Proc. International Conference on Acoustics, Speech, and Signal Processing*, Montereal, Quebec, Canada.

Chu, S., Hsin, Y., Huang, H., Huang, K., & Pan, J. (2005, May). Multiple description watermarking for lossy network. *IEEE International Symposium on Circuits and Systems,* 3990-3993.

Cisco (2006). *Cisco Systems IP Network-Centric Video Surveillance*. White paper.

Clark, D. D. (1988). The design philosophy of the DARPA internet protocols. *ACM SIGCOMM Computer Communication Review, 18*(4), 106-114.

Class UID. (2006). Retrieved May 2006 from http://java.sun.com/j2se/1.4.2/docs/api/java/rmi/server/UID.html

Cole, E. (2003). *Hiding in Plain Sight: Steganography and the Art of Covert Communication.* London: Wiley Publishing Incorporation.

Collberg, C., Thomborson, C., & Low, D. (1997). *A taxonomy of obfuscating transformations.* Technical Report 148, Department of Computer Science, University of Auckland, July 1997

Common Criteria. The Common Criteria for Information Technology Security Evaluation. http://www.common-criteriaportal.org/

Computer Security Institute. (2007). CSI/FBI Computer Crime and Security Survey. http://www.gocsi.com/

Conax (2002). Conax Newsletter 3-2002, Retrieved January 7, 2007, from http://www.conax.com/pdf/newsletter3_2002.pdf

ContentGuard. (2004). MPEG-21 Right Expression Language (MPEG-REL), ISO/IEC 21000-5:2004 standard, http://www.contentguard.com/MPEGREL_home.asp

copyright protection. *ACM SIGCOMM Computer Communications Review, 32*(2), 42–60.

Coral Consortium (whitepaper, 2006). *Coral consortium whitepaper.*

CORAL. (2007). *DRM Interoperability Consortium Invites Steve Jobs to Join*, Coral Consortium, Feb. 9, 2007, http://www.coral-interop.org/main/news/pr20070209.html

Costa, M. (1983). Writing on Dirty Paper. *IEEE Transactions on Information Theory, 29*(3), 439–441.

Cox, B. (1994). *Superdistribution.* Wired Magazine, September 1994, pp 89.92.

Cox, B. (1996). *Superdistribution Objects as Property on the Electronic Frontier*, Addison-Wesley.

Cox, I. J., & Linnartz, J.-P. (1998). Some general methods for tempering with watermarks. *IEEE Journal of Selected Areas in Communication, 16*(4), 587-593.

Cox, I. J., & Miller, M. L. (2001). Electronic watermarking: the first 50 years. In *Proc. IEEE Fourth Workshop on Multimedia Signal Processing*, pp. 225-230.

Cox, I. J., Bloom, J., Miller, M., & Cox, I. (2001). *Digital watermarking: Principles & Practice.* Morgan Kaufmann.

Cox, I. J., Kilian, J., Leighton, F. T., & Shamoon, T. (1997). Secure spread spectrum watermarking for multimedia. *IEEE Transactions on Image Processing, 6*(12), 1673-1687.

Cox, I. J., Miller, M. L., & Bloom, J. A.. (2000). Watermarking applications and their properties. *Proc. IEEE International Conference on Information Technology, Coding and Computing.* Las Vegas, Nev, USA. 6–10.

Cox, I. J., Miller, M. L., & Bloom, J.A. (2002). *Digital Watermarking.* London: Morgan Kaufmann.

Cox, I. J., Milller, M., & McKellips, A. (1999). Watermarking as communications with side information. *Proceedings of the IEEE, 87*(7), 1127–1141.

Cox, I., Bloom, J., & Miller, M. (2001). Digital watermarking: Principles & practice. *The Morgan Kaufmann Series in Multimedia and Information Systems.* Morgan Kaufmann.

Cox, I., Kilian, J., Leighton, T., & Shamoon, T. (1997, December). Secure spread spectrum watermarking for multimedia. *IEEE Transactions on Image Processing, 6*, 1673-1687.

Coyle, K., (2004, February). *Rights Expression Languages.* The Library of Congress, Retrieved from www.loc.gov/standards/relreport.pdf.

Crowcroft, J., Handley, M., & Wakeman, I. (1999). *Internetworking Multimedia.* Morgan Kaufmann, 1999

Cryptography. (2008). Retrieved January 8, 2008, from http://dictionary.reference.com/browse/cryptography.

CSA (2007). CSA – known facts and speculations. Retrieved February 29, 2008, from http://csa.irde.to/

Curran, K., & Bailey, K. (2003). An Evaluation of Image Based Steganography Methods. *International Journal of Digital Evidence 2(2),* 1-40.

Cvejic, N., & Seppanen, T. (2002). A wavelet domain LSB insertion algorithm for high capacity audio steganography. *Proceedings of 10th IEEE Digital Signal Processing Workshop and 2nd Signal Processing Education Workshop*, 53- 55.

Cvejic, N., & Seppanen, T. (2004). Channel capacity of high bit rate audio data hiding algorithms in diverse transform domains. *Proceeding of 2004 IEEE International Symposium on Communications and Information Technology (ISCIT 2004), vol.1*, 84- 88.

Daemen, J., and Rijmen, V. (2002). The Design of Rijndael: AES – The Advanced Encryption Standard. Springer-Verlag.

Dai, J. (2006). QuickPay: *Protocol for online payment*. Graduate Project. Retrieved October 2006 from http://www.cs.sjsu.edu/faculty/stamp/students/QuickPayReport.pdf

Dai, Y., Thiemert, S., & Steinebach, M. (2004). Feature-based watermarking scheme for MPEG-I/II video authentication. In *Proc. SPIE, Security and Watermarking of Multimedia Contents VI, San Jose, 5306*, 325-335.

Dai, Y., Zhang, L., & Yang, Y. (2003). A new method of MPEG video watermarking technology. In *Proceedings of ICCT*, 1845-1847.

Damiani, E., De Capitani di Vimercati, S., Paraboschi, S., & Samarati, P. (2002). A Fine-Grained Access Control System for XML Documents. *ACM Transactions on Information and System Security, 5*(2).

Damiani, E., De Capitani, S., Paraboschi, S., Samarati, P., & Violante, F. (2002). A Reputation-Based Approach for Choosing Reliable Resources in Peer-to-Peer Networks. In *Proc. of the 9th ACM Conf. on Computer and Communications Security*, 207-216.

Dang, P. P., & Chau, P. M. (2000). Image encryption for secure Internet multimedia applications. IEEE Transactions on Consumer Electronics, 46(3), 395-403.

Daniel, C., & Bijan, M. (2002). Watermarking for self-authentication of compressed video. In *IEEE International Conference on Image Processing 2002, Vol. II*, (pp 913–916), Rochester, New York, USA.

Daswani, Garcia-Mollia, & Yang. (2002). Open problems in data-sharing peer-to-peer systems. *Proceedings of the 9th International Conference on Database Theory, 2572*, pp. 1–15.

Daswani, N., & García-Molina, H. (2004). Pong-Cache Poisoning in GUESS. In *Proc. of the 11th ACM Conf. on Computer and communications security*, 98-109.

Dawei, A., Guanrong, C., & Wenbo, L. (2004). A chaos based robust wavelet-domain watermarking algorithm. *Chaos, Solitons and Fractals, 22*, 47-54.

Day, M., Lee, S., & Jou, I. (2007). Robust multirate lattice quantization index modulation watermarking resilient to multiple description transmission channel. *SPIE Optical Engineering, 46*(3), 037005.

Defigueiredo, D., Garcia, A., & Kramer, B. (2002). Analysis of Peer-to-Peer Network Security using Gnutella. University of California Technical Report.

Deguillaume, F., Voloshynovskiy, S., & Pun, T. (2002). A method for the estimation and recovering from general affine transforms in digital watermarking applications. *Proceedings of the SPIE Security and Watermarking of Multimedia Contents IV, 4675*, 313-322.

Desmedt, Y. (1997). Some Recent Research Aspects of Threshold Cryptography. In *Proc. of the 1st. Int. Workshop on Information Security, LNCS 1196*, 58-173. Springer-Verlag.

Desset, C., Macq, B., & Vandendorpe, L. (2002). Block error-correcting codes for systems with a very high BER: Theoretical analysis and application to the protection of watermarks. *Signal Processing: Image Communication, 17*, 409-421.

Dhondt, Y., Lambert, P., & Walle, R. V. d. (2006). A Flexible Macroblock Scheme for Unequal Error Protection. *Paper presented at the Int'l Conf. on Image Processing*.

Dhondt, Y., Mys, S., Zutter, S. D., & Walle, R. V. d. (June 2007). An Alternative Scatter Pattern for Flexible Macroblock Ordering in H.264/AVC. *Paper presented at the International Symposium on Image Analysis and Multimedia Interactive Services*.

Diao, Y., & Franklin, M. (2003). High-performance XML filtering: An overview of filter. *Int. Conf. on Data Engineering*.

Diffie, W., & Hellman, M. (1976). New directions in cryptography. *IEEE Transactions on Information Theory 22*(6), 644–654.

Diffie, W., Oorschot, P. C. V., & Wiener, M. J. (1992). Authentication and authenticated key exchanges. *Des. Codes Cryptography 2*(2), 107–125.

Diggavi, S. N., Sloane, N. J. A., & Vaishampayan, V. A. (2002, May). Asymmetric multiple description lattice vector quantizers. *IEEE Transactions on Information Theory, 48*(1), 174-191.

Digimarc Corporation. (2007). *Digimarc (DMRC)*, Retrieved December 12, 2007, from http://www.digimarc.com/.

Dinitz, J. H., & Stinson, D. R. (1992). Contemporary Design Theory: A Collection of Surveys, New York: Wiley, 1992.

Distributed Computing Industry Association. (2004). Proposed business models for digital music distribution. Retrieved January 2006 from http://www.dcia.info/model.ppt

Dittman, J., Steinmetz, A., & Steinmetz, R. (1999), Content based digital signature for motion pictures authentication and content-fragile watermarking. In *IEEE International Conference on Multimedia Computing and Systems, Vol. II, 1999,* (pp 209), Firenze, Italy.

Dittmann, J., Fiebig, T., Steinmetz, R., et al. (2000). Combined video and audio watermarking: Embedding content information in multimedia data. In *Proc. SPIE Electronic Imaging'00, Security and Watermarking of Multimedia Content II*, San Jose, 2000, pp. 397-408.

DMCA. (1998). *The Digital Millennium Copyright Act of 1998* - U.S. Copyright Office Summary. http://www.copyright.gov/legislation/dmca.pdf

Doctorow, C. (2002). EFF Consensus at Lawyerpoint, Hollywood want to plug the 'analog hole', May 23, 2002, http://bpdg.blogs.eff.org/archives/000113.html

Doërr, G., & Dugelay, J. (2003). Video Watermarking: Overview and Challenges. *Handbook of Video Databases: Design and Applications, Chapter 42,* by Furht, B., & Marques, O. (Editors), CRC Press.

Doërr, G., & Dugelay, J. (2004). Security Pitfalls of Frame-by-Frame Approaches to Video Watermarking.

IEEE Transactions on Signal Processing, Supplement on Secure Media, 52(10), 2955-2964.

Doërr, G., & Dugelay, J. L. (2003). A Guide Tour of Video Watermarking. *Signal Processing: Image Communication, 18(4).* 263-282.

Douceur, J. R. (2002). The Sybil Attack. In *Proc. of the 1st Int. Workshop on Peer-to-Peer Systems*, 251-260.

Drahos, P., & Maher, I., (Eds.), (2004). *Information Economics and Policy. Special Issue.* Elsevier.

Du, R., & Fridrich, J. (2002). Lossless authentication of MPEG-2 video. In *IEEE International Conference on Image Processing, Vol. II,* (pp 893–896), Rochester, NY, USA.

Duda, R., & Hart, P. (1973). Pattern classification and scene analysis. New York, NY: John Wiley.

Dugelay, J. L., & Petitcolas, F. A. (2000). Possible counter-attacks against random geometric distortions. In *SPIE Electronic Imaging, Security and Watermarking of Multimedia Contents II, Vol. 3971.* (pp 338–345), San Jose, CA, USA.

Dulce, R. H.-M., Raul, R.-C., & Claudia, F.-U. (2007). *Adaptive steganography based on textures.* Paper presented at the Proceedings of the 17th International Conference on Electronics, Communications and Computers, Washington, DC, USA.

Dumitrescu, S., Wu, X., & Wang, Z. (2002). Detection of lsb steganography via sample pair analysis. In 5th int. workshop on information hiding (Vol. 2578). Springer Berlin / Heidelberg.

Dyer, J., G., Lindemann, M., Perez, R., Sailer, R., van Doorn, L., Smith, S. W., & Weingart, S. (2001). Building the IBM 4758 Secure Coprocessor. *IEEE Computer, 24*(10).

Eason, R. (2003). A tutorial on BPCS steganography and its applications. *Proceedings of IEEE Pacific-Rim Workshop on Digital Steganography*, 18-31

ECB – European Central Bank. (2002). *The Euro – Our Money.* Retrieved December 20, 2007 from http://www.ecb.int/pub/pdf/other/eurobren.pdf.

Eggers, J., & Girod, B. (2002). *Informed Watermarking.* Boston, MA: Kluwer Academic Publisher.

Eiamjumrus, N., & Aramvith, S. (Dec. 2006). New Rate-Control Scheme based on Cauchy Rate-Distortion Optimization Model for H.264 Video Coding. *Paper presented at the IEEE International Symposium on Intelligent Signal Processing and Communication Systems*, Japan.

Eiamjumrus, N., & Aramvith, S. (Dec. 2006). Rate-Control Scheme based on Cauchy Rate-Distortion Optimization Model for H.264 under Low Delay Constraint. *Paper presented at the IEEE International Conference on Intelligent Information Hiding and Multimedia Signal Processing*, USA.

Eilam, E. (2005). *Reversing: Secrets of Reverse Engineering*. John Wiley & Sons, Inc.

Einhorn, M., A., & Rosenblatt, B. (2005). *Peer-to-Peer networking and digital rights management*. Retrieved January 2006 from http://www.cato.org/pub_display.php?pub_id=3670.

El-Gamal, A., & Cover, T. (1982, November). Achievable rates for multiple descriptions. *IEEE Transactions on Information Theory, 28*, 851-857.

El-Gamal, T. (1984). *Cryptography and logarithms over finite fields*. Ph. D. thesis, Elec. Eng. Dept., Stanford Univ., Stanford, CA.

Emmanuel, S., & Kankanhalli, M. S. (2003). A digital rights management scheme for broadcast video. *Multimedia Systems Journal, 8*, 444–458. ACM-Springer Verlag.

Enabler Release Definition for DRM V2.0. (2003). Open Mobile Alliance, Retrieved from http://xml.coverpages.org/OMA-ERELD_DRM-V2_0_0-20040401-D.pdf.

Eschenauer, L., Gligor, V. D., & Baras, J. (2004). On Trust Establishment in Mobile Ad-Hoc Networks. *Security Protocols, LNCS, 2845*, 47-66. Springer-Verlag.

ETSI (1996). ETSI ETR 289: *Digital Video Broadcasting (DVB); Support for use of scrambling and Conditional Access (CA) within digital broadcasting systems.*

ETSI (2003). ETSI EN 301 192: *DVB Specification for Data Broadcasting*

ETSI (2005). ETSI TS 102 367 V1.1.1: *Digital Audio Broadcasting (DAB); Conditional access.*

Fairplay (2006). *Wikipedia.* Retrieved on August 21, 2006 at http://en.wikipedia.org/wiki/FairPlay

Fairplay. (2006). Retrieved February 2006 from http://en.wikipedia.org/wiki/FairPlay

Fan, W., Chan, C. Y., & Garofalakis, M. (2004). Secure XML Querying with Security Views. *ACM SIGMOD Int. Conf. on Management of Data.*

Fan, Z., & Hongbin, Z. (2004). Capacity and Reliability of Digital Watermarking. *Proceedings of the International conference on the Business of Electronic Product Reliability and Liability*, 162-165.

Farber, N., & Girod, B. (October 1997). Robust H.263 compatible video transmission for mobile acess to video servers. *Paper presented at the IEEE Conf. on Image Processing (ICIP)*, Santa Barbara, CA.

Farid, H. (2001). *Detecting steganographic message in digital images.* Technical Report, TR2001-412, Computer Science, Dartmouth College.

Farkash, S., Raz, S., & Malah, D. (1991). Analog speech scrambling via the Gabor representation. *Proc. of the 17th Convention of Electrical and Electronics Engineers in Israel.* 365–368.

Farrell, S., & Housley, R. (2002). *An Internet Attribute Certificate Profile for Authorization. RFC 3281*, IETF.

Feldman, P. (1987). A practical scheme for non- interactive verifiable secret sharing. In *Proc. of the 28th FOCS*, pp. 427–437. IEEE.

Felten, E. W. (2005). *DRM and Public Policy*, Inside Risks 181, CACM 48, July 7, 2005, http://www.csl.sri.com/users/neumann/insiderisks05.html#181

Ferraiolo, D. F., & Kuhn, D. R. (1992). Role Based Access Control. *15th National Computer Security Conference.*

Fiat, A., & Naor, M. (1994). Broadcast encryption. In Proc. of the 13th Annual Int. *Cryptology Conference on Advances in Cryptology*, 480-491.

Fioravanti, F., Spinu, M., & Campanai, M. (2007). AX-MEDIS as the Service Oriented Architecture for the Media: Is It Feasible?. In *Axmedis* (pp. 264-269).

Fisher, Y. (Ed.). (1995). Fractal Image Compression: Theory and Applications, New York: Springer Verlag.

Fisher, Y., Rogovin, D., & Shen, T. P. (1994). Fractal (self-VQ) encoding of video sequences. Proceedings of SPIE, Vol. 2308, pp. 1359-1370.

Fitzek, F. H. P., & Reisslein, M. (2001) MPEG-4 and H.263 video traces for network performance evaluation. *IEEE Network, 15*(6), 40-54.

Florescu, I., A. Myasnikov and A. Mahalanobis (2007) Statistical analysis of the Diffie-Hellman key exchange protocol in a finite group. arXiv:math/0702155v1

Forrest S. (2006). *Introduction to Deogol*. http://www.wandership.ca/projects/deogol/, last visited: January 23, 2008.

Fox, G. (2001). Peer-to-Peer Networks. *Computing in Science & Engineering, 3*(3).

France, J. (2007). Rhapsody 3.0, Retrieved on April 7, 2007 at http://reviews.cnet.com/Rhapsody_3_0/4505-9239_7-20050753.html?tag=also.

France, Moore, & Dreier. (2007). *Napster*, Retrieved on April 7, 2007 at http://reviews.cnet.com/Napster/4505-3669_7-31302303.html.

France, Viksnins, & Kim. (2007). *eMusic*, Retrieved on April 7, 2007 at http://reviews.cnet.com/eMusic/4505-9240_7-30974740.html?tag=also.

Freeman, J. P. (2001). 2001 report on the closed circuit TV & video surveillance market. In A. Laurin, *Impressive CCTV growth but analog technology lags behind, Axis Company Leaflet*. Available at: http://www.axis.com/documentation/whitepaper/video/2460_article.pdf

Fridrich, J. (1998). Combining low-frequency and spread spectrum Watermarking. *Proceedings of SPIE Symposium on Optical Science, Engineering and Instrumentation, 3456*.

Fridrich, J. (1999). Applications of data hiding in digital images. *Proceeding of ISSPA'99*, 22-25.

Fridrich, J. (2002). Security of fragile authentication watermarks with localization. In *Proc. SPIE Photonic West, 4675*, Electronic Imaging 2002. Security and Watermarking of Multimedia Contents IV. San Jose, 2002, pp. 691-700.

Fridrich, J. (2004). Feature based steganalysis for jpeg images and its implications for future design of stegano-graphic schemes. In 6th int. workshop on information hiding (Vol. 3200). Springer Berlin / Heidelberg.

Fridrich, J., & Goljan, M. (2000). Robust hash functions for digital watermarking. In *International Conference on Coding and Computing*. (pp 178–183), Las Vegas, USA.

Fridrich, J., & Goljan, M. (2003). Digital image steganography using stochastic modeling. In Security, steganography, and watermarking of multimedia content V (Vol. 5020, p. 191-202).

Fridrich, J., & Lisoněk, P. (2007). Grid Coloring in Steganography. *IEEE Transactions on Information Theory, 53*(4), 1547-1549.

Fridrich, J., & Soukal, D. (2006). Matrix embedding for large payloads. *IEEE Transactions on Information Security and Forensics, 1*(3), 390-394.

Fridrich, J., Goljan, M., & Hogea, D. (2002). Attacking the outguess. In ACM workshop on multimedia and security.

Fridrich, J., Goljan, M., & Hogea, D. (2002). Steganalysis of jpeg images: Breaking the F5 algorithm. In 5th int. workshop on information hiding (Vol. 2578, p. 310-323). Springer Berlin / Heidelberg.

Fridrich, J., Goljan, M., & Hogea, D. (2003). New methodology for breaking steganographic techniques for JPEGs. In *Proc. EI SPIE*, Santa Clara, CA, 143-155.

Fridrich, J., Holotyak, T. S., & Soukal, D. (2005). Maximum likelihood estimation of secret message length embedded using +/-k steganography in spatial domain. In Security, Steganography, and Watermarking of Multimedia Content VII (Vol. 5681, p. 595-606). IS&T/SPIE.

Friedl, M., Provos, N., & Simpson, W. (2006). Diffie-Hellman group exchange for the secure shell (SSH) transport layer protocol. Internet proposed standard RFC 4419.

Friedlander, J., & Shparlinski, I. (2001). On the distribution of Diffie-Hellman triples with sparse exponents. *SIAM Journal on Discrete Mathematics, 14*, 162–169.

Fulton, S. M. III (2007). Jupiter analyst: Interoperable drm won't solve music industry dilemma. *BetaNews*, February 16, 5:58 PM 2007. Retrieved October 1, 2007, from http://www.betanews.com/article/Jupiter_Analyst_Interoperable_DRM_Wont_Solve_Music_Industry_Dilemma/1171664985/1

Futureproof. (2006*). JHymn project*, Retrieved on August 24, 2006 at http://hymn-project.org/jhymndoc/.

Gabillon, A. (2004). An Authorization Model for XML DataBases. *ACM Workshop on Secure Web Services.*

Gabillon, A., & Bruno, E. (2001). Regulating access to XML documents. *IFIP Conf. on Database and Application Security.*

Galand, F., & Kabatiansky, G. (2003). Information hiding by coverings. *Proceedings of 2003 IEEE Information Theory Workshop*, 151-514.

Gallager, R. (1965). A simple derivation of the coding theorem and some applications. *IEEE Transactions on Information Theory, 11*(1), 3–17.

Gallery, E., & Tomlinson, A. (2005). Conditional Access in Mobile Systems: Securing the Application. In *The First International Conference on Distributed Frameworks for Multimedia Applications DFMA 05*, France: IEEE.

Gallery, E., & Tomlinson, A. (2007). *Secure delivery of conditional access applications to mobile receivers*. In Leung, A., Yau, P.W., & Mitchell, C.J. (2007).

Gang, L., Akansu, A. N., & Ramkumar, M. (2001). MP3 resistant oblivious steganography. *Proceedings of 2001 IEEE International Conference on Acoustics, Speech, and Signal Processing (ICASSP'01), 3*, 1365-1368.

Gapper, J. (2007). *Why digital music should be set free*, Financial Times, Asia edition, Comment, February 12, 2007, p. 17.

Gasser, M., Goldstein, A., Kaufman, C., & Lampson, B. (1989). The Digital distributed system security architecture. In *Proceedings of the 12th National Computer Security Conference* (pp. 305-319). Baltimore: NIST/NCSC.

Ge, Q., Lu, Z., & Niu, X. (2003). Oblivious Video Watermarking Scheme with Adaptive Embedding Mechanism. *Proceedings of the Second International Conference on Machine Learning and Cybernetics*, (pp. 2876-2881), Xian, China.

Gehrke, N., & Schumann, M. (2002). Constructing electronic marketplaces using peer-to-peer technology.

Proceedings of the 36th Hawaii International Conference on System Sciences.

Gemmell, D.J., Vin, H. M., Kandlur, D. D., Venkat Rangan, P., & Rowe, L. A. (1995). Multimedia storage servers: a tutorial. *IEEE Computer, 28*(5), 40-49.

Generic Authentication Architecture. *Generic Bootstrapping Architecture (Release 6), 3rd Generation Partnership Project*. Technical Specification 3GPP TS 33.220. http://www.3gpp.org/

Gennaro, R., & Rohatgi, P. (1997). How to sign digital streams. In Burton S. Kaliski Jr. (Ed.): *Advances in Cryptology – CRYPTO 1997.*

Gennaro, R., Krawczyk, H., & Rabin, T. (2004). Secure hashed diffie-hellman over non-ddh groups. In *Advances in Cryptology - EUROCRYPT 2004*, Lecture Notes in Computer Science, pp. 361–381. Springer Berlin / Heidelberg.

Gentry, C., Hevia, A., Jain, R., Kawahara, T., & Ramzan, Z. (2005). End-to-End Security in the Presence of Intelligent Data Adapting Proxies: The Case of Authenticating Transcoded Streaming Media. *Journal of Selected Areas of Communication, Q1, 2005.*

Gersho, A., & Grey, R. M. (1992). Vector Quantization and Signal Compression, Boston, MA: Kluwer.

Giguère, E. (2001). Mobile Data Management: Challenges of Wireless and Offline Data Access. *Int. Conf. on Data Engineering.*

Gilbert, E. N. (Sept. 1960). Capacity of Burst-noise Channel. *Bell Systems Technical Journal, 39*, 1253-1266.

Gnutella clients. (2006). Retrieved January 2006 from http://www.gnutella.com/connect

Gnutella. (2006). Retrieved January 2006 from http://en.wikipedia.org/wiki/Gnutella

Gnutella. Retrieved Jan 18, 2008 from Vanguard Gnutella Web site: http://www.gnutella.com

Goldblatt, R. (1987). *Logics of time and computation, 7*. Center for the Study of Language and Information, Stanford, CA, USA.

Goldreich, O. (2001). *Foundations of Cryptography: Basic Techniques, 1*. Cambridge University Press.

Goldwasser, S., & Micali, S. (1984). Probabilistic encryption. *Journal of Computer and System Sciences, 28,* 270–299.

Golle, P., & Modadugu, N. (2001). Authenticated streamed data in the presence of random packet loss. In *Proceeding of Network and Distributed System Security Symposium (NDSS)*, San Diego, CA, Feb. 2001.

Gopalan, K. (2003). Audio steganography using bit modification. *Proceedings of the IEEE International Conference on Acoustics, Speech, and Signal Processing, (ICASSP '03), 2,* 421-424.

Gortz, N., & Leelapornchai, P. (2003, March). Optimization of the Index Assignment for Multiple Description Vector Quantizers. *IEEE Transactions on Communications, 51*(3), 336-340.

Goyal, V. (2001, September). Multiple description coding: Compression meets the network. *IEEE Transactions on Signal Processing, 18,* 74-93.

Green, T., Gupta, A., Miklau, G., Onizuka, M., & Suciu, D. (2004). Processing XML streams with deterministic automata and stream indexes. *ACM Transaction on Database Systems, 29*(4).

Grimen, G., Mönch, C., & Midtstraum, R. (2006). Building secure software-based DRM systems. *Norsk informatikkonferanse.*

Grimm, R., & Nützel, J. (2002). Security and business models for virtual goods. In *Proceedings of the 2002 ACM Multimedia Security Workshp* (pp. 75–79). ACM.

Grimm, R., & Nützel, J. (2003). Potato system and signed media format — an alternative approach to online music business. In *Proceedings of the 3rd International Conference on Web Delivering of Music (WEDELMUSIC 2003)* (pp. 23–26). IEEE Press.

Gui, G.-F., Jiang, L.-G., & Chen, H. (2006). A New Asymmetric Watermarking Scheme for Copyright Protection. *IEICE TRANS. FUNDAMENTALS, 89,* 611-614.

Guignard, B. (2002). *How secure is PDF?* http://www.cs.cmu.edu/~dst/Adobe/Gallery/PDFsecurity.pdf

Gunter, C., Weeks, S., & Wright. A. (2001). *Models and Languages for Digital Rights.* In HICSS '01: Proceedings of the 34th Annual Hawaii International Conference on System Sciences (HICSS-34), 9, p. 9076, Washington, DC, USA.

Guo Y. B., & Ma, J. F. (2004). Practical Secret Sharing Scheme Realizing Generalized Adversary Structure. *Journal of Computer Research and Development, 19*(4), 564-569 (In Chinese).

Guo, H., & Georganas, N. D. (2003). A novel approach to digital image watermarking based on a generalized secret sharing schemes. Multimedia Systems, 9, 249-260.

Guo, J., & Shi, P. F. (2002, December). Object-based watermarking scheme robust to object manipulations. *Electronics Letter, 38*(25), 1656 –1657.

Guo, Y. B., Ma, J. F., & Wang, Y. D. (2005). An Efficient Secret Sharing Scheme Realizing Graph-Based Adversary Structures. *Journal of Computer Research and Development, 42*(5), 877-882 (In Chinese).

Guth, S. (2003). A sample DRM system. *In Digital Rights Management, LNCS 2770,* 150-161. Springer.

Guth, S., (2003). *Rights Expression Languages.* In Digital Rights Management, *2770/2003,* pp. 101–112. Springer Berlin / Heidelberg.

Hacigumus, H., Iyer, B., Li, C., & Mehrotra, S. (2002). Executing SQL over encrypted data in the database-service-provider model. *ACM SIGMOD Int. Conf. on Management of Data.*

Haitsma, J., & Kalker, T. (2002). A highly robust audio fingerprinting system. In *Proceedings of the 3rd International Conference on Music Information Retrieval.*

Halpern, J. Y., & Weissman, V. (2008). *A Formal Foundation for XrML.* Journal of ACM, 55(1), 1–42.

Halpern, J. Y., & Weissman, V. (2004, June). *A Formal Foundation for XrML Licenses.* In Proceedings of the 17th IEEE Computer Security Foundations Workshop, pages 251–265, Asilomar, CA, USA.

Halsall, F. (2001). Multimedia Communications: Applications, Networks, Protocols, and Standards. Reading, MA: Addison-Wesley.

Hamilton, S., & Lodder, R. (2002). Hyperspectral imaging technology for pharmaceutical analysis. In *Proceedings of the Society of Photo-Optical Instrumentation Engineers Conference, 4626*, 136-147.

Han, et. al. (2004). A mutual anonymous peer-to-peer protocol design. *Proceedings of the 19th IEEE International Parallel and Distributed Processing Symposium*, p. 68.

Hantanong, W., & Aramvith, S. (August 2005, August 2005). Analysis of Macroblock-to-slice Group Mapping for H.264 Video Transmission over Packet-based Wireless Fading Channel. *Paper presented at the 48th Midwest Symposium on Circuits and Systems.*

Harel, D. (1979*). First-Order Dynamic Logic.* Springer-Verlag New York, Inc., Secaucus, NJ, USA.

Harmsen, J., & Pearlman, W. (2003). Steganalysis of additive noise modelable information hiding. In Security, Steganography, and Watermarking of Multimedia Content V (Vol. 5020, p. 131-142). IS&T/SPIE.

Harrison, M. A., Ruzzo, W. L., & Ullman, J. D. (1976). Protection in Operating Systems. *Communication of the ACM, 19*(8).

Hartung, F. (1999*). Digital watermarking and fingerprinting of uncompressed and compressed video.* Ph.D. dissertation, University Erlangen-Nurnberg.

Hartung, F., & Girod, B. (1997). Copyright Protection in Video Delivery Networks by Watermarking of Pre-Compressed Video. *Proceedings of the Second European Conference on Multimedia Applications, Services and Techniques, Springer Lecture Notes in Computer Science, 1242*, 423436, Springer, Heidelberg, Milan, Italy.

Hartung, F., & Girod, B. (1998). Watermarking of uncompressed and compressed video. *Signal Processing, 66*(3), 283–301.

Hartung, F., & Kutter, M. (1999). Multimedia Watermarking Techniques. *Proceedings of the IEEE, 87,* 1079-1107.

Haskel, P., & Messerschmitt, D. (1992, 1992). Resynchronization of motion compensated video affected by ATM cell loss. *Paper presented at the ICASSP.*

Hassan, M., & Krunz, M. (August 2007). Video Streaming over Wireless Packet Networks: An Occupancy-Based Rate Adaptation Perspective. *IEEE Trans. on Ckts. and Sys. for Video Tech, 17*(8).

Håstad, J., Impagliazzo, R., Levin, L. A., & Luby, M. (1999). A pseudorandom generator from any one-way function. *SIAM J. Comput., 28*(4), 1364–1396.

Hauer, E., & Thiemert, S. (2004). Synchronization techniques to detect MPEG video frames for watermarking retrieval. *Proceedings of the SPIE Security and Watermarking of Multimedia Contents IV, 5306*, pp. 315-324.

Hauser, T., & Wenz, C. (2003). DRM under attack: Weaknesses in existing systems. In *Digital Rights Management: Technological, Economic, Legal and Political Aspects, LNCS 2770*, 206-223. Springer.

He, D., Sun, Q., & Tian, Q (2003). A semi-fragile object based video authentication system. In *IEEE International Symposium on Circuits and Systems, Vol. III*, (pp 814–817), Bangkok, Thailand.

He, J., & Wang, M. (2001). Cryptography and relational database management systems. *Int. Database Engineering and Applications Symposium.*

Hembrooke, E. F. (1961). *Identification of sound and like signals.* United States Patent, 3,004, 104.

Hernández, J. R., & Pérez-González, F. (1999). Statistical Analysis of Watermarking Schemes for Copyright Protection of Images. *Proceedings of IEEE, Special Issue: Identification and Protection of Multimedia Information*, 1142-1166.

Heron, A., & MacDonald, N. (1992). Video Transmission over a radio link using H.261 and DECT. *Paper presented at the IEE Conference.*

Herrigel, A., Oruanaidh, J., Petersen, H., Pereira, S., & Pun, T. (1998). Secure copyright protection techniques for digital images. In second Information Hiding Workshop (IHW), LNCS 1525, Springer-Verlag, 1998.

Hilty, M., Pretschner, A., Basin, D., Schaefer, C., & Walter, T. (2007, September). *A Policy Language for Distributed Usage Control.* In Proceedings of the 12th European Symposium On Research In Computer Security, pages 531–546, Dresden, Germany.

HIPS (2005), HIPS Systems, ShadowText, http://home.apu.edu/~jcox/projects/HtmlStego1, last visited: 29 July 2005.

Holankar, D., & Stamp, M. (2004). Secure streaming media and digital rights management. *Proceedings of the 2004 Hawaii International Conference on Computer Science*. Honolulu, Hawaii, January 2004

Holland, J. H. (1975). *Adaptation in Natural and Artificial Systems*. The University of Michigan Press.

Holt, L., Maufe, B. G., & Wiener, A. (1988). *Encoded Marking of a Recording Signal*. U.K. Patent GB 2196167A.

Holzer, M., Katzenbeisser, S., & Schallhart, C. (2004). *Towards Formal Semantics for ODRL*. In ODRL Workshop, pages 137–148, Vienna, Austria.

Hopcroft, J., & Ullman, J. (1979). *Introduction to Automata Theory, Languages and Computation*. Addison-Wesley Ed.

Hopfield, J. (1982). Neural networks and physical systems with emergent collective computational abilities. *Proceedings of the National Academy of Sciences. USA, 79*(4), 2554–2558.

Horne, B., Matheson, L., Sheehan, C., & Tarjan, R. E. (2002). Dynamic self-checking techniques for improved tamper resistance. In *Security and privacy in digital rights management*, LNCS 2320, 141-159. Springer.

Hou, J.C. (2003) Visual cryptography for color images. Pattern Recognition, 36(7), 1619-1629

Hsia, Y., Chang, C., & Liao, J. (2004, October). Multiple-description coding for robust image watermarking. *International Conference on Image Processing, 4*, 2163-2166.

Hsu, C.-T., & Wu, J.-L. (1999). Hidden digital watermarks in images. IEEE Transactions on Image Processing, 8(1), 58-68.

Hsu, C.-Y., Ortega, A., & Khansari, M. (May 1999). Rate Control for robuts video transmission over burst-error wireless channels. *IEEE Journal on Selected Areas in Communications, 17*(5), 756-773.

Hu, V.C., Ferraiolo, D. F., & Kuhn, D. R. (2006). Assessment of Access Control Systems. *NIST Technology Administration,* NIST Technical Report NISTIR 7316.

Hu, Y., Kwong, S., & Huang, J. (2004). Using Invisible Watermarks to Protect Visible Watermarked Images. *Proceedings of the IEEE International Conference on Circuit and Systems*, 584-587.

Huang, D., & Yan, H. (2001). Interword Distance Changes Represented by Sine Waves for Watermarking Text Images. *IEEE Transactions on Circuits and Systems for Video Technology, 11*(12), 1237-1245.

Huang, X., & Wu, X. (2006, March). Optimal index assignment for multiple description lattice vector quantization. *IEEE Proceedings Data Compression Conference*, 272-281.

Huth, M., & Ryan, M. (2000). *Logic in Computer Science: Modelling and Reasoning about Systems.* Cambridge University Press, Cambridge, England, 2000.

Hwang, R. J., & Chang, C. C. (1978). An On-Line Secret Sharing Scheme for Multi-Secrets. *Computer Communications of the ACM, 21*(13), 1170-1176.

Iannella, R. (2000, August). *Open Digital Rights Language (ODRL)*, Version 0.5, Retrieved from http://odrl.net/ODRL-05.pdf

Iannella, R. (2002, August). *Open Digital Rights Language (ODRL)*, Version 1.1, Retrieved from http://odrl.net/1.1/ODRL-11.pdf.

IFPI. International Federation of Phonographic Industry. http://www.ifpi.org/

Imaizumi, S., Watanabe, G., Fujiyoshi, M., & Kiya, H. (2005). Generalized hierarchical encryption of JPEG 2000 codestreams for access control. Proc. IEEE International Conference on Image Processing, 2, 1094-1097.

<indecs>rdd White Paper. (2002, May). <indecs>rdd, Retrieved from http://xml.coverpages.org/IndecsWhitePaper200205.pdf.

Indigo Group. (2006). Fairplay: effectiveness and weaknesses of Apple's digital rights management technology, Retrieved on August 20, 2006 at http://www.simson.net/ref/2005/csci_e-170/p1/indigo.pdf#search=%22indigo%20fairplay%22.

Information technology — Coding of audio-visual objects – Part 12: ISO Base Media File Format. (2005, April). *International Organisation for Standardisation*, ISO/IEC 14496-12, Second Edition.

Information technology — multimedia framework (MPEG-21) — part 1: Vision, technologies and strategy. (2001, July). Reference number of working document: ISO/IEC JTC1/SC29/WG11 N 4333.

Inoue, H., Miyazaki, A., & Katsura, T. (2000). Wavelet-Based watermarking for Tamper Proofing of Still Images. *IEEE International Conference on Image Processing, 2*, 88-91.

In-Stat (2006). *In-Sights: Video Surveillance Systems on the Move to IP*. Industry Report.

International Standardization Organization. (1999). Integrated Circuit(s) Cards with Contacts - Part 7, ISO/IEC 7816-7, 1999.

Internet Streaming Media Alliance Encryption and Authentication, Version 2.0. Release version, http://www.isma.tv/

IP Datacast over DVB-H: Service Purchase and Protection (SPP), Digital Video Broadcasting™, DVB Document A100, December 2005. http:// www.dvb.org/

iPod + iTunes. (2006). Retrieved March 2006 from http://www.apple.com/itunes/

iPod News. (2006). QTFairUse6 circumvents iTunes DRM, Retrieved on August 30, 2006 at http://www.ipodnn.com/articles/06/08/30/itunes.drm. circumvented/.

ISO, International Organization for Standardization (published standard, 2004). *ISO/IEC 13818-7:2004 Information technology – Generic coding of moving pictures and associated audio information – Part 7: Advanced Audio Coding (AAC).*

ISO, the International Organization for Standardization (published standard, 1999). *ISO/IEC TR 13818-5:1997/ Amd 1:1999 Advanced Audio Coding (AAC).*

ISO/ICE: JTCI/SC29/WG11. (1997). *Text of ISO/ICE 14496-2 MPEG-4 Video VM ver. 8.0*. Stockhome: Video Group.

ISO/IEC 14496-1:2001 Information Technology - Coding of Audio-Visual Objects- Part 1: Systems

ISO/IEC 14496-2:2003 Information Technology - Coding of Audio-Visual Objects- Part 2: Visual

ISO/IEC. (1995). Coding of moving pictures and associated audio for digital storage media at up to about 1.5 Mbit/s – Part 3 Audio: ISO/IEC 11172-3.

ISO/IEC. (1995). MPEG-2 Standard: Generic coding of moving pictures and associated audio information: Video: ISO/IEC 13 818-2.

ISO/IEC. (1997). Generic coding of moving pictures and associated audio information - Part 7: Advanced Audio Coding (AAC): ISO/IEC 13818-7.

ISO/IEC. (1998). Coding of Moving Pictures and Associated Audio and Digital Storage Media of up to about 1.5 Mbit/s: ISO/IEC 11172.

ISO/IEC. (2002). International Standard Coding of Still Pictures (JPEG 2000): ISO/IEC 15444-1:2004.

ISO/IEC. (2003). Information technology -- Coding of audio-visual objects -- Part 14: MP4 File Format: ISO/IEC 14496-14.

ISO/IEC. (2004). MPEG-4 High Efficiency AAC (HE AAC): ISO/IEC 14496-3, Amd.2.

Ito, M., Saito, A., & Nishizeki T. (1987). Secret Sharing Scheme Realizing General Access Structure. *Proceedings of 1987 IEEE Global Telecommunications Conference (GLOBECOM 1987)*, 99-102.

ITU. (1993). Video codec for audiovisual services at p x 64 kbit/s ITU-T Recommendation: H.261.

ITU. (1995). Video Coding for Low Bit Rate Communications: ITU-T Recommendation H.263.

ITU. (March 2005). Advanced Video Coding for generic audiovisual services: ITU-T Recommendation H.264.

ITU. (Sept. 1992). Digital Compression and Coding of Continuous-Tone Still Images - Requirements and Guidelines: ITU-T Recommendation T.81.

iTunes. (2006). 1 billion served. Retrieved February 2006 from http://abcnews.go.com/Technology/story?id=1653 881&technology=true

Iwan, S., & Lagendijk, R. L. (2001). Low bit-rate video watermarking using temporally extended differential energy watermarking (DEW) algorithm. In *Proc. SPIE, Security and Watermarking of Multimedia Contents III. San Jose, 2001, 4314*, pp. 73-84.

Iwata, T., Takehito, A., Ueda, K., & Sunaga, H. (2003). A DRM system suitable for P2P content delivery and the study on its implementation. *Proceeding of the 9th Asia-Pacific Conference on Communications (APCC 2003.)*

Jacob, M., Boneh, D., & Felten, E. (2003). Attacking an obfuscated cipher by injecting faults. *Lecture Notes in Computer Science, 2696*, 16-31. Springer

Jacquin, A. E. (1993). Fractal image coding: a review. Proceedings of IEEE, 81(10), 1451-1465.

Jain, K., Padhye, J., Padmanabhan, V. N., & Qiu, L. (2005). Impact of Interference on Multi-Hop Wireless Network Performance. *Springer Wireless Networks, 11*(4), 471-487.

Jamil, T. (1999). Steganography: The art of hiding information in plain sight. *IEEE Potentials 18(1),* 10-12.

Jamkhedkar, P. A., & Heileman, G. L. (2004, October). *DRM as a Layered System.* In Proceedings of the Fourth ACM Workshop on Digital Rights Management, pages 11–21, Washington, DC, USA.

Jamkhedkar, P. A., Heileman, G. L., & Martinez-Ortiz, I. (2006, November). *The Problem with Rights Expression Languages.* In Proceedings of the Sixth ACM Workshop on Digital Rights Management, pages 59–67, Alexandria, VA, USA.

Jar Files. (2006). *Packaging programs in jar files.* Retrieved April 2006 from http://java.sun.com/docs/books/tutorial/deployment/TOC.html#jar

Jelinek, F., Bahl, L., Cocke, J., & Raviv, J. (1974). Optimal decoding of linear codes for minimizing symbol error rate. *IEEE Transactions on Information Theory, IT-20, no. 2,* 284-287.

Jeong, J., & Choe, Y. (Feb. 2007). A Rate Control Scheme for H.264/AVC CBR Transmission. *Paper presented at the Fourth International Conference on Signal Processing, Pattern Recognition and Applications.*

Jin, D., Yan, W. Q., & Kankanhalli, M. S. (2005). Progressive color visual cryptography. Journal of Electronic Imaging, 14(3), 033019.

Jobs, S. (2007). *Thoughts on Music.* Apple Inc. Web site, February 6, 2007, http://www.apple.com/hotnews/thoughtsonmusic/

Jobs, S. (2007). Thoughts on music. Open Letter, February 6 2007. Retrieved December 23, 2007, from http://www.apple.com/hotnews/thoughtsonmusic/

John, C. (2004), Steganography - Hiding messages in the Noise of a Picture, http://www.codeproject.com/csharp/steganodotnet.asp, last visited: January 23, 2008.

Johnson, N. F., & Jajodia, S. (1998). Steganalysis: The investigation of Hidden Information. *Proceedings of IEEE Information Technology,* 113-116.

Johnson, N. F., Duric, Z., & Jajodia, S. (2001). Information Hiding, Steganography and Watermarking – Attacks and Countermeasures, Kluwer, Boston.

Johnson, N. F., Duric, Z., & Jojodia, S. (2000). *Information Hiding: Steganography and Watermarking - Attacks and Countermeasures,* London: Kluwer Academic.

Johnson, N., & Jajodia, S. (1998). Exploiting steganography: Seeing the unseen. IEEE Computers, 31 (2), 26-34.

Johnson, N., & Jajodia, S. (1998). Steganalysis of images created using current steganography software. In Second Int. Workshop on Information Hiding (Vol. 1525, p. 273-279). Springer Berlin / Heidelberg.

Jondet, N. (2006) *La France v. Apple: who's the dadvsi in DRMs?*, (2006) 3:4 SCRIPT-ed 473, http://www.law.ed.ac.uk/ahrc/script-ed/vol3-4/jondet.asp

Jonker, H. L. (2004). *Security of Digital Rights Management systems.* Unpublished Master's thesis. Technische Universiteit Eindhoven.

Jordan, F., Martin, K., & Touradj, E. (1997). Proposal of a watermarking technique for hiding/retrieving data in compressed and decompressed video. ISO/IEC JTC1/SC29/WG11 MPEG97/M2281, 1997.

Joumaa, H., & Davoine, F. (2005). An ICA based algorithm for video watermarking. In Proc. ICASSP 2005, II, 805-808.

Joux, A., & Nguyen, K. (2003). Separating Decision Diffie-Hellman from Computational Diffie-Hellman in cryptographic groups. *Journal of Cryptology, 16,* 239–247.

JSSE (2006). Java Secure Sockets Extension. Retrieved January 2006 from http://java.sun.com/products/jsse/

JSSE. (2006). *Java Secure Sockets Extension Reference Implementation.* Retrieved March 2006 from http://java.sun.com/j2se/1.4.2/docs/guide/security/jsse/JSSERefGuide.html#SSLOverview

Judge, J. C. (2001). Steganography: Past, Present, Future. *SANS white paper,* November 30, 2001. Retrieved January 23, 2008, from http://www.sans.org/rr/papers/index.php?id=552

Judge, P., & Ammar, M. (2000, June). WHIM: Watermarking multicast video with a hierarchy of intermediaries. In *Proceedings of the International Workshop on Network and Operation System Support for Digital Audio and Video NOSSDAV'00, 39*(6), 699-712.

Judge, P., & Ammar, M. (2003). CITADEL: A content protection architecture for decentralized peer-to-peer file sharing systems. *Proceedings of IEEE GLOBECOM 2003.*

Juels, A., & Brainard, J. (1999). Client puzzles: A cryptographic defense against connection depletion attacks. In *Proc. of the Networks and Distributed Security Systems*, 151-165.

JVT. (2003). *Proposed Draft of Adaptive Rate Control.* Geneva: Inst. of Computer Technology.

Kahn, D. (1996). *The Codebreakers.* 2nd edition, New York: Macmillan.

Kalker, et. al. (2004). Music2Share: Copyright-compliant music sharing in P2P systems. *Proceedings of IEEE, 92*, 961–970.

Kalker, T., Depovere, G., Haitsma, J., & Maes, M. (1999). A video watermarking system for broadcast monitoring. *Proceedings of SPIE, 3657, Security and Watermarking of Multimedia Content,* 103–112.

Kalker, T., Epema, D., H., J., Hartel, P., H., Lagendijk, R., L., & Steen, M. V. (2004). Music2Share – Copyright-compliant music sharing in P2P systems. *Proceedings of the IEEE.*

Kane, K., & Browne, J. C. (2006). On classifying access control implementations for distributed systems. In *Proc. of the 11th ACM Symposium on Access control models and technologies*, 29-38.

Kang, Z. W., Liu, J., & Yi, Y. G. (2007). Steganography based on wavelet transform and modulus function. *Journal of Systems Engineering and Electronics, 18*(3), 628-632.

Karlof, C., Sastry, N., Li, Y., Perrig, A., & Tygar, J. (2004). Distillation codes and applications to DoS resistant multicast authentication. In *Proceeding of 11th*

Network and Distributed Systems Security Symposium (NDSS'04), San Diego, CA, Feb. 2004.

Karlsson, J. S., Lal, A., Leung, C., Pham, T. (2001). IBM DB2 Everyplace: A Small Footprint Relational Database System. *Int. Conf. on Data Engineering.*

Katz, B., Greenberg, S., Yarkoni, N., Blaunstien, N., & Giladi, R. (March 2007). New Error-Resilient Scheme Based on FMO and Dynamic Redundant Slice Allocation for Wireless Video Transmission. *IEEE Trans. on Broadcasting, 53*(1), 308-319.

Katzenbeisser, S., & Petitcolas, F. A. P. (2000). *Information Hiding Techniques for Steganography and Digital Watermarking.* London: Artech House.

Kaufman, C., Perlman, R., & Speciner, M. (2002). *Network Security: Private Communications in a Public World.* Prentice Hall

Kazaa. (2006). How P2P and Kazaa software works. Retrieved January 2006 from http://www.kazaa.com/us/help/new_p2p.htm

Kerckhoff, A. (1883). La cryptographie militaire. *Journal des sciences militaires, 9,* 5-38.

Kessler, G. (2004). An overview of steganography for the computer forensics examiner. Forensics Science and Communications, 6 (3).

Keytool. (2006). Key and Certificate Management Tool. Retrieved March 2006 from http://java.sun.com/j2se/1.3/docs/tooldocs/win32/keytool.html

Khan, J. Y., & Das, P. (2002). MPEG-4 video over packet switched connection of the WCDMA air Interface. *Proc. of the 13th IEEE International Symposium on Personal Indoor and Mobile Radio Communications, 5.* 2189–2193.

Khansari, M., Jalali, A., Dubois, E., & Memelstein, P. (May 1999). Low bit-rate video transmission over fading channels for wireless microcellular systems. *IEEE Trans. on Ckts. and Sys. for Video Tech, 6*(1), 1-11.

Kiayias, A., & Yung, M. (2003). Breaking and repairing asymmetric public-key traitor tracing. In *Digital Rights Management, LNCS 2320,* 32-50. Springer.

Kiayias, A., Raekow, Y., & Russell, A. (2005). Efficient steganography with provable security guarantees. In 7th

Int. Workshop on Digital Watermarking (Vol. 3727, p. 118-130). Springer Berlin / Heidelberg.

Kim, J., Kwon, S., Hwang, H., Kwon, K., & Kim, D. (2002). Adaptive Digital Watermarking Based on Wavelet Transform Using Successive Subband Quantization and Perceptual Model. In *The International Technical Conference Computers and Communications, 1,* 1240–1243. USA: SPIE Press.

Kim, Y., Moon, K., & Oh, I. (2003). A Text Watermarking Algorithm based on Word Classification and Inter-word Space Statistics. *Proceedings of the Seventh International Conference on Document Analysis and Recognition (ICDAR'03),* (pp. 775–779), Edinburgh, Scotland.

Kirovski, D., & Malvar, H. S. (2003). Spread-spectrum watermarking of audio signals. *IEEE Transaction on Signal Processing, 51*(4), 1020- 1033.

Ko, Y., Shankarkumar, V., & Vaidya, N. H. (2000). Medium access control protocols using directional antennas in adhoc networks. In *Proceedings of the Annual Joint Conference of the IEEE Computer and Communications Societies (INFOCOM), 1,* 13-21.

Koblitz, N., & Menezes, A. J. (2004). Another look at "Provable Security". Technical report, http://eprint.iacr.org/2004/152.

Komatsu, N., & Tominaga, H. (1998). Authentication System Using Concealed Images in Telematics. *Memoirs of the School of Science and Engineering, Waseda University, 52,* 45-60.

Konstantas, D., & Thanos, D. (2000). Commercial dissemination of video over open network: Issues and approaches. *Technical report, LAND, Center Univeritaire d'Informatique of University of Geneva,* Object Systems Group.

Korejwa, J. (2007). *Jsteg shell 2.0.* http://www.tiac.net/users/korejwa/steg.htm.

Kosch, H., Böszörményi, L., Döller, M., Libsie, M., Schojer, P., & Kofler, A.. (2005). The Life Cycle of Multimedia Metadata. *IEEE MultiMedia, 12*(1), 80-86.

Koutsakis, P., Psychis, S., & Paterakis, M. (2005). Integrated wireless access for videoconference from MPEG-4 and H.263 video coders with voice, E-mail, and Web traffic. *IEEE Transactions on Vehicular Technology, 54*(5), 1863-1874.

Krohn, M. N., Freedman, M. J., & Mazires, D. (2004). On-the-Fly Verification of Rateless Erasure Codes for Efficient Content Distribution. *IEEE Symposium on Security and Privacy (S&P'04),* California, USA.

Kullback, S., & Leibler, R. A. (1951). On information and sufficiency. *Annals of Mathematical Statistics,* (22), 79–86.

Kumgollu, F., Bouridane, A., Roula, M. A., & Boussaktd, S. (2003). Comparison of Different Wavelet Transforms for fusion based watermarking applications. *Proceedings of IEEE International Conference on Electronics, Circuits and Systems, 3,* 1188-1191.

Kundur, D. (2001). Watermarking with diversity: Insights and implications. *IEEE multimedia, 8*(4), 46-52.

Kundur, D., & Karthik, K. (2004, June). Video fingerprinting and encryption principles for digital rights management. *Proceedings of the IEEE, 92*(6), 918–932.

Kung, C. H., et al. (2003). Video watermarking using motion vector. The 16th IPPR Conference on Computer Vision, Graphics and Image Processing, 2003, pp. 547-551.

Kuntze, N., Schmidt, A. U. (2006): Transitive trust in mobile scenarios. In Günter Müller (Ed.), *Proceedings of the International Conference on Emerging Trends in Information and Communication Security (ETRICS 2006),* Lecture Notes in Computer Science, 3995, 73-85), Berlin: Springer-Verlag.

Kuntze, N., Schmidt, A. U. (2007): Trusted Ticket Systems and Applications. In: *Proceedings of the IFIP sec2007* (pp. 49-60), Boston: Springer.

Kuntze, N., Schmidt, A. U. (2007): Trustworthy content push. In: *Proceedings of the Wireless Communications and Networking Conference, WCNC 2007, Hong Kong, 11-15 March 2007* (pp. 2909-2912), IEEE Press.

Kuo, C. –T., & Cheng, S. -C. (2007). Fusion of color edge detection and color quantization for color image watermarking using principal axes analysis. *Pattern Recognition, 40,* 3691-3704.

Kutter, M., & Petitcolas, F. A. P. (1999, January). A fair benchmark for image watermarking systems. In *Proceedings of the SPIE Security and Watermarking of Multimedia Contents, 3657,* 226–239.

Kutter, M., Voloshynovskiy, S., & Herrigel, A. (2000). The Watermark Copy Attack. *Proceedings of SPIE, Security and Watermarking of Multimedia Content, 3971*, 1-10.

Kwon, D.-K., Shen, M.-Y., & Kuo, C.-C. J. (May 2007). Rate Control for H.264 Video with Enhanced Rate and Distortion Models. *IEEE Trans. on Ckts. and Sys. for Video Tech, 17*(5).

Kwon, G. R., Lee, T. Y., Kim, K. H., Jin, J. D., & Ko, S. J. (2005). Multimedia digital right management using selective scrambling for mobile handset. *LNAI, 3802*, 1098-1103.

Lacy, J. (2007). *Coral Consortium Letter to Steve Jobs*, Feb. 9, 2007, http://www.coral-interop.org/20070209_Coral_Letter.html

Lam, W.-M., Reibman, A. R., & Lin, B. (1993). Recovery of lost or erroneously received motion vectors. *Paper presented at the ICASSP.*

Lamport, L., Shostak, R., & Pease, M. (1982). The Byzantine General Problem. *ACM Transactions on Programming Languages and Systems, 4*(3), 382-401.

Lancini, R., Mapelli, F., & Tubaro, S. (2002). A robust video watermarking technique in the spatial domain. IEEE Symposium on Video/Image Processing and Multimedia Communications, pp. 251-256.

Langelaar, G. C., Lagendijk, R. L., & Biemond, J. (1997). Real-time labelling methods for MPEG compressed videos. In *Proceedings of the Eighteenth Symposium on Information Theory in the Benelux*, pp. 25-32.

Langelaar, G. C., Lagendijk, R. L., & Biemond, J. (1998, December). Real-time labelling of MPEG-2 compressed video. *Journal of Visual Communication and Image Representation, 9*(4), 256-270.

Langelaar, G., Setyawan, I., & Lagendijk, R. (2000). Watermarking digital image and video data: a state of the art overview. *IEEE Signal Processing Magazine, 17*, 20-46.

Lee, C. –H., & Lee, H. –K. (2005). Geometric attack resistant watermarking in wavelet trasform domain. *Optics Express, 13*, 1307-1321.

Lepro, R. (2003). Cardea: Dynamic access control in distributed systems. *NASA Advanced Supercomputing (NAS) Division*, NAS Technical Report NAS-03-020.

Lepsoy, S., Carlini, P., & Oien, G.E. (1998). On fractal compression and vector quantization, in Y. Fisher (ed.), Fractal Image Encoding and Analysis: A NATO ASI Series Book, Chapter 2, Springer Verlag

Lessig, L. (1996). *Opening Keynote, LinuxWorld*, San Francisco, August 15, 2006.

Leung, A., Yau, P. W., & Mitchell, C. J. (2007). Using Trusted Computing to Secure Mobile Ubiquitous Enviroments. To be published in: *Security and Privacy in Wireless Networking*. Leicester, UK: Troubador Publishing Ltd.

Levine, B. N., & Shields, C. (2002). Hordes: A Protocol for Anonymous Communication Over the Internet. *Computer Security, 10*(3), 213-240.

Li, N., Mitchell, J. C., & Winsborough, W. H. (2005). Beyond Proof-of-Compliance: Security Analysis in Trust Management. *Journal of the ACM, 52*(3), 474-514.

Li, T., Wu, Y., Ma, D., Zhu, H., & Deng, R., (2004). Flexible Verification of MPEG-4 Stream in Peer-to-Peer CDN. *6th International Conference on Information and Communications Security (ICICS'04)*, LNCS 3269, Spain, 2004.

Li, T., Zhu, H., & Wu, Y., (2005). Multi-Source Stream Authentication Framework in case of Composite MPEG-4 Stream. *Seventh International Conference on Information and Communications Security (ICICS'05)*, December 10-13, 2005, Beijing, China. LNCS 3783, 389-401.

Li, W. (2001). Overview of fine granularity scalability in MPEG-4 video standard.

Li, W., Hu, X., & Leung, H. (2004). Performance evaluation of digital audio watermarking algorithms. *IEEE Trans. on Aerospace and Electronic Systems, 40*, 12–26.

Li, Y., Gao, X., & Ji, H. (2003). A 3D Wavelet Based Spatial-Temporal Approach for Video Watermarking. In Proc. 8th International Conference on Computational Intelligence and Multimedia Applications, 2003.

Lian, S., Sun, J., Zhang, D., & Wang, Z. (2004). A selective image encryption scheme based on JPEG2000 codec, Lecture Notes in Computer Science, 3332, 65-72.

Lie, J., & Ngan, K. N. (2005, 2005). An Error Sensitivity-based Redundant Macroblock Strategy for Robust

Wireless Video Transmission. *Paper presented at the Int'l Conf. on Wireless Networks, Comms. and Mobile Computing.*

Liese, S., Wu, D., & Mohapatra, P. (2006). Experimental characterization of an 802.11b wireless mesh network. In *Proceedings of the 2006 ACM international conference on Wireless communications and mobile computing (IWCMC)*, 587-592.

Lin C. C., & Tsai, W. H. (2005). Secret image sharing with capability of share data reduction. Optical Engineering, 42(8), 2340-2345

Lin, C. Y., & Chang, S. F. (1999). Issues and solutions for authenticating MPEG video. In Proc. SPIE Photonic West, 3657, Security and Watermarking of Multimedia Contents IV. San Jose, 1999, pp. 54-65.

Lin, C. Y., & Chang, S. F. (1999). Issues and solutions for authenticating MPEG video. *SPIE Electronic Imaging, Vol. 3657,* (pp. 54–65), San Jose, CA, USA.

Lin, C. Y., & Chang, S. F. (2000). Semi-fragile watermarking for authenticating JPEG visual content. In *SPIE Security Watermarking of Multimedia Contents IV, Vol. 4675.* (pp 512–519). San Jose, CA, USA.,

Lin, C. Y., & Chang, S. F. (2001). Zero-error Information Hiding Capacity of Digital Images. In *IEEE International Conference on Image Processing, 3,* 1007–1010. USA: IEEE Press.

Lin, C.-Y. (2000). *Watermarking and Digital Signature Techniques for Multimedia Authentication and Copyright Protection*, PhD Thesis - Columbia University.

Lin, E. (2005). Video and Image Watermark Synchronization. CERIAS Tech Report 2005-56.

Lin, E. T., & Delp, E. J. (2004, October). Temporal synchronization in video watermarking. IEEE Transactions on Signal Processing: Supplement on Secure Media, 52(10), 3007-3022.

Lin, E.T., Eskicioglu, A. M., Lagendijk, R. L., & Delp, E. J. (2005). Advances in digital video content protection. Proceedings of IEEE, 93(1), 171-183

Lin, S., Costello, D. J., & Miller, M. J. (1984). Automatic repeat error control schemes. *IEEE Communications Magazine, 22,* 5-17.

Lin, W. K., Chiu, D. M., & Lee,Y. B. (2004). Erasure Code Replication Revisited. In *Proc. of the 4th IEEE Int. Conf. on Peer-to-Peer Computing.*

Linde, Y., Buzo, A., & Gray, R. (1980, January). An Algorithm for Vector Quantizer Design. *IEEE Trans. Communication, 28*(1), 84-95.

Linnartz, J. P., & Dijk, M. V. (1998). Analysis of the sensitivity attack against electronic watermarks in images. In *Workshop on Information Hiding*, Portland, 15-17 April, 1998.

Linux (2007). http://www.drfruitcake.com/linux/stest.html

Liu, G. J., Wang, J. W., Lian, S. G., Dai, Y. W., & Wang, Z. Q. (2006). Data hiding in neural network predictioni errors. *Lecture Notes in Computer Scence: ISNN2006, 3973,* 273-278.

Liu, H., Chen, N., Huang, J., et al. (2002). A robust DWT-based video watermarking algorithm. *IEEE International Symposium on Circuits and Systems, 3*(26-29), 631-634.

Liu, M., & Zhu, C. (2007, July). Multiple description video coding using hierarchical B pictures. *2007 IEEE International Conference on Multimedia & Expo,* Beijing, China, 1367-1370.

Liu, M., Zhu, C., & Wu, X. (2006, May). Index assignment design for three-description lattice vector quantization. *IEEE International Symposium on Circuits and Systems,* 3101-3104.

Liu, Y., Li, Z. G., & Soh, Y. C. (January 2007). A Novel Rate Control Scheme for Low Delay Video Communication of H.264/AVC Standard. *IEEE Trans. on Ckts. and Sys. for Video Tech, 17*(1).

Lookabaugh, T., & Sicker, D. C. (2004). Selective encryption for consumer applications. IEEE Communication Magazine, 42(5), 124-129

Lopez, J., Oppliger, R., & Pernul, G. (2004). Authentication and Authorization Infrastructures (AAIs): A Comparative Survey. *Computer Communications, 27*(16), 1608-1616.

Low, S. H., Maxemchuk, N. F., Brassil, J. T., & O'Gorman L. (1995). Document marking and identification using both line and word shifting. *Proceedings of the Four-teenth Annual Joint Conference of the IEEE Computer and Communications Societies (INFOCOM '95), 2,* 853 - 860.

Lu, C. S., Huang, S. K., Sze, C. J., & Liao, H. Y. M. (2000, December). Cocktail watermarking for digital image protection. *IEEE Transactions on Multimedia, 2*(4), 209-224.

Lu, C., Chen, J., Liao, H. M., & Fan, K. (2002). Real-Time MPEG2 Video Watermarking in the VLC Domain. *Proceedings of 16th International Conference on Pattern Recognition, 2,* 552-555.

Luby, M., Mitzenmacher, M., Shokrollahi, A., Spielman, D., & Stemann, V. (1997). Practical loss-resilient codes. In *Proceeding of 29th Annual ACM Symposium on Theory of Computing (STOC)*, El Paso, TX, May 1997.

Luh, W., & Kundur, D. (2005). Digital Media Fingerprint-ing - Techniques and Trends. In Furht B., & Kirovski D. (Ed.), *Multimedia Security Handbook - Techniques and Trends* (pp. 577–603). CRC Press.

Luh, W., & Kundur, D. (2005, June). New paradigms for effective multicasting and fingerprinting of enter-tainment media. In *IEEE Communications Magazine, 43*(6), 77–84.

Lukac, R., & Plataniotis, K. N. (2004). Colour image secret sharing. IEE Electronics Letters, 40(9), 529-530

Lukac, R., & Plataniotis, K. N. (2005). A cost-effective encryption scheme for color images, Real-Time Imaging. *Special Issue on Multi-Dimensional Image Processing,* 11(5-6), 454-464

Lukac, R., & Plataniotis, K. N. (2005). Bit-level based secret sharing for image encryption. *Pattern Recogni-tion,* 38(5), 767-772

Lukac, R., & Plataniotis, K. N. (2005). Digital im-age indexing using secret sharing schemes: A unified framework for single-sensor consumer electronics. *IEEE Transactions on Consumer Electronics,* 51(3), 908-916

Lukac, R., & Plataniotis, K. N. (2005d). Image repre-sentation based secret sharing, Communications of the CCISA. Special Issue on Visual Secret Sharing, 11(2), 103-114

Lukas, J., Fridrich, J., & Goljan, M. (2006). Digital camera identification from sensor pattern noise. *IEEE Transactions of Information Forensics and Security,* 1(2), 205–214.

Lysyanskaya, A., Micali, S., Reyzin, L., & Shacham, H. (2004). Sequential Aggregate Signatures from trapdoor one-way permutations. In Christian Cachin, Jan Cam-enisch (Eds.): *Advances in Cryptology - EUROCRYPT 2004.*

Lysyanskaya, A., Tamassia, R., & Triandopoulos, N. (2004). Multicast Authentication in Fully Adversarial Networks. *IEEE Symposium on Security and Privacy (S&P'04)*, California, USA.

Lyu, S., & Farid, H. (2006). Steganalysis using higher-order image statistics. IEEE Transactions on Information Forensics and Security, 1 (1), 111-119.

Ma, Y., & Wang, D. (2005). An Approach to Fair Re-source Sharing in Peer-to-Peer Systems. In *Proc. of the 4th International Conference on Networking, LNCS 3421,* 643-652. Springer-Verlag.

Malik, H. (2008). Steganalysis of QIM Steganography Using Irregularity Measure. In 10th ACM Multimedia and Security Workshop, 2008. (submitted)

Malik, H., Chandramouli, R., & Subbalakshami, K., (2008). Steganalysis: trends and challenges. In Multi-media Forensics and Security, Ed. Chang-Tsun Li, Idea Group Inc.

Malik, H., Subbalakshami, K., & Chandramouli, R. (2007). Nonparametric steganalysis of quantization in-dex modulation based steganography using approximate entropy. *IEEE Transactions on Information Forensics and Security.* (submitted)

Malik, H., Subbalakshami, K., & Chandramouli, R. (2007). Steganalysis of quantization index modulation based steganography using kernel density estimation. In *9th ACM Multimedia and Security Workshop,* 2007.

Malik, H., Subbalakshami, K., & Chandramouli, R. (2007). Nonparametric steganalysis of quantization index modulation based steganography using kernel density estimaton. *IEEE Transactions on Information Forensics and Security.* (submitted)

Malik, H., Subbalakshami, K., & Chandramouli, R. (2008). Nonparametric steganalysis of quantization index modulation based steganography using approximate entropy. In *Security, Steganography, and Watermarking of Multimedia Contents IX*. IS&T/SPIE.

Malvar, H. S., & Florencio, D. A. F. (2003, April). Improved spread spectrum: A new modulation technique for robust watermarking Improved spread spectrum: A new modulation technique for robust watermarking. *IEEE Transactions on Signal Processing, 51*(4), 898-905.

Maniatis, P., Giuli, T. J., Roussopoulos, M., Rosenthal, D. S. H., & Baker, M. (2004). Impeding Attrition Attacks in P2P Systems. In *Proc. of the 11th ACM SIGOPS European Workshop*.

Mannak, Ridder, & Keyson. (2004). The human side of sharing in peer-to-peer net-works. *ACM International Conference Proceeding Series, 84*, 59–64.

Mao, Y., & Mihcak, M. K. (2005). Collusion-resistant international de-synchronization for digital video finger-printing. *IEEE Conference on Image Processing*.

Marlin Developer Community (whitepaper, 2006). *Marlin architecture overview*.

Marti, S., & Garcia-Molina, H. (2006). Taxonomy of trust: Categorizing P2P reputation systems. *Computer Networks, 50*, 472-484.

Martin, K., Lukac, R., & Plataniotis, K. N. (2005). Efficient encryption of wavelet-based coded color images. Pattern Recognition, 38(7), 1111-1115

Marvel, L. M., Boncelet, Jr. C. G., & Retter, C. T. (1999). Spread spectrum image steganography. *IEEE Transactions on Image Processing*, 1075-1083.

Marvel, L., Boncelet, C., & Retter, C. (1999). Spread spectrum image steganography. IEEE Transactions on Image Processing, 8 (8), 1075-1083.

Mastercard Inc. MasterCard Open Data Storage (MODS). https://hsm2stl101.mastercard.net/public/login/ebusiness/smart_cards/one_smart_card/biz_opportunity/mods

Matsunaga, A., Koga, K., & Ohkawa, M. (1989). An analog speech scrambling system using the FFT technique with high level security. *IEEE Trans. on Selected Areas in Communications, 7*(4), 540–547.

Matsuoka, H. (2006). Spread spectrum audio steganography using subband phase shifting. In Int. Conf. on Intelligent Information Hiding and Multimedia, (p. 3-6).

Maurer, U. M., & Wolf, S. (1999). The relationship between breaking the diffie–hellman protocol and computing discrete logarithms. *SIAM J. Comput., 28*(5), 1689–1721.

McCarty, L. T. (1989). *A Language for Legal Discourse I. Basic Features*. In ICAIL '89: Proceedings of the 2nd international conference on Artificial intelligence and law, pages 180–189, New York, NY, USA.

McEliece, R., Posner, C., Rodemich R., & Santosh, R. (1987). The capacity of the Hopfield associative memory. *IEEE Transactions on Information Theory, 33*(4), 461–482.

Meerwald, P. (2001). Digital Image Watermarking in the Wavelet Transform Domain, *PhD Thesis: Univeristy of Salzburg*.

Meerwald, P., & Uhl, A. (2001). A Survey of Wavelet domain Watermarking Algorithms. *Proceedings SPIE, Electronic Imaging, Security and Watermarking of Multimedia Contents III, 4314*.

Melton, J. A., & Simon, R. (1993). *Understanding the new SQL: A Complete Guide*. Morgan Kaufmann Ed.

Menezes, A. J., van Oorschot, P. C., & Vanstone, S. A. (1997). *Handbook of Advanced Cryptography*. CRC Press.

Menezes, A. J., Vanstone, S. A., & Oorschot, P. C. V. (1996). *Handbook of Applied Cryptography*. CRC Pr Llc.

Mennecke, T. (2005). *Anti-DRM Demonstration Takes Place in New York City*, Oct. 28, 2005, http://www.slyck.com/news.php?story=969

Merabti, M., & Llewellyn-Jones, D. (2006). Digital rights management in ubiquitous computing. *IEEE Multimedia*, 13(2), 32- 42. DOI: 10.1109/MMUL.2006.27

Merkle, R. (1989). A Certified Digital Signature. *Advances in Cryptology*.

Merkle, R. C. (1989). A certified digital signature, Crypto'89, *Lecture Notes on Computer Science, Vol. 0435*, pp. 218-238, Springer-Verlag, 1989.

Michiels, S., Verslype, K., Joosen, W., & Decker, B. D. (2005). Towards a software architecture for DRM. *Proceedings of the Fifth ACM Workshop on Digital Rights Management.*

Micklitz, H.-W., Monazzahian, B., & Rößler, C. (1999). *Door-to-door selling — pyramid selling — multilevel marketing.* Study commissioned by the European Commission. Contract No. A0/7050/98/000156. Retrieved October 7, 2007 from http://europa.eu.int/comm/dgs/ health_consumer/ library/surveys/sur10_en.html

Micropayment Markup. (2006). Common markup for micropayment per-fee-links. Retrieved October 2006 from http://www.w3.org/TR/Micropayment-Markup/#Basic.

Microsoft Inc. Windows Microsoft Media 9. http://www. microsoft.com/windows/windowsmedia/.

Microsoft. (2006). *Next generation secure computing base.* Retrieved on March 17, 2006 at http://www.microsoft.com/resources/ngscb/default.mspx.

Microsoft. (2007). *Peer-to-peer file sharing: Help avoid breaking copyright laws and getting unwanted software.* Retrieved on April 3, 2007 at http://www.microsoft.com/athome/security/online/p2p_file_sharing.mspx.

Miklau, G., & Suciu, D. (2002). Cryptographically Enforced Conditional Access for XML. *Int. Workshop on the Web and Databases.*

Miklau, G., & Suciu, D. (2003). Controlling access to published data using cryptography. *Int. Conf. on Very Large Data Bases.*

Miner, S., & Staddon, J. (2001). Graph-based authentication of digital streams. In *Proceedings of the IEEE Symposium on Research in Security and Privacy,* pages 232-246, May 2001.

Ming, Y., & Hong-yuan, W. (2006). A rate-control scheme for H.264 video under low bandwidth channel. *Journal of Zhejiang University SCIENCE A, 6.*

Mintzer, F. (1998). Developing Digital Libraries of Cultural Content for Internet Access. *IEEE Communications Magazine,* 92-98.

Mintzer, F. C., Boyle, L. E., Cazes, A. N., Christian, B. S., Cox, S. C., Giordano, F. P., Gladney, H. M., Lee, J. C., Kelmanson, M. L., Lirani, A. C., Magerlein, K. A.,

Pavani, A. M. B., & Schiattarella, F. (1996). Toward on-line, worldwide access to Vatican Library materials. *IBM Journal of Research and Development, 40,* 139-162.

Mishra, P., & Stamp, M. (2003). Software uniqueness: how and why. *Proceedings of ICCSA 2003,* P.P. Dey, M.N. Amin and T.M. Gatton, editors, July 2003

Mitchell, C.J. (Ed.) (2005). *Trusted Computing.* IEE Press (2005)

Mobasseri, B. (1998). Direct sequence watermarking of digital video using m-frames. In International Conference on Image Processing, ICIP'98, 1998.

Mobasseri, B. G., & Evans, A. E. (2001). Content-dependent video authentication by self-watermarking in color space. In *SPIE Security and Watermarking of Multimedia Content III, Vol. 4314,* (pp 35–44), San Jose, CA, USA.

Mobasseri, B. G., Sieffert, M. J., & Simard, R. J. (2000). Content authentication and tamper detection in digital video. *IEEE International Conference on Image Processing, Vol. I,* (pp 458–461), Vancouver, BC, Canada.

Model-View-Controller. (2006). Retrieved March 2006 from http://ootips.org/mvc-pattern.html

Moerland, T. (2003). Steganography and Steganalysis, *Leiden Institute of Advanced Computing Science,* Retrieved January 23, 2008, from www.liacs.nl/home/tmoerlan/privtech.pdf

Mohanty, S. P., Ramakrishnan, K. R., & Kankanhalli, M. (1999). A dual watermarking technique for images. *Proceedings of the seventh ACM International Conference on Multimedia,* 49-51.

Mohr, A. E., Riskin, E. A., & Ladner, R. E. (2000). Unequal loss protection: Graceful degradation of image quality over packet erasure channels through forward error correction. *IEEE Journal on Selected Areas in Communications, 18*(6), 819-828.

Molina, M., Castelli, P., & Foddis, G. (2000). Web traffic modeling exploiting TCP connections' temporal clustering through HTML-REDUCE. *IEEE Network, 14* (3), 46-55.

Montgomery Advertiser. (2007). *iTunes slowdown.* Retrieved on January 3, 2007 at http://www.montgomeryadvertiser.com/apps/pbcs.dll/frontpage

Mooney, A. & Keating, J. G., & Pitas, I. (2008). A Comparative Study of Chaotic and White Noise Signals in Digital Watermarking. *Chaos, Solitons and Fractals, 35,* 913-921.

Mooney, A., & Keating, J. G. (2003). An Optical and Digital Technique for Watermark Detection. *Proceedings of SPIE International Symposium on Optical Science and Technology, 5202,* 97-105.

Mooney, A., & Keating, J. G. (2004). The impact of the theoretical properties of the Logistic Function on the generation of optically detectable watermarks. *Proceedings of SPIE, Technology for Optical Countermeasures, Optics/Photonics in Security and Defence, 5615,* 120-129.

Mooney, A., & Keating, J. G. (2005). Generation and Detection of Watermarks Derived from Chaotic Function. *Proceedings of Opto-Ireland, Proceedings SPIE, 5823,* 58-69.

Mooney, A., & Keating, J. G., & Heffernan, D. M. (2006). A Detailed Study of the Generation of Optically Detectable Watermarks using the Logistic Map. *Chaos, Solitons and Fractals, 30,* 1088-1097.

Mori, R., & Kawahara, M. (1990, July). *Superdistribution: The Concept and the Architecture.* Transaction of the IEICE, E *73*(7), 1133-1146.

Mori, R., & Tashiro, S. (1987). *The Concept of Software Service System (SSS).* Transaction of the IEICE, J70-D.1, Jan 1987, pp. 70-81

Morin, J.-H., & Pawlak, M. (2007) *From Digital Rights Management to Enterprise Rights and Policy Management: Challenges and Opportunities.* Advances in Enterprise Information Technology Security, F. Herrmann and D. Khadraoui (Eds), Information Science Reference, IGI Global, July 2007, pp. 169-188.

Morin, J.-H., & Pawlak, M. (2007). *A Model for Credential Based Exception Management in Digital Rights Management Systems,* First International Conference on Global Defense and Business Continuity, ICGD&BC 2007, Second International Conference on Internet Monitoring and Protection, IEEE, July 1-6, 2007, Silicon Valley, USA.

Morin, J.-H., & Pawlak, M. (2008). *Exception-Aware Digital Rights Management Architecture Experimentation,* 2008 International Conference on Information Security and Assurance, (ISA 2008), IEEE, April 24-26, 2008, Busan, Korea, pp. 518-526.

Moulin, P., & Koetter, R. (2005). Data-Hiding Codes. *Proceedings of IEEE, 93*(12), 2083--2126, December 2005.

Moulin, P., & Mihcak, M. (2002). A Framework for Evaluating the Data-Hiding Capacity of Image Sources. *IEEE Transactions on Image Processing, 11*(9), 1029–1042.

MPEG-21 Requirements for a Rights Data Dictionary and a Rights Expression Language. (2001, July). International Organization for Standardization. ISO/IECJTC1/SC29/WG11 N4336, Sydney, Austraila.

Mulligan, D. K., Han, J., & Burstein, A. J. (2003). How DRM-based content delivery systems disrupt expectations of "personal use'. In *Proceedings of the ACM workshop on Digital Rights Management* (pp. 77–89). ACM.

Munawar, M. A., & Ward, P. A. S. (2005). Are two interfaces better than one? In *Proceedings of the IEEE International Conference on Wireless And Mobile Computing, Networking And Communications (WiMob), 2,* 119-125.

Murata, M., Tozawa, A., & Kudo, M. (2003). XML Access Control Using Static Analysis. *ACM Conference on Computer and Communications Security.*

Nandiraju, N., Nandiraju, D., Santhanam, L., He, B., Wang, J., & Agrawal, D. P. (2007). Wireless Mesh Networks: Current Challenges and Future Directions of Web-In-The-Sky. *IEEE Wireless Communications, 14*(4), 79-89.

Naor, M., & Reingold, O. (1997). Number-theoretic constructions of efficient pseudo-random functions. In *FOCS '97: Proceedings of the 38th Annual Symposium on Foundations of Computer Science (FOCS '97),* Washington, DC, USA, pp. 458. IEEE Computer Society.

Naor, N., & Shamir, A. (1995). Visual Cryptography. Advances in Cryptography: Eurocrypt'94, Lecture Notes in Computer Science, Vol. 950 (pp. 1-12)

Napster. (2006). How the old Napster worked. Retrieved January 2006 from http://computer.howstuffworks.com/napster.htm

Narasimha M., Tsudik G. & Yi J.H. (2003). On the Utility of Distributed Cryptography in P2P and MANETs: The Case of Membership Control. In *Proc. of the 11th IEEE Int. Conf. on Network Protocols*, 336-345.

Nascimento, J. C., & Marques, J. S. (2006). Performance Evaluation of Object Detection Algorithms for Video Surveillance. *IEEE Transactions on Multimedia, 8*(4), 761-774.

Navakitkanok, P., & Aramvith, S. (2004). Improved Rate Control for Advanced Video Coding (AVC) Standard under low-delay contraints. *Paper presented at the Intn'l Conf. on Info. Tech.: Coding and Computing (ITCC'04).*

NeoByte Solutions (2008). *Invisible Secrets 4.* http://www.invisiblesecrets.com, last visited: January 23, 2008.

Neubauer, C., Herre, J., & Brandenburg, K. (1998). Continuous steganographic data transmission using uncompressed audio. *Proc. Information Hiding Workshop.* Portland, OR, pp. 208–217, 1998.

Newman, C. (1988). Memory capacity in neural networks, *Neural Network, 1*(1), 223–238.

Next Generation Secure Computing Base. (2007). http://www.microsoft.com/resources/ngscb/default.mspx

Ngan, K. N., Yap, C. W., & Tan, K. T. (2001). *Video Coding for Wireless Communication Systems.* New York: Marcel Dekker, Inc.

NGSCB. (2006). *Next Generation Secure Computing Base.* Retrieved October 2006 from http://www.microsoft.com/resources/ngscb/default.mspx

Niimi, M., Minewaki, S., Noda, H., & Kawaguchi, E. (2003). A Framework of Text-based Steganography Using SD-Form Semantics Model. *IPSJ Journal, 44*(8).

Nikolaidis, A., & Pitas, I. (2000). Robust watermarking of facial images based on salient geometric pattern matching. *IEEE Trans. Multimedia, 2*, 172-184, Sept. 2000.

Niu, X., Schmucker, M., & Busch, C. (2002). Video watermarking resisting to rotation, scaling, and translation.

In *SPIE Security Watermarking of Multimedia Contents IV. Vol.* 4675, (pp 512–519), San Jose, CA, USA.

Norman, B. (1973). *Secret Warfare.* Washington, DC: Acropolis Books.

Norris, C., McCahill, M., & Wood, D. (2004). The Growth of CCTV: a global perspective on the international diffusion of video surveillance in publicly accessible space. Surveillance & Society. *CCTV Special. 2*(2/3), 376-395.

Ó Ruanaidh, J. J. K., & Pun, T. (1998) Rotation, scale and translation invariant spread spectrum digital image watermarking. *Signal Processing, 66*, 303-317.

OASIS standard, eXtensible Access Control Markup Language (XACML), http://www.oasis-open.org/committees/xacml.

ODRL. The Open Digital Rights Language Initiative. http://odrl.net/.

Ogunfunmi, T., & Huang, W. C. (May 2005, May 23-26). A Flexible Macroblock Ordering with 3D MBAMAP for H.264/AVC. *Paper presented at the IEEE International Symposium on Circuits and Systems.*

Ohm, J.-R. (1994, September). Three-dimensional subband coding with motion compensation. *IEEE Transactions on Image Processing, 3*, 559-571.

OMA Broadcast Mobile Services v1.0 enabler, Open Mobile Alliance™. http://www.openmobilealliance.org/

OMA Digital Rights Management v2.0 enabler (2004, June 15). Open Mobile Alliance™, Approved Version 1.0, http://www.openmobilealliance.org/

OMA Digital Rights Management v2.1 enabler. Open Mobile Alliance™, http://www.openmobilealliance.org/

OMA, the Open Mobile Alliance (2004). OMA-DRM-ARCH-V2 0-20040715-C DRM architecture.

Open Digital Rights Language (ODRL), Version 1.1. (2002, August 8). http://odrl.net/1.1/ODRL-11.pdf or http://www.w3.org/TR/odrl/

Open Digital Rights Language ODRL Version 2 Requirements. (2005, February). ODRL, Retrieved from http://odrl.net/2.0/v2req.html.

Open Mobile Alliance. http://www.openmobilealliance.org/

OpenSSL (2007). http://www.openssl.org

Oracle Corp. (2002). Oracle 9i Lite - Oracle Lite SQL Reference. Oracle Documentation.

Ortega, A., Ramchandran, K., & Vetterli, M. (1994). Optimal trellis-based buffered compression and fast approximations. *IEEE Trans. on Image Processing, 3*(1), 26-40.

Osborn, S., Ravi Sandhu, R. S., & Munawer, Q. (2000). Configuring role-based access control to enforce mandatory and discretionary access control policies. *ACM Transactions on Information and System Security, 3*(2,) 85-106.

Ostergaard, J., Jensen, J., & Heusdens, R. (2006, May). N-channel entropy-constrained multiple-description lattice vector quantization. *IEEE Transactions on Information Theory, 52*(5), 1956-1973.

Palomar, E., Estevez-Tapiador, J. M., Hernandez-Castro, J. C.& Ribagorda, A. (In press, 2007). Secure content access and replication in pure P2P networks. Computer Communications.

Pan, D.. (1995). A Tutorial on MPEG/Audio Compression. *IEEE Multimedia*, Summer, pp. 60-74.

Pang L. J., Li, H. X., & Wang, Y. M. (2006). Secret Sharing Scheme with General Access Structures Based on LUC and its Security. *Computer Science, 33*(5), 121-123 (In Chinese).

Pang, L. J., Jiang, Z. T., & Wang, Y. M. (2006). A Multi-Secret Sharing Scheme Based on the General Access Structure. *Journal of Computer Research and Development, 43*(1), 33-38 (In Chinese).

Pannetrat, A., & Molva, R. (2003). Efficient multicast packet authentication. In *Proceeding of Network and Distributed System Security Symposium (NDSS)*, San Diego, CA, Feb. 2003.

Panyavaraporn, J., Cajote, R. D., & Aramvith, S. (Nov. 2007, Nov. 2007). Performance Analysis of Flexible Macroblock Ordering using Bit-count and Distortion Measure for H.264 Wireless Video Transmission. *Paper presented at the Int'l Workshop on Smart Info-Media Systems*, Bangkok, Thailand.

Papapanagiotou, K., Kellinis, E., Marias, G. F., & Georgiadis, P. (2005). Alternatives for Multimedia Messaging System Steganography. *Proceedings the IEEE International Conference on Computational Intelligence and Security (CIS 2005), Part II, LNAI 3802,* (pp. 589-596), Xian, China.

Park, J. M., Chong, E. K., & Siegel, H. J. (2002). Efficient multicast packet authentication using signature amortization. In *Proceedings of the IEEE Symposium on Research in Security and Privacy,* pages 227-240, May 2002.

Park, J., & Sandhu, R. (2004). *The UCON$_{ABC}$ Usage Control Model*. ACM Transactions on Information and Systems Security, 7(1), 128–174.

Park, K., & Lee, H. (2001). On the effectiveness of route-based packet filtering for distributed DoS attack prevention in power-law internets. *ACM SIGCOMM Computer Communication Review, 31*(4), 15-26.

Park, Y.-R., Kang, H.-H., Shin, S.-U., & Kwon, K.-R. (2005). A steganographic scheme in digital images using information of neighboring pixels. *Lecture Notes in Computer Scence: ICNC2005, 3612,* 962-967.

Park, Y.-R., Kang, H.-H., Shin, S.-U., & Kwon, K.-R. (2005). An image steganography using pixel characteristics. *Lecture Notes in Artificial Intelligence: CIS2005,* 581-588.

Parrott, D. (2001, June). *Requirements for a Rights Data Dictionary and Rights Expression Language*. Reuters, Retrieved from https://xml.coverpages.org/RLTC-Reuters-Reqs.pdf.

Parviainen, R., & Parnes, P. (2001). Large scale distributed watermarking of multicast media through encryption. In *Proceedings of IFIP Communications and Multimedia Security 2001*. Norwell MA: Kluwer Academic Publishers, pp.149-158, 2001.

Pathak V. & Iftode L. (2006). Byzantine Fault Tolerant Public Key Authentication in Peer-to-Peer Systems. *Computer Networks, 50*(4), 579-596. Elsevier.

Pedersen, T. P. (1991). Distributed provers with applications to undeniable signatures. In *Advances in Cryptology - EUROCRYPT '91: Workshop on the Theory and Application of Cryptographic Techniques*. Lecture Notes in Computer Science, Brighton, UK, pp. 221–242.

Peer Impact (2007). Web Site. Retrieved June 5, 2007 from http://www.peerimpact.com/

Peer-to-peer (2006). *Wikipedia*. Retrieved on October 7, 2006 at http://en.wikipedia.org/wiki/Peer-to-peer

Pei, D. Y., & Zhu, Y. F. (2002). *Algorithm and Number Theory*. Beijing: Science Press, 127-129 (In Chinese).

Pereira, S., Voloshynovskiy, S., & Pun, T. (2000). Effective channel coding for DCT watermarking. In *Proceedings of the IEEE International Conference on Image Processing, 3*, 671–673. USA: SPIE Press.

Pereira, S., Voloshynovskiy, S., & Pun, T. (2001). Optimal transform domain watermark embedding via linear programming. *Signal Processing, 81*(6), 1251–1260.

Perez-Gonzalez, F., Hernandez, J., & Balado, F. (2001). Approaching the capacity limit in image watermarking: A perspective on coding techniques for data hiding applications. *Signal Processing, 81*, 1215-1238.

Perez-Gonzalez, F., Hernandez, J., & Felix, B. (2001). Approaching the capacity limit in image watermarking, A perspective on coding techniques for data hiding applications. *Signal Processing, 81*(6), 1215–1238.

Perrig, A., Canetti, R., Tygar, J. D., & Song, D. (2000). Efficient authentication and signature of multicast streams over lossy channels. In *Proceedings of the IEEE Symposium on Research in Security and Privacy*, pages 56-73, May 2000.

Pestoni, F., Lotspiech, J. B. & Nusser, S. (2004). xCP: Peer-to-Peer Content Protection. *IEEE Signal Processing Magazine, 21*(2), 71-81.

Petitcolas, F. A., Anderson, R. J., & Kuhn, M. G.. (1999). Information hiding: a survey. *Proceedings of the IEEE, 87*(7). 1062–1078.

Pi, M. H., Li, C. H., & Li, H. (2006). A novel fractal image watermarking. IEEE Transactions on Multimedia, 8(3), 488-499

PictureMarc. (2007). *Embed Watermark*. v 1.00.45, Digimarc Corporation.

Pinet, A. (2007), SecurEngine Professional 1.0, http://securengine.isecurelabs.com, last visited: 12 January 2007.

Piva, A., Barni, M, Bartolini, F., & Cappellini, V. (1998). Threshold Selection for Correlation-Based Watermark Detection. *Proceedings of COST254 Workshop on Intelligent Communications*, 67-72.

Piva, A., Barni, M., Bartolini, F., & Cappellini, V. (1997). DCT-based watermark recovery without resorting to the uncorrupted original image. *Proceedings IEEE International Conference on Image Processing, 1*, 520-523.

Piva, A., Bartolini, F, & Barni, M. (2002). Managing copyright in open networks. *IEEE Internet Computing, 6*(3). 18–26.

Podilchuk, C. I., & Delp, E. J. (2001). Digital watermarking: algorithms and application. IEEE Signal Processing Magazine, 18(4), 33-46

Podolsky, M., McCanne, S., & Vetterli, M. (1998). Soft ARQ for layeres streaming media, *Technical Report UCB/CSD-98-1024*. University of California, Berkeley: Computer Science Division.

Popescu, B .C., Kamperman, F. L. A. J., Crispo, B., & Tanenbaum, A. S. (2004). A DRM security architecture for home networks. In *DRM '04: Proceedings of the 4th ACM workshop on Digital Rights Management*, 1-10. ACM Press.

Pouloudi, A. (1999). Aspects of the stakeholder concept and their implications for information systems development. In R.H. Sprague (Ed.), *Proceedings of the 32nd Hawaii International Conference on System Sciences*, Los Alamitos, CA: IEEE Computer Society Press.

Prechelt, L., & Typke, R. (2001). An interface for melody input. *ACM Transactions on Computer-Human Interaction, 8*(2), 133-149.

Prieto-Digitalaz, R. (1990). Domain analysis: An introduction. *Software Engineering Notes, 15*(2), 47-54.

Provos, N. (2001). Defending against statistical steganalysis. In 10th usenix security symposium.

Provos, N., & Honeyman, P. (2001). Detecting steganographic contents on the internet (Tech. Rep. No. CITI 01-1a). University of Michigan Tech. Rep.

Provos, N., & Honeyman, P. (2003). Hide and seek: An introduction to steganography. IEEE Security and Privacy Magazine, 1 (3), 32-44.

Provos, N., & Honeyman, P. (2003). Hide and Seek: An Introduction to Steganography. *Security & Privacy Magazine,* 32-44.

Pucella, R., & Weissman, V. (2002, June). *A Logic for Reasoning about Digital Rights.* In Proceedings of the 15th IEEE Computer Security Foundations Workshop, pages 282–294, Nova Scotia, Canada.

Pucella, R., & Weissman, V. (2006, January). *A Formal Foundation for ODRL,* Cornell University, Ref: arxiv. org/abs/cs/0601085.

Pucheral, P., Bouganim, L., Valduriez, P., & Bobineau, C. (2001). PicoDBMS: Scaling down database techniques for the smartcard. *VLDB Journal,* 10(2-3).

Puri, R., & Ramchandran, K. (1999, October). Multiple description source coding using forward error correction codes. *33rd Asilomar Conf. on Signals, Systems and Computers 1999, 1,* Pacific Grove, CA, 342-346.

Puri, R., Lee, K.W., & Bharghavan, V. (2001, May). Forward error correction (FEC) codes based multiple description coding for internet video streaming and multicast. *Signal Processing: Image Communication, 16*(8), 745-762(18).

Qi, X., & Qi, J. (2005). *A feature-point-based RST resistant watermarking scheme.* Signal and Image Processing 2005, pp. 255-258.

Qiao, L., & Nahrstedt, K. (1998). Comparison of MPEG encryption algorithms. *Computers and Graphics, 22*(4), 437–448.

Quisquater, J.-J., & Joye, M. (1997). Authentication of sequences with the SL$_2$ hash function: Application to video sequences. *Journal of Computer Security,* 5(3), 213–223.

Quisquater, J.-J., & Joye, M. (1997). Practical solutions to authentication of images with a secure camera. *SPIE 97,* Dallas, Texas. In: *SPIE International Conference on Storage and Retrieval for Image and Video Databases, Vol. 3022,* (pp 290–297), San Jose, CA, USA.

Rabah, K. (2004). Steganography-The Art of Hiding Data. *Information Technology Journal, 3(3),* 245-269.

Radhakrishnan, R., Xiong, Z., & Memon, N. D. (2003). On the security of visual hash functions. In *SPIE*

International Conference Annual Symposium on Electronic Imaging: Science and Technology, Vol. 5020, (pp 644–652), Santa Clara, CA, USA.

Ramanathan, R., & Redi, J. (2002). A brief overview of ad hoc networks: challenges and directions. *IEEE Communications Magazine, 40*(5), 20-22.

Ramkumar, M., & Akansu, A. N. (1999). A Capacity Estimate for Data Hiding in Internet Multimedia. *Symposium on Content Security and Data Hiding in Digital Media,*

Rand Corporation, (1970). *Security Controls for Computer Systems. Report of Defense Science Board Task Force on Computer Security.* Retrieved December 23, 2007, from http://seclab.cs.ucdavis.edu/projects/history/papers/ware70.pdf

Rao, K. R., Bojkovic, Z. S., & Milovanovic, D. A. (May 2002). *Multimedia Communication Systems: Techniques, Standards and Networks*: Prentice Hall PTR.

Ray, I., Ray, I., & Narasimhamurthi, N. (2002). A Cryptographic Solution to Implement Access Control in a Hierarchy and More. *ACM symposium on Access control models and technologies.*

Raymond, D. R., Tompa, F. W., & Wood, D. (1995, March). *Markup Reconsidered.* Department of Computer Science, The University of Western Ontario, Retrieved from http://xml.coverpages.org/raymmark.ps

Real-time Transport Protocol (RTP), RFC 1889. (2007). http://www.faqs.org/rfcs/rfc1889.html

Rencher, A. C. (1995). *Methods of Multivariate Analysis.* New York: John Wiley, ch. 6, 10.

Reti, T., & Sarvas, R. (2004). DiMaS: Distributing Multimedia on Peer-to-Peer File Sharing Networks. *Proceedings of ACM Multimedia.*

Ribas-Corbera, J., & Lei, S. (1999). Rate Control in DCT Video Coding for Low-Delay Video Communications. *IEEE Trans. on Ckts. and Sys. for Video Tech, 9*(1), 172-185.

Rivest, R. L., Shamir, A., & Adleman, L. M. (1978). A method for obtaining digital signatures and public-key cryptosystems. *Communications of the ACM, 21(2),* 120-126.

Roche, S., & Dugelay, J.-L. (1998). Image watermarking based on the fractal transform: a draft demonstration. 1998 IEEE Second Workshop on Multimedia Signal Processing, pp. 358-363

Rodrigues, Liskov, & Shrira. (2002). Peer-to-peer: The design of a robust P2P system. *Proceedings of the 10th ACM SIGOPS European Workshop: Beyond the PC*, pp. 117–124.

Rokhlin, V. A. (1967). Lectures on the entropy theory of measure-preserving transformations. *Russian Mathematical Survey, 22*(5), 1–52.

Rosenblatt, B. (2003). *Integrating DRM with peer-to peer networks.* Retrieved January 2006 from http://www.giantstepsmts.com/drm_p2p.htm.

Rosenblatt, B. (2007). DRM: 2007 Year in Review, Part 2. Retrieved December 12, 2008 from http://www.drmwatch.com/watermarking/article.php/3718651

Rosenblatt, B. Trippe, B., & Mooney, S. (2001). *Digital Rights Management: Business and Technology*, New York: Hungry Minds/John Wiley & Sons, 2001.

Rowaihy, H., Enck, W., McDaniel, P., & La Porta, T. (2005). *Limiting Sybil Attacks in Structured Peer-to-Peer Networks.* Network and Security Research Center, Department of Computer Science and Engineering, Pennsylvania State University, USA.

Rowlnd, Craig H. (1997) Covert Channels in the TCP/IP Protocol. First Monday, Vol.2 No.5 - 5 May 1997.

RSA. (2006). Retrieved February 2006 from http://en.wikipedia.org/wiki/RSA

Ruanaidh, J., & Pun, T. (1998). Rotation, scale and translation invariant spread spectrum digital image watermarking. *Signal Processing, 66*(3), 303-317, 1998.

Rubin, A. D. (1997). Method for the secure distribution of electronic files in a distributed environment. *Patent number, 5,* 638-446.

Sadourny, Y., & Conan, V. (2003). A proposal for supporting selective encryption in JPSEC. IEEE Transactions on Consumer Electronics, 49(4), 864-849

Safavi-Naini, R., & Wang, Y. (2003). Traitor Tracing for Shortened and Corrupted Fingerprints. In *Digital Rights Management*, LNCS 2320, 32-50. Springer

Saha, S. (2000). Image Compression - from DCT to Wavelets: A Review. *ACM Crossroads Magazine, 6(3)*, 12–21, Retrieved January 23, 2008, from http://www.acm.org/crossroads/xrds6-3/sahaimgcoding.html

Salama, P., & King, B. (2005). Efficient secure image transmission: compression integrated with encryption, Proceedings of SPIE, 5681, 47-58

Sallee, P. (2003). Model-based steganography. In 6th Int. Workshop on Digital Watermarking (Vol. 3929, p. 154-167). Springer Berlin / Heidelberg.

Sanchez, M., López, G., Cánovas, O., Juan, A. Sánchez, J. A., & Gómez-Skarmeta, A. F. (2006). An Access Control System for Multimedia Content Distribution. A.S. Atzeni and A. Lioy (Eds.): *EuroPKI, LNCS 4043*, 169-183.

Sandhu R.S. & Zhang X. (2005). Peer-to-peer access control architecture using trusted computing technology. In *Proc. of the 10th ACM Symposium on Access control models and technologies*, 147-158.

Sandhu, R. S., & Samarati, P. (1994). Access Control: Principles and Practice. *IEEE Communications Magazine, 32*(9), 40-48.

Sandhu, R. S., (1993). Lattice-Based Access Control Models. *IEEE Computer, 26*(11), 9-19.

Sandhu, R. S., Coyne E.J., Feinstein H.L. & Youman C.E. (1996). *Role-based access control models. Computer, 29*(2), 38-47.

Sandhu, R., Coyne, E. J., Feinstein, H. L., & Youman, C. E. (1996). Role-based access control models. *IEEE Computer, 29*(2).

Sandhu, R.S., & Munawer, Q. (1998). How to Do Discretionary Access Control Using Roles. In *Proc. of the ACM Workshop on Role-Based Access Control*, 47-54.

Santosa, R. A., & Bao, P. (2005). Audio-to-image wavelet transform based audio steganography. *Proceedings of 47th International Symposium ELMAR*, 209- 212.

Santosh, A. N., & Atul, N. (2006). A filtering based approach to adaptive steganography. *Proceedings of 2006 IEEE Region 10 Conference*, 1-4.

Sarnoff Corporation. (2005). *Sarnoff Watermarking Technologies*, Retrieved December 12, 2007, from http://www.sarnoff.com/products_services/video_vision/digital_watermarking/index.asp.

Saroiu, Gummadi, & Gribble. (2002). A measurement study of peer-to-peer file sharing systems. *Multimedia Computing and Networking, 153*, 156–170.

SAX. A Simple API for XML. http://www.saxproject.org/.

Sayood, K. (2006). Introduction to Data Compression – Third Edition, San Francisco/CA, Elsevier/Morgan Kaufmann.

Schechter, S. E., Greenstadt, R. A., & Smith M.D. (2004). Trusted Computing, Peer-to-Peer Distribution, and The Economics of Pirated Entertainment. *Economics of Information Security, 12*, 1568-2633. Springer.

Schmidt, A. U. (2006). Multi-level markets and incentives for information goods. *Information Economics and Policy*, 18(2), 125–138.

Schmidt, A. U. (2008) Free riding and competition in network markets for digital goods. In: *Proceedings of the 41st Annual Hawaii International Conference on System Sciences* (HICSS-41), January 7-10.

Schmidt, A. U., & Kuntze, N. (2006). Trusted Computing in Mobile Action. In: *Peer-reviewed Proceedings of the ISSA 2006 From Insight to Foresight Conference*, Sandton, South Africa: ISSA.

Schmidt, A. U., Kuntze, N., & Abendroth, J. (2008). Trust for Location-based Authorisation. To appear in: *Proceedings of the Wireless Communications and Networking Conference WCNC 2008*, Las Vegas: IEEE.

Schmidt, A. U., Kuntze, N., & Kasper, M. (2008). On the deployment of Mobile Trusted Modules. To appear in: *Proceedings of the Wireless Communications and Networking Conference WCNC 2008*, Las Vegas: IEEE.

Schneier, B. (1996). *Applied Cryptography, 2nd Edition*. John Wiley & Sons Ed.

Schneier, B. (2000). *Secrets & Lies: Digital Security in a Networked World*. Wiley.

Schwarz, H., Marpe, D., & Wiegand, T. (2006, July). Analysis of hierarchical B pictures and MCTF. *2006 IEEE International Conference on Multimedia & Expo*, Toronto, Canada, 1929-1932.

Secure RTP. (2007). http://srtp.sourceforge.net

Sedky, M. H., Moniri, M., & Chibelushi, C. C. (2005). Classification of smart video surveillance systems for commercial applications. In *Proceedings of the IEEE Conference on Advanced Video and Signal Based Surveillance (AVSS)*, 638-643.

Selcuk, A. A., Uzun, E. & Pariente, M. R. (2004). A Reputation-Based Trust Management System for P2P Networks. In *Proc. of the 4th IEEE/ACM Int. Symposium on Cluster Computing and the Grid*, 251-258.

Serrão, C., Naves, D., Barker, T., Balestri, M., & Kudumakis, P. (2003). Open SDRM – An open and secure digital rights management solution.

Servetto, S. D., Podilchuk, C. I., & Ramchandran, K. (1998). Capacity Issues in Digital Image Watermarking. In *IEEE International Conference on Image Processing, 1*, 445–449. USA: IEEE Press.

Servetto, S. D., Ramchandran, K., Vaishampayan, V. A., & Nahrstedt, K. (2000, May). Multiple description wavelet based image coding. *IEEE Transactions on Image Processing, 9*(5), 813-826.

Servetto, S. D., Vaishampayan, V. A., & Sloane, N. J. A. (1999, March). Multiple description lattice vector quantization. *Proc. Data Compression Conference, 29*(31), 13-22.

Seshadri, P. (1999). Honey, I Shrunk the DBMS: Footprint, Mobility, and Beyond. *ACM SIGMOD Int. Conf. on Management of Data*.

Setyawan, I., Kakes, G., & Lagendijk, R. L. (2002). Synchronization-insensitive video watermarking using structured noise pattern. *Proceedings of the SPIE Security and Watermarking of Multimedia Contents IV, 4675*, 520-530.

SHA-1 (1995). National Institute of Standards and Technology. *Secure Hash Standard (SHS)*, FIPS Publication 180-1, 1995.

Shamir, A. (1979). How to Share a Secret. *Communications of the ACM, 22*(11), 612-613.

Shamir, A., & van Someren, N. (1999). Playing "hide and seek" with stored keys. *Lecture Notes in Computer Science, 1648*, 118-124. Springer

Shannon, C. E. (1948). A Mathematical Theory of Communication. *Bell System Technical Journal, 27,* 373-423.

Shannon, C. E. (1959). Coding Theorems for a discrete source with a fidelity criterion.

Shapiro, W., & Vingralek, R. (2002). How to manage persistent state in DRM systems. In Security and Privacy in Digital Rights Management, LNCS 2320, 176-191. Springer.

Shi, C., & Bhargava, B.(1998). A fast MPEG video encryption algorithm. In *The Sixth ACM International Conference on Multimedia,* (pp 81–88), Bristol, UK.

Shieh, S. P., & Sun, H. M. (1994). On Constructing Secret Sharing Schemes. *Proceedings of IEEE International Conference on Computer Communications (INFOCOM 1994),* 1288-1292.

Shih, F. Y. (2007). *Digital watermarking and Steganography: Fundamentals and Techniques,* CRC Press, Boca Raton, FL.

Shih, F. Y., & Wu, Y.-T. (2005). Enhancement of image watermark retrieval based on genetic algorithm. *Journal of Visual Commu. and Image Repre., 16,* 115-133.

Shirali Shahreza, M. (2005, July). An Improved Method for Steganography on Mobile Phone. *WSEAS Transactions on Systems, 4(7),* 955-957.

Shirali-Shahreza, M. (2005, December). A New Method for Steganography in HTML Files. *Proceedings of the International Joint Conference on Computer, Information, and Systems Sciences, and Engineering (CISSE 2005),* (pp. 247-251), Bridgeport, CT.

Shirali-Shahreza, M. (2006, April). Stealth Steganography in SMS. *Proceedings of the third IEEE and IFIP International Conference on Wireless and Optical Communications Networks (WOCN 2006),* Bangalore, India.

Shirali-Shahreza, M. (2006, February). Steganography in Wireless Application Protocol. *Proceedings of the IASTED International Conference on Internet and Multimedia Systems and Applications (EuroIMSA 2006),* (pp. 91-95), Innsbruck, Austria.

Shirali-Shahreza, M. (2007). Steganography in Artistic Websites. *International Reviews on Computers and Software (IRECOS),* 2(1), 25-29.

Shirali-Shahreza, M. H., & Shirali-Shahreza, M. (2006). A New Approach to Persian/Arabic Text Steganography. *Proceedings of the 5th IEEE/ACIS International Conference on Computer and Information Science (ICIS 2006),* (pp. 310-315), Honolulu, HI, USA.

Shneidman, J. & Parkes, D.C. (2003). Rationality and Self-Interest in Peer to Peer Networks. In *Proc. of the 2nd Int. Workshop on P2P Systems,* 139-148. Springer-Verlag.

Simmons, G. J. (1983). The prisoner's problem and the subliminal channel. *Proceedings of Crypto'83,* 51-67.

Simon, M. K., & Hinedi, M. K., & Lindsey, W. C. (1995). *Digital Communication Techniques: Signal Design and Detection.* London: Prentice-Hall.

Sinha, A., & Singh, K. (2005). Image encryption by using fractional Fourier transform and jigsaw transform in image bit planes. Optical Engineering, 44(5), 057001

Smith, C. L., & Robinson, M. (1999). The understanding of security technology and its applications. In *Proceedings of the IEEE International Carnahan Conference on Security Technology,* 26-37.

Sommerville, I. (2004). *Software Engineering.* Pearson.

SourceForge. (2006). AtomicParsley, Retrieved on September 16, 2006 at http://atomicparsley.sourceforge.net/.

Spanos, G., & Maples, T. (1995). Performance study of a selective encryption scheme for the security of networked, real-time video. *Proc. of 4th International Conference on Computer Communications and Networks.* Las Vegas. Nevada.

Spaulding, J., Noda, H., Shirazi, M. N., & Kawaguchi, E. (2002). BPCS steganography using EZW lossy compressed images. *Pattern Recognition Letters, 23*(13), 1579-1587.

Srinivasan, M. (1999). Iterative Decoding of Multiple Descriptions. *Data Compression Conference,* 463-472.

Srisawaivilai, N., & Aramvith, S. (2005). Improved H.264 Rate-Control using Channel Throughput Estimate for ARQ-based Wireless Video Transmission. *Paper presented at the IEEE Symposium on Intelligent Signal Processing and Communications,* Hongkong.

Stadler, M. (1996). Publicly verifiable secret sharing. In *Advances in Cryptology - EUROCRYPT '96,* 1070 of *Lecture Notes in Computer Science,* pp. 190–199.

Stallings, W. (2003). *Cryptography and Network Security: Principles and Practices.* Prentice Hall

Stamp, M. (2002, September). Risks of digital rights management, Inside Risks 147, *Communications of the ACM, 45*(9), 120

Stamp, M. (2003). Digital rights management: For better or for worse? Extreme Tech, May 20, 2003, Retrieved July 3, 2007 at http://www.extremetech.com/article2/0,3973,1051610,00.asp

Stamp, M. (2003). Digital rights management: the technology behind the hype. *Journal of Electronic Commerce Research, 4*(3), 102-112, http://www.csulb.edu/web/journals/jecr/issues/20033/paper3.pdf

Stamp, M. (2003). Digital rights management: For better or for worse? *ExtremeTech,* May 1, 2003, http://www.extremetech.com/article2/0,3973,1051610,00.asp

Stamp, M. (2004). Risks of monoculture, Inside Risks 165, *Communications of the ACM, 47*(3), 120.

Stamp, M. (2005). *Information Security: Principles and Practice.* John Wiley & Sons, Inc.

Stamp, M., & Dai, J. (2006). *Micropayment token making schemes.* Retrieved October 2006 from http://www.cs.sjsu.edu/faculty/stamp/students/dai.htm

Stamp, M., Mathur, A., & Kim, S. (2006). Role based access control and the JXTA peer-to-peer network. *Proceedings of 2006 International Conference on Security & Management.*

Stefik, M. J., & Casey, M. M. (1994, November). *System for Controlling the Distribution and Use of Digital Works.* Xerox Corporation, U.S. Patent No. 5,629,980.

Steinbach, E., Farber, N., & Girod, B. (Dec. 1997). Standards compatible extension of H.263 for robust video transmission in mobile environments. *IEEE Trans. on Ckts. and Sys. for Video Tech, 7*(6), 872-881.

Stenborg, K-G. (2005). Distribution and Individual Watermarking of Streamed Content for Copy Protection, Licentiate thesis, Department of Electrical Engineering, Linköping University, Sweden.

Stevens, W. R. (1994). TCP/IP Illustrated, Volume 1 - The Protocols. Addison-Wesley.

Stewart, D., & Lerner, E. A. (2007). *IBM - Think Research,* Retrieved December 20, 2007 from http://domino.watson.ibm.com/comm/wwwr_thinkresearch.nsf/pages/solutions299.html.

Stini, M., Mauve, M., & Fitzek, F.H.P. (2006). Digital Ownership: From Content Consumers to Owners and Traders. *IEEE Multimedia, 13*(4), 1- 6. DOI: 10.1109/MMUL.2006.79

Stinson, D. R. (1995). *Cryptography: Theory and Practice.* New York: CRC Press, 343-350.

Sudharsan, S. (2005). Shared key encryption of JPEG color images. IEEE Transactions on Consumer Electronics, 51(4), 1204-1211

Sullivan, K., Bi, Z., Madhow, U., Chandrasekaran, S., & Manjunath, B. (2004). Steganalysis of quantization index modulation data hiding. In Int. Conf. on Image Processing (icip'04) (Vol. 2, p. 1165-1168).

Sun Developer Network. (2007). Remote method invocation, Retrieved on March 12, 2007 at http://java.sun.com/javase/technologies/core/basic/rmi/index.jsp

Sun, H. M., & Shieh, S. P. (1996). An Efficient Construction of Perfect Secret Sharing Schemes for Graph-Based Structures. *Journal of Computers and Mathematics with Applications, 31*(7), 129-135.

Sun, H. M., & Shieh, S. P. (1997). Secret Sharing in Graph-Based Prohibited Structures. *Proceedings of IEEE International Conference on Computer Communications (INFOCOM 1997),* 9-13.

Sun, Q., & Chang, S. (2004). Signature Based Media Authentication. In *Multimedia Security Handbook,* CRC Press, 2004.

Sun, Q., Chang, S. F., Kurato, M., & Suto, M. (2002). A new semi-fragile image authentication framework combining ECC and PKI. In *IEEE International Symposium on Circuits and Systems, Vol. 2,* (pp 440–443), Phoenix, USA.

Suzuki, T., *et al.*, (2004). A system for end-to-end authentication of adaptive multimedia content. *Eighth IFIP TC-6 TC-11 Conference on Communications and Multimedia Security (CMS'04)*, Sept. 2004.

SVP Alliance. Secure content anywhere, anytime. http://www.svpalliance.org/

Swanson, M. D., Kobayashi, M., & Tewfik, A. H. (1998a, June). Multimedia Data-Embedding and Watermarking Technologies. *Proc. IEEE, 86*(6), 1064-1087.

Swanson, M. D., Zhu, B., Tewfik, A. H., & Boney, L. (1998b). Robust audio watermarking using perceptual masking. *Signal Processing, 66*(3), 337-355.

Sweene, P. (1991). *Error Control Coding (An Introduction)*, Prentice-Hall International Ltd., Englewood Cliffs, NJ.

Swing. (2006). Project Swing (Java Foundation Classes). Retrieved April 2006 from http://java.sun.com/j2se/1.5.0/docs/guide/swing/

Szepanski, W. (1979). A Signal Theoretic Method for Creating Forgery proof Documents for Automatic Verification. *Carnahan Conference on Crime Countermeasures*, 101-109.

Tanaka, K., Nakamura, Y., & Matsui, K. (1990). Embedding secret information into a dithered multi-level image. *Proceedings of IEEE Military Communications Conference*, 216-220.

Tang, L. (1996). Methods for encrypting and decrypting MPEG video data efficiently. *Proc. ACM Multimedia, 96*. Boston. 219–230.

Tanin, Nayar, & Samet. (2005). An efficient nearest neighbor algorithm for P2P settings. *Proceedings of the 2005 National Conference on Digital Government Re-search, 89*, 21–28.

Tefas, A., Nikolaidis, A., Nikolaidis, N., Solachidis, V., Tsekeridou, S., & Pitas, I. (2001). Performance Analysis of Watermarking Schemes based on Skew Tent Chaotic Sequences, *NSIP'01, 51*, 1979-1994.

Tefas, A., Nikolaidis, A., Nikolaidis, N., Solachidis, V., Tsekeridou, S., & Pitas, I. (2003). Markov Chaotic Sequences for Correlation Based Watermarking Schemes. *Proceedings of Chaos, Solitons and Fractals, 17*, 567-573.

The IETF TLS Workgroup Retrieved Jan 18, 2008 from Transport Layer Security Web site: http://www.ietf.org/html.charters/tls-charter.html

The MPEG-21 Rights Expression Language – A White Paper. (2003, July). Rightscom Ltd. Retrieved from http://www.xrml.org/reference/MPEG21_REL_white-paper_Rightscom.pdf

The PRISM Rights Language Name Space. (2005, February). PRISM, Retrieved from http://xml.coverpages.org/PRISM-RightsNamespaceV12.pdf.

Thomos, N., Argyropoulos, S., Boulgouris, N. V., & Strintzis, M. G. (Nov. 2005). Error Resilient Transmission of H.264/AVC streams using Flexible Macroblock Ordering. *Paper presented at the EWIMT05*, London, UK.

Tian, C., & Hemami, S. S. (2005, April). A new class of multiple description scalar quantizer and its application to image coding. *IEEE Signal Processing Letters, 12*, 329-332.

Tian, C., & Hemami, S.S. (2004, May). An embedded image coding system based on Tarp filter with classification. *Proc. Int. Conf. Acoustics, Speech, Signal Process, 3*, 49-52, Montreal, QC, Canada.

Tian, J. (2003). Reversible data embedding using a difference expansion. *IEEE Transaction on Circuits and Systems for Video Technology, 13*(8), 890-896.

Tilo, T., & Olmo, G. (2004, November). A novel multiple description coding scheme compatible with the JPEG2000 decoder. *IEEE Signal Processing Letters, 11*(11), 908-911.

Tiny httpd (2007). http://www.acme.com/software/thttpd/thttpd_man.html

Tolone, W., Ahn, G., Pai, T. & Hong, S. (2005). Access Control in Collaborative Systems. *ACM Computing Surveys, 37*(1), 29-41.

Torralba, A., & Olivia, A. (2003). Statistics of natural image categories. IOP Network: Computation in Neural Systems, 14, 391-412.

Tran, H., Hitchens, M., Varadharajan, V., & Watters, P. (2005). A Trust based Access Control Framework for P2P File-Sharing Systems. In *Proc. of the 38th Hawaii Int. Conf. on System Sciences*.

Trappe, W., Wu, M., Wang, Z. J., & Liu, K. J. R. (2003). Anti-collusion fingerprinting for multimedia. *IEEE Trans. Signal Processing, 51*, 1069-1087.

Trivedi, S., & Chandramouli, R. (2005). Secret key estimation in sequential steganalysis. IEEE Transactions on Signal Processing: Supplement on Secure Media, 53 (2), 746-757.

Trusted Computing Group (2007). TCG TPM Specification Version 1.2 Revision 103. Retrieved February 29, 2008, from https://www.trustedcomputinggroup. org/groups/tpm/

Trusted Computing Group (2007). Mobile Trusted Module Specification 1.0. Retrieved February 29, 2008, from https://www.trustedcomputinggroup.org/groups/mobile/

Tsai, C. S., & Chang, C. C. (2004). A new repeating color watermarking scheme based on human visual model. Eurasip Journal on Applied Signal Processing, 2004(13), 1965-1972

Tsekeridou, S., Solachidis, V., Nikolaidis, N., Nikolaidis, A., Tefas, A., & Pitas, I. (2001). Theoretic Investigation of the Use of Watermark Signals derived from Bernoulli Chaotic Sequences, *SCIA2001.*

Tsekeridou, S., Solachidis, V., Nikolaidis, N., Nikolaidis, A., Tefas, A., & Pitas, I. (2001). Bernoulli Shift Generated Watermarks: Theoretic Investigation. *Proceedings of IEEE International Conference on Acoustics, Speech and Signal Processing, 3*, 1989-1992.

Tseng, Y. C., & Pan, H. K. (2001). Secure and Invisible Data Hiding in 2-Color Images. *Proceedings of Twentieth Annual Joint Conference of the IEEE Computer and Communications Societies (INFOCOM 2001) Vol. 2,* (pp. 887-896), Anchorage, Alaska, USA.

Tseng, Y. C., Chen, Y. Y., & Pan, H. K. (2002). A Secure Data Hiding Scheme for Binary Images. *IEEE Transaction on Communications, 50*(8), 1227-31.

Tu, Y.-K., Yang, J.-F., & Sun, M.-T. (May 2007). Rate-Distortion Modeling for Efficient H.264/AVC Encoding. *IEEE Trans. on Ckts. and Sys. for Video Tech, 17*(5).

Tzeng, C. H., & Tsai, W.-H. (2001). A new technique for authentication of image/video for multimedia applications. In *ACM Multimedia and Security Workshop,* Ottawa, Canada.

Tzou, K. (November 1989). Post filtering for Cell loss Concealment in Packet Video. *SPIE Visual Communications and Image Processing IV, 1199,* 1620-1628.

United States Computer Emergency Readiness Team. (2006). *Risks of file-sharing technology.* Retrieved on November 3, 2006 at http://www.us-cert.gov/cas/tips/ST05-007.html

US Federal Standard (2000). *US Federal Standard 1037C, Telecom Glossary,* Retrieved February 29, 2008, from http://www.its.bldrdoc.gov/fs-1037/dir-018/_2554.htm

Vaishampayan, V. A. (1993, May). Design of multiple description scalar quantizers. *IEEE Transactions on Information Theory, 39,* 821-834.

Vaishampayan, V. A., Sloane, N., & Servetto, S. (2001, July). Multiple-description vector quantization with lattice codebooks: Design and analysis. *IEEE Transactions on Information Theory, 47,* 1718-1734.

van der Schaar, M., & Turaga, D. (2003, September). Multiple description scalable coding using wavelet-based motion compensated temporal filtering. *IEEE International Conference on Image Processing 2003, 2,* Barcelona, 489-492.

Van Schyndel, R. G. (2003). Digital Watermarking and Signal Delay Estimation Using Pseudonoise Sequences. *PhD thesis, School of Physics and Material Science, Monash University, Australia.*

Van, L. T., Chong, K.-S., Emmanuel S., & Kankanhalli M. (2007). A survey on digital camera image forensic methods. In *IEEE International Conference on Multimedia and Expo,* pp 16–19, Beijing, China.

Vasco, M. I. G., Näslund, M., & Shparlinski, I. (2004). New results on the hardness of Diffie-Hellman bits. In *Proc. Intern. Workshop on Public Key Cryptography,* Volume 2947 of *Lect. Notes in Comp. Sci.,* Singapore, pp. 159–172. Springer-Verlag.

Venkataramu, R. (2007). *Analysis and enhancement of Apple's Fairplay digital rights management.* Master's report, Department of Computer Science, San Jose State University, 2007, Retrieved July 3, 2007 at http://www.cs.sjsu.edu/faculty/stamp/students/RamyaVenkataramu_CS298Report.pdf

Violet. (2006). Retrieved October 2006 from http://horstmann.com/violet/

Vogt, H., Rohs, M., Kilian-Kehr, R. (2003). *Middleware for Communications, Chapter 16: Middleware for Smart Cards*. John Wiley and Sons Ed.

Voloshynovshiy, S., Pereira, S., Iquise, V., & Pun, T. (2001). Attacking modelling: towards a second generation watermarking benckmark. *Signal Processing, 81*(6), 1177-1214.

Vovida.org. (2004). *Secure RTP,* http://www.vovida.org/protocols/downloads/srtp/

W3C DOM, DOM: Document Object Model. http://www.w3.org/DOM.

Wada, N. (1989). Selective Recovery of video packet loss using error concealment. *IEEE Journal on Selected Areas in Communications, 7,* 807-814.

Wallace, G. K. (1991). The JPEG still picture compression standard. Communications of the ACM, 34(4), 31-44

Wang, C.-M., Wu, N.-I., Tsai, C.-S., & Hwang, M.-S. (2008). A high quality steganographic method with pixel-value differencing and modulus function. *Journal of Systems and Software, 81*(1), 150-158.

Wang, D., Canagarajah, N., Redmill, D., & Bull, D. (2004, May). Multiple description video coding based on zero padding. *IEEE 2004 International Symposium on Circuits and Systems, 2,* Vancouver, Canada, 205-208.

Wang, H., & Kwong, S. (January 2008). Rate-Distortion Optimization of Rate Control for H.264 with Adaptive Initial Quantization Parameter Determination. *IEEE Trans. on Ckts. and Sys. for Video Tech, 18*(1).

Wang, H., Lu, Z., Pan, J., & Sun, S. (2005). Robust Blind Video Watermarking with Adaptive Embedding Mechanism. *International Journal of Innovative Computing, Information and Control, 1*(2), 247-259.

Wang, R. Z., Lin, C. F., & Lin, J. C. (2001). Image hiding by optimal LSB substitution and genetic algorithm. *Pattern Recognition, 34*(3), 671-683.

Wang, W., Lu, Y., Cui, H., & Tang, K. (2006). Rate control for low delay H.264/AVC transmission over channels with burst error. *Paper presented at the IMACS Multiconference on Computational Engineering on Systems Applications.*

Wang, X. (2005, July). *Design Principles and Issues of Rights Expression Languages for Digital Rights Management.* In Visual Communications and Image Processing 2005, *5960,* 1130–1141.

Wang, Y., & Moulin, P. (2006). Optimized feature extraction for learning-based image steganalysis. IEEE Transactions on Information Forensics and Security, 1 (2), 31-45.

Wang, Y., & Tan, K. L. (2001). A Scalable XML Access Control System. *Int. World Wide Web Conf.*

Wang, Y., Orchard, M., Vaishampayan, V. A., & Reibman, A. (2001, March). Multiple description coding using pairwise correlating transforms. *IEEE Transactions on Image Processing, 10,* 351-366.

Wang, Y., Reibman, A., & Lin, S. (2005, January). Multiple description coding for video delivery. *Proceedings of the IEEE, 93,* 57-70.

Wang, Z. J., Wu, M., Trappe, W., Liu, K. J. R. (2005). Group-oriented fingerprinting for multimedia forensics. Preprint, 2005.

Wang, Z., & Bovik, A. C. (2002). A universal image quanlity index. *IEEE Signal Processing Letters, 9*(3), 81-84.

Wang, Z., Bovik, A. C., Sheikh, H. R., & Simoncelli, E. P. (2004). Image quality assessment: From error visibility to structural similarity. *IEEE Transaction on Image Processing, 13*(4), 600-612.

Watson, A. B. (1993). DCT quantization matrices optimized for individual image. Human Vision Visual Processing, and Digital Display IV, 1993, SPIE 1913, 202-216.

Watson, A. B., & Yang, G. Y. (1997). Visibility of wavelet quantization noise. *IEEE Transactions on Image Processing, 6*(8), 1164–1174.

Weatherspoon, H., Moscovitz, T. & Kubiatowicz, J. (2002). Introspective failure analysis: Avoiding correlated failures in peer-to-peer systems. In *Proc. of the Int. Workshop on Reliable Peer-to-Peer.*

Web services security rights expression languages token profile 1.1. (2006). OASIS, Retrieved from http://docs.oasis-open.org/wss/oasis-wss-rel-token-profile-1.1.pdf.

Weinmann, R.-P., & Wirt, K. (2005). Analysis of the DVB Common Scrambling Algorithm. In *Proceedings of the IFIP sec2005* (pp. 195-207), Boston: Springer.

Welsh, B., & Farrington, D. (2002). *Crime prevention effects of closed circuit television: A systematic review.* London: Home Office Research, Development and Statistics Directorate.

Wen, H. (2006). *JHymn goes behind atoms and Apple to bring DRM-free music.* Retrieved on September 14, 2006 at http://osdir.com/Article3823.phtml

Wen, J., Severa, M., Zeng, W. J., Luttrell, M. H., & Jin, W. (2002). A format-compliant configurable encryption framework for access control of video. IEEE Transactions on Circuits and Systems for Video Technology, 12(6), 545-557

Wenger, S., & Horowitz, M. (May 2002). *FMO: Flexible Macroblock Ordering.* Fairfax (USA).

Westfeld, A. (2001). F5 -a steganographic algorithm high capacity despite better steganalysis. In Fifth Information Hiding Workshop (Vol. 2137, p. 289-302). Springer Berlin / Heidelberg.

Westfeld, A. (2002). Detecting low embedding rates. In 5th information hiding workshop (Vol. 2578, p. 324-339). Springer Berlin / Heidelberg.

Westfeld, A., & Pfitzmann, A. (1999). Attacks on steganographic systems breaking the steganographic utilities EzStego, Jsteg, Steganos, and S-Tools and some lessons learned. In *Proc. 3rd International Workshop on Information Hiding*, Dresden, Germany, 61-76.

Wheeler, D., & Needham, R. (1994). *TEA, a tiny encryption algorithm*, http://www.ftp.cl.cam.ac.uk/ftp/papers/djw-rmn/djw-rmn-tea.html

Wiegand, T., Sullivan, G. J., Bjontegaard, G., & Luthra, A. (2003). Overview of the H.264/AVC video coding standard. *IEEE Transactions on Circuits and Systems for Video Technology, 13*(7), 560-576.

Wierzbicki, A. (2005). Peer-to-peer direct sales. *Proceedings of the Fifth IEEE International Conference on Peer-to-Peer Computing.*

Windows Media Digital Rights Management Offering. (2004). http://www.microsoft.com/windows/windowsmedia/wm7/drm/offering.aspx

Wise, A. P. (2007). *Memory encryption for digital video.* U.S. Patent US2007140477 (A1). 2007-06-20.

Wolf, B. (2007). StegoDos - Black Wolf's Picture Encoder v0.90B, Public Domain. ftp://ftp.csua.berkeley.edu/ pub/ cypherpunks/ steganography/ stegodos.zip.

Wolf, J. K., Wyner, A. D., & Ziv, J. (1980, October). Source coding for multiple descriptions. *Bell System Technical Journal, 59,* 1417-1426.

Wolf, W., Ozer, B., & Lv, T. (2002). Smart cameras as embedded systems. *IEEE Computer, 35*(9), 48–53.

Wong, C. K., & Lam, S. S. (1998). Digital signatures for flows and multicasts. In *Proceeding of IEEE International Conference on Network Protocols*, Austin, TX, Oct. 1998.

Wong, P. W., & Memon, N. (2000). Secret and public key authentication watermarking schemes that resist vector quantization attack. In *Proc. SPIE, Security and Watermarking of Multimedia Contents II.* San Jose, 2000, pp. 417-427.

Woolley, S. (2007). Introduction to Multimedia Coding. John Wiley & Sons Inc, 2007.

Wu M., & Liu, B. (2004). Data Hiding in Binary Image for Authentication and Annotation. *IEEE Transaction on Multimedia,* 6(4), 528-538.

Wu, C.P. & Kuo, C.-C.J. (2005). Design of Integrated Multimedia Compression and Encryption Systems. IEEE Transactions on Multimedia, 7(5), 828-839

Wu, D. C., & Tsai, W. H. (2003). A steganographic method for images by pixel-value differencing. *Pattern Recognition Letters, 24*(9-10), 1613-1626.

Wu, H. C., & Chang, C. C. (2003). **Hiding digital watermarks using fractal compression technique. Fundamenta Informaticae, 58(2), 189-202**

Wu, M., Tang, E., & Liu, B. (2000). Data hiding in digital binary image. *Proceedings of IEEE International Conference on Multimedia & Expo 2000 (ICME 2000), vol. 1,* (pp. 393 – 396), New York, USA.

Wu, M., Trappe, W., Wang, Z. J., & Liu, R. (2004). Collusion-resistant fingerprinting for multimedia. *IEEE Signal Processing Magazine*, March 2004, pp. 15-27.

Compilation of References

Wu, T-. L., & Wu, S. F. (1997, June). Selected encryption and watermarking of MPEG video. In *International Conference on Image Science, Systems, and Technology CISST'97.*

Wu, Y. R., Wang, G. J., & Shi, R. H. (in press). Designing Secret Sharing Scheme with a Plane-Based General Access Structure. *Computer Engineering* (In Chinese).

Wu, Y., & Shih F. Y. (2004). An adjusted-purpose digital watermarking technique. Pattern Recognition, 37(12), 2349-2359.

Wu, Y., & Shih F. Y. (2006). Genetic algorithm based methodology for breaking the steganalytic systems. *IEEE Trans. SMC, Part B, 36*(1), 24-31.

Xiang, H., Wang, L., Lin, H., & Shi, J. (1999). Digital watermarking systems with chaotic sequences. *Proceedings of Security and Watermarking of Multimedia Contents*, 449-457.

Xiang, J., Bjorner, D., & Futatsugi, K. (2008, April). *Formal Digital License Language with OTS/CafeOBJ Method.* In Proceedings of the sixth ACS/IEEE International Conference on Computer Systems and Applications, Doha, Qatar.

XMCL. (2001). XMCL - The eXtensible Media Commerce Language. http://www.xmcl.org/specification.html

XML (2006). Extensible Markup Language. Retrieved April 2006 from http://www.w3.org/XML/

XrML 2.0 Technical Overview, version 1.0. (2002, March). Retrieved from http://www.xrml.org/reference/XrMLTechnicalOverviewV1.pdf.

XrML, eXtendible rights Markup Language. http://www.xrml.org/.

Xu, C. X., Chen, K., & Xiao, G. Z. (2002). A Secure Vector Space Secret Sharing Scheme. *Acta Electronica Sinica, 30*(5), 715-718 (In Chinese).

Yan, W.-Q., & Kankanhalli, M. S. (2003). Motion trajectory based video authentication. In *IEEE International Conference on Acoustics, Speech, and Signal Processing, Vol. III,* (pp 810–813), Bangkok, Thailand.

Yang, C. Y., & Lin, J. C. (2006). Image hiding by base-oriented algorithm. *Optical Engeering, 45*(11), 117001_117001-117001_117010.

Yang, J., Gao, L., & Zhang, Y. (2005). Improving Memory Encryption Performance in Secure Processors. *IEEE Transactions on Computers,* 54, 630- 640.

Yao, A. C. (1982). Theory and application of trapdoor functions. In *Proceedings of the 23rd IEEE Symposium on Foundations of Computer Science,* pp. 80–91.

Ye, S., Sun, Q., & Chang, E.-C. (2007). Detecting digital image forgeries by measuring inconsistencies of blocking artifact. In *IEEE International Conference on Multimedia and Expo,* pp 12–15, Beijing, China.

Yeh, C., & Kuo, C. (1999). Digital watermarking through quasi m-arrays. *Proc. IEEE Workshop on Signal Processing Systems.* Taipei, Taiwan. 456–461.

Yeo, J.-C., & Guo, J.-I. (2000). Efficient hierarchical chaotic image encryption algorithm and its VLSI realisation. IEE Proceedings on Vision, Image and Signal Processing, 147(2), 167-175

Yeung, M. M., & Mintzer, F. (1997). An invisible watermarking technique for image verification. In Proc. of ICIP, 1997.

Yi, X., & Ling, N. (May 2005). Improved H.264 Rate Control by Enhanced MAD-based frame complexity prediction. *Journal of Visual Communication and Image Representation.*

Yin, P., & Yu, H. H. (2001). Classification of video tampering methods and countermeasures using digital watermarking. In *SPIE's International Symposium: ITCOM 2001,* Denver, CO, USA.

Yin, P., & Yu, H. H. (2002). A semi-fragile watermarking system for MPEG video authentication. In *International Conference on Acoustic, Speech and Signal Processing, Vol. IV,* (pp 3461–3464), Orlando, FL, USA.

Yodaiken, V. ELEC (2000). http://www.linuxdevices.com/articles/AT3792919168.html

Youtube. (2006). *Broadcast yourself.* Retrieved October 2006 from http://www.youtube.com

Zeng, W., & Lei, S. (2003). Efficient frequency domain selective scrambling of digital video. *IEEE Trans. on Multimedia,* 5, 118–129.

Zeng, W., Lan, J., & Zhuang, J. (2006).Security for multimedia adaptation: architectures and solutions. *IEEE Multimedia,* 13(2), 68- 76. DOI: 10.1109/MMUL.2006.42.

Zerfiridis, K. G., & Karatza, H. D. (2004). File distribution using a peer-to-peer network — a simulation study. *Journal of Systems and Software, 73*, 31–44.

Zhang, G., & Stevenson, R. (2004, October). Efficient error recovery for multiple description video coding. *IEEE International Conference on Image Processing 2004, 2*, Singapore, 829-832.

Zhang, L., Ahn, G. & Chu, B. (2003). A Rule-Based Framework for Role-Based Delegation and Revocation. *ACM Transactions on Information and System Security, 6*(3), 404-441.

Zhang, X. P., & Wang, S. Z. (2005). Steganography using multiple-base notational system and human vision sensitivity. *IEEE Signal Processing Letters, 12*(1), 67-70.

Zhang, X. P., & Wang, S. Z. (2006). Efficient Steganographic Embedding by Exploiting Modification Direction. *IEEE Communication Letters, 10*(11), 781-783.

Zhang, X., Chen, S. & Sandhu, R. (2005). Enhancing Data Authenticity and Integrity in P2P Systems. IEEE Internet Computing, 42--49.

Zhang, Y., Lin, L. & Huai, J. (2007). Balancing Trust and Incentive in Peer-to-Peer Collaborative System. Int. Journal of Network Security, 5(1), 73-81.

Zhao, B.Y., Kubiatowicz, J.D. & Joseph A.D. (2001). Tapestry: An Infrastructure for Fault-tolerant Wide-area Location and Routing. (Tech. Rep. No.UCB/CSD-01-1141). University of California at Berkeley, CA.

Zhao, H. V., & Liu, K. J. R. (2006, January). Fingerprint Multicast in Secure Video Streaming. In *IEEE Transactions on Image Processing, 15*(1), 12-29.

Zheng, D., Zhao, J., & Saddik, A. E. (2003, August). RST-Invariant digital image watermarking based on log-polar mapping and phase correlation. IEEE Transactions on Circuits and Systems for Video Technology, 13(8), 753-765.

Zhu, C., & Liu, M. (2008). Multiple description video coding based on Hierarchical B pictures. *IEEE Transactions on Circuits and Systems for Video Technology*, to be published.

Ziliani, F. (2005). The importance of 'scalability' in video surveillance architectures. In *Proceedings of the IEE International Symposium on Imaging for Crime Detection and Prevention (ICDP)*, 29-32.

Zimmermann P. (1995). The Official PGP User's Guide. MIT Press, Cambridge, Massachusetts.

Zollner, J., Federrath, H., Klimant, H., Pfitzmann, A., Piotraschke, R., Westfeld, A., et al. (1998). Modeling the security of steganographic systems. In Second int. Workshop on Information Hiding (Vol. 1525, p. 345-355). Springer Berlin / Heidelberg.

About the Contributors

Shiguo Lian got his PhD degree in multimedia security from Nanjing University of Science and Technology, China, in July 2005. He was a research assistant in City University of Hong Kong in 2004. He has been with France Telecom R&D (Orange Labs) Beijing since July 2005. He is the author or co-author of more than 50 refereed journal and conference papers covering topics of multimedia security, network security and intelligent services, including lightweight cryptography, digital rights management (DRM), secure content sharing, intelligent multimedia services and security, etc. He has contributed 9 chapters to books and held 7 filed patents. He is a member of IEEE (Institute of Electrical and Electronics Engineers), SPIE (The International Society for Optical Engineering), EURASIP (The European Association for Signal Image Processing) and Chinese Image and Graphics Association. He is a member of IEEE ComSoc Communications & Information Security Technical Committee (CIS TC), IEEE Computer Society's TC on Security and Privacy and multimedia communications Technical Committee (MMTC). He is on the editor board of International Journal of Universal Computer Science, International Journal of Multimedia and Ubiquitous Engineering, and International Journal of Security and Its Applications. He is a co-editor of special issue on "Secure Multimedia Communication" in Journal of Security and Communication Network, and co-editor of special issue on "Multimedia Security in Communication (MUSIC)" in Journal of Universal Computer Science. He is also a member of Technical Committees of some refereed conferences, including IEEE ICC2008, IEEE GLOBECOM2008, MoMM'2008, IPMC'08, UIC-08, MUSIC'08, CASNET 2008, SAM'08 and SecPri_WiMob 2008, etc. He is also the reviewer of some refereed international journals and conferences.

Yan Zhang received the BS degree in communication engineering from the Nanjing University of Post and Telecommunications, China; the MS degree in electrical engineering from the Beijing University of Aeronautics and Astronautics, China; and a PhD degree in School of Electrical & Electronics Engineering, Nanyang Technological University, Singapore. He is associate editor of Security and Communication Networks (Wiley); on the editorial board of International Journal of Network Security, Transactions on Internet and Information Systems (TIIS), International Journal of Autonomous and Adaptive Communications Systems (IJAACS) and International Journal of Smart Home (IJSH). He is currently serving the Book Series Editor for the book series on "Wireless Networks and Mobile Communications" (Auerbach Publications, CRC Press, Taylor and Francis Group). He has served as co-editor for several books. He serves as organizing committee chairs and technical program committee for many international conferences. He received the Best Paper Award and Outstanding Service Award as symposium chair in the IEEE 21st International Conference on Advanced Information Networking and Applications (IEEE AINA-07). From August 2006, he is working with Simula Research Laboratory, Norway. His research interests include resource, mobility, spectrum, data, energy, and security management in wireless networks and mobile computing. He is a member of IEEE and IEEE ComSoc.

* * *

Nicolas Anciaux is a researcher at INRIA, France. He received his PhD in computer science from the University of Versailles in 2004. After one year at University of Twente, Netherlands, he joined the SMIS (Secured and Mobile Information Systems) at INRIA Rocquencourt. His main research area is embedded data management and privacy, in particular in the context of ambient intelligence. He has co-authored about fifteen journal and conference papers.

Supavadee Aramvith received the BS (first class honors) degree in computer science from Mahidol University, Bangkok, Thailand, in 1993. She received the MS and PhD degrees in electrical engineering from the University of Washington, Seattle, USA, in 1996 and 2001, respectively. She is currently an assistant professor at Department of Electrical Engineering, Chulalongkorn University, Bangkok, Thailand. Her research interests include video object segmentation, detection, and tracking, rate-control for video coding, joint source-channel coding for wireless video transmissions, and image/video retrieval techniques. Dr. Aramvith is a senior member of IEEE.

Pradeep K. Atrey is a post-doctoral research fellow at the Multimedia Communications Research Laboratory, University of Ottawa. He obtained PhD in computer science from National University of Singapore in 2006. He was a lecturer at the Delhi College of Engineering, University of Delhi and at the Deenbandhu Chhotu Ram University of Science and Technology, Murthal in India (1992-2002). His research interest includes multimedia surveillance and security, smart environment, and Web. He has authored and co-authored more than 30 refereed journal and conference papers.

Leonardo Badia received the Laurea Degree (cum laude) in electrical engineering and the PhD in Information Engineering from the University of Ferrara, Italy, in 2000 and 2004, respectively. During 2002 and 2003 he was on leave at the Radio System Technology Labs (now Wireless@KTH), Royal Institute of Technology of Stockholm, Sweden. After having been with the Engineering Department of the University of Ferrara, Italy, he joined in 2006 the "Institutions, Markets, Technologies" (IMT) Lucca Institute for Advanced Studies, in Lucca, Italy, where he is currently a research fellow. He also collaborates with DEI, University of Padova, Italy. His research interests include energy efficient ad hoc networks, transmission protocol modeling, admission control and economic modeling of radio resource management for wireless networks. Dr. Badia serves as reviewer for several periodicals in the communication area.

Anja Becker studied mathematics with major computer sciences at the Technical University Darmstadt, Germany. She specialized on IT-security and cryptography and obtained her Diploma with a thesis on elliptic curve cryptography. As a project manager at the Fraunhofer Institute for Integrated Circuits (IIS) in Erlangen, Anja coordinates the Fraunhofer IIS contribution to a research project initiated by the German Federal Ministry of Economy and Technology.

Luc Bouganim is a director of research at INRIA Rocquencourt. He obtained a PhD and the Habilitation à Diriger des Recherches, both from the University of Versailles in in 1996 and 2006, respectively. He worked as an assistant professor from 1997 to 2002 when he joined INRIA. Luc co-authored more than 60 conference and journal papers, an international patent and was the recipient of 3 international awards. Since 2000, Luc is strongly engaged in research activities on ubiquitous data management and data confidentiality. He is currently the vice-head of the SMIS (Secured and Mobile Information Systems) research team.

574

Deepali Brahmbhatt earned her Master's degree in computer science from San Jose State University, San Jose, CA. She graduated in December 2003 and her research focus was on networking and security. Deepali's background includes a bachelor's degree in electronics and communications engineering from L.D. College of Engineering, Gujarat University, India. In addition, she has worked as a member of the technical staff at Barmag (India), Omisystems (Los Altos, California) and Cisco Systems, Inc. (San Jose, California).

Rhandley D. Cajote received the BS in electrical engineering (1998) and MS degree in electrical engineering major in computers and communication (2004) from the Department of Electrical and Electronics Engineering, University of the Philippines, Diliman. He is a faculty member of the University of the Philippines and a PhD student at Chulalongkorn University.

Hsuan T. Chang received his BS degree in electronic engineering from National Taiwan University of Science and Technology, Taiwan, in 1991, and MS and PhD degree in electrical engineering (EE) from National Chung Cheng University, Taiwan, in 1993 and 1997, respectively. He currently is a full professor in EE Department, National Yunlin University of Science and Technology. Dr. Chang's interests include multimedia signal processing, optical information processing/computing, and bioinformatics/genomic signal processing. Dr. Chang is senior member of Institute of Electrical and Electronics Engineers (IEEE), a member of International Society for Optical Engineering (SPIE), Optical Society of America (OSA), and The Chinese Image Processing and Pattern Recognition (IPPR) Society.

Yuewei Dai received the ME,and Dr Eng degrees from Nanjing University of Science and Technology (NUST) in 1987 and 2002 respectively. He works in Automation Department in NUST till now from 1987, and now is the professor. His research interest includes automation control, information technology and information security including data encryption and information hiding, and he has co-authored more than 60 papers. He is the secretary-general of System Engineering Academy of Jiangsu Province in China.

Alessandro Erta graduated (cum laude) in computer systems engineering from the University of Pisa, Italy, in February 2005. He received his PhD from IMT Lucca Institute for Advanced Studies in April 2008. In 2006, he was a visiting student at Rice University, Houston, TX. Currently, he is R&D project manager with Fluidmesh Networks, Inc., developing solutions for wireless mesh networks. He has been involved in national projects, as well as research projects supported by private industries. His research interests include quality of service in wireless networks, the design and performance evaluation of MAC protocols and scheduling algorithms for wireless mesh networks.

Ionut Florescu is an assistant professor with Stevens Institute of Technology. He was born in Bucharest, Romania, and is a graduate of "Facultatea de Matematica" of the University of Bucharest. His PhD is in Statistics from Purdue University. His main area of study is Mathematical Finance but any applied problems in which randomness play an important role seem to be of interest for him.

Harald Fuchs received a diploma in electrical engineering from the University of Erlangen-Nuremberg, Germany in 1997. He has 10 years experience in video coding and transport, and developed software solutions for broadcast, internet and communication services. Today he concentrates on the interaction between multimedia-coding, -transport and -security topics. He coordinates the application- and system-level standardization work of Fraunhofer IIS in the areas of Mobile TV, IPTV and DRM. He is a member of IEEE and actively contributes to several standardization organizations including MPEG, DVB, ISMA and OMA.

Bert Greevenbosch acquired his MSc in mathematics at the University of Leiden in the Netherlands. After graduation, he started working at the Fraunhofer Institute for Integrated Circuits (IIS) in Germany. He specializes in multimedia security technologies, especially in the development and maintenance of the Open Mobile Alliance (OMA) Digital Rights Management standards, as well the associated standards OMA Secure Removable Media and OMA Secure Content Exchange. Since June 2008, Bert chairs the OMA DRM working group.

Gregory L. Heileman received the BA degree from Wake Forest University in 1982, the MS degree in biomedical engineering and mathematics from the University of North Carolina-Chapel Hill in 1986, and the PhD degree in computer engineering from the University of Central Florida in 1989. In 1990 he joined the Department of Electrical and Computer Engineering at the University of New Mexico, Albuquerque, NM, where he is currently professor and associate chair. During 1998 he held a research fellowship at the Universidad Carlos III de Madrid, and in 2005 he held a similar position at the Universidad Politénica de Madrid. His research interests are in digital rights management, information security, the theory of computing and information, machine learning, and data structures and algorithmic analysis. He is the author of the text *Data Structures, Algorithms and Object-Oriented Programming*, published by McGraw-Hill in 1996.

Julio C. Hernandez-Castro is associate professor at the Computer Science Department of Carlos III University of Madrid. He has a BSc in mathematics, a MSc in coding theory and network security, and a PhD in computer science. His interests are mainly focused in cryptology, network security, steganography and evolutionary computation.

Chih-Chung Hsu received his BS degree in information management from Ling-Tung University of Science and Technology, Taiwan, in 2004, and MS degree in electrical engineering (EE) from National Yunlin University of Science and Technology, Taiwan, in 2007, respectively. He currently is a PhD student in EE department, National Tsing Hua University, Taiwan. His research interests include image processing, image compression, image protection/watermarking and cryptography-related topics.

Pramod A. Jamkhedkar received the BE degree in computer engineering from the University of Mumbai in 2002, and the MS degree in computer science from the University of New Mexico in 2005. He is currently pursuing his PhD at the Electrical and Computer Engineering Department at the University of New Mexico. His research interests include digital rights management, networking, systems, security, and logic-based modeling and reasoning of languages and systems. He has several publications in the area of digital rights management systems.

Mercè Serra Joan holds a technical degree in telecommunication engineering from the Technical University of Catalunya (UPC) (Spain) and a Master's degree in electrical engineering from the Friedrich-Alexander University of Erlangen-Nürnberg (Germany). During the last years, she has been working as a research engineer in the Fraunhofer Institute for Integrated Circuits in Erlangen. Her work focused on the development of security technologies for broadcast applications and digital rights management. She was involved in the standardization work of the "Digital Rights Management" and "Mobile Broadcast Services" standards of the Open Mobile Alliance.

Hugo Jonker (1978) received his Master's degree from the Eindhoven University of Technology (TU/e) in 2004. He started his PhD at the end of the same year, during which his research branched out in diverse areas in security, such as e-voting and digital rights management. This has led to several publications in peer-reviewed conferences and workshops. Today, Mr. Jonker is affiliated with both the TU/e and the University of Luxembourg. As a security researcher, his current research interests include privacy, electronic voting (evoting), and DRM.

Mohan S. Kankanhalli is a professor at the Department of Computer Science of the School of Computing at the National University of Singapore. He obtained his BTech (electrical engineering) from the Indian Institute of Technology, Kharagpur, and his MS and PhD (computer and systems engineering) from the Rensselaer Polytechnic Institute. He has worked at the Institute of Systems Science in Singapore and at the Department of Electrical Engineering of the Indian Institute of Science, Bangalore. His current research interests are in multimedia signal processing (sensing, content analysis, retrieval) and multimedia security (surveillance, digital rights management and forensics). He is on the editorial board of several journals including the IEEE Transactions on Multimedia and the IEEE Transactions on Information Forensics and Security.

Sung-Jea Ko received the PhD degree in 1988 and the MS degree in 1986, both in electrical and computer engineering, from State University of New York at Buffalo. In 1992, he joined the Department of Electronic Engineering at Korea University where he is currently a professor. He is also a senior member of IEEE.

Stefan Krägeloh has 20 years of experience in developing hardware and software solutions for a broad range of audio and video related systems including contributions to MP3, IOSONO, DAB and Worldspace. Today his focus is on audio watermarking and interoperable digital rights management solutions based on open standards. He heads the group Multimedia Security Technologies at Fraunhofer IIS.

Nicolai Kuntze received his Diploma of computer science from the Technical University of Darmstadt 2005. Since April 2005 he is employed at the Fraunhofer Institute for Secure Information Technology as a researcher. His focus is in the area of mobile systems and applied trusted computing. He has worked on several industry projects concerned with trusted computing which also lead to publications. He is involved in the standardization in this area as well monitoring the activities of the Trusted Computing Group. As a second focus he works in the area of VoIP security where he is part of the team which developed the signatures on VoIP (VoIPS). Aside these he also worked on research projects for the German BSI and the FP6 Project Hydra.

Goo-Rak Kwon received the PhD degree at the Department of Mechatronic Engineering of Korea University in 2007 and the MS degree in the School of Electrical and Computer Engineering at the Sung-KyunKwan University in 1997. He has also served as chief executive officer and director of Dalitech Co. Ltd. from May 2005 to Feb. 2007. At present, he joined the Department of Information and Communication Engineering at Chosun University where he is currently a full-time instructor.

Tieyan Li is currently a research scientist at Institute for Infocomm Research (I²R, Singapore). He obtained his dual BSc degrees in 1994 at Nan Kai University, China and his PhD degree in 2003 at School of Computing, NUS, Singapore. He has been with I²R since Oct. 2001, and is active in academic security research fields with tens of journal and conference publications and several patents. Prior to this, he had solid working experiences on practical system developments such as networking, system integration and software programming. Currently his areas of research are in applied cryptography and network security, as well as security issues in RFID, sensor, multimedia and tamper resistant hardware/software, etc. Dr. Li has served as the associate editor, PC member and reviewer for a number of security conferences and journals.

Guangjie Liu got his PhD degree in multimedia security from Nanjing University of Science and Technology, China, in 2006. He has been a PostDoc with School of Computer of Nanjing University of Science and Technology since Sep. 2007, focusing on information hiding, digital forensics and perceptual image hashing. He has contributed more than 30 papers in digital watermarking, steganography and intelligent multimedia forensics.

Minglei Liu received the BS degree and MS degree both in communication engineering from Harbin Institute of Technology, Harbin, China, in 2001 and 2003, respectively. He is currently pursuing the PhD degree in information engineering at Nanyang Technogical University, Singapore. His research interests include multiple description image/video coding and multiple description quantization.

Umberto Malesci is president and co-founder of Fluidmesh Networks, a Boston-based technology company that manufactures wireless mesh products specifically designed for security and video applications. He obtained a Master's of Engineering and a Bachelor's of Science in electrical engineering and computer science at MIT. He started his professional career working as a management consultant at McKinsey & Company in Milan, Italy. He also worked as researcher at MIT CSAIL in Cambridge (USA) where he studied innovative routing and MAC protocols to deploy large-scale sensor networks for environmental monitoring. Umberto started Fluidmesh Networks in early 2005 and he currently maintains overall responsibility on the company strategic direction and he is leading sales and business development in Europe and in the US.

Hafiz Malik is an assistant professor the Department of Electrical and Computer Engineering at the University of Michigan – Dearborn. He received his PhD in electrical and computer engineering from the University of Illinois at Chicago, in 2006. He then joined Electrical and Computer Engineering Department at Stevens Institute of Technology as a postdoctoral research fellow. Dr. Malik has served as the Session Chair for 2nd *Secure Knowledge Management Workshop* 2006, lead organizer for special track on *Doctoral Dissertation in Multimedia, IEEE Int. Sym. on Multimedia* (*ISM*) 2006, Member Technical Program Committee for IEEE AVSS 2008, IEEE CCNC 2006, 2007, IEEE ICC 2007, IEEE ICME 2006, 2007, 2008, IEEE ICIP 2008, ChinaCom 2008, Int. Workshop FITs 2004, 2005, 2006. His current research interests lie in the areas of information security, biometric security, digital forensics, DRM, cryptography, cybersecurity multimedia systems, digital signal processing, and data mining.

Sjouke Mauw (1961) received his Master's degree in mathematics (1985) and his PhD degree in computer science (1991) from the University of Amsterdam. He was associate professor at the TU/e, and senior researcher at the Center of Mathematics and Computer Science in Amsterdam. As of 2007, he is full professor of Security and Trust of Software Systems at the University of Luxembourg. His research encompasses many fields in Computer Science, and is characterized by a firm belief in the value of formal methods. Current research interests include privacy, evoting, embedded devices security, DRM, security assessment, and trust&risk management.

Geyong Min is a senior lecturer in the Department of Computing at the University of Bradford, United Kingdom. He received the PhD degree in computing science from the University of Glasgow, United Kingdom, in 2003, and the BSc degree in computer science from Huazhong University of Science and Technology, China, in 1995. His research interests include performance modelling and evaluation, mobile computing and wireless networks, multimedia systems, and information security. He serves on the editorial board of four international journals and as the guest editor for 10 international journals. He was the chair or vice-chair of 16 international conferences/workshops.

Aidan Mooney is a lecturer in the Computer Science Department at the National University of Ireland, Maynooth, Ireland. He completed his PhD entitled "The Generation and Detection of Chaos-Based Watermarks" in 2005 and subsequently took up his current position. His areas of interest include digital watermarking, chaos and image processing. He has published his research in the journal "Chaos, Solitons and Fractals" and at various international conferences.

Jean-Henry Morin is associate professor at Korea University Business School. He holds a PhD and a degree in information systems from University of Geneva where is Chargé de Cours in the Object Systems Group since 2000. He is co-founder of PebbleAge SA, a Geneva based company specialized in corporate performance management solutions where he was director of research and development until 2004. He has published in international conferences and journals and has worked on many European research projects. His research interests include digital rights and policy management (DRM/DPM), corporate information asset management, compliance, corporate governance, electronic commerce and services, peer-to-peer computing, mobile objects (agents), electronic publishing and information services over open networks.

Esther Palomar is assistant professor at the Computer Science Department of Carlos III University of Madrid. She holds a MSc in computer science (2004) from Carlos III University of Madrid. Before joining the university, she worked as forensic analyst for a well-known firm in the field. Currently, she belongs to the Cryptography and Information Security Group, where she is performing her PhD studies. Her research interests are focused on security in peer-to-peer and ad hoc networks.

Pallavi Priyadarshini is a staff software engineer in the DB2 development team at IBM Silicon Valley Labs, California. She has prior experience with IBM Global Services in Singapore and IPDynamics and Infomosaic in California. She completed her undergraduate degree in computer engineering from Nanyang Technological University in Singapore and completed her Master's degree in computer science from San Jose State University in California. Pallavi is interested in working on new solutions in information management, security and enterprise software.

Philippe Pucheral is professor at the University of Versailles, currently in secondment at INRIA Rocquencourt where he is heading the SMIS (Secured and Mobile Information Systems) research team. He obtained a PhD in computer science from the University Paris 6 in 1991 and the Habilitation à Diriger des Recherches from the University of Versailles in 1999. He (co-) authored more than 60 conference and journal papers, 4 international patents, 4 books and was the recipient of 4 international awards (EDBT'92, VLDB'2000, e-gate'2004, SIMagine'2005). His domain of interest covers database systems, mobile and embedded databases and database security.

Arturo Ribagorda is full professor at Carlos III University of Madrid, where he is also the head of the Cryptography and Information Security Group and currently acts as the director of the Computer

Science Department. He has a MSc in telecommunications engineering and a PhD in computer science. He is one of the pioneers of computer security in Spain, having more than 25 years of research and development experience in this field. He has authored 4 books and more than 100 articles in several areas of information security. Additionally, he is member of the program committee of several conferences related to cryptography and information security.

Abdulmotaleb El Saddik is university research chair and professor at the SITE, University of Ottawa and he is recipient of, among others, the Friedrich Wilhelm-Bessel Research Award from Germany's Alexander von Humboldt Foundation (2007) the Premier's Research Excellence Award (PREA 2004). He is the director of the Multimedia Communications Research Laboratory and of the ICT cluster of the Ontario Research Network on E-Commerce. He is leading researcher in interactive haptics audio visual environments and ambient media systems. He has authored and co-authored three books and more than 180 publications. His research has been selected for the BEST Paper Award 2 times. He is an IEEE distinguished lecturer.

Andreas U. Schmidt is senior researcher at the Fraunhofer Institute for Secure Information Technology SIT in Darmstadt, Germany. After studying mathematics and physics at the University Frankfurt, Germany, he received his doctorate in the field of mathematical physics in 1999. Research stays led him to Durban, South Africa, and Pisa, Italy. In his 8 years at SIT, Andreas worked on a broad spectrum of research subjects ranging from long-term security of digital documents to information economy and market models for digital goods. His current interests focus on the creation and mediation of trust between technical systems and humans in mobile situations. Andreas is an active member of the Trusted Computing Group, published numerous research papers on TC, is a co-inventor on some patents in communication security. He initiated EU FP7 projects and is currently task leader in one.

Ronghua Shi received the BSc degree in computer software from the Changsha Railway University in 1986, and the MSc degree in Computer Science from the Central South University of Technology in 1989, and the PhD degree in computer science from the Central South University in 2007. He is currently a professor and a vice dean in School of Information Science and Engineering, Central South University, China. His research interests include authentication, access control, cryptology, and key management.

Frank Y. Shih received BS from National Cheng-Kung University, Taiwan, in 1980, MS from the State University of New York at Stony Brook, in 1984, and PhD from Purdue University, West Lafayette, Indiana, in 1987. He is presently a professor of Computer Science at New Jersey Institute of Technology, Newark, NJ. Dr. Shih is on the editorial board of the International Journal of Pattern Recognition, Journal of Pattern Recognition Letters, Journal of Pattern Recognition and Artificial Intelligence, Journal of Recent Patents on Engineering, Journal of Recent Patents on Computer Science, Journal of Internet Protocol Technology, and Journal of Internet Technology. He holds the research fellow for the American Biographical Institute and the IEEE senior membership. He has published a book, seven chapters and over 200 technical papers, including 95 in prestigious journals. His research interests include image processing, computer vision, sensor networks, pattern recognition, bioinformatics, information security, robotics, fuzzy logic, and neural networks.

M. Hassan Shirali-Shahreza is an assistant professor in the Computer Engineering Department, Yazd University, Yazd, IRAN. He was educated at Isfahan University of Technology, Isfahan, Iran (BSc, Computer Hardware Engineering, 1986), Sharif University of Technology, Tehran, Iran (MSc, Computer

Hardware Engineering, 1988), and Amirkabir University of Technology (Tehran Polytechnic), Tehran, Iran (PhD Computer Hardware Engineering, 1996). In 1994 he was a visiting research scholar in the Electrical Engineering Department, Southern Methodist University (SMU), Dallas, Texas, USA. His interesting fields are genetic algorithm, neural networks, OCR (optical character recognition), and pattern recognition. He is a member of Iranian Computer Society, Iranian Society of Cryptology and a senior member of IEEE.

Mohammad Shirali-Shahreza is an undergraduate student in computer science at Sharif University of Technology in Iran. He got his diploma from Allameh Helli high school, Tehran, Iran, that is a school for exceptional talents students. He is selected as "Iranian Distinguished University Student" in 2008. His project on steganography won the best prize of 5th Iranian Khwarizmi young festival. He has 64 accepted papers in international conferences, nine published papers in journals, one book and one Iranian patent. He was selected as Iranian Distinguished University Student by the Ministry of Science, Research and Technology of Iran for academic year 2006-2007. He won the "undergraduate youngest research award" from Iranian Society of Cryptology (2006), "the young researcher award" of IEEE ICTTA 2006 conference and "the young researcher award" of the 11th International CSI Computer Conference. He is a student member of IEEE and Iranian Computer Society. His research background includes steganography, CAPTCHA, mobile programming, and e-learning.

Mark Stamp spent more than seven years at the National Security Agency working on classified security projects. He left NSA with the goal of getting rich by developing a digital rights management system for a small Silicon Valley startup company. That did not work out quite as planned. Nevertheless, Dr. Stamp was able to broaden his security experience and perspective. Since 2002, Dr. Stamp has been a faculty member in the Department of Computer Science at San Jose State University, where he teaches courses in information security, conducts research in security, and publishes an occasional textbook. Many of his former students are doing security-related work at leading Silicon Valley companies.

K-G Stenborg was born in Edsbyn, Sweden, in 1974. He received the MS degree in applied physics and electrical engineering from Linköping University in 1999. In 2005 he received a Licentiate in Engineering degree from the Image Coding Group, Linköping University. Since 2007 he is working at the Swedish Defence Research Agency.

Juan M.E. Tapiador is associate professor at the Computer Science Department of Carlos III University of Madrid. He holds a MSc in computer science from the University of Granada (2000), where he obtained the Best Student Academic Award, and a PhD in Computer Science (2004) from the same university. His research is focused on cryptography and information security, especially in formal methods applied to computer security, design and analysis of cryptographic protocols, steganography, and some theoretical aspects of network security.

Ramya Venkataramu graduated from San Jose State University with an MS degree in computer science in May 2007. She is currently at Hewlett-Packard, working on developing innovative digital media solutions for emerging products.

Guojun Wang received his BSc degree in geophysics, MSc degree in computer science, and PhD degree in computer science, from the Central South University, in 1992, 1996, 2002, respectively. He is currently a professor (2005-) in School of Information Science and Engineering, Central South University, China. He was a research fellow (2003-2005) in the Hong Kong Polytechnic University, Hong Kong. He was a visiting researcher (2006-2007) in the University of Aizu, Japan. His research interests include trusted computing, mobile computing, pervasive computing, and software engineering. He has published more than 130 technical papers and books/chapters in the above areas.

Zhiquan Wang received the BE degree from Harbin Military Engneering Collage in 1962. He has been working in Nanjing University of Science and Technology from 1962. He has been a professor at Automation Department of NUST since 1991. His research covers control theory, fault-tolerance control, fault detection and diagnosis in complex large system, chaos control and information security. He is the author and co-author of more than 300 papers. He is the director of Automation Academy in China and the deputy-president of Jiangsu Auotmation Academy.

Yirong Wu received his BSc degree in computer science from the Nan Hua University in 2005, and he is now a graduate student in School of Information Science and Engineering, Central South University, China. His research interests include network and information security.

Yi-Ta Wu was born in Taipei, Taiwan. He received the BS degree in physics from Tamkang University, Taipei, Taiwan, in 1995, and the MS degree in computer science from National Dong-Hwa University, Hualien, Taiwan, in 1997. Dr. Wu received PhD from Department of Computer Science, New Jersey Institute of Technology, in May 2005. He was a research fellow at University of Michigan, Ann Arbor. He currently works for the Industry Technology Research Institute in Taiwan. His current research interests include image/video processing, mathematical morphology, image watermarking, steganography, surveillance system, robot vision, pattern recognition, shortest path planning, and artificial intelligence.

Fan Zhang received the BS degree from North China University, China, in 1989, the MS degree from Jiangsu University, China, in 2001, and the PhD degree in computer science from Beijing University of technology (with the highest honors), China, in 2005. Now, he is the associate professor of the College of Computer & Information Engineering, Henan University, China, and the College of Electronic & Information Engineering, Tianjin University, China. His research interests include pattern recognition, image processing, information security and multimedia database.

Ce Zhu is an associate professor at School of Electrical & Electronic Engineering, Nanyang Technological University, Singapore. His research interests include image/video coding and communications, and multimedia signal processing. He has published over 60 papers in referred journals and conferences. As a principle investigator or project leader, Dr. Zhu has successfully completed a few research and industrial projects on image/video coding and processing. He has served over 20 international conferences as a member of Technical Program Committee/Organizing Committee or track/session chair. He is currently a member of the Technical Committee on Multimedia Systems and Applications, IEEE CAS Society, and a senior member of IEEE.

Index

A

A/V codec 430
A/V scrambling 430
access control, dynamic policy management
    169
access control list 90
access control model 157–180
adaptive image steganography 454–471
adaptive steganography 457
Advanced Encryption Standard (AES) 515
analogue conversion 76
Apple 41, 72, 86, 137
asymmetric multiple description lattice vector
    quantization (AMDLVQ) 497
audio and video (A/V) processing software 425
audio encryption 432
audio steganography 246
authentication 67, 94, 305, 315
authentication, and P2P networks 390
authentication, basics 317–319
authentication, message 317
authentication, multimedia 318
authorization 159

B

Bayes classifier 362
BCAST 62
benign operation 303
bit error rate (BER) 258
Black Wolf's Picture Encoder 442
Blindside 356

blokiness 362
BOBE attacks 95
BOBE resistance 25, 90
broadcast streams 65
Byzantine Agreement protocols 394

C

capacity 378, 379, 381, 538, 570
capacity, and detection error rate 267
certificate authority (CA) 59
Chameleon 344
chaotic watermark 287
Chi-square tests 362
CITADEL 90
classification 358
client-server network architecture 87
closed circuit teleVision (CCTV) 120
COiN-video 343
collusion attack 476
commercial watermarking 283
compression 337
conceptual process model 75
confidentiality 316
content creator 74, 77
content distribution, and P2P networks 387
content encapsulation 76
content encryption key (CEK) 57
content extraction 76
content protection 45
content provider 427
content rendering environment 6